Bureaucracies at War

Why do states start conflicts they ultimately lose? Why do leaders possess inaccurate expectations of their prospects for victory? *Bureaucracies at War* examines how national security institutions shape the quality of information upon which leaders base their choice for conflict – which institutional designs provide the best counsel, why those institutions perform better, and why many leaders fail to adopt them. Jost argues that the same institutions that provide the best information also empower the bureaucracy to punish the leader. Thus, miscalculation on the road to war is often the tragic consequence of how leaders resolve the trade-off between good information and political security. Employing an original cross-national data set and detailed explorations of the origins and consequences of institutions inside China, India, Pakistan, and the United States, this book explores why bureaucracy helps to avoid disaster, how bureaucratic competition produces better information, and why institutional design is fundamentally political.

Tyler Jost is Assistant Professor of Political Science at Brown University. He is also Associate in Research at the Fairbank Center for Chinese Studies at Harvard University. His research explores bureaucracy, national security decision-making, and Chinese foreign policy. He earned his doctorate from the Department of Government at Harvard University and received postdoctoral fellowships from the Harvard Kennedy School of Government, Columbia University, and Dartmouth College. While writing this book, he conducted research in nineteen archives and libraries across China, India, Pakistan, Taiwan, the United Kingdom, and the United States.

Cambridge Studies in International Relations

EDITORS
Evelyn Goh
Christian Reus-Smit
Nicholas J. Wheeler

EDITORIAL BOARD
Jacqueline Best, Karin Fierke, William Grimes, Yuen Foong Khong, Andrew Kydd, Lily Ling, Andrew Linklater, Nicola Phillips, Elizabeth Shakman Hurd, Jacqui True, Leslie Vinjamuri, Alexander Wendt

Cambridge Studies in International Relations is a joint initiative of Cambridge University Press and the British International Studies Association (BISA). The series aims to publish the best new scholarship in international studies, irrespective of subject matter, methodological approach or theoretical perspective. The series seeks to bring the latest theoretical work in International Relations to bear on the most important problems and issues in global politics.

166 *Jack Donnelly*
Systems, Relations, and the Structures of International Societies

165 *Jason Ralph*
On Global Learning
Pragmatic Constructivism, International Practice and the Challenge of Global Governance

164 *Barry Buzan*
Making Global Society
A Study of Humankind Across Three Eras

163 *Brian Rathbun*
Right and Wronged in International Relations
Evolutionary Ethics, Moral Revolutions, and the Nature of Power Politics

162 *Vincent Pouliot and Jean-Philippe Thérien*
Global Policymaking
The Patchwork of Global Governance

161 *Swati Srivastava*
Hybrid Sovereignty in World Politics

Series list continues after index

Bureaucracies at War
The Institutional Origins of Miscalculation

Tyler Jost
Brown University

Shaftesbury Road, Cambridge CB2 8EA, United Kingdom

One Liberty Plaza, 20th Floor, New York, NY 10006, USA

477 Williamstown Road, Port Melbourne, VIC 3207, Australia

314–321, 3rd Floor, Plot 3, Splendor Forum, Jasola District Centre, New Delhi – 110025, India

103 Penang Road, #05–06/07, Visioncrest Commercial, Singapore 238467

Cambridge University Press is part of Cambridge University Press & Assessment, a department of the University of Cambridge.

We share the University's mission to contribute to society through the pursuit of education, learning and research at the highest international levels of excellence.

www.cambridge.org
Information on this title: www.cambridge.org/9781009307208
DOI: 10.1017/9781009307253

© Tyler Jost 2024

This publication is in copyright. Subject to statutory exception and to the provisions of relevant collective licensing agreements, no reproduction of any part may take place without the written permission of Cambridge University Press & Assessment.

When citing this work, please include a reference to the DOI 10.1017/9781009307253

First published 2024

A catalogue record for this publication is available from the British Library

Library of Congress Cataloging-in-Publication Data
Names: Jost, Tyler, 1986– author.
Title: Bureaucracies at war : the institutional origins of miscalculation / Tyler Jost.
Description: Cambridge, United Kingdom ; New York, NY : Cambridge University Press, 2024. | Series: Cambridge studies in international relations ; 167 | Includes bibliographical references and index.
Identifiers: LCCN 2023050333 (print) | LCCN 2023050334 (ebook) | ISBN 9781009307208 (hardback) | ISBN 9781009307253 (ebook)
Subjects: LCSH: International relations – Decision making. | Bureaucracy. | China – Foreign relations – 1949–1976. | China – Foreign relations – 1976– | India – Foreign relations – 1947–1984. | Pakistan – Foreign relations – 1947–1971. | United States – Foreign relations – 1945–1989.
Classification: LCC JZ1253 .J67 2024 (print) | LCC JZ1253 (ebook) | DDC 327.09/045–dc23/eng/20240110
LC record available at https://lccn.loc.gov/2023050333
LC ebook record available at https://lccn.loc.gov/2023050334

ISBN 978-1-009-30720-8 Hardback
ISBN 978-1-009-30722-2 Paperback

Cambridge University Press & Assessment has no responsibility for the persistence or accuracy of URLs for external or third-party internet websites referred to in this publication and does not guarantee that any content on such websites is, or will remain, accurate or appropriate.

History is a catalogue of mistakes.

Liddell Hart

Plans are worthless, but planning is everything.

Dwight D. Eisenhower

兼听则明，偏信则暗 | Listen to both sides and you will be enlightened. Believe only one and you will be ignorant.

Traditional Chinese Idiom

Contents

List of Figures	*page* viii
List of Tables	ix
Acknowledgments	x
List of Abbreviations	xiii

1	Introduction	1
2	An Institutional Theory of Miscalculation	21
3	The World of National Security Institutions	54
4	China under Mao	82
5	China after Mao	128
6	India	177
7	Pakistan	226
8	The United States during the Early Cold War	259
9	Conclusion	325

Appendix A National Security Institutions Data Set	339
Appendix B Archival and Interview Data Collection	342
Bibliography	348
Index	370

Figures

2.1	Types of national security institutions	*page* 27
2.2	A model of institutional design choices	47
3.1	Share of states by type of national security institution	59
3.2	National security institutions and regime type	60
3.3	Leaders and changes in institutional design	61
3.4	Interaction between leader experience and regime type	73
4.1	China's national security decision-making, 1949–1976	88
4.2	China's national security coordination, 1949–1976	92
4.3	Mao's changing threat perceptions, 1949–1965	94
4.4	Institutional change in Politburo decision-making, 1949–1965	96
5.1	China's national security decision-making, 1976–1988	136
5.2	Size of the Central Military Commission, 1949–2015	139
6.1	Information flow under Nehru, 1958–1962	187
6.2	Indian defense budget, 1947–1966	190
6.3	Terrorist violence in Jammu & Kashmir, 1990–2005	219
8.1	Venues for U.S. national security decision-making, 1953–1968	267
8.2	Bureaucratic representation in U.S. national security decision-making, 1953–1968	276

Tables

2.1	Informational demands in international crisis	*page* 32
2.2	Theoretical predictions regarding miscalculation	40
3.1	Examples of institutional types	58
3.2	Crisis performance across institutional types	65
3.3	National security institutions and international crisis performance	68
3.4	The political origins of institutional design	71
3.5	Summary of data collection	75
3.6	Overview of the case studies on decision-making	77
4.1	Evolution of China's institutional design under Mao	85
4.2	China's crisis performance under Mao, 1949–1976	101
4.3	Summary of the KMT invasion scare and Sino-Soviet border conflict	103
5.1	Evolution of China's institutional design after Mao	131
5.2	China's crisis performance after Mao, 1976–2012	150
5.3	Summary of the Sino-Vietnamese War and EP-3 reconnaissance aircraft incident	152
6.1	Evolution of India's institutional design	181
6.2	India's crisis performance, 1947–2015	198
6.3	Summary of the Sino-Indian War and Twin Peaks Crisis	200
7.1	Evolution of Pakistan's institutional design	229
7.2	Pakistan's crisis performance, 1947–2015	242
7.3	Summary of the Kargil War	244
8.1	Evolution of U.S. institutional design, 1953–1968	264
8.2	U.S. crisis performance, 1953–1968	281
8.3	Summary of the Second Taiwan Strait Crisis and Vietnam War	283
9.1	Summary of case analysis: Institutional design	330
9.2	Summary of case analysis: Decision-making	331

Acknowledgments

True to the spirit of its argument, this book is the product of an iterative dialogue with many advisers, mentors, and colleagues who have shaped my thoughts on bureaucracy, international politics, and the discipline of social science. When I was an undergraduate at West Point, Ruth Beitler, Suzanne Nielsen, and Tino Perez sparked my interest in political science and China. At SOAS University of London, Julia Strauss supported my application to doctoral programs.

As a graduate student, I was fortunate to have five mentors oversee my dissertation, which was an early attempt at articulating the ideas presented here. Iain Johnston taught me the fundamentals of how to study Chinese foreign policy. Josh Kertzer, beyond reading countless versions of this manuscript, was a model of productivity, creativity, and empathy that I will surely never match. Vipin Narang jumped institutional silos to join the committee. Liz Perry pushed me to think more like a comparativist. Steve Rosen was the model of a dissertation committee chair, generous with his time and patient with my ideas. Other faculty and colleagues whose feedback aided this project include Graham Allison, Dan Altman, Bob Bates, Don Casler, Allison Carnegie, Jon Caverley, Mark Bell, Matt Blackwell, Risa Brooks, Ryan Brutger, Austin Carson, Dan Carpenter, Binn Cho, Chris Clary, Dara Cohen, Zack Cooper, Dale Copeland, Fiona Cunningham, Alex Debs, Mac Destler, David Edelstein, Ryan Evans, Jeff Frieden, Jeff Friedman, Julia Gray, Naima Green-Riley, Sheena Chestnut Greitens, Mike Goldfien, Avery Goldstein, Steve Goldstein, Peg Hermann, Connor Huff, Bob Jervis, Michael Kenwick, Sulmaan Khan, Sarah Kreps, Marika Landau-Wells, Melissa Lee, Chris Lucas, Dan Mattingly, Oriana Mastro, Nuno Monteiro, Jim Morrow, Eric Min, Andy Nathan, Rich Nielsen, Cullen Nutt, Rachel Esplin Odell, John Owen, Barry Posen, Abby Post, Mike Poznansky, Brian Rathbun, Steve Saideman, Anne Sartori, Rob Schub, Todd Sechser, Beth Simmons, Victor Shih, Austin Strange, Yeling Tan, Kai Thaler, Joseph Torigian, Stephen Van Evera, Alex Weisiger, Jessica Chen Weiss, Arne Westad, Peter White, Keren Yarhi-Milo, and Jack Zhang.

Acknowledgments

Over the course of my field research, the Fairbank Center for Chinese Studies, Harvard Law School Program on Negotiation, Smith Richardson Foundation, United States Institute of Peace, and Weatherhead Center for International Affairs provided financial support. I also thank academic colleagues at the Academia Sinica in Taipei, the School of International Studies at Peking University, the Centre for Policy Research in New Delhi, and the Center for International Strategic Studies in Islamabad for hosting me while I was abroad. Faculty and fellows at the George Washington University Institute for Security and Conflict Studies – Steve Biddle, Alex Downes, Charlie Glaser, Dan Jacobs, Michael Joseph, Elizabeth Saunders, Caitlin Talmadge, and Ketian Zhang – provided feedback and friendly support while I was working in the archives in Washington, DC.

I was fortunate to have time and space to turn my dissertation into a book while a postdoctoral fellow at the Belfer Center and the China and the World Program. Through the former, Steve Miller, Sean Lynn-Jones, and Steve Walt were supportive and insightful. Fred Logevall provided helpful feedback, particularly on the Vietnam case. Susan Lynch welcomed me to Belfer. Nick Anderson, Paul Behringer, Rebecca Gibbons, Kelly Greenhill, Mariya Grinberg, Phil Martin, Reid Pauly, Brad Potter, and Ben Zala helped workshop the theory chapter. Adele Carrai, Andrew Chubb, Andrew Erickson, Courtney Fung, Yinan He, Scott Kastner, Alison Kaufman, Wendy Leutert, Adam Liff, Dalton Lin, and Min Ye offered helpful comments on the empirical chapters on China.

This project was completed at Brown, where the Department of Political Science and Watson Institute were endlessly supportive. I am especially indebted to Wendy Schiller and Ed Steinfeld for their advice and support for this project, to Peter Andreas, Rob Blair, Mark Blyth, Jeff Colgan, Rose McDermott, and Nina Tannenwald for their feedback, to Patti Gardner for helping me navigate the transition to being an assistant professor, as well as to many other colleagues and graduate students at Brown who sharpened my ideas. Brown generously hosted a workshop for the manuscript, during which feedback from Tom Christensen, Taylor Fravel, Mike Horowitz, Jessica Weeks, Bill Wohlforth, and my colleagues at Brown was instrumental in testing the argument. The workshop would not have happened without the help of Deirdre Foley.

I am particularly indebted to individuals who helped, in very different ways, to make data available for this project. Nancy Hearst was unbelievably patient with my never-ending requests for Chinese-language materials at the Fung Library. Chuck Kruas provided access to a collection of archival documents from the Chinese Ministry of Foreign Affairs housed by the Wilson Center's History and Public Policy Program. John Wilson at the LBJ Presidential Library was particularly helpful with fielding document requests during the pandemic. Merle Pribbenow graciously shared his translations of numerous Vietnamese documents and memoirs, which greatly assisted the analysis of cases on the Vietnam War and Sino-Vietnamese War. Several chapters in this book would not exist without their assistance. Caroline Deitch and Mila Hanauer helped by translating Russian language materials on the Sino-Soviet border crisis. Omar Afzaal did the same for a memoir in Urdu discussing the Kargil War. Kimberly Silva and Svetlana Rukhelman helped source countless inquiries of foreign legislation needed for the cross-national data set. I was beyond fortunate to have a team of research assistants to build the cross-national data set: Maya Gros, Eiichiro Kuno, Orianne Mountabin, Hope Ndhlovu, Phillip Ramirez, Namsai Sethpornpong, and Gina Sinclair. Max Kuhelj Bugaric and Eileen Phou went above and beyond in coding these and other resources. Additional help came from Prottoya Chowdhury, Ellyse Givens, Bhanu Joshi, Alex Lee, Yucong Li, Dan Post, and Sanne Verschuren. Some of the ideas presented in Chapters 4 and 5 were first published in the summer 2023 issue of *International Security*. I am grateful to the editors for providing the necessary permissions. Finally, I am particularly indebted to John Haslam and Carrie Parkison, who shepherded the manuscript through the publication process at Cambridge University Press.

Many friends – Adam Jannetti, Aroop Mukharji, Brian Palmiter, Mel Sanborn, Paul Shinkman, and Brad Wilson – provided wise counsel. My wife, Tina, was a sounding board for every page of this book. Her decision to marry me was the best moment of my life. This book is dedicated to my parents, Carl and Susan.

Abbreviations

CCRG	Central Cultural Revolution Group
CIA	Central Intelligence Agency
CID	Central Investigation Department
CMC	Central Military Commission
CMLA	Chief Martial Law Administration
CCP	Chinese Communist Party
CCNS	Cabinet Committee on National Security
CCS	Cabinet Committee on Security
CNSC	Central National Security Commission
DCC	Defence Committee of the Cabinet
DDEL	Dwight D. Eisenhower Presidential Library
DRV	Democratic Republic of Vietnam
ECC	Emergency Committee of the Cabinet
FALSG	Foreign Affairs Leading Small Group
FRUS	*Foreign Relations of the United States*
GHQ	General Headquarters
GSD	General Staff Department
IB	Intelligence Bureau
ISI	Inter-Services Intelligence
JCS	Joint Chiefs of Staff
JCL	Jimmy Carter Presidential Library
JFKL	John F. Kennedy Presidential Library
KMT	Nationalist Party (Kuomintang)
LBJL	LBJ Presidential Library
MBVM	McGeorge Bundy Vietnam Manuscript
MEA	Ministry of External Affairs
MFA	Ministry of Foreign Affairs
MSS	Ministry of State Security
NSA	National Security Advisor
NSC	National Security Council
NSLSG	National Security Leading Small Group
OCB	Operations Coordinating Board

List of Abbreviations

OHT	Oral History Transcript
PAC	Political Affairs Committee
PP	Pentagon Papers
PLA	People's Liberation Army
PRC	People's Republic of China
R&AW	Research and Analysis Wing
RNL	Richard Nixon Presidential Library
RVN	Republic of Vietnam
SWJN-SS	Selected Works of Jawaharlal Nehru (Second Series)
TLSG	Taiwan Affairs Leading Small Group
USSR	Union of Soviet Socialist Republics (Soviet Union)
VCSJVA	Vietnam Center and Sam Johnson Vietnam Archive
WBVM	William Bundy Vietnam Manuscript

1 Introduction

One of the tragedies of international conflict is that so often it achieves so little.[1] History is replete with examples of states charging headfirst into international confrontations that left them no better off – and often much worse off – than when they started. The Indian Forward Policy against China in 1961, the United States escalation in Vietnam in 1965, China's border conflict with the Soviet Union in 1969, and Pakistan's attempted seizure of the Kargil heights in 1999 all illustrate a common tendency. States frequently initiate costly international conflicts in which they fail to advance their strategic objectives. In fact, since the end of World War II, states have fallen short of achieving their goals in over half of the international crises that they initiated.[2] What makes these conflicts tragic is not only that they impose devastating human and economic costs on societies, but also that those who pay these costs have little to show for it when the smoke clears.

Miscalculation offers one important answer as to why states enter international conflicts in which they ultimately fail to achieve their goals.[3] Inaccurate propositions about the state of the world lead decision-makers to choose strategies anticipating outcomes more favorable than the ones that eventually materialize. Optimism rooted in inaccuracy leads decision-makers to see more benefits and fewer costs than international conflict turns out to deliver. Each one of the examples discussed earlier illustrates this phenomenon. Indian Prime Minister Jawaharlal Nehru, for

---

[1] Geoffrey Blainey, *Causes of War*, 3rd ed. (New York: The Free Press, 1988), 35–56; Stephen Van Evera, *Causes of War: Power and the Roots of Conflict* (Ithaca: Cornell University Press, 1999), 14–34; Richard Ned Lebow, *Between Peace and War: The Nature of International Crisis* (Baltimore: Johns Hopkins University Press, 1984), 57–97; Fred Charles Iklé, *Every War Must End*, 2nd ed. (New York: Columbia University Press, 2005), 17–37; Alex Weisiger, *Logics of War: Explanations for Limited and Unlimited Conflicts* (Ithaca: Cornell University Press, 2013), 33–42.

[2] Author's calculations discussed in Chapter 3.

[3] Jack S. Levy, "Misperception and the Causes of War: Theoretical Linkages and Analytical Problems," *World Politics* 36, no. 1 (1983): 76–99; Robert Jervis, "War and Misperception," *The Journal of Interdisciplinary History* 18, no. 4 (1988): 676.

instance, believed that establishing military outposts in contested territory along the border with China would solidify India's territorial claims, in part because he thought that China was unlikely to retaliate. American President Lyndon Johnson concluded that escalation in Vietnam offered the United States the last best hope to "win the war." Chinese leader Mao Zedong assessed that ambushing Soviet forces along the border would prompt Moscow to ease rising tensions brought on by the Sino-Soviet split. Pakistani Prime Minister Nawaz Sharif believed that Pakistani incursions into Kashmir would not elicit a strong diplomatic response from the international community. In all these cases, however, the premises on which leaders based their decisions for costly international conflict proved fundamentally flawed.

It is tempting to conclude that, in questions of war and peace, such miscalculations inevitably happen due to the structural uncertainty pervading international politics. Well-meaning policymakers sometimes make decisions with limited information and, through no fault of their own, get things wrong due to pernicious restrictions on their ability to know how adversaries will react and how conflicts will turn out. Hindsight may be twenty-twenty, but a decision-maker's view at the time is often blurry.

Yet there is considerable variation in the quality of judgment that states exhibit when considering the use of force. Different states at different times display systematically different levels of susceptibility to miscalculation. Why are some states more prone than others to miscalculate in international conflict?

The central argument of this book is that variation in national security institutions – a set of rules that define the roles, constraints, and expectations of bureaucracies charged with advising leaders – shapes the propensity for leaders to miscalculate as they choose to initiate conflict. Leaders frequently start conflicts that end disastrously not simply because they lack information, but because they do not effectively aggregate the information that the bureaucracy has or might easily obtain. While uncertainty is a fact of life in international politics, miscalculation is not a fixed consequence. Some states are better positioned than others to manage the uncertainty of international politics. The fog of war may be ever-present, but some institutional choices make it thicker than it need be.

The cases referenced illustrate this pattern. As India adopted the Forward Policy, Nehru's defense advisers feared that Chinese military deployments along the border made it untenable to hold India's new outposts. As the United States began its strategic bombing campaign, multiple iterations of wargame simulations forecasted that escalation would fail to compel Vietnam to end support for the insurgency in South Vietnam.

As China lashed out against the Soviet Union, Chinese diplomats quietly questioned the severity of the Soviet threat and that alternatives to conflict might better serve Mao's goals. As Pakistani forces crossed the line of control in Kashmir, diplomats knew that the international community was unlikely to brook the gambit. And in each case, institutions prevented bureaucratic information from effectively flowing to the leader.

A trade-off between good information and political security leads to institutional variation. For leaders, bureaucracy is both a resource and a liability. Adopting institutions that integrate bureaucrats into competitive deliberations tends to yield higher quality information than leaders can obtain on their own. Yet such institutions also empower bureaucrats in ways that can threaten the leader's political agenda and survival. In short, the institutions that provide the best information also empower the bureaucracy to punish the leader. How leaders resolve this institutional trade-off has profound consequences for whether and how information flows inside the state and, in turn, for the risk of miscalculation on the road to war.

Why Study National Security Institutions?

Bureaucracy is nearly synonymous with modern government.[4] In many ways, states are defined by their capacity to extract taxes, plan economies, regulate markets, and provide public administration.[5] In both democracies and autocracies, politicians make up only a small part of the state. For better or worse, a "realistic study of government has to start with an understanding of bureaucracy," as political theorist Carl Friedrich notes, "because no government can function without it."[6]

---

[4] Max Weber, *Economy and Society: An Outline of Interpretive Sociology* (Berkeley: University of California Press, 1978 [1921]); Anthony Downs, *Inside Bureaucracy* (Boston: Little, Brown & Company, 1967); Stephen Skowronek, *Building a New American State: The Expansion of National Administrative Capacities, 1877–1920* (New York: Cambridge University Press, 1982); James Q. Wilson, *Bureaucracy: What Government Agencies Do and Why They Do It* (New York: Basic Books, 1989); Daniel P. Carpenter, *The Forging of Bureaucratic Autonomy: Reputations, Networks, and Policy Innovation in Executive Agencies, 1862–1928* (Princeton: Princeton University Press, 2001); Ezra N. Suleiman, *Dismantling Democratic States* (Princeton: Princeton University Press, 2013).

[5] Samuel P. Huntington, *Political Order in Changing Societies* (New Haven: Yale University Press, 1968); Barbara Geddes, *Politician's Dilemma: Building State Capacity in Latin America* (Berkeley: University of California Press, 1994); Theda Skocpol, *Protecting Soldiers and Mothers: The Political Origins of Social Policy in the United States* (Cambridge: Harvard University Press, 1995); Susan L. Moffitt, *Making Policy Public: Participatory Bureaucracy in American Democracy* (New York: Cambridge University Press, 2014); Yuen Yuen Ang, *How China Escaped the Poverty Trap* (Ithaca: Cornell University Press, 2016).

[6] Carl J. Friedrich, *Constitutional Government and Democracy* (Boston: Ginn, 1950), 57. See also Downs, *Inside Bureaucracy*, 44.

National security bureaucracy – a set of diplomatic, defense, and intelligence organizations that specialize in foreign and defense affairs – is a widespread component of state capacity in the modern world. Most states and all major powers possess these bureaucracies in some form or fashion. They enable diplomatic representation in embassies and international organizations abroad; they allow states to defend territory and political interests by force; and they collect and process a voluminous array of intelligence available in the international system.

These bureaucracies can (and do) shape decision-making. National security bureaucracies do not make the most important decisions in international politics. Leaders (presidents, prime ministers, and dictators) hold the final say in matters of war and peace.[7] While leaders make decisions, however, bureaucracies can (and often do) inform those decisions. This division of labor introduces a series of gaps between and among leaders and the bureaucracy, which create islands of information within the state. Just because one actor in the system is aware of a piece of information does not mean that all others are. Gaps require bridges.

States use rules to create different types of bridges across these organizational divides. Some bridges are wide, granting access for bureaucrats to relay information to leaders, setting conditions for bureaucrats to speak candidly, and encouraging bureaucrats to share information with one another. Other bridges are narrow or non-existent, insulating decision-making from bureaucratic input, discouraging bureaucrats from speaking truth to power, or prohibiting bureaucrats from sharing information.

National security institutions are a set of rules that shape how information flows across these organizational gaps. Social scientists offer a range of definitions for institutions.[8] Here, national security institutions refer to a comparatively stable and connected set of formal and informal rules that prescribe the roles that bureaucracies play, constrain their actions, and shape their expectations. Institutions do not refer to any single organization, such as a specific bureaucracy or advisory body, but rather the rules that govern how such organizations interact with the leader. If democratic and autocratic institutions are the rules shaping how political

---

[7] On the executive's close relationship with the national security bureaucracy, see Amy B. Zegart, *Flawed by Design: The Evolution of the CIA, JCS, and NSC* (Stanford: Stanford University Press, 2000), 21–40; Carpenter, *The Forging of Bureaucratic Autonomy*, 12.

[8] This definition draws on Robert O. Keohane, "International Institutions: Two Approaches," *International Studies Quarterly* 32, no. 4 (1988): 32. See also Douglass C. North, *Institutions, Institutional Change and Economic Performance* (New York: Cambridge University Press, 1990), 4. For alternative definitions emphasizing patterns of expectation and behavior, see Huntington, *Political Order in Changing Societies*, 9; Wolfgang Streeck and Kathleen Thelen, *Beyond Continuity: Institutional Change in Advanced Political Economies* (New York: Oxford University Press, 2005), 11–12.

leaders are selected for office, national security institutions are the rules shaping how leaders manage the national security bureaucracy.

These institutions are as pervasive in international politics as their designs are distinct from one another. Consider how three different institutional designs created systematically different patterns of information flow in three different countries. In the Soviet Union during much of Nikita Khrushchev's tenure, neither the foreign ministry nor the intelligence agency, the KGB, were appointed as members of important advisory and coordination bodies, such as the Presidium or the Defense Council. With few political protections and limited access, bureaucrats struggled to speak candidly during key crises during the early Cold War. A quite different pattern of information flow emerged from a different institutional design in Pakistan during the 1990s. The Defence Committee of the Cabinet created a routine forum by which diplomatic, defense, and intelligence officials could relay information to the prime minister. Below the decision-making level, however, there were few mechanisms to ensure information sharing between bureaucrats. Finally, a still different pattern in information flow began to emerge in India after the establishment of its National Security Council in the late 1990s. In contrast to the Pakistani system, a series of institutional devices, ranging from coordinators to information sharing committees, increased the state's capacity to not only relay information to leaders, but also to exchange information with one another.

While these institutional differences exist as a matter of fact, we know comparatively little about them. What effect, if any, does institutional design have on patterns of miscalculation? Do designs that incorporate the bureaucracy into national security decision-making deliver better results than those that keep it at arm's length? Can some designs make bureaucracy an asset, rather than a hindrance, to good judgment? Or does the institutional relationship between politicians and bureaucrats, however structured, have little bearing on the most consequential questions in international politics, such as war and peace? We presently have a poor understanding of the answers to these questions. Academic interest in bureaucracy in foreign policy decision-making has declined since the first wave of scholarship began to explore the topic over a half century ago.[9] Moreover, at present, we have comparatively few studies that

---

[9] Michael C. Horowitz, "Leaders, Leadership, and International Security," in *The Oxford Handbook of International Security* (New York: Oxford University Press, 2018), 253; Emilie M. Hafner-Burton et al., "The Behavioral Revolution and International Relations," *International Organization* 71, no. S1 (2017): 19. Even Allison and Zelikow note that information provision is an understudied aspect of bureaucratic politics, calling scholars to devote more attention to procedures affecting its acquisition, distribution, and use. See Graham T. Allison and Philip Zelikow, *Essence of Decision: Explaining*

examine bureaucracy cross-nationally, with most existing work focusing on the United States.[10] This lack of attention has led to two common, but ultimately misleading conclusions about how bureaucracy shapes the judgment of states.

The first is that bureaucratic participation in foreign policy decision-making tends to increase the chance of miscalculation. In this view, bureaucracy is fundamentally and intrinsically flawed.[11] Even in everyday language, the terms "bureaucracy" and "bureaucratic" are used to describe inefficiency, red tape, and excessive formality that get in the way of common-sense solutions to even simple problems. While the charges against bureaucratic organizations are many, one common indictment centers on the idea that their parochial interests give rise to narrow-minded lobbying, pressures for social conformity, and logrolling.[12] The unwieldiness of the bureaucracy stands in contrast to the wisdom of individual leaders, who instead "act decisively and purposefully" in support of more "important" and "long term" goals.[13] As such, incorporating bureaucrats into the leader's decision-making process can easily degrade judgment. As the saying goes, when you ask a committee to design a horse, you end up with a camel.

One of the assumptions underpinning this conclusion is that institutional design offers few remedies to curb bureaucratic pathologies in foreign policy decision-making. Graham Allison's canonical work, for instance, casts considerable doubt on institutional solutions to bureaucratic problems, suggesting that the "layers of complexity" inside the

---

the *Cuban Missile Crisis*, 2nd ed. (New York: Longman, 1999), 266. On first-wave scholarship, see I. M. Destler, *Presidents, Bureaucrats and Foreign Policy: The Politics of Organizational Reform* (Princeton: Princeton University Press, 1972); Morton H. Halperin and Priscilla Clapp, *Bureaucratic Politics and Foreign Policy*, 2nd ed. (Washington, DC: Brookings Institution Press, 2006); Alexander L. George, *Presidential Decisionmaking in Foreign Policy: The Effective Use of Information and Advice* (Boulder: Westview Press, 1980). On appraising Allison's models, see Jonathan Bendor and Thomas H. Hammond, "Rethinking Allison's Models," *American Political Science Review* 86, no. 2 (1992): 301–322; David A. Welch, "The Organizational Process and Bureaucratic Politics Paradigms: Retrospect and Prospect," *International Security* 17, no. 2 (1992): 112–146. See also Scott D. Sagan, *The Limits of Safety: Organizations, Accidents, and Nuclear Weapons* (Princeton: Princeton University Press, 1995).

[10] Welch, "The Organizational Process and Bureaucratic Politics Paradigms," 128–129.
[11] Zegart, *Flawed by Design*, 10.
[12] Allison and Zelikow, *Essence of Decision*; Irving L. Janis, *Victims of Groupthink: A Psychological Study of Foreign-Policy Decisions and Fiascoes* (Boston: Houghton Mifflin, 1972); Jack Snyder, *Myths of Empire: Domestic Politics and International Ambition* (Ithaca: Cornell University Press, 1991). For a recent critique, see Stephen M. Walt, *The Hell of Good Intentions: America's Foreign Policy Elite and the Decline of US Primacy* (New York: Farrar, Straus & Giroux, 2018).
[13] Daniel L. Byman and Kenneth M. Pollack, "Let Us Now Praise Great Men: Bringing the Statesman Back In," *International Security* 25, no. 4 (2001): 142.

state apparatus are essentially beyond repair.[14] Another review of the field similarly summarizes, "Since the Cold War, we have learned that good judgment does not depend on having smart advice" or "a coherent, well-run bureaucratic organization [...] no one organizational structure is best."[15] Many policymakers agree. Former U.S. National Security Advisor Henry Kissinger, for instance, argues that "a large bureaucracy, *however organized* [...] confuses wise policy with smooth administration."[16]

A second common misconception is that bureaucracy shapes international behavior in ways that are too idiosyncratic to draw systematic conclusions.[17] In many cases, country specialists have performed the Herculean task of documenting the byzantine details of specific bureaucratic organizations at particular moments in time. We know much about, for example, bodies like the National Security Council in the United States, the Committee of Imperial Defence in the United Kingdom, and the Central Military Commission in China.[18] Yet we know comparatively little about such organizations in aggregate, in large part because the field has yet to establish a theoretical framework by which to systematically compare the most consequential attributes of their design.

Both conclusions require revision. First, this book's theory and findings call into question the view that bureaucracy necessarily degrades foreign policy judgment. The findings instead show that, under a specific set of institutional conditions, the information that bureaucracy collects and processes tends to *help* leaders avoid miscalculation when deciding between war and peace. This perspective aligns with what scholars of other bureaucratic domains have long noted: institutional design and

---

[14] Allison and Zelikow, *Essence of Decision*, 273.
[15] Deborah Welch Larson, "Good Judgment in Foreign Policy: Social Psychological Perspectives," in *Good Judgment in Foreign Policy: Theory and Application* (New York: Rowman & Littlefield, 2003), 3–4. See also Patrick J. Haney, *Organizing for Foreign Policy Crises* (Ann Arbor: University of Michigan Press, 1997), 125.
[16] Henry Kissinger, *White House Years* (Boston: Little, Brown & Company, 1979), 39. Emphasis added.
[17] Allison and Zelikow, *Essence of Decision*, 257; John P. Burke and Fred L. Greenstein, *How Presidents Test Reality: Decisions on Vietnam, 1954 and 1965* (New York: Russell Sage Foundation, 1989), 274–275. Alternatively, some argue that bureaucracy simply does not matter in the most important decisions in international politics. For the classic articulation, see Stephen D. Krasner, "Are Bureaucracies Important? (or Allison Wonderland)," *Foreign Policy*, no. 7 (1972): 159–179.
[18] John Gans, *White House Warriors: How the National Security Council Transformed the American Way of War* (New York: W.W. Norton & Company, 2019); Nicholas d'Ombrain, *War Machinery and High Policy: Defence Administration in Peacetime Britain, 1902–1914* (New York: Oxford University Press, 1973); David M. Lampton, ed., *The Making of Chinese Foreign and Security Policy in the Era of Reform, 1978–2000* (Stanford: Stanford University Press, 2001).

structure matter for performance.[19] The institutional levers for managing the national security bureaucracy are no rustier than those managing core domestic issues. Thus, certain types of institutions indeed feature the pathologies that dominate our understanding of bureaucracy in the study of international relations, but other types ameliorate them.

Second, these differences in the institutional relationships between leaders and their national security bureaucracies are systematic. Institutional differences establish predictable patterns of how bureaucrats comport themselves and, in turn, how foreign policy decision-making proceeds. Just as scholars of comparative politics have been able to study systematic differences in state capacity in other domains, we can make systematic comparisons across the institutional relationships between leaders and their national security bureaucracy.[20] Unpacking these differences improves our understanding of the conditions under which international conflict rooted in inaccurate assessments is more likely to occur.

The Argument in Brief

National security institutions help explain when and why states miscalculate on the road to war. These periods of international crisis do not usually emerge by happenstance. They are more commonly the result of deliberate decisions by political leaders who weigh costs and benefits. On the one hand, some crises allow states to advance their goals, prompting adversaries to make concessions. On the other hand, crises raise the risk of broader conflict and, for those that escalate, can impart devastating

---

[19] On domestic bureaucracy, see John D. Huber and Charles R. Shipan, *Deliberate Discretion? The Institutional Foundations of Bureaucratic Autonomy* (New York: Cambridge University Press, 2002); Sean Gailmard and John W. Patty, *Learning While Governing: Expertise and Accountability in the Executive Branch* (Chicago: University of Chicago Press, 2012); Mai Hassan, *Regime Threats, and State Solutions: Bureaucratic Loyalty and Embeddedness in Kenya* (New York: Cambridge University Press, 2020). On bureaucracy in international organizations, see Michael N. Barnett and Martha Finnemore, "The Politics, Power, and Pathologies of International Organizations," *International Organization* 53, no. 4 (1999): 699–732; Tana Johnson, *Organizational Progeny: Why Governments Are Losing Control over the Proliferating Structures of Global Governance* (New York: Oxford University Press, 2014); Julia Gray, "Life, Death, or Zombie? The Vitality of International Organizations," *International Studies Quarterly* 62, no. 1 (2018): 1–13.

[20] Peter B. Evans, Dietrich Rueschemeyer, and Theda Skocpol, *Bringing the State Back In* (New York: Cambridge University Press, 1985); Peter Evans and James E. Rauch, "Bureaucracy and Growth: A Cross-National Analysis of the Effects of 'Weberian' State Structures on Economic Growth," *American Sociological Review* 62, no. 5 (1999): 748–765; Carl Dahlström and Victor Lapuente, *Organizing Leviathan: Politicians, Bureaucrats, and the Making of Good Government* (New York: Cambridge University Press, 2017).

human and economic costs. As a general rule, decision-makers prefer to avoid triggering crises that fail to accomplish their goals because such crises impart costs but do not deliver benefits. Variation in institutional design shapes the likelihood that decision-makers make these decisions about crisis initiation based on inaccurate propositions about the state of the world.

National security institutions can be divided into different types, each of which shapes the likelihood of miscalculation in different ways. The first design type, *integrated* institutions, establishes two types of state capacity. First, integrated institutions ease the leader's costs of searching for information during decision-making. Inclusive bodies for decision-making and coordination create opportunities for bureaucrats to shape policy and motivate them to search for information that leaders demand. Further, such bodies reduce the costs of relaying information from one actor to another. Together, lowering information search costs allows the bureaucracy to provide more information critical to assessing a state's prospects, such as the probable outcome, the expected costs, and the alternative strategies available to decision-makers.

Second, integrated institutions allow bureaucracies to access each other's information. This is important because a leader's access to *more* information does not necessarily mean their access to *quality* information. Lowering the costs of information sharing throughout the machinery of the state helps bureaucrats know when their own information is valuable to leaders, particularly when its value is set against the background of what other bureaucracies know. Just as important, it allows bureaucrats to police each other, serving as a check on the information passed on by bureaucracies to the leader. These two design features work in tandem to provide more and higher quality information. Leaders sitting atop integrated institutions are thus best positioned to determine which crises are likely to advance the state's goals. In short, institutions that force bureaucracies to battle internally tend to avoid unsuccessful battles externally.

In comparison, other types of national security institutions raise the risk of miscalculation in international crises. Each design deviates from integrated institutions by removing one of their key features. One alternative design is a *siloed* institution, which impedes horizontal information flow between bureaucracies. Although leaders receive more information, it tends to be of lower quality because bureaucrats can neither access nor check each other's reporting. This creates a distinct pathway to miscalculation, in which leaders initiate international crises based on inaccurate bureaucratic information.

A second alternative design is a *fragmented* institution, which insulates the leader's decision-making processes from the bureaucracy and raises costs for bureaucrats to relay information to leaders. This lowers the bureaucracy's motives to search for information and develop expertise, as no amount of effort can shape the leader's decision-making. Erosion of competence and expertise discourages bureaucrats from speaking truth to power. Fragmented institutions thus create a distinct pathway to miscalculation by delivering a less complete set of information to leaders. Bits of readily available information fail to reach leaders deciding between peace and conflict. Taken together, the theoretical framework suggests that domestic constraints on a leader's information created by siloed and fragmented institutions make miscalculation more likely than when integrated institutions are present.

Why do some states possess national security institutions that increase the likelihood of miscalculation? The answer is that leaders wield considerable power to shape their institutions and, as such, their choices are deeply political. This discretion is greatest at the apex of the state system. While leaders cannot necessarily create or destroy national security bureaucracies at will, they retain an outsized influence over whether and how the bureaucracy is or is not integrated into their decision-making process.

For leaders making these institutional choices, integrated institutions are both a resource and a liability. On the one hand, integrated institutions empower bureaucrats to provide more and better information that helps the leader derive more accurate assessments and make foreign policy blunders less likely. On the other hand, integrated institutions empower the bureaucracy to shape broader debates between leaders and their domestic audiences.[21] More competent bureaucrats might offer better information, but competence could also be deployed to harm the leader's political prospects. Competent bureaucrats can more easily imperil the leader's agenda (and potentially survival), sometimes through opposing the leader in debates with other elites and the mass public – and sometimes through violently removing the leader from office. Thus, despite the benefits they offer to effective decision-making, integrated institutions can also have underlying risks.

Leaders resolve this trade-off based on two aspects of their political environment. That is, different leaders choose different institutions at different times based on how they perceive the costs and benefits of bureaucratic advice. First, leaders tend to choose integrated institutions only when they believe a well-informed bureaucracy does not threaten their political prospects. Under such conditions, the leader's

---

[21] On how advisers can punish leaders through weighing in on policy debates among leaders, legislators, and the mass public, see Elizabeth N. Saunders, "Leaders, Advisers, and the Political Origins of Elite Support for War," *Journal of Conflict Resolution* 62, no. 10 (2018): 2118–2149.

trade-off is easily resolved in favor of the higher quality information that integrated institutions offer. By contrast, leaders opt out of integrated institutions when they believe that the bureaucracy possesses the capability and intent to politically harm them. Despite their inefficiencies, siloed and fragmented institutions are appealing to such leaders, as a restricted information flow helps to neutralize the threat that well-informed bureaucracies pose.

Second, once deciding to deviate from integrated institutions, leaders face a choice between siloing and fragmentation. One of the most important considerations underpinning the leader's choice is the substance of their agenda. Leaders are more likely to choose fragmented institutions when their political survival hinges on domestic issues. A domestic focus reduces the value of bureaucratic advice on national security matters, meaning leaders profit less from the quality advice. The leader's preference changes when international issues become more salient, particularly when threats from abroad raise the costs of miscalculation. Siloed institutions therefore offer leaders a middle ground that hedges against both the threat they perceive from the bureaucracy and the international issues upon which their agenda hinges. Leaders accept a bit of political vulnerability in exchange for better, though not the best, information available.

In sum, variation in the type of institutions that a leader chooses reflects their resolution of a trade-off between good information and political survival, which has important downstream consequences for the risk that leaders miscalculate.

Contributions

While our understanding of the politics of national security institutions is still in its early stages, some existing scholarship provides a few alternative perspectives with which this the theory and findings presented here are in dialogue.

Bureaucracies, Information, and Competitive Dialogue

Perhaps the most prominent theoretical tradition on the national security bureaucracy emphasizes the deleterious effects of its parochial interests. This "interest group model" posits that bureaucracies can degrade judgment by taking actions that leaders have not approved or by compelling leaders to adopt policies they believe unwise.[22]

---

[22] Allison and Zelikow, *Essence of Decision*, 260; Destler, *Presidents, Bureaucrats and Foreign Policy*, 57–59; Halperin and Clapp, *Bureaucratic Politics and Foreign Policy*, 25–27. See

While the interest group model has undoubtedly produced valuable insights, particularly into military organizations, it also has several noteworthy limitations that the book helps to address.[23] First and foremost, the field's conventional focus on how bureaucracies disobey leaders overlooks perhaps its most important pathway to shaping foreign policy decision-making: the ability to inform and persuade leaders. On matters of war and peace, decision-making is fundamentally hierarchical – and leaders have the final say. Bureaucratic influence manifests through the capacity to inform a leader's choices. What information, recommendations, and counsel reaches a leader's desk has profound implications for how they understand the situation they face. Bureaucratic power is the power to shape the leader's thinking.

Second, institutions play a pivotal role in determining whether leaders can effectively transform bureaucratic influence into a force for good in foreign policy decision-making. Configurations that set bureaucracies in competition effectively prevent any single perspective from dominating. To underscore this point, consider the traditional civil-military application of the interest group model, which argues that suboptimal assessments are more likely when a leader lacks control over the military.[24] Yet the logic of national security institutions suggests that mere dominance over a single bureaucracy is an insufficient condition for acquiring quality information. Leaders need institutions that incorporate multiple bureaucratic actors in order to mitigate the risk of biased counsel.

---

also Jean A. Garrison, *The Games Advisors Play: Foreign Policy in the Nixon and Carter Administrations* (College Station: Texas A&M University Press, 1999), 21–26; Daniel W. Drezner, *The Ideas Industry* (New York: Oxford University Press, 2017).

[23] On civil-military relations and international conflict, see among others Samuel P. Huntington, *The Soldier and the State: The Theory and Politics of Civil-Military Relations* (Cambridge: Harvard University Press, 1957), 69–70; Morris Janowitz, *The Professional Soldier: A Social and Political Portrait* (Glencoe: The Free Press, 1960), 230–231; Jack Snyder, *The Ideology of the Offensive: Military Decision Making and the Disasters of 1914* (Ithaca: Cornell University Press, 1989), 24–30; Michael C. Desch, *Civilian Control of the Military: The Changing Security Environment* (Baltimore: Johns Hopkins University Press, 1999), 17–19; Richard K. Betts, *Soldiers, Statesmen, and Cold War Crises* (New York: Columbia University Press, 1991), 3–15; Elizabeth Kier, *Imagining War: French and British Military Doctrine between the Wars* (Princeton: Princeton University Press, 1997), 27–32; Eliot A. Cohen, *Supreme Command: Soldiers, Statesmen and Leadership in Wartime* (New York: The Free Press, 2002), 208–224; Peter D. Feaver, *Armed Servants: Agency, Oversight, and Civil-Military Relations* (Cambridge: Harvard University Press, 2003), 63–68; Ryan Grauer, *Commanding Military Power* (New York: Cambridge University Press, 2016), 35–43.

[24] Risa Brooks, *Shaping Strategy: The Civil-Military Politics of Strategic Assessment* (Princeton: Princeton University Press, 2008), 45. Brooks notes that assessment quality stems from the balance of power between civilian and military actors, rather than the "efficiency-enhancing properties" of institutions to which this book draws attention. See 19–20.

This perspective shifts the focus from conventional frameworks highlighting the interplay between civilian leaders and military subordinates to a broader consideration of how civilian bureaucrats participate in the leader's decision-making. The integration of various types of civilian bureaucracies, including diplomatic and intelligence ministries, emerges as a pivotal determinant of whether leaders receive the quality counsel they seek.

This logic complements and extends insights from related literature on group decision-making, which proposes that increasing the number of participants improves the group's judgment.[25] Yet simply having multiple players integrated into national security institutions proves to be insufficient. Instead, two characteristics of integrated institutions are critical to delivering better information to leaders.

First, participants must possess information and expertise to contribute to crisis decision-making.[26] While every crisis is different, several informational demands are common to all: knowing the adversary's willingness to stand firm and the state's corresponding options at the negotiating table, as well as the balance of material capabilities and options on the battlefield. Each type of information clusters in different corners of the government – the former in diplomatic bureaucracies and the latter in defense bureaucracies.[27] Thus, at a minimum, leaders tend to benefit from institutions that facilitate consultation with these specific bureaucracies before starting international confrontations.

Second, participants must have different ways of seeing the world. Inclusion of diplomatic and defense bureaucracies is helpful in this regard because each tends to house individuals with quite different perspectives and worldviews. Whereas diplomatic ministries tend to attract and train individuals in the art of compromise and negotiation, defense ministries tend to select and socialize individuals to think about the less cooperative

---

[25] George, *Presidential Decisionmaking in Foreign Policy*, 191–208; Allison and Zelikow, *Essence of Decision*, 265, 271; Mark Schafer and Scott Crichlow, *Groupthink versus High-Quality Decision Making in International Relations* (New York: Columbia University Press, 2010), 65; Paul 't Hart, Eric Stern, and Bengt Sundelius, *Beyond Groupthink: Political Group Dynamics and Foreign Policy-Making* (Ann Arbor: University of Michigan Press, 1997). For an alternative account emphasizing the limits of larger and more diverse groups, see Alex Mintz and Carly Wayne, "The Polythink Syndrome and Elite Group Decision-Making," *Political Psychology* 37, no. S1 (2016): 3–21.

[26] Existing scholarship on "multiple advocacy" provides comparatively little insight into which types of players are important – and whether bureaucracy is even necessary at all. Alexander George, for instance, notes that there should be representatives from "different parts" of the government, but does not specify which organizations these include. See Alexander L. George, "The Case for Multiple Advocacy in Making Foreign Policy," *American Political Science Review* 66, no. 3 (1972): 751.

[27] Robert Schub, "Informing the Leader: Bureaucracies and International Crises," *American Political Science Review* 116, no. 4 (2022): 1460–1476.

and more violent side of international politics. Such differences in perspective prove critical to generating meaningful communication between the national security bureaucracy and the leader. It is precisely because these bureaucracies have different ways of seeing international politics that they are more likely to contest each other's arguments. Leaders thus end up possessing more and better quality information because of the competitive dialogue to which integrated institutions give rise. In sum, leaders gain a clearer picture of the wars they are considering fighting when they put bureaucracies "at war" with one another beforehand.

These insights complement two adjacent literatures as well. First, they speak to a well-developed strand of research examining the relationship between military coup-proofing and battlefield performance in authoritarian regimes. Most notably, Caitlin Talmadge finds that dictatorships perform poorly on the battlefield when they structure their military in ways that prevent coups.[28] One of the tensions that this literature leaves unanswered, however, is why such dictatorships often *initiate* conflicts despite the weakness that coup-proofing imposes on military effectiveness. The logic of national security institutions offers an intuitive answer to this puzzle. Coup-proofing strategies do not simply make some dictatorships less powerful. They also make them less effective in identifying the weakness of their bargaining position.[29] Moreover, the political logic of national security institutions extends to a range of situations far broader than the current literature on authoritarian coup-proofing appreciates. We shall see much the same logic apply in democracies and autocracies in which the threat of military coup is low, but leaders nevertheless fear other types of sanctions from diplomatic, defense, and intelligence bureaucrats.[30]

This theory and findings also contribute to a wide body of scholarship examining the quality of intelligence assessments.[31] Existing studies

[28] Caitlin Talmadge, *The Dictator's Army: Battlefield Effectiveness in Authoritarian Regimes* (Ithaca: Cornell University Press, 2015), 13–18. More broadly, see Victor Shih, *Coalitions of the Weak: Elite Politics in China from Mao's Stratagem to the Rise of Xi* (New York: Cambridge University Press, 2022).

[29] For a case study of inaccurate assessments in Iraq under Saddam Hussein, see Kevin M. Woods et al., *Iraqi Perspectives Project* (Norfolk: U.S. Joint Center for Operational Analysis, 2006), 25–38.

[30] On military coup-proofing, see Donald L. Horowitz, *Ethnic Groups in Conflict* (Berkeley: University of California Press, 1985), 532–559; James T. Quinlivan, "Coup-Proofing: Its Practice and Consequences in the Middle East," *International Security* 24, no. 2 (1999): 134–135; Erica De Bruin, "Preventing Coups d'État: How Counterbalancing Works," *Journal of Conflict Resolution* 62, no. 7 (2018): 1433–1458.

[31] On intelligence failures, see Roberta Wohlstetter, *Pearl Harbor: Warning and Decision* (Stanford: Stanford University Press, 1962); Richard K. Betts, "Analysis, War, and Decision: Why Intelligence Failures Are Inevitable," *World Politics* 31, no. 1 (1978): 61–89; Uri Bar-Joseph and Rose McDermott, *Intelligence Success and Failure: The Human Factor* (New York: Oxford University Press, 2017). See also the literature on the

on intelligence emphasize the conditions under which organizations produce accurate assessments, but has comparatively little to say about how this can shape the crisis strategies that leaders choose.[32] The theory presented here instead suggests that intelligence organizations matter only under a specific set of institutional conditions that allows information to flow effectively from the bureaucracy to the leader. In order for intelligence to shape decision-making, leaders need institutional structures that instill confidence in the soundness of the information that intelligence organizations deliver.

Information and Accountability

The logic of national security institutions also shows how political accountability in both democratic and authoritarian regimes is insufficient to explain why states miscalculate. Conventional wisdom holds that democracies (and dictatorships under collective rule) should be less prone to blunder because political leaders fear they will be punished by domestic audiences.[33] But just because leaders are held accountable for policy outcomes does not mean that they are equally well positioned to assess which policies are likely to work. The relationship between leaders and bureaucracies plays a centrally important role in identifying which foreign policies are likely to fail before they are tried. Without effective institutions, even accountable leaders are prone to choosing foreign policies that seem promising for securing their survival in office, but in fact end up resulting in strategic quagmires that instead contribute to their political demise.

---

psychological of intelligence analysis and the procedures for managing intelligence production (e.g., standardization of language regarding certainty and probability). Loch K. Johnson, *Secret Agencies: US Intelligence in a Hostile World* (New Haven: Yale University Press, 1996); Robert Jervis, *Why Intelligence Fails: Lessons from the Iranian Revolution and the Iraq War* (Ithaca: Cornell University Press, 2010); Philip E. Tetlock and Barbara A. Mellers, "Intelligent Management of Intelligence Agencies: Beyond Accountability Ping-Pong," *American Psychologist* 66, no. 6 (2011): 542–554; Jeffrey A. Friedman, *War and Chance: Assessing Uncertainty in International Politics* (New York: Oxford University Press, 2019).

[32] For an important exception, see Erik J. Dahl, *Intelligence and Surprise Attack: Failure and Success from Pearl Harbor to 9/11 and Beyond* (Washington, DC: Georgetown University Press, 2013), 23. Dahl focuses on leader "receptivity" rather than the institutions that make bureaucratic information provision more likely to shape leader choices.

[33] Bruce Bueno De Mesquita et al., "An Institutional Explanation of the Democratic Peace," *American Political Science Review* 93, no. 4 (1999): 791–807; Bruce M. Russett and John R. Oneal, *Triangulating Peace: Democracy, Interdependence, and International Organizations* (New York: Norton, 2001); Kenneth A. Schultz, *Democracy and Coercive Diplomacy* (New York: Cambridge University Press, 2001); Dan Reiter and Allan C. Stam, *Democracies at War* (Princeton: Princeton University Press, 2002); Jessica L. Weeks, *Dictators at War and Peace* (Ithaca: Cornell University Press, 2014).

In a general sense, these two theoretical perspectives are complementary. The risk of miscalculation is curbed not simply by punishing leaders for poor policy outcomes but also by providing them with the best possible information to avoid misadventure in the first place. But the agency that leaders retain – and the possibility that some leaders see the bureaucracy as a potential challenger to their political survival – means that not all leaders are well situated to adopt the institutions that curb the risk of miscalculation.[34] As a result, some democracies possess siloed and fragmented institutions, while some dictatorships feature integrated ones. This means that bureaucratic politics in democratic states may at times exhibit many of the same pathologies found in authoritarian states, while bureaucratic politics in dictatorships can sometimes yield quite effective bureaucratic advice.

The Political Origins of National Security Institutions

Finally, the theory and findings contribute to existing scholarship on the origins of national security institutions. In this regard, past studies offer two, diametrically opposed intuitions. One perspective emphasizes the overwhelming stability and inflexibility of institutional design. For example, Amy Zegart's pathbreaking study of the American national security bureaucracy argues that initial design choices (or "birthmarks") dominate institutional evolution. As Zegart writes, these "founding moments" in a state's history "loom large" in subsequent years, such that initial design choices are "difficult to change."[35]

A second perspective suggests that leader personality dominates, if not determines, institutional design.[36] Popular images of John F. Kennedy

---

[34] On leader agency to make such choices, see Susan D. Hyde and Elizabeth N. Saunders, "Recapturing Regime Type in International Relations: Leaders, Institutions, and Agency Space," *International Organization* 74, no. 2 (2020): 363–395; Elizabeth N. Saunders, "Elites in the Making and Breaking of Foreign Policy," *Annual Review of Political Science* 25 (2022): 219–240.

[35] Zegart, *Flawed by Design*, 42–43. While Zegart notes that the preferences of political leaders and "exogenous events" may also shape institutional design, she is careful to rank the importance of initial design above either concern.

[36] For recent work on leaders, see Rose McDermott, *Presidential Leadership, Illness, and Decision Making* (New York: Cambridge University Press, 2007); Alexandre Debs and Hein E. Goemans, "Regime Type, the Fate of Leaders, and War," *American Political Science Review* 104, no. 3 (2010): 430–445; Elizabeth N. Saunders, *Leaders at War: How Presidents Shape Military Interventions* (Ithaca: Cornell University Press, 2011); Jeff D. Colgan, "Domestic Revolutionary Leaders and International Conflict," *World Politics* 65, no. 4 (2013): 656–690; Keren Yarhi-Milo, *Knowing the Adversary: Leaders, Intelligence, and Assessment of Intentions in International Relations* (Princeton: Princeton University Press, 2014); Weeks, *Dictators at War and Peace*; Matthew Fuhrmann and Michael C. Horowitz, "When Leaders Matter: Rebel Experience and Nuclear Proliferation," *The Journal of Politics* 77, no. 1 (2014): 72–87; Michael C. Horowitz, Allan C.

standing alone in the Oval Office and of Harry Truman's desk placard inscribed with the motto "the buck stops here" capture the common intuition that it is leaders who chart a state's path.[37] The personalities and management styles that leaders bring with them into office motivate leaders to shape institutions in ways that suit their managerial predilections. Decision-making processes are, as I. M. Destler argues, simply a "chameleon" that takes its color from the "character and personality" of the leader.[38]

Yet these insights into the origins of institutional design are incomplete. When we widen the analytical aperture to consider national security institutions across the full range of states in the modern world, we find that changes in institutional design are strikingly frequent. In fact, the empirical analysis shows that nearly two in five leaders since 1946 modified their institutions substantially enough to shift from one type to another. Moreover, it finds that these changes were not predetermined by leader dispositions. The empirical analysis shows that, of the leaders that changed their institutions, the majority did so years into their tenure and over one-third did so more than once.

In short, initial institutional choices and leader characteristics may shape design, but they do not predetermine it. Examining the political trade-offs that leaders face helps explain both continuity and change. On the one hand, when political conditions remain constant, national security institutions are more likely to remain the same even across leaders with dissimilar personalities. On the other hand, sharp changes in the political environment can prompt change even during the same leader's tenure.

Stam, and Cali M. Ellis, *Why Leaders Fight* (New York: Cambridge University Press, 2015); Sarah E. Croco, *Peace at What Price?* (New York: Cambridge University Press, 2015); Jonathan Renshon, *Fighting for Status: Hierarchy and Conflict in World Politics* (Princeton: Princeton University Press, 2017); Marcus Holmes, *Face-to-Face Diplomacy: Social Neuroscience and International Relations* (New York: Cambridge University Press, 2018); Brian C. Rathbun, *Reasoning of State: Realists, Romantics and Rationality in International Relations* (New York: Cambridge University Press, 2019); Roseanne W. McManus, "Crazy Like a Fox? Are Leaders with Reputations for Madness More Successful at International Coercion?," *British Journal of Political Science* 51, no. 1 (2021): 275–293; Rachel Elizabeth Whitlark, *All Options on the Table: Leaders, Preventive War, and Nuclear Proliferation* (Ithaca: Cornell University Press, 2021).

[37] Richard E. Neustadt, *Presidential Power and the Modern Presidents: The Politics of Leadership from Roosevelt to Reagan* (New York: Simon & Schuster, 1991), 17; Burke and Greenstein, *How Presidents Test Reality*, 289.

[38] I. M. Destler, "National Security Advice to US Presidents: Some Lessons from Thirty Years," *World Politics* 29, no. 2 (1977): 143. See also George, *Presidential Decisionmaking in Foreign Policy*, 145–168; Burke and Greenstein, *How Presidents Test Reality*, 23, 272; Thomas Preston, *The President and His Inner Circle: Leadership Style and the Advisory Process in Foreign Policy Making* (New York: Columbia University Press, 2001), 7–12.

Plan of the Book

The chapters that follow ask two key questions about national security institutions. First, what explains why different leaders at different times adopt different institutional designs? Second, what are the consequences of this institutional variation for the risk of miscalculation on the road to war? This book answers these questions through a combination of theory, cross-national statistical analysis, and in-depth tracing of historical cases.

Chapter 2 develops the theoretical argument in detail. Chapter 3 introduces the *National Security Institutions Data Set*, an original, cross-national resource on national security institutions from 1946 to 2015 across 152 countries. The data set is the first of its kind to systematically code institutional variation in how states manage the broad array of national security bureaucracies common in the world today. These data allow us not only to examine just how much the management of national security bureaucracies has changed over the past seven decades but also facilitate the first systematic, cross-national analysis of how bureaucracy shapes crisis behavior.

Exploring these data yields three significant findings. First, states change their institutions more frequently than many traditional accounts would suggest. These changes often happen when there is no leader turnover transition or transition between democracy and autocracy, suggesting that neither leader personality nor regime type is a sufficient explanation for the institutional variation we observe. Second, a series of statistical tests provides evidence suggesting that, across the modern world, states with integrated institutions perform better in international crises than siloed and fragmented institutions. Specifically, states with integrated institutions are significantly less likely than those with fragmented or siloed institutions to initiate international crises in which the state fails to achieve their core strategic objectives. Finally, an additional set of statistical analyses show that institutional designs change systematically in response to the leader's political environment.

The quantitative analysis provides a point of departure for detailed tracing of the origins and consequences of national security institutions in four case countries: China, India, Pakistan, and the United States. This methodological versatility is important because one might rightly wonder if broad statistical patterns help us explain individual historical cases. The case studies aim to provide a granular and nuanced picture of institutions, while still connecting idiosyncrasy back to theoretical principles. The cases rely extensively on interviews and archival materials collected across China, India, Pakistan, Taiwan, the United Kingdom, and the United States. Furthermore, the chapters on China, India, and the United States introduce new microlevel institutional data detailing the frequency of meetings and correspondence between leaders and bureaucratic advisers within each country.

The four case countries – China, the United States, India, and Pakistan – were chosen to demonstrate the theory's broad applicability across different regimes (i.e., democracy and dictatorship). Each chapter focuses on shifts in the design of national security institutions *within* the same underlying regime. It first analyzes the reasons why the institutional change occurred. The analysis then explores episodes of crisis decision-making under different institutional designs within the same regime. Each case seeks to illustrate that the miscalculation might have been avoided with information that the bureaucracy possessed at the time and that the national security institution was the reason this information was not incorporated into the leader's strategic choice.

The case analysis begins with an environment in which existing research on political accountability predicts that bureaucracy should exert little effect: personalist dictatorship. Chapter 4 shows how Mao Zedong integrated China's national security institutions early in his tenure but fragmented them as he began to worry about the loyalty of the party's bureaucracy toward the end of his life. The chapter compares China's bargaining with the United States in 1962 to that with the Soviet Union in 1969, showing how fragmented institutions led to several miscalculations in 1969, whereas integrated institutions helped to avoid similarly inaccurate conclusions in 1962.

Chapter 5 then examines two periods after Mao's death, both characterized by nonpersonalist rule. Suboptimal national security institutions persisted for decades after Mao's death in part because political leaders continued to view the bureaucracy with suspicion. China's leaders initially guarded against bureaucratic threats with fragmented institutions, which provided political cover for the transformational economic reforms of the post-Mao era. Then, in the 1980s, the postrevolutionary generation of Chinese leaders, whose domestic agendas were less ambitious, instead settled on siloed institutions. The chapter argues that these institutional designs help explain miscalculations during both the 1979 Sino-Vietnamese War and the 2001 EP-3 Crisis.

Chapters 2–4 turn to democratic and military regimes. Chapter 6 shows that, despite having inherited institutions modeled on the United Kingdom's Committee of Imperial Defense – the same body that served as the blueprint for the U.S. National Security Council – Indian Prime Minister Jawaharlal Nehru redesigned his country's national security institutions in order to protect his domestic political agenda and ensure control over the national security bureaucracy. As the risk of praetorianism subsided, however, India gradually shifted toward a more integrated design. The chapter argues that fragmented institutions hindered

Nehru's calculations during bargaining with China, ultimately resulting in defeat during the Sino-Indian War in 1962. The analysis then contrasts India's miscalculations during the 1962 Sino-Indian War with its more effective institutional performance during the 2001–2002 Twin Peaks Crisis.

Chapter 7 extends the argument to military regimes, while also presenting a counterfactual to the Indian case. Persistent threat from the national security bureaucracy in Pakistan precluded the possibility of institutional reforms. Even after civilian leaders took control of the country in the late 1980s, pathologies associated with siloed institutions led to miscalculations on the basis of which Prime Minister Nawaz Sharif launched the 1999 Kargil War.

Chapter 8 applies the theory to the United States. While most U.S. presidents chose to adopt or maintain integrated institutions during the early Cold War, the combination of Johnson's perceived threat from the bureaucracy and his transformative domestic agenda led to an institutional setup unusually fragmented for a stable democracy. This institutional choice helps explain why the information that Johnson received on the eve of the escalation in Vietnam was less complete and of lower quality than what other U.S. leaders worked with during other crises earlier in the Cold War.

Finally, Chapter 9 concludes by reviewing the empirical analyses and discussing avenues for future research. Most broadly, the findings collectively show that states do not suffer equally from the pathologies that we commonly associate with national security bureaucracy. A set of institutional remedies exists to make bureaucracy a more effective contributor to decision-making. The crux of this institutional remedy is healthy competition between multiple bureaucracies during deliberations before states charge headfirst into international conflict. Such institutions reduce the chance that leaders base their choices on inaccurate expectations of what they will achieve after the fighting begins. Unfortunately, the institutions that are best situated to deliver the best advice also make leaders the most politically vulnerable. This political trade-off suggests that states may be more resistant to institutional reform than we might hope.

2   An Institutional Theory of Miscalculation

This chapter presents an institutional theory explaining why some leaders are more likely to miscalculate on the road to war. The central proposition is that leaders face a trade-off. They can design institutions that ensure they receive the best possible advice or they can design institutions that ensure the bureaucracy is powerless to threaten them.

This trade-off is discussed in two parts. The chapter first develops a simple theoretical framework describing how different national security institutions shape the availability of quality information to leaders. The framework identifies two dimensions along which these institutions vary: their capacity to search for information and the bureaucracy's access to information elsewhere within the state. It argues that leaders are best positioned to avoid miscalculation when they possess integrated institutions that increase search capacity and permit wide inter-bureaucratic access to information.

The theory next turns to the question of why leaders adopt nonintegrated institutions. After all, why choose an institution that degrades judgment? The reason is that while integrated institutions offer informational benefits, they can also impose political costs. By motivating bureaucrats to develop expertise and granting access to information, integrated institutions empower bureaucrats to use their competence and access to punish the leader. Leaders thus face a trade-off between high-quality bureaucratic information and vulnerability to bureaucratic sanction. Leaders resolve this trade-off based on their political environment. As such, different leaders adopt different institutions at different times.

Leaders, Bureaucracy, and International Crises: A Theoretical Framework

Why do some states miscalculate more often than others as they choose to initiate international crises? To answer this question, we must begin by examining how states initiate crises in the first place. International crises are situations in which decision-makers perceive a time-sensitive threat to their interests and a heightened possibility of military hostility.[1] They are the result of strategic choices made by states. More specifically, crises are the result of choices made by leaders – presidents, prime minister, dictators – who enjoy an outsized degree of authority in determining whether initiating an international crisis can achieve benefits at an acceptable cost.

Leaders make choices about crisis initiation in a purposeful manner. Namely, they weigh the benefits that they expect to reap from initiating a crisis against the costs that crisis will impose. All crises are gambles in which states struggle to show that they are willing to pay higher costs than their adversary to achieve their goals. On the one hand, international crises can advance the state's interests. States may use international crises to seize territory, to improve the balance of power, or to compel adversaries to make bargaining concessions. On the other hand, crises can also impose costs. International crises that escalate to fighting on the battlefield inflict a human and economic toll, detracting from the state's capacity to fight in the future and to provide economic benefits to society. Even in crises that do not escalate to violence, states pay costs to signal their willingness to fight if their demands are not met, whether through military mobilizations that drain state coffers or through public declarations that put the national honor on the line.

A leader's choice for crisis initiation is informed by judgments and projections about the situation they face. That is, leaders consider how international confrontations are likely to end before they make the fateful decision to start them. The nature of international crises implies that three types of information are central to a leader's choice. First, leaders need information about their *strategic options*, such as the different possible military and diplomatic strategies they might pursue. These include both the different strategies for which the leader can opt within a crisis, as well as the alternatives the state can pursue without triggering a crisis.

Second, leaders judge how costly potential crisis strategies will be relative to the strategies available apart from confrontation. Leaders presumably know the value that they assign to achieving their goals in a crisis. Yet leaders must project the countervailing *costs* that the crisis is likely to impose. Some crises require paying costs that exceed

---

[1] Michael Brecher and Jonathan Wilkenfeld, *A Study of Crisis* (Ann Arbor: University of Michigan Press, 1997), 3. On crisis bargaining, see James D. Morrow, "Capabilities, Uncertainty, and Resolve: A Limited Information Model of Crisis Bargaining," *American Journal of Political Science* 33, no. 4 (1989): 941–972; James D. Fearon, "Rationalist Explanations for War," *International Organization* 49, no. 3 (1995): 379–414; Christopher F. Gelpi, "Winners or Losers? Democracies in International Crisis, 1918–94," *American Political Science Review* 95, no. 3 (2001): 633–647; Todd S. Sechser, "Goliath's Curse: Coercive Threats and Asymmetric Power," *International Organization* 64, no. 4 (2010): 627–660.

the leader's limits. With perfect projections, leaders could choose to steer away from international confrontations in which the ultimate price exceed the amount the leader is willing to pay.

Finally, leaders judge the *probable outcomes* of the available strategies. That is, leaders project whether they are likely to be successful during the crisis and possible escalations to battlefield conflict, as well as whether such confrontations will translate into desired concessions from the adversary. With perfect projections about crisis outcomes, leaders can choose to avoid international crises in which the outcome does not advance the leader's interests beyond the status quo.[2]

The Leader's Informational Challenge

One of the central challenges that leaders face is that they lack complete information about the outcome and costs of initiating a crisis relative to other strategic alternatives available to the state.

Part of the leader's informational challenge is structural in nature. Uncertainty pervades international politics generally and international crises specifically. Crisis outcomes depend not only on chance events that no leader can anticipate but also on complex strategic interactions with adversaries whose motives and future choices are never perfectly known.[3] Adversaries obfuscate their capabilities, making it difficult to gauge the balance of power before international confrontations begin.[4] As William Wohlforth summarizes, "many interpretations" of the balance of power are "always possible."[5] Similarly, leaders lack complete information about their adversaries' resolve to resist the leader's demands during crisis.[6] That is, leaders do not know for sure the value that adversaries assign to territories or policies over which they are bargaining – and what costs they are willing to bear in order to get what they want.

---

[2] George suggests that leaders need to acquire information, to consider how policies will affect their interests, as well as to search for a range of options, to weigh costs and benefits, and to consider challenges to implementation. See George, *Presidential Decisionmaking in Foreign Policy*, 109.

[3] See, among others, Kenneth N. Waltz, *Theory of International Politics* (New York: McGraw-Hill, 1979), 91–92; Robert Jervis, "Cooperation under the Security Dilemma," *World Politics* 30, no. 2 (1978): 201; John J. Mearsheimer, *The Tragedy of Great Power Politics* (New York: W.W. Norton & Company, 2001), 31–32; Andrew H. Kydd, *Trust and Mistrust in International Relations* (Princeton: Princeton University Press, 2005), 10–11 Charles L. Glaser, *Rational Theory of International Politics: The Logic of Competition and Cooperation* (Princeton: Princeton University Press, 2010), 55.

[4] Branislav L. Slantchev, "Feigning Weakness," *International Organization* 64, no. 3 (2010): 357–388; David Lindsey, "Military Strategy, Private Information, and War," *International Studies Quarterly* 59, no. 4 (2015): 629–640.

[5] William Curti Wohlforth, *The Elusive Balance: Power and Perceptions during the Cold War* (Ithaca: Cornell University Press, 1993), 303.

[6] Fearon, "Rationalist Explanations for War."

Another part of the challenge stems from the leader's human limitations. The structure of the international system does not preclude leaders from attempting to manage it as best they can by searching for information. Yet leaders are constrained in their ability to perform the time-intensive task of searching for information concerning their crisis prospects.[7] As one report from the United Kingdom observes, leaders "cannot themselves be expected to be deep experts" on foreign and defense issues.[8] One historian notes that even in the early twentieth century, Austro-Hungarian Emperor Franz Joseph "found it impossible to master the oceans of information that came to his desk."[9] Soviet leader Leonid Brezhnev once remarked that his ability to look out at the world from the Kremlin depended entirely on "the papers" that reached his desk.[10] Even the available strategic options are often not immediately obvious to leaders.[11] In the wake of Iraq's invasion of Kuwait, for example, George H. W. Bush later admitted that he "had no idea what [U.S.] options were."[12] In short, information is costly for leaders to acquire.[13]

Constraints on information acquisition can cause leaders to miscalculate, which is defined as choosing a strategy based on an inaccurate proposition about the state of the world.[14] In the context of international crisis, miscalculation refers to situations in which leaders initiate an international confrontation based on inaccurate beliefs about the expected outcome. For instance, leaders might initiate a conflict believing

---

[7] James G. March and Herbert A. Simon, *Organizations* (New York: Wiley, 1958), 136–171; Allison and Zelikow, *Essence of Decision*, 143–158; Neustadt, *Presidential Power and the Modern Presidents*, 130; Ivo H. Daalder and I. M. Destler, *In the Shadow of the Oval Office: Profiles of the National Security Advisers and the Presidents They Served* (New York: Simon & Schuster, 2009), 181.

[8] United Kingdom House of Commons Defence Committee, "Decision-Making in Defence Policy: Eleventh Report of Session 2014–15," March 18, 2015, 37.

[9] Christopher Clark, *The Sleepwalkers: How Europe Went to War in 1914* (New York: Penguin, 2012), 183.

[10] Vladislav M. Zubok, *A Failed Empire: The Soviet Union in the Cold War from Stalin to Gorbachev* (Chapel Hill: University of North Carolina Press, 2009), 201.

[11] Irving L. Janis and Leon Mann, *Decision Making: A Psychological Analysis of Conflict, Choice, and Commitment* (New York: Free Press, 1977), 371; George, *Presidential Decisionmaking in Foreign Policy*, 23–24.

[12] George H. W. Bush and Brent Scowcroft, *A World Transformed* (New York: Alfred A. Knopf, 1998), 315.

[13] Downs, *Inside Bureaucracy*, 3.

[14] Note that miscalculation is similar to misperception in that both emphasize inaccurate propositions, but the former emphasizes beliefs that are linked to strategic choices. See Robert Jervis, *Perception and Misperception in International Politics* (Princeton: Princeton University Press, 1976); Yaacov Y. I. Vertzberger, *The World in Their Minds: Information Processing, Cognition, and Perception in Foreign Policy Decisionmaking* (Stanford: Stanford University Press, 1990); Charles A. Duelfer and Stephen Benedict Dyson, "Chronic Misperception and International Conflict: The US-Iraq Experience," *International Security* 36, no. 1 (2011): 75–76.

that their military enjoys an overwhelming numerical advantage in the number of troops deployed to the battlefield, when in fact the local balance of power is at parity. Similarly, leaders might start a crisis believing that their adversary will yield to their demands, when in fact the other state escalates the confrontation and imposes unanticipated costs.

Thus, the idea of miscalculation does not simply refer to the presence of uncertainty in the international system. Rather, the idea of miscalculation suggests that given the constraints of uncertainty, leaders sometimes derive beliefs that are at odds with the information available in the international system, information which a single leader cannot effectively collect and process on their own.

Bureaucracy offers one solution to alleviate the human limitations of information acquisition.[15] Leaders cannot alter the fundamental uncertainty of the international system, but they can delegate information collection and processing tasks to state organizations with capacities that extend beyond the leader's human limitations.[16] Moreover, leaders can further divide labor among bureaucrats to foster task specialization, allowing bureaucrats to develop knowledge and expertise in specific domains. In short, leaders need information and bureaucracies can supply it.[17]

Although a division of labor among bureaucracies can afford leaders with more and potentially better information than they could obtain on their own, it can also introduce a new set of pathways to miscalculation. First, leaders might miscalculate because they lack information that bureaucrats possess or could easily possess. Second, leaders might miscalculate because the information that bureaucrats provide is of low-quality. Bureaucrats might search halfheartedly, fail to identify what information is valuable for leaders to know, or distort the information they relay.

These pathways draw attention to two questions. First, how costly (i.e., how easy) is it for leaders to search for information? Second, what are the incentives for and constraints on the bureaucracy to provide quality information? The next section argues that the answers to these questions depend on the state's national security institutions. While there is always a baseline risk of initiating crises that fail to achieve the anticipated goals – either because of private information or cognitive resistance to belief

---

[15] Downs defines bureaucracy as a government organization exhibiting four characteristics: large size, permanent employees, deliberate selection, and performance evaluation outside the market. See Downs, *Inside Bureaucracy*, 24–26.
[16] Herbert A. Simon, *Administrative Behavior*, 4th ed. (New York: The Free Press, 1997), 92.
[17] For a similar point, see Schub, "Informing the Leader," 1460.

revision – some leaders face institutional constraints on the information available that others do not.[18]

National Security Institutions and Miscalculation

States differ in their capacity to perform the functions of governance. In the context of foreign policy decision-making, state capacity to collect and process information is established by *national security institutions*: a set of rules and procedures that define the roles, constraints, and expectations of the bureaucracies responsible for informing and advising leaders.[19] These institutions shape how information flows between and among leaders and the bureaucracy. They influence how information is taken in, how it is distributed and condensed, and how it leaves the state system.[20]

National security institutions differ along two key dimensions. First, institutions differ in their capacity to assist leaders in their search for information. Some states feature inclusive structures that build bureaucratic capacity to collect information and reduce costs for information to flow vertically from the bureaucracy to the leader.[21] Other states instead feature insular structures that reduce bureaucratic capacity and obstruct vertical information flow. Second, states differ in their capacity to facilitate information sharing between bureaucracies. Some states feature open structures that ease the costs of horizontal information flow, while others feature closed structures that prevent bureaucracies from accessing each other's information. Thus, as illustrated in Figure 2.1, there are four types of national security institutions that a state might possess: inclusive, open institutions (*integrated*); inclusive, closed

---

[18] Fearon, "Rationalist Explanations for War"; Jervis, *Perception and Misperception in International Politics*.

[19] Allison and Zelikow draw attention to the importance of "action channels" (or "regularized means of taking government action on a specific kind of issue") and "rules of the game," but do not specify a relationship between specific rules and specific outcomes. See Allison and Zelikow, *Essence of Decision*, 300–302. See also Downs, *Inside Bureaucracy*, 185; Destler, *Presidents, Bureaucrats and Foreign Policy*, 61; George, *Presidential Decisionmaking in Foreign Policy*, 98–99; Halperin and Clapp, *Bureaucratic Politics and Foreign Policy*, 127–135. On administrative procedures as a tool of bureaucratic management, see Mathew D. McCubbins, Roger G. Noll, and Barry R. Weingast, "Administrative Procedures as Instruments of Political Control," *Journal of Law, Economics, and Organization* 3, no. 2 (1987): 244; Kathleen Bawn, "Political Control Versus Expertise: Congressional Choices about Administrative Procedures," *American Political Science Review* 89, no. 1 (1995): 62.

[20] Downs, *Inside Bureaucracy*, 77–78, 112; Richard M. Cyert and James G. March, *A Behavioral Theory of the Firm* (Englewood Cliffs: Prentice-Hall, 1963), 103–112.

[21] Structure here denotes the organization or design of the state system.

		Leader information search capacity	
		Inclusive	Insular
Bureaucratic access to information	Open	Integrated	Dictatorial
	Closed	Siloed	Fragmented

Figure 2.1 Types of national security institutions

institutions (*siloed*); insular, closed institutions (*fragmented*); and insular, open institutions (*dictatorial*).[22]

The remainder of this section develops a theory explaining when and why states are likely to miscalculate along the pathways discussed earlier. The theory makes three core claims. First, miscalculation is least likely under integrated institutions and most likely under fragmented institutions, with the likelihood of miscalculation under siloed institutions falling somewhere in between. Second, siloed and fragmented institutions lead states to miscalculate along systematically different pathways. Third, states with dictatorial institutions tend to miscalculate in ways similar to fragmented institutions, but these institutional designs are rare.

Information Search Capacity: Inclusive and Insular Structures

The first dimension is the institution's capacity to search for information. States differ considerably in this regard. At one end of the spectrum are inclusive structures that provide leaders with a more complete understanding of their environment. Broadly speaking, states expand information search capacity in many ways, ranging from increasing the size of bureaucratic organizations to establishing rules that emphasize merit-based appointment.[23] This study is particularly interested in the

---

[22] An important theoretical tradition emphasizes "decision-making units," which are defined as "an individual, group of individuals, or multiple actors" who possess the ability to commit government resources and the authority to prevent others from reversing that allocation of resources. These differ from national security institutions in two ways. First, national security institutions are a comparatively stable characteristic of the state. Second, whereas national security institutions are focused on the interactions between leaders and the bureaucracy, decision-making units cover a wide array of government and societal actors. See Margaret G. Hermann and Charles F. Hermann, "Who Makes Foreign Policy Decisions and How: An Empirical Inquiry," *International Studies Quarterly* 33, no. 4 (1989): 363; Juliet Kaarbo, "A Foreign Policy Analysis Perspective on the Domestic Politics Turn in IR Theory," *International Studies Review* 17, no. 2 (2015): 206–207.

[23] Evans and Rauch, "Bureaucracy and Growth: A Cross-National Analysis of the Effects of 'Weberian' State Structures on Economic Growth"; David E. Lewis, *The Politics*

capacity to channel information from the bureaucracy to the leader, such as through the creation and design of advisory bodies on which senior bureaucratic officials sit.

Inclusive bodies for decision-making shape the information available to leaders in two ways.[24] First, they reduce transaction costs of channeling information from the bureaucracy to the leader. Information, in short, is "more cheaply available" when states possess these capacities.[25] Second, inclusive decision-making bodies motivate bureaucrats to look for information. Foreign policy information is costly to acquire. In inclusive structures, the opportunity to shape the leader's choices encourages bureaucrats to pay these costs.[26] In sum, bureaucrats in inclusive structures should both be driven to uncover more information and have an easier time relaying that information to the leader.

At the other end of the institutional spectrum are states with insular structures, which have a limited capacity to relay information to leaders. Information outside the state system, as well as bureaucratic expertise within it, is less likely to be incorporated into a leader's information set. This might be because transaction costs are higher or because bureaucrats have limited motives to provide counsel.

Several historical examples illustrate how insular structures create incomplete information sets for leaders. Prior to institutional reforms in the United States after World War II, for example, only a small fraction of diplomatic reporting from abroad reached the Oval Office.[27] In Wilhelmine Germany, the *Immediatstellen* – the rules regulating who

---

of *Presidential Appointments: Political Control and Bureaucratic Performance* (Princeton: Princeton University Press, 2008).

[24] For an overview of information search models, see Jonathan Bendor, Amihai Glazer, and Thomas Hammond, "Theories of Delegation," *Annual Review of Political Science* 4, no. 1 (2001): 249–252.

[25] Armen A. Alchian and Harold Demsetz, "Production, Information Costs, and Economic Organization," *The American Economic Review* 62, no. 5 (1972): 795. Note that the emphasis on institutional capacity differs from other process-based arguments that see poor information search stemming from a wide array of group traits, ranging from illusions of invulnerability to teamwork. See Schafer and Crichlow, *Groupthink versus High-Quality Decision Making in International Relations*, 12, 65.

[26] This intuition builds on Gilligan and Krehbiel's study of administrative procedures in legislatures, in which a parent body can encourage a subordinate committee to expend efforts to search for information by restricting the parent body's ability to alter the committee's proposals. See Thomas W. Gilligan and Keith Krehbiel, "Collective Decisionmaking and Standing Committees: An Informational Rationale for Restrictive Amendment Procedures," *Journal of Law, Economics, & Organization* 3, no. 2 (1987): 288. See also Sean Gailmard and John W. Patty, "Slackers and Zealots: Civil Service, Policy Discretion, and Bureaucratic Expertise," *American Journal of Political Science* 51, no. 4 (2007): 873–889.

[27] David Kahn, "U.S. View of Germany and Japan," in *Knowing One's Enemies: Intelligence Assessment before the Two World Wars*, ed. Ernest R. May (Princeton: Princeton University Press, 1984), 487.

had direct access to the Kaiser – afforded disproportionate access to German defense officials at the expense of diplomats, such that the information that the Kaiser received on the eve of World War I overwhelmingly focused on military capabilities rather than diplomacy.[28] Indeed, one review of European intelligence agencies prior to World War I and World War II found that less successful intelligence performance was characterized by poor information flow and unstable processes.[29]

Quality of Bureaucratic Information: Open and Closed Structures

Having established that some states possess more search capacity than others, we now turn to the *quality* of information that leaders receive. Here, high quality refers to the most accurate information available given the constraints of the international system. The key insight here is that quality emerges from the incentives and constraints that institutional structure imposes on the bureaucracy. As historian Ernest May notes in the context of Tsarist Russia, the "extent to which" policymakers failed to ask probing questions when deciding between war and peace cannot simply be attributed to "dull-wittedness," but rather to the structures that dissuaded "the exposure of issues."[30]

Specifically, the quality of information a leader receives hinges in large part on a second dimension of national security institutions: *a bureaucracy's access to information elsewhere in the state*. This capacity might be built through the establishment of coordination bodies that reduce costs of information exchange, by ensuring that key bureaucracies are all appointed to the same bodies, and by appointing managers and staffs that expand capacity for oversight of information sharing.

Access to information in other parts of the state (or horizontal information flow) is crucial for two reasons. First, horizontal information flow allows bureaucrats to identify when their own information needs to be relayed to the leader. Bureaucrats must choose which pieces of information are valuable enough for the leader to know. This can be challenging when meaning is interdependent – that is, when the value of two pieces of information changes when evaluated together than when considered

---

[28] Lebow, *Between Peace and War*, 125–128; Clark, *The Sleepwalkers*, 178; Holger H. Herwig, "Imperial Germany," in *Knowing One's Enemies: Intelligence Assessment before the Two World Wars*, ed. Ernest R. May (Princeton: Princeton University Press, 1984), 89–90; Ernest R. May, "Cabinet, Tsar, Kaiser: Three Approaches to Assessment," in *Knowing One's Enemies: Intelligence Assessment before the Two World Wars*, ed. Ernest R. May (Princeton: Princeton University Press, 1984), 31.

[29] Ernest R. May, ed., *Knowing One's Enemies: Intelligence Assessment before the Two World Wars* (Princeton: Princeton University Press, 1984), 533–534.

[30] May, "Cabinet, Tsar, Kaiser," 26.

apart.³¹ Consider a situation in which two signals are received simultaneously. A diplomat receives a bargaining demand from an adversary and a military commander observes an increase in the adversary's border forces. Each bureaucracy's report suggests that the adversary is resolved, but neither independently meets the minimum value necessary to report it to the leader. Institutions affect whether bureaucrats can solve the puzzle. If the system is closed, the bureaucrat sees only half the picture and, as such, cannot properly assess the value of their own data. If the system is instead open, the bureaucrat can put the two pieces together and, in turn, choose to report their observations to the leader.

Second, horizontal information flow affects incentives for the bureaucracy to intentionally withhold or distort information to suit their parochial interests. In open systems, bureaucrats know what conclusions other bureaucrats have drawn and have passed to leaders. This awareness allows dissenting bureaucrats to relay their own information to initiate a debate. Consider a situation in which the foreign and defense ministry possess different projections about the costs and benefits of triggering a crisis. The defense ministry prepares a report for the leader emphasizing the benefits. The foreign ministry can choose to rebut the report, but many only deem it worthy of the leader's attention if they are aware of the defense ministry's assessment.³² As Anthony Downs summarizes, the "classic antidote" of a monopoly on information is "competition."³³

This ability to police one another's information shapes the incentives of bureaucrats for providing quality information in the first place. Each bureaucracy knows that debate is in the offing. Anticipation of deliberation encourages provision of the information with the best odds of winning the debate. The back-and-forth discussion between advisers results in a leader that is more fully informed and better positioned to identify inaccuracies in the information that bureaucrats provide.³⁴ In sum, leaders

---

³¹ Samuel N. Fraidin, "When Is One Head Better than Two? Interdependent Information in Group Decision Making," *Organizational Behavior and Human Decision Processes* 93, no. 2 (2004): 102–113.

³² This intuition is similar to a "fire alarm" model, in which a third party informs a principal that an agent has acted against their wishes. Mathew D. McCubbins and Thomas Schwartz, "Congressional Oversight Overlooked: Police Patrols versus Fire Alarms," *American Journal of Political Science* 28, no. 1 (1984): 165–179. This intuition has been applied in the context of different military services monitoring each other's behavior (e.g., the navy reporting on the army's actions), as well as in the context of bureaucrats informing the public of leader's foreign policy choices (e.g., leaking a report). Feaver, *Armed Servants*, 80–82; Elizabeth N. Saunders, "War and the Inner Circle: Democratic Elites and the Politics of Using Force," *Security Studies* 24, no. 3 (2015): 474.

³³ Downs, *Inside Bureaucracy*, 119.

³⁴ Thomas W. Gilligan and Keith Krehbiel, "Asymmetric Information and Legislative Rules with a Heterogeneous Committee," *American Journal of Political Science* 33, no.

sitting atop institutions with open access between bureaucracies tend to have access to higher-quality information as they make decisions about peace and conflict.

Having explained the fundamental intuition behind the two dimensions of national security institutions, we can now turn to how the four potential combinations shape the propensity for miscalculation in international crisis. The remainder of this section first discusses integrated institutions, which are best suited to avoid miscalculation. It then compares integrated institutions to three other institutional types – siloed, fragmented, and dictatorial – which make miscalculation more likely relative to integrated alternatives.

Integrated Institutions: The Benefits of Being Informed. The combination of inclusive information search and open bureaucratic access in integrated institutions tends to decrease the risk of miscalculation through competitive dialogue.[35] Open structures improve the quality of information that bureaucrats possess, and inclusive search capacity affords them opportunities to easily relay their counsel. The combination of the two dimensions is critical. Even the highest quality intelligence report will not shape state behavior if it cannot reach the leader.

While one might assume that the presence of multiple actors in a leader's decision-making process is a sufficient condition to yield better information provision, the idea of integrated institutions hinges on the inclusion of three specific types of bureaucracies: diplomatic, defense, and intelligence. There are two reasons for this. The first is that leaders need access to specific types of information and expertise. The previous discussion noted that leaders have three informational demands when considering an international crisis: strategic options, costs, and probable outcomes. As summarized in Table 2.1, the data that inform these leader judgments tend to cluster in different bureaucracies. As one American official pithily notes, "where you sit usually determines what you see closely."[36] The effectiveness of integrated institutions depends upon including representatives who can provide the right types of information.

Some critical information clusters in defense ministries. Defense bureaucrats collect and process information on battlefield capabilities and

---

2 (1989): 459–490; Vijay Krishna and John Morgan, "A Model of Expertise," *The Quarterly Journal of Economics* 116, no. 2 (2001): 747–775.

[35] For brief discussion of open systems, rather than institutional structures, see Allison and Zelikow, *Essence of Decision*, 265; George, *Presidential Decisionmaking in Foreign Policy*, 194; Schafer and Crichlow, *Groupthink versus High-Quality Decision Making in International Relations*, 65. Note that "integration" is used differently than in Dahlström and Lapuente, *Organizing Leviathan*, 30.

[36] McGeorge Bundy, *Vietnam Manuscript Notes*, 11. Box 224, John F. Kennedy Presidential Library. See also Schub, "Informing the Leader."

Table 2.1 *Informational demands in international crisis*

Informational demand	Type of bureaucracy	
	Defense	Diplomatic
Strategic options	Battlefield strategies	Peaceful bargains
Costs	Human and material losses	Adversary willingness to bear costs
Probable outcomes	Battlefield victory/defeat	Adversary concessions

contextualize this information with knowledge about their own state's military strength.[37] For leaders, this expertise is vital to identifying the available battlefield strategies, projecting the costs of each, and assessing the likelihood of successful battlefield outcomes. Defense bureaucracies can leverage expertise on the balance of military capabilities to estimate how many casualties battlefield fighting is likely to inflict, helping leaders to determine the limits of what can be accomplished through force.

Other critical information clusters in foreign ministries. Diplomats collect and process information about the adversary's history, culture, and domestic politics, all of which constrain the policies that adversaries choose.[38] This expertise is important not only to identifying the possible negotiated settlements the state might pursue, but also in projecting the adversary's willingness to bear costs and make concessions. An adversary's response in an international crisis depends on whether they are willing to pay costs and run risks rather than back down.[39] Political characteristics of the regime shape these reactions. These include the intrinsic stakes of the issue (e.g., the cost of losing strategic territory), the dispositions of their leaders (e.g., patience, risk tolerance, and time horizons), and the strategic beliefs, ideologies, and culture of domestic audiences.[40] In short, diplomatic bureaucracies, which specialize in

---

[37] On information in defense bureaucracies, see Betts, *Soldiers, Statesmen, and Cold War Crises*, 3–16; Feaver, *Armed Servants*, 234–282.

[38] William C. Fuller Jr., "The Russian Empire," in *Knowing One's Enemies: Intelligence Assessment before the Two World Wars*, ed. Ernest R. May (Princeton: Princeton University Press, 1984), 123; Clark, *The Sleepwalkers*, 221. On information in diplomatic bureaucracies, see also Matt Malis, "Conflict, Cooperation, and Delegated Diplomacy," *International Organization* 75, no. 4 (2021): 1018–1057; Schub, "Informing the Leader"; David Lindsey, *Delegated Diplomacy: How Ambassadors Establish Trust in International Relations* (New York: Columbia University Press, 2023). On diplomacy broadly, see Brian C. Rathbun, *Diplomacy's Value: Creating Security in 1920s Europe and the Contemporary Middle East* (Ithaca: Cornell University Press, 2014).

[39] Thomas C. Schelling, *Arms and Influence* (New Haven: Yale University Press, 1966).

[40] On stakes, see Bruce W. Jentleson, "The Pretty Prudent Public: Post Post-Vietnam American Opinion on the Use of Military Force," *International Studies Quarterly* 36,

acquiring and analyzing this type of information, can help leaders know the bounds of what adversaries will accept during crisis negotiations.

The second reason why the effectiveness of integrated institutions depends on inclusion of these specific bureaucracies pertains to their organizational perspectives and worldviews. For one, diplomatic and defense bureaucracies tend to possess systematically different foreign policy perspectives.[41] Elite surveys find that hawkish individuals tend to cluster in defense bureaucracies, while dovish individuals cluster in diplomatic ones.[42] Analysis of policy deliberations during the Cold War shows that hawkish and dovish advisers tend to emphasize different topics, with the latter drawing attention to adversary interests and diplomatic engagement.[43] In short, a dialogue between diplomatic and defense actors helps curb the risk that all members view problems the same way.[44] As a result, we would expect that integration of both diplomatic and defense bureaucracies would deliver higher quality information to the leader through more competitive dialogue.

no. 1 (1992): 49–74. On leader dispositions, see among others Saunders, *Leaders at War*; Horowitz, Stam, and Ellis, *Why Leaders Fight*; Joshua D. Kertzer, *Resolve in International Politics* (Princeton: Princeton University Press, 2016). On strategic culture, see Alastair Iain Johnston, *Cultural Realism: Strategic Culture and Grand Strategy in Chinese History* (Princeton: Princeton University Press, 1998). On domestic audiences, see James D. Fearon, "Domestic Political Audiences and the Escalation of International Disputes," *American Political Science Review* 88, no. 3 (1994): 577–592; Schultz, *Democracy and Coercive Diplomacy*; Jessica L. Weeks, "Autocratic Audience Costs: Regime Type and Signaling Resolve," *International Organization* 62, no. 1 (2008): 35–64.

[41] This intuition also implies why integrated institutions should be less prone to groupthink, a phenomenon identified by social psychologists in which collective deliberation raises social pressures for conformity. See Janis, *Victims of Groupthink*; George, *Presidential Decisionmaking in Foreign Policy*, 88–96; Allison and Zelikow, *Essence of Decision*, 283–284.

[42] See also Bernard Mennis, *American Foreign Policy Officials: Who They Are and What They Believe Regarding International Politics* (Columbus: Ohio State University Press, 1971), 167–168; Lloyd S. Etheredge, *A World of Men: The Private Sources of American Foreign Policy*. (Cambridge: MIT Press, 1978), 24–34; Ole R. Holsti and James N. Rosenau, "The Domestic and Foreign Policy Beliefs of American Leaders," *Journal of Conflict Resolution* 32, no. 2 (1988): 248–294; Peter D. Feaver and Christopher Gelpi, *Choosing Your Battles: American Civil-Military Relations and the Use of Force* (Princeton: Princeton University Press, 2004); Tyler Jost, Kaine Meshkin, and Robert Schub, "The Character and Origins of Military Attitudes on the Use of Force," *International Studies Quarterly* 66, no. 2 (2022).

[43] Tyler Jost et al., "Advisers and Aggregation in Foreign Policy Decision-Making," *International Organization* 78, no. 1 (2024): 1–37.

[44] Note that diversity here refers to what organizational theorists term "functional diversity," in that groups are diverse when they contain representatives from bureaucracies possessing different sets of information and perspectives. For a review of how functional diversity shapes task performance, see Daan Van Knippenberg and Michaéla C. Schippers, "Work Group Diversity," *Annual Review of Psychology* 58 (2007): especially, 527–528. For the traditional view of representative bureaucracy, see Kenneth John Meier, "Representative Bureaucracy: An Empirical Analysis," *American Political Science Review* 69, no. 2 (1975): 526–542.

A similar logic underlies the reason why integrated institutions benefit from the inclusion of intelligence bureaucracies as well. One of the potential challenges of information provided by diplomatic and defense ministries is that both have substantial roles in policy implementation. This means that the information they provide could potentially be biased depending on the way in which the policy affects their interests as leader decisions are enacted. In contrast, intelligence bureaucrats are often separated from implementation, meaning that they have limited organizational stakes in the leader's choice. As such, the information that they provide regarding the probable outcomes, costs, and strategic options might provide an additional check on diplomatic and defense reporting. We would thus expect that integration of intelligence bureaucracies yields higher quality information that complements the dialogue between diplomatic and defense bureaucracies.[45]

Evidence from experimental settings provide some insight into the foundations by which integrated institutions work. Groups tend to perform better than individuals in geopolitical forecasting and identifying more effective bargaining strategies, for example.[46] Diverse teams of randomly selected individuals outperform teams of even the best performing individuals in problem-solving tasks.[47] Scholars of organizational behavior have similarly found that structure improves group learning by creating stable expectations.[48] For example, Michaéla Schippers and coauthors show how improving common knowledge of goals, processes,

---

[45] One potential question concerns whether bureaucrats could potentially exploit coordination mechanisms in order to collude in their information provision. Two characteristics of integrated institutions suggest that, as a general rule, this should not be the case. First, diplomatic and defense bureaucracies tend to have different information and perspectives, which should tend to decrease the risk of collusion based on shared interests. Second, some institutional mechanisms in integrated systems, such as a third-party coordinator appointed by the leader who sits atop coordination bodies, should further curb the risk of bureaucratic collusion.

[46] Brad L. LeVeck and Neil Narang, "The Democratic Peace and the Wisdom of Crowds," *International Studies Quarterly* 61, no. 4 (2017): 867–880.

[47] Michael Horowitz et al., "What Makes Foreign Policy Teams Tick: Explaining Variation in Group Performance at Geopolitical Forecasting," *The Journal of Politics* 81, no. 4 (2019): 1388–1404; Lu Hong and Scott E. Page, "Groups of Diverse Problem Solvers Can Outperform Groups of High-Ability Problem Solvers," *Proceedings of the National Academy of Sciences* 101, no. 46 (2004): 16385–16389.

[48] Amy C. Edmondson, Richard M. Bohmer, and Gary P. Pisano, "Disrupted Routines: Team Learning and New Technology Implementation in Hospitals," *Administrative Science Quarterly* 46, no. 4 (2001): 685–716; J. Stuart Bunderson and Peter Boumgarden, "Structure and Learning in Self-Managed Teams: Why 'Bureaucratic' Teams Can Be Better Learners," *Organization Science* 21, no. 3 (2010): 609–624; Henrik Bresman and Mary Zellmer-Bruhn, "The Structural Context of Team Learning: Effects of Organizational and Team Structure on Internal and External Learning," *Organization Science* 24, no. 4 (2013): 1120–1139.

and outcomes decreases team-level bias and information processing failures.[49]

These theoretical intuitions are in tension with the common perspective that integrating the bureaucracy into foreign policy decision-making tends to raise the risk of miscalculation by leading to in-fighting between bureaucratic actors with different parochial interests – and that institutional devices are unable to attenuate these pathologies. The logic of integrated institutions instead suggests that the effects of bureaucratic participation in decision-making can make states "smarter" under integrated institutions.

Siloed Institutions: The Costs of Uninformed Bureaucracies. Siloed institutions, in contrast to integrated alternatives, tend to raise the risk of miscalculation as leaders initiate international crises. While inclusive structures increase the amount of information available to leaders, the bureaucracy's limited access to it impairs their ability and incentives to provide high-quality information. This decrease in information quality results from two factors, both of which complement the logic of integrated institutions.[50]

First, siloed institutions constrain the bureaucracy's ability to identify which bits of information are valuable for the leader to know. Under Joseph Stalin, for instance, the Soviet military possessed only a fraction of the government's intelligence reports, which undermined the defense leadership's ability to assess the likelihood of a German invasion in 1941. As one Soviet general later reflected, Soviet defense officials "probably did not do enough to convince Stalin that war with Germany was inevitable in the very near future."[51]

Second, bureaucrats are more likely to provide leaders with information that reflects their parochial interests. Unlike in integrated institutions, a limited horizontal information flow constrains bureaucracies' ability to police one another. Knowing that their information will not be scrutinized, bureaucrats submit biased reports, mainly with an eye to achieving their own organizational goals. Under siloed institutions in the

---

[49] Michaéla C. Schippers, Amy C. Edmondson, and Michael A. West, "Team Reflexivity as an Antidote to Team Information-Processing Failures," *Small Group Research* 45, no. 6 (2014): 731–769.

[50] For a discussion of siloing in intelligence organizations, see Luis Garicano and Richard A. Posner, "Intelligence Failures: An Organizational Economics Perspective," *Journal of Economic Perspectives* 19, no. 4 (2005): 161–163; Jervis, *Why Intelligence Fails*, 132; Amy B. Zegart, *Spying Blind: The CIA, the FBI, and the Origins of 9/11* (Princeton: Princeton University Press, 2009), 1–14.

[51] John Erickson, "Threat Identification and Strategic Appraisal by the Soviet Union, 1930–1941," in *Knowing One's Enemies: Intelligence Assessment before the Two World Wars*, ed. Ernest R. May (Princeton: Princeton University Press, 1984), 421.

Soviet Union, for instance, bureaucracies rarely questioned each other's information. Historian Vladislav Zubok suggests that Foreign Minister Gromyko had "the first say in diplomatic affairs," whereas Defense Ministers Grechko and Ustinov had "a virtual monopoly in military matters." It is unsurprising, then, that prior to the Soviet invasion of Afghanistan in 1979, the Foreign Ministry did not question the "amazingly tenuous" reporting of the KGB and the Defense Ministry.[52]

Under siloed institutions, the information available to leaders thus tends to be less complete and less accurate than under integrated institutions. Given the discussion earlier, it is natural to consider how siloing might raise the risk of miscalculation by limiting access to three types of information that leaders need. First, leaders might receive incomplete or low-quality information about the probable outcome of a crisis, primarily in the form of inaccurate assessments about the likelihood of battlefield victory or adversary concessions. Second, leaders might receive incomplete or low-quality information about the potential costs of a crisis, failing to accurately identify the price that the country will pay for initiation. Third, leaders might receive incomplete or low-quality information about the options available to them. That is, they might not receive an assessment of the alternative means whereby they could achieve their goals.

Numerous historical examples illustrate the logic of how siloed institutions lead to leader miscalculation. For instance, Russia triggered a crisis in 1908 when Foreign Minister Alexander Izvolsky intimated his approbation of Austria-Hungary's annexation of Bosnia. While the Tsar had approved the Foreign Ministry's strategy, he did so without information from the other ministries in Moscow, which undermined his ability to identify the weakness of the Russian military position. Similarly, prior to World War I, the same siloed system allowed the Russian War Minister to develop a defense policy that was at odds with its diplomatic commitments to France.[53]

In sum, states with siloed institutions are more likely to miscalculate than states with integrated ones. This occurs for a specific reason: leaders sitting atop siloed institutions lack access to interdependent information and make decisions with information that is biased by parochial perspectives. Constraints on the bureaucracy's access to information matter because bureaucrats can relay information to the leader. The interaction of inclusive information search and closed bureaucratic access to information work together to raise the risk of miscalculation.

---

[52] Zubok, *A Failed Empire*, 251, 263.
[53] Clark, *The Sleepwalkers*, 177, 188, 219.

Fragmented Institutions: The Costs of Uninformed Leaders. Fragmented institutions also tend to raise the risk of miscalculation, but for different reasons. One reason is that they introduce the possibility of functional failures in information exchange between the bureaucracy and the leader. For instance, exclusion of defense bureaucracies might limit access to information regarding the prospects of winning on the battlefield, the costs of fighting, or the possible battlefield strategies the state might employ. Exclusion of diplomatic bureaucracies might limit access to information about the prospects of adversary concessions, likely adversary reactions, or possible negotiated settlements.

Yet fragmented institutions lead to miscalculation for another reason as well. They cause bureaucrats to censor their counsel and manipulate the information that they supply to match the leader's beliefs. Fragmentation does not simply create barriers to information provision. It also shapes a bureaucrat's understanding of the types of behaviors that the leader deems appropriate and will therefore reward for two broad reasons.

First, the decision to fragment institutions in itself conveys that leaders will not permit deliberation or dissent within the administration – and may punish bureaucrats who speak truth to power. Seeing some bureaucrats shut out leads others to shut down. Consider a bureaucrat choosing between relaying candid information and withholding or manipulating information. The institutional design shapes the bureaucrat's understanding of which type of behavior the leader deems appropriate. Whereas the decision to integrate institutions conveys that leaders value genuine deliberation, the choice for fragmentation instead signals that leaders prefer that bureaucrats remain silent. Fragmented institutions thus shut down genuine debate. As Michael Geyer notes in his analysis of Nazi Germany's intelligence system, "By fragmenting his intelligence network [...] Hitler reshaped and transformed the role of intelligence much more radically than by simply demanding one or another ideological bias."[54]

Second, fragmented institutions strip bureaucrats of the status and authority that assists them in speaking truth to power.[55] Bureaucrats with low status fear arbitrary punishment at the hands of the leader for reporting what the leader does not want to hear. As a result, they might protect themselves by only providing information they know the leader already believes. Instead of expending effort to gain information on the true state

---

[54] Michael Geyer, "National Socialist Germany: The Politics of Information," in *Knowing One's Enemies: Intelligence Assessment before the Two World Wars*, ed. Ernest R. May (Princeton: Princeton University Press, 1984), 340.

[55] Destler terms this "stature" and "confidence," whereas George calls it "status" and "standing." See Destler, *Presidents, Bureaucrats and Foreign Policy*, 256; George, *Presidential Decisionmaking in Foreign Policy*, 194.

of the world, bureaucrats instead expend effort determining what the leader already believes and tailoring their reporting to match it.[56] On the eve of the First World War, for instance, German diplomats distorted and omitted important details in their reporting in order to relay what Berlin "wanted to hear," even when "they knew it to fly in the face of reality."[57] Bureaucrats might also protect themselves through excessively vague reporting that can be interpreted in multiple ways, such that their reporting matches the leaders belief regardless of whether it changes in the future. This strategy is particularly useful when bureaucrats cannot deduce what the leader is thinking, as is often the case in in fragmented systems.

These arguments raise important questions about the consequences of informational biases in fragmented institutions relative to siloed ones. Namely, are leaders better off with access to comparatively low-quality information or with no information at all? There are some reasons to believe that leaders stand to benefit more from siloed institutions as opposed to fragmented ones. For one, as noted earlier, the opportunity to shape policy in siloed institutions itself encourages bureaucrats to provide accurate information. Bureaucrats in integrated institutions have two motivations to provide quality information: the opportunity to influence policy and inter-bureaucratic policing. Bureaucrats in siloed institutions possess the former, but not the latter. Bureaucrats in fragmented institutions possess neither. For another, leaders may be able to supplement institutional monitoring devices with personal oversight of the bureaucracy's information provision. Franklin Roosevelt, for instance, prided himself on personally cross-checking the information he received from his advisers.[58] In sum, the quality of information provision in fragmented institutions should thus be worse than in siloed institutions.

Finally, it is worth considering whether fragmented institutions are simply an outgrowth of personalist dictatorship. Certainly, many personalist dictatorships feature sycophantic advisers who fear speaking truth to power.[59] Yet there are numerous examples of non-personalist regimes

---

[56] Georgy Egorov and Konstantin Sonin, "Dictators and Their Viziers: Endogenizing the Loyalty–Competence Trade-Off," *Journal of the European Economic Association* 9, no. 5 (2011): 906–909. See also Victor Chung-Hon Shih, "'Nauseating' Displays of Loyalty: Monitoring the Factional Bargain through Ideological Campaigns in China," *The Journal of Politics* 70, no. 4 (2008): 1177–1192; Christopher A. Cooper, "Encouraging Civil Servants to be Frank and Fearless: Merit Recruitment and Employee Voice," *Public Administration* 96, no. 4 (2018): 721–735.

[57] Lebow, *Between Peace and War*, 125–128.

[58] Neustadt, *Presidential Power and the Modern Presidents*, 132.

[59] Weeks, *Dictators at War and Peace*, 31. See also Målfrid Braut-Hegghammer, "Cheater's Dilemma: Iraq, Weapons of Mass Destruction, and the Path to War," *International Security* 45, no. 1 (2020): 51–89.

that featured nearly identical patterns. For instance, even after the death of the personalist dictator Joseph Stalin, Soviet bureaucrats recalled that diplomatic cables were "so full of orthodox Soviet diatribes" that they "could have appeared in the Soviet press as a standard polemic for public consumption."[60] Moreover, as discussed later, there are some conditions under which even personalist dictators might prefer integrated institutions.

Dictatorial Institutions: Costly but Rare. The final possible combination, a dictatorial institution, features both insularity and open bureaucratic access. For instance, North Vietnam in the late 1960s established comparatively strong mechanisms for bureaucratic information sharing, while also restricting the capacity for relaying bureaucratic information to the leader. The combination of insularity and open access inherent in dictatorial institutions implies an outcome quite similar to fragmented institutions. Limited search capacity means that leaders should be more likely to miscalculate because they base their decisions on incomplete information. Yet dialogue and information sharing between bureaucracies should have comparatively little effect on the likelihood of miscalculation because higher quality information cannot reach the leader.

Dictatorial institutions thus imply a somewhat paradoxical design. It requires that bureaucrats pay the costs of horizontal information sharing without an expectation that the higher quality information can inform better choices. Yet states should have few incentives to improve the quality of bureaucratic information if there is limited vertical information flow in the first place.[61] As such, relative to other institutional alternatives, we would expect to find comparatively few states with dictatorial institutions.

As summarized in Table 2.2, the theory offers a set of predictions regarding the relationship between national security institutions and the frequency of miscalculation.

---

[60] Arkady N. Shevchenko, *Breaking with Moscow* (New York: Alfred A. Knopf, 1985), 33.
[61] One alternative possibility is that dictatorial institutions might allow bureaucrats with aligned interests to collude. For example, bureaucrats might share information with one another in order to present an artificially united front to the leader or in order to take independent actions without the leader's authorization. We should expect such situations to be rare, however. First, as noted in note 45, interest alignment should be uncommon given that defense and diplomatic bureaucracies tend to view policy issues from different perspectives. Second, restrictions on vertical information flow under dictatorial institutions mean that even an artificially unified set of bureaucrats have few opportunities to relay information to the leader. Third, leaders tend to retain decision-making authority regarding crisis initiation, meaning that it would be comparatively difficult for bureaucrats to cooperate in order to initiate a crisis without the leader's approval.

Table 2.2 *Theoretical predictions regarding miscalculation*

	Institutional type		
	Integrated	Siloed	Fragmented*
Propensity for miscalculation	Low	Medium	High
Information provision	More complete: high motivation; interdependent information identification	Less complete: high motivation; interdependent information loss	Least complete: low motivation; interdependent information loss
Information quality	High: competitive dialogue	Low: parochial bias	Low: self-censorship

* Theoretical predictions for dictatorial and fragmented institutions are the same.

Alternative Explanations for Miscalculation

Existing scholarship offers several explanations why some states might be more prone to miscalculation than others. Three of the most prominent perspectives merit attention. The section below briefly discusses each with an eye to identifying their observable implications in the empirical analysis.

One perspective, which might be termed the "interest group" model of bureaucratic politics, suggests that states are likely to miscalculate when hawkish bureaucracies are influential in the decision-making process. The core proposition of the interest group model is that the same policy can affect the interests of two bureaucracies differently, such as that each lobbies for the state to pursue different courses of action.[62] In this view, the choices states make reflect the interests of the bureaucracy that "triumphs over other groups fighting for alternatives."[63] A hawkish bureaucracy, for instance, might advocate for a conflictual policy because it advances the organization's interests regardless of whether the strategy succeeds.

Several empirical predictions follow from the interest group model. First, we would expect leaders to exhibit signs of having limited ability to resist the bureaucracy's recommended course of action. Leaders should base their choices on the strategies that bureaucrats recommend (e.g., use force), not the information on which they base it (e.g., coercion will yield adversary concessions). Second, we would expect that patterns of miscalculation follow from the inclusion and exclusion of

---

[62] Allison and Zelikow, *Essence of Decision*, 271.
[63] Ibid., 256. See also Brooks, *Shaping Strategy*, 19–20.

hawkish bureaucracies, such as defense organizations, whose preferences over issues like the use of force the interest group model suggests should remain stable over time.

In contrast, the core proposition of the institutional theory of miscalculation advanced here is that leaders, not bureaucrats, make the most important decisions in international crisis. Bureaucracies matter not because of what they want, but because of the information they provide. Whereas the interest group model would suggest marginalizing hawkish bureaucracies reduces the risk of miscalculation, the institutional model would instead posit that so long as these bureaucracies possess information the leader needs, exclusion raises the risk of error.

Thus, in contrast to the interest group model, the institutional theory posits that information provided by bureaucracies will shape the leader's beliefs. As such, the presence or absence of information about probable outcomes, costs, and alternatives – rather than what bureaucracies recommend – should be pivotal to the leader's decision. We would also expect that the presence of institutional devices, such as competitive dialogue between bureaucrats, will attenuate biases in the information that leaders receive.

Another alternative perspective, which merits equal consideration, underscores the role that leader worldviews play in decision-making, emphasizing the ways in which the broad foreign policy beliefs that leaders bring with them into office may lead them to resist new information that the bureaucracy supplies. In essence, this viewpoint posits that states may err in their calculations because they apply general schemas for international politics, such as their predispositions toward the use of force or international cooperation, to each specific circumstance they encounter regardless of whether it is the most effective in advancing their goals.[64] According to this perspective, the counsel that national security bureaucracies supply should be of secondary importance in comparison to the beliefs leaders hold when they enter office.[65] If true, we would expect that leaders rarely change their beliefs in response to information their bureaucracies provide under all types of institutions.

By contrast, the institutional theory of miscalculation suggests that the propensity for leader beliefs to evolve in response to new information hinges on the design of the institutions in place. Under integrated and siloed institutions, the theory predicts that leader beliefs will update in line with the counsel supplied by advisers. This is because bureaucracies

---

[64] Horowitz, Stam, and Ellis, *Why Leaders Fight*, 10. On the effect of stress during crisis on leader beliefs, see George, *Presidential Decisionmaking in Foreign Policy*, 49.

[65] This could be moderated by other leader attributes, such as "open-mindedness" or "cognitive complexity." See Vertzberger, *The World in Their Minds*, 134; Preston, *The President and His Inner Circle*, 9.

operating within such structures are more inclined to present dissenting views, which increases the likelihood that leaders have the information available to change their beliefs. Conversely, under fragmented institutions, structural barriers to information flow and incentives to avoid dissent create an environment where leader views cannot update. Echo chambers mean that, try as they might, leaders lack the information necessary to properly revise their beliefs. This implies a diminished responsiveness to new information emerging in the international system, making leader beliefs persistently anchored to their preexisting worldviews. In short, how much prior leader beliefs matter depends on the institutional environment in which decision-making unfolds.

A third alternative perspective, termed accountability theory for ease of reference, emphasizes variation in the costs of punishing political leaders for poor performance. In democracies, for example, elections allow voters to hold leaders accountable for policy failures. The threat of political accountability could motivate leaders to, as Reiter and Stam argue, "produce better estimates of the probability of victory" and obtain "higher quality, less biased information."[66] In contrast, because authoritarian regimes, particularly personalist dictatorships, lack the ability to punish leaders after foreign policy failures, leaders may receive information that is based on less careful analysis.[67] In sum, accountability theory would predict that the quality of bureaucratic counsel hinges on whether the regime is a democracy rather than the design of national security institutions.

The Politics of Institutional Design

If the theory's proposition about the relationship between institutions and miscalculation is correct, it suggests a puzzle. Why would states adopt anything other than integrated institutions?

This section argues that in order to answer this puzzle, we must look to the incentives of political leaders. These incentives prove important because leaders retain considerable authority to shape rules and procedures at the apex of national security decision-making. Leaders can issue executive orders establishing and modifying their advisory and coordination bodies. They can expand and reduce the size of staffs that support these

---

[66] Reiter and Stam, *Democracies at War*, 23. See also discussion of how organizational efficiency in democracies and highly centralized autocracies affects wartime economic resource allocation, 126–129.

[67] Weeks, *Dictators at War and Peace*, 31.

bodies. They can integrate diplomatic, defense, and intelligence bureaucracies by appointing their senior officials to these bodies. Leaders can marginalize these same bureaucracies by removing those same officials or shifting decision-making into ad hoc venues. Finally, leaders can refuse to fill senior advisory positions, or take on the portfolio of the defense or foreign ministers themselves.

These institutional choices are colored by a leader's fundamentally political character. Leaders make decisions that maximize the likelihood of remaining in office. Political survival is not determined solely by avoiding miscalculation in international crises. It is also determined by winning political debates about their performance in office.

Integrated institutions present a trade-off to leaders trying to meet both sets of demands.[68] On the one hand, integration improves the quality of information on which leaders base their foreign policy decisions. On the other hand, integration increases the power of bureaucrats, who can then use their competence and access to information in ways that can create political problems for leaders. This insight builds on previous scholarship emphasizing how bureaucratic power stems in part from its ability to punish political officials. The key difference here is that leaders have institutional remedies at their disposal to reduce a bureaucracy's ability to punish them, but these same remedies degrade the quality of information available during foreign policy decision-making.[69] In short, leaders have good reasons for not always choosing institutions that minimize the risk of miscalculation.

How leaders reconcile these competing priorities depends on their political environment. Leaders weigh the benefits that could accrue from higher quality foreign policy information against the costs that bureaucrats can impose. Two aspects of a leader's political environment shape when the benefits of integration outweigh the costs: the political threat that bureaucrats pose and the focus of the leader's agenda.

This section first specifies two types of costs that integrated institutions can levy. It then develops a logic of the political conditions under which leaders choose each type of national security institution.

---

[68] For the classic articulation of the trade-off between political control and expertise, see Bawn, "Political Control versus Expertise." George acknowledges that leaders face a trade-off between good advice and political "acceptability, consensus, and support," but offers few insights as to how they might resolve it. See George, *Presidential Decisionmaking in Foreign Policy*, 2.

[69] For earlier work, see Graham T. Allison and Peter L. Szanton, *Remaking Foreign Policy: The Organizational Connection* (New York: Basic Books, 1976), 73–74; George, *Presidential Decisionmaking in Foreign Policy*, 205; Bendor and Hammond, "Rethinking Allison's Models," 315; Garrison, *The Games Advisors Play: Foreign Policy in the Nixon and Carter Administrations*, 23; Saunders, "War and the Inner Circle," 480.

The Costs of Integrated Institutions

Integrated institutions allow bureaucrats to impose two types of political costs on leaders. While the specific mechanisms whereby bureaucrats leverage this power depend on the nature of the regime, the underlying logic looks quite similar in both democracies and autocracies.

First, integrated institutions arm bureaucrats with more information and expertise, which they can choose to relay to other elites or the public, leaning on their expert reputation to sway their opinions against the leader. The inclusive nature of information search affords the bureaucracy information about the leader's decision-making. Open access to information means that any single bureaucracy is not only armed with its own information, but with information from other bureaucracies as well. While integrated institutions mean that leaders are better informed during foreign policy decision-making, they also mean that leaders are more politically vulnerable because bureaucrats can leverage their information and competence to sanction the leader.

In democratic regimes, the power to remove leaders rests with the public. The public prefers that the leader choose effective policies but often lacks information about the details of foreign policy, both because citizens tend to be cognitive misers and because the nature of foreign policy is such that much of what happens in international politics is hidden from public view.[70] The public thus needs access to information in order to determine whether or not to remove the leader. To form opinions on leader performance, citizens tend to rely on information from sources they deem trustworthy.[71] This might come from other politicians with aligned preferences (i.e., a conservative voter forms their opinions based on information from a conservative politician), but it might also come from individuals the public perceives to possess unique competence and authority in the realm of foreign policy.[72] Bureaucrats can meet this demand by supporting or criticizing the leader's foreign policy choices.[73]

---

[70] John R. Zaller, *The Nature and Origins of Mass Opinion* (New York: Cambridge University Press, 1992).

[71] Arthur Lupia and Mathew D. McCubbins, *The Democratic Dilemma: Can Citizens Learn What They Need to Know?* (New York: Cambridge University Press, 1998).

[72] Adam J Berinsky, *In Time of War: Understanding American Public Opinion from World War II to Iraq* (Chicago: University of Chicago Press, 2009).

[73] On the leader's inner circle, see Saunders, "War and the Inner Circle"; Saunders, "Leaders, Advisers, and the Political Origins of Elite Support for War." See also James Golby, Peter D. Feaver, and Kyle Dropp, "Elite Military Cues and Public Opinion about the Use of Military Force," *Armed Forces & Society* 44, no. 1 (2018): 44–71; Erik Lin-Greenberg and Theo Milonopoulos, "Private Eyes in the Sky: Emerging Technology and the Political Consequences of Eroding Government Secrecy," *Journal of Conflict Resolution* 65, no. 6 (2021): 1067–1097.

While all bureaucrats can theoretically intervene in the broader political debate, however, integrated institutions enable them to be more effective in it. Bureaucrats cannot leak information they do not possess. More access to information means more information to share. More expertise means a higher degree of sway over the target audience.[74] Experimental evidence shows, for instance, that the public is more likely to defer to foreign policy recommendations from more experienced and credentialed diplomatic, defense, and intelligence advisers.[75] As such, the competence that follows from integrated institutions is critical to the bureaucracy's capacity for shaping the opinions of individuals who can remove leaders from office. Integrated institutions thus raise the costs that the bureaucracy can impose on the leader through criticism in front of the leader's domestic audience. In short, integrated institutions are costly in democracies because they allow bureaucrats to shape public opinion.

Several historical examples of political leaders who feared information sharing within the bureaucracy illustrate how leaders see the trade-off inherent in integrated institutions. U.S. President Richard Nixon, for instance, worried that convening the National Security Council would increase the risk of bureaucratic leaks. "Because of leaks – no NSC mtg on SALT talks," Nixon's chief of staff recorded in his diary.[76] Jimmy Carter similarly recalled that he was "leery of channeling" staff work through the State Department, even on some of the most important policy decisions of his administration, because he feared it would leak to the press.[77]

A quite similar logic holds in some authoritarian regimes, in which leaders are selected and removed from office by a small group of elites who, in an analogous manner, evaluate the leader's performance. Of course, the ways in which bureaucrats coordinate with the leader's domestic audience differ considerably from democracies.[78] For example, policy debates occur in much smaller forums, such as a meeting with

---

[74] Dennis Chong and James N. Druckman, "Framing Public Opinion in Competitive Democracies," *American Political Science Review* 101, no. 4 (2007): 637–655.

[75] Tyler Jost and Joshua D. Kertzer, "Armies and Influence: Elite Experience and Public Opinion on Foreign Policy," *Journal of Conflict Resolution*, 2023. See also Michael R. Kenwick and Sarah Maxey, "You and Whose Army? How Civilian Leaders Leverage the Military's Prestige to Shape Public Opinion," *The Journal of Politics* 84, no. 4 (2022): 1963–1978.

[76] Daalder and Destler, *In the Shadow of the Oval Office*, 68.

[77] Jimmy Carter, Zbigniew Brzezinski, and Richard N. Gardner, "Being There," *Foreign Affairs* 78, no. 6 (1999): 164–165.

[78] On the similarities between foreign policy debates in democracies and autocracies, see Weeks, *Dictators at War and Peace*; Jessica Chen Weiss, *Powerful Patriots: Nationalist Protest in China's Foreign Relations* (New York: Oxford University Press, 2014).

members of a politburo. Yet the core logic remains the same: competence shapes the ability of the bureaucracy to inform the elite audience's evaluation of the leader's performance.

The second type of political cost is the ability of bureaucrats to remove leaders directly through coup. One of the unique features of many national security bureaucracies, particularly the state's defense and intelligence organizations, is their parallel control over the coercive levers of the state.[79] As with political debates, this logic is not exclusive to autocracies. Coups can overthrow both elected and unelected officials.[80] Yet the ease with which bureaucracies can depose leaders again depends on the design of institutions. Competent and well-informed bureaucrats tend to be more effective in planning coups.[81] Reputation for expertise similarly bolsters the legitimacy of their decision to oust the leader from office.[82] Consider two possible coup plots, the first organized by a respected technocrat and the second organized by one of a leader's crony. The competent bureaucrat should not only be able to better plan a successful coup but also be more likely to gain the support of other elites who respect the bureaucrat's competence. In contrast, the incompetent bureaucrat is not only less capable of planning a coup but is also unlikely to acquire the requisite level of support for it in the first place. Thus, integrated institutions are costly to dictators because they produce the types of well-respected subordinates that can more effectively challenge the leader's authority and rule.

Choosing between Institutional Designs

Two questions help explain how leaders reconcile the costs and benefits of integrated institutions. First, how secure are leaders from bureaucratic punishment? Second, which issues help leaders stay in office? As illustrated in Figure 2.2, we can think of leaders forming their preferences by answering these two questions in sequence.[83] When bureaucrats pose

---

[79] Milan W. Svolik, *The Politics of Authoritarian Rule* (New York: Cambridge University Press, 2012), 4–5.

[80] These considerations may be particularly salient in personalist dictatorships, in which leaders can only be removed through force, meaning that coercive bureaucracies play an especially pivotal role.

[81] See Naunihal Singh, *Seizing Power: The Strategic Logic of Military Coups* (Baltimore: John Hopkins University Press, 2014), 6; Erica De Bruin, *How to Prevent Coups d'État: Counterbalancing and Regime Survival* (Ithaca: Cornell University Press, 2020), 15–17.

[82] On bureaucratic reputations, see Carpenter, *The Forging of Bureaucratic Autonomy*.

[83] Following existing work, the political theory of institutional design employs a decision tree to weight the relative effects of the two explanatory variables, even though the theory itself remains probabilistic. While stylized, ranking explanatory variables in a decision sequence provides clear and falsifiable predictions about when leaders should be more likely to change their institution. For similar approaches, see Vipin Narang,

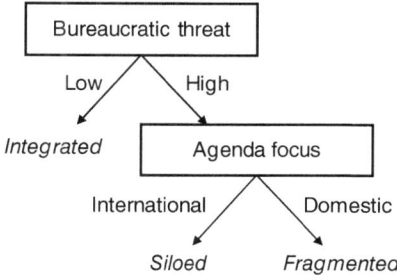

Figure 2.2 A model of institutional design choices

a limited threat to political survival, leaders can adopt integrated institutions regardless of what issues keep them in office. When the level of bureaucratic threat is high, however, how leaders respond depends on the issues that are most important to them. Leaders whose agendas prize domestic issues can choose fragmented institutions to neutralize the threat posed by national security bureaucrats, curbing both their access to the leader's decision-making and to information in other bureaucratic silos. Leaders whose agenda is instead dominated by international issues choose the middle path of siloed institutions. They accept some political risk of censure via more competent and well-informed bureaucrats in order to get better advice, but restrict the amount of information which the bureaucracy might use to inflict political damage. This section discusses each factor in turn.

Bureaucratic Threat: How Leaders Choose Between Integrated and Non-Integrated Institutions. The first factor that explains a leader's institutional choices pertains to the threat that leaders believe the bureaucracy poses to their political survival. Threat is the capability and intent to cause harm. Here, bureaucratic threat refers to the leader's understanding of whether diplomatic, defense, or intelligence bureaucrats both possess the intent to challenge the leader and the capability to successfully do so. Bureaucratic threat is high when leaders believe that bureaucrats have both the motive to politically challenge them and a low probability of surviving such a challenge. Bureaucratic threat is low when leaders believe the bureaucracy either lacks the motive or capability to successfully challenge them.

Nuclear Strategy in the Modern Era: Regional Powers and International Conflict (Princeton: Princeton University Press, 2014), 32; Sheena Chestnut Greitens, *Dictators and Their Secret Police: Coercive Institutions and State Violence* (New York: Cambridge University Press, 2016), 19.

What shapes perception of bureaucratic intent to challenge the leader? Much of this depends on the leader's level of trust in the bureaucracy. One way that such trust might form is through prior behavior. Leaders should be less likely to trust bureaucracies that have censured the leader in the past, either through public criticism, leaks of damaging information, or plotted coups. The more frequently that bureaucratic censure occurs, the less likely leaders are to trust the bureaucracy. Trust can also form because leaders believe the bureaucracy shares their interests. This might emerge because the political preferences of the leader happen to align with those of the bureaucracy. It might also emerge as a product of norms against bureaucratic participation in political debates. If the country's bureaucracy believes, for instance, that it is inappropriate to challenge political leaders, leaders should be less likely to fear a challenge.

What shapes perceptions of bureaucratic capability to challenge the leader? One important determinant of a leader's strength stems from their prior experience in foreign or defense affairs.[84] The reason for this is that experienced leaders are better positioned to win public debates with bureaucrats. Experience confers a reputation for expertise on the leader, which helps to maintain an even playing field between leaders and a competent bureaucracy in political debate. If both leaders and the bureaucracy are "expert," bureaucrats no longer enjoy an advantage over the leader. Experienced leaders are thus better positioned to withstand bureaucratic criticism.[85]

Consider a bureaucrat who publicly criticizes two hypothetical leaders, the first possessing decades of experience in foreign affairs and the second a complete novice. The leader responds with their own public statement. In the case of the experienced leader, however, both leader and bureaucrat enjoy expert reputations. The debate is a draw, and the leader does not lose political support. The situation changes, however, if the leader is inexperienced. Since the inexperienced leader does not enjoy the same reputation for competence, their counterargument does not have the same persuasive power in the eyes of the domestic audience. The audience defers to the bureaucracy and the leader loses political support. Analogous dynamics should play out in non-personalist autocracies, although bureaucrats might criticize the leader's choices in more private settings. Yet the balance of experience between leaders and the

---

[84] Note that this logic differs from existing accounts that emphasize how experience can improve a leader's ability to monitor the bureaucracy, rather than withstand a political challenge from it. See Elizabeth N. Saunders, "No Substitute for Experience: Presidents, Advisers, and Information in Group Decision Making," *International Organization* 71, no. S1 (2017): 219–247.

[85] Several other factors may also shape leader perceptions, such as the strength of their public approval, vulnerability to sanction for illegal activity, or the leader's personality.

bureaucracy should matter most in more democratic states that permit political debates.

This suggests that leaders are free to adopt integrated institutions when they believe that the bureaucracy poses a limited threat to their political survival. Secure leaders judge that bureaucrats are unlikely to use the competence and information that integrated institutions bestow to challenge the leader. Even if bureaucrats do attempt to censure, leaders judge that they can withstand the challenge. Leaders prefer to reap the decision-making benefits that integrated institutions offer. Thus, as depicted in Figure 2.2, the first node of the decision tree predicts that leaders are likely to choose integrated institutions when levels of bureaucratic threats are low.

Agenda Focus: How Leaders Choose between Siloed and Fragmented Institutions. When the level of bureaucratic threat is high, leaders can use the design of national security institutions to attenuate the risk that bureaucrats pose to their political survival. The typology of national security institutions suggests that there are two institutional strategies available to leaders whereby they might address bureaucratic threats. On the one hand, leaders could adopt siloed institutions, restricting only access to other bureaucracies' information. On the other hand, they could adopt fragmented institutions, curtailing information search capacity more broadly.[86]

What informs a leader's choice between these two options? One important consideration is the *focus of the leader's agenda*. Leaders whose political survival primarily depends on domestic issues are less dependent on the information that the national security bureaucracy might provide. That is, an emphasis on domestic issues, as opposed to foreign policy, lowers the expected benefits of quality bureaucratic information. This is particularly the case when leaders possess expansive domestic goals aimed at what other scholars term transforming or revolutionizing their country's domestic programs. A transformative agenda can be defined as an aim to implement a fundamental change to the state or society, such

---

[86] Some scholars of civil-military relations draw attention to external and domestic threats. The theoretical intuition here is different in three ways. First, unlike some existing models, the theory of national security institutions implies that international threats (and by extension an international focus) are not sufficient to prompt leaders to adopt the most effective institutions (integrated). Second, agenda focus encompasses a broader range of political considerations (beyond physical threat) that inform the leader's institutional choice. Leaders may have expansive international agendas even when they are not directly threatened. Third, the theory emphasizes that leaders also care about the bureaucracy's intention to challenge the leader, rather than simply their capability to do so. On external threats in civil-military relations, see Desch, *Civilian Control of the Military*, 12; Talmadge, *The Dictator's Army*, 18–23.

as through major redefinitions to the state's political, economic, or social institutions. Under such conditions, leaders have less need for sound foreign policy advice because their survival depends on what happens domestically.

Fragmented institutions offer an institutional remedy that allows leaders to advance the domestic agenda they prize by reducing the costs that bureaucrats can impose. First, fragmented institutions prevent bureaucrats from developing reputations for expertise and competence.[87] This lowers the status of the bureaucracy, thereby blunting the persuasiveness of adviser criticism. Second, fragmented institutions limit the bureaucracy's access to information. This means that bureaucrats possess only a small fraction of the state's knowledge, which neutralizes the amount that they can share with the leader's domestic audience.

A leader's institutional preference changes when their agenda prioritizes international issues. When a leader's survival hinges on foreign policy, the costs of miscalculation in international conflict increase. Leaders benefit from the quality information that the national security bureaucracy can provide. This is particularly the case when the leader's focus on foreign policy stems from a salient security threat, which raises the probability of crisis bargaining in the future and the expected costs of defeat. At extreme values, the leader's physical, rather than just political, survival may also be at stake. Under such conditions, leaders demand effective foreign policy performance to a greater degree than when their agenda focuses on domestic issues. Historical shocks to a state's international threat level illustrate this point. Defeat in the Russo-Japanese War, for instance, prompted Tsar Nicholas II to establish a Council of State Defense.[88]

Siloed institutions offer leaders a design to reconcile the threats that bureaucrats might pose with their demand for the information that they can provide. Because siloed designs still maintain a high information search capacity, leaders can still benefit from access to more information than they could collect on their own.

---

[87] Note that this differs from the way that theories of civil-military relations typically conceptualize expertise, in which the bureaucrat is assumed to always possess more expertise regardless of the leader's choices. See Feaver, *Armed Servants*, 69–70. The notion here is closer to the distinction that Huntington draws between professional and unprofessional militaries. See Huntington, *The Soldier and the State*, 11–14. This also departs from past scholarship on the politicization of intelligence, which tends to focus on how leaders undermine the effect of specific assessments. Here, leaders instead adopt an organizational strategy that minimizes the bureaucracy's competence writ large. On intelligence politicization, see Joshua Rovner, *Fixing the Facts: National Security and the Politics of Intelligence* (Ithaca: Cornell University Press, 2011), 29–35.

[88] Fuller, "The Russian Empire," 99.

Yet siloed institutions also help to partially, though not fully, curtail the threat that the bureaucracy poses in two ways. First, closing off bureaucratic access to information helps restore balance during debates in front of domestic audiences. Since no single bureaucracy can access all of the state's information, the leader enjoys an informational advantage in the public debate about the soundness of their decisions. For instance, Harry Gelman finds that Leonid Brezhnev was "well aware" that the Soviet Defense Council "segregated information" but preferred this type of institutional design because it solidified his "primacy" over other political elites on national security matters.[89]

Second, siloing can placate bureaucrats by offering them organizational autonomy in exchange for political security. Siloed designs maintain each bureaucracy's turf and minimize the resources each bureaucracy must expend on coordination.[90] Thus, bureaucracies tend to prefer the autonomy associated with siloed institutions. For example, William Fuller finds that the military in Tsarist Russia marginalized civilian ministries from "crucial knowledge of military policy" in order to "deny its rivals ammunition for argument," which left the Ministry of Foreign Affairs "ignorant of the real state of the army."[91] Thus, bureaucrats might be less motivated to politically challenge leaders when they can operate freely under siloed institutions.

Of course, many leaders care about both domestic and international issues, thereby introducing countervailing incentives. Fragmented institutions may offer marginal advantages that break the tie under such circumstances. For one, fragmented institutions buy time. Domestic audiences may eventually punish the leader for foreign policy miscalculations, but it often takes time for the public to learn about these failures. In wartime, for instance, it may become clear that a leader is making poor choices only after numerous battlefield defeats. In contrast, the political costs of bureaucratic criticism are immediate.

Thus, agenda focus should shape the leader's choice between siloed and fragmented institutions.[92] The second node of the decision tree in Figure 2.2 predicts that leaders are more likely to choose fragmented institutions when domestic issues dominate but are more likely to choose siloed institutions when international issues dominate.

---

[89] Harry Gelman, *The Brezhnev Politburo and the Decline of Détente* (Cornell: Cornell University Press, 1984), 63–64.
[90] Downs, *Inside Bureaucracy*, 71; Destler, *Presidents, Bureaucrats and Foreign Policy*, 69; Wilson, *Bureaucracy: What Government Agencies Do and Why They Do It*, Chapter 10; Halperin and Clapp, *Bureaucratic Politics and Foreign Policy*, 38.
[91] Fuller, "The Russian Empire," 100, 125.
[92] Note that this political explanation of siloing differs from existing accounts, which attribute siloing to the institutional inertia introduced by the inherent nature of organizations. See Zegart, *Spying Blind*, 49–58.

Alternative Explanations for Institutional Design

The existing literature identifies three prominent theoretical perspectives about the origins of institutions, which do not emphasize the political considerations outlined earlier. One possibility emphasizes path dependence or, more simply, the absence of institutional change.[93] This theoretical perspective would predict stasis and continuity in institutional design rather than change responding to the political environment.

Another possibility is that institutional design follows the leader's style of management. Some existing literature emphasizes the role of leader personality rather than the political environment.[94] As Alexander George argues, personality influences not only the design of formal institutions but how that formal structure operates "in practice."[95] I. M. Destler similarly argues that decision-making processes are "at the mercy" of leaders.[96] Two empirical predictions follow from this perspective. First, we would expect institutional design to change as new leaders come into office. Second, the leader's decision-making processes in matters of national security should be similar to those in other issue areas, such as the economy.

A third alternative perspective emphasizes international diffusion. Diffusion is a process whereby the adoption of a state trait or practice in one population increases the probability that others will adopt the same trait or practice.[97] Institutional diffusion would posit that states choose institutional designs because certain high-status or high-affinity states already possess them.[98] The institutions that high-status states adopt establish norms of appropriateness that motivate their emulation elsewhere.[99] Two empirical predictions proceed from a diffusion account. First, states would seek out information regarding other states' institutional design. Second, states would tend to adopt the institutions of high-status states, such as those of major powers.

---

[93] Paul Pierson, "Increasing Returns, Path Dependence, and the Study of Politics," *American Political Science Review* 94, no. 2 (2000): 251–267.

[94] Existing literature tends to divide these into three types: formalistic, competitive, and collegial. See Richard Tanner Johnson, *Managing the White House* (New York: HarperCollins Publishers, 1974); George, *Presidential Decisionmaking in Foreign Policy*, 149–158. See also James M. Goldgeier, *Leadership Style and Soviet Foreign Policy: Stalin, Khrushchev, Brezhnev, Gorbachev* (Baltimore: Johns Hopkins University Press, 1994), 2–11.

[95] George, *Presidential Decisionmaking in Foreign Policy*, 147.

[96] Destler, "National Security Advice to US Presidents," 160.

[97] David Strang, "Adding Social Structure to Diffusion Models: An Event History Framework," *Sociological Methods & Research* 19, no. 3 (1991): 325.

[98] Alastair Iain Johnston, *Social States: China in International Institutions, 1980–2000* (Princeton: Princeton University Press, 2014), 1–45.

[99] Alexander Wendt, "Driving with the Rearview Mirror: On the Rational Science of Institutional Design," *International Organization* 55, no. 4 (2001): 1024–1029.

Conclusion

This chapter has made the case that bureaucratic politics looks fundamentally different depending on the institutional context. It detailed a theoretical framework for thinking about these differences. Each of the four types of national security institutions shapes the propensity of miscalculation in international crisis. Avoiding miscalculation in international crisis requires leaders to be capable of effectively managing a vast array of information within the state. Leaders can better manage information by adopting integrated institutions that encourage bureaucrats to provide more complete and higher-quality information. Yet not all leaders adopt these practices for effective information management. Some opt for institutions that restrict the bureaucracy's capacity to relay information to the leader. Others choose institutions that constrain or incentivize the bureaucracy to provide low-quality information. Politics drives these institutional choices. The next chapter offers an empirical strategy for testing these propositions.

3   The World of National Security Institutions

This chapter empirically probes the theory developed in Chapter 2. It offers a strategy to measure the types of national security institutions a state possesses. It then leverages the *National Security Institutions Data Set*, an original cross-national resource offering the first systematic measurement of national security decision-making and coordination bodies across the globe from 1946 to 2015, to test the theory's intuitions.

Analyzing these data yields three important findings. First, the data show that national security institutions are more malleable than previous scholarship has suggested. While the analysis finds some evidence of stability and institutional inertia, it also shows how national security institutions have been redesigned hundreds of times in just the past seven decades alone. These changes frequently occurred within the same regime and, in many cases, even within the same leader. Second, the statistical analysis finds support for the institutional theory of miscalculation. Using the comparative rate of initiating international crises that fail to achieve a state's goals as a proxy for miscalculation, the analysis shows that integrated institutions tend to perform better than nonintegrated alternatives. Finally, the analysis suggests that the leader's political environment is associated with the type of institution a state possesses. Siloed and fragmented institutions are more common in states whose leaders have good reasons to fear the bureaucracy. Among states with nonintegrated institutions, siloed designs are more frequently found under leaders facing salient international security threats, while fragmented designs are more commonly seen under leaders confronting domestic unrest or who possess an ambitious domestic political agenda. The chapter concludes by laying out an empirical strategy for the remainder of the book, discussing case selection and methodology.

The National Security Institutions Data Set

What do we already know empirically about the institutions connecting political leaders and their bureaucratic advisers? A number of existing data sets provide insight into political leaders.[1] Some of these sources focus on the experiences that presidents, prime ministers, and dictators bring with them into office.[2] Others document how leaders are selected for office, the size of the leadership group, and constraints on the leader's authority.[3] While these existing approaches are well positioned for testing other theories, however, they are not well suited to test hypotheses regarding relations between the leader and the national security bureaucracy. As such, existing data cannot systematically evaluate the effects that bureaucratic institutions have on foreign policy. In fact, the canonical models of bureaucratic politics remain cross-nationally untested in the half century since their introduction to political science.[4]

Measurement Strategy and Data Collection

The *National Security Institutions Data Set* helps to address these gaps by collecting and coding data on the bureaucratic and organizational characteristics of 152 countries since the end of World War II.[5] The data set is arranged into country-year observations. This means that there are separate data points for the United States in, for example, 1955 and 1956, as well as for China in those same two years. This allows us to examine institutional differences both within and between countries.

The data set focuses on observable organizational design features that capture the two dimensions of the theory: information search capacity and inter-bureaucracy information access. In particular, two types of bodies provide the building blocks to code each country-year according to the institutional typology. The first is the state's *decision-making body*, by which leaders may receive information from advisers and vice versa. A

---

[1] Hein E. Goemans, Kristian Skrede Gleditsch, and Giacomo Chiozza, "Introducing Archigos: A Dataset of Political Leaders," *Journal of Peace Research* 46, no. 2 (2009): 269–283.

[2] Cali Mortenson Ellis, Michael C. Horowitz, and Allan C. Stam, "Introducing the LEAD Data Set," *International Interactions* 41, no. 4 (2015): 718–741.

[3] Barbara Geddes, Joseph Wright, and Erica Frantz, "Autocratic Breakdown and Regime Transitions: A New Data Set," *Perspectives on Politics* 12, no. 2 (2014): 315; Weeks, *Dictators at War and Peace*, 179–181.

[4] The closest approach to date has been the *Wartime Civil-Military Relations Data Set*, which documents whether the country possessed an institutionalized forum in which civilian and military leaders could exchange information *immediately* prior to interstate war. However, even this measure is limited because it only records the existence of such a body, rather than the design features that distinguish bodies from one another. See Vipin Narang and Caitlin Talmadge, "Civil-Military Pathologies and Defeat in War: Tests Using New Data," *Journal of Conflict Resolution* 62, no. 7 (2018): 12.

[5] Following Geddes et al., the sample includes all states between 1946 and 2015 with populations greater than one million. This intentionally excludes small-population states, whose national security functions are qualitatively different from most other states.

state's decision-making body must meet two criteria for inclusion in the data set. First, the leader must be a member of the organization. Second, it must possess authority to make decisions regarding national security strategy. These coding rules do not necessarily mean that decisions are made by vote. For example, the U.S. National Security Council (NSC) qualifies as a decision-making body in that its members advise the national security decisions that the American president has the authority to make. Examples of decision-making bodies include cabinets, politburos, as well as other bodies such as France's Defense and National Security Council and the United Kingdom's National Security Council.

The second body of interest is the state's *coordination body*, by which bureaucratic advisers may share information with one another. To be included in the data set, a coordination body must possess the authority to exchange information regarding national security strategy.[6] Examples include the Soviet Union's Defense Council, the United Kingdom's Defence and Overseas Policy Committee, Japan's Security Council, and the U.S. NSC Principals Committee. For coding purposes, the coordination body must be distinct from the decision-making body. Coordination bodies typically reside *below* the decision-making body in the state's organizational hierarchy, sometimes as a distinct body but sometimes as a subcommittee of the decision-making body.

For each country, a team of research assistants collected data from a diverse array of sources, including political and diplomatic yearbooks, encyclopedias, foreign constitutions and laws, as well as secondary sources.[7] These resources contained detailed information regarding each country's executive branch, including both descriptions of the bodies in which executive decision-making authority rested, as well as by-name membership for each body in a given year. Research assistants consulted materials in a variety of languages, including Arabic, Belorussian, Czech, Chinese, English, French, German, Indonesian, Italian, Japanese, Korean, Macedonian, Portuguese, Russian, Serbo-Croatian, Slovak, Slovenian, Spanish, Thai, and Ukrainian. When possible, original texts of the legislation or policy that established or modified the body were collected from legal databases and gazettes. In total, the process of data collection, translation, and coding took over three years.

To measure information search capacity, a team of research assistants coded four key characteristics of decision-making bodies: diplomatic

---

[6] In cases in which a state possessed more than one body meeting those criteria, the body with the most senior membership was selected.
[7] The three resources primarily consulted were: *The Council on Foreign Relations Political Handbook of the World* (1946–1952), *International Year Book and Statesmen's Who's Who* (1953–1959), and *The Europa World Yearbook* (1960–2015).

ministry representation, defense ministry representation, foreign intelligence adviser representation, and whether the body was supported by a dedicated staff.[8] To measure bureaucratic access to information, the same team of research assistants coded four characteristics of coordination bodies: whether both defense and diplomatic representatives sat on the coordination body, whether the coordination body was supported by a staff, whether the body was chaired by a leader-appointed representative above the foreign or defense ministry, and whether the state possessed a national security advisor who could coordinate the body.[9] An additional measure coded whether either body actually convened, convened only in crisis, or was simply aspirational.[10]

A simple index score sums the answer to each set of coding questions. States with diplomatic, defense, intelligence representation on a staffed decision-making body thus receive the highest possible score along the information search dimension. States that exclude all three bureaucratic constituencies on a non-staffed decision-making body receive the lowest score. States that possess some, but not all of these characteristics receive an index score that falls in between. Following the same process, states receive the highest possible score for bureaucratic information access when they possess coordination bodies featuring both diplomatic and defense representation, these bodies are supported by a staff and designated coordinator, and possessed a national security advisor to oversee it. States receive the lowest possible score when they lack these organizational design features, with the scores of states possessing some but not all of these features falling in between. To map these index scores onto the typology, states are then binned into one of four institutional types – integrated, siloed, fragmented, and dictatorial – for each year using a score of 0.5 as the cut point for both dimensions. Table 3.1 provides illustrative examples for each category of institution, including both the country and leader name, as well as the specific years for instances in which institutions changed within the same leader's tenure. Several of these examples – such as Saddam Hussein during the Iran–Iraq War and

---

[8] For the complete codebook, see Tyler Jost, "Decision by Design: Leaders, Bureaucracies, and International Crisis Performance," Working Paper, 2024.

[9] The last three variables were only coded as "yes" if the coordination body had both defense and diplomatic representation – and thus could work to facilitate inter-bureaucratic information exchange.

[10] The coarseness of the measure stems from the paucity of data on meeting frequency in many countries. Representation on either body was coded as zero for non-utilized bodies, when the position was vacant, or when the leader held the post of foreign or defense minister. Missingness for the core variables ranged between 1 percent and 6 percent. This highlights one of the principal advantages of the measurement strategy: consistently observable and comparatively objective organizational features. For summary statistics, see Jost, "Decision by Design."

Table 3.1 *Examples of institutional types*

Integrated	Dictatorial
1,149 country-years	220 country-years
United States: Dwight Eisenhower, JFK (1962–63)	Ghana: Jerry Rawlings (1982–91)
China: Mao Zedong (1950–54; 1958–62)	Thailand: Prem Tinsulandond (1979–88)
South Korea: Kim Dae-jung, Roh Moo-hyun	DRC: Mobutu Sese Seko (1969–77, 1979–1989), Laurent Kabila
United Kingdom: Margaret Thatcher, John Major	Argentina: Juan Carlos Onganía; Alejandro Agustín Lanusse
Thailand: Sarit Thanarat, Thaksin Shinawatra	Yugoslavia: Josip Tito (1963–79); Slobodan Milosevic (1989–91)
Japan: Junichiro Koizumi, Shinzo Abe	Turkey: Cemal Gursel; Turgut Ozal
India: Atal Bihari Vajpayee (1999–2004)	Poland: Stanislaw Kania (1981), Wojciech Jaruzelski (1982–83, 1986)

Siloed	Fragmented
4,583 country-years	2,591 country-years
United States: Harry Truman (1946–1950), JFK (1961)	USSR: Nikita Khrushchev (1956–64), Leonid Brezhnev (1965–73)
USSR: Leonid Brezhnev (1974–82)	China: Mao Zedong (1967–76), Hua Guofeng (1977–78)
China: Jiang Zemin, Hu Jintao	India: Jawaharlal Nehru (1951–63)
Iraq: Saddam Hussein (1983–88), Nuri al-Maliki	Iraq: Saddam Hussein (1980–82; 1989–2002)
Israel: Golda Meir; Ariel Sharon	Israel: David Ben Guiron (1950–53; 1957–62)
India: Lal Bahadur Shastri, Indira Gandhi (1966–1977)	North Korea: Kim Il-sung (1973–83), Kim Jong-il (1997–2011)
United Kingdom: Clement Attlee (1947–51), Harold Macmillan	France: Georges Bidault

John F. Kennedy upon entering office – have been documented in the existing research, which helps to validate the measurement approach.[11]

Institutional Variation across Time and Space

These data illustrate three of the central propositions advanced in Chapter 2. First, national security institutions vary considerably across the

---

[11] Talmadge, *The Dictator's Army*, 150–164; Daalder and Destler, *In the Shadow of the Oval Office*, 12–56.

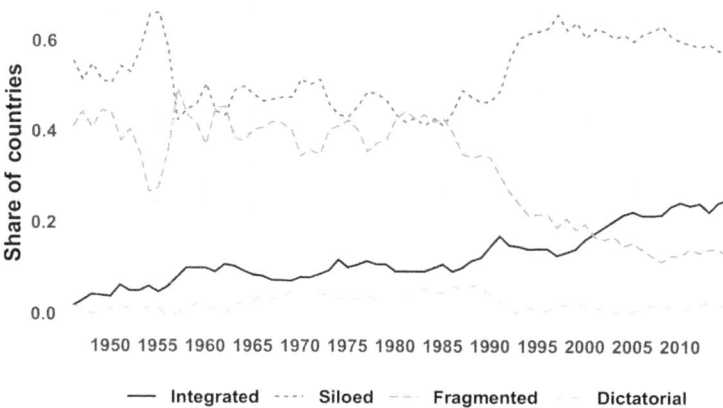

Figure 3.1 Share of states by type of national security institution

modern world. Figure 3.1 shows the distribution of national security institutions across time. In 1946, roughly 56 percent of states possessed siloed institutions while 41 percent possessed fragmented institutions. Only 2 percent of states possessed integrated institutions. Since then, the share of states possessing integrated institutions has gradually risen to about 25 percent. By 2015, the share of states with fragmented institutions had fallen to only 13 percent, while the share with siloed institutions returned to 59 percent. Consistent with the theory's predictions, dictatorial institutions have been historically uncommon. The share of states peaked at 6 percent in the 1980s, but had fallen to 2 percent by 2015.

Institutional variation is also evident across major powers, such as the United States, Soviet Union/Russia, China, the United Kingdom, and France. Even among the world's most powerful states, there is no singular structure by which political leaders relate to diplomatic, defense, and intelligence bureaucracies. For example, U.S. institutions have featured periods of siloing under Harry Truman and John F. Kennedy, prior to the institutionalization of coordinating bodies such as the NSC Principals Committee. Both the United States and France experienced fragmented periods during Lyndon Johnson and Georges Bidault, respectively. By comparison, fragmented institutions have been more common in China, the Soviet Union, and Russia, spanning across Joseph Stalin, Nikita Khrushchev, Leonid Brezhnev, Mao Zedong, and Hua Guofeng.

Second, the data illustrate how national security institutions are conceptually distinct from regime type – and that regime type does not necessarily determine the relationship between political leaders and the bureaucracy. Figure 3.2 shows how the typology of national security

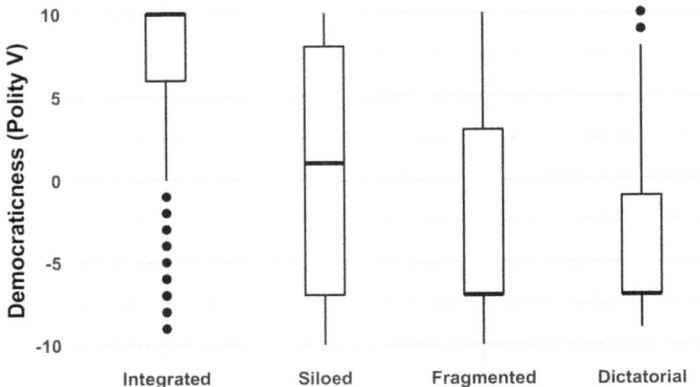

Figure 3.2 National security institutions and regime type
Note: Plot of level of democracy within each type of national security institution, based on Polity V scores. Higher values correspond to more democratic states and lower values correspond to more autocratic states. The black dots indicate outliers.

institutions map onto combined *Polity* scores, one of the most common measures for a state's level of democracy, on a scale from −10 to 10. More autocratic states receive lower *Polity* scores, while more democratic states receive higher ones. The figure highlights the considerable variation both within and across institutional types. The typical *Polity* score among states with integrated institutions (median = 10; mean = 6.74) is higher than those with siloed (median = 1; mean = 0.76) and fragmented (median = −7; mean = −2.84) ones. Yet the upper hinge (75th percentile) of the siloed boxplot is well above the lower hinge (25th percentile) of the integrated boxplot – and the lower hinge of the siloed boxplot is comparable to those of dictatorial and fragmented institutions. The whiskers of these plots (95 percent confidence interval) show that some authoritarian countries possess integrated institutions, while some consolidated democracies have fragmented ones. This strongly suggests that factors beyond regime type shape a state's national security institutions.

Finally, these data illustrate both continuity and change in institutional design. Contrary to theories positing that institutions are like a "chameleon" reflecting the leader's personality, panel (a) of Figure 3.3 shows that the majority of leaders between 1946 and 2015 kept the institutions that they inherited. Contrary to accounts that emphasize institutional path dependence, however, another 38 percent of leaders pursued organizational changes during their tenure large enough to alter the institutional type. The timing and frequency of these changes suggest

Institutional Variation across Time and Space 61

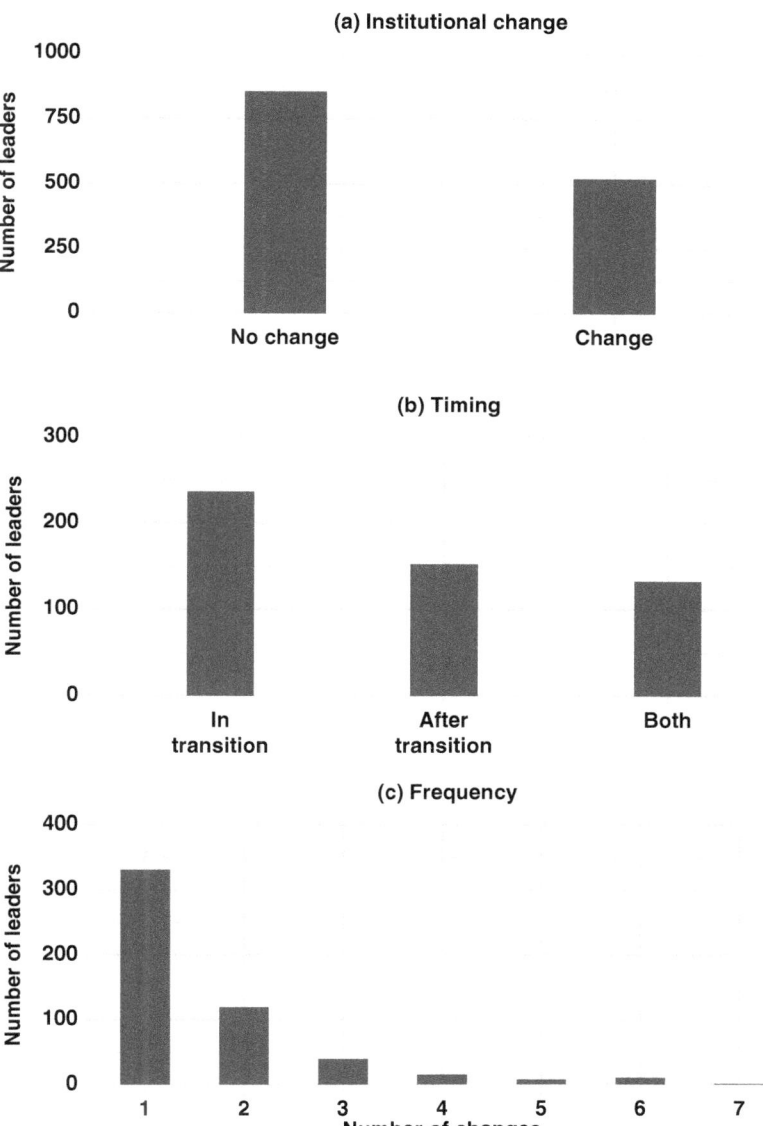

Figure 3.3 Leaders and changes in institutional design
Note: Plots of the institutional design choices of world leaders from 1946 to 2012. Panel (a) shows the breakdown of leaders who changed their institutional design in comparison to those who retained the design they inherited. Panels (b) and (c) report the distribution of leaders who changed their institution by timing and frequency, respectively.

that institutional choices were not simply a reflection of the leader's management style. Panel (b) of Figure 3.3 shows that approximately 55 percent changed their institutions *after* their transition into power. Leonid Brezhnev, for instance, shifted from fragmented to siloed institutions in 1974, over a decade after taking office. In many cases, a single leader changed their institutional design multiple times during their tenure. In fact, panel (c) of Figure 3.3 shows how 191 leaders – roughly 37 percent of leaders since 1946 who changed their institutions – did so more than once. Collectively, these data suggest both that leaders enjoy considerable flexibility in modifying their national security institutions to their liking, and that factors beyond personality shape those choices.

Testing the Institutional Theory of Miscalculation

How can we test the institutional theory of miscalculation? One approach is to examine the frequency with which states start international crises that ultimately fail to advance their objectives. Studying institutional performance in this way has several benefits. The most important advantage of this empirical strategy is that it directly identifies instances in which states initiated crises in which the benefits (i.e., the state's goals) failed to offset the costs.

Of course, leaders sitting atop integrated institutions will not always succeed in crisis – and just because a state failed to achieve its goals does not necessarily mean that there was an institutional miscalculation. For one, any individual crisis may unfold differently than the leader anticipated in ways that the information available beforehand did not suggest. For another, leaders may occasionally initiate crises despite low likelihoods of success because they assign a sufficiently high value to the issue at hand, see their prospects for success declining over time, or derive an ancillary benefit from fighting. When risk-acceptant leaders lose, it is not necessarily because of an institutional pathology. It could also be because a low-chance gamble made sense given the value they placed on the issues at stake.

As such, a statistically significant relationship between the type of national security institution a state possesses and the frequency of such crisis failures would support the core theoretical intuition that institutional pathologies increase the likelihood that leaders miscalculate when choosing to opt into international crises. If, on the other hand, institutional type had no bearing on the quality of decision-making, we would instead expect to find no systematic relationship between institutional type and crisis failures. Thus, the theory would expect that, *relative* to states with integrated institutions, states with siloed, fragmented, and dictatorial institutions should more frequently initiate crises that fail to achieve their goals.

Mapping miscalculation onto observable behavior, such as crisis performance, also requires assumptions about the nature of leader predispositions and of bureaucratic inaccuracies. These assumptions are important because some inaccurate assessments could theoretically push states toward peace rather than conflict.[12] Two specific assumptions are required. First, we must stipulate how leaders are prone to act in the absence of bureaucratic information. For instance, if leaders tended to underestimate their prospects for crisis success under these circumstances, then there might be no difference in the observed frequency of crisis failures between fragmented and integrated institutions. In this case, leaders would opt out of crises because they skew pessimistic in the absence of information.

Second, we must similarly stipulate the direction in which low-quality bureaucratic information skews. For example, if inaccurate information in siloed institutions tended to underestimate crisis prospects, we would expect no difference between siloed and integrated institutions. In this case, leaders would opt out because their information was accurate. Collectively, this would mean that we might find no systematic relationship between the miscalculations that institutions produce and the frequency of poor crisis outcomes.

The analysis of crisis performance proceeds on the assumption that leader predispositions and inaccurate bureaucratic information skew toward overestimating the odds of crisis success, underestimating the costs of crisis, and neglecting the alternatives to crisis. There are several reasons why this behavioral conjecture is warranted. First, decision-makers are prone to making self-serving assessments that inflate their prospects of winning in a wide variety of contexts.[13] Most people believe that they are better than average in performing routine tasks, like driving, as well as more complex ones, like negotiation. This tends to spill over into forecasts about the future, as decision-makers tend to think that their likelihood of positive outcomes is higher than average.[14] Dominic Johnson and colleagues have found not only that decision-makers tend

---

[12] For a discussion of such peace-inducing miscalculations and conflict, see Arthur A. Stein, "When Misperception Matters," *World Politics* 34, no. 4 (1982): 505–526; Levy, "Misperception and the Causes of War"; Jervis, "War and Misperception."

[13] For a review, see Shelley E. Taylor and David A. Armor, "Positive Illusions and Coping with Adversity," *Journal of Personality* 64, no. 4 (1996): 873–898. For applications in political science, see Jervis, *Perception and Misperception in International Politics*, 344–348; Dominic D. P. Johnson and James H. Fowler, "The Evolution of Overconfidence," *Nature* 477, no. 7364 (2011): 317–320; Kertzer, *Resolve in International Politics*, 149; Dominic D. P. Johnson, *Strategic Instincts: The Adaptive Advantages of Cognitive Biases in International Politics* (Princeton: Princeton University Press, 2020), 48–84.

[14] Jonathan Renshon and Daniel Kahneman, "Hawkish Biases and the Interdisciplinary Study of Conflict Decision-Making," in *Advancing Interdisciplinary Approaches to International Relations* (London: Palgrave Macmillan, 2017), 81.

to exhibit overconfidence in crisis simulations, but also that decision-makers exhibiting overconfidence are more likely to start conflicts.[15] Other studies find similar trends in the historical record.[16] Second, decision-makers are prone to underestimating the costs of confrontation and overestimating their own ability. Decision-makers often fail to account for the ways in which hostility during crisis may shape adversary perceptions of their belligerence and unwillingness to compromise in the face of aggression.[17]

In sum, we have good reasons to believe that leaders are more likely to overestimate their odds of success in crisis when they sit atop institutions that provide incomplete or low-quality information. This would suggest that the propensity to miscalculate along the institutional pathways outlined above should degrade a state's record of performance in international crisis. All else being equal, nonintegrated institutions should be more likely to initiate crises that fail to advance the state's goals.

To identify instances of international crisis failure, the analysis turns to the *International Crisis Behavior Data Set* (ICB), which provides a comprehensive list of international crises in the modern era. The ICB contains 367 international crises between 1946 and 2015. Examples include the 1948 Berlin Blockade, the 1962 Cuban Missile Crisis, and the 1998 India–Pakistan nuclear tests. On average, there have been just over five international crises per year since 1945.[18]

The ICB also identifies whether states achieved their objectives during the crisis. A crisis is identified as a success if the observed outcome was either a victory, in which the state achieved its basic goals – or a compromise, in which the state at least partially achieved its basic goals. A crisis is identified as a failure if the observed outcome was either a defeat, in which the state yielded or surrendered to an adversary – or stalemate, in which the crisis had no effect on the state's basic goals.

The ICB's accompanying narrative of each episode, as well as supplemental primary and secondary sources, were reviewed for two reasons. First, the ICB narratives were used to identify first movers in the crisis,

---

[15] Dominic D. P. Johnson et al., "Overconfidence in Wargames: Experimental Evidence on Expectations, Aggression, Gender and Testosterone," *Proceedings of the Royal Society B: Biological Sciences* 273, no. 1600 (2006): 2513–2520.

[16] Van Evera, *Causes of War*, 14–34; Dominic D. P. Johnson, *Overconfidence and War* (Cambridge: Harvard University Press, 2004).

[17] Renshon and Kahneman, "Hawkish Biases," 84–85.

[18] The analysis intentionally departs from another commonly used measures of international conflict, the militarized interstate disputes (MIDs). Past scholarship identifies measurement error in the MID data set that is not distributed at random, but rather clusters in geographic areas outside Europe and North America. See Alastair Iain Johnston, "What (If Anything) Does East Asia Tell Us About International Relations Theory?," *Annual Review of Political Science* 15 (2012): 53–78.

Table 3.2 *Crisis performance across institutional types*

		Type of national security institution			
	Outcome	Integrated	Siloed	Fragmented	Dictatorial
All crises	Success	130 (76%)	218 (54%)	159 (45%)	12 (55%)
	Failure	40 (24%)	185 (46%)	194 (55%)	10 (45%)
Initiated crises	Success	61 (74%)	107 (44%)	73 (32%)	4 (40%)
	Failure	21 (26%)	137 (56%)	153 (68%)	6 (60%)

Note: Cross-tabulations for crisis outcomes by institutional type. Percentages report the column-wise proportions for each institutional category.

thereby accounting for situations in which states were not proximately responsible for triggering the crisis. This is important because states sometimes end up in crisis due to policy choices beyond their control, meaning that there was not necessarily a miscalculation. First-mover status is assigned to states whose policy choices most directly precipitated the international crisis. For example, the Soviet Union is coded as the first mover during the 1958 Berlin Crisis because of its demands for the Western powers to demilitarize the city. Second, the ICB narratives and supplemental sources were used to check the accuracy and consistency of the original codings. In 93 percent of cases, the original outcome coding was supported by the evidence reviewed. Inaccuracies or discrepancies, in which nearly identical circumstances in another crisis were coded differently, were identified and recoded in the remaining cases.[19]

Analysis

Table 3.2 offers a simple analysis of the relationship between national security institutions and crisis performance by reporting cross-tabulations of outcomes for all international crises across the four types of national security institutions. While the success rate is about even (51 percent) for siloed institutions, it is substantially higher for integrated institutions (76 percent) and lower for fragmented institutions (45 percent). The trends are even clearer if we subset the sample to only look at crises that the state was responsible for initiating the crisis. States with integrated institutions were successful in achieving their goals in 74 percent of such crises. In contrast, states with siloed and fragmented institutions fared considerably worse, achieving their goals in only 44 percent and 32 percent,

---

[19] Justification for each coding adjustment, including supporting sources, is detailed in the supplemental appendix. See Jost, "Decision by Design."

respectively. The rate of success for dictatorial institutions is similarly poor, although there are comparatively few cases by which to measure their performance.

Taken together, this offers some preliminary evidence in support of the institutional theory of miscalculation. Across the modern world, states that have adopted integrated institutions tend to achieve their goals in international crisis more frequently than states with other institutional designs that the theory suggests may be prone to incomplete and biased information provision.

We can further probe the theory through a statistical model of the relative frequency of international crisis failure. This is useful because the data reported in Table 3.2 do not account for the amount of time that states possessed each institutional type or the other state characteristics that might have made them more likely to experience an international crisis ending in failure. The dependent variable is thus coded as 1 if the state initiated a crisis that failed to achieve the state's goals and a 0 otherwise. As the dependent variable is dichotomous, the analysis employs logistic regression, using several methods to address temporal and geographic dependence. First, pooled analyses cluster standard errors on the state. This ensures that no single country skews the results. Second, separate models are estimated using country fixed effects, which helps to correct for unobservable characteristics of any given state.[20] Third, all models include a measure of the number of years since the country experienced an international crisis, as well as polynomial terms of this quantity.[21]

Another advantage of a statistical model is that it allows us to account for other variables commonly thought to shape a state's risk of initiating a crisis that fails to advance its objectives, many of which may also be associated with institutional design. The first set of control variables measure demographic characteristics of the leader, such as gender, time in office, and prior military and/or combat experience. This is helpful because existing research finds that such demographic characteristics may be associated with the leader's risk profile, but might also be associated with a leader's style of management.[22] A second set of controls accounts

---

[20] Donald P. Green, Soo Yeon Kim, and David H. Yoon, "Dirty Pool," *International Organization* 55, no. 2 (2001): 441–468.

[21] Year counts begin in 1918, which is the first year for which there is ICB data available. On the method, see David B. Carter and Curtis S. Signorino, "Back to the Future: Modeling Time Dependence in Binary Data," *Political Analysis* 18, no. 3 (2010): 271–292.

[22] Weeks, "Strongmen and Straw Men: Authoritarian Regimes and the Initiation of International Conflict," *American Political Science Review* 106, no. 2 (2012): 326–347; Michael C. Horowitz and Allan C. Stam, "How Prior Military Experience Influences the Future Militarized Behavior of Leaders," *International Organization* 68, no. 3

for the type of regime the state possesses. Less democratic regimes, for instance, could be prone to select into risky crises because leaders are not held accountable for performance, but they might also make leaders less likely to adopt certain institutional arrangements in the first place. The analysis thus uses Polity V scores to account for a state's level of democraticness. More democratic regimes take on higher values and more autocratic regimes take on lower values of the variable.[23] Two dichotomous variables codes whether the state is a military or personalist dictatorship. A final set of controls accounts for material capabilities of the state. States with material advantages may be emboldened to coerce adversaries through military means and thus more likely to select into risky crises but might also be more likely to adopt certain institutional structures. The analysis accounts for material advantages first through a measure of the state's economic and military powers (the *Composite Indicator of National Capability* score), as well as whether the state was an ally of the United States, as identified by the *Alliance Treaty Obligations and Provisions* data set.[24]

The statistical analysis begins by estimating the relationship between national security institutions and international crisis failure. Because the theory's predictions are *relative*, the primary explanatory variable is a categorical variable with integrated set as the base category. This is important because there might be some instances in which states did the best they could with the information they had and still failed in crisis. In other words, there is always some baseline risk that states fail to achieve their crisis goals. It is thus important to test whether there is a statistically significant difference between integrated institutions' rate of failure relative to nonintegrated alternatives. If the theory were correct, we would expect to find that, relative to integrated institutions, states with siloed, fragmented, and dictatorial institutions are more likely to initiate international crises that fail to advance their objectives.

Table 3.3 reports the results. Models 1 and 2 estimate pooled and fixed effects models using the full set of covariates. In both models, states with siloed institutions are more prone to international crisis failure than states with integrated institutions. One interpretation of this finding is

---

(2014): 527–559. The analysis relies on an updated version of the *LEAD* data set. See Jost, "Decision by Design."

[23] Monty G. Marshall, Ted Robert Gurr, and Keith Jaggers, *Polity IV Project: Political Regime Characteristics and Transitions, 1800–2016* (Center for Systemic Peace, 2017). Transitioning states are recoded to the median value in the main analysis and dropped as a robustness check.

[24] J. David Singer, Stuart Bremer, and John Stuckey, "Capability Distribution, Uncertainty, and Major Power War, 1820–1965," in *Peace, War, and Numbers*, ed. Bruce Russett (Beverly Hills: Sage, 1972); Brett Leeds et al., "Alliance Treaty Obligations and Provisions, 1815–1944," *International Interactions* 28, no. 3 (2002): 237–260.

Table 3.3 *National security institutions and international crisis performance*

	Outcome variable: international crisis failure		
	(1)	(2)	(3)
Siloed	0.92*** (0.29)	1.26*** (0.41)	1.22*** (0.42)
Fragmented	1.43*** (0.32)	1.67*** (0.42)	1.61*** (0.43)
Dictatorial	0.61 (0.46)	0.78 (0.58)	0.66 (0.57)
Male	0.62 (0.81)	0.91 (0.77)	1.00 (0.77)
Military experience	0.72*** (0.25)	0.55** (0.22)	0.60** (0.24)
Combat experience	−0.41 (0.26)	−0.50** (0.24)	−0.72*** (0.26)
Time in office	−0.01 (0.01)	−0.02 (0.01)	−0.01 (0.01)
Military regime	−0.30 (0.35)	−0.20 (0.35)	−0.11 (0.38)
Personalist regime	0.25 (0.22)	0.50* (0.27)	0.58** (0.29)
Democraticness	−0.01 (0.02)	−0.03* (0.02)	−0.02 (0.02)
Material capabilities	9.07*** (2.03)	2.25 (5.15)	5.56 (5.29)
U.S. ally		−0.14 (0.28)	−0.14 (0.31)
Size of the decision-making body			−0.02 (0.01)
Military share			0.33 (0.65)
Observations	7,931	7,931	7,269
Pseudo R^2	0.123	0.242	0.252
Cluster robust SEs	✓		
Fixed effects		✓	✓
Regional controls	✓		
Time polynomials	✓	✓	✓

*p <0.1; **p <0.05; ***p <0.01

Note: Results of logistic regressions with country-year as the unit of analysis. *Integrated* serves as the base category for national security institutions. Model 1 reports results with robust standard errors clustered on the country. Models 2 and 3 reports results with country fixed effects. Model 3 includes additional controls for size of the decision-making body, as well as the share of representatives on the decision-making body who were military officers.

that, across the modern world, leaders are prone to miscalculate on the road to war when their state lacks capacity to facilitate inter-bureaucratic information sharing. In addition, states with fragmented institutions are similarly more prone to international crisis failures than integrated institutions. This finding is again consistent with the theory's proposition that leaders are prone to miscalculate when core bureaucratic constituencies lack access and incentive to relay quality information to political leaders. As suggested by the relative magnitude of the coefficients, states with fragmented institutions tend to perform worse than those with siloed institutions. Resetting the reference category reveals a statistically significant difference between siloed and fragmented institutions (p = 0.002). Finally, dictatorial institutions also appear to be prone to international crisis failures, although the statistical relationship is weak, perhaps as a result of the small number of countries with such designs.

One potential question is whether integrated institutions perform better because they include more individuals, regardless of whether they are affiliated with the core bureaucracies the theory posits are critical to supplying leaders with the information they need when considering the costs and benefits of crisis initiation. That is, leaders may simply receive better information in *larger* groups, as opposed to groups into which key bureaucracies participate. Model 3 probes this possibility by controlling for the size of the decision-making body. The results show that while larger bodies are negatively associated with crisis failure, the relationship is not statistically significant. Moreover, including this control does not change the main findings regarding national security institutions.

The direction of the coefficients in these models also allow us probe some of the alternative explanations discussed in Chapter 2. Congruent with accountability theory, the coefficients of a state's level of democracy is negative, suggesting that more democratic states are more likely to "look before they leap" into risky international confrontations. Similarly, the coefficients of personalist dictatorships are positive, suggesting that such states are also more prone to miscalculation. However, the estimated relationships between these regime attributes and international crisis failure are not statistically significant in most model specifications. In addition, the magnitude of the effects is substantively smaller than that of national security institutions. This suggests that transitioning from an integrated to a fragmented institution, for example, exerts a larger effect on a state's propensity for miscalculation than transitioning from a non-personalist to personalist dictatorship. While this does not rule out the possibility that accountability may affect the types of national security institutions states are likely to adopt, the results suggest that accountability alone may be insufficient to explain why states miscalculate.

Consistent with theories emphasizing leader beliefs, heads of state with prior military experience are more likely to initiate international crisis failures in both models. Leaders with combat experience are less likely to do so, although the relationship is only statistically significant in Model 2. Yet even when controlling for these aspects of a leader's risk profile, the models show that national security institutions still exert a large and statistically significant effect on international crisis behavior. In short, leader beliefs are necessary but insufficient to explain why states blunder.

Finally, these results are in tension with the interest group model of bureaucratic politics, which would expect states to miscalculate at higher rates when hawkish constituencies, such as the military, wield more political influence. Models 1 and 2 find no consistent or statistically significant relationship between military dictatorships and international crisis failure. Model 3 further probes the interest group model by including a measure of the share of military officers on the state's decision-making and coordination bodies. Higher (lower) values correspond to a greater (lesser) share of the representatives appointed to these bodies. Inconsistent with the interest group model, states in which military officers enjoy a higher rate of representation are not associated with a higher risk of crisis failure. Again, this suggests that traditional models of bureaucratic politics are insufficient to explain when states miscalculate.

Related work extends these models through alternative model specifications, as well as a series of robustness checks, such as: using continuous measures of the two dimensions; controlling for additional domestic political factors (e.g., time since last coup and transformative domestic agendas); using multinomial models to disaggregate observations in which no crisis was initiated and ones in which the state initiated and succeeded; including gross domestic product and trade, which are excluded from the analysis above due to missingness over the study period; dropping the United States, the Soviet Union/Russia, and China from the analysis; dropping regimes during domestic political transitions; and controlling for the Cold War period.[25]

Testing the Political Theory of Institutional Design

Next, we can use these data to systematically probe the factors shaping the design of national security institutions. Chapter 2 proposed two important considerations stemming from the leader's political environment: bureaucratic threat and the focus of the leader's agenda. It also argued that leaders tend to think about these considerations in sequence, choosing integrated institutions when bureaucratic threat is low, and then choosing between fragmented and siloed institutions based on if the agenda is focused on domestic or international issues. Finally, it reviewed other important factors that might shape institutional design in parallel: regime type, international diffusion, and path dependence.

Table 3.4 explores these candidate explanations of institutional design through three regression models. The theory proposes that a number of different considerations might shape the threat that bureaucracies pose to a leader's survival, many of which will be extremely context-specific. For purposes of a cross-national analysis, however, we can use two proxy variables: the duration of time since the last coup and the number of years of experience in office possessed by the leader. The first variable captures the theory's proposition that leaders distrust bureaucracies that have

---

[25] See Jost, "Decision by Design."

Table 3.4 *The political origins of institutional design*

	Outcome variable:		
	Choosing integrated over nonintegrated institutions		Choosing siloed over fragmented/dictatorial institutions
	(1)	(2)	(3)
Times since last coup (years)	0.06*** (0.01)	0.07*** (0.01)	
Leader experience (years)	0.06*** (0.01)	0.08*** (0.01)	
Transformative domestic agenda			−0.64*** (0.11)
Defense budget (log)			0.14*** (0.03)
Democraticness	0.15*** (0.02)	0.09*** (0.02)	0.11*** (0.01)
Leader experience × democraticness		0.01*** (0.002)	
U.S. ally	0.26 (0.26)	0.21 (0.26)	
Leader inherited integrated institutions	2.70*** (0.19)	2.75*** (0.19)	1.01*** (0.18)
Leader inherited siloed institutions			1.01*** (0.09)
Constant	−3.12*** (0.50)	−3.02*** (0.50)	−3.72*** (0.79)
Observations	8,253	8,253	5,753
Pseudo R^2	0.745	0.749	0.428
Country fixed effects	✓	✓	✓

*p <0.1; **p <0.05; ***p <0.01

Note: Logistic regression with country-year as the unit of analysis. In Models 1 and 2, the outcome variable is coded as "1" if the state possessed an integrated institution and "0" if the state possessed a siloed, fragmented, or dictatorial institution. Model 3 omits "integrated" country-years and the outcome variable is coded as "1" if the state possessed a siloed institution and "0" if the state possessed a fragmented or dictatorial institution.

challenged leaders in the recent past. The second variable reflects the theory's intuition that more experienced leaders may feel better positioned to withstand criticism from the bureaucracy during policy debates.

Model 1 of Table 3.4 uses a simple logistic regression, where the outcome variable is coded as "1" if the state possessed an integrated institution and "0" otherwise. The model controls for the state's level of democracy, whether the state was an ally of the United States, and whether the leader inherited an integrated institution. The first control accounts for existing accounts arguing that more democratic regimes may be predisposed to choose more effective decision-making institutions. The second control accounts for the intuition that integrated institutions may have been more likely to diffuse from high-status countries, such as the United States, when the two countries can share information about institutional design through defense partnerships.[26] The third control variable incorporates the insight that path dependence may shape institutional design. The model also includes country fixed effects to help account for unobservable attributes of the state.

The results align with the theory's claims. There is a positive and significant relationship between the amount of time since there was a coup in the state and integrated institutions. The relationship between leader experience and integrated institutions is similarly positive and statistically significant. This suggests that leaders are more likely to adopt high performing institutions when they feel confident that the bureaucracy does not present a threat to their political survival. As bureaucratic threats increase, leaders prefer to sacrifice the good advice that integrated institutions afford in exchange for political protection.

We can further explore these findings by looking at the interaction between leader experience and the level of democracy within the state. If the theory's contention that experience shapes the ability of leaders to withstand bureaucratic challenges during public debates is correct, we would expect that the effect of leader experience is partly conditional on democratic restraints that protect public debate in the first place. Model 2 thus replicates the analysis in Model 1 but adds an interaction term between leader experience and the state's democraticness. As reported in Table 3.4, the interaction between these variables is statistically significant. Figure 3.4 plots the results for ease of interpretation. The plot shows that the marginal effect of leader experience on choosing an integrated institution is largest in highly democratic states. While this relationship between leader experience and integrated institutions remain

---

[26] As in the previous analyses, democracy scores are taken from the Polity V data set and alliances are taken from the *Alliance Treaty Obligations and Provisions* data set.

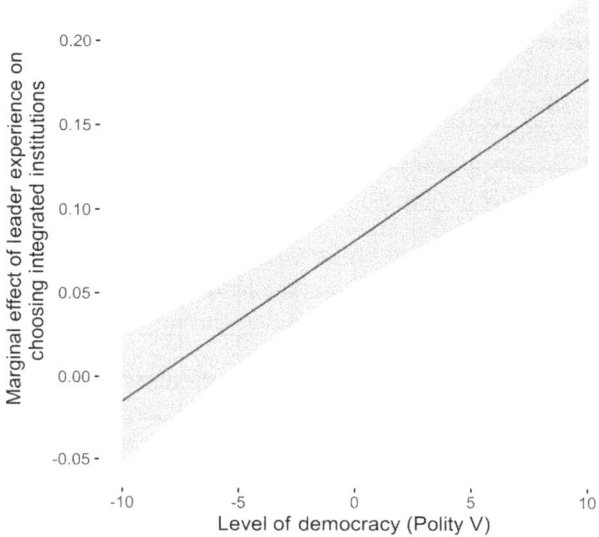

Figure 3.4 Interaction between leader experience and regime type
Note: Plot of the interaction between leader experience (in years) and the state's level of democracy. In highly autocratic states, the marginal effect of leader experience is indistinguishable from zero. As the level of democracy increases, the marginal effect of leader experience becomes positive and statistically significant.

statistically significant in weakly autocratic states as well, the magnitude of the effect is smaller by comparison. In contrast, the marginal effect of experience is statistically indistinguishable from zero in highly autocratic states featuring curtailed space for policy debates.

We can next turn to the choice between different types of nonintegrated institutions. The theory proposes that a major consideration shaping this choice is the leader's agenda focus. Leaders who confront salient international threats should be more likely to adopt the siloed institutions that accept a modicum of political risk in exchange for better bureaucratic information provision. In contrast, leaders whose survival depends on addressing domestic crises or implementing transformative domestic policies may instead opt for fragmented or dictatorial institutions. Much like bureaucratic threat, knowing a specific leader's agenda depends on a number of context-specific factors, but for purposes of a cross-national analysis, we can use two variables that proxy for these considerations. To proxy for the salience of international security issues, the analysis uses the size of the state's defense budget.[27] To proxy for the salience of transformative domestic issues, the analysis includes a variable measuring whether the leader sought to implement a revolutionary change in the official state ideology, property rights, gender rights, ethnic rights, or state religion.[28]

Model 3 of Table 3.4 again employs a simple logistic regression, where the outcome variable is coded as a "1" if the state possessed siloed institutions, and "0" if the state possessed fragmented or dictatorial. The sample of country-years omits states with integrated institutions, allowing us to focus on the choice that leaders face between different pathological configurations. The model includes the same controls as Models 1 and 2.

The results again align with theoretical predictions. There is a positive and statistically significant relationship between larger defense budgets and siloed institutions. Siloed institutions appear to be most useful when leaders face an international environment that makes national security advice more valuable. In contrast, there is a negative and statistically significant relationship between possessing a transformative domestic agenda and siloed institutions. Leaders focused on domestic issues appear to be more likely to choose fragmented institutions that help insulate them from bureaucratic sanction. Taken together, the results are consistent with the theory's core claims that leaders face a trade-off between better advice and political security and that they resolve this trade-off based on the characteristics of their political environment.

Finally, the analysis finds that this political trade-off appears to operate in parallel to other factors emphasized by the existing literature. There is a positive and statistically significant relationship between being allied with the United States and adopting integrated institutions, suggesting that institutional designs may diffuse through strong defense partnerships. There is also a strong positive relationship between the type of institution that leaders inherit and the type that they keep, suggesting that institutions are "sticky" – or resistant to change. Finally, there is a strong positive relationship between democracy and integrated institutions. One interpretation of this finding is that leaders are motivated to choose integrated institutions when they are held politically

---

[27] This variable is taken from the Correlates of War's *National Material Capabilities* data set.
[28] These correspond to five of the seven categories of revolutionary change coded in the *Revolutionary Leaders Data Set*. Two of the original categories – change to formal constitution and creation of a revolutionary council – are omitted because these variables are conceptually similar to the underlying measures of national security institutions. See Colgan, "Domestic Revolutionary Leaders and International Conflict."

accountable. Another possibility more closely aligned with the theory's propositions, however, is that democracies also tend to feature the types of professionalized bureaucracies that make them less politically threatening to the leader. As such, the regime type requires further exploration in the case studies in Chapters 4–8.

Empirical Strategy for the Case Studies

The quantitative analysis provides evidence consistent with the theory's predictions regarding the origins and consequences of national security institutions. While this is useful in establishing broad patterns, however, cross-national statistical analysis leaves open important questions regarding the causal relationship between institutions and miscalculation.

Qualitative analysis in subsequent chapters offers a fruitful method of inquiry to, illustrate the theory's causal mechanisms. To show the broad applicability of the theory's intuitions, the analysis examines four case countries – China, India, Pakistan, and the United States. As summarized in Table 3.5, each case draws from archival documents, government records, memoirs, and interviews. These countries are analytically useful because they are representative of the most prominent types of political regimes: personalist, collectivist, and military dictatorships, as well

Table 3.5 *Summary of data collection*

	Micro-level institutional data: meetings and information flow		
	Record Type	Measures	Source
China	Meetings	Frequency & affiliation	Leader records (年谱)
India	Correspondence	Frequency & affiliation	*Selected Works of J. Nehru*
Pakistan	Not available	Not available	Not available
United States	Meetings	Frequency, affiliation, & duration	Presidential daily dairies
	General sources		
	Archives	Interviews	Published sources
China	Foreign Ministry, provincial	Summer 2016, Spring 2017	Memoirs, official histories
India	Nehru Memorial Library	Winter 2017; oral histories	Memoirs, government reports
Pakistan	Not available	Fall 2017	Memoirs
United States	Eisenhower, JFK, LBJ Libraries	Oral histories	*FRUS*, memoirs

as presidential and parliamentary democracies. Additionally, as summarized in Table 3.6, there is institutional variation *within* the same type of regime. This variation helps to show how the theory illuminates the politics of national security institutions across quite different regime types.

Tracing the Effects of the Political Environment on Institutions

Each chapter begins by testing the political theory of institutional design. The theory has two explanatory variables: the level of *bureaucratic threat* to the leader's political survival and *focus* of the leader's agenda.

Establishing indicators for each variable before examining institutional features is critical to testing the theory's causal mechanisms. To measure bureaucratic threat, we can assess perceptions of the bureaucracy's capability and intent to politically sanction the leader through coup or through shaping broader policy debates between the leader and political opponents. The capability component is measured by evaluating whether the leader had prior experience managing the national security bureaucracy, as experienced leaders are expected to enjoy advantages in navigating and debating bureaucratic advisers aiming to sanction leaders. The intent aspect is measured by determining whether the leader perceived conflicting interests among bureaucratic advisers that were motivating them to sanction the leader.

We can gauge leader focus by examining their beliefs regarding political survival, often directly evidenced their own statements in the historical record. Each case also seeks supporting indicators that the leader's agenda was predominantly focused on international or domestic issues. Agendas are coded as domestically focused when the leader pursues transformative policies aiming to fundamentally alter the country's economic social, or political order. Perceiving few or no hostile foreign adversaries threatening the country's security and territorial integrity similarly provides evidence of domestic focus.[29] Conversely, perceptions of hostile foreign adversaries provide evidence of an international agenda focus.

Each case uses three coding questions to measure *institutional design* within the respective case countries, thereby offering a more detailed

---

[29] These measures raise important questions about whether a leader's threat perceptions are accurate and, if not, whether the source of the inaccuracy stems from poor information or disposition. Where possible, the analysis attempts to show that threat perceptions are rooted in objectively verifiable concerns, but leaves open the possibility that leaders may inflate the severity of these threats. See also Greitens, *Dictators and Their Secret Police*, 35–36.

Table 3.6 Overview of the case studies on decision-making

Regime type	Country (Leader) & Institutional Type	Case Study (Year)
Personalist dictatorship	China (Mao) – integrated	Nationalist invasion scare (1962)
	China (Mao) – fragmented	Sino-Soviet border conflict (1969)
Collectivist dictatorship	China (Deng) – fragmented	Sino-Vietnamese War (1979)
	China (Jiang) – siloed	EP-3 reconnaissance aircraft incident (2001)
Parliamentary democracy	India (Nehru) – fragmented	Sino-Indian War (1962)
	India (Vajpayee) – integrated	Twin Peaks Crisis (2001–2002)
	Pakistan (Sharif) – siloed	Kargil War (1999)
Presidential democracy	The United States (Eisenhower) – integrated	Second Taiwan Strait Crisis (1958)
	The United States (Johnson) – fragmented	Vietnam War (1965)

picture of state's institutions than is possible in a cross-national analysis. The first question assesses whether the state's rules and processes for national security decision-making were inclusive of diplomatic, defense, and intelligence bureaucracies. Indicators for this coding include the appointment and participation of these constituencies on apex decision-making bodies. A second question investigates if the state's rules and processes permitted or restricted information sharing between bureaucracies. Key indicators include the presence of coordination bodies below the apex level, inclusive membership and agendas within these bodies, as well as designated coordinators and staffs to oversee information sharing. A third measure examines whether the historical record shows signs of incomplete or biased information provision. Each case looks for evidence whether bureaucrats possessed access to the leader in practice and whether they engaged in genuine deliberation.

The cases incorporate several sets of micro-level institutional data. In the case on China, archival records from the administrations of Mao Zedong and Deng Xiaoping measure the frequency of and participation in meetings of key bodies such as the Politburo, Central Military Commission, and Foreign Affairs Leading Small Group, as well as numerous informal meetings spanning from 1949 to 1989. The case on the United States complements this process for the Eisenhower, Kennedy, and Johnson administrations by coding data from the Presidential Daily Dairies, which outline the bureaucratic advisers with whom the president met each day in office. The case on India follows a similar approach, measuring the flow of memoranda and correspondence within the Nehru administration. Additional details on this aspect of the data collection process are provided in Appendix B.

Micro-level institutional data offer several advantages. First, they help to validate cross-national measures of national security institutions, ensuring that they shaped decision-making processes as suggested. Second, they enhance confidence that inferences drawn about decision-making are not idiosyncratic or based on outlier episodes. This addresses a common empirical challenge in existing research, where decision-making process is only examined in the same episode for which performance is assessed.[30] Studying the effects of decision-making *during* the Cuban Missile Crisis on outcome might overlook other factors shaping both decision-making and crisis outcome. The approach employed here, inspired by recent studies of leaders,[31] aims to first measure patterns in

---

[30] For an exploration of the connection between process and outcome, see Schafer and Crichlow, *Groupthink versus High-Quality Decision Making in International Relations*.
[31] For example, see Saunders, *Leaders at War*; Keren Yarhi-Milo, *Who Fights for Reputation: The Psychology of Leaders in International Conflict* (Princeton: Princeton University Press, 2018).

decision-making processes broadly before evaluating how they may have shaped crisis behavior.

Tracing the Effects of Institutions on Decision-Making

The second half of each chapter delves into the consequences of the state's institutional design. This begins with a medium-n analysis of all international crises to which the country was party during the study period. The medium-n analysis first considers general patterns in institutional performance, comparing the relative frequency at which the state advanced its goals. To code the state's goals, a supervised team of research assistants reviewed each crisis, identified the leader's objectives, and then evaluated whether they were achieved by the end of the crisis.[32] In parallel with the cross-national statistical analysis, the theory predicts that states with fragmented institutions will be less likely to achieve their goals relative to states with integrated designs. States with siloed institutions are expected to perform better than integrated alternatives, but better than fragmented ones. The medium-n analysis then considers the quality of information flow and deliberation decision-making processes across the full sample of international crises. This helps to ensure that leaders did not set aside institutional processes on the eve of crisis.

The remainder of the analysis focuses on illustrating the theorized mechanisms linking national security institutions to miscalculation. The analysis selects a specific set of crises, summarized in Table 3.6, with three broad considerations in mind. First, cases are selected based on the availability of rich data detailing the decision-making process. Second, cases are selected with prominent alternative explanations in mind. The analysis evaluates several cases that occurred before and after institutional design changes, but under the same regime type. Similarly, the cases on the 1962 Nationalist invasion scare and the 1969 Sino-Soviet border conflict compare decision-making before and after institutional changes under the same leader. Third, the analysis prioritizes cases in which decision-makers perceived high "stakes" to the resolution of the issue at hand. Each chapter discusses country-specific case selection considerations and concludes by exploring alternative explanations for the origin of miscalculations.

Each case study follows a two-step process. The first step codes whether a miscalculation occurred according to the definition outlined in the theoretical framework. This coding procedure begins by examining

---

[32] Narrative codings of crisis objectives and outcomes are provided in the Online Appendix. The tables in the text report the outcome for the state's primary objective during the crisis.

the logic of the leader's decision: what projections and beliefs led the decision-maker to adopt a policy that altered the status quo? What (if anything) did the leader anticipate their choices would accomplish? Leader statements made in private serve as the most compelling evidence in this regard. The coding procedure then evaluates leader projections and beliefs against the actual outcome. Combining these elements, a case is coded as a miscalculation if the leader's projections proved different from the observed outcome.

Evaluating leader projections involves considering several ways that leader projections can prove inaccurate. First, they might be wrong about whether their strategy can achieve their objectives. For instance, a projection that the state will be able to take and hold a piece of territory would prove inaccurate if the state fails to do so. Second, the specific reasons underpinning why leaders think they will succeed at a particular cost may be inaccurate. In the case of India's Forward Policy in the fall of 1961, a key assessment was that China would not use force to dislodge India's new posts along the border. This projection proved incorrect when China attacked Indian positions the following year.

Evaluating leader projections can be especially challenging in some situations. One challenge arises when the leader's strategy was to shape an adversary's beliefs, such as by demonstrating their resolve. The cases adopt two steps to address this challenge. The first is to examine source material from inside the *adversary's* decision-making process in order to assess whether a belief change occurred. In case on the 1979 Sino-Vietnamese War, for instance, Chinese leaders hoped the war would showcase their military superiority over Vietnam. The analysis thus examines Vietnamese primary sources to assess whether the war indeed shaped Hanoi's beliefs as Chinese leaders intended. The second approach involves looking for behavioral indicators of belief change. In the case of the 1979 Sino-Vietnamese War, we can observe whether Vietnamese military behavior was more cautious after the war, suggesting a new estimate of China's military strength.

An additional challenge pertains to what adversaries might have done had no crisis occurred. In the Sino-Soviet border conflict, for instance, one important assessment was that Moscow planned to strike if China did not preempt a Soviet attack. Given that we cannot observe what Soviet decision-makers would have done if China had not attacked Soviet forces, the analysis relies on Soviet records, such as decision-maker diaries, to gauge intentions. Leader projections are coded as inaccurate when the adversary's documentary record does not confirm those beliefs.

The second step of each case study is to consider whether leader (mis)calculations can be attributed to the type of national security institution. The theory would expect that, under integrated institutions, wide information search coupled with competitive dialogue will yield generally accurate leader projections. Conversely, the theory expects that, under fragmented institutions, narrow information search and restrictions on bureaucratic deliberation will cause leaders to miscalculate. In such cases, incomplete information tends to align with the leader's existing beliefs, which remain unchecked during decision-making. Finally, the theory predicts that, unlike fragmented institutions, siloed institutions should encourage bureaucrats to supply information reflecting their organizational biases and parochial interests.

Finally, it is important to consider how to assess whether nondisclosure of information is influenced by factors beyond institutional design. The absence of information could stem from the constraints of the international system or from the rational prioritization of a large volume of state information. The analysis follows two steps to confirm that these considerations are not the sole determinates of poor information. First, each case considers whether the bureaucracy had, or could easily have obtained, more accurate information at the time than the leader possessed. Second, each case examines motivations underpinning the bureaucracy's information provision. Under siloed institutions, the theory would expect bureaucrats to withhold information because they were unaware of what other advisers were telling the leader. Under fragmented institutions, the theory would expect bureaucrats to withhold information because they feared political retribution for speaking truth to power. In both cases, limitations on the leader's access to information arises from institutional considerations.

Conclusion

This chapter offered an empirical strategy to identify different types of national security institutions across the modern world. Leveraging the *National Security Institutions Data Set*, the analysis provided evidence in support of three central propositions advanced in Chapter 2. First, the data showed that there is widespread variation in institutional design across states, which was not predetermined by regime transition or leadership turnover. Second, the chapter offered statistical evidence suggesting that states with integrated institutions tend to achieve their goals in international crises at higher rates than states with nonintegrated alternatives. Third, the chapter illustrated a general connection between institutional type and the domestic political environment. The chapter concluded by laying out a qualitative research design to qualitatively probe these broad patterns, paying special attention to the theoretical mechanisms developed in Chapter 2. The subsequent chapters execute that strategy, beginning with the People's Republic of China under Mao Zedong.

4 China under Mao

On March 2, 1969, China launched a punishing ambush against Soviet troops patrolling on Zhenbao Island, a tract of disputed territory in a remote area along China's northeastern border. In Beijing, reports that the Soviet Union was planning for offensive action against China led decision-makers to conclude that its best available option was to demonstrate its resolve through a show of force.[1] Yet China's ambush at Zhenbao backfired. Instead of deterring Soviet escalation, it provoked it. The Soviet Union ordered a military mobilization, violently retaliated against the Chinese positions along the border, and issued veiled nuclear threats that prompted China to evacuate Beijing.

China's decision to attack Soviet forces on Zhenbao was based on two inaccurate conclusions that its leader, Mao Zedong, had drawn. First, Mao's assessments about the prospects for an attack were wrong. There is little evidence that the Soviet Union was preparing for an attack on China prior to the crisis. Second, Mao mistakenly believed that the Soviet leadership would perceive the ambush as testament to China's resolve, rather than as a security threat. Even before the crisis, however, Soviet decision-makers were intensely concerned about the military threat posed by China. The border clashes confirmed its fears and prompted reactions that Mao had not anticipated. In short, Mao miscalculated.

Mao's strategic judgment was not always so poor. His decision in 1969 to attack a world superpower directly, overtly, and without warning was based on far less complete and accurate information than during earlier international crises.[2] In 1962, for instance, Mao received intelligence reports showing that the Nationalist government in Taiwan was planning a major military operation against the mainland. In part because

---

[1] Thomas J. Christensen, *Worse Than a Monolith: Alliance Politics and Problems of Coercive Diplomacy in Asia* (Princeton: Princeton University Press, 2011), 181–220; Lorenz M. Lüthi, *The Sino-Soviet Split: Cold War in the Communist World* (Princeton: Princeton University Press, 2008), 273–339.

[2] Allen S. Whiting, *The Chinese Calculus of Deterrence: India and Indochina* (Ann Arbor: University of Michigan Press, 1975), 240.

the United States had signed a mutual defense treaty with the Nationalist government in 1954, it was possible that the United States might support the gambit. Mao's strategic response in 1962, however, was markedly different from his decision-making in 1969. Rather than lashing out with military action, Mao moved cautiously. A combination of well-coordinated military and diplomatic signals helped China secure a commitment from U.S. decision-makers to restrain Nationalist plans.

Mao's strategy in 1962 was informed by more complete and high-quality reporting. For one, the Nationalists were indeed planning military action, as archival records from both the United States and Taiwan now confirm. More important, the information that Mao received early in the crisis – before China used military force – shaped his beliefs. The available evidence suggests that early in the crisis Mao genuinely feared a large-scale military attack by Taiwan and the United States. By the end of the crisis, however, Chinese decision-makers concluded that the threat was not as severe as initially feared.

Why was the information on which Mao based his decisions of higher quality in 1962 than in 1969? This chapter argues that the answer to this puzzle lies in changes to China's national security institutions. In 1962, the Chinese Communist Party's diplomatic, defense, and intelligence bureaucracies offered Mao a steady stream of quality counsel. Shortly thereafter, however, Mao began to plan for political succession. He grew concerned that China's bureaucrats would reject his revolutionary agenda once he was gone. In response, Mao preemptively and systematically dismantled the bureaucracy. Chinese diplomats, soldiers, and intelligence analysts were caught in the crossfire. In the process of securing the political succession that he wanted, Mao had to forgo the quality bureaucratic support that had served him well early during his leadership. While China's bureaucrats hinted at the time that the premises behind the ambush were wrong, many were systematically excluded from the decision-making process before the crisis – and the bureaucrats left behind knew the political costs of speaking candidly. Mao's miscalculation was not simply a gamble gone wrong. It was in part a product of his own institutional making.[3]

---

[3] For existing scholarship arguing that China miscalculated, see Whiting, 240; Gerald Segal, *Defending China* (New York: Oxford University Press, 1985), 192–193; Yang Kuisong, "The Sino-Soviet Border Clash of 1969: From Zhenbao Island to Sino-American Rapprochement," *Cold War History* 1, no. 1 (2000): 35; Thomas J. Christensen, "Windows and War: Trend Analysis and Beijing's Use of Force," in *New Directions in the Study of China's Foreign Policy*, ed. Alastair Iain Johnston and Robert S. Ross (Stanford: Stanford University Press, 2006), 69–71; M. Taylor Fravel, *Strong Borders, Secure Nation: Cooperation and Conflict in China's Territorial Disputes* (Princeton: Princeton University Press, 2008), 211–214; Xu Yan, "1969 nian ZhongSu bianjie chongtu [The 1969 Armed Conflict on the Sino-Soviet Border]," *Dangshi yanjiu ziliao*

This chapter is divided into two main sections. The first discusses the political logic of institutional design in China from 1949 to 1976, focusing on the transformation from integrated to fragmented institutions in the early 1960s. The second section explores institutional effects, both through a medium-n analysis of China's crisis performance across this period and through two detailed case studies on Mao's decision-making during the 1962 Nationalist invasion scare and the 1969 Sino-Soviet border conflict.

The Politics of Institutional Design in Mao's China

When the People's Republic of China was founded on October 1, 1949, Mao enjoyed overwhelming power and authority within the Chinese Communist Party. In the mid-1940s, Mao secured formal and informal authority to make decisions unilaterally.[4] While such power did not necessarily mean that Mao always restricted debate or deliberation, senior party organs could not overrule decisions even when Mao was in the minority. As a result, Mao generally controlled appointments to senior political offices, allowing him to promote or dismiss party elites as he saw fit. Thus, the central feature of early elite politics was "the dominant, unchallenged position of Mao."[5]

Mao's absolute political power provides fruitful ground to illustrate the political theory of institutional design. This section shows how changes to the domestic political environment within a single personalist dictatorship shaped China's institutional choices. It first examines the period between 1949 and 1962, in which low levels of bureaucratic threat led to comparatively integrated institutions. It next considers institutional changes in the mid-1960s, at which time Mao's concerns about the loyalty of the bureaucracy during political succession led him to adopt fragmented institutions. Table 4.1 summarizes codings of each element of the political theory of institutional design.

[Research Materials on Party History], no. 5 (1994): 2–13. For alternative accounts that emphasize domestic political mobilization, rather than miscalculation, see Lyle J. Goldstein, "Return to Zhenbao Island: Who Started Shooting and Why It Matters," *The China Quarterly*, no. 168 (2001): 985–997; Li Danhui, "Zhengzhi doushi yu dishou: 1960 niandai ZhongSu bianjie guanxi [Political Fighters and Rivals: Sino-Soviet Border Relations in the 1960s]," *Shehui kexue* [Journal of Social Sciences] 2 (2007): 146–167.

[4] Frederick C. Teiwes, "The Establishment and Consolidation of the New Regime, 1949–1957," in *The Politics of China: Sixty Years of the People's Republic of China*, 3rd ed., ed. Roderick MacFarquhar (New York: Cambridge University Press, 2011), 14.

[5] Frederick C. Teiwes, "The Study of Elite Political Conflict in the PRC: Politics Inside the 'Black Box'," in *Handbook of the Politics of China*, ed. David S. G. Goodman (Northampton, MA: Elgar, 2015), 26–27.

Table 4.1 *Evolution of China's institutional design under Mao*

Period	Bureaucratic threat	Leader agenda	National security institution	Theory support
1949–1962	*Low*: leader with experience managing party bureaucracy; limited intent to challenge Mao's agenda	*Domestic & International*: Cold War tensions with US and USSR; domestic mobilization programs (e.g., Great Leap Forward)	*Integrated*: Inclusive bureaucratic representation on Politburo; coordination through CMC and Secretariat; informal coordinators (Zhou Enlai; Deng Xiaoping)	Strong
1963–1976	*Medium*: experienced leader; perceived bureaucratic threat to agenda after succession	*Domestic*: Cultural Revolution; political succession	*Fragmented*: Insular Central Cultural Revolution Group and Politburo; restricted appointment on CMC; elimination of Secretariat	Strong

The Political Environment in the Early Mao Period, 1949–1962

Mao entered office with a national security bureaucracy that posed comparatively little threat to his rule. From 1949 to 1962, there is little evidence that the national security bureaucracy possessed either the capability or intent to challenge him. By the time that the PRC was established in 1949, Mao had already spent decades overseeing the party apparatus.[6] Mao gained considerable experience managing the national security bureaucracy during World War II and the Chinese Civil War. Mao's experience was complemented by an informal authority stemming from his role in unifying the country, which would have made it difficult for subordinates to justify removing him. Frederick Tewies, for example, suggests that Mao "approximated the ideal charismatic leader" whose

---

[6] Pang Xianzhi and Jin Chongji, ed., *Mao Zedong zhuan* [Biography of Mao Zedong] (Beijing: Zhongyang wenxian chubanshe, 2011), Vol. II; Alexander V. Pantsov and Steven I. Levine, *Mao: The Real Story* (New York: Simon & Schuster, 2012), 185–362.

position could simply not be challenged, as doing so would constitute an attack on the regime itself.

Mao displayed few fears of a challenge by the national security bureaucracy. There was a firm pattern of subordination to party authority, even among the most powerful bureaucratic organizations. Senior officers within the People's Liberation Army (PLA) had not seriously challenged Mao's authority during World War II or the subsequent civil war with the Nationalist (KMT) party.[7] While Mao brought the Chinese military into government administration to establish local political control during the PRC's early years, Chinese defense leaders also smoothly handed power back to civilian authority. Even during a notable split within the party in 1953, for instance, the Chinese military does not appear to have used the opportunity to challenge Mao's rule.[8] In June 1958, Mao further noted that he had not "interfered in military affairs for four years."[9] As late as the summer of 1962, Mao directly complimented the efficiency and dependability of both the defense and diplomatic bureaucracy.[10]

Integrated Institutions under Mao, 1949–1962

The theory predicts that leaders are likely to adopt integrated institutions when the national security bureaucracy possesses neither the capability nor the intent to challenge the leader. As predicted by the theory, the design of China's national security institutions was generally integrated during the first decade of Mao's rule. This can be divided into two components: inclusive information search and a moderately high level of bureaucratic access to information.

Inclusive Information Search Capacity. Several institutional devices established capacity to relay information to Mao. At the decision-making level, the Politburo of the Chinese Communist Party was chaired by Mao Zedong and included both senior military and diplomatic officials. In fact, of the thirteen Politburo members in 1949, nearly half held responsibilities in defense or foreign policy. On the military side, this included Zhu De, Peng Dehuai, and Lin Biao – all of whom held concurrent administrative or operational responsibilities in the Chinese military, the People's

---

[7] Teiwes, "The Establishment and Consolidation of the New Regime," 30.
[8] Ibid., 29–30, 46–51.
[9] M. Taylor Fravel, *Active Defense: China's Military Strategy since 1949* (Princeton: Princeton University Press, 2019), 81.
[10] Pang Xianzhi and Feng Hui, ed., *Mao Zedong nianpu, 1949–1976* [Chronicle of Mao Zedong, 1949–1976] (Beijing: Zhongyang wenxian chubanshe, 2013), Vol. V, 115.

Liberation Army (PLA).[11] On the diplomatic side, China's first foreign minister, Zhou Enlai, was the Politburo's fourth-ranking member. Zhou's replacement, Chen Yi, similarly held a seat on the body into the 1960s.

Mao routinely used the Politburo to discuss defense and foreign policy. Figure 4.1 reports the annual average number of formal and informal meetings attended by Mao in which the agenda touched on either defense or foreign policy.[12] The top panel demonstrates that between 1949 and 1962 Mao convened the Politburo over ten times per year on average to discuss these issues. The bottom panel of Figure 4.1 illustrates that Mao's national security decision-making routinely included both defense and diplomatic officials during this period.

The available evidence suggests that integrated institutions yielded reasonably complete and high-quality information provision. As Xia Yafeng notes, these meetings helped Mao "weigh the pros and cons of major foreign policy decisions."[13] Politburo meetings served as a vehicle to relay reports, even in sensitive areas such as defense policy. On May 27, 1953, for instance, Mao instructed Defense Minister Peng Dehuai and Chief of General Staff Huang Kecheng to provide routine reports from the CMC:

There should be an outline of the Central Military Commission [for the Politburo] once or twice every month. [...] The method is to write up [a report] concisely and give it to Comrade Yang Shangkun to publish, enter into the agenda, and have Huang give a short explanation during a meeting.[14]

Mao further noted that "important matters in other departments," presumably including the Foreign Ministry, should follow a similar procedure. Mao was aware that his senior defense advisers were preparing similar reports for circulation into the late 1950s.[15] He instructed ambassadors to dispatch cables on recent developments, such as troop mobilizations and public opinion, that would help him to gauge foreign intentions.[16]

---

[11] Unless otherwise noted, data on the organization and membership of Chinese government institutions are taken from CCP records. See Zhonggong zhongyang zuzhibu, ed., *Zhongguo gongchandang zuzhi shi ziliao* [Materials on the organizational history of the Chinese Communist Party] (Beijing: Zhonggong dangshi chubanshe, 2000).

[12] Unless otherwise noted, all descriptions of patterns in China's decision-making use the *PRC National Security Decision-Making Data Set*. Sources and coding rules for these data are included in Appendix B.

[13] Xia Yafeng, "China's Elite Politics and Sino-American Rapprochement, January 1969–February 1972," *Journal of Cold War Studies* 8, no. 4 (2006): 5.

[14] Li Jie et al., ed., *Jianguo yilai Mao Zedong junshi wengao* [The Military Manuscripts of Mao Zedong since the Founding of the State] (Beijing: Zhongyang wenxian chubanshe, 2010), Vol. II, 341.

[15] Ibid., Vol. II, 341.

[16] Pang and Feng, *Mao Zedong nianpu*, Vol. I, 99–101.

88   China under Mao

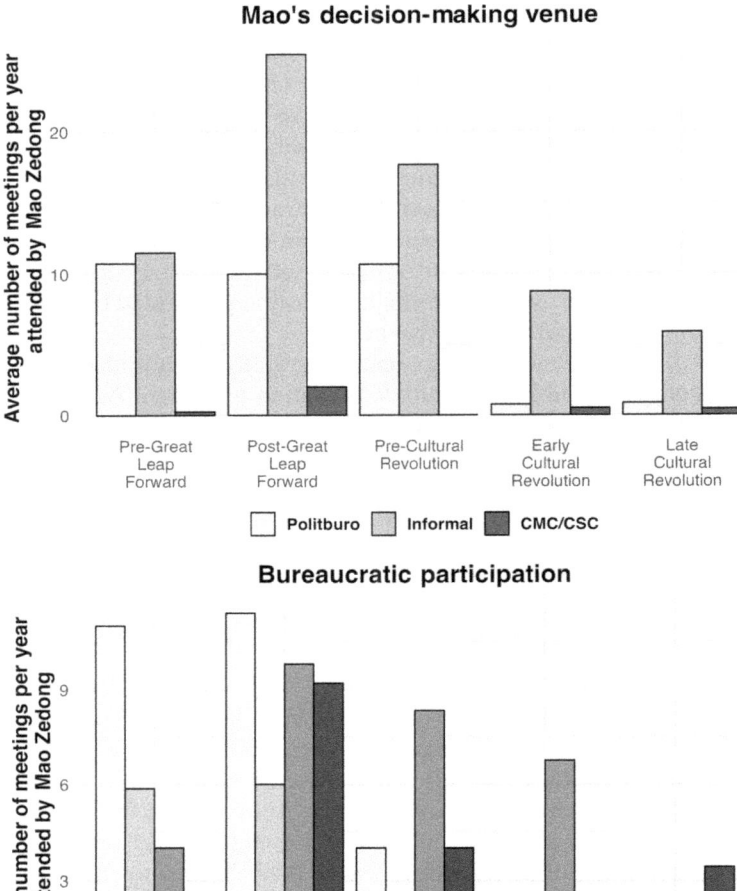

Figure 4.1 China's national security decision-making, 1949–1976
Note: Figures report the average annual frequency of meetings attended by Mao Zedong discussing foreign or defense policy across five periods: (1) pre-Great Leap Forward (1950–1957); post-Great Leap Forward (1958–1962); (3) pre-Cultural Revolution (1963–1965); (4) early Cultural Revolution (1966–1969); and (5) late Cultural Revolution (1970–1976). The top and bottom panels report frequency by venue and type of bureaucratic participation, respectively. Coding details provided in Appendix B.

Outside these meetings, integrated institutions channeled information from the bureaucracy to the leader. Mao received routine diplomatic reports from the Foreign Ministry,[17] as well as intelligence reports from the party's intelligence arm on topics ranging from Japan's reactions to China's diplomatic statements to American domestic politics.[18] Other reports leveraged information collected from government journalists, which Mao routinely consumed.[19] In sum, as one Chinese source summarizes, foreign affairs decision-making in the initial years of the PRC allowed bureaucratic stakeholders to "provide advice and intelligence" and participate in "frequent and procedural" discussions.[20]

Finally, inclusiveness and open access created the conditions for "blunt talk" between Mao and his advisers.[21] As one Chinese source notes, advisers from the national security bureaucracy often provided differing opinions, deliberated across bureaucratic lines, and delivered foreign policy advice before decisions were reached by Mao.[22] Other Chinese scholars note that senior advisers "offered recommendations to the central government on important questions" and bureaucracies "indirectly affected decision-making" through routine submission of reports circulated to the senior leadership.[23] Senior bureaucratic advisers during this period, such as Wang Jiaxiang, were more than "yes men."[24] They could gain "trust and access" with Mao and gave "important counsel" on international affairs.[25]

Open Bureaucratic Access to Information. Inter-bureaucratic information sharing during Mao's early years was comparatively high. Several bodies below the Politburo used for information sharing and coordination included a diverse set of bureaucratic representatives. The Central Military Commission (CMC) included both military and diplomatic appointees for most of this period. Premier and Foreign Minister Zhou Enlai chaired

[17] Pang and Feng, *Mao Zedong nianpu*, Vol. IV, 14.
[18] Ibid., Vol. II, 435.
[19] Bo Yibo, *Ruogan zhongda juece yu shijian de huigu* [Reflections on Certain Major Decisions and Events], Revised Edition (Beijing: Renmin chubanshe, 1997), Vol. II, 801.
[20] Zhang Lili, *Waijiao juece* [Foreign Policy Decision-Making] (Beijing: Shijie zhishi chubanshe, 2007), 125–126.
[21] Michel C. Oksenberg, "Policy Making under Mao Tse-tung, 1949–1968," *Comparative Politics* 3, no. 3 (1971): 337.
[22] Zhang, *Waijiao juece*, 109.
[23] Gong Li, Men Honghua, and Sun Dongfang, "Zhongguo waijiao juece jizhi bianqian yanjiu [Changes and Evolution in China's Foreign Policy Decision-Making Mechanisms, 1949–2009]," *Shijie jingji yu zhengzhi* [World Economics and Politics], no. 11 (2009): 46.
[24] Xia Yafeng, "Wang Jiaxiang: New China's First Ambassador and the First Director of the International Liaison Department of the CCP," *American Journal of Chinese Studies* 16, no. 2 (2009): 155.
[25] Ibid., 140, 153.

numerous meetings as a formal member in the early 1950s.[26] Even after handing over responsibility for routine CMC affairs to Defense Minister Peng Dehuai near the end of the Korean War, Zhou continued to periodically chair CMC meetings throughout the 1950s and early 1960s.[27] Zhou's authority to oversee inter-ministerial coordination persisted in part due to his chairmanship of the State Council, on which the senior military leadership – including Peng Dehuai, Nie Rongzhen, Lin Biao, and Luo Ruiqing – sat during the early years of the PRC. Similarly, even after resigning as foreign minister, Zhou continued to receive routine briefings from senior diplomatic officials.[28]

In the mid-1950s, many coordination functions transitioned to the CCP Secretariat, chaired by Deng Xiaoping.[29] Oversight responsibilities of the Secretariat included defense, international affairs, and intelligence.[30] Like the Politburo, its membership included senior figures from the military and diplomatic bureaucracy.[31] It also included Yang Shangkun, who oversaw China's intelligence organization, the Central Investigation Department (CID).[32] The Secretariat's coordination was further supported by a series of "leading small groups," such as the Taiwan Affairs Leading Small Group (TLSG) and the Foreign Affairs Leading Small Group (FALSG).[33]

---

[26] Li Ping and Ma Zhisun, ed., *Zhou Enlai nianpu, 1949–1976* [Chronicle of Zhou Enlai, 1949–1976] (Beijing: Zhongyang wenxian chubanshe, 1997), Vol. I, 41; Nie Rongzhen, *Nie Rongzhen huiyilu* [Memoirs of Nie Rongzhen] (Beijing: Jiefangjun chubanshe, 2007), 568–569.

[27] For examples of CMC meetings in which Zhou participated, see Li and Ma, *Zhou Enlai nianpu*, Vol. I, 557, 581; Vol. II, 461; Vol. III, 147, 155. On Zhou's resignation, see Pang and Feng, *Mao Zedong nianpu*, Vol. I, 571.

[28] See, for example, Zhou's meetings with the Foreign Ministry in *Zhou Enlai nianpu*, Vol. II, 213, 274. On Zhou's early years, see Wu Xiuquan, *Eight Years in the Ministry of Foreign Affairs: Memoirs of a Diplomat* (Beijing: International Book Trading Corporation, 1985), 41–42.

[29] Lu Ning, *The Dynamics of Foreign-Policy Decisionmaking in China*, 2nd ed. (Boulder: Westview Press, 1997), 11.

[30] Yang Shengqun and Yan Jianqi, ed., *Deng Xiaoping nianpu, 1904–1974* [Chronicle of Deng Xiaoping, 1904–1974] (Beijing: Zhongyang wenxian chubanshe, 2009), Vol. II, 1318–1319.

[31] Zhonggong zhongyang zuzhibu, *Zhongguo gongchandang zuzhi shi ziliao*, Vol. IX, 41–42.

[32] For examples of Yang's meetings with the CID, see Yang Shangkun, *Yang Shangkun riji* [Diary of Yang Shangkun] (Beijing: Zhongyang wenxian chubanshe, 2001), Vol. I, 165, 337, 359, 368, 372, 384, 387.

[33] On the TLSG, see Huang Yao and Zhang Mingzhe, ed., *Luo Ruiqing zhuan* [Biography of Luo Ruiqing] (Beijing: Dangdai Zhongguo chubanshe, 1996), 425. On the FALSG, see Zhonggong zhongyang zuzhibu, *Zhongguo gongchandang zuzhi shi ziliao*, Vol. XIV, 611–613, 628–629. The TLSG composition included both military and civilian intelligence representatives. The FALSG included only diplomatic and intelligence representatives, but senior military officials attended at least some of its meetings. See Zhou Junlun, ed., *Nie Rongzhen nianpu* [Chronicle of Nie Rongzhen] (Beijing: Renmin

The available evidence suggests there was a comparatively high level of horizontal information sharing facilitated through Zhou Enlai and Deng Xiaoping. Figure 4.2 reports the annual average number of formal and informal meetings chaired by Zhou or Deng in which the agenda touched on either defense or foreign policy. The top panel shows that between 1949 and 1962, formal meetings of the State Council or Secretariat touching on these issues occurred about once per month on average. In addition, there were informal norms encouraging bureaucrats to share information. Military leaders recall maintaining "close contact" with senior diplomatic and intelligence officials, exchanging reports and viewpoints.[34] Foreign Ministry reports and cables were routinely circulated to the military and intelligence bureaucracies, as well as other relevant departments.[35]

The Political Environment in the Late Mao Period, 1963–1976

Mao's perceptions of bureaucratic threat changed during the early 1960s. While it is not clear that the bureaucracy's capability to challenge the leader increased, there were clear changes in Mao perceptions of its intent to challenge his political agenda, particularly after his death.

Mao's shifting perceptions of bureaucratic intentions can be traced to the Great Leap Forward, an economic and social mobilization campaign launched by Mao in 1958. The strategy proved to be a disaster, sparking policy discussions within the party elite about how to restore basic economic welfare for the country. Diplomatic and defense officials, many of whom enjoyed considerable status and respect within the party, played a central role in a series of meetings held at Lushan, in which the party questioned whether the Great Leap Forward had yielded the results for which they had hoped. In particular, Defense Minister Peng Dehuai and Vice Foreign Minister Zhang Wentian, were among those who suggested that China might change its economic course.[36]

---

chubanshe, 1999). On early FALSG reporting, see Li and Ma, *Zhou Enlai nianpu*, Vol. II, 326, 445.

[34] Lei Yingfu, "KangMei yuanChao zhanzheng huiyi pianduan [Fragmentary Recollections of the Korean War]," in *Zongcanmoubu: huiyi shiliao, 1927–1987* [General Staff Department: Recollections and Historical Materials, 1927–1987] (Beijing: Jiefangjun chubanshe, 1995), 365.

[35] Author's review of a diplomatic cables available in the Archives of the Ministry of Foreign Affairs. For a different perspective, see Carol Lee Hamrin, "Elite Politics and the Development of China's Foreign Relations," in *Chinese Foreign Policy: Theory and Practice*, ed. Thomas W. Robinson and David Shambaugh (Oxford: Clarendon Press, 1994), 83.

[36] Mao had easily dismissed Peng Dehuai and Zhang Wentian for their tempered and initially private suggestions about the Great Leap Forward's failures. On the Lushan Conference, see Roderick MacFarquhar, *The Origins of the Cultural Revolution: The*

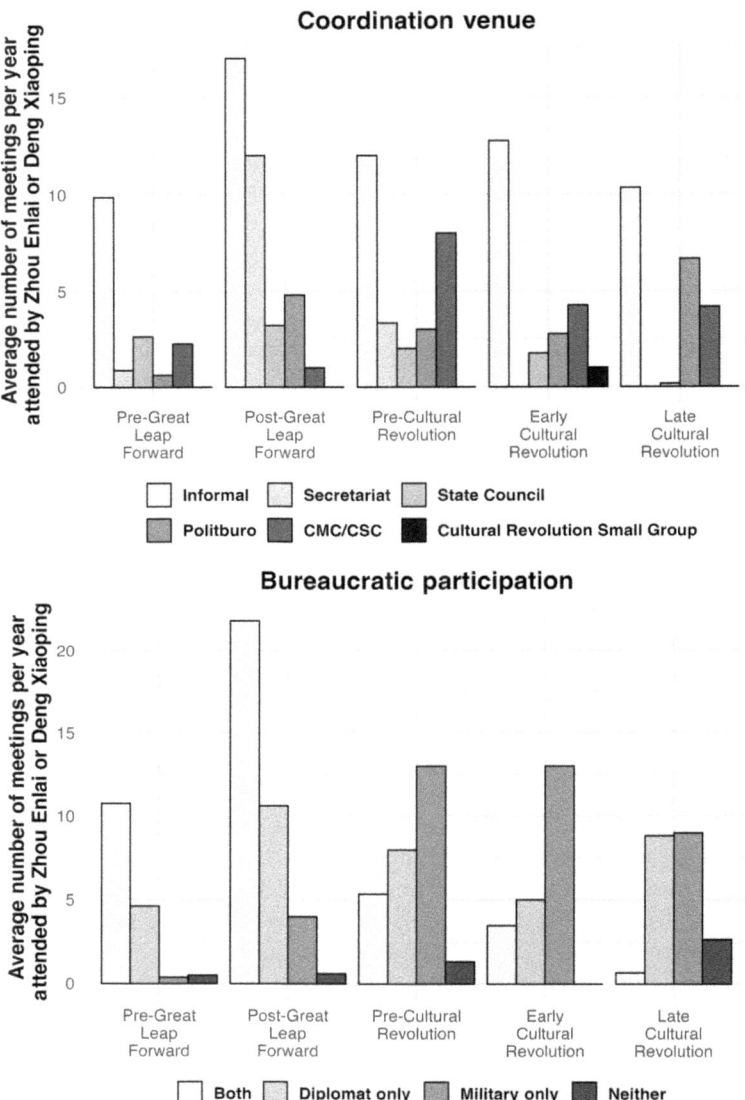

Figure 4.2 China's national security coordination, 1949–1976
Note: Figures report the average annual frequency of coordination meetings discussing foreign or defense policy across five periods: (1) pre-Great Leap Forward (1950–1957); post-Great Leap Forward (1958–1962); (3) pre-Cultural Revolution (1963–1965); (4) early Cultural Revolution (1966–1969); and (5) late Cultural Revolution (1970–1976). Coordination meetings are those in which Zhou Enlai and/or Deng Xiaoping participated but Mao Zedong did not. The top and bottom panels report frequency by venue and type of bureaucratic participation, respectively. Coding details provided in Appendix B.

These events shaped Mao's views of what the bureaucracy would do during and after succession. The lack of revolutionary zeal displayed at Lushan was, in Mao's mind, a serious challenge to sustaining his agenda in the long term. Mao's fear was that the views expressed by party leaders during the Great Leap Forward signaled that they would be unwilling to uphold his revolutionary agenda after he handed power to a successor. As Mao put the problem, "What will happen after I die?"[37]

The fall of 1962 appears to have marked a turning point in Mao's perceptions of "revisionism" – a term Mao used to label subordinates he believed would not uphold his agenda. In discussions with his inner circle at Beidaihe in August 1962, Mao charged that even if revisionism did not appear in the next generation, it might appear in the one after that.[38] Mao made the charge more directly at the Tenth Plenum of the Eighth Central Committee the following month, noting that "we, the Chinese people, also have contradictions with domestic revisionism."[39] Mao reiterated this point repeatedly over the next four years. In May 1963, Mao noted that China might change its color.[40] In October 1963, he commented that "measures must be taken" to curb the spread of revisionism.[41] The following summer, Mao charged that revisionism would emerge if the party did not pay attention to it – and might emerge even if it did.[42] Figure 4.3 summarizes this trend more systematically by examining the frequency of the different phrases Mao used to describe threats in his speeches and written communications with party leaders. It shows that Mao's references to domestic threats increased during the early 1960s – and did so using the new language of "revisionism."

Mao expressed particular concern about China's Foreign Ministry. He commented that diplomats needed to devote attention to the "connection between revisionism at home and abroad" or else they would "definitely be taken in" by it. Mao instructed the foreign affairs system to "heighten their vigilance."[43] In the following years, Mao described Chinese diplomats as "intellectuals" and as leading a "bourgeois" lifestyle.[44]

Great Leap Forward, 1958–1960 (New York: Columbia University Press, 1983), 187–254.
[37] Andrew G. Walder, *China under Mao* (Cambridge: Harvard University Press, 2015), 184.
[38] Pang and Feng, *Mao Zedong nianpu*, Vol. V, 133.
[39] Ibid., Vol. V, 152.
[40] Ibid., Vol. V, 221.
[41] Ibid., Vol. V, 270.
[42] Ibid., Vol. V, 360–361.
[43] Mao Zedong, *Jianguo yilai Mao Zedong wengao* [The Manuscripts of Mao Zedong since the Founding of the State] (Beijing: Zhongyang wenxian chubanshe, 1987), Vol. X, 199.
[44] Chen Jian and David L. Wilson, "All under the Heaven Is Great Chaos: Beijing, The Sino-Soviet Border Clashes, and the Turn Toward Sino-American Rapprochement,

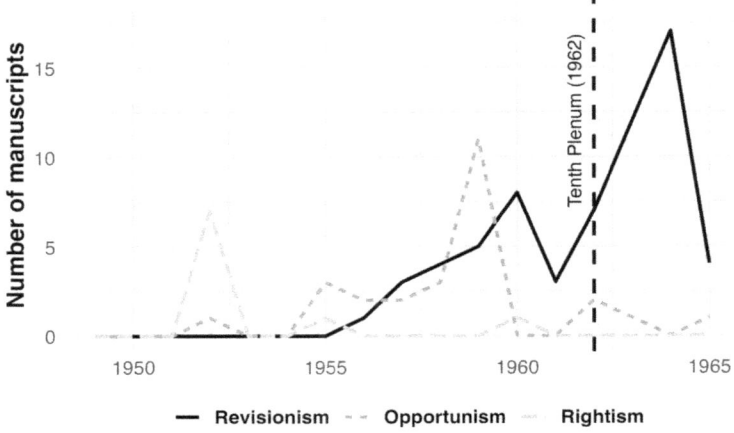

Figure 4.3 Mao's changing threat perceptions, 1949–1965
Note: plot reports the frequency of manuscripts written or edited by Mao Zedong containing references to (1) revisionism (修正主义), (2) opportunism (机会主义), or (3) rightism (右倾思想). Vertical line indicates the Tenth Plenum of the Eight Central Committee in September 1962. Source: *Jianguo yilai Mao Zedong wengao*, Vol. I–XI.

In parallel to elevated threat perceptions, Mao's attention shifted toward domestic matters. By March 1964, Mao commented that he had turned his focus "back to domestic issues."[45] In 1965, Mao hinted at more drastic measures to reshape the party. "If revisionism emerges in the party center," Mao cautioned, "we should rebel."[46] Mao's rectification of the party culminated with the Cultural Revolution, a mass campaign from 1966 and 1976 that mobilized Chinese society to purge members of the Chinese Communist Party who were judged to be at odds with its ideology. Zhou Enlai's summary of the strategy of the Cultural Revolution illustrates the culmination of Mao's shift in emphasis from international to domestic priorities: "target the center, rather than the localities, *the domestic rather than the international one*, inside rather than outside the party, and higher levels rather than lower levels."[47]

1968–69," *Cold War International History Project Bulletin*, no. 11 (1998): 156; Song Yongyi, *Jimi dang'an zhong xin faxian deMao Zedong jianghua* [Speeches of Mao Zedong Newly Discovered in Secret Archives] (Deer Park, NY: Guoshi chubanshe, 2018), 412; Barnouin Barbara and Changgen Yu, *Chinese Foreign Policy during the Cultural Revolution* (London: Kegan Paul International, 1998), 13.

[45] Pang and Feng, *Mao Zedong nianpu*, Vol. V, 324.
[46] Ibid., Vol. V, 534.
[47] Roderick MacFarquhar and Michael Schoenhals, *Mao's Last Revolution* (Cambridge: Harvard University Press, 2006), 41. Emphasis added.

It is worth emphasizing that Mao's concern seems to have primarily been the costs that the Chinese bureaucracy could impose on his political legacy, rather than a coup that would directly seize power.[48] Mao took issue with a speech in which Defense Minister Lin Biao warned against a "counterrevolutionary coup" in which political power might be "usurped."[49] Mao instead felt that any power seizure would prove "short-lived" because the Chinese people "would not tolerate it." Mao's focus remained on the long-term threat that revisionism posed after succession: "Our present task is to [...] topple the rightists in the whole party and entire country. And in seven or eight years there will be another movement to sweep away evil people of all kinds, and still more purges thereafter."[50] In short, the core issue was not how Mao could protect himself against a coup; the issue was how Mao could shape the policy debates that Mao anticipated would ensue after his death.

Fragmented Institutions under Mao, 1963–1976

Elevated threat perceptions and domestic focus lead Mao to sweeping change China's national security institutions. In contrast to Mao's early years, the fragmented institutions that emerged in the early 1960s featured insular information search and restricted bureaucratic access to information. These institutional modifications degraded both the completeness and quality of bureaucratic information.

Insular Information Search Capacity. Mao systematically redesigned China's institutions in ways that curtailed capacity for information search. First, Mao changed the locus of national security decision-making from the more inclusive Politburo to its more restrictive Standing Committee, on which there were no representatives from the Foreign Ministry. As illustrated in Figure 4.4, prior to the Tenth Plenum in the fall of 1962, nearly seventy percent of Politburo meetings touching on foreign or defense affairs were regular or expanded sessions that included more than the core group of party elites. From 1963 to the eve of the Cultural Revolution in 1965, however, participation in over 78 percent of Politburo meetings was restricted to the Standing Committee.

The launch of the Cultural Revolution in the spring of 1966 expanded these preliminary moves. As depicted in Figure 4.1, the Politburo was

---

[48] For a nuanced account, see MacFarquhar and Schoenhals, 51.
[49] For Lin's views, see Pang and Feng, *Mao Zedong nianpu*, Vol. V, 587. For Mao's reaction, see Vol. V, 596–597.
[50] Ibid., Vol. V, 597.

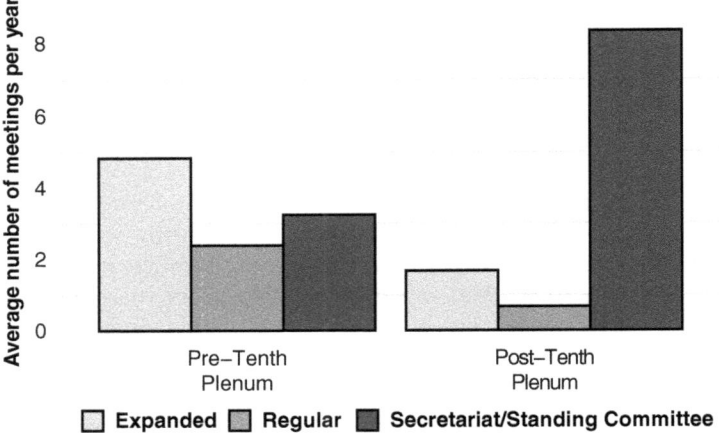

Figure 4.4 Institutional change in Politburo decision-making, 1949–1965
Note: Figure reports the average annual frequency of Politburo meetings by type: (1) expanded session, (2) regular session, or (3) Standing Committee session. Coding details provided in Appendix.

first sidelined and then disbanded.[51] In its place, Mao established a new body called the Central Cultural Revolution Group (CCRG), which "overrode" the Politburo and Secretariat as the "central management mechanism" for the party.[52] The CCRG was less bureaucratically inclusive, excluding representatives from the Foreign Ministry from the leader's inner circle.[53]

During the Cultural Revolution, Mao restricted capacity to search for information within China's bureaucracies as well. Nearly three-quarters of the diplomatic personnel stationed overseas were recalled. All but one ambassador returned to China.[54] Seventy percent of Foreign Ministry officials in Beijing were "sent down" to the countryside to learn from the revolutionary spirit of the peasants.[55] Through the end of 1969, the

---

[51] Pang and Feng, *Mao Zedong nianpu*, Vol. VI, 56.
[52] Zhonggong zhongyang zuzhibu, *Zhongguo gongchandang zuzhi shi ziliao*, *Zhongguo gongchandang zuzhi shi ziliao*, Vol. X, 60.
[53] Liu Zhijian, himself a senior military officer, was from the military's propaganda department and did not have operational responsibilities. See *Jiefangjun jiangling zhuan* [Biographies of People's Liberation Army Generals] (Beijing: Jiefangjun chubanshe, 1995), Vol. XIV, 115.
[54] Liu Xiaohong, *Chinese Ambassadors: The Rise of Diplomatic Professionalism since 1949* (Seattle: University of Washington Press, 2001), 117.
[55] Zhonggong zhongyang zuzhibu, *Zhongguo gongchandang zuzhi shi ziliao*, *Zhongguo gongchandang zuzhi shi ziliao*, Vol. XV, 502.

full-time task of most of the professional diplomatic staff in the Foreign Ministry, especially the diplomats who were forced to return from embassies abroad, was to study propaganda and write self-criticisms.[56] Mao similarly curtailed China's intelligence capacity. In the spring of 1967, the CID was first put under military administration and then completely disbanded.[57]

Mao also removed several senior advisers, particularly within the party's diplomatic arm. Prior to the Cultural Revolution, Mao sidelined one of China's senior diplomats, Wang Jiaxiang, for a foreign policy report he had authored.[58] During the Cultural Revolution, one of the principal targets was Foreign Minister Chen Yi, who opposed the instability of the Cultural Revolution during deliberations within the party elite.[59] Mao relieved Chen of his diplomatic responsibilities in October 1968 and did not appoint a replacement from the Foreign Ministry to assume his responsibilities.[60] Technically on "sick leave," Chen was sent to Nankou Locomotive and Rolling Stock Machinery Factory, a "model unit" for thought reform where he was largely ignored.[61] While Mao formally appointed a new foreign minister, Ji Pengfei, in 1972, neither Ji nor his successor, Qiao Guanhua, were granted membership on key decision-making bodies.

Restricted information search capacity degraded information flow. This particularly affected Mao's interactions with the Foreign Ministry. As illustrated in the bottom panel of Figure 4.1, diplomatic participation in Mao's formal and informal meetings dramatically decreased beginning in 1963. More broadly, party records of Mao's meetings during the early Cultural Revolution contain scant references to information provision or deliberation. Outside these meetings, the volume of information on foreign affairs supplied to Mao also decreased, as reports from party journalists became the sole window to the outside world.[62]

---

[56] Ma Jisen, *The Cultural Revolution in the Foreign Ministry of China* (Hong Kong: Chinese University Press, 2004), 75–76.

[57] Pang and Feng, *Mao Zedong nianpu*, Vol. VI, 71, 259; Li and Ma, *Zhou Enlai nianpu*, Vol. III, 138; Li Ke and Hao Shengzhang, eds., *Wenhua dageming zhong de renmin jiefangjun*, 351.

[58] Xu Zehao, ed., *Wang Jiaxiang nianpu, 1906–1974* [Chronicle of Wang Jiaxiang, 1906–1974] (Beijing: Zhongyang wenxian chubanshe, 2001), Vol. II, 491; Xia, "Wang Jiaxiang," 151–152.

[59] Pang and Feng, *Mao Zedong nianpu*, Vol. VI, 53–54.

[60] Jiang Hongbin, ed., *Chen Yi zhuan* [Biography of Chen Yi] (Shanghai: Shanghai renmin chubanshe, 1992), 735; Chen Donglin, Du Pu, eds., *Zhonghua renmin gongheguo shilu* [Record of the People's Republic of China] (Changchun: Jilin renmin chubanshe, 1994), Vol. III, 365.

[61] Du Yi, ed., *Wenge zhong de Chen Yi* [Chen Yi during the Cultural Revolution] (Shijie zhishi chubanshe, 1997), 195–197.

[62] Zhang, *Waijiao juece*, 117, 153.

There is considerable evidence of self-censorship in the national security bureaucracy as well. For example, Chinese historian Zhang Baijia notes that after 1962, "Mao's subordinates did not dare to suggest changes in Chinese foreign policy."[63] One Chinese diplomat reports that Foreign Ministry was filled with "sycophants" during this period.[64] Another former Chinese diplomat later recalled that there was no policy debate.[65] Mao himself criticized defense assessments from the Chinese military, stating that the CMC "neither participated nor consulted."[66] Even when Mao did attempt to solicit a modicum of discussion at one meeting in 1969, advisers remained too frightened to offer an opinion.[67] Perhaps because he recognized that bureaucrats were self-censoring, Mao questioned the validity of diplomatic reporting that did reach him, commenting that he did not "trust the reports" from the Foreign Ministry and his ambassadors abroad.[68] Zhou Enlai similarly lamented that the old Chinese adage of "even when right, a [civilian] official can never win an argument with a military man" had been turned on its head: "When coming into contact with [civilian] officials, the military cannot persuade even when speaking with reason."[69]

Closed Bureaucratic Access to Information. A second component of these institutional changes was to eliminate many of the coordination mechanisms on which the party had previously relied to share information between the bureaucracies. The Secretariat and FALSG ceased to function soon after the Cultural Revolution.[70] Meetings of the State Council discussing foreign or defense affairs were rare during this period.[71]

Mao also restricted informal coordination functions that Deng Xiaoping and Zhou Enlai had previously performed. Deng was placed under

---

[63] Zhang Baijia, "The Changing International Scene and Chinese Policy toward the United States, 1954–1970," in *Re-examining the Cold War: US-China Diplomacy, 1954–1973* (Cambridge: Harvard University Asia Center, 2001), 61.
[64] Ji Chaozhu, *The Man on Mao's Right: From Harvard Yard to Tiananmen Square, My Life Inside China's Foreign Ministry* (New York: Random House, 2008), 237.
[65] Frederick C. Teiwes and Warren Sun, *The End of the Maoist Era: Chinese Politics during the Twilight of the Cultural Revolution, 1972–1976* (New York: Routledge, 2015), 85.
[66] Pang and Feng, *Mao Zedong nianpu*, Vol. VI, 410.
[67] Joseph Torigian, "Elite Politics and Foreign Policy in China from Mao to Xi," Brookings Institution, January 22, 2019.
[68] Song, *Jimi dang'an zhong xin faxian de Mao Zedong jianghua*, 412.
[69] Li and Ma, *Zhou Enlai nianpu*, Vol. III, 252.
[70] Zhou Wang, *Zhongguo "xiaozu jizhi" yanjiu* ["Leading Small Groups" in Chinese Politics] (Tianjin: Tianjin renmin chubanshe, 2010), 40.
[71] Author's review of Li and Ma, *Zhou Enlai nianpu*.

house arrest in 1967.[72] While Zhou retained his position, Mao reduced his responsibilities and administrative support. On June 3, 1968, Mao told Zhou, "Chen Yi has already been brought down and you are nearly there."[73] The Foreign Affairs Office, the secretarial arm of the State Council that had helped Zhou oversee foreign policy, was shut down.[74] Mao also limited Zhou's secretarial staff. "Don't keep too many people around you," Mao told him, "be lean."[75] Zhou himself complained to an Albanian diplomat in August 1968 that he was busier than he had been during the Chinese civil war. Explaining China's inability to keep up with its international activities, Zhou wrote that he could not find "a single minister" in the party's foreign affairs bureaucracy to assist him.[76] Zhou also relinquished his informal responsibilities for overseeing the CMC. In October 1967, he noted that all routine matters of the CMC, including troop deployments, personnel appointments, and weaponry, should be handled by the defense minister.[77] In March 1968, Mao affirmed that the defense minister would directly manage CMC affairs.[78]

Alternative Explanations for Institutional Design

Two alternative explanations for China's institutional evolution under Mao merit attention. First, Mao's leadership style was famously idiosyncratic throughout his tenure.[79] Many of his informal meetings with senior advisers took place by his pool or late into the evening. Leadership style alone, however, struggles to explain the stark differences between how the bureaucracy was integrated into his decision-making process during his early years, but excluded from it during his later years.

Second, while international diffusion contextualizes some of Mao's design choices in the 1950s, there is no evidence that the institutional design that China pursued in the 1960s drew from a foreign example. China's international isolation during the Cultural Revolution meant that there were few cross-national linkages for it to gain new information regarding the design of national security institutions. Advisers from the Soviet Union – the principal channel for international diffusion – were

---

[72] Ezra F. Vogel, *Deng Xiaoping and the Transformation of China* (Cambridge: Harvard University Press, 2011), 43.
[73] Li and Ma, *Zhou Enlai nianpu*, Vol. III, 238.
[74] Lu, *The Dynamics of Foreign-Policy Decisionmaking in China*, 155.
[75] Li and Ma, *Zhou Enlai nianpu*, Vol. III, 227.
[76] Ibid., Vol. III, 252.
[77] Ibid., Vol. III, 194–195.
[78] Pang and Feng, *Mao Zedong nianpu*, Vol. VI, 155–157.
[79] Lucian W. Pye, "Mao Tse-tung's Leadership Style," *Political Science Quarterly* 91, no. 2 (1976): 230–233; Oksenberg, "Policy Making under Mao Tse-tung," 327–328.

withdrawn in 1960.[80] Moreover, even before Soviet advisers departed, Chinese leaders resisted imitation of the Soviet system. Chief of Staff Nie Rongzhen, for instance, believed that Soviet advisers "fundamentally misunderstood" China and noted that their country could not "parrot" the Soviet example.[81]

China's Crisis Performance under Mao

How did national security institutions shape China's crisis behavior under Mao Zedong? First, we can examine China's record of crisis performance over time, which is summarized in Table 4.2.[82] China achieved its primary objective in the vast majority of its crises before 1962. Yet China fared worse after shifting to fragmented institutions, failing to achieve is primary objective in the majority of its crises. The pattern looks similar even when accounting for the fact that China often had more than one goal in a given crisis. On average, China achieved roughly nine in ten crisis goals during integrated periods, but just above one in three crisis goals during fragmented periods.

Patterns in China's crisis decision-making were systematically different during its integrated and fragmented periods. Formal and informal meetings between Mao and the senior diplomatic and defense advisers played an important role during each of the nine international security crisis to which it was party from 1949 to 1962. Formal and informal meetings offered Mao different, and candid, bureaucratic advice. Senior defense official Lin Biao recommended against China's involvement in the Korean War and offered potential ways to mitigate escalation risks during the 1958 Taiwan Strait Crisis.[83] Foreign Minister Zhou Enlai provided counsel critical to nudging Mao to adopt less confrontational policies regarding Vietnam, Taiwan, and the United States in the summer of 1954.[84] Mao consulted with both diplomatic and defense advisers prior to confrontations with India in 1959 and 1962.[85]

---

[80] Lüthi, *The Sino-Soviet Split*, 35–36, 40.
[81] Nie, *Memoirs of Nie Rongzhen*, 582–583.
[82] Detailed codings of China's crisis performance are provided in Tyler Jost, "Institutional Origins of Miscalculation in China's International Crises," *International Security* 48, no. 1 (2023): 47–90.
[83] Chen Jian, *China's Road to the Korean War: The Making of the Sino-American Confrontation* (New York: Columbia University Press, 1994), 281, note 78; Lin Qiang and Lu Bing, ed., *Ye Fei zhuan* [Biography of Ye Fei] (Beijing: Zhongyang wenxian chubanshe, 2007), 602.
[84] Chen Jian, *Mao's China and the Cold War* (Chapel Hill: University of North Carolina Press, 2001), 169–171.
[85] Fravel, *Strong Borders, Secure Nation*, 83–86, 189–197.

Table 4.2 *China's crisis performance under Mao, 1949–1976*

Crisis	Year	Institution	Primary goal	Successful?
Coastal Islands seizure	1950	Integrated	Improve control of offshore islands	✓
Korean War (entry)	1950	Integrated	Prevent U.S. military presence above 38th Parallel	✓
Korean War (termination)	1953	Integrated	Secure favorable prisoner of war agreement	✓
First Taiwan Strait Crisis	1954	Integrated	Deter treaty between the U.S. and Taiwan	✗
Second Taiwan Strait Crisis	1958	Integrated	Mobilize support for Great Leap Forward	✓
Sino-Indian border clashes	1959	Integrated	Seal Tibet's borders	✓
China-Nepal border clashes	1959	Integrated	Seal Tibet's borders	✓
Nationalist invasion scare	1962	Integrated	Deter KMT attack	✓
Sino-Indian War	1962	Integrated	Compel India to abandon "Forward Policy"	✓
Vietnam War	1964	Fragmented	Compete with Soviet Union for influence in Southeast Asia	✗
Sikkim Ultimatum	1965	Fragmented	Compel India to accept ceasefire	✓
Sino-Indian border clashes (Nathu La and Cho La)	1967	Fragmented	Deter Indian military presence along border	✗
Sino-Soviet border conflict	1969	Fragmented	Deter Soviet attack/escalation	✗
Paracel Islands seizure	1974	Fragmented	Improve territorial control of the Paracel Islands	✓

Yet there is no evidence that Mao used meetings with his bureaucratic advisers to deliberate China's potential options in any of its five international crises under fragmented institutions. Some accounts suggest that there was minimal planning by the leadership in Beijing prior to the 1967 border clashes with India.⁸⁶ Even in cases in which China ultimately achieved its crisis objectives, China's decision-making appears to have featured poor information search and sharing. The records available suggest that Mao approved the Sikkim Ultimatum, in which China attempted to compel India to agree to peace negotiations during the 1965 India–Pakistan War, at a dinner party.⁸⁷ China's decision to seize the Paracel Islands in 1974 was handled by an ad hoc group, which excluded the Foreign Ministry.⁸⁸

We can further probe the connection between institutional design and crisis performance by process tracing China's decision-making during two international crises: the 1962 Nationalist invasion scare and the 1969 Sino-Soviet border conflict. Table 4.3 summarizes the key points for each case study. The 1962 crisis helps to illustrate how integrated institutions shaped the availability and quality of information available to Mao during his early years. This case is particularly valuable in part because it illustrates Mao's decision-making at the end of the integrated period. The case is also valuable because the crisis occurred after the Sino-Soviet split was clearly visible in both Beijing and Moscow, as harmony between China and the Soviet Union during the early years of the relationship may have helped to reduce the risk of miscalculation.⁸⁹

By contrast, the 1969 conflict helps to illustrate the connection between China's fragmented institutions and its miscalculations during Mao's later years. This case is a particularly helpful comparison with the 1962 Nationalist invasion scare for two reasons. First, the crisis occurred at the peak of China's institutional fragmentation. The low levels of information search and bureaucratic information access help to clearly illustrate the consequences for crisis decision-making. Second, both crises featured a materially superior adversary. This similarity is useful because the balance of power could potentially induce caution among decision-makers to avoid confrontations with strong opponents, even in the wake of detailed bureaucratic assessments. Alternatively, power imbalances could induce perceptions of vulnerability that could cause China to lash out in order to demonstrate its resolve.

---

⁸⁶ Fravel, *Strong Borders, Secure Nation*, 198–199.
⁸⁷ Yang Gongsu, *Cangsang jiushi nian: yi ge waijiao teshi de huiyi Cangsang jiushi nian: yi ge waijiao teshi de huiyi* [The Vicissitudes of Ninety Years: Recollections of a Diplomatic Envoy] (Haikou: Hainan chubanshe, 1999), 283; Cheng Xiaohe, "Di erci YinBa zhanzheng zhong Zhongguo dui Bajisitan de zhiyuan [Chinese Support to Pakistan during the Second India-Pakistan War]," *Waijiao pinglun* [Foreign Affairs Review] 3 (2012): 83.
⁸⁸ Liu Jixian, ed., *Ye Jianying nianpu, 1897–1986* [Chronicle of Ye Jianying, 1897–1986] (Beijing: Zhongyang wenxian chubanshe, 2007), Vol. II, 1072–1073.
⁸⁹ Christensen, *Worse Than a Monolith*.

Table 4.3 *Summary of the KMT invasion scare and Sino-Soviet border conflict*

Crisis (institution)	Pathway Information provision	Observable implications		
		Leader projections	Outcome	Miscalculation
Nationalist invasion scare (integrated)	*High quality*: extensive information search by MFA and PLA; competitive dialogue between MFA and PLA	Mobilization and diplomacy will deter KMT/U.S. action; U.S. support key to KMT action	KMT does not invade; U.S. restricts support for KMT operations	No
Sino-Soviet border conflict (fragmented)	*Low quality*: limited information search by MFA and PLA; self-censored MFA reporting	PRC ambush will compel USSR to de-escalate; USSR planning attack on PRC	USSR escalates and continues military build-up along border; limited evidence of Soviet plans to strike before crisis	Yes

The 1962 Nationalist Invasion Scare

Since its founding, China has maintained territorial claims on Taiwan, as well as smaller islands off the mainland's shore.[90] After their defeat by CCP forces on the mainland, KMT forces led by Chiang Kai-shek retreated to Taiwan and the offshore islands. China's military plans to retake the contested territory by force were delayed after the Truman administration renewed U.S. commitments to defend the KMT regime, allowing Chiang and the KMT military to regroup and strengthen their position.[91] Even after the retreat to Taiwan, however, the official position

---

[90] For an overview of the change in U.S. policy between 1950 and 1958, see Zhang Shu Guang, *Deterrence and Strategic Culture: Chinese-American Confrontations, 1949–1958* (Ithaca: Cornell University Press, 1992), 46–78, 189–224.

[91] Lin Hsiao-ting, *The Accidental State: Chiang Kai-shek, the United States, and the Making of Taiwan* (Cambridge: Harvard University Press, 2016).

of the KMT government was that it would reunify the country, including the mainland, under its leadership. Throughout the 1960s, hopes that the KMT would "return to the mainland" by way of military attack, subversion, infiltration, or regime change remained central to the KMT's platform.[92]

By 1961, the economic disaster of the Great Leap Forward led Chiang to believe a mainland invasion might be successful.[93] The Ministry of Defense established a National Recovery Operations Office, which explored plans for offensive action, recruitment of forces on the mainland, and post-invasion mobilization.[94] The KMT approved a "Special Tax for National Defense," established a Battlefield Administration Bureau, and established an Economic Mobilization Planning Commission to oversee the budget for the operation.[95]

Mao had several options for how to respond to a possible KMT invasion or KMT-backed insurrection.[96] One option was to attack KMT or U.S. forces, particularly those stationed on Jinmen and Mazu Islands, which were well within striking distance of the mainland's artillery. This option would have followed the "noose" strategy that Mao developed during the 1958 Taiwan Strait Crisis, whereby China could use intermittent attacks on the offshore islands when it needed coercive leverage over policymakers in Washington or Taipei.[97] Another option was to simply ignore the KMT military preparations.

China instead chose to pursue coercive diplomacy. In early June, China deployed approximately 100,000 troops to southeast China and placed them on alert.[98] Alongside military mobilization, China used

---

[92] Jay Taylor, *The Generalissimo: Chiang Kai-shek and the Struggle for Modern China* (Cambridge: The Belknap Press of Harvard University Press, 2009), Chapters 10–11.
[93] Lin Hsiao-ting, *Taihai, lengzhan, Jiang Jieshi: Jiemi dang'an zhong xiaoshi de Taiwan shi* [Taiwan Strait, Cold War, Chiang Kai-shek: Taiwan's Hidden History in Declassified Records] (Taipei: Lianjing chuban shiye gufen youxian gongsi, 2015), 158.
[94] Lin Zhengyi, "Jiang Jieshi, Mao Zedong, Kennidi yu 1962 Taihai weiji [Chiang Kai-shek, Mao Zedong, Kennedy and the 1962 Taiwan Strait Crisis]," in *Jiang Zhongzheng yu Minguo waijiao* [Chiang Kai-shek and the Republic's Diplomacy], ed. Wu Zusheng and Chen Liwen (Taipei: Guoli zhongzheng jiniantang guanlichu, 2013), 295–296; Lin, *Taihai, lengzhan, Jiang Jieshi*, 150–156.
[95] Lin, *Taihai, lengzhan, Jiang Jieshi*, 155–156.
[96] For an overview of the events in 1962, see Xia Yafeng, *Negotiating with the Enemy: US-China Talks during the Cold War, 1949–1972* (Bloomington: Indiana University Press, 2006), 112–119; Nancy Bernkopf Tucker, *Strait Talk: United States-Taiwan Relations and the Crisis with China* (Cambridge: Harvard University Press, 2009), 19–21; Fravel, *Strong Borders, Secure Nation*, 249–252; Wang Dong, "1962 nian Taihai weiji yu Zhong-Mei guanxi [The 1962 Taiwan Strait Crisis and Sino-American Relations]," *Zhonggong dangshi yanjiu* [Research on CCP Party History], no. 7 (2010): 60–69.
[97] Chen, *Mao's China and the Cold War*, 185–187.
[98] Li et al., *Mao Zedong junshi wengao*, Vol. III, 138–140.

diplomatic channels with the United States in Warsaw to probe American intentions and signal China's concern.[99] The goal of Mao's strategy was twofold. First, China hoped to deter major military action by the KMT against the mainland. Second, China sought to limit U.S. support for any military operation the KMT might pursue.

The Logic of Mao's Decision. Mao's choice for coercive diplomacy was based on two projections. First, Mao judged that the KMT was genuinely contemplating military action against the mainland.[100] For Mao, the KMT preparations were not simply tough talk. They were a real threat of military action.

Second, Mao judged that coercive diplomacy would help convince the United States not to support Chiang's proposals. Initially, Mao worried that U.S. support for the operation might be forthcoming.[101] Yet the mutual defense treaty between the United States and Taiwan offered China an avenue to push U.S. policymakers to restrain their ally. Because the treaty required agreement prior to any military action, convincing decision-makers in Washington to withhold support would short-circuit any KMT gambit.

China's Outcome. The projections on which Mao based his choices during the Nationalist invasion scare proved generally accurate. First, internal records from Taiwan strongly suggest that Chiang Kai-shek was seriously contemplating military action in the spring of 1962. Chiang felt that a major operation might succeed in the wake of the Great Leap Forward, noting in his diary that there was "clear proof" that public support for the Communist regime was waning.[102] Indeed, Chiang confided that this was his "only favorable opportunity" for an offensive against the mainland.[103] Internal records of deliberations between Chiang and his advisers similarly document how the KMT was planning a large-scale airdrops followed by an amphibious landing.[104] Chiang reportedly believed the United States would not "raise serious objections" to a KMT assault

---

[99] Fravel, *Strong Borders, Secure Nation*, 249–252.
[100] Huang and Zhang, *Luo Ruiqing zhuan*, 368–370.
[101] Wang, "1962 nian Taihai weiji yu ZhongMei guanxi," 61.
[102] Lu Fangshang, ed., *Jiang Zhongzheng nianpu changbian* [Chronicle of Chiang Kai-shek] (Taipei: Guoshiguan, 2014), Vol. 11, 537.
[103] Ibid., Vol. 11, 545.
[104] "Minutes of the 8th Military Talks," April 17, 1962, Chiang Kai-shek Collection, Academia Historica Archives, File 602-680200-604.

on the mainland.¹⁰⁵ The CIA similarly observed that KMT planning and preparation had taken a "new degree of urgency and credibility."¹⁰⁶

Second, China's mobilization shaped the U.S. decision to withhold support for large-scale KMT operations. Some U.S. officials initially voiced support for the KMT's military plans. On March 30, 1962, the U.S. embassy in Taiwan recommended "a program of substantially increased [...] probing activity against the mainland" that would "cover as broad a spectrum as possible."¹⁰⁷ U.S. President John F. Kennedy was briefed on possible KMT operations on March 31 and May 17.¹⁰⁸ Kennedy "did not want to dismiss" the possibility of supporting KMT plans altogether, as he felt that if the Communist regime "could be destroyed, it would tremendously alter the situation in Asia to the advantage of the Free World."¹⁰⁹ Even in the wake of the disaster of the Bay of Pigs, Kennedy was willing to approve "probing operations" and "close liaison" with the KMT to plan and prepare for "larger scale clandestine operations on a contingent basis involving up to a maximum of 200 men in a single airdrop."¹¹⁰

After China's mobilization, however, the NSC staff realized that the White House had "made a mistake" by supporting KMT proposals for airdrops and that the United States should "stop short of deliberately supplying an offensive capability under circumstances which makes it possible for others to take the ultimate decision away from us."¹¹¹ By November 1962, the NSC Policy Planning Council stated that U.S. policy would "avoid ourselves, and insist that the Nationalists avoid, military operations against the mainland" on any large scale. While "small-scale probes and clandestine operations" might facilitate additional intelligence collection and test the "temper of communist-armed forces," the United States would not sanction any additional escalation. The United States would instead "gradually make clear" to Chiang that the "only

---

¹⁰⁵ Central Intelligence Agency, "Mainland Recovery Preparations," May 10, 1962. National Security File, Box 25, John F. Kennedy Presidential Library (hereafter JFKL).
¹⁰⁶ "Prospects for Early Chinese Nationalist Military Action against the Mainland," July 27, 1961. National Security File, Box 22, JFKL. See also Nancy Bernkopf Tucker, *China Confidential: American Diplomats and Sino-American Relations, 1945–1996* (New York: Columbia University Press, 2001), 175–176.
¹⁰⁷ "Telegram from the Embassy in the Republic of China to the Department of State," March 30, 1962. *FRUS 1961–1963 Volume XXII, Northeast Asia*.
¹⁰⁸ "White House Meeting on GRC Plans," March 31, 1962. *FRUS 1961–1963 Volume XXII*.
¹⁰⁹ "White House Briefing on China," May 17, 1962. *FRUS 1961–1963 Volume XXII*.
¹¹⁰ "Memorandum to the Chief of the Central Intelligence Agency Station in Taipei (Cline)," March 31, 1962. *FRUS 1961–1963 Volume XXII*.
¹¹¹ "Memorandum from Michael Forrestal of the White House Staff to the President's Special Assistant for National Security Affairs (Bundy)," August 3, 1962. *FRUS 1961–1963 Volume XXII*.

circumstance" that the United States would consider supporting major military action would be if the KMT had "in effect been invited to do so by strong forces within China, which had already declared themselves against the communist regime."[112]

The tightening of U.S. policy helped to restrain KMT plans. Between late June and early July, the U.S. State Department issued instructions that "it is most important that [the KMT] not give the Communists any pretext for such attack either by any public statements by [KMT] officials or by any [KMT] actions."[113] As one historian notes, "pressure on Taiwan played a considerably important role" in the "sudden halt" to the KMT's large-scale invasion plans.[114] In the summer of 1962, KMT media reports on a mainland invasion "suddenly went quiet" and instead began to emphasize the need for political, military, and economic preparation.[115] While small-scale military operations persisted throughout the mid-1960s, they did not compare in scale to the 1962 mobilization.[116] In sum, as one Chinese scholar summarizes, Mao was able to effectively communicate his "intentions and policy bottom lines," while simultaneously avoiding "formal misjudgment or conflict escalation."[117]

Institutional Origins of Mao's Decision. The theory predicts that leaders sitting above integrated institutions are more likely to receive complete and accurate information upon which they can base their choices on the road to international conflict. Congruent with this prediction, China's national security bureaucracies supplied a range of high-quality counsel that shaped Mao's decision-making during the KMT invasion scare.[118]

Part of Mao's decision-making was informed by intelligence and analysis from his defense bureaucracy. Military intelligence provided early warning of KMT mobilization.[119] Defense information flowed freely within the Chinese state system, supported by a variety of decision-making and coordination bodies. The CMC discussed incoming intelligence and possible military options.[120] Chief of General

---

[112] "Paper Prepared in the Policy Planning Council," November 30, 1962. *FRUS 1961–1963 Volume XXII*.
[113] "Telegram from the Department of State to the Embassy in the Republic of China," June 19, 1962. *FRUS 1961–1963 Volume XXII*.
[114] Lin, *Taihai, lengzhan, Jiang Jieshi*, 158.
[115] Ibid., 164.
[116] Yang Guihua, ed., *Zhongguo renmin jiefangjun junshi* [Military History of the Chinese People's Liberation Army] (Beijing: Junshi kexue chubanshe, 2010), Vol. V, 317.
[117] Wang, "1962 nian Taihai weiji yu ZhongMei guanxi," 69.
[118] Pang and Feng, *Mao Zedong nianpu*, Vol. V, 104–105.
[119] Huang and Zhang, *Luo Ruiqing zhuan*, 368–370, 666.
[120] Huang and Zhang, *Luo Ruiqing zhuan*, 368–369. Luo was in Shanghai with Mao to discuss the military's recommendations on China's defense strategy. See Pang and Feng, *Mao Zedong nianpu*, Vol. V, 103.

Staff Luo Ruiqing instructed both the Deputy Chief of Staff for Operations Lei Yingfu and Deputy Chief of Staff for Intelligence Zhang Ting to brief Premier Zhou Enlai and Defense Minister Lin Biao.[121] At Zhou Enlai's direction, Wang Bingnan, China's diplomatic representative at the U.S.–China ambassadorial talks in Warsaw, met with Luo Ruiqing to exchange information between the CMC and Foreign Ministry. The CMC appears to have played a particularly important role in assessing the possibility of a KMT attack,[122] with both senior military and diplomatic leaders providing input during its assessment process. In parallel, the Strategic Research Small Group analyzed China's strategy and offer policy recommendations. Civilian officials from the State Council participated in its proceedings.[123] The threat of invasion was subsequently discussed at a special meeting of the senior party leadership on June 1. Senior military officials briefed the party leadership at Politburo meetings on May 18, June 2, and June 6 – and again in conjunction with Foreign Minister Chen Yi in a broader venue on June 20.[124]

Mao's decision-making process was influenced not only by input from Chinese defense officials but also by diplomatic information that added context to the military's perspective. Although both diplomatic and defense advisers concurred on the seriousness of the threat posed by a KMT invasion, Mao's diplomatic advisers observed that the KMT's decision was contingent on support from the United States.[125]

Moreover, it was unclear to Chinese diplomats that the United States was willing to provide support. Foreign Minister Chen noted in May that while KMT or U.S.-KMT military action was possible, the United States might not support more ambitious KMT action. "It is more likely," Chen explained, "that Chiang Kai-shek has ignored U.S. restraints." In the Foreign Minister's view, the United States would "dare not take the risk" of a major war. Chen's views circulated widely throughout the Chinese

[121] Huang and Zhang, *Luo Ruiqing zhuan*, 369–370.
[122] Ibid., 369; Zhang Zishen, ed., *Yang Chengwu nianpu, 1914–2004* [Chronicle of Yang Chengwu, 1914–2004] (Beijing: Jiefangjun chubanshe, 2014), 364.
[123] Tan Jingqiao, "Wuliushi niandai de zongcan zuozhanbu [The General Staff Operations Department in the 1950s and 1960s]," in *Zongcanmoubu: huiyi shiliao, 1927–1987* [General Staff Department: Recollections and Historical Materials, 1927–1987] (Beijing: Jiefangjun chubanshe, 1995), 425.
[124] Yang and Yan, *Deng Xiaoping nianpu, 1904–1974*, Vol. III, 1708, 1711; Pang and Feng, *Mao Zedong nianpu*, Vol. V, 104; Yang Qiliang et al., ed., *Wang Shangrong jiangjun* [General Wang Shangrong] (Beijing: Dangdai Zhongguo chubanshe, 2000), 485; Huang and Zhang, *Luo Ruiqing zhuan*, 371. Sun Yi, ed., *Zhou Enlai junshi huodong jishi, 1918–1975* [Record of Zhou Enlai's Military Activities, 1918–1975] (Beijing: Zhongyang wenxian chubanshe, 2000), Vol. 2, 564. Zhou also participated in CMC discussions in February.
[125] Yang et al., *Wang Shangrong jiangjun*, 485. Zhou Enlai, *Zhou Enlai junshi wenxuan* [Military Works of Zhou Enlai], ed. Liu Wusheng (Beijing: Renmin chubanshe, 1997), Vol. IV, 433–434.

government, including Mao Zedong, Zhou Enlai, as well as the defense and intelligence bureaucracies.[126]

China's diplomatic envoys played a critical role in supporting Chen's analysis, especially during a significant U.S.–China ambassadorial meeting in Warsaw on June 23. During the engagement, the American ambassador explicitly assured China's envoy that the United States "had no intention" of supporting a KMT attack on mainland China.[127] Furthermore, the U.S. ambassador stressed that any KMT invasion of the mainland required the consent of U.S. policymakers, who would refuse such support. Under these circumstances, the KMT was unlikely to engage in aggression against the mainland.[128]

In his report to the party leadership, Chinese envoy Wang Bingnan drew a number of conclusions from the diplomatic engagement. He highlighted the existing "contradictions" between decision-makers in Washington and Taipei regarding a mainland attack, emphasizing that the United States would not "risk releasing Chiang for fear of disaster." Wang's report circulated widely within the bureaucracy in Beijing and directly affected Mao's thinking. As Wang later recalled:

The position of the United States was now quite clear and this was exactly what we anxiously needed to know. This important development would directly affect the party leadership's formulation of frontline combat deployments. I quickly reported the contents of the conversation with [the U.S. ambassador]. Afterwards, the central leadership promptly requested [additional] intelligence from me in order to understand the U.S. attitude. They were extremely satisfied and *this had a major effect on decision-making at the time.*[129]

China's diplomatic reporting appears to have reshaped thinking widely across the state. By July, Mao reportedly believed that China no longer

---

[126] "Chen Yi fu zongli jiejian Sulian zhuhua dashi Qierwonianke tanhua jilu [Record of Conversation between Vice Premier Chen Yi and Soviet Ambassador to the PRC Chervonenko]," May 12, 1962. PRC Foreign Ministry Archive, File 109-03803-09. On the distribution of this report, see the attached routing sheet.

[127] Prior to the talks, President Kennedy approved a U.S. State Department policy to reassure China that the United States would not support an invasion. The goal was to ensure that China did not "act under a misunderstanding of [U.S.] intentions." See "Memorandum from Acting Secretary of State Ball to President Kennedy," June 21, 1962. *FRUS 1961–1963 Volume XXII*, Document 124, note 0.

[128] This paragraph is based on the PRC and U.S. meeting summaries. "Telegram from the Embassy in Poland to the Department of State," June 23, 1962. *FRUS 1961–1963 Volume XXII*; "Guanyu yu Meiguo dashi fei zhengshi huitan qingkuang [Cable from Warsaw to Beijing: On the Informal Meeting with the U.S. Ambassador]," June 23, 1962. PRC Foreign Ministry Archive, File 111-00605-01. See also Wang Bingnan, *ZhongMei huitan jiunian huigu* [Nine Years of Sino-American Talks in Retrospect] (Beijing: Shijie zhishi chubanshe, 1985), 87–90.

[129] Wang, *ZhongMei huitan jiunian huigu*, 90. Emphasis added.

needed to "create tension."[130] Indeed, China's diplomatic reporting appears to have reshaped thinking widely across the state. Zhou Enlai noted that the United States aimed to avoid "entanglement" and steer clear of a war with China.[131] In November, the Foreign Affairs Work Conference predicted continuation of the "status quo" with the United States.[132]

In sum, China's integrated institutions – particularly the interactive deliberations between its diplomatic and defense bureaucracies – allowed Mao to make decisions based on high-quality information during the 1962 Nationalist invasion scare. The access and status that both diplomatic and defense bureaucrats enjoyed yielded candid assessments that informed Mao's choices.

Alternative Explanations. It is helpful to consider three alternative explanations for Mao's decision-making during the 1962 Nationalist invasion scare. One possibility consistent with the interest group model of bureaucratic politics might suggest that China's behavior reflected the dominant influence of a single bureaucracy over the leader. In this case, however, there is no evidence that Mao believed he had no choice but to accept the recommendations of either his defense or diplomatic advisers. On the contrary, multiple bureaucracies provided information that proved critical to the choices that Mao made. In particular, the case suggests that reporting from Chinese diplomats – both the foreign minister and diplomatic representatives abroad – shaped Mao's thinking about the possibility of American support for a mainland invasion.

Another possibility is that the strategy China chose simply reflected intransigent leader beliefs. Yet Mao's choices throughout the episode reflected the information that his bureaucracy supplied. Mao's decision to mobilize the Chinese military was informed by accurate intelligence reporting regarding the KMT's invasion planning, while Mao's choice not to further escalate the crisis reflected information that Chinese diplomats supplied. If anything, Mao's restrained choices during the crisis are at odds with his general belief in the efficacy of military force.[133] Whereas Mao used violence to pursue China's objectives in both the 1954 and 1958 Taiwan Strait Crises, he opted for a more diplomatic approach in 1962.

[130] "Chen Yi fu zongli jiejian Sulian zhuhua dashi Qierwonianke tanhua jilu," June 28, 1962. PRC Foreign Ministry Archives, File 109-03803-09.
[131] Zhou Enlai, *Zhou Enlai junshi wenxuan* [Military Works of Zhou Enlai], ed. Liu Wusheng (Beijing: Renmin chubanshe, 1997), Vol. IV, 433–434.
[132] "Main Points of the Sixth National Foreign Affairs Conference," November 1962. Jiangsu Provincial Archives, File 3124–0145.
[133] Andrew Kennedy, *The International Ambitions of Mao and Nehru: National Efficacy Beliefs and the Making of Foreign Policy* (New York: Cambridge University Press, 2012).

A final possibility is that Mao might have been unusually prudent in the summer of 1962 because of a heightened threat of elite accountability. While such a threat would have been uncommon under Mao's strongman rule, it is possible that Mao felt he was losing his grip on power in the wake of the economic disaster of the Great Leap Forward. Yet there are several reasons why this alone would not explain the choices China made during this crisis. First, there is scant evidence available suggesting that Mao believed he might be removed from office if he did not resolve the tensions across the Taiwan Strait effectively. Second, Mao's patterns of decision-making discussed in Figure 4.1 do not show substantive changes in the period between 1958 and 1962. Mao continued to convene the Politburo – and to meet with both his diplomatic and defense advisers – with about the same frequency as prior to the Great Leap Forward.

The 1969 Sino-Soviet Border Conflict

In contrast to the 1962 Nationalist invasion scare, the Sino-Soviet border conflict illustrates how fragmented institutions can cause leaders to miscalculate. In the mid-1960s, the Soviet Union and China were locked in a broad competition for international leadership within the Communist bloc.[134] In addition, the two sides had lingering disagreements concerning territorial features in the Amur and Ussuri Rivers. Negotiations between China and the Soviet Union to reach a peaceful settlement to these disputes stalled in 1964.[135] Both sides instigated clashes along the border in the late 1960s.[136] On February 16, 1967, senior authorities in Beijing ordered the military leadership in Jilin province to "engage in a tit-for-tat struggle with all provocative schemes of Soviet revisionism." While the central leadership asked local authorities to show restraint and did not approve armed conflict, decision-makers in Beijing instructed local authorities to persist in "verbal struggles" (文斗) aimed at the Soviet side. Soviet reports suggest that in the beginning of 1967, the number of border violations by Chinese authorities, including forward patrolling on the islands, increased. Soviet border forces began preventing Chinese border guards from conducting patrols, but their orders were reportedly to "avoid armed collisions."[137] These border clashes reflected

---

[134] For an overview, see Lüthi, *The Sino-Soviet Split*.
[135] Fravel, *Strong Borders, Secure Nation*, 119–123; Nikita Sergeyevich Khrushchev, *Memoirs of Nikita Khrushchev*, ed. Sergei Khrushchev (University Park: Penn State University Press, 2004), Vol. III, 475; Lüthi, *The Sino-Soviet Split*, 276–277.
[136] Li and Hao, *Wenhua dageming zhong de renmin jiefangjun*, 317–318.
[137] "Waijiaobu, zongcanmoubu: Guanyu dangqian zhong Su bianjing douzheng de ruogan wenti [Foreign Ministry, General Staff Department: Some issues concerning the current Sino-Soviet border struggle]," February 16, 1967. Jilin Provincial Archives,

112   China under Mao

the escalating Sino-Soviet rivalry.[138] As Zhou Enlai noted, negotiations with the Soviet Union over the border were "inseparable from the overall situation" in the bilateral relationship.[139]

In the early months of 1969, Mao had several options available. First, Mao could order troops along the border to refrain from forward patrolling and perhaps de-escalate tensions through negotiations with Soviet leaders, who remained open to such talks.[140] Second, Mao could order Chinese forces to continue small-scale clashes along the border, but to prohibit them from using violence against the Soviet side.[141] A third option, and the one that Mao ultimately chose, was to directly attack Soviet forces. Field commanders in the Shenyang and Beijing Military Regions received orders to prepare operational plans on January 24, 1968.[142] Shortly thereafter, supported by analysis from the Chinese military, Mao approved plans to attack Soviet forces along the border.[143] The CMC tasked the Shenyang and Beijing Military Regions to "choose a politically-favorably time, place, and situation" to "attack in a focused and planned manner."[144] On March 2, 1969, China ambushed Soviet forces on Zhenbao Island, resulting in 91 Chinese and approximately 200 Soviet casualties.[145]

The Logic of Mao's Decision. Mao's decision to ambush Soviet forces in March 1969 rested on three assessments. First, Mao judged that an ambush would reduce the chance of a Soviet attack.[146] Mao did not believe that the ambush would lead the Soviet Union to escalate.[147] On the

Collection 77, Catalog 13, Vol. I; "Soviet Report to East German Leadership on Sino-Soviet Border Clashes," March 2, 1969, Wilson Center Digital Archive, SAMPO-BArch J IV 2/202/359. Translated by Christian F. Ostermann.

[138] Christensen, *Worse Than a Monolith*, 202–208.
[139] Chai Chengwen, "Zhou Enlai lingdao women jinxing ZhongSu bianjie tanpan [Zhou Enlai Led Our Sino-Soviet Border Negotiations]," in *Zhonggong dangshi zhongda shijian shushi* [An Account of Major Events in CCP History], Expanded Edition, ed. Yang Shengqun and Chen Jin (Beijing: Renmin chubanshe, 2008), 220.
[140] Melvin Gurtov and Byong-Moo Hwang, *China under Threat: The Politics of Strategy and Diplomacy* (Baltimore: Johns Hopkins University Press, 1980), 206; Oleg B. Borisov and B. T. Koloskov, *Soviet-Chinese Relations, 1945–1970* (Bloomington: Indiana University Press, 1975), 343.
[141] Li, "Zhengzhi doushi yu dishou," 158.
[142] Li and Hao, eds., *Wenhua dageming zhong de renmin jiefangjun*, 318.
[143] Wu Faxian, *Wu Faxian huiyilu* [Memoirs of Wu Faxian] (Hong Kong: Beixing chubanshe, 2006), Vol. II, 758. See also Li Zuopeng, *Li Zuopeng huiyilu* [Memoirs of Li Zuopeng] (Hong Kong: Beixing chubanshe, 2011), Vol. II, 637.
[144] Xu, "1969 Nian ZhongSu bianjie chongtu."
[145] Fravel, *Strong Borders, Secure Nation*, 201–202.
[146] Christensen, "Windows and War," 69–71; Fravel, *Strong Borders, Secure Nation*, 211–214.
[147] Li, "Zhengzhi doushi yu dishou," 158; Xu Yan, *Xu Yan jianggao zixuanji* [Selected Works from Xu Yan's Lectures] (Beijing: Guofang daxue chubanshe, 2014), 267.

contrary, Mao seems to have assessed that China's ambush would be perceived by the Soviet Union as a defensive measure. Indeed, Mao judged that the "Soviets know that we will not invade their country as it is so cold there."[148]

Second, Mao concluded that Soviet leaders were contemplating an invasion – and, as in the 1962 Nationalist invasion scare, Mao was apprehensive about the formidable strength of the Soviet military.[149] In October 1964, Mao suggested that the Soviet Union might use military force to occupy Xinjiang, Heilongjiang, or Inner Mongolia.[150] In 1967, orders from Beijing told local military commanders that Tsarist Russia had "always regarded Xinjiang, Inner Mongolia, and Heilongjiang as their spheres of influence" and the current leadership in Moscow had "completely inherited this tsarists ambition."[151] On November 28, 1968, Mao stated that both the United States and the Soviet Union had "the capacity to start a war" and feared that "a war might begin."[152] On February 19, 1969, Mao asserted that international matters had been "somewhat strange," noting reports from foreign newspapers claiming that "the Soviet Union plans to deploy troops."[153] Shortly after the crisis erupted, Mao told his inner circle that "We cannot say that the Soviet Union and the United States do not wish to occupy Europe and Asia, including inside China."[154] Just over a week later, Mao ordered the northern areas of China to prepare for a Soviet and U.S. invasion.[155] While the Soviet Union might not initiate a war immediately, the actions on the border were "just the beginning" and now China could "see the prospects." Indeed, Mao reasoned that the United States and the Soviet Union had colluded in the past, expanded their arms, and hoped to divide up the world anew.[156]

---

[148] "Mao Zedong's Talk at a Meeting of the Central Cultural Revolution Group (Except)," March 15, 1969. Chen and Wilson, "All under the Heaven Is Great Chaos," 162.
[149] Xu, *Xu Yan jianggao zixuanji*, 275.
[150] Yang, "The Sino-Soviet Border Clash of 1969," 24.
[151] "Cable from the Foreign Ministry and General Staff Department to the Jilin Military Region: Some Issues Concerning the Current Sino-Soviet Border Struggle," February 16, 1967.
[152] "Conversation between Mao Zedong and E. F. Hill," November 28, 1968. In Chen Jian and David L. Wilson, "All under the Heaven Is Great Chaos: Beijing, The Sino-Soviet Border Clashes, and the Turn Toward Sino-American Rapprochement, 1968–69," *Cold War International History Project Bulletin*, no. 11 (1998): 161. The Soviet invasion of Czechoslovakia in August 1968 likely exacerbated Mao's fears. See Li, "Zhengzhi doushi yu dishou," 157.
[153] Wang Yongqin, "1966–1976 nian ZhongMeiSu guanxi jishi (lianzai yi) [Chronicle of Sino-American-Soviet Relations (1)]," *Dangdai Zhongguo shi yanjiu* [Research on Contemporary Chinese History], no. 4 (1997): 118.
[154] Pang and Feng, *Mao Zedong nianpu*, Vol. VI, 232.
[155] Li et al., *Mao Zedong junshi wengao*, Vol. III, 355–357.
[156] Ibid., Vol. III, 356–358.

The final assessment suggested that China had few alternatives to international conflict. In particular, Mao judged that rapprochement with the United States did not yet offer an alternative route to balance against the perceived Soviet threat. While there are some indications that Mao was interested in improving U.S.–China relations, particularly as U.S. President Richard Nixon entered office, Mao did not foresee improvement.[157] On February 7, shortly before initiating the Sino-Soviet border crisis, Mao told the CCRG that "for the time being there will not be any major changes" in the Nixon administration's policy toward China.[158] On the contrary, Mao told his inner circle that the new U.S. president was "engaged in military expansion and preparing for war."[159] Even some of the signals that Nixon had sent to Mao prior to assuming office seem to have been interpreted negatively. Mao complained that China did not appreciate the U.S. initiative to "pull [China] into the United Nations" or to "bring the Chinese people into the world community."[160]

China's Outcome. Mao's projections proved inaccurate. First, the ambush contributed to Soviet escalation, rather than de-escalation, of tensions along the border. The ambush triggered a Soviet military mobilization, retaliation against the Chinese positions at Zhenbao, and additional border clashes along the western border. Only *after* the attack did Soviet decision-makers begin to seriously consider offensive action against China, sounding out whether the United States would accept a limited Soviet strike on China.[161] Even after the crisis abated, the Soviet Union expanded deployments along the Sino-Soviet border.[162] These trends continued throughout the 1970s, as the Soviet Union held military exercises, including the largest ever proximate to the border.[163] In short, as Chinese historian Yang Kuisong notes, Mao miscalculated the Soviet response, as the effects of China's actions went "beyond Mao's worst expectations."[164]

---

[157] Chen, *Mao's China and the Cold War*, 245.
[158] Pang and Feng, *Mao Zedong nianpu*, Vol. VI, 229.
[159] Li et al., *Mao Zedong junshi wengao*, Vol. III, 357.
[160] Pang and Feng, *Mao Zedong nianpu*, Vol. VI, 214.
[161] Shevchenko, *Breaking with Moscow*, 165; "Memcon: Linkov and Holdridge," September 26, 1969. NSC Files: Name Files, Holdridge [1969–1972], Box 818, Richard Nixon Presidential Library (hereafter RNL); "Memorandum from the President's Assistant for National Security Affairs (Kissinger) to President Nixon," September 29, 1969. *FRUS 1969–1976, Volume XII, Soviet Union, January 1969–October 1970.*
[162] Fravel, *Strong Borders, Secure Nation*, 205.
[163] Central Intelligence Agency, "Sino-Soviet Exchanges, 1969–84: A Reference Aid," April 1984, 2.
[164] Yang, "The Sino-Soviet Border Clash of 1969," 35. Allen Whiting similarly concludes that Chinese decision-makers "almost certainly miscalculated the magnitude

Second, the available evidence suggests that Soviet decision-makers were not considering attacking prior to the Chinese ambush in March 1969. On the contrary, Soviet leaders feared the superiority of numbers in the Chinese military might lead to an invasion of the Soviet Union.[165] The Soviet Politburo reportedly feared China's military's superiority in manpower.[166] Thus, from the perspective of decision-makers in Moscow, the motivation behind Soviet military deployments along the border was primarily defensive.[167] In his diary, Brezhnev initially downplayed the Chinese ambush, initially writing that "there was no need to dramatize" the fighting. Instead, Brezhnev appears to have feared that the incident would signal discord between China and the Soviet Union – and that Nixon would "take advantage of this."[168] One Chinese military officer notes that "it is clear that China overestimated the threat" from the Soviet Union.[169] In sum, as Chinese historian Xu Yan argues, both China and the Soviet Union "made serious misjudgments [...] believing the other side was going to aggressively attack the other."[170]

Third, Mao misread the United States. There is considerable evidence that Richard Nixon entered office with a keen interest in improving relations with China.[171] In November 1968, Nixon told incoming National Security Advisor Henry Kissinger that the United States needed "to re-evaluate our policy toward Communist China."[172] Nixon revisited the topic shortly after entering office, telling Kissinger that now was "the moment to establish normal relations with Communist China," and ordering his subordinates to move in that direction.[173] As early as January 11, the American bureaucracy was considering options for policy

of Russian reaction." See Whiting, *The Chinese Calculus of Deterrence*, 239. See also Christensen, "Windows and War," 71.

[165] David Holloway, "Assessing China's Nuclear Policy" (Unpublished manuscript, 2010), 19–20.
[166] Lüthi, *The Sino-Soviet Split*, 299.
[167] Shevchenko, *Breaking with Moscow*, 164–165; Sergei Goncharov and Victor Usov, *O Kitae Srednevekovom i Sovremennom: Zapiski Raznykh Let* [On Medieval and Modern China: Notes from Various Years] (Novosibirsk: Nauka, 2006), 315.
[168] Leonid Brezhnev, *Rabochie i dnevnikovye zapisi* [Work and Diary] (Moscow: IstLit, 2016), Vol. I, 368–369.
[169] Wang Zhongchun, "The Soviet Factor in Sino-American Normalization, 1969–1979," in *Normalization of U.S.-China Relations: An International History*, ed. William C. Kirby, Robert S. Ross, and Gong Li (Cambridge: Harvard University Asia Center, 2005), 153.
[170] Xu, *Xu Yan jianggao zixuanji*, 267.
[171] The timing of U.S. policy is important, as one might evaluate Mao's judgment differently if Mao had foreseen that a border conflict would catalyze rapprochement.
[172] Richard Nixon, *RN: The Memoirs of Richard Nixon* (New York: Grosset & Dunlap, 1978), 340–341, 370–374.
[173] Alexander M. Haig, *Inner Circles: How America Changed the World*, (New York: Warner Books, 1992), 257.

readjustment toward China and scheduling them for consideration by the NSC.[174] On February 1, 1969, Nixon felt that the United States "should give every encouragement" that the administration was "exploring possibilities of raprochement [sic] with the Chinese."[175] Days later, Kissinger issued National Security Study Memorandum 14, which requested a study on U.S. policy toward China.[176] Diplomatic talks offered China and the United States an opportunity to seek "a modus vivendi with the Communist Chinese which provides greater stability for East Asia." While Kissinger later claimed that the crisis helped shape his views on rapprochement, his writings at the time suggested that the White House was already "implicitly moving in this direction" by mid-February 1969.[177]

More broadly, although China's local control over Zhenbao improved, the crisis did little to resolve the border dispute. By the fall of 1969, China dropped preconditions for resuming diplomatic negotiations with the Soviet Union – Moscow's first and primary demand.[178] Moreover, over the course of fifteen rounds of border talks between October 1969 and June 1978, Soviet negotiators made few concessions.[179] Soviet envoys rebuffed Chinese requests to categorize the contested area as "disputed."[180] They also refused to accept Chinese proposals for interim measures to stabilize the border. As one Chinese diplomat recounts, the "two sides exchanged delegation heads numerous times, but in the end did not reach an agreement." Despite Chinese protests, the Soviet military "continued to cross the border into China."[181] Finally, while China's tactical control over Zhenbao Island improved, the Soviet Union had

---

[174] "Memorandum from Richard Sneider to Henry Kissinger," January 11, 1969. NSC Files: Name Files, Sneider [Jan 69–Jun 70], Box 818, RMNL.
[175] "Memorandum from President Nixon to his Assistant for National Security Affairs (Kissinger)," February 1, 1969. *FRUS 1969–1976, Volume XVII, China, 1969–1972*.
[176] "National Security Study Memorandum 14," February 5, 1969. *FRUS 1969–1976, Volume XVII*.
[177] "Memorandum from the President's Assistant for National Security Affairs (Kissinger) to President Nixon," February 12, 1969. *FRUS 1969–1976, Volume XVII*.
[178] Sergei Goncharov and Victor Usov, "Kosygin-Zhou Talks at Beijing Airport," *Far Eastern Affairs*, nos. 4–6 (1992): 57.
[179] Li Fenglin, "Mosike ershi nian [Twenty Years in Moscow]," in *Dangdai Zhongguo shijie waijiao shengya* [The Diplomatic Careers of Contemporary Chinese Envoys] (Beijing: Shijie zhishi chubanshe, 1996), Vol. IV, 294; Chai, "Zhou Enlai lingdao women jinxing ZhongSu bianjie tanpan," 220–222; Li Lianqing, ed., *Waijiao yingcai Qiao Guanhua* [Talented Diplomat Qiao Guanhua] (Nanjing: Jiangsu renmin chubanshe, 2000), 167–173.
[180] Goncharov and Usov, "Kosygin-Zhou Talks at Beijing Airport," 53.
[181] Li Lianqing, *Leng nuan sui yue: Yibosanzhe de ZhongSu guanxi* [Warm and Cold Years: The Ups and Downs of Sino-Soviet Relations] (Beijing: Shijie zhishi chubanshe, 1999), 379–380.

offered to cede control in 1964 as part of a border settlement, which was nearly identical to the final agreement reached by the two sides in 1991.[182]

Institutional Origins of Mao's Miscalculation. Fragmented institutions help to explain Mao's miscalculation in 1969. The theory predicts that leaders sitting atop fragmented institutions should receive incomplete information that biases toward the leader's prior beliefs. While China's integrated national security institutions provided Mao with generally complete and accurate information in 1962, fragmented institutions relayed low-quality information in 1969.[183] Specifically, we can trace Mao's inaccurate projections regarding the costs of peace, the probability of success, and the availability of alternatives to institutional pathologies within the Chinese bureaucracy.

Information supplied by the Chinese military shaped Mao's conclusions regarding the severity of the Soviet threat. Throughout 1969, the senior military leadership "overestimated the possibility of war" and assessed that "the possibility of a large-scale invasion by the Soviet Union was extremely high."[184] Firsthand accounts note that the intelligence section of the General Staff Department obtained reports suggesting that "the Soviet Union might be considering a surprise attack on China."[185] Chinese military intelligence reportedly intercepted radio communications between newly deployed Soviet forces and freshly established missile bases. Chief of General Staff Huang Yongsheng warned of "large numbers of troops" stationed along the border and the intensification of "armed provocations against China."[186] Internal reports drew attention to recent Soviet military drills and suggested that China had become the "number one" enemy of the Soviet Union.[187] The military leadership was "particularly anxious" about the rising number of Soviet infantry divisions deployed east of the Ural Mountains.[188] The senior military leadership repeatedly forwarded reports to Mao from subordinate

---

[182] Fravel, *Strong Borders, Secure Nation*, 122.
[183] Lorenz M. Lüthi, "Restoring Chaos to History: Sino-Soviet-American Relations, 1969," *The China Quarterly*, no. 210 (2012): 396.
[184] Zheng Qian, "Zhonggong jiu-da qianhou quanguo de zhanbei gongzuo [National War Preparations before and after the Ninth Party Congress]," in *Zhonggong dangshi ziliao* [Materials on Party History] (Beijing: Zhonggong dangshi chubanshe, 1992), 41, 211.
[185] Wu, *Wu Faxian huiyilu*, Vol. II, 761.
[186] Whiting, *The Chinese Calculus of Deterrence*, 237–239.
[187] Guolin Yi, *The Media and Sino-American Rapprochement, 1963–1972: A Comparative Study* (Baton Rouge: Louisiana State University Press, 2020), 78.
[188] Wang, "The Soviet Factor in Sino-American Normalization," 150.

118   China under Mao

military commands requesting permission to adopt defensive measures along the border.[189]

In contrast, fragmented institutions increased the costs of broader information search, particularly the flow of information from the Foreign Ministry. In the months before the 1969 Sino-Soviet crisis, Mao's decision-making process restricted the participation of diplomatic advisers. Mao himself directly noted that the Chinese Politburo did not deliberate before China launched the attack.[190] Instead, Mao convened at least fifteen informal meetings with members of the CCRG in 1968. While foreign affairs were discussed in roughly one-third of those meetings, Foreign Minister Chen Yi attended only one.[191] Senior MFA diplomats were similarly excluded from Mao's decision-making.[192] According to one diplomat, the Foreign Ministry was "very busy studying the materials" of the Ninth Party Congress.[193] The PRC ambassador to the Soviet Union, Pan Zili, had been recalled and diplomatic activities of the roughly twenty Chinese personnel remaining in Moscow were "reduced to a minimum."[194]

The increased costs of bureaucratic information provision prevented the flow of two important bits of information from the Foreign Ministry. The first was indications that the Soviet Union was not preparing to attack. Diplomats in the Foreign Ministry suggested that "the situation inside and outside the Soviet Union was not advantageous for war" and that "the Soviet Union feared that a situation was emerging in which it would have to cope with both China and the United States as enemies."

---

[189] Wu, *Wu Faxian huiyilu*, Vol. II, 757; Li, *Li Zuopeng huiyilu*, Vol. II, 637; Deng Liqun, *Deng Liqun guoshi jiangtanlu* [Record of Deng Liqun's Lectures on National History] (2000), Vol. VI, 491.

[190] Wang, "1966–1976 nian ZhongMeiSu guanxi jishi," 119, emphasis added; interview T111, Beijing, China, Spring 2017.

[191] See Pang and Feng, *Mao Zedong nianpu*, Vol. VI.

[192] For example, the Foreign Ministry appears not to have drafted a diplomatic démarche in advance of the Chinese ambush on March 2. After they were informed of the attack, Zhou asked Chinese diplomats to craft one, but it was not delivered to the Soviet embassy until later that afternoon and *after* the Soviet Foreign Ministry had delivered a note on the incident to the chargé d'affaires of the Chinese embassy. In the common Chinese saying, "the villain sued the victim before he could be prosecuted" (恶人先告状). Qiao and Li were criticized for their "lack of energy" in handling the matter. Li Lianqing, *Da waijiaojia Zhou Enlai* [The Great Diplomat Zhou Enlai] (Beijing: Renmin chubanshe, 2016), Vol. VI, 141–142. The MFA's lack of preparation contextualizes the fact that although the MFA had approved the military's operational plans, the MFA likely did not play an important role in the decision-making process. See Li and Hao, *Wenhua dageming zhong de renmin jiefangjun*, 319.

[193] "Note about the 'Club Meeting' of the Ambassadors and Acting Ambassadors of the Fraternal Countries," June 6, 1969, WCDA, PA AA, C 1365/74. Translated by Bernd Schaefer.

[194] Li, "Mosike ershi nian," 288–290.

At the same time, just as China was struggling to understand Soviet intentions, so too was the Soviet Union struggling to "clearly understand China's attitude."[195]

Fragmented institutions also obstructed the flow of diplomatic signals from the Soviet Union suggesting that no Soviet attack was imminent. One senior diplomat in the MFA recalls that Soviet leaders "tried to directly approach the Chinese leadership in order to defuse the border conflict and seek out the Chinese attitude before making a decision." The first attempt came through a phone call on the Sino-Soviet hotline requesting to connect Brezhnev to Mao.[196] The Chinese operator refused to transfer the call. On March 21, the Chinese operator similarly refused to connect Soviet Premier Alexei Kosygin to Zhou Enlai, calling the Soviet leader a "revisionist."[197] Kosygin confided to the Soviet ambassador in Beijing that he had orders from the Politburo to "talk personally with Comrades Mao Zedong and Zhou Enlai" but "some boor sitting at the telephone board in Beijing answered rudely and refused to connect me to them." Soviet leaders had hoped to communicate that it did not seek to escalate the conflict.[198] As one Chinese diplomat notes, "a potential dialogue at the highest levels between China and the Soviet Union had come to an untimely end."[199]

A second set of bureaucratic assessments pertained to the alternatives available to China. In December 1968, sidelined Foreign Minister Chen Yi noted that China might be able to capitalize on tensions between the United States and the Soviet Union.[200] Indeed, diplomatic signals from the United States suggested its openness to realignment at the time. As early as 1966, the Johnson administration signaled receptivity to warmer relations with China. In February 1966, U.S. Secretary of State Dean Rusk told the ambassador in Poland that the United States sought to take "small steps" in the Warsaw talks to demonstrate "reasonableness and our desire to move toward some lessening of tensions."[201] NSC staff members similarly noted that the objective of these "flexible initiatives"

---

[195] Li, *Da waijiaojia Zhou Enlai*, Vol. VI, 145.
[196] Gao Wenqian, *Wannian Zhou Enlai [Zhou Enlai's Later Years]* (Hong Kong: Mingjing chubanshe, 2003), 403.
[197] Li, *Da waijiaojia Zhou Enlai*, Vol. VI, 145.
[198] Goncharov and Usov, *O Kitae Srednevekovom i Sovremennom*, 317.
[199] Li, *Da waijiaojia Zhou Enlai*, Vol. VI, 145; Gao Wenqian, *Wannian Zhou Enlai* [Zhou Enlai's Later Years] (Hong Kong: Mingjing chubanshe, 2003), 403.
[200] Quoted in Chen Xiaolu, "Dangdai jiechu de waijiaojia Chen Yi [The Illustrious Diplomat of Our Era]," in *Huanqiu tongci liangre: Yi dai lingxiumen de guoji zhanlüe sixiang* [It Is the Same Temperature around the Globe: International Strategic Thinking of First-Generation Leaders] (Beijing: Zhongyang wenxian chubanshe, 1993), 155.
[201] "Letter from Secretary of State Rusk to the Ambassador to Poland (Gronouski)," February 5, 1966. *FRUS 1964–1968, Volume XXX, China*.

was to "gradually to help break down China's acutely distorted view of the outside world that plots her encirclement and destruction."[202]

U.S. signals were received by Chinese diplomats in Warsaw but failed to shape decision-making in Beijing. According to PRC ambassador Wang Guoquan, there was a "leap" forward during the talks when the United States referred to the Chinese side as the "government of the People's Republic of China" for the first time.[203] As Wang recalls, U.S. signals at the meeting were "the first hint that the United States was moving toward recognizing" the Communist regime, which "implied a clear change in the direction of U.S. domestic and foreign policy." Unfortunately, as Wang's account documents, the signal was lost:

[...] after I reported the change in the U.S. side back [to Beijing], it did not receive sufficient emphasis or timely discussion and we missed a favorable opportunity to move U.S.–China relations forward in a timely fashion. It must be said that this is a regrettable incident in the history of diplomacy.[204]

The failure in signal reception was tied to China's fragmented institutions. Like the other Chinese ambassadors discussed above, Wang Guoquan was recalled from Warsaw in the summer of 1967 to participate in the Cultural Revolution.[205] In an unusually frank assessment, Wang reflected that "if the Cultural Revolution had not occurred, China would have adjusted its foreign policy and the normalization of U.S.–China relations would perhaps not have been delayed until 1972."[206] As one historian writes, American initiatives "led nowhere because China's Cultural Revolution intensified."[207] Subsequent rounds of talks were repeatedly delayed.[208] In May 1968, for example, the Foreign Ministry claimed that the Chinese ambassador would be unable to "return to his

---

[202] "Memorandum from James C. Thomson, Jr., of the National Security Council Staff to the President's Special Assistant (Valenti)," March 1, 1966. *FRUS 1964–1968, Volume XXX*.

[203] According to Wang's recollections, a member of the American party drew attention to this phrase in a subsequent conversation after the meeting. Wang Guoquan, "Wo de dashi shengya [My Ambassadorial Career]," in *Dangdai Zhongguo shijie waijiao shengya* [The Diplomatic Careers of Contemporary Chinese Envoys] (Beijing: Shijie zhishi chubanshe, 1995), Vol. II, 153–154.

[204] Ibid., 155.

[205] Luo Yisu, "Zai Bolan de suiyue [Years in Poland]," in *Dangdai Zhongguo shijie waijiao shengya* [The Diplomatic Careers of Contemporary Chinese Envoys] (Beijing: Shijie zhishi chubanshe, 1996), Vol. IV, 177; Wang, "Wo de dashi shengya," 156.

[206] Wang, "Wo de dashi shengya," 155.

[207] Xia, *Negotiating with the Enemy*, 130–131.

[208] Zhang Baijia and Jia Qingguo, "Steering Wheel, Shock Absorber, and Diplomatic Probe in Confrontation: Sino-American Ambassadorial Talks Seen from the Chinese Perspective," in *Re-examining the Cold War: US-China Diplomacy, 1954–1973* (Cambridge: Harvard University Asia Center, 2001), 193; Kenneth T. Young, *Negotiating with the Chinese Communists: The United States Experience, 1953–1967* (New York: McGraw-Hill, 1968), 296.

post."[209] Nixon later remarked that Chinese decision-makers "ignored" the "signals of interest" that the United States sent them during his first year in office.[210] In short, fragmented institutions curtailed the information collected and supplied to Mao during one of the most important moments of China's Cold War. China's channels for information collection had been constricted by redesigning the linkages connecting Mao to his bureaucracy.[211]

Fragmented institutions also degraded the quality of information that Mao received, as it became politically untenable for his advisers to provide new or conflicting information. China's bureaucrats, its diplomats in particular, were "primarily concerned with their own survival" and strove to signal political loyalty during decision-making in order to secure it.[212] Instead of looking for signals from the international environment, Chinese officials looked for clues as to what Mao was already thinking. According to firsthand accounts, bureaucratic reports produced in 1969 "were all more or less what the higher ups had already said."[213] One Chinese historian similarly notes that advisers, particularly diplomats, "did not dare to express genuine ideas" for fear of making an "ideological mistake."[214]

The assessments produced by a small, ad hoc group of diplomatic and defense officials, often referred to as the "Four Marshals" group, provide an interesting counterfactual about the quality of information that might have been supplied to Mao prior to the Zhenbao ambush under more integrated institutions. In the summer of 1969, Mao temporarily allowed a group of four senior officials – Chen Yi, Ye Jianying, Nie Rongzhen, and Xu Xiangqian – to assess China's international situation. The group drew three conclusions that contradicted the assessments that had led China to initiate the crisis.

The first conclusion suggested that the costs of peace were low. The group noted that "in the foreseeable future it is unlikely that U.S. imperialists and Soviet revisionists will launch a large-scale war against China, either jointly or separately." Both the United States and the Soviet Union were preoccupied with other foreign policy endeavors elsewhere

---

[209] Gurtov and Hwang, *China under Threat*, 206.
[210] Nixon, *The Memoirs of Richard Nixon*, 545.
[211] Lüthi, "Restoring Chaos to History," 396.
[212] Gurtov and Hwang, *China under Threat*, 187.
[213] Xiong Xianghui, *Wo de qingbao yu waijiao shengya* [My Intelligence and Diplomatic Career] (Beijing: Zhongxin chubanshe, 2019), 210.
[214] Gong Li, "Chinese Decision Making and the Thawing of U.S.-China Relations," in *Re-examining the Cold War: US-China Diplomacy, 1954–1973* (Cambridge: Harvard University Asia Center, 2001), 325.

in Europe and Asia.[215] Any war with China would lead to a "protracted ground war" that the Soviet Union could not win. Their conclusion was that the Soviet Union would "dare not start a major war against China."

Second, the group emphasized domestic political factors motivating Soviet behavior, rather than an intent to attack China. The group concluded that despite Soviet deployments and threats, decision-makers in Moscow could not do anything due to "political considerations." The "main purpose" of the Soviet Union's mobilization, according to the group, was "to consolidate their political control and to suppress resistance to them at home and in Eastern Europe." Thus, while the Soviet Union was deploying troops eastward, "it does not mean that its strategic emphasis is also moving eastward."

Third, the group identified an available alternative to deal with the Soviet threat: improving relations with the United States. The group noted that the United States had "expressed their willingness to improve relations with China," including the resumption of ambassadorial talks that could "bring about results of strategic significance." Indeed, the Soviet Union was "scared by the prospect that we might ally ourselves with the U.S. imperialists to confront them," and it had rushed to issue a diplomatic statement on the first day of Nixon's trip to Asia in July. In fact, one of the group's members, the ousted Foreign Minister Chen Yi, recommended that China should elevate the Warsaw talks to the minister level without preconditions. As Chen noted, the "situation has changed today" and, as such, it was necessary for China to "utilize the contradiction between the United States and the Soviet Union in a strategic sense, and pursue a breakthrough in the Sino-American relations."

Yet the group's assessments had a limited effect on Mao's decision-making, particularly during the early stages of the crisis. First, the group began meeting only *after* Mao had decided to attack Soviet forces along the border.[216] As a result, the decision to initiate conflict with the Soviet Union had already been made when the group began to convene.

---

[215] The following paragraphs are based on excerpts of two of the reports authored by the Four Marshals. See "A Preliminary Evaluation of the War Situation," July 11, 1969 and "Our Views about the Current Situation," September 17, 1969. Chen and Wilson, "All under the Heaven Is Great Chaos," 166–171.

[216] Pang and Feng, *Mao Zedong nianpu*, Vol. VI, 231; Yan Yongchun, ed., *Xu Xiangqian nianpu* [Chronicle of Xu Xiangqian] (Beijing: Jiefangjun chubanshe, 2016), Vol. II, 250; Liu, *Ye Jianying nianpu*, Vol. II, 981–982. Available records indicate the first meeting was on March 1.

Moreover, the group appears not to have taken part in deliberations of the central leadership between the summer and fall of 1969.[217]

Second, the group was at first reticent to supply original analysis.[218] The group initially noted that offering a "different way of thinking" would be "easier said than done" because anything new might be criticized as dissenting with Mao's views.[219] As a result, while the Four Marshals group discussed the national defense situation in a series of meeting in March 1969, their initial analysis offered by the group repeated their interpretation of what they perceived to be Mao's desired conclusions.[220] It was only after Mao and Zhou pushed for new thinking that the group began to offer more thoughtful analysis.

Third, particularly in the first half of 1969, fragmented institutions restricted the group's access to information within the bureaucracy. By virtue of being purged, the members' access to sensitive information had been cut off. Chen Yi, for instance, "did not attend meetings nor was he provided official documents, as documents were only issued according to the specifications of the Central Committee." While group members technically retained appointments on the CMC Standing Committee, the body "existed only in name" and "did not concern itself with [actual] work nor play any role."[221] Materials from the Foreign Ministry were not made available to them until May.[222] The group continued to confront obstacles to obtaining the information required for their analysis as late as June 1969.[223]

Finally, fearing punishment for original analysis, other bureaucrats resisted the group's conclusions. In early September 1969, for example, the Foreign Ministry was unwilling to change its assessment on the threat the United States posed to China or discuss diplomatic negotiations. Instead, it encouraged the Four Marshals group "not to discuss anything

---

[217] Liu, Vol. II, 983–987; Zhang Tingdong, *Wo pei Ye shuai zou wan zuihou shiqi nian: yi wei shenbian mishu de huiyi* [Accompanying Marshal Ye for the Last Seventeen Years: A Memoir of a Secretary by his Side] (Beijing: Zhonggong dangshi chubanshe, 1999), 53–54.
[218] Li et al., *Mao Zedong junshi wengao*, Vol. III, 351–352.
[219] Xiong Xianghui, "Dakai ZhongMei guanxi de qianzhou [Prelude to the Opening of Sino-American Relations]," *Zhonggong dangshi ziliao* [Materials on Party History], no. 42 (1992): 61.
[220] Zhou, *Nie Rongzhen nianpu*, 1107; Yan, *Xu Xiangqian nianpu*, Vol. II, 250.
[221] Du, *Wenge zhong de Chen Yi*, 207.
[222] Wang, "1966–1976 nian ZhongMeiSu guanxi jishi," 121; Xiong, *Wo de qingbao yu waijiao shengya*, 207–210.
[223] *Zhou Enlai junshi huodong jishi, 1918–1975*, Vol. II, 394.

specific" for fear that bolder recommendations would be labeled a "rightist deviation."[224]

Fragmented institutions also offer some tentative reasons why the assessments that the Four Marshals group produced were substantially different from those produced by the military leadership. One reason may have been that the military leadership was simply unwilling to offer analysis different from Mao. The assessments that the CMC Office produced in 1969 generally reiterated conclusions that Mao had provided the party leadership at the Ninth Party Congress.[225] Another reason is that diplomatic information may not have been shared with the military in full. CMC Office member Wu Faxian reflected that while the military *later* learned that the Soviet leadership had been divided at the time of the crisis, the CMC leadership was unaware that Soviet leaders, such as Soviet Premier Kosygin, were advocating diplomatic dialogue.[226] Yet these basic facts would have been known by the Foreign Ministry by the time of the refused Soviet phone calls in March.

In addition, there appears to have been little interaction between the Four Marshals group and the military leadership over the summer of 1969. Unlike the inclusive information sharing and coordination exhibited in 1962, the Four Marshals group appears not to have participated in CMC conferences and symposia in the summer of 1969 that analyzed plans against the Soviet Union. On the contrary, Mao reportedly had "no intention of letting [the Four Marshals] dip their fingers" back into military affairs.[227] The Four Marshals group were even prohibited from bringing their secretaries to internal meetings for fear that the discussions would leak and "stir up disaster among the elite."[228] While the group met more than twenty times between June and October and authored numerous reports, most never circulated beyond Mao.[229]

Alternative Explanations. While fragmented institutions help to explain Mao's miscalculation during the 1969 Sino-Soviet border conflict, several alternative accounts are worth considering. One alternative explanation is that China's choices reflected the coercive influence of the Chinese military during the peak of the Cultural Revolution. Indeed,

---

[224] Xiong, *Wo de qingbao yu waijiao shengya*, 225.
[225] See especially Huang Yongsheng's speech in *"Jiu-da" zilao huibian* [Collection of Materials from the "Ninth Congress"] (Ji'nan: Ji'nan tieluju Ji'nan cheliangduan wuqi zhongxue, 1969).
[226] Wu Faxian, *Wu Faxian huiyilu [Memoirs of Wu Faxian]* (Hong Kong: Beixing chubanshe, 2006), Vol. II, 761.
[227] Gao, *Wannian Zhou Enlai*, 407.
[228] Xiong, *Wo de qingbao yu waijiao shengya*, 207.
[229] Liu, *Ye Jianying nianpu*, Vol. II, 982.

the CMC Office's hawkish assessments during the summer of 1969 are consistent with an interest group model of bureaucratic politics, in which defense advisers are more likely to perceive international threats and recommend risk-acceptant responses.[230] Yet Mao remained firmly in charge throughout the Cultural Revolution; there is scant evidence that Mao felt he needed to make policy concessions to appease military leaders. Defense Minister Lin Biao, for instance, consistently deferred to Mao.[231] If anything, Mao's demonstrated ability to remove party elites during the Cultural Revolution suggests that military leaders feared a similar fate and provided information and policy recommendations that catered to Mao's preferences.

China's behavior during the Sino-Soviet border conflict is also consistent with theories emphasizing political accountability and leader beliefs. Part of Mao's inaccurate judgments in 1969 could be attributed to the party elite's inability to impose costs for a failed foreign policy. Mao's miscalculation is also consistent with a leader-centric account, given that his general worldview tended to emphasize the utility of military strategies in achieving international goals.[232] From this perspective, Mao may have been resistant to quality bureaucratic information even if his advisers had the opportunity and incentive to supply it. While both of these alternative theoretical perspectives offer insights into this case, however, they do not offer straightforward explanations for why Mao miscalculated during the 1969 Sino-Soviet border conflict but not the 1962 Nationalist invasion scare.

A final alternative perspective, unique to this case, is that Mao's primary aim during the 1969 border conflict was to mobilize the country to bring an end to the domestic chaos of the Cultural Revolution. For example, Mao noted in a speech in the spring of 1969 that "it is advantageous to mobilize and prepare" and that "if the enemy does not come, that does not matter." Yet the context of Mao's statements suggests that he felt mobilization was necessary because of a genuine Soviet threat rather than because of domestic upheaval.[233] Even if the hypothesis explains why Mao launched a propaganda campaign, it does not explain why Mao evacuated the party leadership from Beijing or other urban

---

[230] See Thomas M. Gottlieb, *Chinese Foreign Policy Factionalism and the Origins of the Strategic Triangle* (Santa Monica, CA: Rand, 1977), 84–121; John W. Garver, *China's Decision for Rapprochement with the United States: 1968–1971* (Boulder: Westview Press, 1982), 108–148.
[231] MacFarquhar and Schoenhals, *Mao's Last Revolution*, 48, 107–108, 328.
[232] Kennedy, *The International Ambitions of Mao and Nehru*, 45–55.
[233] Liu Zhinan, "1969 nian, Zhongguo zhanbei yu dui MeiSu guanxi de yanjiu he tiaozheng [1969, China's War Preparations and its Research and Adjustment in Relations with the United States and the Soviet Union]," *Dangdai Zhongguo shi yanjiu* [Research on Contemporary Chinese History], no. 3 (1999): 43.

centers – measures that Mao had not taken during past domestic mobilizations.[234] Finally, even if one of Mao's objectives in the crisis was indeed domestic mobilization, the campaign proved less successful than previous campaigns, such as the Great Leap Forward.[235]

Conclusion

This chapter illustrated the trade-off between sound bureaucratic advice and political security in the context of a personalist dictatorship. During his early years, Mao Zedong was able to adopt inclusive and open institutions because the bureaucracy possessed minimal capability and intent to challenge his leadership. Integrated institutions performed well across the majority of China's international crises, as illustrated by the comparatively complete and high-quality information that Mao received during the 1962 Nationalist invasion scare.

China's national security institutions shifted as Mao's perceptions of bureaucratic threat changed. While fragmented institutions secured the political succession that Mao desired, they also came at a cost to the quality of information that the bureaucracy supplied. The 1969 Sino-Soviet border conflict illustrated how the incomplete and biased information that fragmented institutions supplied contributed to Mao's miscalculations.

The chapter advances the book's overall argument in two ways. First, it illustrated the theory of national security institutions in a personalist dictatorship. Existing scholarship suggests that bureaucracy should have minimal effect on policymaking when a single leader holds unchecked power.[236] Instead, the chapter showed that even personalist dictators can build integrated institutions to solicit candid policy advice and deliberation when bureaucratic threats are low.

Second, it showed that patterns of bureaucratic politics can change dramatically even within the same regime under the same leader. While existing scholarship on foreign policy decision-making has traditionally prioritized the role of personality and leadership style, the analysis shows how the politics of institutional design help to explain variation in the quality of bureaucratic information provision within the same leader's tenure.

---

[234] Fravel, *Strong Borders, Secure Nation*, 214.
[235] Yang, "The Sino-Soviet Border Clash of 1969," 41–42; MacFarquhar and Schoenhals, *Mao's Last Revolution*, 316–217. On the successful use of the Great Leap Forward to mobilize the Chinese public, see Thomas J. Christensen, *Useful Adversaries: Grand Strategy, Domestic Mobilization, and Sino-American Conflict, 1947–1958* (Princeton: Princeton University Press, 1996), 205.
[236] Weeks, *Dictators at War and Peace*, 32.

Conclusion

In sum, this chapter showed both how politics inside personalist regimes shapes institutional design and how institutions shape the risk of miscalculation. To explain Mao's missteps in the Sino-Soviet border conflict, we must first account for the institutional environment in which Mao made his decisions. The next chapter extends the argument to China after Mao's rule, exploring whether the same dynamics hold during a period of less personalistic rule. We will see not only that pathological institutions persisted even after Mao's death, but that these institutional pathologies help to account for China's miscalculations during the 1979 Sino-Vietnamese War and the 2001 EP-3 Crisis.

5 China after Mao

On February 17, 1979, China invaded the Democratic Republic of Vietnam. In a war that lasted just under a month, some 300,000 Chinese soldiers fought their former Communist brethren in order to "teach a lesson" to leaders in Hanoi.[1] Chinese decision-makers believed that such a lesson would pressure Vietnam to begin withdrawing troops from Cambodia and curtail its defense cooperation with the Soviet Union. Yet the conflict had the opposite result of what Chinese decision-makers anticipated. Poor performance on the battlefield demonstrated the toll that the Cultural Revolution had taken on China's military power. As Vietnamese Prime Minister Pham Van Dong noted, the war ironically taught China the lesson that it had hoped to teach Vietnam.[2]

Over two decades later, on April 1, 2001, Chinese leaders made a similar, though less costly, mistake when a Chinese fighter jet collided with an American reconnaissance plane off the coast of Hainan Island. In the wake of the collision, Chinese Communist Party (CCP) General Secretary Jiang Zemin chose to detain the crew, who had made an emergency landing in Hainan. Jiang demanded that the United States accept responsibility for the incident, end its reconnaissance program along China's borders, and apologize for the collision. The United States refused. U.S. reconnaissance missions resumed in early May 2001 and, throughout the episode, American officials maintained that China bore responsibility for the accident. After several rounds of negotiations, the U.S. Department of State eventually released a public statement that, while conciliatory, fell short of China's demands. China released the crew having achieved little.

---

[1] On the size of the invasion force, see Zhang, Xiaoming. "China's 1979 War with Vietnam: A Reassessment." *The China Quarterly* 184 (2005): 865.

[2] "Conversation between Jambyn Batmunkh and Pham Van Dong," December 2, 1979, Wilson Center Digital Archive, Mongol Ulsyn Zasgiin Gazryn Arkhiv: fond 1, tov'yog 28, kh/n 19 (1980 on), khuu 21–55. Obtained and translated by Sergey Radchenko with the assistance of Onon Perenlei.

What connects these two seemingly disparate events? In both cases, Chinese leaders based their choices on incomplete and low-quality information. In the case of the 1979 Sino-Vietnamese War, newly available evidence introduced in this chapter suggests not only that China's decision-makers mistook how China's use of force would shape the beliefs and behaviors of Vietnamese decision-makers, but also that this miscalculation was rooted in China's fragmented institutions.[3] In the case of the 2001 EP-3 reconnaissance aircraft incident, this chapter uses recently declassified documents to illustrate not only that low-quality information led Jiang to conclude that his coercive leverage over the United States was stronger than it was, but also how inaccurate reporting traced back to institutional design.

In addition, analyzing these episodes illustrates the different pathways by which fragmented and siloed institutions lead decision-makers to miscalculate. Prior to the Sino-Vietnamese War, China's fragmented institutions featured few mechanisms for information sharing. The politically precarious position of bureaucrats curtailed their willingness to offer candid views. In contrast, prior to the 2001 EP-3 incident, Chinese bureaucrats did not distort reports because they feared contradicting their leader. Instead, the absence of competitive dialogue between diplomatic and defense bureaucracies degraded information provision. The reports upon which Jiang made his initial decisions came directly from the Chinese defense bureaucracy and were not evaluated by diplomatic or intelligence counterparts. Both institutions led to poor information on the eve of confrontation, but for systematically different reasons.

Neither institutional design emerged by chance. Both were a product of China's political environment at the time. In the late 1970s, the party

---

[3] Existing scholarship on the Sino-Vietnamese War tends to characterize the war as a strategic failure for China. Past accounts, however, have comparatively little to say about why China initiated a conflict that ended poorly. On the conflict, see Harlan W. Jencks, "China's 'Punitive' War on Vietnam: A Military Assessment," *Asian Survey* 19, no. 8 (1979): 801–815; Segal, *Defending China*, 226; Allen S. Whiting, "China's Use of Force, 1950–96, and Taiwan," *International Security* 26, no. 2 (2001): 120; Christensen, "Windows and War," 74; Henry J. Kenny, "Vietnamese Perceptions of the 1979 War with China," in *Chinese Warfighting: The PLA Experience since 1949*, ed. Mark A. Ryan, David M. Finkelstein, and Michael A. McDevitt (New York: M.E. Sharpe, 2003), 232; Xiaobing Li, *A History of the Modern Chinese Army* (Lexington: University Press of Kentucky, 2007), 259; Edward C. O'Dowd, *Chinese Military Strategy in the Third Indochina War: The Last Maoist War* (New York: Routledge, 2007); Joseph Torigian, "Prestige, Manipulation, and Coercion: Elite Power Struggles and the Fate of Three Revolutions" (PhD diss., Massachusetts Institute of Technology, 2016), 420–423. On China's options, see Robert Ross, *The Indochina Tangle: China's Vietnam Policy, 1975–1979* (New York: Columbia University Press, 1988), 265; Christensen, "Windows and War," 75. For a revisionist account arguing that China succeeded in obtaining its strategic goals, see Xiaoming Zhang, *Deng Xiaoping's Long War: The Military Conflict between China and Vietnam, 1979–1991* (Chapel Hill: University of North Carolina Press, 2015).

was in the midst of a power struggle between Hua Guofeng and Deng Xiaoping. Fragmented institutions were temporarily helpful to neutralize bureaucratic threats, particularly those from the military, until the power struggle had resolved. Similarly, the siloed institutions over which Jiang Zemin presided reflected apprehensions among a new generation of political leaders concerning the threat of bureaucratic challenges from more experienced officials at the apex of the national security bureaucracy. Whereas a clear prioritization of transformative domestic reforms in the late 1970s made fragmented institutions appealing to party leaders, however, new international threats and China's integration into the global economy made siloed institutions more attractive to Jiang and his successors.

This chapter is divided into two main sections. The first charts the evolution of China's national security institutions from Mao's death in 1976 to the contemporary era. It shows how domestic political considerations led China's leaders to retain the fragmented institutions they inherited. It then discusses the possible motivations behind China's transition to siloed institutions in the 1980s. The second section turns to the consequences of these institutional choices through detailed case studies on the 1979 Sino-Vietnamese War and 2001 EP-3 reconnaissance aircraft incident.

The Politics of Institutional Design in China, 1976–2012

After Mao Zedong's death on September 9, 1976, China transitioned to a period of less personalistic rule.[4] While competition for power remained intense, Chinese supreme leaders – Hua Guofeng, Deng Xiaoping, Jiang Zemin, and Hu Jintao – did not enjoy the same level of power and authority within the party that Mao had possessed.[5] One clear indicator of relative levels of power can be found in the density of personal connections that the supreme leader enjoyed within the party. In 1949, Mao had personal connections with roughly 70 percent of the Central Committee, an elite organization of several hundred of the CCP's most important cadres. In comparison, the share of Central Committee members with

---

[4] Vogel, *Deng Xiaoping*, 240–245; David M. Lampton, *Following the Leader: Ruling China, from Deng Xiaoping to Xi Jinping* (Berkeley: University of California Press, 2013), 53; Susan L. Shirk, "China in Xi's 'New Era': The Return to Personalistic Rule," *Journal of Democracy* 29, no. 2 (April 2018): 22–36. See also Weeks, *Dictators at War and Peace*, 40; Barbara Geddes, Joseph Wright, and Erica Frantz, *How Dictatorships Work* (New York: Cambridge University Press, 2018), 83.

[5] Note that non-personalist here refers to a regime in which the balance of power among elites is closer to parity. For an alternative conceptualization of non-personalist rule, see Joseph Torigian, *Prestige, Manipulation, and Coercion: Elite Power Struggles in the Soviet Union and China after Stalin and Mao* (New Haven: Yale University Press, 2022), 11.

Table 5.1 *Evolution of China's institutional design after Mao*

Period	Bureaucratic threat	Leader agenda	National security institution	Theory support
1976–1981	*High*: politicized bureaucracy with conservative preferences on post-Mao agenda	*Domestic*: Opening and Reform program; political succession	*Fragmented*: insular Politburo with no diplomatic representation; minimal coordination capacity	Strong
1982–1988	*Low*: experienced leader with firm control over bureaucracy	*Domestic*: Opening and Reform program; reduction in perceived international threat level	*Siloed*: irregular but inclusive decision-making processes; segregation of diplomatic and defense agenda between FALSG and CMC; no diplomatic/ intelligence representation in CMC	Weak
1989–2012	*Medium/high*: inexperienced leaders coupled with concerns over bureaucratic loyalty after Tiananmen	*International*: perceived threat from US, Taiwan independence, and territorial disputes	*Siloed*: inclusive representation on Politburo; decision-making role for leading small groups; continued siloing between FALSG and CMC	Strong

whom Chinese leaders after Mao had personal connections was much lower, ranging from 20 percent to 35 percent.

The period between 1976 and 2012 in China thus provides fruitful ground to explore the politics of institutional design within a non-personalist autocracy.[6] Table 5.1 summarizes the key components of the theory for the case across three political periods: the power struggle between Hua Guofeng and Deng Xiaoping (1976–1981); Deng's rule

---

[6] The analysis intentionally sets aside the period under Xi Jinping, for which there remains insufficient material on national security decision-making processes to render conclusive judgments.

through his lieutenants (1982–1988); and the rule of Deng's successors, Jiang Zemin and Hu Jintao (1989–2012).

The Political Environment in the Hua-Deng Period, 1976–1981

The political environment after the death of Mao Zedong was marked by two key features pertinent to the theory. First, bureaucratic threats were comparatively high. Party histories often describe the years following Mao's death as one in which the party had to "restore order from chaos."[7] Leaders like Hua Guofeng and Deng Xiaoping warned that "radical" cadres within the bureaucracy, who had been promoted during the Cultural Revolution, might be used by senior leaders to coordinate against them and in support of a leadership challenge.[8] Indeed, party elites referred to both defense and intelligence bureaucracies as "disaster areas."[9]

These problems were particularly salient within the military.[10] In July 1975, Deng Xiaoping suggested that there was "a certain amount of conceit" among military officers, who had become "arrogant and overbearing" since the Cultural Revolution began.[11] In December 1977, Deng noted that some within the military were "now bent on building small circles of supporters."[12] In January 1979, Deng argued that problems were both widespread and "even more serious," suggesting that trust between superiors and subordinates had been "destroyed."[13]

One reason that the military was potentially threatening was their political conservatism, which party leaders saw as a possible roadblock to desired economic reform.[14] In July 1979, Deng argued that one third of officers at the PLA Political Academy "do not understand, doubt,

---

[7] Feng Changson, ed., *Zhongguo renmin jiefangjun guanli shi* [History of PLA Management] (Beijing: Guofang daxue chubanshe, 2013), 216–239.
[8] Teiwes and Sun, *The End of the Maoist Era*, 446.
[9] Zhang Sheng, *Cong zhanzheng zhong zoulai: Liangdai junren de duihua* [Emerging from War: A Conversation between Soldiers of Two Generations] (Beijing: Shenghuo, dushu, xinzhi sanlian shudian chubanshe, 2013), 571; Guo Xuezhi, *China's Security State: Philosophy, Evolution, and Politics* (New York: Cambridge University Press, 2012), 362.
[10] Interview J127, Beijing, Spring 2017.
[11] "Speech at a CMC Meeting," July 14, 1975. Deng Xiaoping, *Selected Works of Deng Xiaoping (1975–1982)* (Beijing: Foreign Languages Press, 1984), Vol. II, 30.
[12] "Speech at a Plenary CMC Meeting," December 28, 1977. *Selected Works of Deng Xiaoping*, 100.
[13] "Jiejue jundui jigou yongzhong wenti [Solving the Problem of the Military's Institutional Bloating]," January 2, 1979. *Deng Xiaoping junshi wenji* [Selected Military Works of Deng Xiaoping] (Beijing: Junshi kexue chubanshe, 2004), Vol. III, 145–148.
[14] Fravel, *Active Defense*, 153–154; Roderick MacFarquhar, "The Succession to Mao and the End of Maoism, 1969–1982," in *The Politics of China: Sixty Years of the People's Republic of China*, 3rd ed. (New York: Cambridge University Press, 2011), 332.

or are dissatisfied" with the reform policies that the party was pursuing.[15] Deng further suggested that roughly the same share of the entire military shared these views.[16] In short, as historian Xiao Donglian summarizes, there were serious challenges in compelling the military to "accept guidelines and policies" of opening and reform.[17]

Perceptions of bureaucratic threat extended to the intelligence and diplomatic organizations as well.[18] In his final months, Mao had attacked the Foreign Ministry's "right tendencies," especially Foreign Minister Qiao Guanhua.[19] The campaign caused the Foreign Ministry's standing to precipitously decline. Party leaders complained of the "arrogance" of senior diplomats.[20] Mao's successor, Hua Guofeng, visited the Foreign Ministry to condemn its connections to radical groups.[21] In 1978, the party launched another "deep-going campaign to expose and criticize every individual" connected to radical groups.[22] One party leader instructed diplomats to attend to the "problems" remaining in their ministry.[23] The problem of factionalism "persisted under the surface" until 1982.[24]

The way in which the bureaucracy might have potentially imposed political costs on the leadership was not simply the threat of removal by coup. It also included the ability to shape debates within the party about economic reform. As Roderick MacFarquhar notes, "mobilization of elite opinion through the press" proved critical in the power struggle between party elites.[25] The national security bureaucracy's intervention into these debates seems to have played an important role. For example, the *People's Liberation Army Daily* newspaper's decision to republish a single key article had dramatic consequences for the power struggles between party elites.[26]

---

[15] Torigian, *Prestige, Manipulation, and Coercion*, 179.
[16] Ibid., 181.
[17] Quoted in ibid., 181–182.
[18] Teiwes and Sun, *The End of the Maoist Era*, 521; Guo, *China's Security State*, 363.
[19] Ji, *The Man on Mao's Right*, 261, 293; Lu, *The Dynamics of Foreign-Policy Decisionmaking in China*, 56–57.
[20] Zhang Hanzhi, *Wo yu Qiao Guanhua* [Qiao Guanhua and I] (Beijing: Zhongguo qingnian chubanshe, 1994), 93. See also Lee Kuan Yew, *From Third World to First: The Singapore Story, 1965–2000* (New York: HarperCollins, 2000), 584.
[21] Ji, *The Man on Mao's Right*, 288; Zhang, *Wo yu Qiao Guanhua*, 99; Ma, *The Cultural Revolution in the Foreign Ministry of China*, 386.
[22] "Huang Hua's Report on the World Situation," *Issues and Studies* 14, no. 1 (1978): 107.
[23] Wang Weicheng, ed., *Li Xiannian nianpu* [Chronicle of Li Xiannian] (Beijing: Zhongyang wenxian chubanshe, 2011), Vol. V, 665.
[24] Lu, *The Dynamics of Foreign-Policy Decisionmaking in China*, 58. See also Ji, *The Man on Mao's Right*, 281–282; Liu, *Chinese Ambassadors*, 159.
[25] MacFarquhar, "The Succession to Mao and the End of Maoism," 315.
[26] Torigian, *Prestige, Manipulation, and Coercion*, 186.

The second characteristic of the political environment after Mao's death was the emphasis that party leaders placed on domestic issues. Deng Xiaoping noted that "Everything depends on our doing the work in our own country well. [...] Of course, we have to handle our many other affairs well too, but economic development is primary."[27] Similarly, when discussing budget priorities, Deng argued that economic programs had to be prioritized over national defense ones.[28] In the near future, Deng noted in March 1980, China would "cut down military spending so as to strengthen national construction."[29]

The economic program that the party was undertaking was both transformative in scope and vulnerable to political opposition. Deng described his domestic reforms as "a great and profound revolution" in the party's policy. Deng also noted that the domestic agenda would "not be easy to introduce" and would likely "meet with numerous obstacles." In particular, he noted that the party would need to "overcome the evils of bureaucracy" in order to implement the program.[30]

A second aspect of the party elite's domestic focus was the struggle for power itself. After the Cultural Revolution, there were four informal, but distinct groups within the party. Individuals from each group tended to possess common backgrounds and career paths, which gave each different sets of social connections and claims to leadership.[31] Mao Zedong's successor, Hua Guofeng, was part of a "beneficiary" group, composed of cadres who were rapidly promoted toward the end of the Cultural Revolution. Another group, known as the "radicals," had also been promoted during the Cultural Revolution but had done so toward its beginning and with a mandate from Mao to attack the party apparatus. A third group, known as the "veterans," had been promoted prior to the Cultural Revolution and had managed to keep their position through the revolution's tumult. A fourth group of "victims" had lost their positions during the Cultural Revolution and hoped to regain their status after Mao's passing.[32]

---

[27] "The Present Situation and Tasks," January 16, 1980. Deng, *Selected Works of Deng Xiaoping*, 225.

[28] "Speech at a Plenary Meeting of the Military Commission of the Central Committee of the CPC," December 28, 1977. *Selected Works of Deng Xiaoping*, 94.

[29] "Streamline the Army and Raise Its Combat Effectiveness," March 12, 1980. *Selected Works of Deng Xiaoping*, 270.

[30] "Emancipate the Mind, Seek Truth from Facts and United as One in Looking to the Future," December 13, 1978. *Selected Works of Deng Xiaoping, 161, 164*.

[31] Teiwes, "The Study of Elite Political Conflict in the PRC," 32; Vogel, *Deng Xiaoping*, 190.

[32] MacFarquhar, "The Succession to Mao and the End of Maoism," 297; Fravel, *Active Defense*, 151–152.

The first power struggle was between Hua Guofeng and key leaders within the radical group, commonly known as the Gang of Four. As the Gang of Four began to consolidate power, Hua moved preemptively and arrested them.[33] While Hua successfully removed each of the four from their positions, party elites worried that the Gang's supporters throughout the party might mobilize to threaten Hua's position.

A second power struggle emerged between Hua and Deng Xiaoping, part of the victim group. Deng's reinstatement in 1977 marked the beginning of a power struggle between Hua's supporters and Deng's faction, reflecting both cold calculations about power politics and broader debates about the party's future.[34] In short, there were ample reasons for party leaders to prioritize domestic issues in the period after Mao's death.

Fragmented Institutions in the Hua-Deng Period

The combination of a high level of bureaucratic threat and domestic focus help to explain why Chinese leaders sustained a fragmented institutional design featuring curtailed information flow within the Chinese state for roughly half a decade after Mao's death.

China's persisting fragmentation is first observable in structures that limited interaction between political leaders and the bureaucracy. For one, China lacked a stable forum for national security decision-making. The Politburo did not routinely meet to consider national security issues. The top panel of Figure 5.1 illustrates this pattern by plotting the frequency of leader meetings touching on defense or foreign affairs. From 1976 to 1981, the Politburo convened to discuss such matters roughly twice per year. This frequency was much lower than that exhibited during China's integrated period from 1949 to 1962, as discussed in Chapter 4.

In addition, the Politburo's membership kept the status of key national security bureaucracies, particularly the Foreign Ministry, low. Unlike the early Mao period, seats on either the Politburo or its Standing Committee were not allocated to the foreign minister. While the party's defense leadership enjoyed appointment to these bodies, Deng himself served as the Chief of General Staff, meaning that he was in effect his own senior military adviser and unilaterally controlled information coming in and out of the defense bureaucracy.[35]

---

[33] Liu, *Ye Jianying nianpu*, Vol. II, 1109–1116.
[34] On the importance of power politics, see Torigian, *Prestige, Manipulation, and Coercion*, 136–192. On debates about the party's future, see Fravel, *Active Defense*, 153–154; MacFarquhar, "The Succession to Mao and the End of Maoism," 314–315.
[35] Andrew Scobell, *China's Use of Military Force: Beyond the Great Wall and the Long March* (New York: Cambridge University Press, 2003), 138.

136 China after Mao

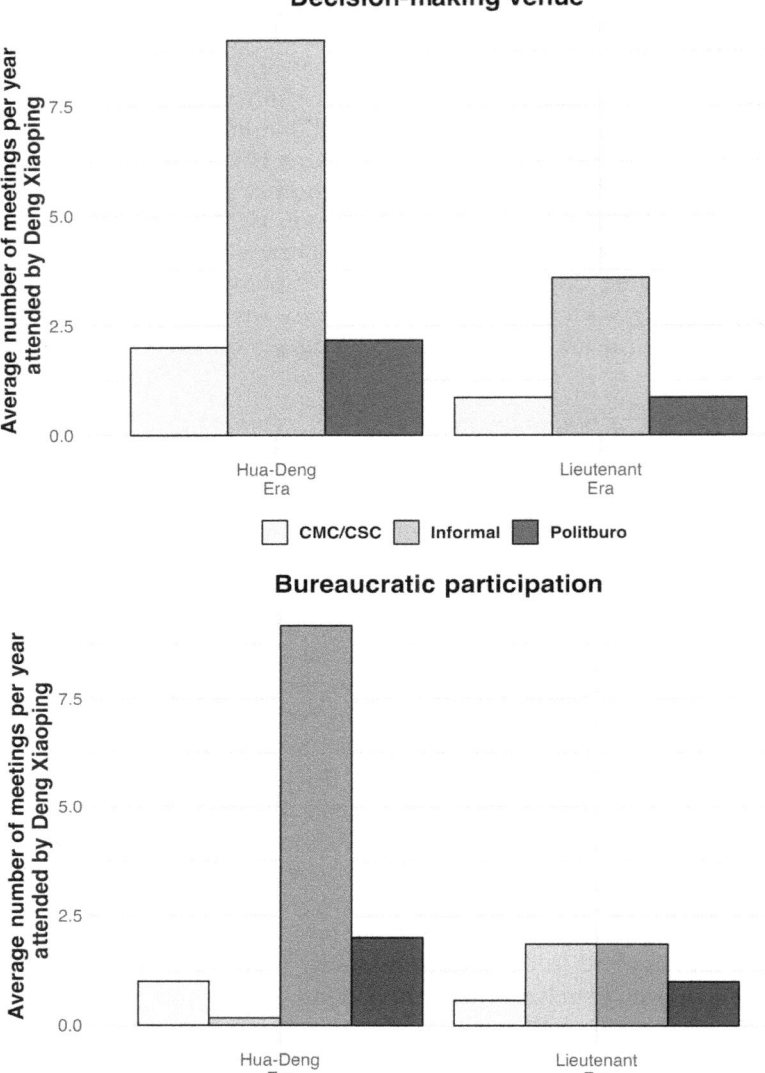

Figure 5.1 China's national security decision-making, 1976–1988
Note: Figures report the average annual frequency of meetings attended by Deng Xiaoping discussing foreign or defense policy across two periods: (1) the Hua-Deng (1976–1981) and (2) the lieutenant era (1982–1988). The top and bottom panels report frequency by venue and type of bureaucratic participation, respectively. Coding details are provided in Appendix B.

Patterns in bureaucratic participation in these meetings further illustrates the marginalization of the Foreign Ministry during this period. The bottom panel of Figure 5.1 shows the low frequency of interaction between the party leadership and the Foreign Ministry in both formal and informal settings from 1976 to 1981. While these data also show that Deng had frequent interaction with the PLA during this period, nearly all such meetings did not include Chinese diplomats. In short, China's institutional structure during this period systematically curtailed deliberative dialogue between diplomatic and defense advisers.

Fragmented institutions shaped the information provided to Chinese leaders. Systematic barriers to interaction between leaders and the bureaucracy signaled that the higher-ups did not value input. One Chinese defense minister felt that "only the highest leaders were qualified to consider strategic issues." For most within the party system, the task was "just to study, understand, and execute."[36] As a result, China's bureaucracy self-censored its reporting.[37] Diplomats reportedly sought to "cater to the leader," creating a type of "intelligence game" in which bureaucrats sought to find out the political leadership's preferences in advance and adjust their reports to match them.[38] As one Chinese ambassador noted, "speaking the truth" was "not easy."[39] Political leaders detected the sycophantic tendencies of the bureaucracy as well, causing them to discredit the information they received. Deng Xiaoping observed that defense officials were failing to fulfill their advisory responsibilities by simply reporting what they had read in party newspapers.[40]

Fragmented institutions also degraded the flow of information between bureaucracies. The Foreign Affairs Leading Small Group (FALSG) was not reestablished until 1981. Similarly, the Central Military Commission (CMC) did not meet routinely between 1977 and 1980.[41] When the CMC did convene, the agenda focused on domestic political issues.[42] As late as 1982, Deng remarked that the CMC was "not very satisfactory."[43]

---

[36] Zhang, *Cong zhanzheng zhong zoulai*, 629–630.
[37] Lampton, *Following the Leader*, 93.
[38] Interview C431, Beijing, Spring 2017. For a similar account, see Teiwes and Sun, *The End of the Maoist Era*, 429.
[39] Peter Martin, *China's Civilian Army: The Making of Wolf Warrior Diplomacy* (New York: Oxford University Press, 2021), 135.
[40] "Speech at a Meeting of the General Staff Headquarters," January 25, 1975 and "Speech at a CMC Meeting," July 14, 1975. *Selected Works of Deng Xiaoping*, Vol. II, 13, 31–32.
[41] Kong Xiangxiu, "Churen junwei mishuzhang, Geng Biao chonghui jundui [Geng Biao Returns to the Army as Secretary General of the CMC]," *Xiang chao*, no. 8 (2013): 23.
[42] Zhang, *Cong zhanzheng zhong zoulai*, 572.
[43] "Speech at a Forum of the CMC," July 4, 1982. *Selected Works of Deng Xiaoping*, 388.

The Political Environment in the Lieutenant Period, 1982–1989

China's political environment had fundamentally changed by the early 1980s. The severity of elite power struggles dropped dramatically. In September 1980, Hua Guofeng resigned his position as premier.[44] Months later, the party leadership convened a series of meetings to criticize Hua and removed him from his post as chairman of the Central Committee and Central Military Commission.[45] A historical resolution passed by the Central Committee in June 1981 detailed the "serious errors" in Hua's leadership.[46] With Mao's designated successor fully sidelined, Deng's position as supreme leader was fully secure. In parallel, the threat that the bureaucracy posed to Deng's rule declined. In the Foreign Ministry, efforts to root out radical sympathizers dissipated as a "new generation of technocrats" assumed control over managing China's diplomatic affairs.[47] Similar trends occurred within the Chinese military as well. As depicted in Figure 5.2, military appointments to the CMC fell precipitously in the early 1980s, at first removing individuals with undesirable political backgrounds, but stabilizing thereafter. The volume of military regulations for discipline and oversight similarly peaked in 1982.[48] In short, the national security bureaucracy of the early 1980s was less threatening than it had been in the late 1970s.

Deng's position was further secured by the impressive array of experience managing the national security bureaucracy with which he entered office. Deng had served in the PLA during the Chinese Civil War and held a number of formal and informal roles during the early Mao period in which he managed various aspects of diplomatic, intelligence, and military affairs. Deng had ample reason to believe his position vis-à-vis the national security bureaucracy was secure by the mid 1980s.

Siloed Institutions in the Lieutenant Period

Given the low level of bureaucratic threat, the theory would predict that China would have transitioned toward integrated institutions in the mid-1980s. Yet the historical record instead suggests that China's institutions fell somewhere closer to a siloed design. More inclusive structures

---

[44] Leng Rong, ed., *Deng Xiaoping nianpu, 1975–1997* [Chronicle of Deng Xiaoping, 1975–1997] (Beijing: Zhongyang wenxian chubanshe, 2004), Vol. I, 672–673.
[45] Ibid., Vol. I, 689–690.
[46] Julian Gewirtz, *Never Turn Back: China and the Forbidden History of the 1980s* (Cambridge: Belknap Press of Harvard University Press, 2022), 28–29.
[47] Liu, *Chinese Ambassadors*, 159.
[48] Shen Jialiang, Gao Yunzhang, Wang Xianhan, eds., *Zhongguo renmin jiefangjun zhengzhi gongzuo: Junshi jiancha gongzuo* [Political Work of the Chinese People's Liberation Army: Military Inspection Work] (Beijing: Jiefangjun chubanshe, 2001), 1–17.

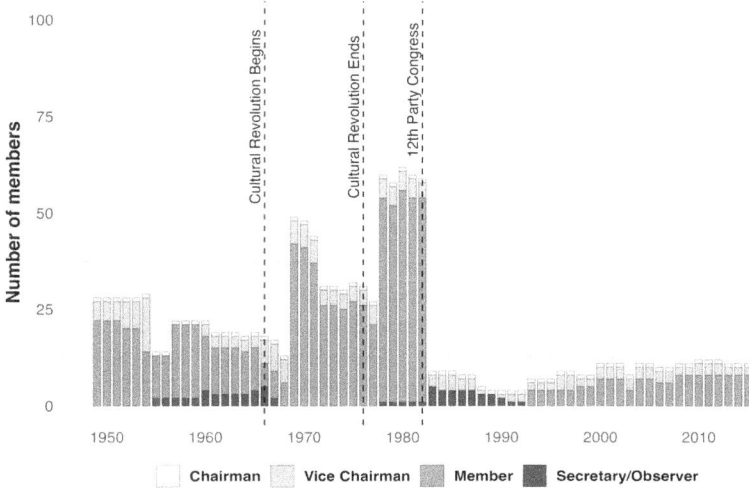

Figure 5.2 Size of the Central Military Commission, 1949–2015
Sources: CMC membership from Zeng Dadu, ed., *Zhongguo gongchandang Zhongguo renmin jiefangjun zuzhishi ziliao* [Materials on CCP Chinese People's Liberation Army Organizational History] (Beijing: Changzheng chubanshe, 1996), Vol. IV, 3–8, Vol. V, 2–8, Vol. VI, 2–10; *Directory of PRC Military Personalities* (Hong Kong: Defense Liaison Office, 1993–2015).

afforded more opportunities for bureaucrats to shape decision-making, while constraints on interministerial coordination impeded horizontal information sharing.

Although the political theory of institutional design does not successfully predict China's institutional choices, there are several possible explanations that are consistent with the theory's intuitions. One possibility is that Deng's past experience during the Cultural Revolution left him unwilling to accept any possibility of a potential rival, even if there was little objective capability or intent to challenge him.

A second possibility is that Deng expected resistance from the defense bureaucracy, whose budget he planned to cut. Senior defense officials noted that it would "not be possible to achieve very great progress in the modernization of our national defense" in the near future.[49] It is possible that Deng anticipated that PLA officers would challenge his agenda as a result if given the opportunity. A related possibility is that Deng did

---

[49] Ellis Joffe, *The Chinese Army after Mao* (Cambridge: Harvard University Press, 1987), 59.

not require more integrated institutions because he perceived international threats as comparatively low. In August 1982, for example, Deng suggested that there might be peace for several decades.[50] Diminished threat levels became official policy in June 1985, when Deng noted that Chinese decision-makers had changed their view that "the danger of war is imminent."[51]

A final possibility is that bureaucratic threats may have been higher for Deng's lieutenants, Hu Yaobang and Zhao Ziyang, to whom Deng delegated responsibilities for routine affairs. In contrast with Mao and Deng, Hu and Zhao had comparatively little experience overseeing the national security bureaucracy. Hu, who became the CCP General Secretary in September 1982, had served in the military's General Political Department in Yan'an, as well as a political commissar. After 1949, however, Hu had little contact with the national security bureaucracy.[52] While Hu was acquainted with some of the top military brass, others viewed him as too inexperienced to oversee military affairs.[53] Hu himself noted there was "a practice of arranging seniority according to length of service in the Army."[54] Zhao's ties to the national security bureaucracy were also comparatively thin. Deng remarked, for instance, that Zhao was "unfamiliar" with the military and that it would take time for him to "get to know" its senior ranks.[55]

More Inclusive Information Search Capacity. Beginning in the early 1980s, Deng made a number of institutional changes that improved information search. First, Deng appointed subordinates to key leadership positions within the defense bureaucracy, rather than retaining the portfolio for himself. Deng relinquished his position as the Chief of General Staff and selected Yang Dezhi to take his place.[56]

---

[50] "Zhongguo dui wai zhengce [China's Foreign Policy]," August 21, 1982. *Deng Xiaoping junshi wenji*, Vol. III, 220–221.

[51] "Speech at an Enlarged CMC Meeting," June 4, 1985. *Deng Xiaoping wenxuan, 1975–1982* [SelectedWorks of Deng Xiaoping, 1975–1982] (Beijing: Renmin chubanshe, 1993), Vol. III, 127.

[52] Vogel, *Deng Xiaoping*, 726–729.

[53] Central Intelligence Agency, "China's Party Conference: The Waning of the *Ancien Regime*," November 1985, 16.

[54] "Hu Yaobang Interviewed by Pai Hing's Lu Keng," FBIS-CHI-85-106, June 3, 1985, W1-W38. For Zhao's commentary on the interview, see Zhao Ziyang, *Prisoner of the State: The Secret Journal of Premier Zhao Ziyang* (New York: Simon & Schuster, 2009), 168.

[55] Liu Huaqing, *Liu Huaqing huiyilu* [Memoirs of Liu Huaqing] (Beijing: Jiefangjun chubanshe, 2007), 530.

[56] Yang Dezhi, "Xin shiqi zongcanmoubu de junshi gongzuo [Military Work of the General Staff Department in a New Era]," in *Zongcanmoubu: huiyi shiliao, 1927–1987* [General Staff Department: Recollections and Historical Materials, 1927–1987] (Beijing: Jiefangjun chubanshe, 1995), 650.

Deng also appointed Yang Shangkun, a senior party civilian, to the CMC and entrusted him with China's routine defense affairs.[57] Both Yang Shangkun and Yang Dezhi enjoyed were Politburo members, which conferred status within the party during formal and informal meetings. To help manage China's diplomatic affairs, Deng appointed Li Xiannian, a Politburo Standing Committee member, as head of the Foreign Affairs Leading Small Group (FALSG), the function of which was to "exchange views, study problems, and communicate" among "all organizations concerned with foreign affairs."[58,59] In 1985, the foreign minister also gained a Politburo seat, which shaped the authority of the diplomatic corps to relay information to the political leadership.[60]

The new structure eased the flow of information from the bureaucracy to the party elite.[61] The Foreign Ministry routinely supplied analysis on international developments through the FALSG.[62] The FALSG's assessments and plans were in turn submitted to the party center,[63] which allowed the FALSG to play a "pivotal role" in the decision-making process.[64] As one Chinese source summarizes, there was "a major change in the atmosphere and form of decision-making" that afforded more "discussion, debate, and differing opinions" under Deng's leadership.[65]

---

[57] The *Rules and Regulations for CMC Work* stipulated that Yang Shangkun would chair CMC Standing Committee meetings. See Zeng Dadu, ed., *Zhongguo gongchandang Zhongguo renmin jiefangjun zuzhishi ziliao* [Materials on CCP Chinese People's Liberation Army Organizational History] (Beijing: Changzheng chubanshe, 1996), Vol. VI, 7–8; Liu, *Liu Huaqing huiyilu*, 619.

[58] Zhao Ziyang Interview Transcript, Arthur Doak Barnett Papers, Box 116, Rare Books & Manuscripts Library, Columbia University.

[59] Cheng Zhensheng, "Li Xiannian yu gaige kaifang chuqi de duiwai gongzuo [Li Xiannian and Foreign Affairs Work during the Early Reform Era]," *Zhonggong dangshi yanjiu* [CCP Historical Research], no. 6 (2009): 93.

[60] Gong, Men, and Sun, "Zhongguo waijiao juece jizhi bianqian yanjiu," 50.

[61] Information search remained low in other ways. Deng's face-to-face interactions with diplomatic and defense officials decreased compared to the previous period (see Figure 5.1). Deng also kept national security decision-making off the agenda the Secretariat and the Politburo. For the agendas of Secretariat meetings under Hu Yaobang, see Zheng Zhongbing and Sheng Ping, ed., *Hu Yaobang nianpu ziliao changbian* [Chronicle Materials of Hu Yaobang] (Hong Kong: Shidai guoji chuban gongsi, 2005). For the agendas of Politburo meetings under Zhao Ziyang, see Zhang Xianyang and Shi Yijun, eds., *Zhao Ziyang Zhongnanhai shinian jishi* [Ten-Year Chronicle of Zhao Ziyang in Zhongnanhai, 1980–1989] (Hong Kong: Shijie kexue jiaoyu chubanshe, 2005). See also Lampton, *Following the Leader*, 60.

[62] For example, see Li Xiannian, *Jianguo yilai Li Xiannian wengao* [Manuscripts of Li Xiannian since the Founding of the State] (Beijing: Zhongyang wenxian chubanshe, 2011), Vol. IV, 227.

[63] Cheng, "Li Xiannian yu gaige kaifang chuqi de duiwai gongzuo," 94–95.

[64] Lu, *The Dynamics of Foreign-Policy Decisionmaking in China*, 12.

[65] Zhang, *Waijiao juece*, 192.

Bureaucracies began advancing differing opinions and were afforded more space to deliberate.[66]

Closed Bureaucratic Access to Information. Despite more inclusive information search, inter-bureaucratic information sharing remained low. The FALSG convened dozens of times throughout the 1980s, discussing issues ranging from U.S. arms sales to Taiwan to political developments in Cambodia. Yet the FALSG was primarily a diplomatic silo.[67] In the early 1980s, the FALSG was composed of senior party leaders, diplomats, and State Council officials.[68] While the Deputy Chief of General Staff for military intelligence was technically appointed to the body, the military was not represented in practice until 1987.[69]

The military had its own silo. Unlike the early Mao era, the CMC's membership did not include the foreign minister. CMC Vice Chairman Yang Shangkun's authority to coordinate across diplomatic-defense silos was minimal compared to that of Zhou Enlai. Yang was not a member of the FALSG, and it appears that Yang and FALSG Chairman Li Xiannian rarely met outside of ceremonial functions.[70] The rest of the civilian party leadership, even Hu Yaobang and Zhao Ziyang, were generally cut off from the CMC's information channels and only informed of CMC decisions "after the fact."[71] When the State Council attempted to increase its oversight of China's defense industry, Defense Minister Zhang Aiping told Zhao that it was "inappropriate for the State Council to unilaterally decide on issues touching on military affairs."[72]

The Political Environment in the Jiang-Hu Period, 1989–2012

China's political environment changed fundamentally after the 1989 Tiananmen protests and the rise of a new generation of party politicians. Two characteristics of the new political environment since 1989 help to explain why China retained the siloed institutions that emerged in the

---

[66] Interview D482, Beijing, Spring 2017.
[67] On the FALSG agenda, see Cheng, "Li Xiannian yu gaige kaifang chuqi de duiwai gongzuo," 94; Bian Yanjun Zhang Wenhe, and Yu Lijuan, eds., *Li Xiannian zhuan*, 1949–1992 [Biography of Li Xiannian, 1949–1992] (Beijing: Zhongyang wenxian chubanshe, 2009), Vol. II, 1231–1238.
[68] On the FALSG membership, see Zou Ximing, ed., *Zhonggong zhongyang jigou yange shilu* [Record of CCP Organizational Evolution: 1921.7–1997.9] (Beijing: Zhongguo dang'an chubanshe, 1998), 132, 144, 160.
[69] Lu, *The Dynamics of Foreign-Policy Decisionmaking in China*, 161.
[70] Author's review of Wang, *Li Xiannian nianpu*.
[71] Richard Baum, *Burying Mao: Chinese Politics in the Age of Deng Xiaoping* (Princeton: Princeton University Press, 1994), 241.
[72] Zhang, *Cong zhanzheng zhong zoulai*, 611–613.

late 1980s: the lack of leader experience managing the national security bureaucracy and the rising salience of international issues.

The generation of party leaders who succeeded Deng Xiaoping, including Jiang Zemin and Hu Jintao, possessed far less experience managing the military, diplomatic, and intelligence bureaucracies than either Mao or Deng.[73] Jiang Zemin, who became head of the party and military in 1989, had a background in engineering. He rose through the party ranks with assignments in the State Import–Export Management Commission, Ministry of Machine Building, and the Ministry Electronics Industry before becoming the mayor of Shanghai.[74] Jiang's successor, Hu Jintao, was also a technocrat whose assignments had been in the provinces, Communist Youth League, and other civilian party organs.[75] China's leaders themselves recognized this deficiency in their pedigrees. In a speech to the CMC in November 1989, for instance, Jiang admitted that his understanding of military affairs was "limited."[76] Deng similarly worried that Jiang's limited contacts with the military could be a political liability.[77]

A second characteristic of the political environment was an increasing focus on international security issues, particularly regarding Taiwan. Deng commented that he had been "disappointed" by the end of the Cold War, as its end coincided with "two new cold wars" directed at the Global South and surviving socialist regimes, such as China.[78] With the collapse of the Soviet Union, China's leaders feared that the "long-term strategic objective" of some in the United States was "to promote peaceful evolution" away from a socialist system.[79] Together, as one senior Chinese diplomat summarized, the disintegration of the Soviet Union "fundamentally shook the strategic foundation" of U.S.–China relations.[80]

---

[73] Lampton, *Following the Leader*, 168.

[74] Joseph Fewsmith, *China since Tiananmen: The Politics of Transition* (New York: Cambridge University Press, 2001), 25–27.

[75] Hu's role in the CMC from 1999 to 2004 was reportedly confined to ceremonial activities. See Andrew J. Nathan and Bruce Gilley, *China's New Rulers: The Secret Files*, 2nd ed. (New York: New York Review of Books, 2003), 77–86, 231–233.

[76] "Ba jundui de jianshe he gaige gao de geng hao [Improving Military Construction and Reform]," November 1989. *Jiang Zeming wenxuan* [Selected Works of Jiang Zemin] (Beijing: Renmin chubanshe, 2006), Vol. I, 74.

[77] Liu, *Liu Huaqing huiyilu*, 576.

[78] Deng, *Deng Xiaoping wenxuan*, Vol. III, 344.

[79] "Waijiao gongzuo yao jianding buyi de weihu guojia he minzu de zui gao liyi [Diplomatic Work Must Firmly Safeguard the Highest Interests of the Nation and People]," July 12, 1993. *Jiang Zemin wenxuan*, Vol. I, 312.

[80] Tang Shubei, "Huiyi Wu Xueqian fu zongli zai Duitai gongzuo shang de zhongyao gongxian [Recollections of Vice Premier Wu Xueqian's Important Contributions on Taiwan]," in *Wu Xueqian jinian wenji* [Selected Works Commemorating Wu Xueqian], ed. Shi Yin (Beijing: Shijie zhishi chubanshe, 2009), 314.

The view of Jiang Zemin, who became General Secretary of the CCP in 1989, was only slightly more sanguine. Jiang suggested that, while another world war was "not imminent," the post-Cold War world would be "far from peaceful."[81] On the contrary, the factors that might induce limited wars and other armed conflicts persisted. Of particular concern was the growing possibility of Taiwan independence. While Jiang hoped for peaceful reunification between Taiwan and the mainland, he also worried about "new complications" that threatened to impede it.[82] First, Taiwan was moving toward democracy, which afforded greater political space for opposition parties to promote independence. Second, Taiwan's leaders were initiating a diplomatic campaign to win broader international recognition. In particular, China feared that the United States might support Taiwan's move toward independence.[83]

In 1991, Jiang warned of "major changes" in the situation in Taiwan, particularly "the spread of 'Taiwan independence' thinking" that required "serious attention and vigilance."[84] The following year, Jiang told a group of China's diplomatic envoys, "For a relatively long time into the future, the United States will remain our diplomatic adversary," noting that the United States was likely to "apply pressure on China" in the area of Taiwan and accusing the United States of taking "an imperious attitude and a posture of hegemonism and power politics in its dealings with China."[85]

Siloed Institutions in the Jiang-Hu Period

The bureaucratic threat, coupled with the rising salience of international security issues, helps explain the persistence of China's siloed design after 1989. First, siloing suited the needs of political leaders, who faced increasingly salient international issues. One senior Chinese official reflected that China's attempts to build mechanisms for information search occurred at "precisely the moment when the international situation and Taiwan's domestic situation began to undergo major changes."[86] Another Chinese source emphasizes that an increasing volume of national security

---

[81] "Speech Excerpts from Three Forums on the Gulf War," June 1991. *Jiang Zemin wenxuan*, Vol. I, 142.
[82] "Speech at an Expanded CMC Meeting," January 13, 1993. *Jiang Zemin wenxuan*, Vol. I, 280–281.
[83] Tang, "Huiyi Wu Xueqian," 314–315; Fravel, *Strong Borders, Secure Nation*, 255–258.
[84] State Council Taiwan Affairs Office, ed., *Jiang Zemin, Li Peng tan Taiwan wenti* [Jiang Zemin and Li Peng on the Taiwan Question] (Beijing: Huayi chubanshe, 1997), 22.
[85] "Waijiao gongzuo yao jianding buyi de weihu guojia he minzu de zui gao liyi," July 12, 1993. *Jiang Zemin wenxuan*, Vol. I, 312. These concerns crystallized during the 1995–96 Taiwan Strait Crisis.
[86] Tang, "Huiyi Wu Xueqian," 313–315.

emergencies necessitated more inclusive decision-making and information search.[87] Second, siloing suited the preferences of bureaucratic officials, over whom Jiang and Hu lacked the "personal relationships born of shared experience" to infringe on organizational turf by forcing information sharing.[88] The political leadership chose not to approve several proposals for institutional reforms during the 1990s and 2000s to establish more robust capacity.[89] One Chinese commentator noted that these efforts to establish a "coordinating agency" failed "due to resistance from the military and factions within the leadership that did not want to cede power."[90]

Inclusive Information Search Capacity. The most significant change in China's institutional design after 1989 was the expansion of information search capacity. At the decision-making level, the Politburo began discussing both foreign and defense affairs.[91] The Politburo convened approximately once every two months and its Standing Committee every two weeks,[92] making decision-making more "systematic and institutionalized."[93] The composition of the Politburo in the late 1980s and 1990s included representatives from both the defense and diplomatic bureaucracies,[94] which elevated the status and influence of key national security bureaucracies, particularly the Foreign Ministry.[95]

---

[87] Interview V309, Beijing, Spring 2017.
[88] Lampton, *Following the Leader*, 185; Alastair Iain Johnston, "The Evolution of Interstate Security Crisis-Management Theory and Practice in China," *Naval War College Review* 69, no. 1 (2016): 53; You Ji, "China's National Security Commission: Theory, Evolution and Operations," *Journal of Contemporary China* 25, no. 98 (2016): 185.
[89] See Hu Ping, *Guoji chongtu fenxi yu weiji guanli yanjiu* [International Conflict Analysis and Crisis Management Research] (Beijing: Junshi yiwen chubanshe, 1993); Zhao Kejin, "China's National Security Commission," Carnegie Endowment for International Peace, July 14, 2015; Hu Guangzheng, *Dangdai junshi tizhi gaige yanjiu* [Research on Reforming the Modern Military System] (Beijing: Junshi kexue chubanshe, 2007); You, "China's National Security Commission," 186–187; Yang Mingjie, ed., *Guoji weiji guanli gailun* [Introduction to International Crisis Management] (Beijing: Shishi chubanshe, 2003); Johnston, "The Evolution of Interstate Security Crisis-Management Theory and Practice in China," 52.
[90] Cited in Gillian Wong, "China's State Security Committee Shows Xi's Clout," *Associated Press*, November 13, 2013.
[91] For example, see Jiang Weimin, ed., *Liu Huaqing nianpu, 1916–2011* [Chronicle of Liu Huaqing, 1916–2011] (Beijing: Jiefangjun chubanshe, 2016), Vol. II, 943, 999, 1002, 1020.
[92] On the frequency of Politburo meetings in the 1990s, see records in Ding, *Liu Huaqing nianpu*. On Politburo meetings in the early 2000s, see Alice L. Miller, "Hu Jintao and the Party Politburo," *China Leadership Monitor* 9 (2004).
[93] Gong, Men, and Sun, "Zhongguo waijiao juece jizhi bianqian yanjiu," 51.
[94] Zhonggong zhongyang zuzhibu, *Zhongguo gongchandang zuzhi shi ziliao*, Vol. VII, 116–117.
[95] Interview I216, Beijing, China, Spring 2017.

Beginning in the 1990s, party leaders began relying on leading small groups to supplement information search outside of Politburo meetings as well. The function of the FALSG, for example, shifted toward what Chinese sources describe as "decision-making consultation," expanding the role of these bodies to include policy formulation.[96] In 2001, China established the National Security Leading Small Group (NSLSG),[97] which established a focal point around which decision-making revolved.[98] Leading small groups featured more bureaucratic participation than they had during the 1980s, such that all members held concurrent appointments in the national security bureaucracy.[99]

As a result, Chinese leaders received a larger volume of information from diplomatic, defense, and intelligence bureaucracies.[100] The Politburo, as well as the FALSG and NSLSG, provided forums for routine briefings by bureaucratic advisers.[101] Diplomatic reports were submitted to the party leadership at Politburo meetings.[102] As Chinese historians note, "the number of information channels" increased, affording decision-makers access to research and advice from across the government.[103]

A more inclusive design also encouraged Chinese bureaucrats to speak more candidly. Jiang himself commented that diplomats ought to "boldly make new comments and suggestions for the central leadership to consider in making policy decisions."[104] The status of key bureaucracies, such as the Foreign Ministry, became "respected, assured, and protected," which in turn promoted a freer exchange of ideas and opinions.[105] Decision-making began to be characterized by a traditional

---

[96] Interview C621, Beijing, China, Spring 2017; Richard C. Bush, *The Perils of Proximity: China-Japan Security Relations* (Washington, DC: Brookings Institution Press, 2010), 129.

[97] Yun Sun, *Chinese National Security Decision-Making: Processes and Challenges* (Washington, DC: Brookings Institution Press, 2013), 12. Others note the limited mandate of the FALSG and NSLSG. See Thomas J. Christensen, "More Actors, Less Coordination? New Challenges for the Leaders of a Rising China," in *China's Foreign Policy*, ed. Gilbert Rozman (New York: Palgrave Macmillan, 2012), 25; You, "China's National Security Commission," 188.

[98] Gong, Men, and Sun, "Zhongguo waijiao juece jizhi bianqian yanjiu," 53.

[99] Zou, *Zhonggong zhongyang jigou yange shilu*, 160, 186.

[100] Lu, *The Dynamics of Foreign-Policy Decisionmaking in China*, 29–33.

[101] For example, see Jiang, *Liu Huaqing nianpu*, Vol. III, 1224, 1234, 1288.

[102] For records of FALSG briefings, see Jiang, *Liu Huaqing nianpu*, Vol. II, 1069; Vol. III, 1254, 1341.

[103] Gong, Men, and Sun, "Zhongguo waijiao juece jizhi bianqian yanjiu," 52–54; Zhang, *Waijiao juece*, 189–190.

[104] "Speech at the Eighth Meeting of Chinese Diplomats Posted Abroad," July 12, 1993. *Jiang Zemin wenxuan*, Vol. I, 315.

[105] Zhang, *Waijiao juece*, 191.

idiom stressing that leaders can distinguish between right and wrong by listening to various opinions.[106]

Closed Bureaucratic Access to Information. China's institutional design, however, maintained high barriers to information sharing between bureaucracies, particularly between civilian and military organizations. As a result, diplomatic and defense decision-making each remained within their own silo.[107] First, while the leading small groups were nominally tasked with inter-ministerial coordination, this did not include the CMC, which remained organizationally separated. The CMC remained the "primary forum" for military input on defense strategy and operational matters.[108] By law, the CMC not only exercised unified command over the PLA, but also "decide[d] on military strategies and form[ed] concepts of operations for the armed forces."[109] Chinese interlocutors report that the CMC's design effectively gave the military its "own system."[110]

China's diplomatic leadership did not participate as equals in defense decision-making. Instead, the Foreign Ministry's "bastion" of influence was the FALSG, in which foreign affairs were routinely discussed but defense matters rarely so.[111] Siloing thus went both ways. Just as the foreign ministers were not members of the CMC, the CMC did not have a "heavy footprint" in the FALSG.[112] For most of this period, the military representative on the leading small groups was the defense minister, who by that time played a limited role in China's operational planning and intelligence analysis. CMC vice chairmen, who formulated policy and managed operations, were not included on the FALSG.

In addition, there was no formal or informal coordinator to facilitate information sharing across diplomatic and defense silos. Unlike the Mao era, in which Zhou Enlai and Deng Xiaoping informally coordinated between the defense and diplomatic sectors, China's leaders kept this role for themselves. The system's design ensured that only the most senior civilian officials were "allowed to touch military affairs."[113]

---

[106] Interview C621, Beijing, Spring 2017. The Chinese idiom is 兼听则明，偏信则暗.
[107] You, "China's National Security Commission," 189.
[108] Bonnie S. Glaser, "The PLA Role in China's Taiwan Policymaking," in *PLA Influence on China's National Security Policy-Making*, ed. Phillip C. Saunders and Andrew Scobell (Stanford: Stanford University Press, 2015), 169; interview T111, Beijing, Spring 2017.
[109] 1997 National Defense Law, Articles 13 and 27.
[110] Interview J127, Beijing, Spring 2017.
[111] Lu, *The Dynamics of Foreign-Policy Decisionmaking in China*, 107–108; interview A323, Beijing, Spring 2017.
[112] Interview J127, Beijing, Spring 2017.
[113] Interview H566, Beijing, Summer 2016.

This siloed configuration impeded information sharing between diplomatic and defense organizations. As one Chinese source noted, the PLA and Foreign Ministry had "no formal communications mechanisms."[114] In other words, the institutional design featured "much vertical interaction with little horizontal influence."[115] The lack of horizontal information sharing between the military and civilian bureaucracies almost guaranteed that "the left hand (the diplomats)" did not always know what "the right hand (the military)" was doing.[116]

Restricted access to information shaped the quality of information that bureaucrats provided to the leader. Different Chinese bureaucracies saw things from "different angles" both because each was filled with different types of personnel and because each was analyzing the situation from "the perspective of their organization's mission, responsibilities, and work."[117] Bureaucrats exploited the lack of horizontal information flow to submit biased reports to superiors reflecting their organizational interests and perspectives.[118] In particular, the CMC directly transmitted intelligence and policy recommendations to the supreme leader and the Politburo.[119] This meant that other bureaucracies typically lacked the opportunity to provide alternative information that could contextualize or contest the defense bureaucracy's reporting. As such, China's diplomats and intelligence officials could not "apprise the civilian leadership of how military activity" might affect other policy domains.[120]

Alternative Explanations for Institutional Design

How much do alternative theories help us account for China's institutional evolution since Mao's death? Perspectives emphasizing the leader's management style would predict institutional change after new leaders take office. Yet there is striking continuity across Chinese leaders during this period. China's national security institutions remained fragmented from the mid-1960s to the early 1980s despite stark differences in leadership style between Mao, Hua, and Deng. There is similar institutional continuity from Deng's later years through Hu Jintao's tenure that leader personality alone struggles to explain.

---

[114] Zhang Qingmin, "Bureaucratic Politics and Chinese Foreign Policy-Making," *The Chinese Journal of International Politics* 9, no. 4 (2016): 454.
[115] Zhang, *Waijiao juece*, 196.
[116] Lampton, *Following the Leader*, 171.
[117] Interview A323, Beijing, China, Spring 2017.
[118] Lampton, *Following the Leader*, 97.
[119] For example, see Jiang, *Liu Huaqing nianpu*, Vol. II, 1069; Vol. III, 1173, 1156, 1239, 1271.
[120] Lampton, *Following the Leader*, 186.

There is mixed evidence in support of international diffusion. While there is no evidence that the choice for fragmentation after Mao's death came from a foreign example, there is some evidence that Chinese decision-makers subsequently examined decision-making structures in Russia, Japan, the United Kingdom, Israel, and South Korea.[121] Jiang Zemin also reportedly expressed interest in the U.S. National Security Council during a visit to Washington.[122] Yet neither policy analysis of foreign models at the bureaucratic level nor interest in foreign systems at the political level led China to adopt more robust coordination structures below the apex level of decision-making.

Two aspects of China's institutional evolution – the persistence of fragmented design after Mao's death and the persistence of a siloed design after Deng relinquished power – are partially consistent with path dependence. Yet the evidence presented suggests that many of the same motivations that led Mao Zedong to fragment institutions in the 1960s persisted past his death. Chinese leaders had ample reason to choose to keep their institutions fragmented, even if path dependence made that choice easier.

Finally, one possibility is that institutional siloing may have stemmed from the unique character of the CCP. In Leninist regimes, firm control over coercive institutions is vital to the party's political survival. Given this, it is tempting to think that an autocratic regime such as the CCP cannot help but keep the Chinese defense establishment segregated from the rest of the civilian bureaucracy. Yet this perspective struggles to explain why Mao Zedong was able to adopt a more integrated design during his early years. The political theory of institutional design draws attention to how variation in bureaucratic threats and leader agendas help to explain this variation.

China's Crisis Performance after Mao's Death

How did China's national security institutions perform after Mao's death? Examining the full record of China's crisis performance under fragmented and siloed institutions from 1976 to 2012 provides some insight into this question.[123] As summarized in Table 5.2, China was party to three international crises during the post-Mao fragmented period. All ended without achieving China's primary goal. Congruent with the theory's predictions, China's siloed institutions fared better than fragmented

---

[121] Yang Mingjie, *Guoji weiji guanli gailun*.
[122] Hu Weixing, "Xi Jinping's 'Big Power Diplomacy' and China's Central National Security Commission," *Journal of Contemporary China* 25, no. 98 (2016): 163–164.
[123] See also Jost, "Institutional Origins of Miscalculation in China's International Crises."

Table 5.2 *China's crisis performance after Mao, 1976–2012*

Crisis	Year	Institution	Primary Goal	Successful?
Sino-Vietnamese War	1979	Fragmented	Demonstrate PRC military strength against DRV	✗
Sino-Vietnamese border clashes (Luojiapingda Mt.)	1980	Fragmented	Compel DRV to announce withdrawal from Cambodia	✗
Sino-Vietnamese border clashes (Faka and Kuolin Mts.)	1981	Fragmented	Compel DRV to announce withdrawal from Cambodia	✗
Sino-Vietnamese border clashes (Lao Mt.)	1984	Siloed	Compel DRV to announce withdrawal from Cambodia	✗
Sino-Indian border standoff (Sumdurong Chu)	1986	Siloed	Deter Indian military presence along border	✗
Spratly Islands clashes (Johnson Reef)	1988	Siloed	Gain control over features in the Spratly Islands	✓
Mischief Reef seizure	1994	Siloed	Occupy Mischief Reef	✓
Third Taiwan Strait Crisis	1995	Siloed	Compel the United States to publicly oppose Taiwan independence	✗
EP-3 Reconnaissance aircraft incident	2001	Siloed	Deter American reconnaissance flights	✗
Scarborough Shoal Crisis	2012	Siloed	Improve control over the Scarborough Shoal	✓
Senkaku Islands Nationalization Crisis	2012	Siloed	Compel Japan to end nationalization of Senkaku Islands	✗

alternatives, but worse than integrated ones. During its siloed period, China failed to achieve its primary objective in half of its crises, higher than the rate of failure under integrated institutions (see Chapter 4), but less than the rate of failure under fragmented ones. These trends look similar when accounting for the fact that China often had multiple goals in each crisis. In the post-Mao era, China achieved roughly one third of its goals during crises under fragmented institutions, but roughly two fifths of its goals during crises under siloed institutions. These trends also look similar when accounting for the duration of time under each institutional type. China was involved in a crisis in which it failed to achieve its objectives about once every eight years under siloed institutions. In comparison, such crisis failures occurred once every fourteen years under integrated institutions, but once every three years under fragmented institutions.

Second, we can probe general patterns in China's decision-making over time. Available sources provide comparatively little evidence of an inclusive and collaborative decision-making process characteristic of the early Mao period. Prior to the 1979 war, decisions were made in insular meetings between Deng Xiaoping and the Chinese military. While there are comparatively few sources on elite decision-making for the 1980 and 1981 crises, those available suggest that decision-making followed a similar process.[124]

The evidence available from China's crises during its siloed period, such as the 1988 Spratly Islands clashes, the 1994 Mischief Reef Seizure, and the Third Taiwan Strait Crisis, similarly suggests that Chinese decision-making followed the key patterns we would expect to find under siloed institutions. At the decision-making level, leaders enjoyed a wide range of bureaucratic advice. Multiple bureaucratic stakeholders supplied assessments and reports prior to the 1988 Johnson Reef seizure.[125] Diplomatic and defense advisers were free to express disagreement during the Third Taiwan Strait Crisis.[126] Yet information flow between bureaucracies was a persistent problem across these crises.[127] Prior to the 1988 Johnson Reef seizure, the military reported operational plans directly to Zhao Ziyang.[128] Similarly, the military had directed access

---

[124] Zhang, *Deng Xiaoping's Long War*, 146–148.

[125] "Haijun Zhang Xunsan fu silingyuan zai Nansha qundao wenti xueshuhui shang de jianghua [Speech by Naval Deputy Commander Zhang Xunshan at the Academic Conference on the Spratly Islands]," January 11, 1988. *Nansha wenti lunwen ziliao huibian* [Compilation of Issue Papers on the Spratly Islands] (Haijun junshi xueshu yanjiusuo, 1988), 3.

[126] Interview V309, Beijing, China, Spring 2017; Jiang, *Liu Huaqing nianpu*, Vol. III, 1195–1200; Michael D. Swaine, "Chinese Decision-Making Regarding Taiwan, 1979–2000," in *The Making of Chinese Foreign and Security Policy in the Era of Reform, 1978–2000*, ed. David M. Lampton (Stanford: Stanford University Press, 2001), 322–323.

[127] On the 1984 clashes with Vietnam, see Zhang, *Deng Xiaoping's Long War*, 148–153. On the 1986–87 border standoff with India, see Ji Wenbo, "1987 nian ZhongYin bianjie weiji huigu yu fansi [The 1987 Sino-Indian Border Crisis in Retrospect]," *Nanya yanjiu* [Research on South Asia] Vol. 1 (2018); Wang Xuedong, *Fu Quanyou zhuan* [Biography of FuQuanyou] (Beijing: Jiefangjun chubanshe, 2015), Vol. I, 447–480.

[128] Jiang, *Liu Huaqing nianpu*, 768–769; Liu, *Liu Huaqing huiyilu*, 539.

Table 5.3 *Summary of the Sino-Vietnamese War and EP-3 reconnaissance aircraft incident*

Crisis (institution)	Pathway	Observable implications		
	Information provision	Leader projections	Outcome	Miscalculation
Sino-Vietnamese War (fragmented)	*Low quality*: limited information search on DRV response; some evidence of PLA and MFA self-censoring	Military operations will demonstrate battlefield superiority; demonstrated strength will compel DRV behavior change	Poor battlefield performance demonstrates DRV strength; minimal change to DRV-USSR cooperation / DRV occupation of Cambodia	Yes
EP-3 reconnaissance aircraft incident (siloed)	*Low quality*: restricted dialogue between PLA, MFA, and MSS; parochial bias in PLA information	Detaining U.S. crew and plane will compel U.S. concessions	Minimal change to U.S. reconnaissance program; U.S. denies responsibility for collision	Yes

to Jiang Zemin during the Third Taiwan Strait Crisis.[129] When Vice Foreign Minister Liu Huaqiu traveled to the United States for talks, the Chinese diplomat was not aware of the details of ongoing military exercises.[130]

Tracing China's decision-making during two episodes – the 1979 Sino-Vietnamese War and the 2001 EP-3 reconnaissance aircraft incident – helps to illustrate the quite different pathways by which fragmented and

---

[129] Guo Xiangjie, *Zhang Wannian zhuan* [Biography of Zhang Wannian] (Beijing: Jiefangjun chubanshe, 2011), Vol. II, 242–245; Jiang, *Liu Huaqing nianpu*, Vol. III, 1173, 1184, 1195, 1207, 1234.

[130] Ashton B. Carter and William J. Perry, *Preventive Defense: A New Security Strategy for America* (Washington, DC: Brookings Institution Press, 2000), 96; Nancy Bernkopf Tucker, *China Confidential*, 483.

siloed institutions lead to miscalculation. Table 5.3 summarizes the key points of each case.

Examining these specific cases is helpful for several reasons. Of China's three crises during its fragmented period, the 1979 case is noteworthy because of the high stakes of the issue. It is also worth noting that while China possessed quantitative material advantages, Vietnam signed a defense treaty in 1978 that committed the Soviet Union to support Vietnam in the event of attack. Thus, while Soviet leaders did not commit their forces to the fighting, Chinese decision-makers made the choice to attack what was in aggregate a materially formidable adversary. Studying the EP-3 reconnaissance aircraft incident is especially worthwhile for different reasons. For one, the incident was the clearest case of miscalculation during China's siloed period. In addition, the comparative low-intensity of the crisis helps to highlight the broad scope of the theory. Institutions do not only help us explain instances of major international conflicts, such as the Sino-Vietnamese War. They also help us understand nonviolent, yet nevertheless consequential crises between major powers.

The Sino-Vietnamese War

The Sino-Vietnamese War was part and parcel of a strategic rivalry between China and the Soviet Union, which had continued past the 1969 border conflict. Particularly after the American intervention in Vietnam ended and U.S. military presence in Southeast Asia declined, both the Soviet Union and China perceived a "vacuum" in the region that the other might attempt to fill. As the Soviet embassy in Hanoi noted in 1971, the Soviet Union would now have "more possibilities for establishing our policy in this region" and that Indochina could become "the key to the whole of Southeast Asia."[131]

Vietnam played a central role in the Sino-Soviet rivalry at the turn of the decade. Financially burdened by the costs of its war against America, Vietnam presented an opportunity for either China or the Soviet Union to gain influence by offering economic or military assistance. Vietnam could either turn to China or the Soviet Union, but the Sino-Soviet rivalry made accepting aid from both difficult, if not impossible.[132] Both

---

[131] Christopher Goscha, "Vietnam, the Third Indochina War and the Meltdown of Asian Internationalism," in *The Third Indochina War: Conflict between China, Vietnam, and Cambodia, 1972–79*, ed. Odd Arne Westad and Sophie Quinn-Judge (New York: Routledge, 2006), 182, note 7.

[132] Wang Taiping, ed., *Zhonghua renmin gongheguo waijiao shi* [Diplomatic History of the People's Republic of China] (Beijing: Shijie zhishi chubanshe, 1998), Vol. III, 59; Ross, *The Indochina Tangle*, 3.

China and the Soviet Union attempted to use assistance to entice Vietnam's alignment, but they were unevenly matched to win Vietnam's favor. The Soviet Union could offer trade credits, aid, and debt forgiveness.[133] As one Vietnamese ambassador later recalled, the Soviet Union "expanded its political, economic and military presence" in the region and "worked to persuade Vietnam and other Indochina countries to follow the Soviet lead in countering the Sino-American alliance."[134] In contrast, China could not match deep Soviet pockets in the wake of the Cultural Revolution. As Hua Guofeng told General Secretary of the Communist Party of Vietnam Le Duan on November 20, 1977, while China pledged to "do its best" to help Vietnam, it was constrained by economic hardships of its own.[135]

Vietnam's tensions with Cambodia also affected its alignment with the Soviet Union. Vietnamese decision-makers grew frustrated by China's continued support for the Khmer Rouge. Vietnam's concerns stemmed from the Khmer Rouge's harassment attacks and "feeler operations" along the border with Vietnam. In December 1978, Vietnam invaded Cambodia with the goal of ending ongoing border skirmishes and overthrowing the Khmer Rouge regime. Vietnam signed a Treaty of Friendship and Cooperation with the Soviet Union in November 1978 to hedge against the possibility of Chinese retaliation.[136] Vietnam also signed a protocol granting the Soviet Union access to Cam Ranh Bay, which allowed the Soviet Union to deploy military assets to Southeast Asia.[137]

In parallel to these developments, border clashes between Chinese and Vietnamese forces increased from 1974 to 1978. While each side blamed the other, both sides likely bear some responsibility.[138] Vietnam's former ambassador to Cambodia recalled that China caused 837 incidents along the border in 1977 alone.[139] CIA assessments noted Chinese border actions, which it believed China was using to signal its position on Cambodia.[140] In the fall of 1978, China launched probes of Vietnamese

---

[133] Stephen J. Morris, *The Soviet-Chinese-Vietnamese Triangle in the 1970s: The View from Moscow* (Woodrow Wilson International Center for Scholars, 1999), 20.

[134] Huynh Anh Dung, *Ghi chep ve Campuchia (1975–1991)* [Notes on Cambodia (1975–1991)], trans. Merle Pribbenow (1995), 24.

[135] Wang, *Zhonghua renmin gongheguo waijiao shi*, Vol. III, 66.

[136] Morris, *The Soviet-Chinese-Vietnamese Triangle*, 37.

[137] Ian Storey and Carlyle A. Thayer, "Cam Ranh Bay: Past Imperfect, Future Conditional," *Contemporary Southeast Asia* 23, no. 3 (2001): 455.

[138] Wang, *Zhonghua renmin gongheguo waijiao shi*, Vol. III, 67–68; Li Min, *ZhongYue zhanzheng shinian* [Ten Years of War between China and Vietnam] (Chengdu: Sichuan daxue chubanshe, 1993), 13–14.

[139] Huynh, *Ghi chep ve Campuchia*, 14.

[140] Central Intelligence Agency, "China and Southeast Asia," May 12, 1978. *FRUS, 1977–1980 Volume XXII, Southeast Asia and the Pacific*.

positions along the border.[141] Vietnamese sources similarly report that border incidents increased from 49 per month in 1978 to 171 in January 1979 and 230 in the first half of February.[142]

China's Options in 1979. Chinese decision-makers had several options by which to respond to expanding Soviet and Vietnamese influence in 1979. First, China could have partnered with the United States to diplomatically and economically isolate Vietnam. In January 1979, for example, U.S. President Jimmy Carter noted that international isolation would prove an effective strategy to counter Vietnam's invasion of Cambodia. Carter's national security advisor, Zbigniew Brzezinski, similarly felt that diplomatic isolation would prove successful and warned that "Chinese military action against Vietnam would jeopardize the gains" the United States had made in the international community.[143]

Second, China could have pursued a war of attrition against Vietnam but without launching its own invasion across the Vietnamese border. In his meeting with Deng, Carter suggested that China could "create problems for Vietnam *even without intrusion*."[144] Before China's invasion, China had secured a private agreement with Thailand's Prime Minister, Kriangsak Chamanand, to covertly support the Khmer Rouge "as part of a wide bid to isolate and wear down the Vietnamese." On January 13, 1979, China encouraged the Khmer Rouge foreign minister to transition toward a guerrilla insurgency that would "progressively weaken" the Vietnamese occupation.[145] In parallel to covert action, China might have, as the U.S. intelligence thought it might, "beef[ed] up its military presence" and "harass[ed] Vietnamese shipping and naval activity" in the Gulf of Tonkin.[146]

A third option, and the one that Deng Xiaoping ultimately chose, was to launch a punitive war against Vietnam. During less than one month of fighting, the Chinese military struggled to seize provincial capitals in

---

[141] O'Dowd, *Chinese Military Strategy in the Third Indochina War*, 54; "Research Paper Prepared in the National Foreign Assessment Center, Central Intelligence Agency: The Sino-Vietnamese Border Dispute," March 1979. *FRUS 1977–1980, Volume XIII, China.*

[142] Kenny, "Vietnamese Perceptions of the 1979 War with China," 227.

[143] "Oral Presentation by President Carter to Chinese Vice Premier Deng Xiaoping," January 30, 1979. *FRUS 1977–1980, Volume XIII*; Jimmy Carter, *Keeping Faith: Memoirs of a President* (Fayetteville: University of Arkansas Press, 1995), 210–213; "Memorandum from Brzezinski to Carter," January 26, 1979. *FRUS 1977–1980, Volume XXII.*

[144] "Oral Presentation by President Carter to Chinese Vice Premier Deng Xiaoping," January 30, 1979. *FRUS 1977–1980, Volume XIII.*

[145] Goscha, "Vietnam, the Third Indochina War and the Meltdown of Asian Internationalism," 176.

[146] Central Intelligence Agency, "Another Cambodian War," December 15, 1978. *FRUS 1977–1980, Volume XXII.*

northern Vietnam. Once the PLA finally captured these targets, China withdrew its invasion force.

The Logic of Deng's Decision. Why would China seize Vietnamese territory only to withdraw a few weeks later? The central premise of Deng Xiaoping's decision to invade Vietnam was to demonstrate Chinese military strength.[147] The war sought to show that China *could* inflict costs on Vietnam if it wished to do so. After it withdrew, China could (and did) threaten another invasion. If the first invasion went well, Vietnam would be more likely to comply with China's demands. In short, China aimed to "teach a lesson" to Vietnam.[148]

Deng believed that demonstrating military strength would advance two goals. The first was to compel Vietnam to withdraw its military forces from Cambodia and end clashes along the Sino-Vietnamese border.[149] In mid-November 1978, for instance, former Chinese Foreign Minister Qiao Guanhua relayed private diplomatic messages through Yugoslavia and East Germany that if Vietnam attacked Cambodia, China would "take measures" against Vietnam. As Deng commented, China's "goal was simple, and that is to let [Vietnamese decision-makers] know that charging about is not permissible." The war was not about Sino-Vietnamese relations per se, Deng noted, but about "global strategy."[150] Even after the war, China continued to demand Vietnam's withdrawal from Cambodia as a precondition for normalizing relations.[151]

The second goal was to curtail Soviet "hegemony" in East Asia. China hoped that demonstrating strength would encourage the Soviet Union and Vietnam to limit their defense cooperation.[152] Chinese leaders noted that the Soviet Union was using Vietnam to "contain China" and achieve its "Asian security system."[153] During his visit to Washington in January,

---

[147] On China's objective to "demonstrate Chinese military superiority over Vietnam" and to "force withdrawals" from Cambodia, see Central Intelligence Agency, "China's Vietnam War: Preparations, Combat Performance, and Apparent Lessons," March 1980, NIC-SAFE-A-9-18-1-6, 9. Jimmy Carter Presidential Library (hereafter JCL).

[148] "Speech by Deng Xiaoping on Sino-Vietnamese Border Operations," March 16, 1979. Available in the Fung Library, Harvard University. See also Scobell, *China's Use of Military Force*, 125.

[149] Deng Liqun, *Deng Liqun guoshi jiangtanlu* [Record of Deng Liqun's Lectures on National History] (2000), Vol. III, 353.

[150] On Qiao's message, see Huynh, *Ghi chep ve Campuchia*, 17. On Deng's comments, see "Deng Xiaoping fuzongli tan Yuenan wenti [Vice Premier Deng Xiaoping Discusses the Vietnam Issue]," March 1, 1979. Fujian Provincial Archives, File 222-12-287.

[151] Tran Quang Co, *Hoi Ky Tran Quang Co* [Tran Quang Co: A Memoir], trans. Merle Pribbenow (2003), 32–35.

[152] Scobell, *China's Use of Military Force*, 136.

[153] "Deng Xiaoping fuzongli tong waibin tan Yuenan wenti [Vice Premier Deng Xiaoping Discusses the Vietnam Issue with Foreign Guests]," February 21, 1979. Fujian Provincial Archives, File 222-12-287.

Deng explained that China's strategic position was "like a barbell" with "a strong Soviet position on two flanks with a thin connecting line between."[154] As such, Chinese leaders felt that military action would make the Soviet Union "discover that supporting Vietnam was too heavy a burden."[155]

Overall, Deng seems to have assessed that a Chinese invasion of Vietnam would advance these goals.[156] He reportedly envisioned a "quick decisive campaign" that would clearly demonstrate China's military strength.[157] In December 1978, Deng noted that the operation would showcase China's "determination and *ability* to break through" the Soviet Union's encirclement of China.[158] Even on March 1, 1979, several days into the fighting, Deng was optimistic that the war would allow China to "damage Soviet strategic deployments."[159] Deng made frequent comparisons between an offensive against Vietnam and the Chinese victory against India in 1962, noting that "some punishment *over a short period of time* will put restraint on Vietnamese ambitions" and that China would not face "too much difficulty" in so doing.[160] In short, as one Chinese historian argues, Deng assessed that the war "as easy as the one Mao launched against India" in 1962.[161]

China's Outcome. The war failed both to demonstrate its military superiority and to extract the concessions from Vietnam that it ultimately sought. The PLA's advance was slow and cumbersome.[162] More than 300,000 Chinese troops struggled to seize three provincial capitals located immediately south of the Sino-Vietnamese border from roughly

---

[154] "Memorandum from Oksenberg to Brzezinski," January 29, 1979. *FRUS 1977–1980, Volume XIII*.
[155] Lee, *From Third World to First: The Singapore Story, 1965–2000*, 601.
[156] "Speech at a Plenary CMC Meeting," December 28, 1977. *Selected Works of Deng Xiaoping*, 93–94. Deng was likely referring to the Soviet Union, which he presumably considered to be stronger than Vietnam.
[157] Vogel, *Deng Xiaoping*, 527.
[158] King C. Chen, *China's War with Vietnam, 1979: Issues, Decisions, and Implications* (Stanford: Hoover Institution Press, 1987), 88. Emphasis added.
[159] "Deng Xiaoping fuzongli tan Yuenan wenti," March 1, 1979.
[160] "Memorandum of Conversation on Vietnam between President Carter and Vice Premier Deng Xiaoping," January 29, 1979. *FRUS 1977–1980, Volume XIII*. Emphasis added.
[161] Ruan Ming, *Deng Xiaoping: Chronicle of an Empire* (Boulder: Westview Press, 1994), 54.
[162] O'Dowd, *Chinese Military Strategy in the Third Indochina War*, 46; Sun Hongxian, *Zai Xu Shiyou shenbian de rizi* [Days Beside Xu Shiyou] (Guangzhou: Guangdong renmin chubanshe, 2011), 233.

50,000 Vietnamese soldiers.[163] China also suffered high casualties in the process. In less than one month of fighting, China lost some 31,000 soldiers.[164] Moreover, China performed poorly despite the fact that Vietnam had held its regular units behind the front lines. At best, the battlefield outcome was not clear enough to unambiguously demonstrate China's military superiority.

On the contrary, the war improved the confidence Vietnamese decision-makers that China's military capabilities had been seriously degraded by the Cultural Revolution. General Secretary Le Duan noted that China "suffered a setback" during the war.[165] Vietnam's leaders drew direct connections between China's poor battlefield performance and its ability to threaten military action in the future. One Vietnamese source noted that Vietnamese decision-makers estimated that China would need at least a million troops to execute a second invasion.[166] Le Duan similarly noted that the tactical challenges associated with China's invasion demonstrated Vietnam's secure position:

If [the Chinese] bring in one million troops, they will only gain a foothold in the north. Descending into the mid-lands, the deltas, and into Hanoi and even further downwards would be difficult. [...] *Even fighting for two, three, or four years [Chinese forces] will still not be able to enter.*"[167]

Senior Vietnamese military officials similarly judged that China's invasion demonstrated its inability to reach Hanoi.[168] In short, as Prime Minister Pham Van Dong concluded in December 1979, "it was not [China] who gave [Vietnam] a 'lesson,' but it was [Vietnam] who gave [China] a 'lesson.'"[169]

Given that the logic of the invasion rested on demonstrating strength on the battlefield, it is not surprising that Vietnamese decision-makers refused to concede to China's demands after the conflict. First, the war had little effect on Vietnam's deployments in Cambodia.[170] Weeks after the Chinese withdrawal, Vietnam launched a major offensive in Cambodia, sending multiple divisions to clear areas controlled by the Khmer

---

[163] On the size of Chinese forces, see Zhang, "China's 1979 War with Vietnam," 865. On the Vietnamese deployments, see O'Dowd, *Chinese Military Strategy in the Third Indochina War*, 54.
[164] Zhang, *Deng Xiaoping's Long War*, 119.
[165] "Comrade B on the Plot of the Reactionary Chinese Clique against Vietnam," 1979, Wilson Center Digital Archive, People's Army Library, Hanoi. Obtained and translated by Christopher Goscha.
[166] O'Dowd, *Chinese Military Strategy in the Third Indochina War*, 92–94.
[167] "Comrade B on the Plot of the Reactionary Chinese Clique against Vietnam." Emphasis added.
[168] Kenny, "Vietnamese Perceptions of the 1979 War with China," 232.
[169] "Conversation between Jambyn Batmunkh and Pham Van Dong," December 2, 1979.
[170] Deng, *Deng Liqun guoshi jiangtanlu*, 353.

Rouge.[171] The memoirs of Vietnam's military commander in Cambodia, Le Duc Anh, suggest that Vietnam did not begin considering withdrawing forces from Cambodia until 1982.[172] On the contrary, China's invasion strengthened Vietnamese determination to remain in Cambodia to ensure that China did not "benefit" from its withdrawal.[173]

Chinese decision-makers privately noted that the war had failed to change Vietnam's behavior. In April 1979, the Chinese Foreign Ministry noted that Vietnam would not "seriously negotiate with [China] to resolve disputes between the two countries" and would be unlikely to resolve "substantive issues."[174] In May, Chinese diplomats commented that "supported by the Soviet global hegemonists, the Vietnamese regional hegemonists will not withdraw from Kampuchea or Laos easily."[175] In August 1979, Deng admitted that "Vietnam is not yet in enough of a difficult position to accept a political solution."[176]

Second, the war did not curtail Soviet hegemony in the region. On the contrary, the war increased Vietnamese reliance on the Soviet Union.[177] In July 1979, Brezhnev told East German leader Erich Honecker that the threat China posed to Vietnam had to be taken seriously: "This obliges all of us, of course, not to weaken in the slightest manner our support and our help for the Vietnamese people as well as the peoples of Laos and Cambodia."[178] Annual arms transfers from the Soviet Union to Vietnam increased by over 350 percent between 1979 and 1984.[179] Soviet military presence in Southeast Asia also expanded. The first Soviet naval flotilla arrived to Vietnam in late March 1979. Between 1979 and 1984, Cam

---

[171] O'Dowd, *Chinese Military Strategy in the Third Indochina War*, 90.
[172] Le, *Cuoc doi va su nghiep cach mang*, 274.
[173] "Conversation between Jambyn Batmunkh and Pham Van Dong," December 2, 1979. For similar conclusions within the Communist bloc, see "Decisions of the NVR from 9 March 1979: Oral Report on China's Aggression against the Socialist Republic of Vietnam," March 27, 1979, Wilson Center Digital Archive, BStU, ZA, AGM 369. Translated by Bernd Schaefer. For an assessment by U.S. intelligence, see Central Intelligence Agency, "China's Vietnam War," iii–v.
[174] "Waijiaobu guanyu juxing ZhongYue liangguo fuwai zhanji tanpan de tongbao [Notice Regarding Holding Sino-Vietnamese Bilateral Talks at the Vice-Ministerial Level]," Fujian Provincial Archives, File 222-12-287, 10–12.
[175] "Summary of the President's Meeting with Ambassador Chai Zemin," May 3, 1979. *FRUS 1977–1980, Volume XIII*.
[176] "Summary of the Vice President's Meeting with PRC Vice Premier Deng Xiaoping," August 27, 1979. *FRUS 1977–1980, Volume XIII*.
[177] Xue Li and Li Wei, "ZhongYue bianjing zhanzheng: Yuanyin tanxi yu Zhongfang shouyi pinggu [The Sino-Vietnamese Border War: Assessment of the Causes and Evaluation of the Gains]," *Zhanlüe juece yanjiu* [Journal of Strategy and Decision], no. 2 (2015): 81.
[178] "Transcript, Meeting of East German leader Erich Honecker and Soviet leader Leonid Brezhnev," July 28, 1979, Wilson Center Digital Archive, Obtained and translated by Christian Ostermann.
[179] Data taken from the *SIPRI Arms Transfers Database*.

Ranh Bay became the Soviet's largest overseas military base outside the Warsaw Pact.[180]

It is worth considering a few alternative goals that might have potentially offset these failures.[181] First, one might wonder whether the fighting at least drew some Vietnamese forces away from the fighting in Cambodia, thereby weakening the strength of its deployed forces. Yet this appears not to be the case. The units that Vietnam sent to augment the northern border were mainly reconstituted from reserve forces rather than those deployed to Cambodia.[182] Moreover, while Vietnam expanded the size of its defense forces along the northern border, few of these units were initially drawn from Cambodia. Most were instead newly mobilized units. Most importantly, Vietnam augmented their deployments to Cambodia by the fall of 1979, meaning that deployments did not cause Vietnam to curtail the size of its occupation force.[183]

Another possibility is that the war might have improved China's relations with the United States, showing that leaders in Beijing were willing to bear costs to support American foreign policy interests. Yet Carter had discouraged China from launching the invasion. In January 1979, U.S. President Jimmy Carter told Deng that it would be "a serious mistake" to initiate a military conflict against Vietnam. A "token action," as Carter described China's military plans, would be insufficient to inflict significant punishment on Vietnam and was "unlikely" to shape Vietnamese actions in Cambodia.[184] On the day of the invasion, Carter condemned the Chinese invasion in a cable to Soviet leader Leonid Brezhnev, describing it as a "serious breach" of the "principle of non-use of force to settle international disputes." Carter informed Brezhnev that the United States "object[s] to the military steps [China has] taken and urge[s] the immediate withdrawal of their force from Vietnam."[185] Cooperation between the United States and China persisted in spite of, not because of, the invasion.

A third possibility is that the war helped to reduce the threats that China faced along its southern border and, as a result, created a more peaceful environment for Chinese economic development. Yet border

---

[180] Storey and Thayer, "Cam Ranh Bay," 456.
[181] For an overview of these alternative objectives, see Zhang, *Deng Xiaoping's Long War*, 120–123.
[182] O'Dowd, *Chinese Military Strategy in the Third Indochina War*, 71–72.
[183] Ibid., 186, note 130; Central Intelligence Agency, "Vietnam's Military Posture and Perceptions of Chinese Threat," September 12, 1979. *FRUS 1977–1980, Volume XXII*; Central Intelligence Agency, "China's Vietnam War," iii.
[184] "Oral Presentation by President Carter to Chinese Vice Premier Deng Xiaoping," January 30, 1979. *FRUS 1977–1980, Volume XIII*.
[185] "Message from President Carter to Soviet General Secretary Brezhnev," February 17, 1979. *FRUS 1977–1980, Volume VI, Soviet Union*.

tensions persisted after the war ended. At the war drew to a close, Deputy Chief of General Staff Wang Shangrong noted that Vietnamese border attacks were likely to continue.[186] In 1980, Chinese authorities claimed that Vietnamese forces had seized and fortified border areas, including Luojiapingda, Faka, and Koulin mountains.[187] In 1983, Beijing protested Vietnamese "provocations and border intrusions."[188] There were minor skirmishes throughout the 1980s, including major fighting on Lao Mountain in 1984.[189] The war, in short, failed to produce a lasting peace.

A final possibility is that the war was successful in the long term, contributing pressure that eventually led Vietnam to withdraw from Cambodia a decade later. Yet the evidence available suggests that neither the war – not the subsequent border fighting between China and Vietnam – were a decisive factor in Vietnam's decision-making regarding Cambodia. American intelligence assessed that Vietnam was confident that it could "absorb and contain costs China imposed on its Cambodian policy."[190] On the contrary, Vietnamese sources point to two factors unrelated to the war as central to its decision to withdrawal. The first was diplomatic pressure from the United States and the Soviet Union to "reach a political solution."[191] The second factor was perceptions that Vietnam's military operations had succeed in improving conditions in Cambodia, which along with improved border fortifications, provided space for Vietnam to announce withdraw of its forces.[192]

Institutional Origins of Deng's Miscalculation. China's fragmented institutions help to explain Deng's miscalculation, the crux of which was to assess that China's military performance would demonstrate its strength and, at least eventually, compel Vietnam to make concessions. China's plans called for battles of quick decision (速决战) that would "annihilate a major part of the Vietnamese army in a quick, decisive campaign that would set back by many years Vietnam's ability to threaten China."[193]

---

[186] "Wang Shangrong guanyu ZhongYue bianjing ziwei fanji zuozhan qingkuang de baogao [Report by Wang Shangrong on the Self-Defense Counterattack between China and Vietnam]," March 16, 1979. Available in the Fung Library, Harvard University.
[187] Fravel, *Strong Borders, Secure Nation*, 218.
[188] O'Dowd, *Chinese Military Strategy in the Third Indochina War*, 97.
[189] Zhang, *Deng Xiaoping's Long War*, 141–168.
[190] "National Intelligence Estimate 14-3-85: Cambodia: Vietnamese Strategy and the New Realities." October 1985.
[191] Huynh, *Ghi chep ve Campuchia*, 29.
[192] Ibid., 31–32.
[193] Vogel, *Deng Xiaoping*, 530; O'Dowd, *Chinese Military Strategy in the Third Indochina War*, 46.

China's leaders anticipated a much shorter campaign than was actually achieved.[194] In short, China overestimated its military strength and underestimated Vietnamese resolve.[195]

Two aspects of China's fragmented design were pivotal to this miscalculation. First, Deng Xiaoping served as the Chief of General Staff inside the military, meaning that Deng was essentially his own military adviser. Important documents were provided directly to him and he made quick and unilateral decisions.[196] Second, questions regarding whether the strategy would work, as well as the alternatives available to China, appear to have been overlooked during China's decision-making. Fragmented institutions failed to search for information and created political incentives for bureaucrats, particularly the military, to stifle concerns that they possessed at the time. In other areas of the government, such as the Foreign Ministry, politically insecure bureaucrats chose to derive their judgments based upon top-down cues from party leaders.

Available accounts suggest that the bureaucracy did not seriously consider whether a limited invasion would compel bargaining concessions from either Vietnam or the Soviet Union. The specific objectives of the operation were not clearly communicated during planning for the war.[197] As such, bureaucratic assessments focused on how military options might help China solve ancillary issues, such as border tensions and the treatment of ethnic Chinese in Vietnam. In September 1978, for instance, the General Staff Department convened a meeting on Vietnam chaired by Deputy Chief of Staff Zhang Caiqian, the task of which was to "advise CCP leaders how to counter Vietnam's mistreatment of ethnic Chinese in Vietnam and the increasing provocations by Vietnamese military and security troops along the China-Vietnam border" – neither of which were central to the objectives that China sought to achieve.[198]

While the CMC might have provided a forum in which broader strategic or political considerations could be deliberated, the body had limited capacity for staff work. During the latter half of 1978, the CMC was without a secretary.[199] It is thus unsurprising that the CMC supplied little additional analysis. During a meeting of the CMC in late November,

---

[194] Central Intelligence Agency, "China's Vietnam War: Preparations, Combat Performance, and Apparent Lessons," March 1980, 9, NLC-SAFE-A-9-18-1-6, JCL.
[195] Zhang, *Deng Xiaoping's Long War*, 131.
[196] Liu, *Liu Huaqing huiyilu*, 394; 'Zhang, *Deng Xiaoping's Long War*, 54; Scobell, *China's Use of Military Force*, 138.
[197] Scobell, *China's Use of Military Force*, 142.
[198] Zhou Deli, *Yige gaoji canmouzhang de zishu* [Memoirs of a High-Ranking Staff Officer] (Nanjing: Nanjing chubanshe, 1992), 239.
[199] Luo Ruiqing died in August 1978 and was not replaced until January 1979. Zeng, *Zhongguo gongchandang Zhongguo renmin jiefangjun zuzhishi ziliao*, Vol. VI, 6.

for example, discussions focused on whether the Soviet Union would retaliate, rather than whether China's military could deliver a battlefield victory clear enough to elicit concessions by decision-makers in Moscow or Hanoi.[200] In December, the CMC again discussed the worsening situation, but assessments continued to focus on the likelihood of Soviet retaliation instead of the likelihood of advancing China's broader strategic goals beyond the battlefield.[201] Yet even without full consideration of these factors, the CMC ordered subordinate units to complete preparations for war by early January.[202]

Finally, fragmented institutions failed to identify the poor state of military readiness until after the senior leadership had approved the war. While Deng probably suspected the military had lost some of its combat capabilities during the Cultural Revolution, the specific implications for China's planned invasion of Vietnam do not appear to have been reported to Deng until January 1979 – *after* he had already brought the invasion to the Politburo. Indeed, these assessments did not come through normal military channels, but rather through informal meetings at Deng's home with PLA officers to whom he was personally connected.[203]

Fragmented institutions also encouraged bureaucrats to provide information that was biased toward Deng's prior beliefs.[204] Several officials, including Defense Minister Xu Xiangqian and CMC Vice Chairman Ye Jianying, reportedly did not support the war.[205] Two pieces of information were central to the military's assessments. For one, the PLA was not prepared, particularly as the Cultural Revolution had shifted the military's focus away from professional training.[206] In comparison, Vietnam had just demonstrated its strength through a short and decisive victory

---

[200] Zhou, *Yi ge gaoji canmouzhang de zishu*, 245; Zhang Zhen, *Zhang Zhen huiyilu* [Memoirs of Zhang Zhen] (Beijing: Jiefangjun chubanshe, 2003), Vol. II, 165–166.
[201] Li, *ZhongYue zhanzheng shinian*, 17; "Deng Xiaoping zai ZhongYue bianjing zuozhan qingkuang baogaohui shang de jianghua [Deng Xiaoping's Speech on a Meeting to Report on the Sino-Vietnamese Border War]," March 16, 1979. Available in the Fung Library, Harvard University. The Foreign Ministry reportedly had a similar analytical focus. See Chen Yali, "The PLA in China's Foreign and Security Policy-Making: Drivers, Mechanisms, and Interactions" (PhD diss., Johns Hopkins University, 2015), 455.
[202] Zhou, *Yi ge gaoji canmouzhang de zishu*, 246.
[203] Inspections were conducted by Yang Yong, Wei Guoqing, and Zhang Zhen. Subsequent informal discussions also included Xu Xiangqian, Nie Rongzhen, and Geng Biao. See Zhang, *Zhang Zhen huiyilu*, Vol. II, 168; Jiang Feng et al., ed., *Yang Yong jiangjun zhuan* [Biography of General Yang Yong] (Beijing: Jiefangjun chubanshe, 1991), 495–496. See also Liu Zhi et al., ed., *Xu Xiangqian zhuan* [Biography of Xu Xiangqian] (Beijing: Dangdai Zhongguo chubanshe, 1991), 549.
[204] Interview C431, Beijing, Spring 2017.
[205] Zhang, *Deng Xiaoping's Long War*, 53–54; Vogel, *Deng Xiaoping*, 532.
[206] Chen, "The PLA in China's Foreign and Security Policy-Making," 474–475.

over Cambodia.[207] For defense officials, the balance of power merited caution and perhaps even a more conciliatory strategy toward Vietnam. CMC Vice Chairman Ye Jianying felt that "one cannot fight at all times," advocating that China consider its shared interests with Vietnam and end the fighting between them.[208]

Yet these concerns were neither made forcefully nor shared outside the defense bureaucracy.[209] One senior military officer recalled that Deng's defense advisers "did not reveal [their objections] to others."[210] The PLA's acquiescence traces back to China's fragmented system. Deng's assumption of operational responsibilities for the General Staff meant that sharing concerns outside the military would represent a breach of their chain of command.

The institutional position of the Foreign Ministry also impeded provision of candid diplomatic assessments. As Ezra Vogel notes, while China's senior diplomats possessed "extensive knowledge of other countries and of past negotiations," they lacked the institutional position to "make important political judgments."[211] Foreign Minister Huang Hua was not a Politburo member and did not play an important role in negotiations with Vietnam or Cambodia. Months prior to the outbreak of conflict, diplomatic staff in Hanoi recall that they did not know "where Sino-Vietnamese relations were heading or what the tasks of the embassy were."[212]

These factors likely colored the information that China's envoys reported. The Foreign Ministry reportedly took its cues from Li Xiannian, a Politburo member who had some responsibility for China's diplomatic affairs at the time. According to interviews with Chinese officials, Li's support for the war "trickled down" through the Foreign Ministry and permeated the Foreign Ministry's reports, which "corroborated and supported" the decision to invade.[213] Chinese diplomats, both in Beijing and in Chinese embassies abroad, appear to have withheld and distorted information as a result. Yang Gongsu, the Chinese ambassador in Hanoi,

---

[207] U.S. intelligence analysts believed that Vietnam's invasion of Cambodia had successfully "demonstrated military preeminence." See "Briefing Memorandum from the Acting Director of the Bureau of Intelligence and Research (Mark) to Secretary of State Vance," January 8, 1979. *FRUS 1977–1980, Volume XXII*.
[208] Liu, *Ye Jianying nianpu*, Vol. II, 1126–1127.
[209] Chen, "The PLA in China's Foreign and Security Policy-Making," 476.
[210] Zhou, *Yi ge gaoji canmouzhang de zishu*, 245.
[211] Vogel, *Deng Xiaoping*, 267.
[212] Yang, *Cangsang jiushi nian*, 320–323.
[213] Li's support for the war is itself surprising given his conciliatory line toward Vietnam in the summer of 1978. See Wang, *Li Xiannian nianpu*, Vol. 5, 620. One possibility is that Li's support may have reflected his weak political position at the time. See Chen, "The PLA in China's Foreign and Security Policy-Making," 490–491; Baum, *Burying Mao*, 54–55.

later admitted that he had been "too optimistic" in his assessments of Cambodia's ability to withstand the Vietnamese offensive. Yet Yang recalls that he based his conclusions on the "speeches of decision-makers" and other top-down reports from the Foreign Ministry.[214] Intelligence reports from China's Southeast Asian outposts were similarly eager to convey the conclusions that the central leadership wanted to hear, regardless of the reliability of their sources.[215]

What information might China's diplomats have provided under a different institutional configuration? The international community of diplomats with whom China's envoys might have easily liaised possessed two key pieces of information about Vietnam's likely response to Chinese military coercion.[216] First, Vietnam's invasion of Cambodia was driven by concerns about attacks by the Khmer Rouge on its border. Vietnam's ambassador to Cambodia later explained, the "primary objective was to draw the Khmer Rouge military forces away from us by getting them to withdraw from the east and back to the west."[217] Prime Minister Pham Van Dong visited Thailand, the Philippines, Indonesia, Malaysia, and Singapore in the fall of 1978 and had offered to sign treaties of nonaggression.[218] Such information militated against the conclusions being drawn by Deng Xiaoping concerning Vietnam's expansionist motives.[219] At the very least, better diplomatic information might have led to the conclusion that Vietnamese expansion was not imminent. China had time to pursue options other than an invasion that might demonstrate its material weakness.[220]

Second, and more important, there were diplomatic alternatives to war. Indeed, as one historian notes, it was "on the diplomatic and economic fronts" that China eventually dealt a "devastating blow" to Vietnam after the war. China was able to, in collaboration with the United States, successfully isolate Vietnam for over a decade.[221] Vietnamese officials suggest that such diplomatic pressure was critical to its eventual decision to withdraw from Cambodia.[222] Yet Chinese diplomats appear

---

[214] Yang, *Cangsang jiushi nian*, 326.
[215] Vogel, *Deng Xiaoping*, 291.
[216] On China's ineffective engagement with the international community during the war, see Xue and Li, "ZhongYue bianjing zhanzheng," 80–81.
[217] Huynh, *Ghi chep ve Campuchia*, 40.
[218] Ibid., 20.
[219] Geng Biao, "Guanyu Yinzhi bandao xingshi baogao [Report on the Situation in the Indochina Peninsula]," *Zhonggong yanjiu* [Studies on Chinese Communism], no. 10 (1980): 142–160.
[220] "Telegram From the Embassy in Thailand to the Department of State," January 24, 1979. *FRUS 1977–1980, Volume XXII*.
[221] Christopher Goscha, *Vietnam: A New History* (New York: Basic Books, 2016), 396.
[222] Huynh, *Ghi chep ve Campuchia*, 31–32.

to have failed to identify this alternative approach, which ultimately cost less and achieved more, before the war began.

Alternative Explanations. Several alternative explanations merit attention. First, the interest group model of bureaucratic politics offers little purchase in explaining China's decision to invade Vietnam. China launched the invasion despite the apprehensions of many senior defense advisers. Although diplomats reportedly supported the invasion, the available evidence does not suggest that the choice for war hinged upon these recommendations. On the contrary, the case finds that it was the lack of information search by the defense and diplomatic bureaucracies, particularly in evaluating whether the war would shape Vietnam's behavior relative to potential alternatives to invasion, that underpinned the decision for war.

Accountability theory similarly struggles to explain the case. Given China's transition to non-personalist leadership after Mao's death, accountability theory would suggest that deliberations among *political* elites might have steered China toward a more effective strategy. Yet fragmented institutions allowed Deng Xiaoping to shape what information other political elites received both before and after the war. The Politburo was not briefed on the military's invasion plans until late December.[223] In his report to the party leadership in Beijing in early February 1979, Deng reportedly told the political leadership that the United States had not expressed strong opposition to China's operational plans – a relatively clear misrepresentation of what Carter said during the visit.[224] One of Deng's foreign policy advisers would even justify the war on *opposite* grounds, arguing that the war was "an important step in showing unity" with the United States, even though Carter opposed the war.[225]

One of the reasons that accountability appears not to have worked is that other party elites were informed by similarly incomplete and low-quality information. For example, when tasked to weigh the pros and cons of invasion, one senior civilian member of the Politburo naturally

---

[223] Zhang, *Zhang Zhen huiyilu*, Vol. II, 165–166; Xie Hainan, Yang Zufa, and Yang Jianhua, ed. *Yang Dezhi yisheng* [The Life of Yang Dezhi] (Beijing: Zhonggong dangshi chubanshe, 2011), 302; interview A323, Beijing, Spring 2017.

[224] Chen, *China's War with Vietnam*, 93. Chen's source refers to this as a CMC meeting, but it was more likely one of two expanded Politburo meetings on February 11 and 14 that discussed "continued armed encroachments into China's border territory." See Zhou, *Nie Rongzhen nianpu*, Vol. II, 1147. Deng also delivered a report on the military action to senior party officials on February 16. See Zhu Jiamu, *Chen Yun nianpu*, Vol. III, 265.

[225] Li Shenzhi, *Li Shenzhi wenji* [Collected Works of Li Shenzhi] (China: n.p., 2004), Vol. II, 335.

turned to the defense bureaucracy leaders to inform his recommendation. As a result, his conclusions were nearly identical to Deng's.[226] Deng's rival, Hua Guofeng, reportedly harbored doubts about the war.[227] Yet it was deliberations among the political elite that convinced Hua to support the gambit.[228] In fact, deliberations among the party elite in December 1978 reportedly led to even more optimistic assessments about China's prospects for advancing its goals through a punitive war.[229]

Fragmented institutions also allowed Deng to shape post-evaluations of the war's success after China withdrew from Vietnam. For example, on the final day of military operations, Wang Shangrong and Deng Xiaoping delivered reports to the Central Committee.[230] Wang reported that the operation had "achieved great victories both politically and militarily." The decision to initiate the conflict, according to Wang, had been "completely correct and most wise."[231] Deng similarly argued that the war was a strategic victory, allowing China to resist Soviet hegemony in Asia, create a stable environment for the four modernizations, and provide the PLA with military experience.[232] A more candid assessment of the war, which admitted that "there were also many problems," was contained within a secret report by the Academy of Military Science.[233] Indeed, Deng continued to claim into the 1980s that the war had yielded "victories both military and political."[234]

China's decision-making prior to the Sino-Vietnamese War is consistent with theoretical accounts emphasizing leader beliefs. Elevated emotions may have predisposed Deng toward a military solution toward Vietnam. Ezra Vogel, for instance, argues that Deng was "passionately upset" by Vietnam's behavior, which affected his choice for war.[235] Conventional wisdom tends to suggest that Deng was less militaristic than

---

[226] Deng, *Deng Liqun guoshi jiangtanlu*, Vol. III, 354; Zhu Jiamu, ed., *Chen Yun nianpu, 1905–1995* [Chronicle of Chen Yun, 1905–1995], Revised Edition (Beijing: Zhongyang wenxian chubanshe, 2015), Vol. III, 264–265.
[227] Teiwes, "The Study of Elite Political Conflict in the PRC," 32.
[228] Zhu Jiamu, *Chen Yun nianpu*, Vol. III, 264–265; "Deng Xiaoping zai ZhongYue bianjing zuozhan qingkuang baogaohui shang de jianghua," March 16, 1979.
[229] Zhang, *Deng Xiaoping's Long War*, 56.
[230] Leng, *Deng Xiaoping nianpu, 1975–1997*, Vol. I, 492–493.
[231] "Wang Shangrong guanyu ZhongYue bianjing ziwei fanji zuozhan qingkuang de baogao," March 16, 1979.
[232] "Deng Xiaoping zai ZhongYue bianjing zuozhan qingkuang baogaohui shang de jianghua," March 16, 1979.
[233] Yan, *Xu Xiangqian nianpu*, Vol. II, 370.
[234] "Speech at a Meeting of the Central Committee," January 16, 1980. Deng, *Selected Works of Deng Xiaoping*, 232.
[235] Vogel, *Deng Xiaoping*, 528.

Mao, however, making a leader-centric account less straightforward.[236] Moreover, Deng's intransigence is also consistent with the logic of fragmented institutions. Miscalculations in such a system tend to reflect the leader's early judgments, which are often based on incomplete information and are never critically examined by the advisory system. The case indeed suggests that Deng's assessments about the imperative for military action against Vietnam rested on information that was less complete and less accurate than was possible at the time.

One extension of this leader-centric account posits that Deng had an ulterior motive for invasion. Namely, while the war may not have achieved its strategic objectives, poor battlefield performance demonstrated the need to reform the military.[237] On the one hand, this account is partially consistent with the idea that fragmented institutions appealed to Deng because he needed to subordinate the military in order to pursue his domestic agenda. On the other hand, there is scant evidence that Deng expected that poor battlefield performance could be used for political gain *prior* to the war.[238] If Deng's strategy was to delegitimize the senior PLA commanders, it is unclear why Deng took an active role in planning and executing the war, thereby linking himself to the poor outcome.

The 2001 EP-3 Reconnaissance Aircraft Incident

On April 1, 2001, a Chinese fighter jet collided with an American EP-3 military aircraft off the coast of Hainan Island. The Chinese pilot, Wang Wei, was killed in the process. The American crew made an emergency landing on Hainan, which Chinese authorities had not approved. The United States requested that China release the crew and return the plane.

China had two primary options after the collision. One option was to grant the U.S. request to return the crew and plane to American custody. Another option was to hold the crew and the plane in order to extract concessions from the United States in the wake of the crash. CCP General Secretary Jiang Zemin ultimately chose the latter option, detaining the crew until April 12th and holding the plane until July 3.[239] This

---

[236] Feng, *Chinese Strategic Culture and Foreign Policy Decision-Making*, 75–78.
[237] Ibid., 55.
[238] The inference that Deng sought to use the war's outcome to subordinate the military relies primarily on speeches given by Wang Shangrong and Deng Xiaoping after the fighting ended. Thus, it is difficult to discern whether they reflect Deng's true beliefs before the war or a *post hoc* justification to explain a poor outcome.
[239] On Jiang's role in the decision, see Susan L. Shirk, *China: Fragile Superpower* (New York: Oxford University Press, 2007), 235.

decision triggered a crisis with the United States, in which senior U.S. decision-makers feared a hostage situation.[240]

The Logic of Jiang's Decision. Central to Jiang's choice to detain the crew was the assessment that the United States bore responsibility for the accident. Specifically, Jiang received reports stating that a "sudden change in direction" by the U.S. plane caused the collision.[241] As noted in one senior party member's diary, decision-makers in Beijing believed that they possessed "iron proof" of U.S. culpability that would allow them to "gain the initiative" in negotiations.[242] When at fault in the recent past, U.S. officials had been quick to make concessions to China. In May 1999, for instance, U.S. President Bill Clinton apologized for an air strike that hit the Chinese embassy in Belgrade, agreeing to provide compensation to the victims and for the damage the strike had caused.[243] Indeed, Chinese officials made explicit comparisons to these accommodations during the 2001 incident.[244]

This assessment regarding responsibility for the accident suggested that detaining the crew might allow China to achieve four objectives. One objective was to compel the United States to change its aerial reconnaissance program along China's border. Since the Cold War, the United States had conducted reconnaissance missions inside China's Exclusive Economic Zone (EEZ) to collect intelligence. While American decision-makers maintained that such missions were permitted under international law, China disputed this legal interpretation and repeatedly demanded that the United States end the program.[245] Jiang used the collision as an opportunity to increase coercive pressure on the United

---

[240] George W. Bush, *Decision Points* (New York: Crown, 2010), 426; John Keefe, *Anatomy of the EP-3 Incident, April 2001* (Alexandria: Center for Naval Analyses, 2002), 7. The U.S. Pacific Command Commander retrospectively noted that the United States might have used a precision military strike to destroy sensitive technology aboard the plane. See Zhang Tuosheng, "The Sino-American Aircraft Collision: Lessons for Crisis Management," in *Managing Sino-American Crises: Case Studies and Analysis*, ed. Michael D. Swaine, Zhang Tuosheng, and Danielle F. S. Cohen (Washington, DC: Carnegie Endowment for International Peace, 2006), 420, note 42.
[241] Wang, *Fu Quanyou zhuan*, Vol. II, 210.
[242] Li Peng, *Heping fazhan hezuo: Li Peng waishi riji* [Peace, Development and Cooperation: Li Peng's Diary on Foreign Affairs] (Beijing: Xinhua chubanshe, 2008), Vol. II, 865.
[243] Katharine Q. Seelye, "Chinese Finally Allow Clinton Time for Telephone Apology," *The New York Times*. May 15, 1999; Elisabeth Rosenthal, "U.S. Agrees to Pay China $28 Million for Bombing," *The New York Times*, December 16, 1999.
[244] Beijing to State, "Ambassador's Meeting with FM Tang," April 4, 2001. FOIA F-2010-07070.
[245] Dennis C. Blair and David V. Bonfili, "The April 2001 EP-3 Incident: The U.S. Point of View," in *Managing Sino-American Crises: Case Studies and Analysis*, ed. Michael D. Swaine, Zhang Tuosheng, and Danielle F. S. Cohen (Washington, DC: Carnegie Endowment for International Peace, 2006), 378.

States. In a public statement on April 3, Jiang demanded that the United States "stop [reconnaissance] flights in China's coastal airspace." China's Foreign Minister, Tang Jiaxuan, relayed these same demands through diplomatic channels, suggesting that U.S. flights were "the root cause of the collision."[246]

Second, Chinese decision-makers aimed to force the United States to accept full responsibility for the collision, which official guidance described as a "resolute struggle against the erroneous behavior" of the United States.[247] On April 2, Assistant Foreign Minister Zhou Wenzhong demanded that the United States must bear "full responsibility for the collision."[248] Even after the crew was released in mid-April, Chinese decision-makers aimed for a "package deal," such that China would return the plane in exchange for a change in the American reconnaissance program or accepting responsibility for the accident.[249]

Third, Chinese decision-makers sought to extract an apology from the United States.[250] Jiang publicly pressed China's demand for an apology in the days after the collision.[251] On April 4, the Chinese foreign minister privately told U.S. Ambassador Joseph Prueher that if the United States "admitted its mistake in clear-cut terms and apologized," China would release the crew.[252]

Finally, Chinese decision-makers sought to maintain "the overall situation of Sino-American relations."[253] The collision came at a "politically sensitive time" for Jiang.[254] The George W. Bush administration took office with apprehensions about China's growing military power.[255] Chinese political leaders feared that the new administration planned to take

---

[246] Tang Jiaxuan, *Jinyu xufeng* [Heavy Storm and Gentle Breeze] (Beijing: Shijie zhishi chubanshe, 2009), 273.
[247] Zhang Tuosheng, "The Sino-American Aircraft Collision: Lessons for Crisis Management," 396.
[248] Beijing to State, "P-3 Incident: Ambassador's April 2 Meeting at MFA," April 2, 2001. FOIA F-2010-07070.
[249] Zhang, "The Sino-American Aircraft Collision," 403; Tang, *Jinyu xufeng*, 282.
[250] Zhou Wenzhong, *Dou Er Bupo: Zhongmei boyi yu shijie zai pingheng* [Fighting without Breaking: The US-China Contest and the Rebalancing of the World] (Beijing: Zhongxin chubanshe, 2017), 16–17.
[251] "Feiji pengzhuang shijian zeren wanquan zai Meifang [The American Side Is Completely at Fault for the Airplane Collision Incident]," *Renmin Ribao*, April 3, 2001; Wu Xinbo, *Managing Crisis and Sustaining Peace between China and the United States*. (Washington, DC: United States Institute of Peace Press, 2008), 17.
[252] Beijing to State, "Ambassador's Meeting with FM Tang," April 4, 2001. FOIA F-2010-07070.
[253] Zhang, "The Sino-American Aircraft Collision," 396; Wu Jianmin, *Waijiao anli* [Case Studies in Diplomacy] (Beijing: Renmin daxue chubanshe, 2007), 324–327.
[254] Interview H566, Beijing, Summer 2016.
[255] "Interview with Stephen J. Hadley," November 1, 2011. Miller Center, University of Virginia, 86.

a more confrontational stance toward China.[256] In March 2001, weeks before the collision occurred, Jiang sent one of his foreign policy advisers, Qian Qichen, to the United States to help improve relations.[257] While the visit made some progress with the Bush administration, however, Jiang hoped to maintain stable relations with the United States as part of his broader strategy for economic development and international engagement.[258]

China's Outcome. Jiang's assessments proved to be inaccurate. With time, it became clear that the initial reports regarding the details of the accident were inaccurate. Given the technical differences between the Chinese fighter jet and the American reconnaissance plane, it is unlikely that that a sudden turn by the American side could have caused the collision.[259] On the contrary, the United States subsequently released evidence documenting that the Chinese pilot involved in the incident had a reputation for risky aerial maneuvers.[260] At minimum, the evidence was sufficiently murky such that U.S. policymakers were not willing to make the same types of concessions they had during the 1999 Belgrade bombing.

As a result, China did not meet its first two objectives during the crisis. U.S. reconnaissance flights resumed in early May.[261] Throughout the episode, U.S. policymakers maintained that the United States had done nothing wrong – and thus did not have reason to accept responsibility or apologize for the collision.[262] The Chinese leadership attempted to claim a symbolic victory after the United States released a statement of regret. Yet the substance of the U.S. statement fell short of China's demands.[263]

---

[256] Interview cited in Weiss, *Powerful Patriots*, 78.
[257] Weiss, *Powerful Patriots*, 72.
[258] Wu, *Waijiao anli*, 324.
[259] Interviews with Chinese interlocutors suggest that the Chinese military eventually recognized the inaccuracy of the early reporting.
[260] For a detailed report regarding the details of the collision, see Department of the Navy, "Investigation Into the Circumstances Connected with the Aircraft Between Fleet Air Reconnaissance Squadron One (VQ-1) EP-3E Buno 156511 and the People's Republic of China (PRC) F-8," March 17, 2003. Digital National Security Archive.
[261] Tang Jiaxuan, *Jinyu xufeng*, 285; Blair and Bonfili, "The April 2001 EP-3 Incident," 388.
[262] Beijing to State, "MGCH01: Chinese Agree to Release Aircrew," April 11, 2001, FOIA F-2010-07070; Beijing to State, "EP-3 Consultations: 4/18 Opening Session," April 18, 2001. FOIA F-2010-07070.
[263] The statement conveyed to the Chinese people and the pilot's family was that the United States was "very sorry" for their loss, but the word that U.S. diplomats used in the translation (惋惜) is better understood as regret for something for which one is not responsible. For a detailed analysis of the language used in the letter, see Hang Zhang, "Culture and Apology: The Hainan Island Incident," *World Englishes* 20, no. 3 (2001): 383–391.

After the release of the letter, U.S. Secretary of State Colin Powell clarified that the United States had done nothing wrong and therefore it was not possible to "apologize."[264]

China paid long-term costs as well. After the crisis began, U.S. Secretary of Defense Donald Rumsfeld wrote to President George Bush to discuss a long-term review of defense strategy.[265] On April 16, U.S. officials met to consider what American relations with China would look like in the wake of the incident.[266] U.S. officials recall that the EP-3 incident hardened the administration's views on China.[267] By the end of April, the U.S. Department of Defense restricted contacts with the Chinese military.[268] The Pentagon began to "pivot" assets toward the Asia-Pacific, even before the policy gained this moniker during subsequent U.S. administrations.[269] While the scope of the damage on U.S.-China relations was curtailed by the September 11th terrorist attacks, the United States approved a new defense strategy that "emphasized the increasing importance of Asia" and "the emergence of China as a growing regional power."[270] One Chinese source suggests that "the negative impact of the crisis on bilateral relations might have been less serious and enduring" had the American crew been expeditiously released by China.[271]

Institutional Origins of Jiang's Miscalculation. Siloed institutions help explain Jiang's miscalculation. In a siloed system, miscalculations tend to occur more frequently because leaders receive information that is both incomplete and that is biased toward the perspective of the bureaucracy from which it originated. Both factors contributed to strategic choices that did not advance China's goals as anticipated.

---

[264] "U.S. Crew Members to Come Home after Detention," CNN Transcript, April 11, 2001.
[265] "Memorandum from Rumsfeld to Bush," April 12, 2001. Rumsfeld Archive.
[266] "NSC Deputies Committee Meeting on China," April 16, 2001. George W. Bush Library, FOIA 2017-0054-M.
[267] "Interview #1 with Evan A. Feigenbaum," November 20, 2020. George W. Bush Oral History Project, 6.
[268] Donald Rumsfeld, *Known and Unknown, A Memoir* (New York: Sentinel, 2011), 314.
[269] See Dennis Wilder, "Memorandum for the Record on China Policy," November 10, 2008. Available in Stephen J. Hadley, ed. *Hand-Off: The Foreign Policy George W. Bush Passed to Barack Obama* (Washington, DC: Brookings Institution Press, 2023), 418; "Memorandum from Andy Marshall to Secretary of Defense on Near Term Actions to Begin Shift of Focus towards Asia," May 2, 2002. Rumsfeld Archive. For an overview, see Nina Silove, "The Pivot Before the Pivot: US Strategy to Preserve the Power Balance in Asia," *International Security* 40, no. 4 (2016): 53–58.
[270] "Memorandum from Rumsfeld to LaPorte," October 18, 2002. MDR 07-M-1968.
[271] Wu Jianmin, *Waijiao anli* [Case Studies in Diplomacy] (Beijing: Renmin daxue chubanshe, 2007), 21.

According to Chinese interlocutors, the inaccurate information that Jiang received stemmed from the "stove-piped" nature of the bureaucratic structure, which gave the military unilateral access to the leader.[272] Jiang's information that a "sudden change in direction" by the U.S. aircraft came from local military commanders to the General Staff Department in Beijing.[273] The information was reported directly to Jiang through the CMC without vetting by other bureaucratic stakeholders. In addition, alternative information channels were "sluggish," particularly at the beginning of the crisis.[274] While the Foreign Ministry was notified that the crisis had occurred, China's diplomats initially lacked context about the "real situation."[275]

Even at the time, the Chinese bureaucracy possessed information that suggested the military's explanation of the crash was not credible. In December 2000, for example, the United States expressed concern about PLA intercepts through a démarche delivered during talks with the Chinese military.[276] It is not clear if the Chinese military relayed the signal to Jiang or other civilian bureaucracies based on currently available evidence. In the four months before the crisis occurred in April, however, China neither responded to the démarche nor modified the nature of these intercepts. Based on the information flow patterns, it is likely that the Foreign Ministry and the PLA did not discuss the strategic implications of the démarche, either because the information was not shared beyond the military's silo or because the Foreign Ministry believed this was a military, rather than diplomatic, issue.[277]

Chinese diplomats also received signals shortly after the collision that militated against the military's interpretation of the facts. In meetings on April 1 and 2, Ambassador Prueher noted that China's description of the collision was "physically impossible" based on the technical properties of the two planes.[278] In his memoirs, Tang draws attention to the fact that Prueher had served in the navy and "could pilot over fifty different types of naval aircraft."[279] Yet the U.S. ambassador later suggested that the Foreign Ministry was not properly "passing the word up the line, perhaps because Chinese diplomats were deferring to military counterparts."[280]

---

[272] Interviews A323, T111, Beijing, Spring 2017; Shirk, *Fragile Superpower*, 235.
[273] Wang, *Fu Quanyou zhuan*, Vol. II, 210.
[274] Zhang Tuosheng, "The Sino-American Aircraft Collision: Lessons for Crisis Management," 410.
[275] Wang, *Fu Quanyou zhuan*, Vol. II, 211; interview cited in Lampton, *Following the Leader*, 176.
[276] Keefe, *Anatomy of the EP-3 Incident*, 2.
[277] Interviews V960 and R816, Beijing, Spring 2017.
[278] Keefe, *Anatomy of the EP-3 Incident*, 5.
[279] Tang Jiaxuan, *Jinyu xufeng*, 272.
[280] "Interview with Joseph Prueher."

After the crisis, Jiang chided the military, questioning its "strategic awareness, scientific and technical knowledge, and international knowledge." The General Staff was asked to "deeply reflect" on the incident, as the military bore responsibility for the "problems in slow emergency response" and "backward command and control measures."[281] A subsequent review by a think tank affiliated with the Chinese intelligence bureaucracy found that one of the core functions that the U.S. National Security Council provided – and, implicitly, that the Chinese system lacked – was a mechanism for "comprehensive processing" of intelligence to ensure that "senior decision-makers do not respond improperly" in the early stages of a crisis.[282] Similarly, the report noted that the government needed to guard against the risk of "organizational biases" undermining the overall situation.[283] Taken together, the review suggests that Chinese interlocutors believed that the assessments that Jiang received might have been different had the military's reporting been vetting by other bureaucratic stakeholders.

Alternative Explanations. While siloed institutions help account for Jiang's miscalculation during the 2001 EP-3 reconnaissance aircraft incident, several alternative explanations should be considered. The interest group model of bureaucratic politics can at best only partially explain the crisis. First, there is little evidence presently available that Jiang was forced to accept the policy recommendations of a single bureaucracy. On the contrary, Jiang reportedly rejected more conflictual recommendations offered by the Chinese military.[284] Instead, the evidence available suggest that incomplete and biased information provided by his defense advisers led Jiang to overestimate the prospects for successive coercion.

Another alternative explanation might posit that Jiang's unwillingness to incorporate new information precipitated the crisis. Yet Jiang's decision-making suggests the opposite. His broader goal in the spring of 2001 was to maintain a cooperative relationship with the United States. Information provided by the defense bureaucracy led Jiang to believe that China might succeed in pressuring the United States to make concessions, even if doing so put Jiang's broader goal at risk.

Finally, accountability theory offers comparatively little insight into China's decision-making during the EP-3 incident. Given collective

---

[281] Wang, *Fu Quanyou zhuan*, Vol. II, 212.
[282] Yang Mingjie, *Guoji weiji guanli gailun*, 253.
[283] Ibid., 257.
[284] Nan Li, "Top Leaders and the PLA: The Different Styles of Jiang, Hu, and Xi," in *PLA Influence on China's National Security Policy-Making*, ed. Phillip C. Saunders and Andrew Scobell (Stanford: Stanford University Press, 2015), 126; Shirk, *Fragile Superpower*, 236.

leadership within the party, accountability theory would predict that Jiang should have avoided such risky confrontations. Yet the political elites that might have held Jiang accountable for a poor outcome were just as dependent on the bureaucracy's assessments.[285] As a result, other political elites seem to have derived similarly inaccurate conclusions regarding the strength of China's bargaining position in the dispute.[286] As such, accountability was only as strong as the counsel that was available.

Conclusion

This chapter explored the trade-off between high-quality bureaucratic information and political security in the context of a non-personalist autocracy. During the late 1970s, a combination of bureaucratic threats and a transformative domestic political agenda pushed Chinese leaders to retain fragmented institutions well past Mao's death in 1976. China's pattern of crisis performance broadly, as well as in its miscalculations during the 1979 Sino-Vietnamese War specifically, illustrated the effects of its persistingly fragmented design.

In the 1980s, China transitioned to siloed institutions. The postrevolutionary generation of party leaders, lacking experience in national security matters, perceived themselves as politically vulnerable to bureaucratic sanction. In addition, these leaders faced a series of international challenges and possessed few goals to radically transform the economy or society. As a result of the institutions they possessed, the information that Jiang Zemin and Hu Jintao received featured biases uncharacteristic of China's integrated period discussed in Chapter 4. The medium-n analysis, as well as the case study of the 2001 EP-3 reconnaissance aircraft incident, suggest that degraded information provision shaped the quality of China's judgment during its international crises.

This chapter advances the book's overall argument in two ways. First, it showed how political accountability in authoritarian regimes is an insufficient condition to avoid miscalculation. Existing theories would anticipate that Chinese leaders, fearing the threat of political sanction for failed crisis outcomes, would have adopted more effective institutions and reached more accurate judgments in 1979 and 2001. The analysis suggests that political accountability alone is insufficient to explain when dictatorships are likely to miscalculate. How decision-makers understand which strategies are likely to succeed or fail depends on their national security institutions.

---

[285] Interviews J127, C621, and V960, Beijing, Spring 2017.
[286] Li, *Li Peng waishi riji*, Vol. II, 865.

Second, the chapter illustrates the theory's proposition that the lack of a competitive dialogue between diplomatic and defense bureaucracies increases the risk of miscalculation. During the 2001 crisis, the evidence suggests that Jiang initially received biased advice because it was not properly vetted by other bureaucratic constituencies. The crux of the problem was not that the military acted independently or compelled the leader to adopt their recommendations. Rather, the problem was that Jiang lacked the institutional support to quickly identify the inaccuracies in the information his defense advisers supplied.

Coupled with Chapter 4, the case of China demonstrates how politics drives institutional design – and that institutional design has downstream consequences for crisis decision-making – in both personalist and non-personalist autocracies. In short, to explain China's miscalculations, including those in major conflicts like the Sino-Vietnamese War, we have to first account for its institutional design. The next chapter applies this same theoretical logic in the context of a democracy: India. Specifically, to understand India's blunders during the 1962 Sino-Indian War, we must first look to the politics of national security institutions.

6   India

In the fall of 1961, Indian Prime Minister Jawaharlal Nehru made one of the most consequential decisions in the history of Indian foreign policy. India was in the midst of an ongoing competition with China to establish control over disputed territory along its borders. In response to Chinese gains, Nehru approved what became known as the Forward Policy. The premise of this strategy was to reclaim the upper hand in negotiations with China by establishing a series of Indian outposts deep into contested land along the border. Nehru believed the strategy would curtail Chinese expansion into territory claimed by India, help push China to withdraw from the positions it had already established, and ultimately improve its coercive leverage for a political settlement on more favorable terms.

The outcome was far from what Nehru envisioned. In response to the Forward Policy, China launched a devastating military assault, marking the start of the 1962 Sino-Indian War. The conflict proved to be a watershed moment for South Asia. For India, it was a decisive battlefield defeat – India's worst outcome of any conflict since gaining independence in 1947. In just over a month of fighting, China easily overran Indian positions. By the end of the fighting, over four thousand Indian soldiers were killed, wounded, or missing. Another four thousand were captured.[1]

The logic of the Forward Policy rested on several inaccurate assessments. Nehru believed that the Forward Policy would not cause China to retaliate, judging that the Sino–Soviet split and the economic disaster of Great Leap Forward had weakened China. As a result, India could negotiate from a position of strength. Yet the Sino–Soviet split actually encouraged China to adopt a more assertive foreign policy to demonstrate its revolutionary credentials within the Communist bloc. Moreover, a successful military mobilization along the border gave China

---

[1] Oriana Skylar Mastro, *The Costs of Conversation: Obstacles to Talks in Wartime* (Ithaca: Cornell University Press, 2019), 173, note 92.

a sizable material advantage over Indian forces that made the Forward Policy tactically unsound.

Existing scholarship offers several explanations for why India made such a consequential error. Some scholars emphasize the role of domestic public opinion.[2] Indeed, the war's outcome was ultimately costly for Nehru, as India's failures supplied his political opponents with ammunition to question his authority and judgment. Although this perspective sheds light on Nehru's motivation to find a more favorable solution, however, it does not explain why India adopted a strategy based on inaccurate projections regarding whether the Forward Policy would achieve the outcomes the Indian public desired. On the contrary, accountability theory would predict that Nehru would have been highly motivated to find an effective strategy that would secure his political survival.[3] As this chapter shows, however, this explanation struggles to explain Nehru's approval choice for a risky military solution.

India's national security institutions offer an answer as to why India miscalculated. In 1947, India inherited inclusive institutions that were near replicas of the British system during World War II. Institutions optimized for the United Kingdom during the mid-twentieth century did not last long once transplanted to a new political environment, however. Nehru came into office focused on uniting the country and transforming the Indian economy. He viewed both the defense and intelligence bureaucracies as potential threats to that political agenda. On one level, Nehru was frustrated by leaks from the national security bureaucracy and was aware of the potential for a military coup d'état. At a deeper level, Nehru worried, perhaps correctly, about establishing political control over India's coercive institutions. Nehru thus adopted fragmented institutions that curtailed the ability of defense and intelligence bureaucracies to contribute to policy. From the perspective of domestic politics, fragmented institutions helped to ensure that India's colonial legacy did not lead to praetorian rule. From the perspective of foreign policy, however, they impaired the quality of information that the bureaucracy delivered to Nehru.

These institutional choices help to explain India's miscalculation on the road to the Sino-Indian War. Fragmented institutions restricted the flow of information from bureaucrats who contested Nehru's assessments regarding the balance of power and the feasibility of implementing the

---

[2] Neville Maxwell, *India's China War*, Revised Edition (Dehra Dun: Natraj, 2015), 42–43; Lebow, *Between Peace and War*, 184–192; Srinath Raghavan, *War and Peace in Modern India* (London: Palgrave Macmillan, 2010), 253.

[3] Other accounts point to Nehru's stubbornness and dovish worldview. See Steven A. Hoffmann, *India and the China Crisis* (Berkeley: University of California Press, 1990); Kennedy, *The International Ambitions of Mao and Nehru*, 139–172.

Forward Policy. Nehru privately admitted that his advisory team had "been found lacking."[4] As one internal government review later summarized, after it became clear that the assessments underpinning the Forward Policy were "no longer valid," no reappraisal took place because India lacked "institutionalised support for decision-making at the national level."[5]

This chapter advances the overall argument of the book in two ways. First, the chapter shows that the trade-offs that leaders face regarding national security institutions look quite similar in both democratic and authoritarian regimes. Bureaucrats often use different strategies to punish political leaders in authoritarian regimes, but the implications of the trade-off look quite similar in both contexts. This insight helps to clarify why democracies can (and do) often adopt ineffective decision-making processes despite the hazards they pose to foreign policy judgment. Second, the Sino-Indian War provides a useful counterpoint to the interest group model of bureaucratic politics. The Indian Foreign Ministry enjoyed greater access to and influence over Nehru than either India's defense or intelligence bureaucracies. Yet diplomatic dominance did not yield discerning (or dovish) decisions. The case illustrates that exclusively relying on bureaucracies that might be predisposed toward international cooperation cannot substitute for deliberative dialogue among bureaucracies about the effectiveness of potential strategies.

The chapter proceeds as follows. The first section applies the political theory of institutional design. It shows that variation in India's political environment helps to explain the evolution of India's national security institutions since independence. During the 1950s, salient domestic political threats led to unmistakably fragmented institutions that restricted information flow within the bureaucracy. As threats from China and Pakistan became more pronounced, however, India's generally weak political leaders transitioned toward siloed institutions. Finally, in the late 1990s, India established a National Security Council (NSC) system, nudging India toward a more integrated design. The subsequent sections turn to institutional consequences, first tracing how fragmented institutions shaped Indian decision-making in the lead-up to the 1962 Sino-Indian War. A second case examines the 2001–2002 Twin Peaks Crisis, illustrating how integrated institutions yielded more complete and accurate information on which Prime Minister Atal Bihari Vajpayee based his decisions.

---

[4] Sarvepalli Gopal, *Jawaharlal Nehru: A Biography* (New Delhi: Oxford University Press, 1979), 224.
[5] P. B. Sinha and A. A. Athale, *History of the Conflict with China, 1962* (New Delhi: Ministry of Defence History Division, 1992), xx–xxi.

The Politics of Institutional Design in India

On August 15, 1947, India gained its independence from the United Kingdom. In the process, India inherited an institutional design that was modeled on the British system. In the months immediately after India's independence, British officers leading the Indian military helped to design the Defence Committee of the Cabinet (DCC). The DCC was intended to be a replica of the British system during World War II. British military officers setting up the DCC obtained "copies of charters for the various subcommittees of the cabinet committees at home," which served "as models" for India's own.[6] As envisioned, the purpose of the DCC was to bring together multiple perspectives on national security. The design afforded unfettered access between the political leadership and India's defense bureaucracy.[7] According to its architects, the reason was that when making decisions about international conflict, it was impossible to "to draw a clear dividing line between what was a military matter and what was not." Its architects noted that the model "had worked extremely well" in the United Kingdom and had already been replicated in other countries.[8]

Yet India's leaders formally and informally modified the institutions they inherited in accordance with their political incentives. To understand these subsequent institutional changes, we must look to the political environment and the domestic and international threats that Indian leaders faced. Table 6.1 summarizes the key components of the theory for the India case.

The Political Environment before 1962

India's first prime minister, Jawaharlal Nehru, perceived a salient threat from the military and, to a lesser extent, from intelligence bureaucracies. First, Nehru worried senior military officers might organize into a political interest group.[9] For example, in January 1948 Nehru expressed concerns about "the tendency of some of our senior officers to dabble in politics." Later that year, Nehru mentioned that he was concerned about the increased frequency of military officers attending political gatherings

---

[6] "Letter from General Sir R.M.M. Lockhart to Lord Ismay," October 2, 1947, MB1/D100/10, Mountbatten Papers.
[7] "Memorandum Originating in the Ministry of Defence, Government of India, Regarding the Creation of Committees Dealing with Matters Affecting the Indian Armed Forces," October 2, 1947, MB1/D139/2, Mountbatten Papers.
[8] "Minutes of a Provisional Defence Committee Meeting," October 1, 1947, MB1/D42/2, Mountbatten Papers.
[9] Anit Mukherjee, *The Absent Dialogue* (New York: Oxford University Press, 2019), 40–46.

Table 6.1 *Evolution of India's institutional design*

Period	Bureaucratic threat	Leader agenda	National security institution	Theory support
1947–1950 (inherited)	*High*: distrust of UK military officers; inexperienced leader	*International*: post-Independence territorial conflicts	*Siloed*: inclusive bureaucratic representation on DCC and JIC	Weak
1951–1962	*Medium*: perceived intent to challenge; more experienced leader	*Domestic*: transformative social and economic programs; low perceived international threat	*Fragmented*: insular Foreign Affairs Committee; retention of diplomatic portfolio; minimal coordination capacity	Strong
1963–1998	*High*: perceived intent to challenge; inexperienced leaders	*International*: territorial challenges by China and Pakistan	*Siloed*: inclusive Political Affairs Committee; delegation of diplomatic and defense portfolios; limited coordination capacity	Strong
1999–2012	*Low-Medium*: low perceived intent to challenge; more experienced leader (Vajpayee)	*International*: nuclear threats from Pakistan; border tensions with China and Pakistan; transnational terrorism	*Integrated*: inclusive CCS; delegation of diplomatic and defense portfolios; national security advisor, staff, and coordination bodies	Strong

in which officers were "discussing their interests or other subjects from a communal point of view." Nehru believed that the development "should be dealt with firmly and without loss of time."[10] Nehru was similarly "anxious to help [former Indian military] personnel to find employment" and worried in September 1955 that any further budget decreases might cause the Army to become a "dissatisfied" and "disgruntled" lot.[11] Nehru distrusted other elements of the national security bureaucracy as well. Nehru entered office suspicious of intelligence organizations, based in part on his prior experience being monitored by British intelligence services.[12]

Second, Nehru worried that senior military officers were leaking information.[13] In January 1948, Nehru believed that senior officers were "discussing military matters and plans with all manner of people."[14] In March 1961, Nehru stated that there had been "far too much loose talk about Army matters," which had been indulged in by senior military officers.[15] Nehru complained that "top secret matters," including the contents of DCC meetings, had been leaked to the press.[16] Formal investigations against the military leadership followed, which Nehru monitored personally.[17] The apprehensions of Indian leaders were not entirely without cause. Senior military officials recall that their colleagues were "in the habit of making tenacious and indiscreet remarks openly against our national leaders."[18] Nehru commented that some military statements had become "almost a public exhibition of disapproval" of their own government.[19]

Nehru's beliefs were possibly rooted in the fact that most Indian military officers had not participated in the independence movement.[20] On the contrary, Indian officials noted that the military "had often been utilized by the British Government to suppress the national movement," which lead to "an essential antagonism" between political leaders and the military after independence.[21] In the senior ranks, there were few Indians

---

[10] Sarvepalli Gopal et al., eds., *Selected Works of Jawaharlal Nehru (Second Series)* (New Delhi: Jawaharlal Nehru Memorial Fund, 1984) (hereafter SWJN-SS), Vol. 7, 519.
[11] Gopal et al., Vol. 7, 528; Vol. 30, 346.
[12] B. N. Mullik, *My Years with Nehru: 1948–1964* (New Delhi: Allied Publishers, 1972), 57.
[13] B. M. Kaul, *The Untold Story* (New York: Allied Publishers, 1967), 317.
[14] Gopal et al., *SWJN-SS*, Vol. 5, 432.
[15] Ibid., Vol. 67, 219.
[16] Ibid., Vol. 7, 521. See also Vol. 66, 352; Vol. 70, 384.
[17] Ibid., Vol. 69, 612–613; Vol. 74, 560; Vol. 75, 508; Vol. 77, 357.
[18] Kaul, *The Untold Story*, 317.
[19] Gopal et al., *SWJN-SS*, Vol. 23, 180–181.
[20] Stephen Peter Rosen, *Societies and Military Power: India and Its Armies* (Ithaca: Cornell University Press, 1996), 198.
[21] P. V. R. Rao, *Defence without Drift* (Bombay: Popular Prakashan, 1970), 3.

but many British officers.²² Post-independence Indian military officers had typically been trained at Sandhurst, the British military academy. In fact, they were previously titled "King's Commissioned Indian Officers" and, as one scholar notes, were "more Anglicized than other Indians of their social class."²³ Finally, military officers who trained and fought alongside India's own before 1947 – but had instead been dispatched to Pakistan after partition – had launched an unsuccessful coup in 1951 and a successful one in 1958. Indian leaders rightly worried whether their Indian counterparts would do the same.

These concerns persisted across Nehru's tenure. In January 1961, Nehru and other senior civilians reportedly had "some inkling" that senior commanders might attempt a coup. General S.P.P. Thorat, for example, was alleged to have criticized the government and to have appealed to the military's "loyalty to the Army Chief, with no word about loyalty to the Government or the Constitution of India."²⁴ As one Ministry of Defence study noted, the Indian military "remained a close-knit professional body deliberately isolated from the citizen" and might have acted "like the Praetorian Guards of the Roman Empire."²⁵

Finally, Nehru's agenda privileged domestic over international issues. As Nehru commented in 1948, "We have many important preoccupations, but the fundamental and basic problem still continues to be the economic problem." For Nehru, the problem was critical to the survival of the country, noting that the economy "may well break us if we cannot deal with it satisfactorily."²⁶ In 1955, Nehru similarly suggested that India's economic situation was "as serious as any war situation and we should look upon it, therefore, from a special point of view and not allow ourselves to remain in very orthodox, set grooves of thought."²⁷ Nehru saw his economic program as transformative. Within a decade, Nehru promised, "our plans will change the picture of the country so completely that the world will be amazed."²⁸ Nehru saw an intimate connection between the first five-year plan, for instance, and the legitimacy of the new government, aiming to make the plan "something living, vital and dynamic, which captures the imagination of our people."²⁹ As Nehru's biographer summarizes, by the mid-1950s, Nehru believed that "it was

---

²² Steven I. Wilkinson, *Army and Nation: The Military and Indian Democracy since Independence* (Cambridge: Harvard University Press, 2015), 102.
²³ Rosen, *Societies and Military Power*, 225–226.
²⁴ S. S. Khera, *India's Defence Problem* (Orient Longmans, 1968), 73–74.
²⁵ Sinha and Athale, *History of the Conflict with China*, xxii.
²⁶ Gopal, *Jawaharlal Nehru*, Vol. II, 96.
²⁷ Ibid., Vol. II, 197.
²⁸ Ibid., Vol. II, 200.
²⁹ Ramachandra Guha, *India after Gandhi: The History of the World's Largest Democracy* (New York: HarperCollins, 2007), 218.

within the country that the real problems lay, and these were more intractable and less responsive to reason and argument than the issues in foreign affairs."[30]

Part and parcel to Nehru's domestic focus was the judgment that the international threats that India faced were comparatively low. While Nehru was cognizant of the potential for military confrontation with Pakistan, the partition between India and Pakistan afforded basic geographic advantages to India, such as contiguous borders and strategic depth. India also inherited a larger share of the forces, infrastructure, and defense factories relative to Pakistan.[31] As Nehru himself summarized early in his tenure, "I am certain that there will be no war in the near future."[32] The share of the central budget focused on defense, for instance, plummeted in the first decade of Nehru's rule. In 1948, the defense budget accounted for roughly 67 percent of the central budget. By 1954, it was less than 23 percent.[33]

Fragmented Institutions before 1962

The political environment, and the threat that the national security bureaucracy posed to the new regime, led Nehru to adopt fragmented national security institutions. As one Indian diplomat recalls, the "basic discernible fact" concerning decision-making under Nehru was that there was "no institutional and structured policy planning mechanisms underpinning the process."[34] The design of India's national security institutions was directly linked to the two components of the theory. First, as noted by one of Nehru's senior military leaders, India's institutional design was aimed at "the prevention of any dictatorship by the Armed Forces."[35] Other scholars note that "administrative and organizational changes introduced after independence" were chosen "for the purpose of reducing the role of the military in the decision-making process."[36] Government publications from the time similarly observed that

---

[30] Gopal, *Jawaharlal Nehru*, Vol. 2, 196.
[31] Wilkinson, *Army and Nation*, 196–197.
[32] Gopal et al., *SWJN-SS*, Vol. 5, 439.
[33] See Budget Papers of 1956–1965, Government of India. Available in the Nehru Memorial Museum and Library (hereafter NMML).
[34] J. N. Dixit, *My South Block Years: Memoirs of a Foreign Secretary* (New Delhi: UBS, 1996), 425.
[35] "Roy Bucher to Neville Maxwell," February 29, 1968, Bucher Papers, United Kingdom National Archives - National Army Museum (hereafter UKNA-NAM), Box 29.
[36] Stephen P. Cohen, *The Indian Army: Its Contribution to the Development of a Nation* (Berkeley: University of California Press, 1971), 171. See also Wilkinson, *Army and Nation*, 21.

the intent of design choices was to make "civilian control supreme over the military wing."[37]

Second, perceptions regarding the salience of international threats relative to domestic priorities appear to have been critical to these choices. P.V.R. Rao, who served as the Indian defence secretary in the 1960s, recalled that after "the establishment in 1948 of the Cease Fire in Kashmir, and India's policy of peace and non-alignment and the belief of Government that [...] India's security was not threatened by any other foreign power," the key decision-making and coordination bodies that India inherited from the British "fell into disuse" and did not play "any effective part in an objective determination of the danger which the county was expose" or the "preparations" required to meet it.[38]

Insular Information Search Capacity. Three design choices created an insular decision-making process. First, Nehru created new decision-making bodies with more restrictive membership. He established a Foreign Affairs Committee (FAC), which became the principal formal body in which national security affairs, including territorial disputes, were discussed.[39] Unlike the DCC, the FAC consisted only of members nominated by the prime minister.[40] While he retained the DCC, Nehru established a "Defence Committee *Members* of the Cabinet," which circumvented the requirement in the DCC's charter that the military service chiefs would be "in attendance" as non-members.[41] As Nehru wrote to Defence Minister Baldev Singh, while there would "inevitably" be some need to consult with the military leadership, Nehru felt that "this consultation should not become widespread."[42] Second, Nehru restricted the DCC's agenda to budgetary and administrative matters.[43] In January 1948, for example, Nehru explained that he saw "no particular advantage in putting up

---

[37] *India: A Reference Annual, 1953*, Government of India, 184.
[38] Rao, *Defence without Drift*, 309. On the DCC's utilization under Nehru, see also Raju G. C. Thomas, *The Defence of India: A Budgetary Perspective of Strategy and Politics* (Delhi: Macmillan, 1978), 87; Jaswant Singh, *Defending India* (New York: St. Martin's Press, 1999), 158; R. Venkataraman, *India's Higher Defence: Organisation and Management* (New Delhi: K.W. Publishers, 2011), 86.
[39] Gopal et al., *SWJN-SS*, Vol. 54, 492; Vol. 57, 430; Vol. 61, 454; Vol. 65, 437–438; Vol. 78, 654. According to one account, a meeting of the FAC might be called if there was a "very considerable raid by Pakistan." See interview with Krishna Menon, available in Michael Brecher, *India and World Politics: Krishna Menon's View of the World* (London: Oxford University Press, 1968), 249. The FAC similarly handled India's policy toward the Portuguese occupation of Goa. See Gopal et al., *SWJN-SS*, Vol. 61, 421–422.
[40] Brecher, *India and World Politics*, 250.
[41] Gopal et al., *SWJN-SS*, Vol. 38, 440–441.
[42] Ibid., Vol. 5, 432.
[43] Ibid., Vol. 30, 349; Vol. 44, 647–648.

[military plans against Pakistan] before the motley crowd that attends the DCC meetings."[44] After receiving a report from the Chief of Army Staff in June 1958, Nehru noted that he preferred to discuss its contents "privately" rather than at the DCC. In particular, Nehru feared that discussions of policy at the DCC would make their way into the press, opening the prime minister to public criticism.[45] From this perspective, meetings of the DCC were risky because they elevated the threat of leaks.[46] Third, Nehru chose to fill the position of foreign minister himself for the duration of his tenure, as well as the position of defence minister for part of the 1950s. In effect, Nehru was his own diplomatic and defense adviser.[47] As Steven Wilkinson summarizes, Nehru changed the institutions overseeing India's decision-making, ensuring that the military "no longer had a seat at the political decision-making table."[48]

These institutional choices constrained both the quantity and quality of bureaucratic information. As shown in Figure 6.1, the vast majority of Nehru's communications with government officials on both foreign *and* defense policy went through the Foreign Ministry. In 1962, Nehru noted that he "hardly ever" received intelligence updates outside those from the Director of the Intelligence Bureau (DIB), India's civilian intelligence chief at the time, such as those originating from the Joint Intelligence Committee (JIC).[49]

India's fragmented institutional design led to self-censorship. The military leadership felt that voicing dissenting views would be "political suicide."[50] One military officer noted that the "direct ways of dealing with all and sundry won't work in this set up." Indian officers would have to become "more of a courtier."[51] Nehru's former cabinet secretary similarly recalled that "a widespread impression prevailed, rightly or wrongly, in the armed forces, especially amongst the senior cadres, that there was a system of favourites."[52] These patterns extended beyond the defense bureaucracy as well. Nehru felt that though he received a number of

---

[44] Gopal et al., *SWJN-SS*, Vol. 5, 200.
[45] Ibid., Vol. 42, 487.
[46] "Nehru to Cabinet Secretary," August 2, 1962, Jawaharlal Nehru Papers, F. No. 736, Part I, No. 366-PMO/62, NMML.
[47] Jeffrey Benner, *Structure of Decision: The Indian Foreign Policy Bureaucracy* (New Delhi: South Asian Publishers, 1984), 63.
[48] Wilkinson, *Army and Nation*, 103.
[49] Gopal et al., *SWJN-SS*, Vol. 75, 507–508.
[50] Maxwell, *India's China War*, 210; J. P. Dalvi, *Himalayan Blunder* (Bombay: Thacker, 1969), 95.
[51] Wilkinson, *Army and Nation*, 107.
[52] Khera, *India's Defence Problem*, 73. Khera served as Cabinet Secretary during the Sino-Indian War.

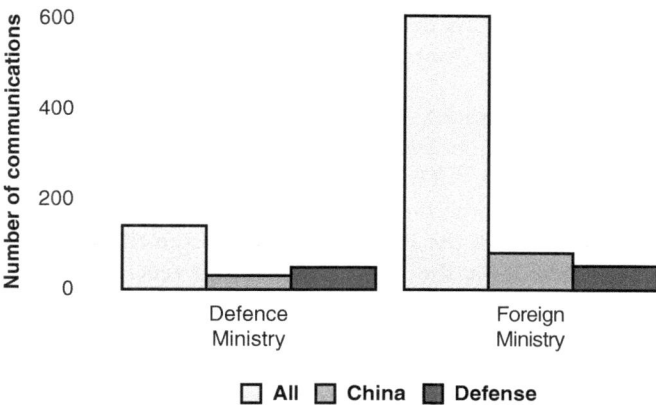

Figure 6.1 Information flow under Nehru, 1958–1962
Note: The left and right sets of bar plots report communications (cables, reports, directives, notes) between Prime Minister Jawaharlal Nehru and officials in the Ministry of Defence and Ministry of External Affairs from October 1958 to October 1962. Within each group, the left bar reports the total number of communications, the middle bar reports the number pertaining to China and Tibet, and the right bar reports the number pertaining to defense and military affairs. Coding details provided in Appendix B. Source: *Selected Works of Jawaharlal Nehru (Second Series)*.

notes from the DIB, their value was limited because they did not convey "any really pertinent information."[53] Even in the Foreign Ministry, Nehru's decision to retain the minister position for himself reportedly encouraged "sycophancy" and " eagerness to please" in India's diplomatic reporting.[54]

Closed Bureaucratic Access to Information. India's coordination bodies were similarly weak. While the inherited system had established a Joint Intelligence Committee (JIC) to share "all the information relating to the situation" among diplomatic, defense, and intelligence bureaucracies, the JIC was "moribund."[55] Similarly, the former Director of Military

---

[53] Gopal et al., *SWJN-SS*, Vol. 75, 507–508.
[54] Maxwell, *India's China War*, 90.
[55] "Minutes of a Provisional Defence Committee Meeting," October 1, 1947, MB1/D42/2, Mountbatten Papers. On dysfunction within the JIC, see P. V. R. Rao, *India's Defence Policy and Organisation since Independence* (New Delhi: United Service Institution of India, 1977), 11–12; "Report by General Sir Roy Bucher," March 17, 1949, Bucher Papers, UKNA-NAM Box 20, 6.

Operations reflected that the military services chiefs were, from an organizational perspective, "not part of the [Defence] Ministry" and did not "function as such."[56]

Fragmented institutions impeded horizontal information flow. Available records suggest that few of Nehru's communications were circulated among the ministries.[57] The Military Wing of the Cabinet, which provided secretarial support for the DCC, did not receive copies of foreign telegrams to and from the Foreign Ministry, even those with a "bearing on defence." Similarly, the DCC staff did not receive copies of "correspondence between any of the Ministries and the Ministry of Defence," even when the contents discussed defense matters.[58] Similarly restricted were memoranda passed between the Ministry of Defence and military service headquarters, as well as assessments and operational orders. As one Indian diplomat recalls, there was "little institutional coordination" between defense, diplomatic, and intelligence bureaucracies.[59] As Defence Minister V. K. Krishna Menon later reflected, "there were large numbers of matters about which" he knew nothing.[60] Even within the Foreign Ministry, there were problems with horizontal information sharing during the policymaking process. One senior diplomat remembered that there was "no policy, no direction" because individual advisers would meet with Nehru, receive the prime minister's "consent for what he wanted and went his way."[61]

Nehru was aware of these organizational deficiencies, but did not rectify them. In the fall of 1947, shortly after Indian independence, the Indian political leadership was informed that India's current intelligence system "was not functioning as efficiently as it used to function."[62] Two months later, the Commander-in-Chief noted that "there was at present a general lack of good and coordinated intelligence."[63] Yet Nehru consistently resisted proposals for reform. On receiving a proposal for a Joint Intelligence Organization in March 1953, Nehru replied that India should only strengthen its intelligence system on a "modest scale" and

---

[56] D. K. Palit, *War in the High Himalaya: The Indian Army in Crisis, 1962* (New York: St. Martin's Press, 1991), 125.

[57] Gopal et al., *SWJN-SS*, Vol. 56, 358; Vol. 70, 555; Vol. 73, 376.

[58] "Report by General Sir Roy Bucher," Bucher Papers, iii.

[59] Dixit, *My South Block Years*, 426.

[60] Brecher, *India and World Politics*, 249. On Menon's relationship with Nehru, see Kaul, *The Untold Story*, 209–210.

[61] Shashi Tharoor, *Reasons of State: Political Development and India's Foreign Policy under Indira Gandhi, 1966–1977* (New Delhi: Vikas, 1982), 33.

[62] "Emergency Committee Paper No. 16," September 24, 1947, MB1/D39/2, Mountbatten Papers.

[63] "Minutes of the Seventeenth Meeting of the Defence Committee," November 28, 1947, MB1/D43/8, Mountbatten Papers.

suggested that the proposed budget should be reduced.[64] In February 1962, Nehru received an internal review documenting the inefficiencies of the Indian intelligence system, noting that "it seems to me clear that the present way of gathering intelligence is not very satisfactory, chiefly because it is not properly coordinated." Yet Nehru also told his aides that he found intelligence bureaucracies unhelpful and was "doubtful" about expanding their bureaucratic capacity.[65]

The Political Environment after 1962

The political environment in India after 1962 was marked by both continuity and change. On the one hand, the level of bureaucratic threat remained high. Indira Gandhi kept retired Chief of Army Staff Cariappa under surveillance for over two decades after his retirement.[66] In 1963, one British adviser noted that Indian officials were wary of increasing the level of coordination, presumably out of a fear of allowing the defense bureaucracy more access to information.[67] Indira Gandhi's principal secretary, P.N. Haksar, similarly noted that India should "resist the temptation" to allow greater authority to integrate civilian and military bureaucracies.[68]

In addition, the prime ministers who immediately followed Nehru – Lal Bahadur Shastri, Indira Gandhi, Morarji Desai, Chaudhary Singh, and Rajiv Gandhi – all lacked experience overseeing the national security bureaucracy. Indira Gandhi's prior experience, for example, amounted to two years overseeing the Information and Broadcasting Ministry.[69] Rajiv Gandhi's cabinet secretary observed that as a "newcomer" in the government, the prime minister "did not know many senior civil servants."[70] As one Indian official recalled, "prime ministerial weakness meant bureaucratic strength" in the Indian government after Nehru's death.[71]

On the other hand, India's wars with China and Pakistan in 1962 and 1965, respectively, dramatically reshaped the importance of international issues for Indian political leaders. In contrast to the uneven division of military forces in 1947 described in the previous section, Pakistani

---

[64] Nehru noted that he did not know who was leading the JIC at the time he received the proposal. Gopal et al., *SWJN-SS*, Vol. 21, 307.
[65] Ibid., Vol. 75, 507–508.
[66] Wilkinson, *Army and Nation*, 143.
[67] "Remarks of Earl Mountbatten at the Military Affairs Committee," May 1, 1963, T. T. Krishnamachari Collection, File 27, NMML.
[68] "Analysis of Kashmir," n.d., P.N. Haksar Collection (III), File 170, NMML.
[69] Tharoor, *Reasons of State*, 50.
[70] B. G. Deshmukh, *From Poona to the Prime Minister's Office: A Cabinet Secretary Looks Back* (New Delhi: HarperCollins, 2004), 143.
[71] Interview J393, New Delhi, Winter 2017.

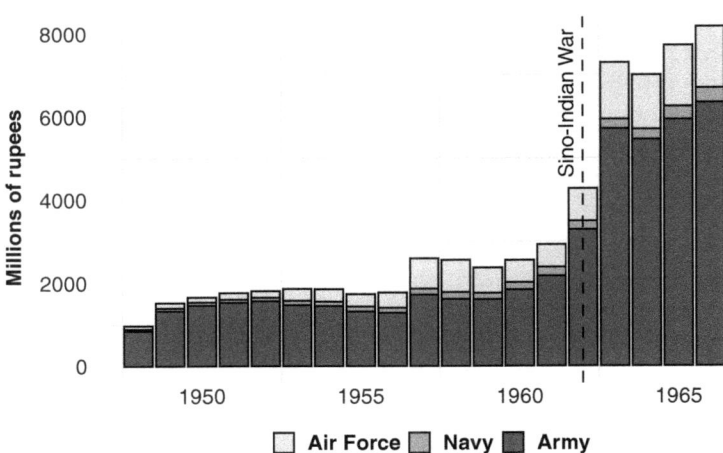

Figure 6.2 Indian defense budget, 1947–1966
Note: The figure reports the annual budget for each service branch in millions of rupees. Source: *Defence Service Estimates* and *Budget Papers* available in the Nehru Memorial Museum and Library.

ground troops had reached near parity with India by the mid-1960s. In 1964, Pakistan possessed seven infantry divisions in comparison to India's nine. Pakistan also possessed nearly two armored divisions, consisting of seventeen Patton, Sherman, and Chaffee tank regiments, nearing parity with the fourteen armored regiments possessed by India.[72] As highlighted in Figure 6.2, changes to India's security environment were reflected in its military spending, which nearly tripled after the war with China.

Siloed Institutions after 1962

The theory predicts that leaders tend to prefer siloed institutions when facing both bureaucratic and international threats. Consistent with theory, Indian leaders modified their institutional design after the 1962 Sino-Indian War to increase the capacity for information search, while keeping coordination mechanisms limited.

Inclusive Information Search Capacity. After the Sino-Indian War, India's decision-making rules and processes became more inclusive. The DCC was replaced by an Emergency Committee of the Cabinet (ECC),

---

[72] S. N. Prasad and U. P. Thapliyal, eds., *The India-Pakistan War of 1965: A History* (New Delhi: Natraj Publishers, 2011), 10.

designed to address national security matters in the wake of the war.[73] Despite its name, the ECC handled both routine matters, such as diplomatic negotiations on the Non-Proliferation Treaty, as well as crisis decision-making, such as that during the 1965 Indo-Pakistani War.[74] In 1970, the ECC and the Foreign Affairs Committee of the Cabinet were merged into the Political Affairs Committee (PAC).[75] In contrast to the DCC, which was routinely "marginalized" prior to 1962, both the ECC and the PAC met on a relatively routine basis.[76] Finally, Indian leaders generally appointed dedicated foreign and defence ministers, instead of keeping these portfolios to themselves as Nehru had.[77] Senior officials noted that the PAC allowed "free and democratic" discussion of foreign policy.[78] Another senior intelligence official found that there was a "continuous and voluminous" intelligence flow to decision-makers.[79] While Indian leaders did not appoint the military service chiefs to the ECC or PAC, they invited them as required.[80] Thus, in contrast to India's earlier institutional design, newly established bodies featured more capacity for provision of bureaucratic advice.

Closed Bureaucratic Access to Information. Below the decision-making level, however, India's institutional design did not substantially change. Initiatives to establish coordination bodies, such as the Committee of Defence Planning and the Foreign and Defence Advisory Committee, failed. The first closed shortly after its formation and the second existed

---

[73] Rao, *India's Defence Policy and Organisation since Independence*, 12.
[74] C. S. Jha, *From Bandung to Tashkent: Glimpses of India's Foreign Policy* (New Delhi: Sangam Books, 1983), 209–210, 301–303. Jha served as India's foreign secretary in the mid-1960s.
[75] P. C. Alexander, *My Years with Indira Gandhi* (New Delhi: Vision Books, 1991), 50–51.
[76] Jayantanuja Bandyopadhyaya, *The Making of India's Foreign Policy: Determinants, Institutions, Processes and Personalities* (New Delhi: Allied Publishers, 2003), 139–140.
[77] While some subsequent prime ministers have directly managed the foreign or defense portfolios for a time, these periods have been short compared with the duration of Nehru's hold over the diplomatic portfolio. Appointments more than one year in duration were Indira Gandhi (minister of external affairs: September 1967–February 1969, defence minister: January 1980–January 1982), Rajiv Gandhi (defence minister: September 1985–January 1987), V.P. Singh (defence minister: December 1989–November 1990), and P.V.N. Rao (defence minister: March 1993–May 1996).
[78] Interview with Swaran Singh, quoted in Bandyopadhyaya, *The Making of India's Foreign Policy*, 92–94.
[79] B. Raman, *The Kaoboys of R&AW: Down Memory Lane* (New Delhi: Lancer, 2007), 10–11.
[80] S. K. Sinha, *Higher Defence Organisation in India* (New Delhi: United Service Institution, 1980), 7–8; S. K. Sinha, *Of Matters Military* (New Delhi: Vision Books, 1980), 39. S.K. Sinha served as the Vice Chief of Army Staff in the mid-1980s. The actual record of military participation is mixed. See Rao, *Defence without Drift*, 309; Thomas, *The Defence of India*, 87; V. A. Pai Panandiker and Ajay K. Mehra, *The Indian Cabinet* (New Delhi: Centre for Policy Research, 1996), 177–178.

only on paper.[81] Instead, coordination responsibilities were delegated to the Ministry of External Affairs. A Policy Planning Committee included the Foreign, Commerce, Defence, and Home Secretaries, but was chaired by the foreign secretary.[82]

In sum, as one former official notes, the "lack of an effective supreme coordinating body was acutely felt" in the decades after Nehru's death.[83] As late as the 1990s, one government evaluation of India's national security system concluded that the country lacked an "institutionalized mechanism for coordination or objective-oriented interaction between agencies and consumers at different levels," as well as a "mechanism for tasking the agencies, monitoring their performance and reviewing their records to evaluate" the quality of their information.[84]

India's Shift to Integrated Institutions

During the 1990s, two changes in India's political environment opened space for institutional reform. First, fears of military intervention into India politics had largely dissipated. The Indian military had become more representative of the general population than it had been in the 1940s.[85] The generation of officers trained in India after independence began reaching senior ranks in the 1990s. Those who had attended the British military academy and served in the colonial-era army gradually retired. Unlike many of India's neighbors, Indian democracy had survived four decades without a coup. Second, India gained a new prime minister in 1998 – Atal Bihari Vajpayee – who had previously served as foreign minister. As discussed later, this level of prior experience overseeing the national security bureaucracy was relatively uncommon among contemporary prime ministers in India.[86]

The combination of a reduced threat of coup coupled with a comparatively experienced prime minister provided a window for India to move toward a more integrated design. This included not only the formation of inclusive decision-making bodies, such as the Cabinet Committee

---

[81] Sushant K. Singh, "Military as an Instrument of India's Foreign Policy," in *Handbook of Indian Defence Policy: Themes, Structures and Doctrines*, ed. Harsh V. Pant (New York: Routledge, 2015), 106–107.

[82] Bandyopadhyaya, *The Making of India's Foreign Policy*, 203–204.

[83] S. D. Pradhan, "National Security System – Evolution," in *India's National Security*, ed. Satish Kumar (New Delhi: Routledge), 436.

[84] *Kargil Review Committee Report*, 217. Available in the Institute for Defence Studies and Analyses Library, New Delhi.

[85] Wilkinson, *Army and Nation*, 177–179.

[86] On Vajpayee's experience, see also Christopher Clary, *The Difficult Politics of Peace: Rivalry in Modern South Asia* (New York: Oxford University Press, 2022), 226; N. P. Ullekh, *The Untold Vajpayee: Politician and Paradox* (Gurgaon: Penguin, 2018), 78–88.

on Security and National Security Council, but also a series of mechanisms below the apex level to facilitate information sharing. Former NSC staff members suggest that the primary motivation behind the reforms was that officials recognized that individual bureaucracies in the existing system were "working in silos." The political leadership needed an institutional mechanism to "hold [decision-making] together and coordinate."[87]

Inclusive Information Search Capacity. Shortly after entering office, Prime Minister Vajpayee formed a new decision-making body, the Cabinet Committee on Security (CCS), which consisted of the prime minister, as well as the home, defence, and external affairs ministers. The military service chiefs and foreign intelligence organization, the Research and Analysis Wing (R&AW), along with the defence and foreign secretaries, attended meetings as required.[88] In April 1998, Vajpayee appointed a task force to outline the role and function of a National Security Council (NSC).[89] On April 16, 1999, the Vajpayee administration released a resolution outlining the NSC system, explaining that "national security management requires integrated thinking and co-ordinated application of the political, military, diplomatic, scientific and technological resources of the State to protect and promote national security goals and objectives." Vajpayee adopted the NSC to provide that function.[90]

At the apex of the new institutional design was the NSC itself.[91] The CCS retained decision-making authority and considered short-term actions, while the NSC was a deliberative body focused on India's long-term national security strategy.[92] India also formed a decision-making body specifically for nuclear matters, the National Command Authority (NCA). The NCA incorporated the prime minister and the CCS into a Political Council, which was advised by an Executive Council, through which the political leadership interacted with the service chiefs and the Commander-in-Chief of Strategic Forces Command.[93] While details on

---

[87] Interview with Satish Chandra, *Strategic News International*, April 16, 2019.
[88] S. Padmanabhan, *A General Speaks* (New Delhi: Manas Publications, 2005), 112.
[89] B. Raman, "National Security Management," *Outlook*, May 20, 2004; P. R. Chari, "India's Nuclear Doctrine: Confused Ambitions," *The Nonproliferation Review* 7, no. 3 (2000): 123–135; George Perkovich, *India's Nuclear Bomb: The Impact on Global Proliferation* (Berkeley: University of California Press, 2002), 297.
[90] "Cabinet Secretariat Resolution No. 281/29/6/98/TS," April 16, 1999, *The Gazette of India*.
[91] Pradhan, "National Security System – Evolution," 438.
[92] Tanvi Madan, "Officialdom: South Block and Beyond," in *The Oxford Handbook of Indian Foreign Policy* (New Delhi: Oxford University Press, 2016), 241.
[93] Gurmeet Kanwal, "Military Dimensions of the 2002 India-Pakistan Standoff: Planning and Preparation for Land Operations," in *The India-Pakistan Military Standoff: Crisis*

the membership of the Executive Council remain classified, informed observers report that it included not only the three military service chiefs, but also intelligence leadership.[94]

More Open Bureaucratic Access to Information. The NSC reforms introduced several institutional changes to inter-bureaucratic information sharing as well. First, the NSC system established a coordination body, the Strategic Policy Group (SPG), envisioned to be "the principal mechanism for inter-ministerial coordination and integration of relevant inputs in the formulation of national security policies."[95] Bureaucratic representation included the three military service chiefs, as well as the foreign and defence secretary. SPG agendas included items offered by the ministries, as well as the NSC Secretariat.[96] The SPG was chaired by the cabinet secretary – and thus provided a neutral arbiter between the ministries. As one former official noted, the SPG proved a "useful organization" to manage subordinate bureaucracies.[97]

The NSC system also established a national security advisor (NSA), a position envisioned for "servicing" the NSC.[98] For example, India's first NSA, Brajesh Mishra, noted that each bureaucratic adviser was "entitled to his say, so let him have his say."[99] Members of the bureaucracy responded by supplying candid opinions, even when they contradicted the government's policy. As one deputy national security advisor later recalled, "There was any number of occasions on which papers submitted by us to the government did express a contrary view" without being penalized by the government in response.[100] Key foreign and national security policy decisions were ultimately made by the prime minister, but

---

and Escalation in South Asia, ed. Zachary Davis (New York: Palgrave Macmillan, 2011), 91.

[94] Harsh V. Pant, "India's Nuclear Doctrine and Command Structure: Implications for India and the World," *Comparative Strategy* 24, no. 3 (2005): 249.

[95] "Cabinet Secretariat Resolution No. 281/29/6/98/TS," April 16, 1999, *The Gazette of India.*

[96] Pradhan, "National Security System – Evolution," 446.

[97] Arvind Gupta, *How India Manages Its National Security* (New Delhi: Penguin, 2018), 340.

[98] "Cabinet Secretariat Resolution No. 281/29/6/98/TS."

[99] A. S. Dulat, *Kashmir: The Vajpayee Years* (Noida: HarperCollins, 2015), 173. Dulat served as the head of R&AW from 1998 to 2000 and remained in the Prime Minister's Office as an adviser on the Kashmir issue through 2004.

[100] Interview with Satish Chandra, *Strategic News International.*

"with the supporting homework being done by the bureaucracy."[101] Others suggest that NSAs "arbitrated differences" between the ministries, sometimes through convening SPG meetings.[102]

Finally, the reforms introduced an NSC Secretariat, which would consolidate information and reports from the ministries. The NSC Secretariat produced monthly intelligence assessments, as well as long-term strategic analyses, which were submitted for inter-ministerial discussion in CCS and SPG meetings.[103] "Notes for the Approval of the CCS" originating from the ministries were first examined by the NSC Secretariat, whose views were relayed to the original ministry and the political leadership.[104] The NSC Secretariat introduced procedures "to encourage the intelligence community to work together more cooperatively and cohesively," such as a system for "annual tasking and evaluation of the agencies."[105] In contrast to typical "turf" battles between the ministries, the NSC Secretariat introduced "neutrality" into the decision-making process.[106] As Tanvi Madan notes, the NSC Secretariat had "the advantage of reflecting different perspectives and including information from various sources."[107]

Alternative Explanations for Institutional Design

What insight do alternative explanations offer into India's institutional evolution? International diffusion helps to explain the institutions that India inherited, but cannot explain the subsequent shifts toward fragmented and siloed institutions. Indian leaders retained elements of the British institutions, but discarded others.[108] For example, Defence Minister Menon called the Foreign Affairs Committee "an Indian invention."[109] In fact, Nehru held many Western institutions in contempt. Nehru commented, for example, that he did not "think much of the

---

[101] Dulat, *The Vajpayee Years*, 176.
[102] Madan, "Officialdom," 235; Pradhan, "National Security System – Evolution," 446.
[103] Satish Chandra, "National Security System and Reform," in *India's National Security Annual Review* (New Delhi: Knowledge World, 2005), 217, 223; Satish Chandra and Rahul Bhonsle, "National Security: Concept, Measurement and Management," *Strategic Analysis* 39, no. 4 (2015): 341.
[104] Pradhan, "National Security System – Evolution," 446.
[105] Chandra, "National Security System and Reform," 216.
[106] Ibid., 217. Interview with Satish Chandra, *Strategic News International*.
[107] Madan, "Officialdom," 235.
[108] Wilkinson, *Army and Nation*, 101.
[109] Brecher, *India and World Politics*, 250.

structure" of the British military and felt that the example of American intelligence organizations was "not an inspiring" one.[110]

International diffusion offers some insight into India's design choices in the 1990s. Prior to establishing the NSC, an Indian task force studied institutional models in countries ranging from the United States to Russia.[111] Nevertheless, India chose not to replicate the design of any single foreign system.[112] More importantly, these examples were observable decades before India chose to investigate them. In the end, India's political environment shaped the willingness of its leaders to explore foreign models.

Nehru's institutional design choices might also be attributed to his style of management. While Nehru may have been predisposed toward informal management, however, he was not opposed to planning or co-ordination generally.[113] Nehru's personal style was more pronounced in managing foreign, as opposed to domestic, policy-making.[114] In contrast to his management of national security affairs, Nehru actively tried to build institutional mechanisms for economic planning and coordination.[115] Moreover, leader style struggles to explain the persistence of siloed institutions across multiple leaders with different methods of management.

Finally, while path dependence cannot account for India's institutional changes, it may help to explain the persistence of CCS and NSC. Vajpayee's successors – Manmohan Singh and Narendra Modi – lacked his same level of prior experience managing the bureaucracy. Yet variation in leader experience may have continued to shape institutional design at the margins. For example, upon entering office, Prime Minister Singh reduced the NSA's rank in government, which may have undermined inter-ministerial coordination.[116] Four years into his tenure, however, Singh's NSA began chairing routinized meetings with SPG members twice per month, which proved "invaluable in improving coordination."[117] A similar trend may have occurred under Prime Minister Modi's government. Several years into his tenure, the SPG was "reconstituted" with NSA Ajit Doval as the chairman.[118]

[110] Gopal et al., *SWJN-SS*, Vol. 42, 488; Vol. 75, 507–508.
[111] Pradhan, "National Security System – Evolution," 438.
[112] B. Raman, "National Security Management," *Outlook*, May 20, 2004.
[113] K. Subrahmanyam, "Neville Maxwell's War," *Strategic Analysis* 37, no. 2 (2013): 279.
[114] Maxwell, *India's China War*, 89.
[115] Gopal, *Jawaharlal Nehru*, Vol. II, 96–99.
[116] Siddharth Varadarajan, "More Effective Externally than Internally," *The Hindu*. January 10, 2010; Siddharth Varadarajan, "It's Strategic Culture That Counts," *The Hindu*. January 22, 2010.
[117] Pradhan, "National Security System – Evolution," 446.
[118] "Strategic Policy Group Reconstituted, Ajit Doval Is Chairman," *The Hindu*. October 10, 2018.

India's Crisis Performance since 1947

How did India's national security institutions perform in crisis? We can first probe this question by examining India's pattern of crisis outcomes from 1947 to 2015.[119] As summarized in Table 6.2, India was party to four crises during its integrated period, but only failed to achieve it primary objective in one (25 percent). India performed much worse during its siloed and fragmented periods. It failed to achieve its primary goal in five of twelve (41 percent) crises under siloed institutions and three of four (75 percent) crises under fragmented institutions. The picture looks similar when we account for India's record of achieving secondary goals. On average, India achieved 81 percent of its goals during crises that occurred during its integrated period. In contrast, India on average achieved only 55 percent and 50 percent of its goals during crises under siloed and fragmented institutions, respectively. Moreover, whereas India only experienced one crisis failure during seventeen years under integrated institutions, it experienced a crisis failure once every eight and four years under siloed and fragmented institutions, respectively. While the small number of cases precludes any definitive judgments, patterns in India's performance is consistent with the theory's prediction that integrated institutions tend to perform better than fragmented ones, with the performance of siloed institutions falling between the other two.

Next, we can examine India's patterns of crisis decision-making from 1947 to 2015. Decision-making processes looked markedly different during each institutional period. India utilized the DCC, along with the supplemental Emergency Committee of the Cabinet, during its first three crises under integrated institutions: the First Indo–Pakistani War and the crises over Junagadh and Hyderabad.[120] After shifting to a fragmented design, Indian decision-making instead followed ad hoc procedures during 1961 Goa crisis as well as the 1959 and 1962 border conflicts with China.[121] In contrast, inclusive decision-making bodies, such as the ECC, PAC, and CCS played an important role during crises during which India possessed siloed institutions, such as the wars with India

---

[119] In addition to international crises listed in the ICB dataset, the sample includes the 1950 Bengal Crisis, the 1984 Siachen Glacier Crisis, and 2008 Mumbai Attacks. It also treats the 2001–2002 Twin Peaks Crisis as a single case, rather than two (as in the original ICB dataset). On 1950 and 1984, see Raghavan, *War and Peace in Modern India*, 148–187; Feroz Hassan Khan, Peter B. Lavoy, and Christopher Clary, "Pakistan's Motivations and Calculations for the Kargil Conflict," in *Asymmetric Warfare in South Asia*, ed. Peter R. Lavoy (Cambridge: Cambridge University Press, 2009), 54–55. On the Twin Peaks Crisis, see Alex Stolar, *To the Brink: Indian Decision-Making and the 2001–2002 Standoff* (Washington, DC: Henry L. Stimson Center, 2008). On the Mumbai attacks, see Narang, *Nuclear Strategy in the Modern Era*, 279–282.

[120] See Raghavan, *War and Peace in Modern India*, 26–148.

[121] On decision-making during Goa, see Brecher, *India and World Politics*, 121–124.

Table 6.2 *India's crisis performance, 1947–2015*

Crisis	Year	Institution	Primary goal	Successful?
Junagadh	1947	Siloed	Gain control of Junagadh	✓
First Indo-Pakistani War	1947	Siloed	Seize key territory within Kashmir	✓
Hyderabad	1948	Siloed	Gain control of Hyderabad	✓
Bengal Crisis	1950	Siloed	Compel Pakistan to sign pact on minority rights	✓
Punjab War Scare	1951	Fragmented	Improve claims in Kashmir	✗
Sino-Indian border crisis	1959	Fragmented	Secure negotiated settlement with China	✗
Goa Crisis	1961	Fragmented	Compel Portuguese withdrawal from Goa	✓
Sino-Indian War	1962	Fragmented	Compel Chinese withdrawal from contested territory	✗
Rann of Kutch	1965	Siloed	Seize contested territory in the Rann of Kutch	✗
Second Indo-Pakistani War	1965	Siloed	Defend Indian-controlled territory in Kashmir	✓
Third Indo-Pakistani War	1971	Siloed	End mass violence in Bangladesh	✓
Siachen Glacier	1984	Siloed	Seize control of Siachen Glacier	✓
Brasstacks Crisis	1987	Siloed	Compel Pakistan to withdrawal support for Sikh insurgency	✗
Sri Lanka Intervention	1987	Siloed	Compel insurgent disarmament	✗
Compound Crisis	1990	Siloed	End Pakistan facilitation of Kashmir insurgency	✗
Nuclear tests	1998	Siloed	Improve Indian power and international reputation	✗
Kargil War	1999	Integrated	Compel Pakistan to withdraw from Indian-administered Kashmir	✓
Twin Peaks Crisis	2001	Integrated	Compel reduction in Pakistani support for cross-border terrorism	✓
Mumbai attacks	2008	Integrated	Prevent military conflict with Pakistan	✓
India–Pakistan border crisis	2014	Integrated	Deter Pakistani support for cross-border terrorism	✗

in 1965 and 1971, Operation Brasstacks, the military intervention in Sri Lanka, the Kargil War, as well as the Parliament and Kaluchak attacks.[122]

We can further probe the connection between India's institutions and the risk of miscalculation through tracing its decision-making during the 1962 Sino-Indian War and the 2001–2002 Twin Peaks Crisis. Table 6.3 summarizes the key details of each case. While both cases are primarily selected to illustrate the theory's mechanisms, these episodes are especially illuminating for several reasons. The Sino-Indian War represents India's worst conflict outcome since its independence, making it substantively interesting case. In addition, the war is a puzzling case for accountability theory. Despite its democratic institutions, India nevertheless miscalculated.

Out of all of India's crises during its integrated period, the Twin Peaks Crisis is particularly helpful to consider, as terrorist attacks on Parliament might easily have motivated retaliatory military action, regardless of the prospects for advancing India's objectives beyond the status quo. As the case shows, Indian decision-makers seriously contemplated responding to the terrorist attacks with military force. In contrast, Pakistan's seizure of disputed territory in Kashmir during the 1999 Kargil War severely constrained the strategic responses that Indian decision-makers considered. Similarly, the limited severity of border tensions in 2014 meant that Indian leaders would have been unlikely to use force given the stakes of the issue.

The Sino-Indian War

The Sino-Indian War began on October 21, 1962, when Chinese forces launched a major assault on Indian positions in two regions along the

---

[122] On the 1965 Indo-Pakistani War, see R. D. Pradhan, *1965 War The Inside Story: Defence Minister Y.B. Chavan's Diary of the India-Pakistan War* (New Delhi: Atlantic, 2007); Farooq Bajwa, *From Kutch to Tashkent: The Indo-Pakistan War of 1965* (London: Hurst Publishers, 2013). On the 1971 Indo–Pakistan War, see Srinath Raghavan, *1971: A Global History of the Creation of Bangladesh* (New Delhi: Permanent Black, 2013); Richard Sisson and Leo E. Rose, *War and Secession: Pakistan, India, and the Creation of Bangladesh* (Berkeley: University of California Press, 1990). On the intervention in Sri Lanka, see V. P. Malik, *India's Military Conflicts and Diplomacy: An Inside View of Decision Making* (Noida: HarperCollins, 2013), Chapter 1; J. N. Dixit, *Assignment Colombo* (Delhi: Konark Publishers, 1998). On Operation Brasstacks, see Kanti Bajpai, *Brasstacks and Beyond: Perception and Management of Crisis in South Asia* (New Delhi: Manohar, 1995); P. R. Chari, Pervaiz Iqbal Cheema, and Stephen P. Cohen, *Four Crises and a Peace Process: American Engagement in South Asia* (Washington, DC: Brookings Institution Press, 2009), 39–79. On the 1990 Compound Crisis, see Chari, Cheema, and Cohen, *Four Crises and a Peace Process*, 80–117. On Kargil, see V. P. Malik, *Kargil: From Surprise to Victory* (Noida: HarperCollins, 2006). There is insufficient evidence available on the 2014 India-Pakistan Border Crisis to assess the decision-making process.

Table 6.3 *Summary of the Sino-Indian War and Twin Peaks Crisis*

Crisis (institution)	Pathway: Information provision	Observable implications: Leader projections	Outcome	Miscalculation
Sino-Indian War (fragmented)	*Low-quality*: limited information search in/outside the DCC; some evidence of self-censorship by defense and intelligence advisers	Minimal PRC response to forward outposts; Forward Policy will improve India's bargaining leverage against PRC	PRC destroys Indian forward positions; no change to PRC bargaining position on border dispute	Yes
Twin Peaks Crisis (integrated)	*High-quality*: extensive information search in the CCS; competitive dialogue between MEA, R&AW, and MoD	Coercive diplomacy will mobilize United States and Pakistan to address terrorism; high costs to Indian escalation	U.S. applies pressure to Pakistan; two public Pakistani commitments to curb terrorism; Pakistan temporarily reduces support for cross-border terrorist activity	No

border. The first was the region of Ladakh, situated in northern India between Jammu and Kashmir province to the west and China to the east. The second was the North-East Frontier Agency (NEFA), now the Indian province of Arunachal Pradesh, located in eastern India between the modern provinces of Assam and Nagaland to the south and China to the north.[123]

The roots of the conflict lay in a failure by China and India to reach a negotiated settlement to their territorial disputes. Both India and China claimed parts of Ladakh and NEFA, as well as parts of the border west

---

[123] The overview of the territorial dispute discussed in this paragraph is based on Raghavan, *War and Peace in Modern India*, 227–233. See also Fravel, *Strong Borders, Secure Nation*, 174–197; Mastro, *The Costs of Conversation*, 63–64.

of Himachal Pradesh and Uttaranchal. While these regions had been disputed since India gained its independence and the Chinese Communist Party rose to power, India and China kept these disputes off the negotiating table through most of the 1950s. After border clashes at Longju and Kongka Pass in 1959 and failed diplomatic talks between Nehru and Chinese Premier Zhou Enlai in April 1960, both India and China attempted to bolster their territorial claims by constructing roads and opening checkposts in disputed border areas.[124]

China's efforts to occupy territory, however, were more successful than India's. By 1961, the situation along the border had changed in China's favor in at least two major ways. First, China had deployed a full division in Ladakh, which tripled the number of forces in the area. These forces were generally positioned within about 25 kilometers of China's claim line, running between Dehra La, Kongka La, Khurnak Fort, and Spanggur. In comparison, India possessed only one brigade, two-thirds of which was made up of militia forces and lacked artillery or mortar support. Indian forces were positioned between Murgo, Tsogstsalu, Phobrang, Chushul, and Demcok. This meant that, by 1961, India's forces were positioned over a hundred kilometers west of its claim line – and Chinese forces stood in between.[125] Second, the Chinese position enjoyed strong supply lines. In 1957, China completed a major highway, which ran through Aksai Chin and connected deployed Chinese forces to logistical support in Xinjiang and Tibet.[126] Between 1959 and 1961, China also finished seven new outposts in Ladakh and twenty-five new outposts in NEFA, which were supported by new roads in both areas.[127] By October 1961, China had established a total of sixty-one new posts.[128] China also had the advantage geographically, as most of China's supply lines in the Aksai Chin ran over flat terrain, whereas India's positions were mostly in mountainous areas that could only be supplied by air drops.

By the end of 1961, India had three general options for addressing its border disputes with China. One option was to seek out diplomatic negotiations. Chinese Premier Zhou Enlai had offered a proposal that called for India to cede territory in Ladakh in exchange for Chinese recognition

---

[124] Raghavan, *War and Peace in Modern India*, 252–273.
[125] T. B. Henderson Brooks and Premindra Singh Bhagat, *Operations Review of the Sino-Indian War of 1962* (New Delhi: Ministry of Defence), 5–7.
[126] Raghavan, *War and Peace in Modern India*, 245–246.
[127] B. N. Mullik, *My Years with Nehru: The Chinese Betrayal* (New Delhi: Allied Publishers, 1971), 313.
[128] Sinha and Athale, *History of the Conflict with China*, 60–61.

of India's claims in NEFA.[129] Chinese representatives also told Indian Foreign Secretary Desai at Geneva in March 1962 that China would be willing to relinquish its claim on NEFA and part of Ladakh, so long as India would relinquish its claim on the Aksai Chin. Similarly, Chinese diplomats in New Delhi affirmed that it would be open to joint use of the Aksai Chin road, demarcation of the Ladakh border by joint commission, and recognition of the McMahon Line.[130] Negotiated settlement would have almost certainly have been difficult to pursue because of domestic opposition, but Nehru nevertheless suggested that he was "agreeable" to compromise in the Aksai Chin "as part of a satisfactory overall settlement."[131] Defence Minister Menon later commented that India "could have considered some adjustments."[132] Nehru himself noted on September 12, 1959 that the border between India and other countries was "a matter for argument."[133] As late as June 1962, Nehru noted that Indian leaders not only "would like a settlement" but also believed that "the mood of the Chinese was in favour" a peaceful resolution as well.[134]

A second option was to maintain the status quo along the border, diplomatically contest China's claims on Aksai Chin, and strengthen its military position in areas it could defend. The overall size of the Indian military would have needed to expand in order to increase the number of troops in Ladakh and NEFA without degrading India's western defense against Pakistan. India would have also needed to expand its defense budget, which had been tightly restricted to fund economic development, in order to sustain the new forces along its border with China. In addition, because India's defense industry was still developing, it would have needed foreign assistance to obtain military platforms, such as cargo airplanes and helicopters, in order to improve its logistical capacity for its outposts along the border. The United States would likely have supported military aid, particularly dual-use military platforms such as the ones that the Indian military needed to improve its logistical capacity.[135]

---

[129] Transcripts of the Zhou-Nehru talks are available in Avtar Singh Bhasin, ed., *India-China Relations, 1947–2000: A Documentary Study* (New Delhi: Ministry of External Affairs, 2018), Vol. 3, 3139–3300.
[130] Central Intelligence Agency, *The Sino-Indian Border Dispute: Section III, 1961–62*, POLO XVI, 1964, 24–25.
[131] Raghavan, *War and Peace in Modern India*, 240.
[132] Brecher, *India and World Politics*, 141.
[133] Hoffmann, *India and the China Crisis*, 73.
[134] Gopal et al., *SWJN-SS*, Vol. 77, 646. Indian diplomats were similarly hopeful for a peaceful settlement. See "R.K. Nehru to T.N. Kaul," May 16, 1962. Bhasin, *India-China Relations, 1947–2000*, Vol. IV, 3683.
[135] Tanvi Madan, *Fateful Triangle: How China Shaped US-India Relations during the Cold War* (Washington, DC: Brookings Institution Press, 2020), 139–142.

A third option – and the option that Nehru ultimately chose in November 1961 – was to deploy Indian forces east of China's claim line to establish new checkposts, some of which extended behind China's own positions. This strategy, later termed the "Forward Policy," had three primary objectives.[136] The first was to curtail further Chinese expansion into Ladakh, thereby preventing "the Chinese from advancing further" along the border.[137] As one Indian diplomat recalls, "it was necessary to see that our forces [...] also moved forward and established small out-posts in areas which the Chinese had not claimed."[138] Second, the Forward Policy sought to compel Chinese forces to withdraw from their positions by "dominating from any posts which [Chinese forces] may have already established in [Indian] territory."[139] Third, the policy aimed to improve India's bargaining leverage, presumably in order to force the Chinese to cede at least some of the territory it had occupied in the Aksai Chin.[140]

The Logic of Nehru's Decision. Nehru's decision to adopt the Forward Policy was rooted in three assessments suggesting that the strategy would improve India's bargaining position. As Nehru summarized, "We will continue to build these [forward outposts] up so that ultimately we may be in a position to take effective action to recover such territory as is in their possession."[141] First, Nehru believed that China's capability to project military power was limited. The Sino–Soviet split, along with the economic devastation inflicted by the Great Leap Forward, meant that Beijing was not able to defend its territorial claims.[142] As such, Nehru suggested that China would be unable to project power into India and, overall, the situation over this time was "changing, from a military point of view and from other points of view, *in our favour*."

The second assessment pertained to the strength of the Indian position. Nehru believed that India possessed adequate military capabilities vis-à-vis China to support the Forward Policy without increasing defense budgets or requesting foreign assistance.[143] Nehru believed he was well-positioned to pursue policies that put India "in a position to take action

---

[136] Maxwell, *India's China War*, 192–193.
[137] Henderson Brooks and Bhagat, *Operations Review of the Sino-Indian War*, 8.
[138] N. B. Menon, "The Integrity of Frontiers as a Function of State Power," in *The State Against People: A Discussion on Authoritarianism and Militarization in India* (Bangalore: ECC, 1982), 48.
[139] Henderson Brooks and Bhagat, *Operations Review of the Sino-Indian War*, 8–9.
[140] Hoffmann, *India and the China Crisis*, 121.
[141] *The Sino-Indian Border Dispute*, 19; Gopal, *Jawaharlal Nehru*, Vol. 3, 209.
[142] Kaul, *The Untold Story*, 339; Mullik, *The Chinese Betrayal*, 302–303.
[143] Hoffmann, *India and the China Crisis*, 113, 120.

to recover such territory as is in their possession."¹⁴⁴ If China was sufficiently weak, India would not need to make drastic or immediate changes to its defense budget or international arms imports. Thus, Indian defense expenditures remained low until the outbreak of war in 1962.¹⁴⁵ In short, Nehru wanted to secure the border by gradually building up "supplies and resources" on the cheap.¹⁴⁶ Nothing was urgent.¹⁴⁷

The third assessment concerned China's probable response to the Forward Policy. Nehru believed that a Chinese invasion was "exceedingly unlikely" because it would "undoubtedly lead to a world war."¹⁴⁸ Conflict with the Chinese would "inevitably contain the risk of great power intervention" and "any major Chinese aggression would trigger a wider war, which would not be fought on India's frontiers alone."¹⁴⁹ Even in 1962, Nehru believed that "it is no small matter to have a war between two of the biggest countries in Asia."¹⁵⁰ Nehru thus concluded that "the Chinese are unlikely to invade India because they know that this would start a world war, which the Chinese cannot want."¹⁵¹ As such, Nehru concluded that Beijing was not prepared to fight and that India should not put too much emphasis on "the brave words" in Chinese diplomatic communications.¹⁵²

India's Outcome. Nehru's projections regarding the Forward Policy proved to be inaccurate. Rather than improve India's bargaining position, it precipitated the Sino-Indian War, which ended in a decisive defeat. In just over a month of fighting, China overran the checkposts that India had established east of China's claim line. In the process, India achieved few of its objectives. China continued to enhance its fortifications along the border in the following decades. China's bargaining offers for settling the underlying territorial disputes did not shift in India's favor as a result of the Forward Policy. On the contrary, the battlefield defeat exacted a reputational toll, particularly in Pakistan's understanding of Indian military power. Pakistan's foreign minister described India as a "defeated nation" shortly after the war.¹⁵³

---

¹⁴⁴ Gopal et al., *SWJN-SS*, Vol. 72, 649.
¹⁴⁵ Ibid., Vol. 53, 489.
¹⁴⁶ Gopal et al., *SWJN-SS*, Vol. 59, 355.
¹⁴⁷ Kaul, *The Untold Story*, 339.
¹⁴⁸ Gopal et al., *SWJN-SS*, Vol. 15 (Part 2), 344.
¹⁴⁹ Sinha and Athale, *History of the Conflict with China*, 279.
¹⁵⁰ Gopal et al., *SWJN-SS*, Vol. 72, 649.
¹⁵¹ Raghavan, *War and Peace in Modern India*, 279.
¹⁵² Gopal, *Jawaharlal Nehru*, Vol. 3, 209.
¹⁵³ Y. D. Gundevia, *Outside the Archives* (New Delhi: Sangam Books, 1984), 246.

The outcome of the war forced India to adopt a course quite similar to the second option available to it before the fighting. By the war's end, India accepted *de facto*, though not *de jure*, Chinese control over the Aksai Chin in exchange for its control over NEFA.[154] India adopted a cautious and comparatively conciliatory attitude toward China. A policy summary placed before the ECC after the fighting argued that India should "do nothing to provoke" China, noting the need for caution in the coming years.[155] In addition, India dramatically increased its military expenditures after the war. In a meeting of the Ministry of Economic and Defence Coordination, senior Indian officers commented that "a high degree of military preparedness would be necessary for a long time to come" and that India would need to dramatically increase defense production by the end of 1963.[156] The Indian defense budget more than doubled.[157] Finally, despite previous beliefs that reliance on American or British military aid might have undermined its preferred policy of non-alignment during the Cold War, the crisis prompted Indian decision-makers to arrive precisely at that conclusion: "If [Chinese] military pressure is extensive, we will have to rely upon the USA and UK coming in heavily [...] to assist us."[158] By the fall, India was urgently requesting "military transportation and communications equipment" from the United States.[159]

Institutional Origins of Nehru's Miscalculation. Fragmented institutions help to explain Nehru's miscalculation. As predicted by the theory, information available at the time suggested major problems with the Forward Policy, but Nehru received incomplete and low-quality bureaucratic reporting that tended to filter out information that was inconsistent with his prior beliefs, particularly for individuals in the defense and intelligence bureaucracies. There were pockets of information within the Indian government which contradicted Nehru's conclusions about the balance of power and China's willingness to initiate a limited conflict with India. Yet fragmented institutions obstructed the flow of this information to the prime minister.

---

[154] Hoffmann, *India and the China Crisis*, 226.
[155] "Paper of the Emergency Committee of the Cabinet," n.d. T.T. Krishnamachari Papers, File 52, NMML.
[156] "Meeting Minutes, Ministry of Economic and Defence Coordination," November 30, 1962. T.T. Krishnamachari Papers, File 26, NMML.
[157] Hoffmann, *India and the China Crisis*, 228.
[158] "Paper of the Emergency Committee of the Cabinet," T.T. Krishnamachari Papers.
[159] "Memorandum from Brubeck to Bundy," October 15, 1962. *FRUS 1961–1963, Volume XIX, South Asia.*

India's fragmented institutions eased costs to relay information from India's diplomats while it increased costs to relay information from its military advisers. As the former Indian defence secretary notes, bodies that might have facilitated information flow, such as the DCC, did not play "any effective part in an objective determination of the danger which the county was exposed [...] and in the preparations to meet it."[160] Instead, preparations for negotiations with Zhou Enlai in early 1960, as well as development of the Forward Policy itself in early 1961, occurred in more restrictive meetings of the FAC.[161] These deliberations were held "very discreetly and were confined to Nehru, his senior cabinet colleagues, and some [diplomatic] officials."[162] Nehru even excluded Indian Defense Minister Krishna Menon from discussions in 1959.[163]

India's institutions channeled diplomatic information from the Foreign Ministry that supported optimistic assessments regarding the probable outcome and likely Chinese response to the Forward Policy.[164] First, India's diplomats believed that India's claims to the Aksai China were strong from the perspective of international law. After a lengthy briefing by the Foreign Ministry in February 1960, Nehru convened a meeting of the FAC. By the end of the meeting, Nehru stated that he was "persuaded" by his diplomats' assessment of the situation. Other cabinet members deferred to Nehru and the Foreign Ministry's analysis.[165] Nehru thus came to believe that a "political solution" could be achieved without concessions.[166]

Second, diplomatic officials assessed that "the Chinese would not engage in hostilities."[167] For example, the Indian foreign secretary noted that "one of the most effective methods" of curbing Chinese border encroachments would be to "given them an occasional knock" during chance encounters.[168] The MEA's principal China analyst, J. S. Mehta, concluded that while China had an "aggressive mood," Beijing was in no place to seriously threaten India.[169]

---

[160] Rao, *Defence without Drift*, 309. See also Dalvi, *Himalayan Blunder*, 69.
[161] "Dutt to Parathasarathy," March 27, 1960. Bhasin, *India-China Relations, 1947–2000*, Vol. IV, 3085; Hoffmann, *India and the China Crisis*, 84.
[162] Raghavan, *War and Peace in Modern India*, 263; Hoffmann, *India and the China Crisis*, 84.
[163] Hoffmann, *India and the China Crisis*, 46
[164] Ibid., 86.
[165] Maxwell, *India's China War*, 126; Hoffmann, *India and the China Crisis*, 83. Both accounts are based on interviews with S. Gopal, the MEA official who briefed Nehru.
[166] Hoffmann, 86. Hoffman's account is based on an interview with J. S. Mehta.
[167] Palit, *War in the High Himalaya*, 96. See also Hoffmann, *India and the China Crisis*, 95.
[168] Palit, *War in the High Himalaya*, 96.
[169] Hoffmann, *India and the China Crisis*, 61. Based on an interview with Mehta.

Yet India's fragmented institutions raised the costs of relaying defense information that suggested more pessimistic conclusions regarding China's likely response to the Forward Policy and the probable battlefield outcome in the event of escalation. By October 1961, China had a full division, equipped with mortars, recoilless weapons, semi-automatic rifles facing an under-strength and ill-equipped Indian brigade in Ladakh.[170] In the Daulat Beg Oldi and Chang Chenmo sectors, the local balance of forces by 1962 was approximately one Chinese regimental group to three Indian companies. India fared only slightly better in the Chushul sector, with a full battalion facing down a Chinese regimental group.[171] In total, China increased the number of battalions deployed along the border from twenty-seven to thirty-six between September 1961 and May 1962.[172] By September 1962, the Indian army assessed that China had deployed an additional six battalions over the summer and that approximately seven of the eight Chinese divisions stationed in Tibet had been dispatched to the border.[173]

Throughout the late 1950s and early 1960s, the military leadership assessed that India's capabilities lagged well behind China's. General K.S. Thimayya, the Indian Chief of Army Staff, could not "envisage taking on China in open conflict" given restrictions that the government had placed on India's defense budget.[174] In October 1960, the Army Headquarters issued a consolidated intelligence review describing that, in Ladakh, China's "ability to deploy against the various sectors had greatly increased."[175] In January 1961, the Indian military service chiefs released a similar assessment, detailing the Indian military's requirements along the border, noting that should a military conflict with China "go beyond that of a limited war," it would be "beyond the capacity of our forces to prosecute the work [...] beyond a short period, because of the limitation on size, the paucity of available equipment and the lack of adequate logistical support."[176]

Subordinate military commands held similar, if not even more pessimistic, views. Like the higher command, operational commanders were concerned about the unfavorable balance of forces along the border. In October 1960, the Indian Western Command convened a wargame, entitled Exercise Sheel, to assess the troop requirements to defend Indian border positions. The exercise concluded that at least one division would

---

[170] Sinha and Athale, *History of the Conflict with China*, 62.
[171] Henderson Brooks and Bhagat, *Operations Review of the Sino-Indian War*, 15.
[172] Sinha and Athale, *History of the Conflict with China*, 63.
[173] Ibid., 74.
[174] Palit, *War in the High Himalaya*, 80.
[175] Henderson Brooks and Bhagat, *Operations Review of the Sino-Indian War*, 6.
[176] Palit, *War in the High Himalaya*, 79–80.

be required to defend Ladakh. The outcome of the wargame was forwarded to the Army Headquarters and a formal request for additional forces was submitted in September 1961.[177] India's Eastern Commander warned that "with the troops, weapons, equipment and communications available at that time, it was difficult to contain or even delay any aggression by China."[178]

Operational commanders also raised concerns about the tactical advisability of the Forward Policy's plan to increase the number of Indian checkposts without increasing the number of forces to occupy them. Dispersing forces in the area into dozens of new "penny packets" of ten to twenty soldiers left each checkpost even more vulnerable to the numerical superiority of Chinese forces.[179] The Western Command assessed in August 1962 that "it is imperative that political direction is based on military means," as failure to do so would create a situation in which India might" lose both in the material and moral sense much more than" it already had. As such, until military strength could be built up, operational commanders recommended that the Forward Policy "should be held in abeyance."[180]

While India's defense establishment attempted to provide this information to Nehru, it was in a "very poor position to register its disquiet."[181] For example, the General Staff submitted threat estimates regarding increased Chinese troops deployments that never reached the prime minister.[182] In February 1961, a study group on border defense submitted a report that remained in the defence minister's secretariat until July 1963.[183] Later that year, the General Staff submitted another paper describing the logistical challenges associated with the Forward Policy that went unanswered.[184] Finally, between late 1961 and mid-1962, the military leadership submitted numerous reports on the "serious shortages in the Army," noting that "these disadvantages *vis-a-vis* our possible aggressors would not permit us to function in the event of war for long."[185] Military leaders requested that these matters be put before the DCC, but

---

[177] Henderson Brooks and Bhagat, *Operations Review of the Sino-Indian War*, 5.
[178] Chandra B. Khanduri, *Thimayya: An Amazing Life* (New Delhi: Knowledge World, 2006), 236.
[179] Henderson Brooks and Bhagat, *Operations Review of the Sino-Indian War*, 13–15; Sinha and Athale, *History of the Conflict with China*, 69–70.
[180] Henderson Brooks and Bhagat, *Operations Review of the Sino-Indian War*, 16.
[181] Maxwell, *India's China War*, 204; Hoffmann, *India and the China Crisis*, 125.
[182] Khanduri, *Thimayya*, 251.
[183] Sinha and Athale, *History of the Conflict with China*, 414.
[184] Palit, *War in the High Himalaya*, 99.
[185] Kaul, *The Untold Story*, 328. Maxwell obtained at least one of these letters. See Maxwell, *India's China War*, 521, note 30. See also Tharpar's letter from the Defence Ministry's Official Records, cited in Sinha and Athale, *History of the Conflict with China*, 82, note 90.

they were not.[186] Without access to these studies, the political leadership severely underestimated India's logistical constraints and, by extension, the probable outcome and costs of a military conflict with China.

Fragmented institutions degraded the quality of information provision as well. Nehru's confidence that China would not escalate tensions in reaction to the Forward Policy was bolstered by analysis from the top of India's intelligence wing. The Intelligence Bureau's (IB) assessment from September 1961 projected that Chinese forces were likely to "come right up to" their claim line in all areas in which India had not established checkposts. It noted, however, that in the past Chinese forces had "kept away" from border areas in which India had "even a dozen men" to protect it. The assessment went on to recommend that the Indian military should establish a series of forward checkposts along the border.[187] If the DIB's assessment was right, the Forward Policy posed minimal risk because China was unlikely to attack the (outnumbered) penny packets of Indian soldiers. This assessment became the "article of faith" on which the Forward Policy was launched.[188]

Yet the DIB made this assessment unilaterally rather than through a deliberative process with other bureaucracies.[189] As one diplomat remembers, there was "little institutional coordination" and no "integrated strategic assessment" provided to the prime minister.[190] The unilateral nature of the IB's assessment was significant because many within India's defense establishment disagreed with the conclusion that Chinese forces would not escalate if India adopted the Forward Policy. The military's annual intelligence review of 1959–1960 "clearly indicated that the Chinese would resist by force any attempt to take back territory held by them."[191] In February 1960, the General Staff warned of "an armed invasion with superior forces" by China.[192] Months later, Chief of General Staff L.P. Sen cautioned that if Indian patrols and checkpost construction intensified in disputed areas, China "might react sharply."[193] In the fall of 1961, the Director of Military Operations was similarly skeptical

---

[186] Kaul, *The Untold Story*, 327–333.
[187] Palit, *War in the High Himalaya*, 97–98.
[188] Raghavan, *War and Peace in Modern India*, 274; Gopal, *Jawaharlal Nehru*, Vol. III, 208.
[189] Raghavan, *War and Peace in Modern India*, 283.
[190] Dixit, *My South Block Years*, 426.
[191] Henderson Brooks and Bhagat, *Operations Review of the Sino-Indian War*, 8. This may have been a departure from a previous military intelligence assessment in September 1959 that concluded a "major incursion" by China was unlikely. Yet this assumed "the present state of development," rather than a significant change in Indian strategy like the Forward Policy. Sinha and Athale, *History of the Conflict with China*, 65.
[192] Palit, *War in the High Himalaya*, 94.
[193] D. R. Mankekar, *The Guilty Men of 1962* (Bombay: Tulsi Shah Enterprises, 1968), 143–144.

of a Forward Policy on grounds that Chinese forces had recently "acted more aggressively than ever before."[194] Others suggested that the "only safe course" was to temporarily endure Chinese positions already in place and "to consolidate the areas still in Indian possession by pushing roads forward, building up strong bases and inducting a division of troops into Ladakh to match the Chinese strength."[195]

Some senior military officers had hoped to utilize the JIC to draft a joint assessment that incorporated information from the military, diplomatic, and intelligence bureaucracies. The Director of Military Operations recalls that if "formal intelligence procedures had been operative" at the time, he would have asked the JIC for a "fresh examination" of China's patterns of behavior. As noted earlier, however, the JIC had "ceased functioning" and was structurally ill-equipped to facilitate proper intelligence assessment.[196] The JIC did not meet once in the period between India's escalation of its Forward Policy in the fall of 1961 and the outbreak of war in 1962.[197] As such, it failed to judge how key events, such as the Sino–Soviet split, the Great Leap Forward, the 1962 Taiwan Strait Crisis, or morale in the Chinese military, might affect China's ability to launch retaliatory military operations.[198] As Director of the Intelligence Bureau (DIB) B. N. Mullik summarized, there was simply "no independent JIC which could weigh impartially the evidence available."[199] Outside observers later found that the Indian intelligence system was "wholly unprepared to develop sound national intelligence estimates" concerning the possibility of a Chinese attack.[200]

Fragmented institutions dissuaded dissent as well. Once the DIB's assessment was issued, the senior military leadership deferred.[201] The military leadership did not produce a new assessment of its own.[202] The Director of Military Operations suggested that the military staff might "dispel some of the illusions that civilians in the MEA and IB appeared to harbour about [India's] operational capability" by providing them a detailed briefing, but Chief of General Staff B.M. Kaul suggested that such briefings would be "presumptuous and therefore counterproductive."[203]

---

[194] Palit, *War in the High Himalaya*, 96.
[195] Sinha and Athale, *History of the Conflict with China*, xxiii.
[196] Palit, *War in the High Himalaya*, 176.
[197] Ibid., 231.
[198] Ibid., 109–110.
[199] Mullik, *The Chinese Betrayal*, 305.
[200] See "Report to the Joint Chiefs of Staff on Indian Military Situation," December 3, 1962, Enclosure I, NSF, Box 111, JFKL.
[201] Palit, *War in the High Himalaya*, 105–106.
[202] Henderson Brooks and Bhagat, *Operations Review of the Sino-Indian War*, 30–32.
[203] Palit, *War in the High Himalaya*, 103.

What did the senior military leadership believe at the time? Some evidence suggests that Chief of General Staff Kaul felt that Indian positions were secure.[204] On September 5, 1962, the General Staff conveyed assurances that large-scale hostilities were unlikely.[205] Nevertheless, the top brass appears to have been more pessimistic in private. Chief of Army Staff Tharpar worried about a Chinese attack in the summer of 1962.[206] Chief of General Staff Kaul was sufficiently concerned about the prospects for a Chinese attack that he bluntly asked one American envoy if India could expect aid in the event of an "armed invasion" and requested secret meetings to discuss India's military plans.[207] Kaul also later claimed that he was "convinced by the end of 1961 that the Chinese might well have a confrontation" with India.[208]

Fragmented institutions offer one explanation for the military's deference despite these private apprehensions. For one, there were systematic impediments to the military's information access. Between July 1954 and July 1961, India and China had exchanged numerous diplomatic notes protesting alleged border violations. From mid-1961 onward, Beijing's notes featured increasingly severe language, describing that China "would not stand idly by" and that "serious" or "grave" consequences would result if China's demands were not met. By April 1962, a diplomatic message from the Ministry of Foreign Affairs delivered to the Indian embassy in Beijing noted that Chinese frontier guards would be "compelled to defend themselves."[209]

Yet there was no arrangement by which the DIB and MEA circulated cables coming from Beijing with the military staff. The JIC chairman, an MEA joint secretary, "seldom contributed information regarding diplomatic or international developments."[210] In fact, the first time the Director of Military Operations saw these diplomatic communications was reportedly on a chance visit to the Ministry of External Affairs in late February 1962. Whereas the Director of Military Operations complained that such information "clearly indicated possible Chinese military action [...] and was therefore of great interest" to the military staff, Chief

---

[204] Sinha and Athale, *History of the Conflict with China*, 82, note 59.
[205] Henderson Brooks and Bhagat, *Operations Review of the Sino-Indian War*, 17.
[206] Sinha and Athale, *History of the Conflict with China*, 416.
[207] Kaul, *The Untold Story*, 341; "Telegram from the Embassy in Pakistan to the Department of State," March 3, 1962. *FRUS 1961–1963, Volume XIX*.
[208] B.M. Kaul Oral History Transcript (hereafter OHT), 148–149, NMML. This account should be viewed with some skepticism, as Kaul may have been misrepresenting his beliefs at the time.
[209] *White Paper No. VI: Notes, Memoranda and Letters Exchanged and Agreements Signed between the Governments of India and China, November 1961–July 1962* (New Delhi: Ministry of External Affairs, 1962), 39.
[210] Palit, *War in the High Himalaya*, 85.

of General Staff Kaul suggested that it pertained to "political matters" outside of the military's bailiwick.[211] The compartmentalization of information did not simply affect the quality of the military's assessments. The MEA's China division was similarly aware of changes in Chinese diplomatic rhetoric, but believed that it should be the IB – or the military – that should evaluate the matter. Because Indian diplomats lacked details regarding operational military matters, however, they "could not readily see how the Chinese were reacting to Indian actions" along the border.[212]

The military's restricted information access undermined its ability to effectively advise Nehru, who repeatedly noted that Indian generals lacked all the information.[213] On two occasions, senior military leaders sought an informal audience to relay concerns about the Chinese threat. In 1959, Chief of Army Staff Thimayya criticized "the apathetic attitude" of India's defence minister in response to China.[214] In a one-on-one meeting with Nehru in November 1961, Kaul argued that because "the Armed Forces had not been strengthened" it was presently "*not* in a position to deal with the Chinese effectively."[215] Yet the information that Thimayya and Kaul provided bore little fruit.[216] Nehru dismissed the military's appeals, replying that its generals "did not quite understand the situation."[217] After all, a fragmented system meant that Indian military leaders lacked key information that Nehru possessed.

These institutional patterns affected the advice that others were prepared to offer. For example, most of the deliberation before the Forward Policy was adopted occurred in extended, one-on-one briefings between Nehru and DIB Mullik. When Nehru convened a meeting with the rest of his advisers, Director of Military Operations Palit inferred that Nehru

---

[211] Palit, *War in the High Himalaya*, 162.
[212] Hoffmann, *India and the China Crisis*, 244.
[213] Ibid., 98.
[214] "Thimayya-Nehru Correspondence," n.d., Thimayya Papers, NMML; Khanduri, *Thimayya*, 251.
[215] Kaul, *The Untold Story*, 279.
[216] Nehru described Thimayya's complaints as "trivial." See "Thimayya-Nehru Correspondence." In fact, Nehru's reaction had less to do with addressing the substance of Thimayya's concerns and more to do with critiquing his method of circumventing the defence minister. Thimayya had bypassed the India's institutional arrangement, which was designed to prevent these types of encounters from occurring. In response, Thimayya submitted a letter of resignation on August 31, 1959, in which he stated that it was impossible "for me and the other two Chiefs of Staff to carry out our responsibilities under the present Defence Minister." Nehru persuaded Thimayya to withdraw his resignation, but then publicly sided with Menon and questioned the appropriateness of senior military officers resigning in protest. The event likely signaled not only that Nehru was uninterested in the military's input on China policy, but also that political repercussions might follow if Nehru's generals argued their case too forcefully.
[217] Kaul, *The Untold Story*, 321.

had "already made up his mind about what steps needed to be taken."[218] It is unsurprising, then, that the military leaders present in the meeting did not argue their point forcefully.[219]

Institutional constraints affected the IB's information and assessments as well. When it came to international politics, it was Nehru who briefed the Indian intelligence community.[220] Nehru's position as his own foreign minister afforded an informational advantage over the DIB, whose intelligence collection Nehru had curtailed. In his memoirs, Mullik recalled that he would "drink deep" from the prime minister during their meetings, comparing Nehru to a "sage" who was explaining "the Truth" to his disciple.[221] As such, the IB sought out "areas of agreement" with Nehru, refusing to "put the facts together in a confrontational way" by which Nehru's judgments or policies might be questioned.[222]

Fragmented institutions thus offer a potential insight into why the IB's assessment of the probability of a major Chinese invasion did not dramatically change over the course of 1962 as it received new information that contradicted its original assessment. The IB's judgment in September 1961 stipulated that a Chinese invasion was unlikely because Chinese forces had not been willing to attack Indian troop concentrations in the past. By the summer of 1962, however, China was doing exactly that. From May to June 1962, the IB received intelligence reports indicating that the Chinese government would "adopt a new line of action toward India," and now considered military action to be "essential" to resolving the situation.[223] While the IB's reports were forwarded to senior leadership, there was no inter-governmental analysis or discussion of these new signals from China.[224] Even if the IB's 1961 assessment had been a sound one, there was no institutional support to reevaluate the changing situation in the summer of 1962.

Alternative Explanations. Several alternative explanations for India's decision-making are worth examining. First, the interest group model of bureaucratic politics offers limited insight into India's miscalculation. The historical record is clear that the Foreign Policy was not imposed

---

[218] Palit, *War in the High Himalaya*, 106.
[219] Kaul, *The Untold Story*, 280; Palit, *War in the High Himalaya*, 105–106; Mullik, *The Chinese Betrayal*, 315–316.
[220] Mullik documents several of Nehru's briefings to the IB in 1960 and 1961. See Mullik, *The Chinese Betrayal*, 263, 302–303. Mullik's memoirs also suggest that Nehru was more interested in the IB's domestic intelligence reports than their reports on international affairs. See Mullik, *My Years with Nehru*, 64.
[221] Ibid., 65.
[222] Hoffmann, *India and the China Crisis*, 240.
[223] Mullik, *The Chinese Betrayal*, 329–330.
[224] Palit, *War in the High Himalaya*, 176.

upon Nehru but was rather chosen because he believed it to be the best option available. Moreover, numerous voices inside India's defense bureaucracy appear to have recommended against the operation. Yet the defense establishment operated in an institutional configuration that curtailed its access to Nehru and deterred it from presenting its case candidly. Instead, it was information provided by India's diplomats, which was not vigorously debated by India's defense or intelligence establishments, that informed Nehru's confidence in the strength of his position on diplomatic, rather than military, grounds.

We might instead posit that Nehru's decisions were the result of a lack of accountability, perhaps owing to the unique (and overwhelming) support he enjoyed as one of India's national founders. Yet Nehru was under considerable political pressure at the time he approved the Forward Policy – and this pressure proved an insufficient motivation for Nehru to improve the decision-making process.[225] Even after opposition leaders in parliament began condemning Nehru's foreign policy performance, Nehru's pattern of information search and deliberation did not change. In short, political accountability, in itself, was an insufficient condition to avoid miscalculation.

A third possible explanation is that Nehru was resistant to new information. Yet this cannot explain how diplomatic advisers, institutionally privileged within Nehru's advisory circle, were able to persuade the prime minister regarding the legal strength of India's claims in the Aksai Chin. A related proposition is that Nehru was, by disposition, naive when it came to defense affairs or averse to the use of military force.[226] Yet this would have made Nehru prone to seek out strategies other than military coercion.

A final alternative explanation, unique to this case, places blame for the miscalculation on the lack of experience and strategic judgment in the Indian military.[227] In some respects, this argument complements the logic of fragmented institutions. The expedited promotion of Indian officers to replace their British predecessors reflected Nehru's distrust of the military's leadership – and highlights another facet of the trade-off leaders face between appointing bureaucrats likely to provide the best advice and those who are sure to remain loyal. Moreover, in addition to their inexperience, the senior military leaders whose promotion Nehru expedited were operating under institutional constraints on their access to information. Senior officials recalled, for example, that the Director of

---

[225] Kennedy, *The International Ambitions of Mao and Nehru*, 235; Raghavan, *War and Peace in Modern India*, 253.
[226] Kennedy, *The International Ambitions of Mao and Nehru*, 202.
[227] Raghavan, *War and Peace in Modern India*, 272, 278.

Military Intelligence "was unable to make threat appreciations based on inside information."[228] After the 1962 Sino-Indian War broke out, both American and British military advisers noted deficiencies in the military's intelligence capacity.[229] In short, Indian military leaders may have been inexperienced, but they were also ill-informed.

The Twin Peaks Crisis

Tracing India's decision-making during its military standoff with Pakistan from December 2001 to June 2002 – often referred to as the Twin Peaks Crisis – helps to illustrate how integrated institutions led to more complete and accurate information provision than fragmented alternatives. The crisis was precipitated by a number of high-profile terrorist attacks on targets in India. On April 20, 2000, a Jaish-e-Mohammed (JeM) suicide bombing targeted Indian military barracks in Kashmir. In December 22, 2000, Lashkar-e-Taiba (LeT) militants fired on the Red Fort in New Delhi, killing two Indian soldiers and a civilian security guard. On October 1, 2001, JeM attacked the Jammu and Kashmir legislative assembly in Srinagar.[230] Between 1998 and 2001, the estimated number of insurgent fighters in Kashmir increased and Indian security force fatalities roughly doubled.[231] Finally, on December 13, 2001, a group of terrorists attacked the Indian Parliament building, in which hundreds parliamentarians were present. The Indian government concluded that the attack was planned by two Pakistan-based terrorist organizations, LeT and JeM. While Pakistan's government denied supporting these attacks, both LeT and JeM had close ties with Pakistan's intelligence service, the Inter-Services Intelligence (ISI).[232]

In the wake of the Parliament attack, India's decision-makers sought to persuade Pakistan to decrease support for cross-border terrorist attacks. As NSA Brajesh Mishra succinctly noted, the "goal was to curb terrorism emanating from Pakistan."[233] Foreign Minister Jaswant Singh

---

[228] Palit, *War in the High Himalaya*, 84.
[229] See "Minutes of the Military Affairs Committee Meeting," May 1, 1963, 12–13, Subject File 27, T.T. Krishnamachari Papers, NMML.
[230] Chari, Cheema, and Cohen, *Four Crises and a Peace Process*, 150.
[231] Praveen Swami, "The Roots of Crisis: Post-Kargil Conflict in Kashmir and the 2001–2002 Near-War," in *The India-Pakistan Military Standoff: Crisis and Escalation in South Asia*, ed. Zachary Davis (New York: Palgrave Macmillan, 2011), 30–33.
[232] Pakistan had provided covert aid to support the incipient insurrection in Kashmir. Pakistan helped to organize LeT during the mujaheddin insurgency in Afghanistan in the 1980s and most likely played a role in founding JeM in the early 2000s.
[233] Interview with Brajesh Mishra, quoted in S. Paul Kapur, "Ten Years of Instability in a Nuclear South Asia," *International Security* 33, no. 2 (2008): 82.

similarly described India's first objective as "to defeat cross-border infiltration/terrorism without conflict," adding that the political leadership also aimed to contain the "national mood" calling for the use of military force against Pakistan and to "destroy and degrade Pakistan's war fighting capabilities" in the event of war.[234] The Defence Ministry likewise stated that India sought to "thwart the active promotion of cross border terrorism and posturing by Pakistan."[235]

To that end, India considered three options in response to the terrorist attacks. The first was to launch limited military strikes across the Line of Control (LoC) in Kashmir.[236] Limited strikes would have attempted to degrade the capacity of the terrorist organizations operating in parts of Kashmir controlled by Pakistan and, perhaps, seize and hold disputed territory. The second option was a large-scale military invasion of Pakistan. By the summer of 2002, India had positioned three offensive "strike corps" along its border with Pakistan, which could attack from Rajasthan across the international border to destroy Pakistani military forces and seize territory in Sindh and Punjab provinces.[237]

The third option, and the one for which Indian Prime Minister Atal Bihari Vajpayee opted, was coercive diplomacy. India demanded that Pakistan curb LeT and JeM's operations and applied diplomatic pressure on the United States in support of those demands. India's ambassador in Washington "worked hard" to communicate the severity of India's concerns.[238] Simultaneously, India initiated its largest Indian military mobilization since 1971, entitled Operation Parakram ("Valor"), which threatened military force if Pakistan did not reduce support for cross-border terrorism.[239]

The Logic of Vajpayee's Decision. Why did Vajpayee ultimately choose coercive diplomacy over military action? The evidence available suggests that Vajpayee's decision was based on two considerations. First, Vajpayee seems to have believed that coercive diplomacy would yield significant progress. Indian decision-makers concluded that if India could appear

---

[234] Jaswant Singh, *In Service of Emergent India: A Call to Honor* (Bloomington: Indiana University Press, 2007), 229.
[235] Government of India, *Ministry of Defence Annual Report, 2002–2003*, 19.
[236] Chari, Cheema, and Cohen, *Four Crises and a Peace Process*, 154; Sumit Ganguly and Michael R. Kraig, "The 2001–2002 Indo-Pakistani Crisis: Exposing the Limits of Coercive Diplomacy," *Security Studies* 14, no. 2 (2005): 302.
[237] Stolar, *To the Brink*, 16; Kapur, "Ten Years of Instability in a Nuclear South Asia," 80–81; V. K. Sood and Pravin Sawhney, *Operation Parakram: The War Unfinished* (New Delhi: Sage Publications, 2003), 73–74.
[238] Interview with Lalit Mansingh, quoted in Stolar, *To the Brink*, 12.
[239] Kanwal, "Military Dimensions of the 2002 India-Pakistan Standoff," 68; Sood and Sawhney, *Operation Parakram*, 62.

willing to risk a conventional war, the United States would pressure Pakistan to make concessions on cross-border terrorism. Second, Vajpayee seems to have ultimately determined that limited military strikes would not substantially degrade terrorist capacity and thus not further India's goals. The political leadership, as one senior Indian diplomat recalls, was hesitant to pursue military action unless the desired objectives "were virtually guaranteed success."[240] On the contrary, as noted by senior Indian officials, Vajpayee "feared that a full-scale military response" to the terror attacks "could precipitate a wider conflagration" and was unwilling to accept the risk of nuclear escalation.[241] Thus, while Indian decision-makers seriously considered initiating military conflict early in the crisis, Vajpayee opted for coercive diplomacy.[242]

India's Outcome. The projections on which Vajpayee based his decision proved generally accurate. Although the outcome of the crisis remains debated, coercive diplomacy did yield results. India's strategy catalyzed the United States to apply pressure on Pakistan, which yielded assurances from leaders in Islamabad. In the wake of its mobilization, the American intelligence community believed the chance of an Indian strike was "high." Although State Department officials disagreed about the likelihood of an intentional Indian strike, they were nevertheless concerned about the possibility of inadvertent escalation. As Vajpayee later recalled, "America gave us the assurance that something will be done by Pakistan about cross-border terrorism."[243] U.S. President George W. Bush pressured Pakistani President Pervez Musharraf to blacklist certain terrorist organizations. Under the advice of U.S. policymakers, Musharraf subsequently delivered a speech announcing a ban on terrorist activities.[244] Consistent with Indian objectives, Musharraf stated that "no organization will be allowed to indulge in terrorism in the name of Kashmir."[245] Shortly thereafter, Pakistani officials briefed the United States that it had

---

[240] T. C. A. Raghavan, *The People Next Door: The Curious History of India's Relations with Pakistan* (London: Hurst, 2019), 259.
[241] Praveen Swami, "A War to End a War: The Causes and Outcomes of the 2001–2 India-Pakistan Crisis," in *Nuclear Proliferation in South Asia*, ed. Sumit Ganguly and S. Paul Kapur (New York: Routledge, 2009), 150.
[242] Narang, *Nuclear Strategy in the Modern Era*, 275.
[243] Interview with Vajpayee, quoted in Kapur, "Ten Years of Instability in a Nuclear South Asia," 82.
[244] Polly Nayak and Michael Krepon, "U.S. Crisis Management in South Asia's Twin Peaks Crisis," in *The India-Pakistan Military Standoff: Crisis and Escalation in South Asia*, ed. Zachary Davis (New York: Palgrave Macmillan, 2011), 154–156. Even scholars who are critical of India's decision-making process acknowledge that Musharraf's speech was a "diplomatic victory" for India. See Chari, Cheema, and Cohen, *Four Crises and a Peace Process*, 161–164.
[245] Raghavan, *The People Next Door*, 255.

jailed thousands of terrorist activists and closed hundreds of jihadi offices after Musharraf's address.[246]

Musharraf's address was critical to India's decision to "postpone any action across the border and the Line of Control."[247] The head of the National Security Advisory Board noted that the signal from Musharraf was "well received."[248] Vikram Sood, the head of R&AW at the time, corroborates this account.[249]

India secured a second set of assurances after a subsequent terrorist attack on an Indian Army garrison at Kaluchak on May 14, 2002. On May 22, Indian NSA Brajesh Mishra told his American counterpart, Condoleezza Rice, that India required a "guarantee" in order to de-escalate the crisis.[250] U.S. Secretary of State Colin Powell called for Pakistan to stop terrorist infiltration in Pakistan.[251] On May 27, Musharraf gave another address in which he stated that "Pakistan will never allow the export of terrorism anywhere in the world from within Pakistan."[252] In early June, U.S. Deputy Secretary of State Richard Armitage traveled first to Pakistan and then to India. Musharraf assured Armitage that "nothing is happening" across the Line of Control. Moreover, Armitage believed he elicited and confirmed Musharraf's assurance that this cessation would be permanent. Armitage then relayed Pakistan's message to the leadership in New Delhi on July 7.[253]

Terrorist activity in Kashmir appears to have declined immediately following the crisis. Musharraf reportedly directed Pakistani intelligence to relocate the main militant camps from Kashmir to western parts of Pakistan.[254] As illustrated in Figure 6.3, the number of terrorist incidents, as well as civilian and Indian security force fatalities, dropped between 2002 and 2005. Other sources suggest that terrorist infiltration fell by 53 percent between 2001 and 2002.[255]

---

[246] David Smith, "The 2001–2002 Standoff: A Real-Time View from Islamabad," in *The India-Pakistan Military Standoff: Crisis and Escalation in South Asia*, ed. Zachary Davis (New York: Palgrave Macmillan, 2011), 198.
[247] Interview with Brajesh Mishra, quoted in Stolar, *To the Brink*, 13.
[248] Interview with C. V. Ranganathan, quoted in Stolar, *To the Brink*, 18.
[249] Interview with V. K. Sood, quoted in Stolar, *To the Brink*, 19.
[250] Swami, "A War to End a War," 152.
[251] Nayak and Krepon, "U.S. Crisis Management in South Asia's Twin Peaks Crisis," 163–164.
[252] Stolar, *To the Brink*, 20–21.
[253] Nayak and Krepon, "U.S. Crisis Management in South Asia's Twin Peaks Crisis," 166–168.
[254] Smith, "The 2001–2002 Standoff," 205.
[255] R. K. Jasbir Singh, ed., *Indian Defence Yearbook* (Dehra Dun: Natraj Publishers, 2003), 56. See also comments of V.P. Malik, cited in Chari, Cheema, and Cohen, *Four Crises and a Peace Process*, 159. Chari et al. dispute these inferences but provide no data.

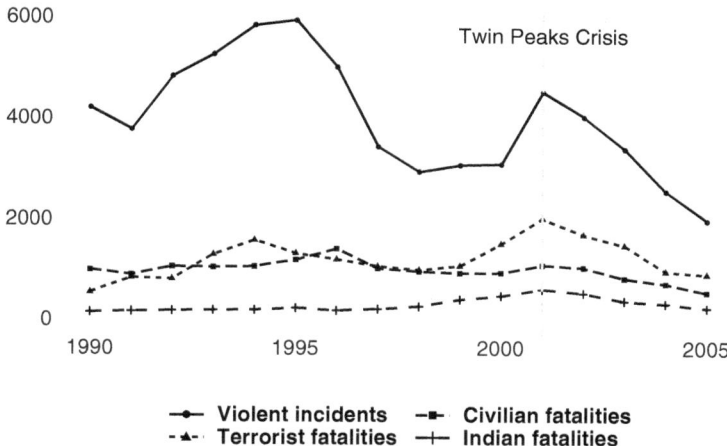

Figure 6.3 Terrorist violence in Jammu & Kashmir, 1990–2005
Source: Praveen Swami, "A War to End a War: The Causes and Outcomes of the 2001–2 India-Pakistan Crisis," in *Nuclear Proliferation in South Asia*, eds. Sumit Ganguly and S. Paul Kapur (New York: Routledge, 2009), 146.

Institutional Origins of Vajpayee's Decision. Integrated institutions help to explain Vajpayee's calculations during the standoff. Under integrated institutions, the theory predicts that leaders should be more likely to receive complete and high-quality information. In contrast to Indian decision-making during the Nehru era, integrated institutions provided a forum in which diplomatic, defense, and intelligence advisers relayed candid advice to the prime minister.[256] The information that Vajpayee's bureaucratic advisers supplied proved critical in shaping the prime minister's judgments.

During the decision-making process, the CCS provided a forum by which Vajpayee received quality information from diplomatic, defense, and intelligence bureaucracies. Vajpayee convened a series of meetings of the CCS to receive briefings and to deliberate India's strategy.[257] Available accounts suggest that Vajpayee's advisers presented different options over whether India should attack.[258] Diplomatic and intelligence advisers had routine access to the prime minister, but the political leadership also

---

[256] Rahul Bedi, "A Strike Staunched," *Frontline*, 19, no. 12, June 2002.
[257] Stolar, *To the Brink*, 13; Sood and Sawhney, *Operation Parakram*, 73.
[258] Srinath Raghavan, "A Coercive Triangle: India, Pakistan, the United States, and the Crisis of 2001–2002," *Defence Studies* 9, no. 2 (2009): 246–247.

"sought military advice on a regular basis."[259] As one military officer recalls, in contrast to "the early practice when the political leadership and the armed forces worked in splendid isolation from each other," there had been "a steady increase in the interaction" between the political and military leadership.[260]

Deliberations between diplomatic and defense advisers helped to identify weaknesses in each other's arguments. To illustrate the way in which the competitive dialogue between Indian diplomatic and defense advisers worked, it is helpful to break the decision-making process into two windows – that is, each of the "twin peaks" – in which Indian officials considered the use of military force. The first window was between the Parliament attacks on December 13, 2001 and Musharraf's address on January 12, 2002. During this time, CCS deliberations were critical in arriving at the conclusion that limited strikes were unlikely to be successful. Vajpayee's defense advisers argued that the targets of these strikes were rudimentary and mobile terrorist camps consisting of "drill squares and firing ranges" that could be easily relocated after a limited strike. Indian Chief of Army Staff Sundararajan Padmanabhan assessed that limited strikes would have been "totally futile."[261] In short, the Indian military questioned the utility of limited military strikes.

While Vajpayee's defense advisers cautioned against limited strikes, however, the information they provided suggested that a large-scale military operation might be successful. In the military's estimate, the only viable option was a "short and swift all-out war which would achieve worthwhile aims."[262] The military thus briefed the top political leadership, including Vajpayee, on the benefits of "proactive action" across the Line of Control to check infiltration.[263] Chief of Army Staff Padmanabhan believed that military gains could have been achieved in January, including "degradation of the other force, and perhaps the capture of disputed territory in Jammu and Kashmir."[264]

The counsel that Vajpayee's diplomatic advisers provided, however, identified the costs associated with the military's plans for large-scale action. Foreign Minister Jaswant Singh advised the CCS that a military strike might diplomatically backfire with the United States. Though reportedly in the minority, Singh made the case that "restraint" could

---

[259] Sood and Sawhney, *Operation Parakram*, 86.
[260] Kanwal, "Military Dimensions of the 2002 India-Pakistan Standoff," 70.
[261] Praveen Swami, "Gen. Padmanabhan Mulls over Lessons of Operation Parakram," *The Hindu*, February 6, 2004; Sumit Ganguly, *Deadly Impasse* (New York: Cambridge University Press, 2016), 68.
[262] Sood and Sawhney, *Operation Parakram*, 77.
[263] Ibid., 73.
[264] Swami, "Gen. Padmanabhan Mulls over Lessons of Operation Parakram."

be a "strategic asset."²⁶⁵ Singh assessed that India had just recently restored good relations with the United States after the 1998 nuclear test. A military strike could threaten India's leverage and, inadvertently, benefit Pakistan.²⁶⁶ The NSC Secretariat submitted a report that the international environment was "not favourable" for military action.²⁶⁷ The NSAB similarly concluded that international public opinion favored India and nothing "provocative" should be done.²⁶⁸

Moreover, there were several factors suggesting that alternative strategies, such as coercive diplomacy, might work.²⁶⁹ Indian diplomats knew, for example, that the United States played a central role in facilitating the ceasefire between India and Pakistan during the Kargil War in 1999. From India's perspective, the U.S. role illustrated how the United States might apply diplomatic pressure on Pakistan in ways that suited its interests. Senior Indian diplomats recall that American decision-makers' "interest in the India-Pakistan face-off was immense and obvious."²⁷⁰ In the wake of September 11th Al-Qaeda attacks, the United States had stronger incentives to stand against international terrorism.²⁷¹ Manipulation of U.S. interests could thus play "an integral component of India's coercive strategy."²⁷²

In short, the information that defense advisers provided identified the limited utility of limited military strikes, while the information that diplomatic advisers offered emphasized the costs that a large-scale military operation would impose in India. This left Vajpayee with the option he chose: coercive diplomacy. As NSA Mishra later summarized, "we debated, we talked, and we came to the conclusion that the threat of military action should be held up."²⁷³

The second window for military action came after the Kaluchak attack in May. The armed forces had remained mobilized since January and were prepared to execute an offensive operation. By the summer, however, Pakistani decision-makers had improved their defense by redeploying units from the 10, 11, and 12 Corps to their eastern border.²⁷⁴ The limited strikes that India had prepared in January no longer appeared feasible. Thus, from early January until June, the Indian armed forces searched for battlefield plans that would "regain the element of

---

²⁶⁵ Singh, *In Service of Emergent India*, 230.
²⁶⁶ Sood and Sawhney, *Operation Parakram*, 97–98.
²⁶⁷ Singh, *Indian Defence Yearbook*, 48.
²⁶⁸ Interview with C. V. Ranganathan, quoted in Stolar, *To the Brink*, 13.
²⁶⁹ There is presently insufficient evidence to know how these assessments were reached.
²⁷⁰ Raghavan, *The People Next Door*, 258.
²⁷¹ Raghavan, "A Coercive Triangle," 243–244.
²⁷² Ibid., 247.
²⁷³ Steve Coll, "The Stand-Off," *The New Yorker*, February 2006.
²⁷⁴ Kanwal, "Military Dimensions of the 2002 India-Pakistan Standoff," 69.

surprise."²⁷⁵ NSA Mishra later pointed out that it would have meant "all-out war."²⁷⁶

Again, the CCS provided a forum by which these plans were briefed to the prime minister. In particular, Vajpayee convened meetings of the CCS on May 18 and 20 in which various options, including military strikes, were discussed.²⁷⁷ As in January, advisers reportedly entered CCS meetings with differing perspectives, particularly between Mishra, Singh, and the military.²⁷⁸ Similarly, the NSC Secretariat felt it had "full freedom" to express their views even when they "went against" the government's policies.²⁷⁹

Several pieces of advice appear to have informed Vajpayee's judgments. First, Foreign Minister Singh continued to draw attention to the potential blowback that military operations would have on India's diplomatic leverage with the United States. Specifically, Singh assessed that "immediate retaliatory action" after the Kaluchak attacks would be "strategically faulty" because of the ongoing conflict in Afghanistan.²⁸⁰

Second, there was even more information available by the summer of 2002 indicating that coercive diplomacy was yielding results. Violent incidents in Kashmir were down 17 percent, attacks on Indian security personnel 20 percent, attacks on civilians 6 percent, and terrorist infiltration 51 percent.²⁸¹ Indian intelligence intercepted communications indicating that Pakistan had indeed instructed terrorist organizations to lie low.²⁸² As one senior intelligence official noted, terrorist activity had not "halted altogether," but it had "come down."²⁸³ Forward military commanders also reported a decrease in terrorist infiltration across the Line of Control after Musharraf's speech. For example, Lieutenant General Ved Patankar, commander of the 15 Corps in Kashmir, observed a "perceptible dip" in cross-border movement.²⁸⁴

---

[275] Sood and Sawhney, *Operation Parakram*, 80–81.
[276] Interview with Brajesh Mishra, quoted in Narang, *Nuclear Strategy in the Modern Era*, 278.
[277] Jay Raina, "Crucial CCS Meet on Saturday," *Hindustan Times*, May 18, 2002; "Pak Told to Recall Envoy – PM to Visit J&K," *Hindustan Times*, May 19, 2002; Saurabh Shukla, "India Puts Forces in Action Mode," *Hindustan Times*, May 20, 2002.
[278] Saurabh Shukla, "PMO, MEA Differ on How to Punish Pak," *Hindustan Times*, May 17, 2002.
[279] S. D. Pradhan, "Contribution of Brijesh Mishra in Strategic Affairs and Security Reforms," *Strategic Analysis* 37, no. 2 (2013): 163.
[280] Singh, *In Service of Emergent India*, 228.
[281] Author's analysis of data from Ganguly and Kraig, "The 2001–2002 Indo-Pakistani Crisis," 304.
[282] Sood and Sawhney, *Operation Parakram*, 99.
[283] Raymond Bonner, "India Believes Pakistan Restrains Militants," *The New York Times*, June 6, 2002.
[284] Interview with Ved Patankar, quoted in Stolar, *To the Brink*, 21.

Third, the deliberations suggested that the window for large-scale military action had closed. With Pakistan's military was "poised in its defences," one military staff member recalled, "it was possible that even a large-scale offensive action may have led only to a stalemate."[285] As Chief of Army Staff Padmanabhan noted, the objectives of such an operation were "more achievable in January, less achievable in February, and even less achievable in March."[286] Sources in Pakistan agreed that the "ground force ratios were insufficient to guarantee a quick Indian victory."[287] Thus, as a senior Indian military officers summarizes, a "major reason" that India did not go to war in 2002 was "the lack of decisive conventional superiority."[288] As such, as one well-placed Indian journalist suggests, Vajpayee eventually concluded that the Indian Army was "in no position to immediately deliver a decisive" victory and that small-scale military strikes, while possible, would not necessarily deliver "useful political outcomes."[289]

Alternative Explanations. What light do alternative explanations shed on India's decision-making during the Twin Peaks Crisis? First, the interest group model of bureaucratic politics offers comparatively little insight. Vajpayee's decisions were ultimately his own, overruling hawkish recommendations that his defense advisers offered. Nevertheless, and unlike Nehru's decision-making process before choosing the Forward Policy, the information that military leadership provided shaped Vajpayee's understanding of the limits of the use of force. In short, the primary way that the bureaucracy shaped decision-making was not by telling Vajpayee what to do, but rather informing his understanding of the strategies that were likely to succeed.

Second, the case suggests that Vajpayee's beliefs were malleable. Vajpayee reportedly favored military strikes against Pakistan immediately after the attack, but was persuaded to delay action by his advisers in the CCS. Bureaucratic information was critical to Vajpayee's change in beliefs: advisers argued that India was not yet able to defend itself against Pakistani retaliation.[290]

Third, although India's accurate projections are consistent with accountability theory, there is comparatively little evidence available that public opinion shaped Vajpayee's choices. Based upon interviews with Indian decision-makers, P.R. Chari and co-authors describe public opinion

[285] Kanwal, "Military Dimensions of the 2002 India-Pakistan Standoff," 69.
[286] Swami, "Gen. Padmanabhan Mulls over Lessons of Operation Parakram."
[287] Smith, "The 2001–2002 Standoff," 199.
[288] Kanwal, "Military Dimensions of the 2002 India-Pakistan Standoff," 88.
[289] Swami, "A War to End a War," 150.
[290] Ibid., 149.

as "irrelevant" to the prime minister's decision-making.[291] If anything, public opinion at the time seemed to favor retaliatory strikes, which meant that the Vajpayee administration may have paid political costs for choosing a more prudent strategy.[292]

Finally, nuclear weapons present an important alternative explanation unique to this case. The possession of nuclear weapons may have militated against large-scale military conflict. For instance, Army Vice Chief of Staff V.K. Sood assessed that Pakistan "would use nuclear weapons" if India were to launch an all-out war.[293] Yet Indian decision-makers seriously considered military strikes – and Vajpayee may have initially favored them – despite the presence of nuclear weapons. One reason for this may have been that Indian decision-makers projected that Pakistan would not resort to nuclear weapons if India's operations were confined to a limited war. As one senior Indian army officer noted, Pakistan would only "turn to use nuclear weapons" when it believed it was "being annihilated," but Indian ground operations could stop short of such a point.[294] This conclusion may have been informed by the Kargil War, in which India and Pakistan had fought a conventional conflict without resorting to nuclear escalation. In sum, Indian decision-makers seriously debated limited military action, despite the presence of nuclear weapons, and appear to have ultimately concluded against based on other considerations.[295]

Conclusion

This chapter illustrated how even democratic leaders face a trade-off between high-quality information and political security. In the case of India, the political leadership inherited institutions that were near replicas of the British system. Yet India charted an institutional path quite distinct from its British legacy. Institutions optimized for the United Kingdom during the mid-twentieth century did not last long in a different political environment. Instead, Jawaharlal Nehru modified India's institutions as part of a strategy to protect the new regime from bureaucratic sanction. While Indian political leaders primarily saw this threat in terms of coup d'état,

---

[291] Chari, Cheema, and Cohen, *Four Crises and a Peace Process*, 177.
[292] Kanti Bajpai, "To War or Not To War: The India-Pakistan Crisis of 2001–2," in *Nuclear Proliferation in South Asia*, ed. Sumit Ganguly and S. Paul Kapur (New York: Routledge, 2009), 167.
[293] Interview with Sood, quoted in Kapur, "Ten Years of Instability in a Nuclear South Asia," 83.
[294] Stolar, *To the Brink*, 28.
[295] In his memoirs, Singh goes so far as to say that "a nuclear dimension just did not exist." Singh, *In Service of Emergent India*, 341. See also Chari, Cheema, and Cohen, *Four Crises and a Peace Process*, 176; Kapur, "Ten Years of Instability in a Nuclear South Asia," 82; Narang, *Nuclear Strategy in the Modern Era*, 278–279.

they also feared the ways that Indian bureaucrats shape broader public debates. As these threats abated, institutional reforms followed.

The medium-n analysis suggested that these institutional choices systematically shaped India's crisis performance. Integrated institutions tended to perform better in crisis than siloed or fragmented institutions, with fragmented institutions performing the worst of all. The case study of the Sino-Indian War supported the theory's claim that fragmented institutions are prone to miscalculate because they degrade the completeness and quality of information that leaders receive. The case study on the Twin Peaks Crisis, in contrast, illustrated the theory's intuition regarding how the competitive dialogue inherent in integrated institutions curbs the risk of miscalculation.

In short, the chapter shows that politics shapes national security institutions – and that these institutions in turn affect the choices leaders make – in both authoritarian and democratic regimes. The origins of the India's miscalculations during the Sino-Indian War, as well as its sound judgment during the Twin Peaks Crisis, rested in the institutions it possessed at the time. More broadly, the Indian case suggests that in order for states to transition to more effective institutions, threats emanating from the national security bureaucracy must be low. The next chapter further illustrates this point by examining a country that in many ways looked quite similar to India, but in which such threats endured: Pakistan. Examining these institutional differences illuminates the origins of Pakistan's miscalculations in the 1999 Kargil War.

7   Pakistan

In the winter months of 1998 and 1999, Pakistan quietly moved troops across the Line of Control between Indian and Pakistani controlled parts of Kashmir. The goal of Pakistan's strategy, entitled Operation Koh Paima, was to seize territory overlooking the city of Kargil, a strategically valuable point along Indian supply lines. The gambit triggered a costly international war with India.

The Kargil War – the only instance of a direct international military conflict between two states possessing nuclear weapons – was a decisive defeat for Pakistan. During the conflict, some 200 to 700 Pakistani soldiers died and still more were wounded.[1] By the time the smoke had cleared, Pakistan had withdrawn from the territory it had attempted to seize, thereby returning the situation along the border to the status quo. Pakistan's prime minister at the time, Nawaz Sharif, later commented that "there was no need to sacrifice so many" soldiers given that the conflict did so little to advance the country's interests.[2] Moreover, the diplomatic consequences of the Kargil conflict were considerable, undermining recent diplomatic initiatives between Pakistan and India that had made substantial progress in the prior year to foster a more stable and peaceful relations between the two countries. Finally, the Kargil War was politically costly for Sharif. In the months after Pakistan's defeat, a domestic political battle over who was to blame ensued between Sharif and the military. Sharif attempted to remove Chief of Army Staff Pervez Musharraf in the fall of 1999, but the military instead rallied behind Musharraf and ousted Sharif through a coup d'état.

---

[1] John H. Gill, "Military Operations in the Kargil Conflict," in *Asymmetric Warfare in South Asia*, ed. Peter R. Lavoy (Cambridge: Cambridge University Press, 2009), 122. Foreign Minister Sartaj Aziz claims that Pakistan suffered 2,700 casualties. Prime Minister Nawaz Sharif claims there were 2,000 fatalities. See Sartaj Aziz, *Between Dreams and Realities: Some Milestones in Pakistan's History*, 2nd ed. (Karachi: Oxford University Press, 2020), 259; Suhail Warriach, *The Traitor Within: The Nawaz Sharif Story in His Own Words* (Lahore: Sagar Publishers, 2008), 126.

[2] Warriach, *The Traitor Within*, 127. This source includes transcripts of interviews with Nawaz Sharif.

Pakistan's failure during the Kargil War is commonly attributed to hawkish military leaders who made unilateral and unauthorized decisions that pushed Pakistan into war.[3] Yet the evidence presented in this chapter suggests a different story. Sharif was not only briefed on the operation, but was persuaded the plan would succeed. The Kargil War began because Sharif believed he would emerge victorious.

What explains the miscalculation that would ultimately cost Sharif the prime ministership? This chapter argues that Sharif's choices were rooted in the incomplete and low-quality information that siloed institutions supplied. Information from a narrow segment of defense advisers proved crucial in shaping Sharif's optimism. A leader's "mind is made by his advisers," one of Sharif's senior diplomats later recalled, so the decision that a leader reaches "depends on what kind of advisers [they] have."[4] Equally important, however, was the advice Sharif did not receive. Numerous diplomatic and intelligence bureaucrats possessed more pessimistic information, but were unaware of the military's plans. Stifled horizontal flow of information *between* Pakistan's bureaucracies undermined the ability of each to identify the value of their own information. Sharif thus miscalculated not simply because the information that his defense advisers provided was incomplete, but because siloed institutions impeded the ability of diplomatic and intelligence bureaucracies to counsel Sharif as to why defense assessments were misguided.

Siloed institutions were ultimately the result of a trade-off that Sharif faced. During the 1990s, salient international threats from India, particularly after the nuclear tests in 1998, demanded a more inclusive decision-making system. Yet the military posed a salient threat to the political survival of Pakistan's civilian prime ministers. To balance these two requirements, Pakistan's leaders left their institutions siloed.

This chapter advances the argument of the book by illustrating the distinct way by which siloed institutions lead states to miscalculate. The analysis builds on the discussion of Chinese decision-making in Chapter 5, illustrating how the pathways by which siloed institutions cause leaders to miscalculate look remarkably similar in democratic and authoritarian contexts. The first section identifies how the threat of coup first led to the fragmentation of the institutions that Pakistan inherited in the late 1940s. It then discusses how shifting agendas shaped the institutional transition to siloed alternatives. The second section considers institutional

---

[3] For example, see Khan, Lavoy, and Clary, "Pakistan's Motivations and Calculations for the Kargil Conflict," 74–80; Brooks, *Shaping Strategy*, 196–209; C. Christine Fair, *Fighting to the End: The Pakistan Army's Way of War* (New York: Oxford University Press, 2014), 150–154.

[4] Interview with Shamshad Ahmad (Foreign Secretary), Islamabad, Fall 2017.

performance since 1947, using the 1999 Kargil War to illustrate the consequences of siloed designs.

The Politics of Institutional Design in Pakistan

In the late 1940s, Pakistan inherited national security institutions akin to those in India. As in India, Pakistan established a Defence Committee of the Cabinet (DCC), the purpose of which was to define the "task of the armed forces in accordance with overall policy of government." The DCC was an inclusive body, including both the defence and foreign ministers, as well as the military service chiefs on invitation.[5]

Pakistan's political leaders set aside the institutions they inherited. As in India, Pakistan's leaders feared the bureaucracy. Unlike India, however, these threats persisted into the contemporary era. As such, integrated institutions were never a viable option for Pakistan's leaders. Instead, the choice was between fragmented and siloed designs. From the 1950s through the 1980s, fragmented institutions better suited the political needs of leaders focused on the threat of secession by East Pakistan and, at moments, the transformation of state and society. After the end of military rule, however, a series of international issues – nuclear crises with India, the Kashmir insurgency, and the threat of cross-national terrorism – prompted a shift to siloed institutions. Table 7.1 summarizes the key components of Pakistan's institutional design since 1947.

The Political Environment under Early Civilian and Military Rule

The political environment in Pakistan featured high bureaucratic threats under both military and civilian regimes. The most salient aspect of this threat was the possibility of military coup. While Pakistan inherited a generally apolitical and professional military officer corps, as Aqil Shah notes, "within a few years of independence, the Pakistani army had developed a political orientation" that made them a threat to incumbent leaders.[6] In 1948, for instance, Muhammad Ali Jinnah commented that "high-ranking" military officers did not understand the "implications of the Oath" they swore to uphold the orders of the civilian government.[7]

---

[5] "Formation of the Sub-Committees of the Defence Committee of the Cabinet," September 25, 1948, Cabinet Secretariat File 172/CF/48, cited in Aqil Shah, *The Army and Democracy* (Cambridge: Harvard University Press, 2014), 35–36 and 305–306. The available evidence suggests that Pakistan lacked the coordination mechanisms initially inherited by India.

[6] Shah, *Army and Democracy*, 33. On the "unthreatening" military, see also Stephen P. Cohen, *The Idea of Pakistan* (Washington, DC: Brookings Institution Press, 2004), 41.

[7] Shah, *The Army and Democracy*, 48.

Table 7.1 *Evolution of Pakistan's institutional design*

Period	Bureaucratic threat	Leader agenda	National security institution	Theory support
1947–1948 (inherited)	*High*: perceived bureaucratic intent to challenge; inexperienced leader	*Domestic & international*: initial peak of Kashmir dispute; domestic crises	*Siloed*: inclusive DCC; minimal coordination mechanisms	Weak
1949–1986; 2000–2008	*Medium to high*: perceived bureaucratic intent to challenge; range of leader experience	*Domestic & international*: threat of E. Pakistan secession; revolutionary agendas (Ayub, Bhutto, Zia)	*Fragmented*: insular decision-making bodies (e.g., Afghan Cell); redesign of DCC under Yahya; minimal coordination mechanisms	Strong
1987–1999; 2009–2015	*High*: perceived intent to challenge; inexperienced civilian leaders	*International*: nuclear crises with India; Kashmir insurgency	*Siloed*: reestablishment of inclusive DCC; minimal coordination mechanisms	Strong

These fears were well founded. The Pakistani military repeatedly demonstrated its capability to coerce leaders, both civilian and military, to step down from office. As a result, political succession in Pakistan was determined almost exclusively by the military, often with the support of the civilian bureaucracy. In total, there were at least five political transitions between 1947 and 1986 that qualify as coups.[8] In October 1958, Pakistan's President, Major General Iskander Mirza, dismissed the civilian government under Firoz Khan Noon and appointed the Pakistan Army Commander-in-Chief, Ayub Khan, as Chief Martial Law Administrator. Later that month, Ayub forced Mirza into exile and formed a new government without a prime minister. The 1958 coup initiated an era of political rule by Ayub Khan from 1958 to 1969. Ayub was ousted

---

[8] The fate of deposed leaders during this period has varied. Firoz Khan Noon and Ayub Khan withdrew from political life. Izkander Ali Mirza and Nawaz Sharif went into exile. Yahya Khan spent the remainder of his life under house arrest. Zulfikar Ali Bhutto was executed.

by another military leader, Yahya Khan, who ruled from 1969 to 1971. Yahya, too, resigned under threat by junior Pakistani military officers, who allowed Zulfikar Ali Bhutto (a civilian) to rule from 1971 to 1977. A coup by Zia ul-Haq in 1977 removed Bhutto from power and led to military rule through Zia's death in 1988.

A number of coup attempts, though unsuccessful, further shaped concerns about the military's intentions. In 1951, a group of military officers plotted a conspiracy in Rawalpindi to overthrow the government.[9] The plot was led by the Chief of General Staff, Akbar Khan, who allegedly told one mid-grade military officer that there was "no reason why the government should not be taken over by the army." The group planned to detain Prime Minister Liaquat Ali Khan and "overthrow the government."[10] In January 1968, twenty-eight persons associated with the Agartala conspiracy were arrested, including senior members of the civil service and mid-grade military officers.[11] The Bhutto administration uncovered another coup plot in March 1973.[12] In 1980, the Zia ul-Haq regime identified a coup conspiracy led by Major General Tajammal Hussain Malik, who was plotting to organize a Revolutionary Command to overthrow the government.[13] Reports of another unsuccessful military coup plot surfaced in March 1984.[14]

A second key attribute of political environment was the extraordinary domestic instability in Pakistan that demanded the political leadership's attention. As Stephen Cohen summarizes, the country was "unstable from the outset."[15] First, Pakistan was initially divided into two geographic areas, East and West Pakistan. The two areas were not only separated geographically by India – some one thousand miles away from one another – but also separated by distinct ethnic identities. By the early 1950s, Bengali political figures in East Pakistan organized the Awami Muslim League, which began proposing policies that foreshadowed what eventually became a separatist agenda. The possibility of secession generated fears among both civilian and military elites in the

---

[9] Shah, *The Army and Democracy*, 42–43.
[10] Testimonies of Lieutenant Colonel Gul Muwaz and Major Eusoph Sethi, *Proceedings of the Rawalpindi Conspiracy Tribunal* (Cabinet Secretariat, Government of Pakistan, 1951) cited in Shah, *The Army and Democracy*, 45.
[11] Altaf Gauhar, *Ayub Khan: Pakistan's First Military Ruler* (Lahore: Sang-e-Meel, 1993), 408–409.
[12] Shah, *The Army and Democracy*, 122–123.
[13] Owen L. Sirrs, *Pakistan's Inter-Services Intelligence Directorate: Covert Action and Internal Operations* (New York: Routledge, 2017), 110–111.
[14] Mary Anne Weaver, "Failed Coup against Pakistan Leader May Have Involved India," *The Christian Science Monitor*, March 19, 1984.
[15] Cohen, *The Idea of Pakistan*, 54.

Pakistan government.[16] Liaquat Ali Khan, for example, noted that "we must kill this provincialism for all times to come."[17] In a cabinet meeting in 1954, Pakistani officials described the possibility of adopting Bengali as a state language as precipitating "the disintegration of Pakistan" and "a triumph for those who wanted to see East Pakistan detached from West Pakistan."[18] Military officers spoke of the "country's rapid drift towards chaos."[19] In short, Pakistan's leaders feared that their country might be permanently divided.

Second, Pakistan's military leaders – particularly Ayub Khan, Zia ul-Haq, and Pervez Musharraf – pursued transformative domestic policies to address this instability.[20] Shuja Nawaz, for instance, describes Ayub as a "revolutionary leader" who sought to "change the socio-political and economic map of the country."[21] Ayub implemented reforms that afforded protection and privileges to Pakistani women, encouraged a new model of export-led economic development, and introduced a new model of local elections throughout the country.[22] Zia similarly hoped to transform the Pakistan to reflect the ideals of Islam. Zia imposed numerous changes to the legal, judicial, and economic systems in Pakistan, imposing policies ranging from criminal punishments according to religious interpretation to the requirement of a religious tax on wealth (*zakat*).[23] Musharraf similarly aimed to bring about, as Stephen Cohen terms it, a "fundamental change in Pakistan's political order."[24] He created a new National Accountability Bureau, tasked with investigating corruption. Musharraf also implemented a new model of local political representation (the *nazim* system).[25]

To be sure, Pakistan also faced a formidable international threat from India during this period. Yet after the First Kashmir War, there was little consensus that Pakistan could change the status quo along the border through its foreign or defense policy.[26] In addition, many leaders concluded that dealing with the country's domestic unrest was more

---

[16] Shah, *The Army and Democracy*, 34, 53, 58–59. See also Cohen, *The Idea of Pakistan*, 55.
[17] Shah, *The Army and Democracy*, 60.
[18] Ibid., 74–75.
[19] Ibid., 85.
[20] Cohen, *The Idea of Pakistan*, 84.
[21] Shuja Nawaz, *Crossed Swords: Pakistan, Its Army, and the Wars Within*, 2nd ed. (Karachi: Oxford University Press, 2017), 172.
[22] Shah, *The Army and Democracy*, 96–97; Nawaz, *Crossed Swords*, 173–174.
[23] Shah, *The Army and Democracy*, 152.
[24] Cohen, *The Idea of Pakistan*, 155.
[25] Shah, *The Army and Democracy*, 188–195; Nawaz, *Crossed Swords*, 529–533.
[26] Cohen, *The Idea of Pakistan*, 53.

important to their political survival. For instance, Jinnah noted that Pakistan could play a more active role in international affairs only if it would "put [its] house in order internally."[27] Upon entering office, Ayub confided in his cabinet that his primary focus would be the "stability in the economic life of the country."[28] Similarly, Zia ul-Huq described his policies to make the Pakistani state more Islamic as of equal importance to "the security of the country's geographical boundaries."[29]

Fragmented Institutions, 1949–1986 and 1999–2008

The political theory of institutional design suggests that leaders who face salient bureaucratic threats and who seek transformative domestic policies should be more likely to adopt fragmented institutions. Pakistan's institutional design from the late 1940s to the late 1980s, as well as another interlude of military rule from 1999 to 2008, was generally congruent with this prediction.

The trade-off between quality information and neutralizing bureaucratic threats shaped the institutions that Pakistan's leaders adopted. For civilian rulers, the crux of the issue to protect themselves from military coup. For military rulers, the crux of the issue was that extreme domestic instability precipitated intervention in Pakistan's political system. Pakistan's military rulers demanded fragmented institutions that afforded flexibility in implementing the types of domestic political changes they believed necessary before returning the government to civilian hands.[30] Thus, Pakistan's national security institutions during period of military rule were, somewhat paradoxically, more fragmented than we might at first anticipate them to be based upon the traditional focus of military organizations on international issues.

Insular Information Search Capacity. The first characteristic of Pakistan's national security institutions during these periods was restricted information search. Despite a Cabinet requirement to convene at least once every two months, the DCC had stopped meeting regularly by 1951.[31] One Pakistani official remembers that Pakistan was unable to sustain

---

[27] Ibid., 44.
[28] Nawaz, *Crossed Swords*, 171.
[29] Cohen, *The Idea of Pakistan*, 84.
[30] Paul Staniland, "Explaining Civil-Military Relations in Complex Political Environments: India and Pakistan in Comparative Perspective," *Security Studies* 17, no. 2 (2008): 349–350.
[31] "Reorganization of the Existing Joint Services Machinery," November 6, 1951, Cabinet Secretariat File 172/CF/48, cited in Shah, *The Army and Democracy*, 315. See also Government of Pakistan, *Report of the Hamoodur Rehman Commission of Inquiry into the 1971 War* (Lahore: Vanguard, 2000), 265.

the defense mechanism that was inherited from the United Kingdom after independence, describing the DCC as in "suspended animation." As a result, national security policymaking was "neither colonial nor democratic nor even totalitarian. It was just hotch-potch."[32]

After Yahya Khan replaced Ayub in 1969, the DCC membership was restructured to formally exclude key elements of the bureaucracy, including the Foreign Ministry. Yahya restricted DCC membership to the president, minister for home affairs, industries, finance and communications.[33] It was renamed the President's Committee for Defence in February 1970, but only included the president, adviser for finance, and secretaries of industries, communications, and home affairs. It was only in October 1971 that the President's Committee on Defence was finally expanded to include the defence and foreign secretaries.[34] Instead, the "nerve center" of Yahya's decision-making was the Secretariat of the Chief Martial Law Administration (CLMA), composed of military officers.[35] Firsthand accounts confirm that "there was no Defence Committee of the Cabinet" and that "there was no institutional framework for co-ordination and consultation between [the CMLA] and the civil governmental machinery."[36]

The domestic priority of Yahya Khan is evident in the design of a National Security Council (NSC) and corresponding national security advisor established during this period. In theory, the NSC was supposed to facilitate policy and intelligence coordination between the military, Foreign Ministry, and ISI, supported by a secretariat entitled the Security Council Division.[37] Yet the body was principally aimed at domestic political surveillance, monitoring opposition political parties, and recommending "policies that might favor the parties committed to the ideology of Pakistan."[38] As Aqil Shah writes, the "main purpose" of Yahya's NSC was to "direct an intelligence operation designed to prevent any political party from winning an overall majority in elections."[39]

These patterns continued after the 1977 coup led by Zia ul-Haq. Zia established a Military Council, consisting of Zia, the chairman of the

---

[32] Fazal Muqueem Khan, *Pakistan's Crisis in Leadership* (Islamabad: National Book Foundation, 1973), 265.
[33] Government of Pakistan, *Hamoodur Rehman Commission Report*, 265.
[34] "Composition of the Defence Committee of the Cabinet," in Government of Pakistan, 276.
[35] Hasan Zaheer, *The Separation of East Pakistan: The Rise and Realization of Bengali Muslim Nationalism* (Karachi: Oxford University Press, 1994), 111.
[36] Ibid., 354–355.
[37] Government of Pakistan, *Hamoodur Rehman Commission Report*, 268–269.
[38] Husain Haqqani, *Pakistan: Between Mosque and Military* (Washington, DC: Carnegie Endowment for International Peace, 2005), 55.
[39] Shah, *The Army and Democracy*, 108.

Joint Chiefs of Staff Committee, as well as the three service chiefs.[40] The most important foreign policy decisions during the 1980s were made in the Afghan Cell – an ad hoc body to deal with Pakistan's national security policy across its western border. Zia restricted the membership of the Afghan Cell and "elbowed out" Minister of State for Foreign Affairs Agha Shahi. One former diplomat notes that "vital decisions" on Afghanistan were made solely on the advice of the ISI.[41] Even after Zia replaced Shahi with his former military colleague, Sahabzada Yaqub Khan, and began to include the Foreign Ministry, Yaqub reportedly "complained that the Foreign Office faced the difficulty of defending Pakistan's Afghan policy," which he felt was formulated by "other departments." Yaqub noted that the ISI was the single organization responsible for "the provision of equipment, as well as planning, implementation, supervision, intelligence, operations, and the analysis of the operational tasks."[42]

Similar patterns reemerged after Pervez Musharraf seized power in 1999. On October 17, just after the coup deposing Nawaz Sharif, Musharraf announced the formation of a new National Security Council (NSC). Despite the body's name, however, the NSC was designed to address a range of domestic issues such as "law and order, corruption, accountability, recovery of bank loans and public debts from defaulters, finance, economic and social welfare, health, education, Islamic ideology, human rights, protection of minorities and women development." The NSC managed issues such as the Federal Public Service Commission, education, government organization, diplomatic delegations, and economic strategy.[43]

As such, Musharraf's NSC was not designed to be bureaucratically inclusive. While Musharraf's original announcement specified that the NSC's composition would include legal, financial, foreign policy and national affairs "specialists," the executive order formally codifying the

---

[40] K. M. Arif, *Working with Zia: Pakistan's Power Politics, 1977–1988* (Karachi: Oxford University Press, 1995), 103; Shahid Javed Burki, "Zia's Eleven Years," in *Pakistan under the Military: Eleven Years of Zia ul-Haq*, ed. Shahid Javed Burki and Craig Baxter (Boulder: Westview Press, 1991), 17–18.
[41] S. M. Koreshi, *Diplomats & Diplomacy: Story of an Era, 1947–1987* (Islamabad: Khursheed Printers, 2004), 330.
[42] Arif, *Working with Zia*, 322.
[43] Ansar Abbasi, "Musharraf Approves Pre-1973 Authority for FPSC," *Dawn*, January 27, 2000; Faraz Hashmi, "Chief Executive Assures Madaris of Non-Interference," *Dawn*, 28 July 2000; "PTCL Merged Into S&T Ministry," *Dawn*, January 5, 2000; Ihtashamul Haq, "Islamabad Hopes for Talks: Pullout of Troops From LoC Completed," *Dawn*, January 5, 2001; M. Ziauddin and Ihtasham ul Haque, "CE Addresses 1st News Conference: Musharraf Hints at Referendum," *Dawn*, November 2, 1999; Ihtasham ul Haque, "All Debts be Cut on Top Priority: Chief Executive," *Dawn*, December 2, 1999.

NSC stipulated that only military leaders would be full members.[44] In 2001, Musharraf issued Chief Executive's Order No. 5, which expanded membership to the four provincial governors and "others nominated by the president."[45] The 2004 National Security Council Act expanded the composition further still to include the president, prime minister, Senate chairman, speaker of the National Assembly, leader of the opposition in the National Assembly, chief ministers of the provinces, the chairman Joint Chiefs of Staff Committee, and the military chiefs of staff. Yet none of these arrangements formally included the foreign minister or foreign intelligence agencies.[46]

Pakistan's fragmented institutions featured poor information flow in several ways. First, there were functional problems with information sharing between political leaders and the bureaucracy. Douglas Gracey described Pakistan's political leadership as "completely [and] abysmally ignorant of what was going on in the military."[47] According to the CMLA chief of staff, Military Council members "did not have access to information and statistics needed to make a meaningful contribution to the decision-making process."[48] With the exception of Zia's finance minister, ministerial leadership was "usually bypassed."[49]

Second, information and intelligence often biased toward the prior beliefs of political leaders. A 1974 intelligence review concluded that the "sole aim" of the bureaucracy was to be the first to report to the prime minister and "to please him."[50] Diplomats became "subservient" and "gave advice which they thought" the leadership wanted to hear. Otherwise, bureaucrats feared that they might "lose their jobs" or "be punished" for holding opposing views.[51] Others recalled that while there was a "sizeable segment of opinion" within the Foreign Ministry that opposed Pakistan's intervention in Afghanistan, dissent was "muted" and officials refrained from putting their opinions in writing.[52]

---

[44] "General Pervez Musharraf's Address to the Nation," October 17, 1999; Chief Executive Order No. 6 of 1999, "Appointment of National Security Council and Oath of Office Order," October 30, 1999.
[45] Hasan-Askari Rizvi, "The National Security Council and Policymaking on Security Affairs in Pakistan," *South Asian Journal*, no. 41 (2013): 58.
[46] "National Security Council Act of 2004, No. F.9(5)/2004," in *Gazette of Pakistan*, April 20, 2004.
[47] Interviews cited in Wilkinson, *Army and Nation*, 204.
[48] Arif, *Working with Zia*, 110.
[49] Mohammad Asghar Khan, *Generals in Politics: Pakistan 1958–1982* (New Delhi: Vikas, 1983), 141.
[50] Rafi Raza, *Zulfikar Ali Bhutto and Pakistan, 1967–1977* (Karachi: Oxford University Press, 1997), 302.
[51] Interview with retired official, Islamabad, Fall 2017.
[52] Interview with retired diplomat, Islamabad, Fall 2017.

Closed Bureaucratic Access to Information. A second key aspect of Pakistan's national security institutions was limited capacity for interbureaucratic access to information. Pakistan's leaders did not appoint coordinators, coordinating staffs, or coordinating bodies to facilitate information sharing. Instead, information flow generally occurred in one-on-one meetings between the chief executive and intelligence, military, or diplomatic leaders.[53] The system "ensured that the three dominant intelligence agencies [...] reported directly" to the president.[54] One senior military officer recalls that the CMLA Secretariat and the GHQ of the military were frequently "unaware of what the other did or failed to do."[55] The aforementioned 1974 intelligence review also revealed that there was "no coordination or exchange of information or views among the various agencies."[56] Pakistan's political leaders were aware of problems with information flow but chose not to fix them. Ayub, Yahya, and Zia all formed committees to review Pakistan's intelligence organization.[57] For example, after the intelligence failures of the 1965 Indo-Pakistani War, Ayub appointed Yaqub Khan to lead a committee on intelligence reform,[58] but Ayub chose not to act on the report's recommendations.[59]

The Political Environment under Late Civilian Rule

After Zia ul-Haq's death in 1988, there have been two prolonged periods of civilian rule in Pakistan: from 1988 to 1999 and from 2008 to present. Pakistan's political environment during these periods was marked by both continuity and change. On the one hand, the threat of coup remained high: the 1999 coup demonstrated the military's continued

---

[53] For examples of individual meetings with intelligence officials, see Ayub Khan diary entries from October 11, 1967 and April 12, 1968. For an example of individual meetings with the military operational leadership, see entries on August 29, 1967. For examples of such meetings, see entries on May 8, 1968. Mohammad Ayub Khan, *Diaries of Field Marshal Mohammad Ayub Khan, 1966–1972* (New York: Oxford University Press, 2007), 140, 164, 211, and 218.

[54] Sirrs, *Pakistan's Inter-Services Intelligence Directorate*, 63.

[55] Arif, *Khaki Shadows: Pakistan 1947–1997* (New York: Oxford University Press, 2001), 135.

[56] Raza, *Zulfikar Ali Bhutto and Pakistan*, 302.

[57] K.M. Sheikh Committee (1960), Fida Hussain Committee (1967), G. Ahmed Committee (1971), Rafi Raza Committee (1974), and Yaqub Khan Committee (1981). See P. C. Joshi, *Main Intelligence Outfits of Pakistan* (New Delhi: Anmol Publications, 2008), 141.

[58] Khan, *Diaries of Ayub Khan*, 69.

[59] Ibid., 422.

political power. Thus, even as the military relinquished formal political positions within government, an informal power-sharing arrangement between civilian politicians and the military leadership emerged. If anything, the vulnerability to bureaucratic sanction was higher because civilian leaders lacked experience managing the national security bureaucracy. Prime Minister Benazir Bhutto, for instance, lacked familiarity with the bureaucratic establishment, which set conditions for the military to dominate her in policy debates.[60]

On the other hand, Pakistan's new civilian leaders lacked the revolutionary programs that characterized military rule. Benazir Bhutto and Nawaz Sharif, for instance, did not seek to transform Pakistan in the same way that Ayub Khan and Zia ul-Haq had. In addition, Pakistan's civilian leaders were increasingly concerned about international issues. One of the most important changes pertained to the completion of Pakistan's nuclear program. Possession of nuclear weapons raised the stakes of international conflicts with India. When combined with a growing insurgency in Kashmir, this shift in the balance of power opened the possibility of renegotiating its disputes with India.[61]

There was a conventional dimension to the growing international imperatives as well. By the 1990s, rudimentary force ratio estimates show that India possessed between a two-to-one to a three-to-one advantage in conventional strength over Pakistan. Support from outside patrons declined as well. During the Cold War, Pakistan benefited from a defense partnership with the United States, whose policymakers viewed Pakistan as an important proxy by which to balance against the Soviet Union, meaning that Pakistani leaders could lean on the United States for support in the event of a serious security crisis with India. With the end of the Cold War, however, the United States turned its attention and support elsewhere, leaving Pakistani leaders vulnerable to Indian coercion.[62]

Siloed Institutions, 1987–1999 and 2009–2015

The political theory of institutional design suggests that leaders are more likely to prefer siloed designs when they confront a combination of bureaucratic threats coupled with a focus on international issues. Congruent with the theory's prediction, Pakistan's system is best characterized as siloed during these periods.

---

[60] Interview, Islamabad, Fall 2017.
[61] Cohen, *The Idea of Pakistan*, 53.
[62] This paragraph relies on Narang, *Nuclear Strategy in the Modern Era*, 55–94.

This institutional choice reflected two countervailing realities of the political environment. First, the international issues that civilian Pakistani leaders faced created elevated demand for quality advice from the national security bureaucracy.[63] Second, civilian leaders feared strengthening coordination mechanisms. Politicians preferred unilateral control over each bureaucratic silo. As one senior Pakistani official later recalled, Nawaz Sharif did not wish to strengthen the DCC because he feared it would be "usurped" by the military.[64] This choice also helped to placate the bureaucracy, which preferred unilateral access to the political leadership. As one Pakistani official recalls, "everyone wanted the prime minister's ear without any interface in-between."[65]

Inclusive Information Search Capacity. The most important change to Pakistan's national security institutions was the expansion of capacity for information search. The DCC was reestablished in the mid-1980s.[66] The restored DCC was inclusive in its bureaucratic participation, including representatives from the Defence Ministry, Foreign Ministry, and foreign intelligence. Under Benazir Bhutto, for instance, the DCC convened as frequently as once or twice per month – and for all the most important policy decisions.[67] Nawaz Sharif routinely used the DCC as well, despite his reported distaste for routinized decision-making processes.[68]

Inclusive search continued after the restoration of civilian control in 2008. President Asif Ali Zardari and Prime Minister Yousuf Raza Gilani convened the DCC up to five times per year between 2008 and 2012.[69]

---

[63] Interview with Talat Massod (Secretary of Defence Production), Islamabad, Fall 2017.
[64] Interview with Shamshad Ahmad (Foreign Secretary), Islamabad, Fall 2017.
[65] Interview with Mahmud Ali Durrani (National Security Advisor), Islamabad, Fall 2017.
[66] The institutional transition date used here is 1987, the first year in which there is evidence of the DCC's use. See Arif, *Khaki Shadows*, 271–272. Zulfikar Ali Bhutto seems to have moved toward a similar reconstitution of the DCC through a *White Paper on Defence Organization* released in May 1976. See "1976 White Paper on Higher Defence Organization," in Hasan-Askari Rizvi, *The Military and Politics in Pakistan: 1947–1997* (Lahore: Sang-e-Meel, 2013), 312.
[67] Interview with Talat Massod (Secretary of Defence Production), Islamabad, Fall 2017.
[68] For examples of DCC meetings during this period cited in available sources, see Benazir Bhutto, *Daughter of the East: An Autobiography* (New York: Simon & Schuster, 2007), 407; Mushahid Hussain and Akmal Hussain, *Pakistan: Problems of Governance* (New Delhi: Konark Publishers, 1993), 104–105; Aziz, *Between Dreams and Realities*, 191–192; Gohar Ayub Khan, *Testing Times as Foreign Minister* (Islamabad: Dost Publications, 2009), 36; interviews with Salmon Bashir (Foreign Secretary) and Shamshad Ahmad (Foreign Secretary), Islamabad, Fall 2017.
[69] Hasan-Askari Rizvi, *Performance of the Defence Committee of the Cabinet* (Islamabad: PILDAT, 2012).

Subsequent institutional reforms made only minor modifications to Pakistan's decision-making body. In August 2013, for instance, Pakistan created a Cabinet Committee on National Security (CCNS).[70] In early January 2014, Prime Minister Nawaz Sharif announced his intention to strengthen and institutionalize the CCNS.[71] Despite the change in name, however, the only significant change was to integrate the military service chiefs as full members on the body. The core feature of inclusive information search remained unchanged. In short, as Foreign Minister Khurshid Mahmud Kasuri summarized, a "consensus" emerged that Pakistan's leaders benefited from more inclusive decision-making bodies.[72]

Siloed institutions featured high levels of information flow between the political leadership and the bureaucracy. Multiple opinions and viewpoints were offered. For instance, Air Chief Marshal Jamal Ahmad Khan recalled that deliberations in the DCC featured "free expression and rigorous examination of every option" and that the "wide-ranging participation" of the forum "helped in preventing the dangerous syndrome of 'Groupthink' from taking hold" among Pakistani decision-makers.[73]

Closed Bureaucratic Access to Information. Expanded capacity for information search was not matched by improved mechanisms for interbureaucratic information sharing. Political leaders neither established a coordination body below the DCC nor appointed coordinators to assist in managing the bureaucracy. For example, upon appointment as foreign minister in 1998, Sartaj Aziz was "struck by the absence of a viable institutional framework that could help military planners to coordinate more effectively with makers of foreign policy."[74] Other Pakistani scholars note that the deficiency of the DCC rested in its limited authority to coordinate national security strategy.[75] One government review of Pakistan's decision-making system found that the DCC was "no substitute" for a stronger and more routinized mechanisms for coordination.[76]

---

[70] "DCC to be Reconstituted as Committee on National Security," *Dawn*, August 22, 2013.
[71] Khaleeq Kiani, "Plan to Strengthen NSC, Says Sharif," *Dawn*, January 2, 2014.
[72] Khurshid Mahmud Kasuri, *Neither a Hawk Nor a Dove: An Insider's Account of Pakistan's Foreign Policy* (London: Penguin, 2015), 484.
[73] Arif, *Khaki Shadows*, 271–272.
[74] Aziz, *Between Dreams and Realities*, 241.
[75] See, for example, Rizvi, *Performance of the Defence Committee of the Cabinet*.
[76] Javaid Iqbal, ed., *Abbottabad Commission Report* (Government of Pakistan, 2013), 320.

The absence of coordination mechanisms reduced information flow between bureaucrats. The military leadership had direct access to political leaders, often without the participation of representatives from diplomatic and intelligence bureaucracies.[77] While there is some evidence of informal coordination between the Foreign Ministry and military, there were few institutional mechanisms to ensure this occurred. A classified government review of Pakistan's intelligence system concluded that there was "no coordination mechanism" between civilian and military intelligence other than "at a personal level on an irregular unorganized and non-institutionalized basis."[78] One former ISI Director General similarly recalled that there was little intelligence sharing between the military intelligence services, the Ministry of Interior, and the Ministry of Defence.[79] A former defence secretary also notes that intelligence sharing "had to be specifically authorized for specific cases."[80] As a result, bureaucracies tended to withhold information when it suited their interests.

Alternative Explanations for Institutional Design

How well do alternative explanations account for the evolution of Pakistan's institutional design? International diffusion offers a strong explanation for Pakistan's initial institutional structure, which was modeled on that of the United Kingdom.[81] Army Commander-in-Chief Frank Messervy set up the General Headquarters (GHQ) "with the same structure as the GHQ in New Delhi."[82] As in the Indian case, however, international diffusion does not account for Pakistan's break from the institutions it inherited. Similarly, path dependence offers comparatively little insight into subsequent shifts between siloed and fragmented designs in the following decades. Finally, leader-centric accounts do not necessarily offer straightforward explanations for institutional continuity across leaders with dissimilar personalities during both Pakistan's fragmented (e.g., Ayub Khan and Yahya Khan) and siloed (e.g., Benazir Bhutto and Nawaz Sharif) periods.

---

[77] The prime minister and the chief of army staff reportedly met approximately seventy times from 2014 to 2015 alone. See Ahmed Bilal Mehboob, "Whither NSC?" *Dawn*, November 29, 2015.
[78] Iqbal, *Abbottabad Commission Report*, 309.
[79] Ibid., 211.
[80] Ibid., 222.
[81] Nagendra Singh, *The Defence Mechanism of the Modern State* (London: Asia Publishing House, 1964), 217.
[82] Nawaz, *Crossed Swords*, 33.

Pakistan's Crisis Performance since 1947

How well did siloed and fragmented institutions perform in Pakistan? We can first probe this question by looking at patterns in Pakistan's crisis performance holistically, which is summarized in Table 7.2.[83] During its fragmented periods (from 1947 to 1986 and from 2000 to 2008), Pakistan was party to thirteen international crises. It failed to achieve its primary goal in nine of them (69 percent). During Pakistan's siloed periods (from 1947 to 1948 and from 1987 to 1990, and from 2009 to 2015), Pakistan was party to seven international crises, during which it similarly failed to achieve its primary objectives in four of them (57 percent). A similar pattern emerges when accounting for Pakistan's secondary crisis goals as well. On average, Pakistan achieved 38 percent of its goals during crises under siloed institutions, but on average achieved only 26 percent of its goals during crises under fragmented institutions. Overall, these patterns are consistent with the theory's proposition that siloed institutions perform slightly better than fragmented ones, although these patterns should be interpreted with caution given the small number of cases.

Given that Pakistan does not have an integrated period to which we can compare these trends, the analysis of India's crisis performance discussed in Chapter 6 provides a helpful comparison to contextualize Pakistan's patterns of crisis outcomes. Pakistan experienced a crisis failure under siloed institutions about three times as frequently as India experienced crisis failure under integrated institutions (once every six and seventeen years, respectively).

Next, we can probe the consequences of siloed and fragmented institutions by looking at decision-making processes during Pakistan's four major international conflicts against India. During the post-Independence conflicts, Pakistani leaders oversaw decision-making through the DCC, although the military enjoyed considerable autonomy during the assessment and planning process.[84] For example, the private secretary of Pakistan's Army Commander-in-Chief recalls that the DCC met to deliberate Pakistan's response to Indian military operations in Hyderabad in 1948.[85]

Crisis decision-making looked different after Pakistan's shift to fragmented institutions. Prior to the 1965 Indo-Pakistani War, deliberations

---

[83] On sample construction, see Chapter 6, note 122. To date, there is insufficient data on the 2008 Mumbai attacks to code Pakistan's goals.
[84] Nawaz, *Crossed Swords*, 42–73. See also Akbar Khan, *Raiders in Kashmir* (Islamabad: National Book Foundation, 1970), 21–27.
[85] James Wilson, "Pakistan Defence: The Early Days," *Army & Defence Quarterly Journal* 121, no. 3 (1991): 303.

Table 7.2 *Pakistan's crisis performance, 1947–2015*

Crisis	Year	Institution	Primary goal	Successful?
Junagadh	1947	Siloed	Gain control over Junagadh	✗
First Indo-Pakistani War	1947	Siloed	Seize key territory within Kashmir	✓
First Pushtunistan crisis	1950	Fragmented	Repel Afghan forces along border	✓
Bengal crisis	1950	Fragmented	Resist Indian demands to sign pact on minority rights	✗
Punjab war scare	1951	Fragmented	Improve claims to Kashmir	✗
Second Pushtunistan crisis	1955	Fragmented	Improve control over Pushtun tribal regions	✓
Third Pushtunistan crisis	1961	Fragmented	Repel Afghan forces along border	✓
Rann of Kutch	1965	Fragmented	Seize contested territory in Rann of Kutch	✗
Second Indo-Pakistani War	1965	Fragmented	Secure contested territory in Kashmir	✗
Third Indo-Pakistani War	1971	Fragmented	Prevent succession of East Pakistan	✗
Invasion of Afghanistan	1979	Fragmented	Deter Soviet invasion of Afghanistan	✗
Soviet-Pakistan crisis	1979	Fragmented	Deter Soviet military action against Pakistan	✓
Siachen Glacier	1984	Fragmented	Seize territory in Siachen Glacier	✗
Brasstacks crisis	1987	Siloed	Deter Indian military action	✓
Compound crisis	1990	Siloed	Compel India to honor United Nations plebiscite	✗
Nuclear tests	1998	Siloed	Demonstrate nuclear capabilities	✓
Kargil War	1999	Siloed	Compel Indian concessions on Kashmir	✗
U.S. invasion of Afghanistan	2001	Fragmented	Maintain favorable regime in Afghanistan	✗
Twin Peaks Crisis	2001	Fragmented	Maintain Pakistan's policies toward the Kashmir insurgency	✗
India–Pakistan border crisis	2014	Siloed	Deter Indian military actions across Line of Control	✗

shifted from the DCC to an insular body known as the Kashmir Cell.[86] Deliberations were intentionally not recorded, as putting anything "on paper" would "not be advisable."[87] Meetings were held in a private residence to "protect the proceedings from bureaucratic curiosity." The secretive nature of the body kept both the diplomatic and defense bureaucracies from contributing to deliberations.[88] The Diplomats lacked the opportunity to "conceive, examine, analyse or plan."[89] Senior diplomats report that diplomatic inquiries received from India were not properly analyzed or contextualized.[90] The Kashmir Cell also left key military organizations, such as the air force, out of the planning process.[91] The Commander-in-Chief of the Army wrote at the time that Pakistan's preparations had been inadequate.[92] Overall, according to a member of Ayub's cabinet, there was no "careful analysis of the pros and cons" in the planning for the war.[93]

The 1971 Indo-Pakistani War exhibited similar patterns in decision-making as the 1965 conflict.[94] Fragmented institutions meant that senior bureaucrats were not involved in the decision-making process. Both the foreign and defence secretaries learned of key decisions through public radio announcement.[95] This curtailed the ability of Pakistan's bureaucracy to relay information to the Chief Executive, Yahya Khan. Foreign Secretary Agha Shahi, for instance, routinely sent reports containing a "realistic diplomatic picture" that "were not finding their way" to the leader. Shahi himself describes the Foreign Ministry as "playing no role" in decision-making during the war.[96] Bureaucrats similarly feared speaking truth to power. One retired foreign minister recalled that "the Foreign Office virtually gave up its role of giving independent advice

---

[86] Gul Hassan Khan, *Memoirs of Lt. Gen. Gul Hassan Khan* (Karachi: Oxford University Press, 1993), 139. Gul Hassan Khan was serving as the Director General of Military Operations at the time. See also Arif, *Khaki Shadows*, 52–53.
[87] Mohammed Musa, *My Version: India-Pakistan War, 1965* (Lahore: Wajidalis, 1983), 5.
[88] Musa, 4–5; Mahmud Ahmed, *Illusion of Victory: A Military History of the Indo-Pakistan War–1965* (Karachi: Lexicon Publishers, 2002), 24.
[89] Arif, *Khaki Shadows*, 48.
[90] Iqbal Akhund, *Memoirs of a Bystander* (Karachi: Oxford University Press, 1997), 82–83.
[91] Mohammad Asghar Khan, *The First Round: Indo-Pakistan War 1965* (New Delhi: Vikas, 1979), 1–11; Khan, *Memoirs of Lt. Gen. Gul Hassan Khan*, 177.
[92] Musa, *My Version*, 5–10.
[93] Bajwa, *From Kutch to Tashkent*, 97–98.
[94] Raghavan, *1971: A Global History of the Creation of Bangladesh*, 34–35, 233–234.
[95] Government of Pakistan, *Hamoodur Rehman Commission Report*, 262.
[96] Zaheer, *The Separation of East Pakistan*, 311.

Table 7.3 *Summary of the Kargil War*

Crisis (institution)	Pathway	Observable implications		
	Information provision	Leader projections	Outcome	Miscalculation
Kargil War (siloed)	*Low quality*: restricted dialogue between military, MoFA, and ISI; parochial bias in military information	Pakistani military will successfully seize Kargil heights; limited international pressure to withdraw	Indian counterattack compels Pakistan to restore territorial status quo ante bellum; international community imposes costs in excess of Pakistan's tolerance	Yes

and contented itself with just carrying out uncritically the policies of the Yahya regime."[97]

Finally, tracing Pakistan's decision-making prior to the 1999 Kargil War helps to illustrate the unique pathway by which siloed institutions lead to miscalculation. Table 7.3 provides an overview of the key components of the case. This case is particularly helpful for two reasons. First, while the discussion of the 1965 and 1971 Indo-Pakistani wars are illuminating, the ineffective decision-making processes might also be attributable to the preferences and dispositions of the military rulers under which they occurred. The Kargil War, in contrast, was launched under civilian leadership, meaning that the outcome cannot be explained by military rule alone. Second, the case illustrates the unique pathways to miscalculation associated with siloed institutions. Whereas the Sino-Indian War discussed in Chapter 6 shows how fragmented institutions led bureaucrats to provide information that was congruent with Nehru's prior beliefs, patterns in bureaucratic information flow prior to the Kargil War were systematically different. Pakistan's bureaucracy did not withhold information because they were afraid to speak truth to

---

[97] Kasuri, *Neither a Hawk Nor a Dove*, 788. See also S. M. Burke, "The Management of Pakistan's Foreign Policy," in *Pakistan: The Long View*, ed. Lawrence Ziring and Ralph Braibanti (Durham: Duke University Press, 1977), 361.

power. Rather, bureaucrats did not speak up because they did not know that Sharif needed their counsel.

The Kargil War

Since the partition of India and Pakistan in 1947, the two sides have contested control of the province of Kashmir, which rests in the far north of India and the northeast of Pakistan. A "Line of Control" divides Pakistan-held territory in the north and west from Indian-held territory in the south and east. The city of Kargil is located on the Indian-held side of the Line of Control. The heights north of Kargil overlook National Highway 1A, the military transit and resupply route between Srinagar and Leh. Kargil has historically represented strategic terrain for both sides, as control of the Kargil heights protects India's ability to resupply its forces east of Srinagar.[98] The strategic importance of Kargil increased after India seized terrain north of Leh in the Siachen glacier in 1984.[99] The Indian position in Siachen was logistically dependent on the highway running below the Kargil heights.[100] Cutting off these supply lines would thus threaten India's stronghold in Siachen. During the 1980s and 1990s, both India and Pakistan engaged in small-scale military operations to establish posts along the Line of Control.[101]

In the winter of 1998, there were at least two strategies available to Pakistan to settle the territorial dispute with India. The first option was to continue diplomatic engagement with India and the international community. After India and Pakistan's nuclear tests in May 1998, there was a window of opportunity for negotiations between the two countries. As the Indian High Commissioner stationed in Pakistan at the time summarized, the Indian government under the newly elected leadership of Prime Minister Atal Bihari Vajpayee made the decision to "reduce tensions" and "bring the temperature down" after the nuclear tests.[102]

Three developments highlight the diplomatic momentum from the summer of 1998 to the spring of 1999. First, both countries expressed willingness to revive diplomatic engagement. On May 30, 1998, Pakistani Foreign Secretary Shamshad Ahmad stated that Pakistan was "prepared

---

[98] "Nawaz Blames Musharraf for Kargil," *The Times of India*, May 26, 2006.
[99] Khan, Lavoy, and Clary, "Pakistan's Motivations and Calculations for the Kargil Conflict," 74.
[100] Nawaz, *Crossed Swords*, 508.
[101] Nasim Zehra, *From Kargil to the Coup: Events That Shook Pakistan* (Lahore: Sang-e-Mee, 2019), 40; Khan, Lavoy, and Clary, "Pakistan's Motivations and Calculations for the Kargil Conflict," 77–79.
[102] Interview with G. Parthasarathi, October 20, 2019, *Strategic News International*.

to enter into discussion with India for taking all steps that are necessary to ensure mutual restraint and equitable measures for nuclear stabilization in the region."[103] On June 6, Nawaz Sharif echoed Ahmad's comments, telling a joint session of Parliament that he was open to diplomatic talks with India.[104] The Pakistani Ministry of Foreign Affairs formally offered to resume a diplomatic dialogue between India and Pakistan on June 11, 1998.[105] The Indian Ministry of External Affairs wrote to accept Pakistan's offers on June 12, 1998 and Vajpayee formally expressed readiness to meet in Colombo in a letter to Sharif on June 14, 1998.[106] While the Colombo meeting was a diplomatic stalemate, both sides agreed to continue talks.[107] The following month, Foreign Minister Sartaj Aziz and Vajpayee met at the Non-Aligned Movement summit in Durban, where the two sides reached an agreement to revive talks at the foreign secretary level. The first of these meetings occurred in Islamabad in October and in New Delhi in November. The Indian and Pakistani prime ministers held a sideline meeting in September 1998 at the UN General Assembly, during which they agreed that Vajpayee would visit Pakistan the following year.[108] These talks were accompanied by a joint statement outlining a framework for issues to be negotiated diplomatically.[109] In October, Foreign Minister Aziz noted that India was "expressing its desire to improve its relations with Pakistan" and that Pakistan was looking forward to a sustained dialogue.[110] Finally, the Indian and Pakistani

[103] "Announcement by Pakistan Foreign Secretary Shamshad Ahmad on the Sixth Test Conducted by Pakistan thereby Completing the Current Series," May 30, 1998, in Avtar Singh Bhasin, ed., *India-Pakistan Relations, 1947–2007: A Documentary Study* (New Delhi: Ministry of External Affairs, 2012), Vol. 6, 4599.
[104] "Statement by Pakistan Prime Minister Nawaz Sharif at the Joint Session of the Parliament Making an Offer of Talks to India," June 6, 1998, in Bhasin, Vol. 5, 3597.
[105] "Press Statement by Pakistan Ministry of Foreign Affairs Offering Resumption of Pakistan-India Dialogue," June 11, 1998, in Bhasin, *India-Pakistan Relations, 1947–2007*, Vol. 5, 3598.
[106] "Press Release Issued by the Ministry of External Affairs regarding Modalities of Official Dialogue between India and Pakistan," June 12, 1998; "Letter from Prime Minister Atal Behari Vajpayee to Pakistan Prime Minister Muhammad Nawaz Sharif," June 14, 1998, in Bhasin, *India-Pakistan Relations, 1947–2007*, Vol. 5, 3599–3600. Sharif affirmatively replied to this note on June 23, 1998.
[107] "Press Statement by Foreign Secretary K. Raghunath on the Rationale for Bilateral, Composite and Broad Based Dialogue to Solve the Outstanding Issues between the Two Countries," July 31, 1998, in Bhasin, *India-Pakistan Relations, 1947–2007*, 3604–3605.
[108] A. G. Noorani, "The Truth about the Lahore Summit," *Frontline* 19, no. 4 (2002).
[109] "Joint Statement Issued at the End of a Summit Meeting between Prime Minister Atal Behari Vajpayee and Pakistan Prime Minister Nawaz Sharif on the Sidelines of the UN General Assembly Session," September 23, 1998, in Bhasin, *India-Pakistan Relations*, Vol. 5, 3606.
[110] Shireen M. Mazari, *The Kargil Conflict 1999: Separating Fact from Fiction* (Islamabad: Institute of Strategic Studies, 2003), 94.

defence secretaries opened negotiations on the Siachen border dispute in November, agreeing to "continue discussions on the issue during the next round of the dialogue process."[111]

Second, and more significantly, Prime Minister Nawaz Sharif and Prime Minister Atal Bihari Vajpayee met for a summit in Lahore. In February 1999, Sharif and Vajpayee signed a landmark agreement establishing a framework for diplomatic negotiations, as well as for further confidence-building measures between the two countries. The Lahore Declaration, as the agreement was called, reflected a compromise between India's preferences for more stable bilateral relations and Pakistan's interest in a fair settlement on the Kashmir issue. A joint statement released on the same day detailed the diplomatic mechanism for negotiating these issues and increased cooperation in a number of other areas, including trade, information technology, international travel, detainees and missing prisoners of war.[112]

Third, diplomatic initiatives yielded new confidence-building measures between India and Pakistan. On January 1, 1999, both sides exchanged lists of nuclear installations.[113] On January 17, the two sides agreed to initiate regular bus service between New Delhi and Lahore. In mid-February, parliamentarians from India and Pakistan met in Islamabad for the first time in fifty years.[114] The Lahore Declaration was accompanied by a memorandum of understanding between the two foreign ministries, which specified a number of areas of bilateral cooperation ranging from commitment to dialogue, consultation, accident notification, and confidence building measures.[115] Just prior to the talks, Pakistani spokesperson Tariq Altaf even indicated that Sharif was open to a reduction of forces in Kashmir.[116]

---

[111] "Joint Press Statement Issued on the Conclusion of 7th Round of Talks between the Defence Secretaries of India and Pakistan on Siachen," November 6, 1998, in Bhasin, *India-Pakistan Relations*, Vol. 6, 5343. "Note Circulated to the Press by the Government of India after the Seventh Round of India–Pakistan Talks on Siachen," November 6, 1998, in Bhasin, *India-Pakistan Relations, 1947–2007*, Vol. 6, 5344–5345.
[112] "Joint Statement Issued by Indian Prime Minister Atal Behari Vajpayee and Pakistan Prime Minister Muhammad Nawaz Sharif," February 21, 1999.
[113] "Note from Pakistan Ministry of Foreign Affairs Listing Its Nuclear Installations," January 1, 1999; "Note from Ministry of External Affairs Listing Indian Nuclear Facilities," January 1, 1999, in Bhasin, *India-Pakistan Relations*, Vol. 6, 4628–4629.
[114] Mazari, *The Kargil Conflict*, 96.
[115] "Memorandum of Understanding Signed by Indian Foreign Secretary K. Raghunath and Pakistan Foreign Secretary Shamshad Ahmad," February 21, 1999.
[116] Ashraf Mumtaz, "Vajpayee Arrives Today: Open-Ended Agenda for Summit," *Dawn Wire Service*, February 20, 1999; Hasan Akhtar, "Nawaz-Vajpayee Agenda Includes Kashmir," *Dawn Wire Service*, February 13, 1999.

Through the spring of 1999, Pakistan's Foreign Ministry continued these diplomatic exchanges and confidence-building measures. On March 9, India and Pakistan signed an agreement relaxing restrictions on business visas. On March 21, the Pakistani and Indian foreign ministers met in Sri Lanka, agreeing to speed up nuclear talks and hold another dialogue in May. Indian accounts from senior R&AW leadership similarly indicate that Vajpayee had authorized the Foreign Minister Jaswant Singh to explore an agreement on Kashmir.[117] As late as May 9, the Pakistani Ambassador in India, Ashraf Jehangir Qazi stated that the "spirit of the Lahore declaration has not evaporated and both sides are committed to it."[118]

A second strategic option, and the one that Pakistan ultimately chose to pursue, was to seize territory in Kashmir in order to compel India to make bargaining concessions. In the 1980s, the Pakistan military had developed contingency plans to seize the heights overlooking Kargil, thereby threatening India's military posture in Kashmir and improving Pakistan's tactical advantage. In late 1998, Chief of Army Staff Pervez Musharraf began planning for a military initiative to seize Kargil.[119] In February 1999, as the Lahore Declaration was being signed, the Pakistani military began troop movements and construction of new military outposts on the border.[120] In March 1999, in the months during which the agreements reached at Lahore were to be executed, the military operation began. By the end of April, the Pakistani military had established over a hundred new posts across the Line of Control.[121]

Sharif oversaw the operation through a series of meetings with the military leadership from January to May.[122] During this period, Sharif retained the ultimate control over the most important strategic decisions. In mid-May, for example, Chief of Army Staff Musharraf told Sharif that he would withdraw Pakistani units if Sharif gave the order. Sharif instead chose to proceed with the military gambit.[123]

---

[117] Dulat, *The Vajpayee Years*, 24–29; see also Joseph R. Gregory, "India, Pakistan: Pledge to Improve Relations," *The New York Times*, March 20, 1999.
[118] Agence France-Presse, "India Reinforces Kashmir Troops," *The New York Times*, May 23, 1999.
[119] Pervez Musharraf, *In the Line of Fire: A Memoir* (London: Simon & Schuster, 2006), 87–88; Zehra, *From Kargil to the Coup*, 96.
[120] Nawaz, *Crossed Swords*, 514.
[121] Mazari, *The Kargil Conflict*, 42–49; Musharraf, *In the Line of Fire*, 90.
[122] On the January 29th briefing, see Mazari, *The Kargil Conflict*, 57; Musharraf, *In the Line of Fire*, 95–96; Khan, Lavoy, and Clary, "Pakistan's Motivations and Calculations for the Kargil Conflict," 85; Zehra, *From Kargil to the Coup*, 134.
[123] Zehra, *From Kargil to the Coup*, 167.

The Logic of Sharif's Decision. The logic of Sharif's choice rested on two assessments. The first pertained to the probable outcome of the crisis. The premise of Operation Koh Paima was that once Pakistani forces were in position, the Indian army would not be able to dislodge them. The hope was that Indian forces would be worn out from the counterinsurgency in Kashmir and from cross-border tensions.[124] Local Indian forces already in Kashmir might thus be unable to take back the Kargil heights. In addition, the covert nature of the operation might catch India by surprise and, as a result, Indian reinforcements might not arrive until late June or early July. By that time, the Pakistan military could furnish reinforcements of their own, thereby securing their hold over contested territory.[125]

The best evidence presently available suggests that Sharif shared these optimistic conclusions. During a briefing by the military leadership on January 29, Sharif argued that "small-scale operations could complement his political and diplomatic efforts to move forward on détente and peace with India."[126] When the military explained the risks associated with the operation, Sharif simply told the military to "fix it."[127] During a pivotal meeting on May 17, in which Sharif gave the green light to continue the operation, the prime minister noted that the plan was moving in the right direction.[128] Sharif remarked that there would be "no withdrawal" and "no surrender of any post" that Pakistan had established along the border. When Sharif asked if Pakistan could hold their new positions, he was reportedly assured that Pakistan's forces could do so.[129] Sharif reportedly remarked that the military operation presented an opportunity to Pakistan that diplomacy alone could not afford: the opportunity to settle the Kashmir issue through force.[130]

The second assessment concerned the probable response from India and the international community. The premise was that, because of the anticipated strength of the Pakistani position, any Indian counteroffensive would entail considerable battlefield costs, which the Indian

---

[124] Feroz Hassan Khan, *Eating Grass: The Making of the Pakistani Bomb* (Stanford: Stanford University Press, 2012), 312.
[125] Khan, Lavoy, and Clary, "Pakistan's Motivations and Calculations for the Kargil Conflict," 86–87; Zehra, *From Kargil to the Coup*, 123–124.
[126] Zehra, *From Kargil to the Coup*, 134.
[127] Interview with Mahmud Ahmed, quoted in Khan, Lavoy, and Clary, "Pakistan's Motivations and Calculations for the Kargil Conflict," 85.
[128] Interview with a Pakistani official who participated in the meeting, Islamabad, Fall 2017.
[129] Interview with Ziauddin Butt, quoted in Nawaz, *Crossed Swords*, 517.
[130] Zehra, *From Kargil to the Coup*, 164–165.

government would be unwilling to pay.[131] In parallel, Pakistan's leaders assessed that the international community would not pressure Pakistan to withdraw.[132] Instead, Pakistan could count on the United States, as well as the international community, to apply pressure on India to settle the Kashmir dispute on terms favorable to Pakistan. At minimum, international pressure would curb the risk of Indian military escalation on the border.[133]

Again, the evidence available suggests that Sharif shared these beliefs. Shortly after the conflict began, Sharif told U.S. President Bill Clinton that he had not expected India to react as strongly as it did.[134] Sharif later recalled that he believed that the operation "would neither cause any trouble nor result in loss of life."[135]

Pakistan's Outcome. The projections on which Nawaz Sharif based his choice to launch the Kargil War proved to be inaccurate. First, India escalated the fighting in Kargil. While initially surprised by the operation, India detected the incursions and ordered military operations in retaliation more quickly than Pakistani decision-makers had expected. India coupled brigade-size ground attacks on Pakistani positions with aerial bombing and artillery strikes. The Indian military was particularly effective in preventing Pakistan's posts from being resupplied. Although Indian progress was slow, it made steady gains on the battlefield throughout June and July. Casualties did not deter Indian politicians, who instead feared backing down before upcoming elections.[136] By the beginning of July, it was clear that Pakistan's battlefield position was tenuous at best. Sharif later recalled that Pakistan was losing its posts "one after the other" and was "on the verge" of a "very disgraceful retreat, and ultimately dishonorable defeat."[137]

Rather than support Pakistan in settling the Kashmir issue on more favorable terms, the international community's reaction was decidedly antagonistic. Sharif found himself under fierce diplomatic pressure, particularly from the United States and the United Kingdom. Both countries were alarmed that Pakistan would initiate a conflict that might escalate to

---

[131] In his memoirs, Musharraf hints at this conclusion by noting that he believed that Indian leaders had "unreasonably escalated" the conflict. See Musharraf, *In the Line of Fire*, 97.
[132] Khan, *Eating Grass*, 312.
[133] Ibid., 317; Khan, Lavoy, and Clary, "Pakistan's Motivations and Calculations for the Kargil Conflict," 72.
[134] Aziz, *Between Dreams and Realities*, 278.
[135] Warriach, *The Traitor Within*, 126.
[136] Chari, Cheema, and Cohen, *Four Crises and a Peace Process*, 141.
[137] Warriach, *The Traitor Within*, 129.

nuclear war and pressured Pakistan to withdraw behind the Line of Control immediately.[138] China quietly pushed Pakistan to resolve the crisis as well.[139] Sharif later recalled that Pakistan found itself "diplomatically isolated."[140] On July 4, Sharif traveled to the United States to seek out a political solution that would allow him to withdraw while saving face. U.S. officials found him "distraught" and "deeply worried" about the direction the crisis was headed.[141] Clinton was clear: if Sharif did not agree to withdraw, the United States would issue a public statement that would "pin the blame" for the crisis on Pakistan.[142] Sharif relented without concessions from the United States.[143] By Sharif's own account, the United States offered nothing in exchange beyond a vague assurance of U.S. interest in settling the Kashmir issue.[144] The deal Sharif struck did not even include a ceasefire, meaning that the Pakistani military suffered the bulk of its casualties as it retreated.[145]

The operation yielded no bargaining concessions in subsequent diplomatic talks with India. If anything, the Kargil operation undermined Pakistan's credibility in future peace talks with Pakistan. Indian Prime Minister Vajpayee told Pakistani Foreign Minister Aziz that the "real casualty" of the war was "the trust" between India and Pakistan.[146] Sharif later recalled that "the whole world held Pakistan responsible for the operation," which "adversely affected" the peace process.[147] Senior Pakistani diplomats similarly note that while discussions with India had achieved a "breakthrough" after the nuclear tests, progress was curtailed by the Kargil operation.[148] India's foreign minister, Jaswant Singh, questioned why "focused aggression in the Kargil sector" was occurring so "soon after the Lahore bus journey," especially when Lahore had inspired a "promise of peace."[149] In a statement released in June, Indian Prime Minister Vajpayee told the leadership in Pakistan that "while I talked

---

[138] Bruce Riedel, "American Diplomacy and the 1999 Kargil Summit at Blair House," in *Asymmetric Warfare in South Asia*, ed. Peter R. Lavoy (New York: Cambridge University Press, 2009), 133–134.
[139] Aziz, *Between Dreams and Realities*, 268.
[140] Warriach, *The Traitor Within*, 135.
[141] Riedel, "American Diplomacy and the 1999 Kargil Summit at Blair House," 138.
[142] Ibid., 140.
[143] Ibid., 141.
[144] Warriach, *The Traitor Within*, 133.
[145] Khan, *Eating Grass*, 314.
[146] Aziz, *Between Dreams and Realities*, 272.
[147] Warriach, *The Traitor Within*, 130.
[148] Interview with Shamshad Ahamad (Foreign Secretary), Islamabad, Fall 2017.
[149] Jaswant Singh, *India at Risk: Mistakes, Misconceptions and Misadventures of Security Policy* (New Delhi: Rainlight, 2013), 182.

peace with you, you were preparing to attack our borders."[150] The war also opened the door to relations between India and the United States, which would assist in India's successful coercive diplomacy during the Twin Peaks crisis.[151]

Institutional Origins of Sharif's Miscalculation. Siloed institutions help to explain Sharif's miscalculation. Under siloed institutions, we would expect that leaders are less likely to receive complete information from their advisers because of restrictions on bureaucratic access to information. The institutional theory of miscalculation expects bureaucrats in siloed institutions to withhold their counsel because they lack access to information available elsewhere in the state. This logic helps to explain why the advice that Pakistan's bureaucracies provided (and failed to provide) led Sharif to mistakenly conclude that India would refrain from escalating the conflict and that the international community would support Pakistan's gambit. Information was available at the time, but siloed institutions impeded its flow. As Pakistan's foreign minister later summarized, if there would have been a stronger "national security committee" in the spring of 1999, the decision-making process "would have been different."[152]

Prior to Sharif's decision to approve Operation Koh Paima, Sharif received little information besides that provided from the small group of military advisers planning the operation. As a result, defense information supplied by the military proved pivotal in Sharif's decision to give Operation Koh Paima the green light. The Director General of Military Operations, for example, assured Sharif that the operation would prove successful, owing to the strength of Pakistan's tactical positions, the lack of Indian resolve, and a conducive international environment.[153] When questioned whether Pakistani forces could hold their positions, the military replied, "Absolutely."[154] The Chief of General Staff reportedly told Sharif that he would "go down in history" as the prime minister under whose tenure the Kashmir issue was "resolved."[155] In fact, the military's assessment posited that the worst possible outcome of the operation was

---

[150] Celia W. Dugger, "Atmosphere Is Tense as India and Pakistan Agree to Talks," *The New York Times*, June 1, 1999.
[151] Riedel, "American Diplomacy and the 1999 Kargil Summit at Blair House," 142–143.
[152] Interview with Sartaj Aziz, Islamabad, Fall 2017.
[153] Zehra, *From Kargil to the Coup*, 162.
[154] Aziz, *Between Dreams and Realities*, 256.
[155] Zehra, *From Kargil to the Coup*, 164–165.

that India would withdraw from Siachen. At best, however, the planners felt that the operation would compel India to enter into a "serious dialogue on Kashmir."[156]

The wider bureaucracy in Pakistan possessed a considerable amount of information that contradicted the assessments that the military provided Sharif. Particularly important was the diplomatic information in the Foreign Ministry, which suggested that the reactions of India and the international community would be much different than the military assumed. Diplomats knew that Pakistan's ties with both the United States and China were comparatively weak and that both had recently moved to improve relations with India.[157] The Foreign Ministry had shouldered the bulk of responsibility for dealing with the diplomatic fall-out from Pakistan's 1998 nuclear tests, which foreshadowed increasing U.S. concern about the prospects for conflict between India and Pakistan.[158] Pakistan's Strategic Policy Review, developed in 1998, noted that Pakistan needed to mitigate the economic impact of nuclear sanctions, which implied that it would be susceptible to international pressure.[159] In addition, the Foreign Ministry assessed that the Vajpayee government in India was constrained by public opinion.[160] Such domestic political concerns would make it difficult for Indians to accept a military *fait accompli*. By May, Pakistani diplomats had received diplomatic warnings from both India and the United States.[161] The Indian High Commissioner in Pakistan, for instance, warned Pakistan's diplomats that India would use air power to regain the Kargil heights.[162]

Pakistan's foreign intelligence agency, the ISI, also seems to have been skeptical of the plan's chances for success. For example, a special team within the ISI reportedly drafted a report in late 1998 or early 1999 that emphasized the costs that a Kargil operation would entail.[163] Indeed, the ISI had harbored concerns on previous occasions when the military had proposed similar operations in Kargil. In the mid-1990s, for instance, the ISI conducted a review of a military plan to seize Kargil, which questioned how the military would translate battlefield gains into bargaining

---

[156] Zehra, *From Kargil to the Coup*, 123. See also Aziz, *Yeh Khamoshi Kahan Tak?* [How Long Will This Silence Remain?] (Islamabad: Seven Springs, 2015), 196.
[157] Khan, *Eating Grass*, 317.
[158] According to one U.S. official, the risk of nuclear conflict between India and Pakistan "dominated American nightmares" about the region. Riedel, "American Diplomacy and the 1999 Kargil Summit at Blair House," 134.
[159] Khan, *Eating Grass*, 308.
[160] Interview with Sartaj Aziz, cited in Nawaz, *Crossed Swords*, 518.
[161] Interview with Riaz Hussain Khokar (Pakistan's Ambassador in the United States), Islamabad, Fall 2017; Zehra, *From Kargil to the Coup*, 166–167.
[162] Interview with G. Parthasarathi, October 20, 2019, *Strategic News International*.
[163] Zehra, *From Kargil to the Coup*, 121.

concessions, particularly given that Pakistan might face international pressure to withdraw.[164]

Critically, however, there was no institutional mechanism to force information exchange between the military, Foreign Ministry, and ISI. Military leaders chose to share and withhold information as suited their interests. As a result, diplomatic and intelligence bureaucrats were systematically disadvantaged to identify the advice that Sharif needed.

As a result, neither the Foreign Ministry nor the ISI provided their information to Sharif until after Pakistani military units had already moved across the Line of Control. The lack of information provision was not linked to unwillingness to contradict Sharif. Rather, key bureaucratic stakeholders were not aware a military operation was underway and did not recognize that their information was needed. Foreign Minister Aziz, for example, was not informed until mid-May.[165] Foreign Secretary Shamshad Ahmad recalls that the Foreign Ministry had not been consulted.[166] ISI Director General, Ziauddin Butt, similarly recalls a lack of dialogue between the military and the Pakistani intelligence wing.[167] Indeed, the head of ISI analysis, Shahid Aziz, recounts that he only became aware of the military operation in May.[168] Meetings in which the Foreign Ministry and ISI were present did not discuss the new military initiative.[169]

Would Sharif's diplomatic and intelligence advisers have provided more information sooner if they had been aware of Operation Koh Paima? Foreign Secretary Ahmad later claimed that if he had been consulted prior to its initiation, he would have advised against it.[170] Foreign Minister Sartaj Aziz similarly reflected that if there had been institutional support for a continuing deliberation and assessment, information flow might have improved and the Foreign Ministry might have been successful in "preempting" the military's operation.[171] Indeed, both the Foreign Ministry and ISI raised concerns after learning of the military operation.[172]

---

[164] Zehra, *From Kargil to the Coup*, 46–47.
[165] Aziz, *Between Dreams and Realities*, 258.
[166] Interview with Shamshad Ahmad (Foreign Secretary), Islamabad, 2017. In his memoir's, Ahmad noted that the operation was "launched without political blessing." See Shamshad Ahmad, *Dreams Unfulfilled* (Lahore: Jahangir Book Depot, 2009), 155.
[167] Nawaz, *Crossed Swords*, 517–518.
[168] Aziz, *Yeh Khamoshi Kahan Tak*, 196.
[169] Aziz, *Between Dreams and Realities*, 253; Zehra, *From Kargil to the Coup*, 156.
[170] Interview with Shamshad Ahmad (Foreign Secretary), Islamabad, Fall 2017.
[171] Interview with Sartaj Aziz (Foreign Minister), Islamabad, Fall 2017.
[172] Aziz, *Between Dreams and Realities*, 258; Zehra, *From Kargil to the Coup*, 164.

Pakistan's decision-making prior to the Kargil War illustrates a second key aspect of siloed institutions: bureaucrats provide low-quality information that skews toward their parochial perspectives. For one, there is considerable evidence that the military did not clearly explain to Sharif that Operation Koh Paima would involve conventional military units, as opposed to mujahideen fighters about which Pakistan would have plausible deniability. While Sharif was aware, in a general sense, of ongoing operations in Kashmir, it appears that the Pakistan's military leadership described the operation as a "tactical maneuver of limited dimensions."[173] As such, it appears that Sharif did not understand that the operation went beyond covert support to mujahedeen fighters, which had been Pakistan's policy throughout that decade.

Why was the information that Sharif's defense advisers provided of such low-quality? One possibility consistent with the logic of siloed institutions would suggest that military leaders anticipated that other bureaucracies would provide input to Sharif on matters beyond military planning. Military leaders indicated on several occasions that the broader implications of Operation Koh Paima, such as "how to deal with the political and diplomatic aspects," would need to be determined by others.[174] The military reportedly noted that political decisions were out of its mandate and resisted providing input.[175]

Another possibility also consistent with the logic of siloed institutions is that is that involvement in the planning of the operation biased the military leadership's assessments regarding its prospects for success. Indeed, others inside Pakistan's defense establishment were skeptical of Operation Koh Paima once they learned of it. An analysis by the Joint Staff, for instance, suggested that India would react by deploying reserves and artillery. Even if the operation was successful in blocking the highway, the analysis concluded, India would likely launch a counterattack elsewhere in Kashmir, which would escalate the conflict and undermine the country's political goals.[176] Yet these core portions of the military staff that would normally evaluate such a plan were not consulted in advance.[177] The Pakistani defence secretary, also excluded from the planning process until May, similarly assessed that Pakistan's Foreign Ministry would

---

[173] Musharraf, *In the Line of Fire*, 98. It is not clear if the military deliberately withheld information from Sharif to obscure the facts of the operation, or if Sharif simply lacked the institutional support to process the information he was presented.
[174] Malik, *Kargil*, 411.
[175] Musharraf, *In the Line of Fire*, 96–97.
[176] Interview with JCS Headquarters staff officer, cited in Nawaz, *Crossed Swords*, 514.
[177] Interview with Ehsan ul Haq (Director General of Military Intelligence), Islamabad, Fall 2017; Aziz, *Yeh Khamoshi Kahan Tak*, 197.

"never be able to handle" the diplomatic fallout from the operation and that India would not accept the *fait accompli* as the military hoped.[178]

Another possible explanation for the low-quality information that the military provided instead suggests that the planners of Operation Koh Paima *intended* the operation to fail, either to sabotage diplomatic negotiations or to instigate a coup against Sharif.[179] Yet the bulk of the evidence does not support this interpretation. The military's confidence appears to have been genuine. In internal discussions with other military leaders in January, operational commanders reportedly were quick to assure Chief of Army Staff Musharraf that Pakistan's battlefield position was strong. Both Musharraf and his subordinates were aware that their careers were on the line if the operation failed.[180] In a private conversation between Musharraf and his Chief of General Staff on May 26, both military leaders suggested that the operation was likely to succeed in catalyzing international pressure for diplomatic negotiations between India and Pakistan, during which Pakistan would presumably have the advantage.[181] In short, the available evidence suggests that Musharraf's rise to power in the aftermath of the Kargil War was an inadvertent byproduct of the war's failed outcome, not the result of a shrewd and Machiavellian strategy to seize control.

Alternative Explanations. Several alternative explanations for the Kargil War are worth examining. Accountability theory struggles to explain the case, as public opinion played no obvious role in Sharif's choice to initiate the war. The prime minister may have suspected that the public would welcome a military victory, but there is no evidence that the public was clamoring for immediate action.

Sharif's choices also do not appear to be the result of entrenched leader beliefs. On the contrary, Sharif came to office primed to pursue a more peaceful relationship with India. Before entering office, for example, Sharif asked one of his advisers, "Are we going to go on fighting? For the last fifty years there has been no way to resolve [the Kashmir issue]. We cannot get a perfect solution. We must find some solution."[182] Yet despite these prior beliefs, military advisers persuaded Sharif that it was in Pakistan's interest to approve a gambit that would derail Sharif's efforts to foster better relations with India.

---

[178] Zehra, *From Kargil to the Coup*, 165–166.
[179] Sharif alleges this to be the case. Warriach, *The Traitor Within*, 128–129.
[180] Zehra, *From Kargil to the Coup*, 120. See also Aziz, *Yeh Khamoshi Kahan Tak*, 196–198.
[181] The telephone conversation was intercepted by India, who subsequently released the transcript. See Malik, *Kargil*, 410–411.
[182] Interview with Sartaj Aziz, quoted in Noorani, "Interview with Sartaj Aziz."

The case is partially consistent with an interest group model of bureaucratic politics, in that biased military information did push Pakistan toward international conflict. Yet the institutional theory of miscalculation explains several points for which traditional civil-military relations models struggle to account. First, inconsistent with the interest group model, Sharif made the most important decisions throughout the operation. While the military may have withheld information from Sharif, they did not take autonomous actions without Sharif's approval. Sharif similarly chose not withdraw Pakistani forces from Kargil when given the opportunity in mid-May – and seems to have done so based on assessments that the plan would succeed.[183] Second, the interest group model does not explain why diplomatic and intelligence advisers failed to relay information to Sharif in early 1999. The logic of siloed institutions helps explain the poor horizontal flow of information that undermined the ability of civilian bureaucrats to identify what information would best serve Sharif's decision-making.

A final alternative explanation unique to this case is that nuclear weapons might have emboldened Pakistani decision-makers to launch the war, anticipating that India would be unable or unwilling to respond in kind.[184] Some operational military planners reportedly believed that nuclear weapons would prevent India from escalating the fighting along the border. Rather than risk a nuclear confrontation, India would simply accept the *fait accompli*.[185] To a large extent, however, these assessments proved to be wrong: nuclear weapons did not prevent India from delivering a sufficiently powerful military response resulting in a Pakistani defeat.[186] Moreover, the available evidence suggests that the potential for nuclear escalation was not evaluated during the military planning process. The planners of Operation Koh Paima had no experience with nuclear deterrence and had no institutional support specializing in this topic.[187] Indeed, Pakistan established a new government organization for nuclear strategy, the Strategic Plans Division, *after* the Kargil War to provide the analysis that Pakistan lacked in 1999. Thus, the implications of the nuclear revolution were not immediately obvious, but rather a product of the low-quality information to which Sharif had access.

---

[183] Zehra, *From Kargil to the Coup*, 167. Musharraf proved true to his word after Sharif decided to end the war in July, despite the military's assessment that they could continue to hold their positions.
[184] Narang, *Nuclear Strategy in the Modern Era*, 267–273.
[185] Khan, Lavoy, and Clary, "Pakistan's Motivations and Calculations for the Kargil Conflict," 87.
[186] Ibid., 88.
[187] Ibid., 90.

Conclusion

This chapter examined the origins and consequences of national security institutions in a regime in which political leaders faced a persistent threat of coup at the hands of the national security bureaucracy. Much like the case of India discussed in Chapter 6, the institutions that Pakistan inherited in 1947 devolved into a less effective system by the 1950s. Leaders resolved the trade-off between quality information and political security in favor of the latter. The institutional strategy that Pakistan's leaders have employed to secure themselves, however, depended on the nature of their political agenda. For Pakistan's military rulers, fragmented institutions complemented the transformational domestic programs they sought to implement. For Pakistan's leaders with circumscribed domestic ambitions, siloed institutions reflected the salient external threats that Pakistan has faced from India.

The siloed institutions that emerged in the late 1980s produced a distinctive pathway to miscalculation. As illustrated by the case on the Kargil War, siloed institutions led to blunders stemming from restrictions on competitive dialogue between bureaucracies that might have curbed parochial information provision. This pathway to miscalculation looked quite similar to the way in which parochial advice caused Jiang Zemin to miscalculate during the 2001 EP-3 reconnaissance aircraft incident discussed in Chapter 5. Diplomats and intelligence analysts failed to provide information to Prime Minister Nawaz Sharif not because of an inaccessible leader or because they feared political punishment. Rather, they failed to provide needed input because they were unaware of the advice that Sharif's defense advisers were offering. As a result, Sharif entered the war holding inaccurate projections of his prospects for success.

The chapter advances the book's broader argument by highlighting the central importance of the competitive dialogue in helping leaders determine when bureaucrats are providing low-quality information. While existing literature commonly attributes Pakistan's failure during the Kargil War to pathological civil-military relations, a deeper look suggests that Sharif approved the gambit. While Sharif remained the final decision-maker, he lacked institutional support to put the advice he received into dialogue with other bureaucracies possessing different information and perspectives. A small number of military advisers won the day not because they acted independently, but because they could persuade the leader that their plan would work. In short, the origins of Pakistan's miscalculation rest within the institutions that its leaders possessed – and the political constraints that necessitated their pathological design. Chapter 8 shows how a similar logic can apply in institutionalized democracies, such as the United States.

8 The United States during the Early Cold War

The American escalation in Vietnam was arguably the costliest foreign policy failure of its history. More U.S. soldiers were killed in Vietnam than during the conflicts in Korea, the Persian Gulf, Iraq, and Afghanistan combined.[1] As many as three million Vietnamese soldiers and civilians lost their lives. The settlement eventually reached between the United States and North Vietnam in January 1973 was not substantially better than the alternatives that had been available to the United States in early 1965. The United States negotiated its withdrawal and, by 1975, the regime in Saigon that the United States had fought so hard to preserve fell to Communist rule.

Unlike so many other decision-makers who deflect blame for failed foreign policies, the American officials who oversaw the decision for escalation in Vietnam were unusually candid about their shortcomings. National Security Advisor McGeorge Bundy admitted that Vietnam was "a war we should not have fought."[2] The "cardinal error" of the war, Bundy reflected, was that the spread of communism in Southeast Asia "could have been contained just about as well as it was at much lower cost."[3] Defense Secretary Robert McNamara agreed, stating that "we were wrong, terribly wrong."[4] "Disengagement," McNamara reflected, "was the course we should have chosen."[5] Even President

---

[1] Korean War: 36,574 deaths; Vietnam War: 58,220 deaths; Persian Gulf War: 383 deaths; Operation Iraqi Freedom: 4,431; Operation Enduring Freedom (Afghanistan): 2,352. See Nese F. DeBruyne and Anne Leland, *American War and Military Operations Casualties: Lists and Statistics* (Washington, DC: Congressional Research Service, 2020); Department of Defense, "Casualty Status," July 25, 2022.

[2] Gordon M. Goldstein, *Lessons in Disaster: McGeorge Bundy and the Path to War in Vietnam* (New York: Holt, 2008), 227.

[3] McGeorge Bundy Vietnam Manuscript (hereafter MBVM), Introduction, 7. Box 224, John F. Kennedy Presidential Library (hereafter JFKL).

[4] Robert McNamara, *In Retrospect: The Tragedy and Lessons of Vietnam* (New York: Vintage, 1996), xx.

[5] Ibid., 164.

Lyndon Johnson would privately admit by the spring of 1968 that he had "goofed" in his decision-making on Vietnam.[6]

What is striking about these reflections from the architects of American escalation is not simply that they believed that they had erred, but also that they believed that the *process* by which they arrived at their decision was fundamentally flawed. McGeorge Bundy, who oversaw the National Security Council at the time, reflected that his "worst mistake" was that he had not pressed for a systematic "study of the prospects of success, of one side's strength and one side's weakness, especially in 1965."[7] Defense Secretary McNamara similarly remembered that Johnson's advisory team "never carefully debated what U.S. force would ultimately be required, what our chances of success would be, or what the political, military, financial, and human costs would be if we provided it. Indeed these basic questions went unanswered."[8] Even at the time, Undersecretary of State George Ball bemoaned the "lacunae" of analytical thought concerning the options available to the United States.

It is puzzling to find such limited analysis and deliberation on the eve of one of the most important foreign policy decisions of the Cold War. Accountability theory suggests that democracy should incentivize politicians to search far and wide for the best information possible in order to avoid policy miscalculations that might get them voted out. It is all the more puzzling when one considers that the ultimate decision-maker, Lyndon Johnson, possessed legendary political acumen.[9] McGeorge Bundy later recalled that the president was "living with his own political survival" each time he examined the issue.[10]

Why did such an ingenious and otherwise savvy politician choose what proved to be what one scholar describes as political "suicide" in slow motion?[11] The logic of national security institutions helps to explain this puzzle. No one factor can explain America's decision to double down rather than cut losses in Vietnam. The claim in this chapter is more circumscribed. It presents new evidence showing that Lyndon Johnson deliberately modified U.S. national security institutions to adopt a remarkably more fragmented system than his predecessors had designed. As a result, the information that Johnson received in the fateful

---

[6] Brian VanDeMark, *Road to Disaster: A New History of America's Descent into Vietnam* (New York: Custom House, 2018), 467.
[7] Goldstein, *Lessons in Disaster*, 178.
[8] McNamara, *In Retrospect*, 107.
[9] Doris Kearns Goodwin, *Lyndon Johnson and the American Dream* (New York: St. Martin's Griffin, 1976); Robert Dallek, *Flawed Giant: Lyndon Johnson and His Times, 1961–1973* (New York: Oxford University Press, 1998).
[10] VanDeMark, *Road to Disaster*, 214.
[11] Larry Berman, *Planning a Tragedy: The Americanization of the War in Vietnam* (New York: W.W. Norton & Company, 1982), 146.

months between November 1964 and March 1965 – when the most consequential decisions on Vietnam were made – was remarkably flawed.

Johnson's choice for fragmented institutions stemmed from a political trade-off. In order to get sound advice on whether escalation would fail – and, thus, whether doubling down in Vietnam might be even more costly to Johnson's political prospects than a graceful exit in 1965 – he needed an open flow of information and candid deliberation. In short, he needed integrated institutions. Yet Johnson feared that easing the costs of information sharing would also increase the risk that bureaucrats would impose immediate political costs by leaking that information. In particular, leaks might put at risk two ambitious goals that defined Johnson's agenda: the Great Society program and civil rights legislation.[12]

Johnson resolved this institutional trade-off in favor of the domestic agenda that he prized. Most consequentially, Johnson effectively shut down policy deliberation in the National Security Council and established an alternative, insular forum known as the Tuesday Luncheon. As historian Fred Logevall summarizes, Johnson's "fear of leaks" led to a "cloistered decision-making system that effectively excluded contrarian voices from the deliberation and discouraged in-depth reexamination of the fundamental issues among those who remained."[13] These choices minimized the immediate political threat that bureaucrats could pose, but they also degraded the quality of information that Johnson received. Information did reach Johnson's desk, but it was incomplete and skewed toward the beliefs that the president already held.

This chapter advances the book's argument regarding the relationship between fragmented institutions and the risk of miscalculation in two ways. First, the chapter applies the theory in the context of an institutionalized democracy. Whereas one might argue that political leaders in newly established democracies, such as India or Pakistan, have more latitude to shape national security institutions to their liking, such changes may be less likely in countries with comparatively strong checks on executive authority. Yet the case highlights that even well-institutionalized democracies can (and do) adopt ineffective decision-making processes despite the hazards they pose to foreign policy judgment. Second, it

---

[12] Others have noted that Johnson worried that his opponents would withhold support if he withdrew from Vietnam without a fight. Brian VanDeMark, *Into the Quagmire: Lyndon Johnson and the Escalation of the Vietnam War* (New York: Oxford University Press, 1991), 162; Francis M. Bator, "No Good Choices: LBJ and the Vietnam/Great Society Connection," *Diplomatic History* 32, no. 3 (2008): 309–340; Saunders, "War and the Inner Circle," 485–490; Alexander B. Downes, "How Smart and Tough are Democracies? Reassessing Theories of Democratic Victory in War," *International Security* 33, no. 4 (2009): 43–46.

[13] Fredrik Logevall, *Choosing War: The Lost Chance for Peace and the Escalation of War in Vietnam* (Berkeley: University of California Press, 2001), 394.

shows that political leaders use similar institutional strategies to protect themselves from bureaucrats aiming to punish leaders by coup or by public criticism.

The analysis also complements and contributes to ongoing debates about the origins of the American failure in Vietnam. For the purposes of this chapter, it is helpful to divide existing scholarship into two broad perspectives. One view suggests that American decision-makers faced a difficult situation, made the best use of the information available, and ultimately failed through no fault of their own.[14] Another school of thought argues that the United States miscalculated due to a number of psychological, organizational, and cultural reasons.[15] Among those who see Vietnam as a miscalculation, many place special blame on Johnson and his dysfunctional advisory system.[16] This chapter's findings side with existing accounts that view Johnson's beliefs and advisory system as central in explaining the U.S. miscalculation, but emphasizes how institutional trade-offs help account for the origins of these decision-making pathologies in the first place.

---

[14] For the canonical account, see Leslie H. Gelb and Richard K. Betts, *The Irony of Vietnam: The System Worked* (Washington, DC: Brookings Institution Press, 1979). See also John E. Mueller, "The Search for the 'Breaking Point' in Vietnam: The Statistics of a Deadly Quarrel," *International Studies Quarterly* 24, no. 4 (1980): 497–519.

[15] Early accounts include David Halberstam, *The Best and the Brightest* (New York: Random House, 1972); Frances FitzGerald, *Fire in the Lake: The Vietnamese and the Americans in Vietnam* (Boston: Little, Brown & Company, 1972); George C. Herring, *America's Longest War: The United States and Vietnam, 1950–1975*, 2nd ed. (Boston: McGraw-Hill, 2002). For later accounts, see VanDeMark, *Into the Quagmire*; Marilyn B. Young, *The Vietnam Wars* (New York: HarperCollins, 1991); David E. Kaiser, *American Tragedy: Kennedy, Johnson, and the Origins of the Vietnam War* (Cambridge: Harvard University Press, 2000); Logevall, *Choosing War*; VanDeMark, *Road to Disaster*. For accounts in political science that have made similar arguments, see Janis, *Victims of Groupthink*; Jervis, *Perception and Misperception in International Politics*; Yuen Foong Khong, *Analogies at War: Korea, Munich, Dien Bien Phu, and the Vietnam Decisions of 1965* (Princeton: Princeton University Press, 1992), Chapter 4; James H. Lebovic, *Planning to Fail: The US Wars in Vietnam, Iraq, and Afghanistan* (New York: Oxford University Press, 2019), Chapter 2. While most accounts suggest that the error was in failing to disengage from Vietnam, another variant suggests that the error stemmed from the American military strategy. See Andrew F. Krepinevich Jr., *The Army and Vietnam* (Baltimore: Johns Hopkins University Press, 1986); H. R. McMaster, *Dereliction of Duty: Lyndon Johnson, Robert McNamara, the Joint Chiefs of Staff and the Lies that Led to Vietnam* (New York: HarperCollins, 1997); Mark Moyar, *Triumph Forsaken: The Vietnam War, 1954–1965* (New York: Cambridge University Press, 2006).

[16] On the former, see George, *Presidential Decisionmaking in Foreign Policy*; Burke and Greenstein, *How Presidents Test Reality*; Lawrence Freedman, *Kennedy's Wars: Berlin, Cuba, Laos, and Vietnam* (New York: Oxford University Press, 2000); Logevall, *Choosing War*; Andrew Preston, *The War Council: McGeorge Bundy, the NSC, and Vietnam* (Cambridge: Harvard University Press, 2006). On the latter, see Berman, *Planning a Tragedy*; David M. Barrett, *Uncertain Warriors: Lyndon Johnson and His Vietnam Advisers* (Lawrence: University Press of Kansas, 1993).

The chapter proceeds as follows. The first section examines the origins of institutional design in the United States during the early Cold War. Studying institutional evolution over time suggests that different advisory processes might have been possible from 1964 to 1965 under different political conditions. The chapter then turns to institutional consequences. The second section uses the 1958 Taiwan Strait Crisis in order to illustrate how integrated institutions shaped Eisenhower's thinking on American strategy toward China and Taiwan. The third section traces in detail how fragmented institutions shaped the information on which Lyndon Johnson made the choice for escalation in Vietnam.

The Politics of Institutional Design in the United States during the Early Cold War

The early Cold War offers a fruitful period for exploring in detail how changes to the president's political environment shaped the evolution of U.S. national security institutions. By the early 1950s, U.S. national security institutions can best be described as integrated. Established in 1947, the U.S. National Security Council served as a mechanism for information exchange to "advise the President with respect to the integration of domestic, foreign, and military policies relating to national security."[17] A subsidiary coordination body, known in the Truman administration as the NSC Senior Staff committee, similarly aimed to increase the flow of information between bureaucracies. Overall, as noted in one government report, the goal of the U.S. system was to "bind together" diplomatic and military bureaucracies by creating "organizational ties," particularly in "the gathering of information and intelligence and its dissemination and use."[18]

This section shows how variation in the political environment lead three American presidents – Dwight D. Eisenhower, John F. Kennedy, and Lyndon Johnson – to adopt distinct national security institutions. While Eisenhower left the institutions that he inherited intact, Kennedy and Johnson each made substantial design changes. For Kennedy, these changes proved short-lived, quickly restoring an integrated system structurally similar to the one he inherited from Eisenhower. For Johnson, however, institutional change was substantial and long-lasting. Table 8.1 summarizes these changes, as well as the two key explanatory variables in the political theory of institutional design – bureaucratic threat and agenda focus.

---

[17] *National Security Act of 1947*, July 26, 1947.
[18] "Unification of the War and Navy Departments and Postwar Organization for National Security," June 19, 1945, 5–6.

Table 8.1 *Evolution of U.S. institutional design, 1953–1968*

Period	Bureaucratic threat	Leader agenda	National security institution	Theory support
1953–1960	*Low*: experienced leader; minimal leak threat	*International*: Cold War tensions; Korean War	*Integrated*: inclusive National Security Council, Planning Board, Operations Coordinating Board	Strong
1961	*Medium*: moderately inexperienced leader; minimal leak threat	*International*: Cold War tensions	*Siloed*: inclusive National Security Council; elimination of Planning Board and Operations Coordinating Board	Mixed
1962–1963	*Low*: more experienced leader; no change to leak threats	*International*: Cold War tensions	*Integrated*: inclusive National Security Council; establishment of the NSC Standing Group	Strong
1964–1968	*High*: highly inexperienced leader; high leak threat	*Domestic*: Great Society & Civil Rights legislation; easing of Cold War tensions	*Fragmented*: insular Tuesday Luncheon; restrictive information sharing	Strong

The Political Environment in the Eisenhower Administration

More than most American presidents, Eisenhower had little reason to believe that the national security bureaucracy posed a threat to his political survival. He came to the White House with a considerable amount of experience dealing with national security matters. During World War II, he served on the General Staff in the Pentagon, and later as the Supreme Allied Commander, military governor of the American occupied zone in Germany, and NATO Supreme Commander. These positions all featured an unusually high level of interaction with diplomatic and intelligence affairs. In short, Eisenhower was "absolutely certain" that he was "qualified to be" the commander-in-chief.[19]

---

[19] John W. Sloan, "The Management and Decision-Making Style of President Eisenhower," *Presidential Studies Quarterly* 20, no. 2 (1990): 298.

In addition, Eisenhower did not believe that the national security bureaucracy harbored the intent to undermine his political prospects. Historians note that there were no clear "cleavages" or factions within his inner circle.[20] One indication of this trust is found in the minimal number of leaks during the Eisenhower administration. While Eisenhower was aware of the possibility of spillage, there were few leaks originating from the NSC.[21] In fact, during one of his last NSC meetings, Eisenhower noted that he could "remember only one occasion when a remark made in the Council room during his Administration had been quoted publicly outside."[22]

Integrated Institutions Under Eisenhower

Given the low bureaucratic threat, the political theory of institutional design would predict that Eisenhower would retain the general features of the integrated system that he inherited. Indeed, he did so.[23] Despite having criticized Truman's NSC before entering office, Eisenhower made only a few changes to institutional design once in office.[24] A policy review approved by Eisenhower recommended comparatively few adjustments to the existing setup.[25] Eisenhower saw a direct connection between his institutional design and the minimal threat that bureaucratic leaks posed to his political survival. Shortly before leaving office, Eisenhower

---

[20] Dwight David Eisenhower, *The White House Years: Mandate for Change, 1953–1956* (New York: Doubleday, 1963), 83–89; Fred I. Greenstein and Richard H. Immerman, "Effective National Security Advising: Recovering the Eisenhower Legacy," *Political Science Quarterly* 115, no. 3 (2000): 343.

[21] "Memorandum of Discussion at the 183rd Meeting of the NSC," February 4, 1954. *FRUS 1952–1954, Indochina, Volume XIII, Part 1*; "Letter from the President to the Acting Secretary of State," October 8, 1956. *FRUS 1955–1957, Suez Crisis, July 26–December 31, 1956, Volume XVI*; "Memorandum of Discussion at the 165th Meeting of the NSC," October 7, 1953. *FRUS 1952–1954, National Security Affairs, Volume II, Part 1*.

[22] "Discussion at the 474th Meeting of the NSC," January 13, 1961. *FRUS 1961–1963, Volumes VII, VIII, IX (Microfiche Supplement)*.

[23] For an overview, see Robert R. Bowie and Richard H. Immerman, *Waging Peace: How Eisenhower Shaped an Enduring Cold War Strategy* (New York: Oxford University Press, 2000), 83–95; Robert Cutler Papers, Box 7, Dwight D. Eisenhower Presidential Library (hereafter DDEL).

[24] Anna Kasten Nelson, "The 'Top of Policy Hill': President Eisenhower and the National Security Council," *Diplomatic History* 7, no. 4 (1983): 308–309; Andrew Preston, "The Little State Department: McGeorge Bundy and the National Security Council Staff, 1961–65," *Presidential Studies Quarterly* 31, no. 4 (2001): 638.

[25] "Memorandum for the President by the Special Assistant to the President for National Security Affairs (Cutler)," March 16, 1953. *FRUS 1952–1954, National Security Affairs, Volume II, Part 1*; Robert Cutler, *No Time for Rest* (Boston: Little, Brown & Company, 1966), 299.

commented that the NSC had been "a body in which views were frankly and openly expressed" because "what was said in the room was secret."[26]

High Information Search Capacity. Integrated institutions under Eisenhower kept the costs of information transmission from the bureaucracy to the president low. The decision-making body, the NSC, included the secretary of state and secretary of defense as members. By rule, the chairman of the Joint Chiefs of Staff and director of the Central Intelligence Agency would always attend NSC meetings. Advisers had "full right" to submit reports to the NSC, as well as the explicit right to express "disagreement on the part of his department or agency with any part of such report."[27]

Exploring the patterns in Eisenhower's utilization of the NSC further shows that the structure of the NSC mattered to the way that decision-making proceeded. Eisenhower wanted the NSC in "constant use" and considered its importance commensurate with that of the Cabinet.[28] As illustrated in Figure 8.1, the NSC convened routinely, affording bureaucratic advisers nearly 600 hours of access to the president in formal meetings alone.[29]

This design shaped the bureaucracy's incentives to provide quality information. Eisenhower's subordinates believed that the president needed "the vital studies, advice and counsel that only a capable and well-developed staff organization" could offer.[30] Eisenhower's advisers also displayed a willingness to express genuine beliefs.[31] As one historian notes, Eisenhower's advisers were not "yes-men."[32] As such, the information that advisers provided could be highly persuasive. Eisenhower recalled that the NSC's debates "never failed" to provide "a deeper understanding of questions" and, on several occasions, successfully persuaded him "to reverse some of my preconceived notions."[33]

---

[26] "Discussion at the 474th Meeting of the NSC," January 13, 1961. *FRUS 1961–1963, Microfiche Supplement.*

[27] "Memorandum for the President by the NSA (Cutler)," March 16, 1953. *FRUS 1952–1954, Volume II, Part 1.* See also Dillon Anderson, "The President and National Security." *Atlantic Monthly*, January 1956, 44–45.

[28] Cutler, *No Time for Rest*, 295.

[29] See also Daalder and Destler, *In the Shadow of the Oval Office*, 5.

[30] Interview with Andrew Goodpaster, cited in "A Forum on the Role of the National Security Advisor," April 12, 2001. Wilson International Center for Scholars.

[31] Cutler, *No Time for Rest*, 298; Greenstein and Immerman, "Effective National Security Advising," 341; Robert H. Ferrell, ed., *The Eisenhower Diaries* (New York: W.W. Norton, 1981), 379.

[32] Nelson, "Top of Policy Hill," 310.

[33] Quoted in Greenstein and Immerman, "Effective National Security Advising," 344.

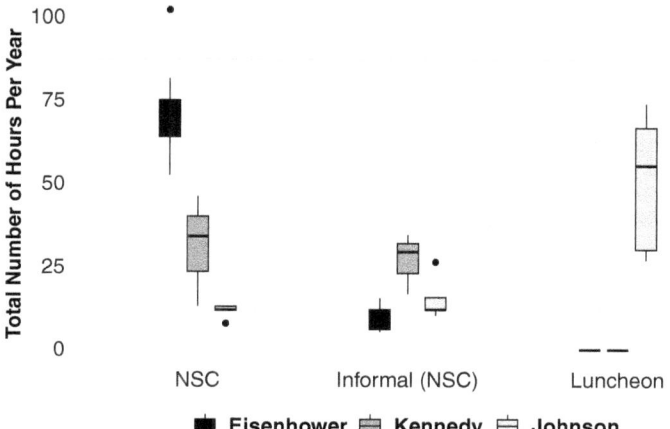

Figure 8.1 Venues for U.S. national security decision-making, 1953–1968
Note: Figure reports the average time per year that Eisenhower, Kennedy, and Johnson spent in NSC meetings, informal meetings with all NSC statutory members/advisers present, and Tuesday Luncheons. Data collected from the Presidential Daily Dairies. For details, see Appendix B.

Open Bureaucratic Access to Information. Integrated institutions also afforded open bureaucratic access to information. Eisenhower's NSC system featured two coordination bodies below the NSC itself. The Planning Board included representatives from a range of diplomatic, defense, intelligence, and economic bureaucracies.[34] Eisenhower later added an additional mechanism, the Operations Coordinating Board, to further expand horizontal information sharing. The NSC Planning Board regularly convened two to three times per week, in addition to routine meetings of the Operations Coordinating Board. This was by design. Eisenhower intuited that "some information would be lost" if it were put into "rigid compartments."[35]

Finally, Eisenhower modified the NSC structure in ways that pushed the U.S. structure toward an even more integrated design. One such change was to establish the position of the Special Assistant for National Security Affairs (NSA), whose primary function was inter-departmental coordination. The NSA led Planning Board meetings "in such manner

---

[34] Eisenhower's Planning Board was largely an organizational "rebranding" of the NSC Senior Staff that he had inherited. Gans, *White House Warriors*, 18.
[35] "Discussion at the 474th Meeting of the NSC," January 13, 1961. *FRUS 1961–1963, Microfiche Supplement.*

as to bring out the most active participation by all present and the most expeditious dispatch of business."[36] The NSA also ensured that information from across the bureaucracy was routinely circulated to all attendees prior to NSC meetings.[37]

Bureaucratic access to information interacted with high information search to yield high-quality information provision by the bureaucracy. One of Eisenhower's advisers described the NSC system as an "acid bath" that "brought every side of every question out into the clear light of day."[38] The institutional design explicitly prohibited disagreements from being "swept under the rug" or "glossed over."[39] In fact, Eisenhower later recalled that, had his advisers presented a unanimous conclusion, he "would have suspected that some important part of the subject was being overlooked, or that [his] subordinates had failed to study the subject."[40]

The Political Environment in the Kennedy Administration

Bureaucratic threat was modestly higher under Kennedy than under Eisenhower. Kennedy came to office with comparatively little experience managing the national security bureaucracy.[41] As historian Robert Dallek notes, Kennedy "anticipated dealing with more experienced Washington hands who would see his youth as a reason to assert their authority over him."[42] This did not mean that Kennedy lacked strong beliefs on or personal interest in foreign policy. He had served in the military during World War II and on the Foreign Relations Committee during his time in the Senate. Yet Kennedy's path to the White House did not feature intimate exposure to the inner workings of the bureaucratic establishment. During the Democratic primary, other candidates criticized Kennedy's inexperience in the area. Kennedy's campaign team took the liability seriously enough to draft memoranda emphasizing Kennedy's foreign travels and knowledge relative to other candidates.[43]

---

[36] "Memorandum for the President by the NSA (Cutler)," March 16, 1953. *FRUS 1952–1954, Volume II, Part 1*; "Executive Order 10483: Establishing the Operations Coordinating Board," September 2, 1953.
[37] Cutler, *No Time for Rest*, 301.
[38] Ibid., 300.
[39] Ibid., 305.
[40] Dwight David Eisenhower, *The White House Years: Waging Peace, 1956–1961* (New York: Doubleday, 1965), 632.
[41] Theodore C. Sorensen, *Kennedy* (New York: Harper, 2010), 281.
[42] Robert Dallek, *An Unfinished Life: John F. Kennedy, 1917–1963* (New York: Little, Brown & Company, 2003), 305–306.
[43] Dallek, *An Unfinished Life*, 264.

Kennedy himself told incoming Secretary of Defense Robert McNamara's that he did not "know how to be president" and stated they would "learn [their] jobs together."[44]

Nevertheless, there is little evidence that Kennedy perceived the national security bureaucracy, particularly at senior levels, as threatening his political prospects. Leaks from the national security bureaucracy were minimal. One NSC official who served in both administrations later noted that the Kennedy administration generally "did not have people fighting policy through the press."[45]

Second, Kennedy entered office with an agenda focused on foreign affairs.[46] Before becoming president, Kennedy noted that the "key thing" for the United States was to develop a "new foreign policy that will break out of the confines of the cold war."[47] Kennedy's advisers described that Kennedy felt that "the Presidency was above all about foreign policy" and described him as its "day-to-day director."[48] While his disposition may have shaped Kennedy's interest in foreign affairs, this interest was also the result of a political calculation. Kennedy believed he stood a better chance of delivering in foreign policy but "doubted" that he could do so in domestic affairs.[49] Kennedy noted that foreign affairs was "the only important issue for a President to handle."[50]

From Siloed to Integrated Institutions Under Kennedy

The moderate level of bureaucratic threat under Kennedy yields an indeterminate prediction for institutional design. Kennedy's inexperience with the bureaucracy offers one potential explanation for why he *initially* adopted siloed institutions. Both Kennedy himself, as well as his staff, described the president as "the center of a wheel" with "spokes out from himself."[51] Kennedy appears to have favored this model in part because of his level of prior experience. One speechwriter observed that several

---

[44] Richard Reeves, *President Kennedy: Profile of Power* (New York: Simon & Schuster, 1994), 25.
[45] Bromley Smith, Oral History Transcript (hereafter OHT). July 23, 1970, JFKL, 18.
[46] On Kennedy's foreign affairs focus, see Dallek, *An Unfinished Life*, 309, 327, 377.
[47] Dallek, *An Unfinished Life*, 237.
[48] Clark Clifford, *Counsel to the President: A Memoir* (New York: Random House, 1991), 656; Arthur M. Schlesinger, *A Thousand Days: John F. Kennedy in the White House* (New York: Houghton Mifflin, 2002), 424.
[49] Dallek, *An Unfinished Life*, 328.
[50] Ibid., 370. Kennedy chose a less ambitious path on most domestic issues, including civil rights and economic programs, relying more on executive action than Congressional legislation. See Dallek, *An Unfinished Life*, 330–334.
[51] Bromley K. Smith, *Organizational History of the National Security Council during the Kennedy and Johnson Administrations* (National Security Council, 1988), 17. Walt W. Rostow, OHT, April 11, 1964, JFKL, 12–13.

"limitations and pressures beset" Kennedy in assembling his advisory team, as most of his "previous contacts and friendships" were in the field of politics rather than the bureaucracy.[52] As Kennedy himself noted, "I can't afford to confine myself to one set of advisers. If I did that, I would be on their leading strings."[53]

High Information Search Capacity. Much as Eisenhower had done, Kennedy kept the costs of information search low. Kennedy did not introduce major institutional changes to the NSC at the decision-making level. Kennedy's advisers suggested keeping the main Council to "provide a regular and relatively formal place for free and frank discussion" and recommended "reasonably regular meetings."[54] Kennedy supplemented his engagement with the core bureaucracy members of the NSC in slightly smaller and more informal settings, as illustrated by Figure 8.1.[55] As shown by Figure 8.2, however, these informal meetings generally mirrored the access afforded by the NSC's design, meaning that the senior members of the bureaucracy were not shut out.

Like Eisenhower's arrangement, this design facilitated a high flow of information from the bureaucracy to the White House. From the beginning, Kennedy "wanted a complete flow of raw information." This channeling of information allowed Kennedy to seek out "independent judgement and recommendation."[56] National Security Advisor McGeorge Bundy claimed that the system allowed even more information "from a wider and more varied circle" to flow up to Kennedy than had under the Eisenhower administration.[57] The system encouraged bureaucratic advisers to be "skeptical and critical" rather than "sycophantic," even at the risk of "displeasing" the president.[58]

What of the Executive Committee (EXCOMM) of the NSC, which Kennedy created during the Cuban Missile Crisis and retained after the crisis abated? While the EXCOMM is sometimes described as a landmark institutional innovation, neither the design nor utilization of the EXCOMM represented a significant departure from the perspective of the theoretical framework. On the contrary, the EXCOMM replicated the core bureaucratic constituencies already represented on the National

---

[52] Sorensen, *Kennedy*, 254.
[53] Dallek, *An Unfinished Life*, 307.
[54] "Memorandum from Bundy to Kennedy," January 24, 1961. *FRUS 1961–1963, Volume XXV, Organization of Foreign Policy.*
[55] On Kennedy's possible motivations, see Michael V. Forrestal, OHT, April 8, 1964, JFKL, 53.
[56] Robert W. Komer, OHT, October 31, 1964, JFKL, 20.
[57] "Memorandum for the President from Bundy," November 16, 1962. National Security Files, Box 283a, NSC Organization (12/27/61–11/22/63), JFKL.
[58] Sorensen, *Kennedy*, 259.

Security Council. The EXCOMM did include additional members from lower tiers of the bureaucracy (e.g., the under secretary of state), but nearly all these bureaucracies already had formally appointed representatives on the National Security Council. The EXCOMM, in short, merely tended to reinforce already low information search costs.[59]

From Closed to Open Bureaucratic Access to Information. While Kennedy kept his institutional structure open at the decision-making level, he approved substantial modifications at lower levels that yielded a structurally siloed system early during his tenure. First, Kennedy abolished the NSC's coordination bodies, such as the Planning Board and Operations Coordinating Board. As Secretary of State Dean Rusk later remembered, "the NSC as such was not downgraded [...] but some of the lower machinery of the NSC was eliminated" when Kennedy came into office.[60] Interdepartmental coordination efforts were transferred back to the State Department.[61] Horizontal information flow between the bureaucracies suffered as a result.[62] Bundy noted that the State Department had "not proved to be as effective" in ensuring coordination between the bureaucracies because they lacked the "necessary standing and authority."[63]

There is some evidence that siloing in the first year of the Kennedy administration may have degraded the quality of information that Kennedy received as well. Bundy admitted that due to the elimination of the coordination mechanisms that Eisenhower had established, policymaking proceeded in a "somewhat haphazard" fashion during Kennedy's first year in office.[64] Another staff member recalled that others did not necessarily know what the president had read or decided because "almost everybody had access" to the president.[65]

Yet Kennedy's institutional changes were short-lived. In mid-1961, Kennedy's advisers began pushing for a coordination body similar to

---

[59] See "National Security Action Memorandum 196," October 22, 1962. *FRUS, 1961–1963, Volume XI, Cuban Missile Crisis and Aftermath.*
[60] David Dean Rusk, OHT, April 27, 1970, JFKL, 271.
[61] "Statement by the President Upon Signing Order Abolishing the Operations Coordinating Board," February 19, 1961. *Public Papers of the Presidents of the United States: John F. Kennedy, 1961* (Washington, DC: US Government Printing Office, 1961), 104–105. "Memorandum for the NSA," March 27, 1961. National Security Files, Box 467, NSC/OCB, JFKL. See also Walt W. Rostow, OHT, April 11, 1964, JFKL, 42.
[62] Smith, *Organizational History of the NSC*, 14.
[63] "Memorandum for the President from Bundy," November 16, 1962. National Security Files, Box 283a, NSC Organization (12/27/61–11/22/63).
[64] "Memorandum for the President from Bundy," November 16, 1962.
[65] Bromley Smith, OHT, July 23, 1970, JFKL, 19.

the one Eisenhower had established.⁶⁶ In January 1962, Kennedy approved the establishment of the NSC Standing Group. The new body was so similar to the coordination structure under Eisenhower that its proposed name was originally the "Plans and Operations Committee" of the NSC – almost identical to the names of Eisenhower's coordination bodies.⁶⁷

What accounts for Kennedy's modifications to coordination bodies below the apex decision-making level? One possibility is that institutional changes reflect Kennedy's steady accumulation of experience in office, which helped to reduce the level of threat that the bureaucracy posed. Another possibility, which is commonly emphasized in organizational histories of the Kennedy administration, is that Kennedy was not aware of the deleterious consequences his institutional modification would have. Once the disaster of the Bay of Pigs demonstrated these deficiencies, Kennedy restored a more integrated model. This account emphasizes that the political environment does not always produce the exact kind of institutional setup the theory predicts, but also that such deviations might not be long-lasting.

The Political Environment in the Johnson Administration

Unlike his predecessors, Lyndon Johnson entered office perceiving an unusually high level of threat from the national security bureaucracy. First, while Johnson possessed a wealth of prior political experience, most of it pertained to domestic, as opposed to foreign policy, issues.⁶⁸ As Doris Kearns Goodwin describes, Johnson lacked "an intimate and detailed command" of international affairs. Critically, this affected Johnson's understanding of his own ability to shape public debates on foreign policy issues. In contrast with his attitudes toward domestic policy, Johnson believed that others better versed in foreign affairs could shape public judgments. Thus, Johnson was vulnerable to criticism by the officials who occupied senior positions within the national security bureaucracy and enjoyed a reputation for expertise in the eyes of the American public.⁶⁹

In addition, Johnson was deeply suspicious of the intentions of his bureaucratic advisers. Some of his misgivings stemmed from the unusual

---

⁶⁶ "Memorandum for the President," June 22, 1961. National Security Files, Box 283a, NSC Organization (2/1/61–5/4/61), JFKL. See also "Memorandum for Bundy from Smith," June 26, 1961. JFKL, National Security Files, Box 283a, NSC Organization (2/1/61–5/4/61).
⁶⁷ See "Draft Memorandum from Bundy to the President," April 2, 1963. JFKL, National Security Files, Box 315.
⁶⁸ For a summary on Johnson's inexperience in foreign affairs, see Preston, *The President and His Inner Circle*, 144–145.
⁶⁹ Goodwin, *Lyndon Johnson and the American Dream*, 256.

circumstances under which he had entered office. After Kennedy's assassination, Johnson believed that he "needed" to keep the advisory team he inherited, rather than appoint his own, in order to maintain his "link" to the fallen president. Without them, Johnson calculated, he would have "absolutely no chance of gaining the support of the media or the Easterners or the intellectuals" and, as a result, would have "no chance of governing the country."[70] Johnson described the bureaucracy as filled with "dividers" who were "waiting to knock me down before I could even begin to stand up."[71] One NSC staff member similarly recalled that "we were not his men."[72]

One indication of the threat that the bureaucracy posed was the administration's persistent obsession with containing leaks. Both Johnson and members of his staff picked up on the risk of information spilling into public debates. The NSC executive secretary later noted that "Kennedy loyalists" had "used leaks consciously to damage the Johnson administration."[73] White House staff noted that the "problem of leaks" worried the administration "to no end."[74]

A second dimension of Johnson's political environment was his focus on domestic issues, especially during his first years in office. Specifically, Johnson's agenda included two ambitious economic and social programs that sought to transform American society: the Great Society Program and the Civil Rights Act. Johnson prized these aspects of his agenda, particularly the Great Society Program, over other foreign policy issues, later describing the latter as "the woman I really loved."[75] Johnson's domestic agenda depended upon Congressional support. Despite a Democratic majority in both the Senate and House of Representatives, Johnson and his aides knew that political coalitions between small-government Republicans, who opposed increased social spending, and Deep South Democrats, who opposed civil rights legislation, threatened to jeopardize the president's domestic programs.[76] In late January 1965, for instance, Johnson described that while he had a "good chance" of getting his domestic agenda passed, he feared losing "power and authority" as time progressed.[77]

---

[70] Goodwin, *Lyndon Johnson and the American Dream*, 178.
[71] Ibid., 170.
[72] Michael Forrestal, OHT, July 29, 1969, LBJ Presidential Library (hereafter LBJL), 22.
[73] Bromley Smith, OHT II, September 25, 1969, LBJL, 13.
[74] Ibid., 11–12; Kai Bird, *The Color of Truth: McGeorge Bundy and William Bundy, Brothers in Arms* (New York: Simon & Schuster, 1998), 299–300.
[75] Goodwin, *Lyndon Johnson and the American Dream*, 251.
[76] Bator, "No Good Choices," 321–322
[77] Ibid., 324.

In contrast, Johnson believed that he had assumed office during a period in which Cold War tensions had temporarily subsided. The end of the Cuban Missile Crisis marked the beginning of a more stable relationship between the United States and the Soviet Union. As Johnson later noted, it was "almost as if the world had provided a breathing space within which I could concentrate on domestic affairs."[78] Of course, this is not to suggest that Johnson devoted no attention to foreign policy; the point, rather, is that he privileged his domestic agenda.

Fragmented Institutions Under Johnson

The combination of high levels of bureaucratic threat and an ambitious domestic political agenda helps to explain Johnson's fragmentation of U.S. national security institutions, particularly during his initial years in office. His most important institutional modification was to create a new decision-making body called the Tuesday Luncheon, which became the "heart" of the advisory process.[79] Johnson's motivations in changing U.S. national security institutions were unequivocally linked to perceived threats from the bureaucracy. As he later recalled:

> The National Security Council meetings were like sieves. I couldn't control them. You knew after the National Security Council meeting that each of those guys would run home to tell his wife and neighbors what they said to the President. That's why I used the Tuesday lunch format instead. That group never leaked a single note. [...] but in those larger meetings, why, every Defense Department official and his brother would be leakers at one time or another.[80]

Other firsthand accounts corroborate that Johnson's motivation in shutting down the NSC system was to "minimize the possibility of leaks."[81] The NSC executive secretary remembered that what Johnson "got out of" the Tuesday Luncheons was assurance that there would be "no public knowledge of the discussions and of the various positions taken."[82]

---

[78] Goodwin, *Lyndon Johnson and the American Dream*, 193.
[79] On the Tuesday Luncheons more generally, see Henry Franklin Graff, *The Tuesday Cabinet: Deliberation and Decision on Peace and War under Lyndon B. Johnson* (Englewood Cliffs: Prentice-Hall, 1970); David C. Humphrey, "Tuesday Lunch at the Johnson White House: A Preliminary Assessment," *Diplomatic History* 8, no. 1 (1984): 81–101; Gans, *White House Warriors*, 29.
[80] Goodwin, *Lyndon Johnson and the American Dream*, 319–320.
[81] Walt Whitman Rostow, *The Diffusion of Power: An Essay in Recent History* (New York: Macmillan, 1972), 360; Smith, *Organizational History of the NSC*, 63.
[82] Bromley Smith, OHT I, July 29, 1969, LBJL, 16.

Moreover, the historical record makes clear that Johnson expressed similar views while in office.[83] After a leak from the State Department in June 1965, for example, Johnson privately noted: "I can't talk to [Secretary of State] Rusk and [...] I can't talk to [Assistant Secretary of State for Far Eastern Affairs] Bill Bundy. I don't think I can talk to [Undersecretary of State] George Ball [...] So that narrows me down in my State Department." Johnson suggested that decision-making would simply have to proceed without advice from his diplomats.[84]

Low Information Search Capacity. Johnson's decision to establish the Tuesday Luncheon dramatically reshaped the structure of U.S. national security institutions. It quickly became clear to bureaucrats that the Tuesday Luncheon was the most important body for national security decision-making in the administration. As illustrated in Figure 8.1, the average time that Johnson spent in NSC meetings per year decreased by 84 percent in comparison to Eisenhower, and 63 percent in comparison to Kennedy. In fact, these data show that Johnson averaged nearly as much time in Tuesday Luncheons as Eisenhower did in NSC meetings. It was thus common knowledge among Johnson's advisers that the NSC only continued to exist in order to "ratify a decision already arrived at by the President."[85] One of Johnson's senior advisers bluntly wrote that the White House should not "pretend the NSC meetings are the occasion" when the president would be making decisions.[86]

The consequences of Johnson's institutional change might have been minimal had the Tuesday Luncheon replicated the NSC in a different setting. Yet Johnston's institutional innovation fundamentally raised information search costs in three ways. First, the Tuesday Luncheon was initially without staff support. Records of conversations were deliberately not kept. As the NSC executive secretary later recalled, even when Johnson requested policy analysis, "There was no machinery to put together papers worthy of the President's attention."[87] Whereas the Kennedy administration had published close to three hundred policy memorandum in less than three years, the Johnson administration would produce only

---

[83] Michael R. Beschloss, ed., *Taking Charge: The Johnson White House Tapes, 1963–1964* (New York: Simon & Schuster, 1997), 74, 147, 165–167, 248.
[84] Michael R. Beschloss, ed., *Reaching for Glory: Lyndon Johnson's Secret White House Tapes, 1964–1965* (New York: Simon & Schuster, 2001), 370.
[85] Bromley Smith, OHT I, July 29, 1969, LBJL, 13. Smith served as the executive secretary of the NSC during the Kennedy and Johnson administrations. See also Rostow, *The Diffusion of Power*, 360.
[86] "Memorandum from the President's Special Assistant (Rostow) and the Executive Secretary of the NSC (Smith) to President Johnson," May 25, 1966. *FRUS 1964–1968, Volume XXXIII, Organization and Management of Foreign Policy.*
[87] Bromley Smith, OHT I, July 29, 1969, LBJL, 12–13.

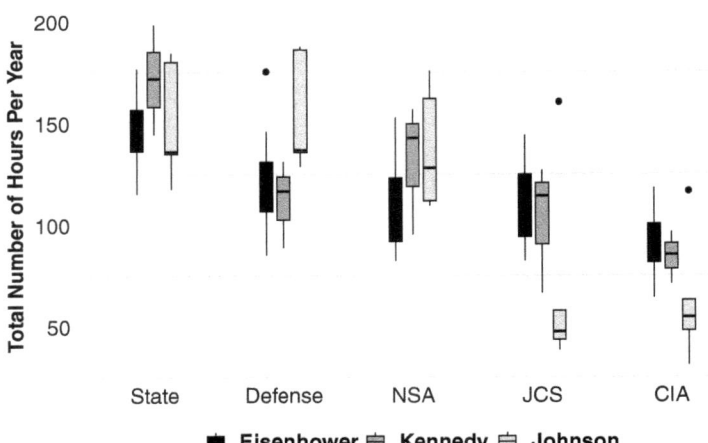

Figure 8.2 Bureaucratic representation in U.S. national security decision-making, 1953–1968
Note: Figure reports the average time per year that Eisenhower, Kennedy, and Johnson spent with senior officials from the Department of State, Department of Defense, National Security Council, Joint Chiefs of Staff (JCS), and Central Intelligence Agency (CIA). The black dots for JCS and CIA representation during the Johnson administration are 1968. Data collected from the Presidential Daily Dairies. For details, see Appendix B.

thirty-nine over five years.[88] One NSC staffer recalled that it was "very hard" to reach the president.[89]

Second, there were no formal appointments to the Tuesday Luncheon, meaning that advisers had no assurance of maintaining access. The list of individuals who typically attended Tuesday Luncheons included some of the core bureaucratic constituencies, such as Secretary of Defense Robert McNamara and Secretary of State Dean Rusk. Yet it also excluded core constituencies that had been integrated into the NSC under both Eisenhower and Kennedy. Of the thirty-eight Tuesday Luncheons held in 1964, for instance, only six included a representative from the CIA; only two included a representative from the Joint Chiefs of Staff (JCS). As visualized in Figure 8.2, access of senior military advisers to Johnson during the first four years of his tenure decreased by 58 percent and 54 percent in comparison to Eisenhower and Kennedy, respectively. The CIA's access to Johnson similarly dropped by 45 percent in comparison to Eisenhower and 42 percent in comparison to Kennedy. CIA

---

[88] *FRUS 1964–1968, Volume XXXIII*, Editorial Note 152.
[89] Michael Forrestal, OHT, 22–23.

Director John McCone was "highly dissatisfied" with his face time with the president, noting that he was unable to conduct intelligence briefings that had been customary under Eisenhower and Kennedy.[90] White House staff would sometimes offer Johnson the option of including a more diverse set of potential participants, but Johnson alone decided who was permitted to attend.[91]

Johnson's institutional choices negatively shaped the bureaucracy's incentives to provide quality information to the president. For example, one NSC staff member later noted that because all parties knew that Johnson made decisions in "smaller, more intimate" settings that the rest of the NSC had not participated in, "gut" issues were "seldom raised and searching questions were seldom asked." The staff member recalled that during NSC meetings, the president would often ask all members present if they agreed with the decision reached:

During the process I would frequently fall into a Walter Mitty-like fantasy: When my turn came I would rise to my feet slowly, look around the room and then directly at the President, and say very quietly and emphatically, "Mr. President, gentlemen, I most definitely do *not* agree." But I was removed from my trance when I heard the President's voice saying, "Mr. Cooper, do you agree?" And out would come a "Yes, Mr. President, I agree."[92]

Closed Bureaucratic Access to Information. Johnson's institutional changes also shaped access to information between bureaucracies. The design of the Tuesday Luncheons created "serious communication problems," as the bureaucracy was uncertain as to what had been decided and what actions should be executed.[93] White House aides noted the "continued confusion and uncertainty."[94] Official paperwork for NSC meetings was discontinued.[95] As one NSC staff member commented at the time, the "setup" was not designed to facilitate information sharing. Bureaucrats received "only the crumbs" the fell from "the senior's table."[96] Johnson

---

[90] "Memorandum for the Record: Breakfast Meeting at the White House," April 22, 1964. John McCone Memoranda, Box 1, Folder 4, LBJL. Under Eisenhower, each NSC meeting opened with a briefing from the CIA. See Cutler, *No Time for Rest*, 304.
[91] "Memorandum from McGeorge Bundy to Jack Valenti," June 28, 1965. National Security Files, Aides Files, McGeorge Bundy, Box 19, Luncheons with the President, Vol. I [Part 1], LBJL.
[92] Chester L. Cooper, *The Lost Crusade: America in Vietnam* (New York: Dodd, Meade & Company, 1970), 223. Emphasis in original.
[93] Daalder and Destler, *In the Shadow of the Oval Office*, 53.
[94] "Memorandum for Record: Daily White House Staff Meeting," January 27, 1964. *FRUS 1964–1968, Volume XXXIII*.
[95] David C. Humphrey, "NSC Meetings during the Johnson Presidency," *Diplomatic History* 18, no. 1 (1994): 33–34.
[96] "Memorandum from Harold Saunders of the NSC Staff to the President's Special Assistant (Rostow)," April 8, 1966. *FRUS 1964–1968, Volume XXXIII*.

also disbanded the NSC Standing Group.[97] Early in his administration, Johnson spoke with President Eisenhower concerning the reestablishing a coordination body similar to the Planning Board, but ultimately decided against it.[98]

Alternative Explanations for Institutional Design

Tracing institutional change across the administrations of three American presidents during the early Cold War helps illustrate that domestic politics – threats to the leader's agenda and the leader's control over the bureaucracy – shape a leader's institutional choices. Contrary to theoretical perspectives emphasizing how path dependence leads to stasis, these cases instead reveal how changes to the political environment push leaders to reconfigure their bureaucratic machinery, both in terms of formal design and de facto decision-making patterns. This is not to suggest that path dependence did not shape the broader set of organizations inside the American national security bureaucracy. Yet when it came to institutions connecting leaders to the bureaucracy, domestic political considerations sparked major adjustments in a relatively short period of time.

An alternative perspective might instead explain institutional evolution by pointing to the leader's personality. Some argue that Eisenhower may have been socialized during his military career to prefer formal and routinized decision-making procedures.[99] In contrast, Johnson's experience in the Senate may have conditioned him to delegate policy deliberations to committees.[100] Yet as noted earlier, Johnson himself stated that he created the Tuesday Luncheon for political reasons: a more insular institutional structure was politically advantageous.[101]

One could argue, however, that Johnson may have been less trusting by disposition and, as a result, more prone to inflating the risk of bureaucrats damaging his political prospects through information leaks. Yet there are reasons to believe that domestic political threats, particularly those that Johnson perceived, were rooted in reality. Johnson's subordinates noted the prominent threat of bureaucratic leaks as well. Both the NSC executive secretary and the deputy national security advisor observed how

---

[97] The final meeting of the NSC Standing Group on record is April 30, 1964. See *FRUS 1964–1968, Volume XXXIII*, Editorial Note 147.
[98] See, for example, "Memorandum for the Record: Discussion with President Johnson," January 5, 1964; "Memorandum for the Record: Discussion with President Johnson," April 29, 1964. John McCone Memoranda, Box 1, Folder 5, LBJL.
[99] Sloan, "The Management and Decision-Making Style of President Eisenhower," 304.
[100] George E. Reedy, *Lyndon B. Johnson: A Memoir* (New York: Andrews & McMeel, 1982), 82.
[101] Goodwin, *Lyndon Johnson and the American Dream*, 319–320.

leaks were used to damage Johnson's political career. As historian Doris Kearns Goodwin summarizes, Johnson's domestic political fears were "not simply pure illusion."

Several additional points further militate against an interpretation that would focus strictly on leader personality. First, at least in the case of Kennedy, the design of the advisory system resulted from a methodical consideration of different options, rather than from habit.[102] In fact, it was Kennedy's aides, rather than force of managerial routines, who persuaded the president to eliminate Eisenhower's coordination bodies.[103] Second, each president, but Johnson in particular, exhibited different management styles when handling domestic, as opposed to foreign policy, issues.[104]

Finally, leadership style struggles to account for the ways that presidents altered their institutions more than once while in office. As discussed earlier, Kennedy made substantial changes to coordination capacity during his presidency. While the changes were not substantial enough to shift the institutional coding, Johnson also modified his institutions over time. For example, the Tuesday Luncheon became more inclusive and "structured" during his later years in office.[105] By the end of 1968, one Johnson staffer remarked that "the Tuesday lunch is, in effect, a regular NSC meeting."[106] CIA and military participation in the Tuesday Luncheon increased substantially beginning in the fall of 1967. As illustrated in Figure 8.2, by 1968, intelligence and military representation in meetings with Johnson *exceeded* average representation rates from both the Eisenhower and Kennedy administrations.[107] If institutional design followed directly from stable features of the leader's personality, we would instead have expected to find a uniform design within each administration.

U.S. Crisis Performance in the Early Cold War

How did variation in national security institutions shape U.S. crisis performance during the early Cold War? First, we can examine the United

---

[102] "Memorandum for Kennedy from Neustadt," December 8, 1960. Richard E. Neustadt, *Preparing to be President: The Memos of Richard E. Neustadt* (Washington, DC: American Enterprise Institute, 2000); Bird, *The Color of Truth*, 185–186.
[103] Walt W. Rostow, OHT, JFKL. April 11, 1964, 42. See also Robert Komer, OHT, October 31, 1964, JFKL, 18; McGeorge Bundy, OHT, November 30, 1970, JFKL, 4.
[104] Goodwin, *Lyndon Johnson and the American Dream*, 256.
[105] Bromley Smith, OHT I, July 29, 1969, LBJL, 13–14.
[106] "Information Memorandum from the President's Special Assistant (Rostow) to President Johnson," December 5, 1968. *FRUS 1964–1968, Volume XXXIII*.
[107] See also Humphrey, "Tuesday Lunch at the Johnson White House," 90.

States' record of achieving its strategic objectives during international crises. Between 1953 and 1968, the United States was party to twenty-three crises, as summarized in Table 8.2. Of the eleven crises that occurred during periods of institutional integration under Eisenhower and Kennedy, the United States failed to achieve its goals in only two (18 percent). Put slightly differently, the United States experienced a crisis failure about once every five years under integrated institutions. A similar pattern holds when accounting for the fact that the United States often had more than one goal in each crisis. Across these crises, the United States on average achieved over 72 percent of its goals in crises occurring under integrated institutions.

The picture is different for periods in which the United States moved away from integrated institutions. Of the twelve crises that occurred under siloed or fragmented institutions, the United States failed to achieve its objectives in five (42 percent). Similarly, on average, the United States achieved only 39 percent of its goals during crises during siloed and fragmented periods. The United States experienced a crisis failure about once a year under fragmented and siloed institutions. These include some of the more notable miscalculations of the Cold War, such as the attempted invasion of Cuba at the Bay of Pigs in April 1961. While the small number of cases precludes definitive judgment, this nevertheless provides suggestive evidence that the United States was less likely to miscalculate when U.S. leaders presided over integrated institutions rather than siloed and fragmented ones.

Second, we can probe the record of American decision-making across this period. An expert survey conducted by Gregory Herek, Irving Janis, and Paul Huth is particularly helpful in this regard.[108] In the study, Herek and co-authors identified the four international crises in each U.S. administration during the early Cold War that ranked highest in terms of importance and severity.[109] The study then asked a panel of outside experts to assess the quality of decision-making across seven criteria: omissions in surveying alternatives; omissions in surveying objectives; failure to examine costs and risks; poor information search; selective bias in information processing; failure to reconsider rejected alternatives;

---

[108] Gregory M. Herek, Irving L. Janis, and Paul Huth, "Decision Making during International Crises: Is Quality of Process Related to Outcome?," *Journal of Conflict Resolution* 31, no. 2 (1987): 203–226.

[109] The sample of crises included: Eisenhower – Dien Bien Phu, First Taiwan Strait Crisis, Suez Nationalization, Second Taiwan Strait Crisis; Kennedy – Laos, Berlin Wall, Cuban Missile Crisis; Johnson – Gulf of Tonkin, Vietnam Strategic Bombing; Vietnam Ground War; Arab-Israeli War. The study only examined three crises during the Kennedy administration due to lack of available data on the fourth episode (the 1962 Taiwan Strait Crisis).

Table 8.2 *U.S. crisis performance, 1953–1968*

Crisis	Year	Institution	Primary goal	Successful?
Korean War termination	1953	Integrated	Break political and military stalemate with PRC and North Korea	✓
Guatemala	1954	Integrated	Install a pro-American government	✓
Dien Bien Phu	1954	Integrated	Prevent spread of Communism to Vietnam	✗
First Taiwan Strait Crisis	1954	Integrated	Maintain KMT control of Jinmen and Mazu Islands	✓
Suez nationalization	1956	Integrated	Compel UK and France to end military intervention in Sinai Peninsula	✓
Syria-Turkey	1957	Integrated	Facilitate regime change in Syria	✗
Iraq-Lebanon	1958	Integrated	Preserve pro-American regime in Lebanon	✓
Second Taiwan Strait Crisis	1958	Integrated	Deter PRC attack on Offshore Islands	✓
Berlin Ultimatum	1958	Integrated	Maintain status quo in West Berlin	✓
First Laos Crisis	1961	Siloed	Prevent Laos from falling to Pathet Lao	✓
Bay of Pigs invasion	1961	Siloed	Install a pro-American regime in Cuba	✗
Berlin Crisis	1961	Siloed	Maintain a pro-Western Berlin and West Germany	✓
Viet Cong Insurgency	1961	Siloed	Reduce insurgent threats to the South Vietnam regime	✓
Second Laos Crisis	1962	Integrated	Prevent communist takeover of Laos	✓
Cuban Missile Crisis	1962	Integrated	Compel removal of nuclear missiles from Cuba	✓
Panama Flag	1964	Fragmented	Maintain U.S. position regarding control of Panama Canal	✗
Gulf of Tonkin	1964	Fragmented	Compel DRV to end support for insurgency in RVN	✗
Second Congo Crisis	1964	Fragmented	Rescue hostages from Stanleyville	✓
Pleiku crisis	1965	Fragmented	Compel DRV to end support for insurgency in RVN	✗
Dominican Republic	1965	Fragmented	Restore order in Dominican Republic	✓
Six Day War	1967	Fragmented	Deter Soviet intervention in conflict	✓
USS Pueblo seizure	1968	Fragmented	Compel North Korea to return the USS Pueblo crew	✓
Tet Offensive	1968	Fragmented	Compel DRV to accept U.S. demands to end war	✗

and failure to work out implementation, monitoring, and contingency plans.[110]

The results of the expert survey show striking differences between the quality of decision-making across the three institutional types. Decision-making pathologies were comparatively rare under integrated institutions. In assessing the seven criteria across the five crises that occurred while the United States possessed integrated institutions, the survey found evidence of only four (of thirty-five possible) symptoms of pathological decision-making.

In contrast, assessing the four crises that occurred under fragmented institutions on the same seven dimensions, the survey found evidence of eighteen symptoms of decision-making pathologies. While the survey found only one symptom of pathological decision-making in the two crises the United States faced under siloed institutions, the frequency of a crisis featuring at least one pathology was slightly higher for siloed institutions (one per year) than for integrated institutions (one every three years). As with the general trends in U.S. crisis outcomes, the small number of cases means that we should interpret these results with caution. Nevertheless, the observed patterns in decision-making accord with what we would expect to find under different types of national security institutions.

Finally, we can trace U.S. decision-making processes in some of these cases in order to illustrate the theory's propositions about how national security institutions shape the risk of miscalculation. To that end, the subsequent sections examine two episodes in detail: the 1958 Taiwan Strait Crisis and the 1965 escalation in Vietnam. Table 8.3 summarizes the key elements of each case.

While the primary purpose of each case study is to illustrate the theory's mechanisms, examining these specific crises is particularly helpful for several additional reasons. For one, both cases rank among the most substantively important in U.S foreign policy during the Cold War. In addition, there are some similarities to the underlying dynamics associated with each. In both cases, the United States was attempting to contain the spread of communism in East Asia through a third-party ally that was in the middle of an ongoing civil conflict with a communist state (with whom the United States lacked direct diplomatic ties). Unlike other prominent crises, such as Dien Bien Phu or the Suez nationalization, decision-makers perceived that American reputation was directly

---

[110] See Janis and Mann, *Decision Making*, 371. Note that the original study was concerned with understanding the consequences of decision-making process generally, rather than testing whether different institutional designs are associated with systematically distinct patterns of decision-making.

U.S. Crisis Performance in the Early Cold War

Table 8.3 *Summary of the Second Taiwan Strait Crisis and Vietnam War*

Crisis (institution)	Pathway — Information provision	Observable implications — Leader projections	Outcome	Miscalculation
Second Taiwan Strait Crisis (integrated)	*High quality*: extensive information search by NSC; competitive dialogue between State and Defense	U.S. support to KMT will deter further PRC action; PRC strategy depends on U.S. action	No PRC assault on Offshore Islands; PRC motives included probing U.S. resolve	No
Vietnam War (fragmented)	*Low quality*: limited information search by NSC; self-censorship, particularly outside Tuesday Luncheon	Escalation will improve U.S. bargaining leverage against DRV; costs of escalation within bounds of U.S. tolerance; collapse of RVN prohibitively costly	Minimal improvement in U.S. bargaining position; costs exceed U.S. resolve; RVN collapse does not precipitate fall of non-communist regimes in Southeast Asia	Yes

at stake. Moreover, in both cases, American decision-makers were motivated by concerns that concessions to the adversary would erode the domestic legitimacy of a U.S.-backed regime, risking the viability of its political survival. Finally, neither Taiwan nor Vietnam involved a direct threat to the American homeland, as was the case with other high-stakes episodes, such as the Cuban Missile Crisis.

One important difference between the cases is that the timeline along which the United States expected to pay costs if it failed was substantially shorter for Vietnam than for Taiwan. Whereas the Eisenhower administration did not anticipate that the Nationalist regime's immediate survival was at stake in 1958, the Johnson administration believed that withholding additional U.S. support would lead the regime in Saigon to collapse in the near future. Yet it is not clear how the immediacy of costs should shape the risk of miscalculation. One might make the case, for instance, that the costs of defeat should have increased Johnson's incentives to institute a more effective decision-making process. In short, although the purpose of this section is not to draw inferences based on the comparison of nearly identical crises, some basic similarities between the two cases provide fertile ground to illustrate the theoretical mechanisms posited in Chapter 2.

The 1958 Taiwan Strait Crisis

On August 23, 1958, the People's Republic of China began a massive artillery barrage against Nationalist (KMT) forces stationed on Jinmen and Mazu islands. In the following days, mainland Chinese forces clashed with the KMT on Dongding Island and initiated a blockade of the offshore islands. The mainland's attack presented a serious challenge for the Eisenhower administration, as the United States had played an integral role in the defense of Taiwan during the early Cold War.

In response to the deteriorating situation in the Taiwan Strait, Eisenhower had several options available. First, the United States could have approved KMT proposals for escalatory military action against the mainland, such as covert raids or preemptive strikes on airfields. This might have degraded the mainland's military capability and signaled U.S. resolve, but risked the onset of conflict between the United States and China.[111] The United States might also have insisted on bolstering KMT presence on the offshore islands. Second, the United States could have refused to support the KMT. This would have curtailed the possibility of violent confrontation between China and the United States, but it would have jeopardized KMT resupply missions to the offshore islands and might have shaped China's beliefs about American resolve.

Instead, Eisenhower chose a strategy of coercive diplomacy that fell between these two alternatives. It consisted of three main components. First, Eisenhower approved an increase in U.S. military capabilities in the Taiwan Strait in order to deter China from seizing the offshore islands. Early intelligence warnings allowed the United States to begin deploying additional air and naval assets to the Taiwan Strait even before the shelling had begun.[112] Eisenhower directed the aircraft carrier USS *Essex*, along with four accompanying destroyers from the Mediterranean Sea to the Taiwan Strait and placed U.S. strategic bombers in Guam

---

[111] Robert Accinelli, "'A Thorn in the Side of Peace': The Eisenhower Administration and the 1958 Offshore Islands Crisis," in *Re-examining the Cold War: US-China Diplomacy, 1954–1973* (Cambridge: Harvard University Asia Center, 2001), 137.

[112] Morton H. Halperin, *The 1958 Taiwan Straits Crisis: A Documented History* (Santa Monica, CA: Rand, 1966), 65.

on alert. Once in position, Eisenhower authorized the Seventh Fleet to "escort and protect" KMT ships that needed to run the Communist blockade in order to resupply the offshore islands.[113]

Second, in parallel to its military mobilization, the United States sent diplomatic signals that it was prepared to defend the offshore islands if China attempted an invasion. On August 23, Secretary of State John Foster Dulles stated that it would be "highly hazardous" for China to assume that an attempt to change the status quo on the offshore islands would "be a limited operation."[114] On August 27, Eisenhower held a press conference emphasizing the importance of the offshore islands. On August 28, the State Department reiterated Dulles' statement, warning against a mainland seizure of Jinmen. Over the same period, the military held defense exercises and conducted patrols in the area.[115] Dulles issued a more direct warning on September 4, stating that U.S. defense commitments included "securing and protecting" Jinmen and Mazu islands.[116]

Third, the United States quietly pressured Chiang Kai-shek to decrease KMT military presence on the offshore islands and scale back his plans to use military force. As Dulles detailed, the United States sought "some peaceful modus vivendi" with mainland China.[117]

The Logic of Eisenhower's Decision. Eisenhower's strategic choices rested on three assessments.[118] The first pertained to the probable outcome of the crisis. Eisenhower believed that the United States could deter a mainland invasion of the offshore islands. In Eisenhower's view, China was probing the United States and was not intent on retaking the islands. In mid-August, Eisenhower did not feel an "attack on Taiwan was probable."[119] He later wrote that he was by "no means convinced that the Chinese Communists would be willing to risk war with us."[120]

Instead, Eisenhower felt that the United States and China were in a "war of nerves," in which the mainland "may be seeing how far they can go if we do not react." China's strategy would depend on the U.S. response, leading to Eisenhower's conclusion that "if the Communists were convinced that we would come to the aid of Quemoy, they would

---

[113] Zhang, *Deterrence and Strategic Culture*, 249.
[114] Halperin, *The 1958 Taiwan Straits Crisis*, 95.
[115] Ibid., 134–135 and 139.
[116] "White House Press Release," September 4, 1958. *FRUS 1958–1960, Volume XIX, China.*
[117] "Memorandum from Secretary of State Dulles to Acting Secretary of State Herter and the Assistant Secretary of State for Far Eastern Affairs (Robertson)," August 23, 1958. *FRUS 1958–1960, Volume XIX.*
[118] Accinelli, "A Thorn in the Side of Peace," 119.
[119] "Memorandum for the Record," August 14, 1958. *FRUS 1958–1960, Volume XIX.*
[120] Eisenhower, *Waging Peace*, 295.

probably refrain from outright attack, confining their actions, at least partially, to blockade and interdiction tactics."[121] In short, China was probing the United States.

The second assessment concerned the costs of conflict. Eisenhower believed that if Chinese forces did attempt an invasion, the United States could successfully prevent it.[122] In some respects, this belief was a remarkable one. While Eisenhower concluded that the United States may be able to temporarily hold off a mainland assault through conventional weapons, the contingency plans Eisenhower approved would have relied heavily on at least limited nuclear strikes targeting mainland China. Nevertheless, in his memoirs, Eisenhower suggests that he was prepared to follow through.[123]

The third assessment concerned the availability of alternatives to international conflict. Eisenhower believed that the United States could use the crisis to restrain Taiwan's position on the offshore islands, which possessed "no strategic value" and had come at considerable cost to the United States.[124] Eisenhower noted that, in and of themselves, the islands did little to further a mainland attack on Taiwan.[125] Eisenhower felt that "something must be done to make Chiang more flexible in his approach" and asked for plans to "get him out of the offshore islands."[126] Eisenhower hoped that Chiang could be persuaded to remove "all or nearly all his garrison from the offshore islands."[127] Eisenhower's "preferred solution" was thus to solicit "Chiang's voluntary decision" to make the offshore islands "lightly defended, dispensable outposts or to quit them entirely."[128]

The U.S. Outcome. The projections on which Eisenhower based his choices during the 1958 Taiwan Strait Crisis proved to be generally

---

[121] Ibid., 294–295; "Memorandum for the Record," August 14, 1958. *FRUS 1958–1960, Volume XIX.*
[122] Halperin, *The 1958 Taiwan Straits Crisis*, 292.
[123] Eisenhower, *Waging Peace*, 295.
[124] "Memorandum for the Record," August 14, 1958. *FRUS 1958–1960, Volume XIX.*
[125] "Memorandum of Conference with President Eisenhower," August 12, 1958. *FRUS 1958–1960, Volume XIX.*
[126] "Memorandum of Conference with President Eisenhower," September 29, 1958. *FRUS 1958–1960, Volume XIX.* Eisenhower held this opinion before the shelling began. Eisenhower noted on August 14 that "he did not agree with the logic of putting all the Chinese Nationalist strength on these two off-shore islands." See "Memorandum for the Record," August 14, 1958. *FRUS 1958–1960, Volume XIX.* By October 13, Eisenhower hoped the KMT would agree to "withdraw at least two-thirds of the Chinese Nationalist troops from Quemoy." See "Memorandum of Conference with President Eisenhower," October 13, 1958. *FRUS 1958–1960, Volume XIX.*
[127] "Memorandum from President Eisenhower to Secretary of State Dulles," October 7, 1958. *FRUS 1958–1960, Volume XIX.*
[128] Accinelli, "A Thorn in the Side of Peace," 128.

accurate. The United States strategy proved generally successful. The mainland did not attempt to seize the offshore islands. On September 6, Chinese Premier Zhou Enlai offered to reenter diplomatic talks with the United States. China declared a unilateral ceasefire on October 6th.[129] While shelling resumed in late October, artillery quickly shifted from firing live ammunition to propaganda leaflets beginning in November.[130] Chinese sources suggest that this outcome was shaped, at least in part, by Eisenhower's strategy. Toward the end of the crisis, Mao explained to another senior party official that China was "not unwilling to seize Jinmen and Mazu," but that China had to give:

special consideration to the U.S. position. [...] At present the United States concentrated six out of its twelve aircraft carriers in the Taiwan Strait, three heavy cruisers, forty destroyers, and two air divisions. Its strength is quite powerful and should not be underestimated. It should be taken seriously.[131]

In addition, Chinese sources suggest that Eisenhower's conclusions regarding Mao's intentions were at least partially correct. Mao was indeed using the crisis to probe the scope of the mutual defense treaty between the United States and Taiwan, which came into force on March 3, 1955. As Mao himself noted in a Politburo Standing Committee meeting on August 25, "we only mean to probe" U.S. intentions. As the treaty did not "clearly stipulate whether the American defense perimeter includes Jinmen and Mazu," China needed to "observe whether the Americans will carry these two burdens [the offshore islands] on their backs." Mao explicitly stated that he wanted "to gauge the resolve of the Americans."[132] Even before the shelling began, Mao told Defense Minister Peng Dehuai on August 18 that while the bombardment would directly target the KMT, it would be "indirectly aimed" at the United States.[133] In fact, over the course of the crisis, Chinese military plans took pains to avoid direct confrontation with the United States. China's initial military plans called only for an artillery barrage and a blockade rather than an amphibious invasion of the offshore islands. Mao rejected

---

[129] Zhang, *Deterrence and Strategic Culture*, 261.
[130] Halperin, *The 1958 Taiwan Straits Crisis*, 473.
[131] Wu Lengxi, *Yi Mao zhuxi* [Recalling Chairman Mao] (Beijing: Xinhua, 1995), 82. It is not clear whether U.S. public statements affected Mao's decision. On the day that Dulles' statement was released, the Politburo still felt that the United States might be "afraid of war" and was "not certain whether [the United States] would dare contest Jinmen and Mazu with China." See Jin Chongji, ed., *Zhou Enlai zhuan* [Biography of Zhou Enlai], 2nd ed. (Beijing: Zhongyang wenxian chubanshe, 2008), Vol. III, 1288.
[132] Wu, *Yi Mao zhuxi*, 76.
[133] Pang and Feng, *Mao Zedong nianpu*, Vol. III, 413.

proposals for air strikes on Jinmen on grounds that it could trigger a confrontation with the United States.[134]

While it is clear that Mao also had domestic political motivations for initiating the crisis, it is likely that China preferred to seize the islands if the United States was willing to cede them.[135] As Mao stated, China "would land [on the islands] if given the chance. Why shouldn't China seize Jinmen and Mazu if the opportunity arose?"[136] Before doing so, however, Mao needed to see how American policymakers would respond. On August 20, Mao told Defense Minister Peng that he was unsure whether the KMT would withdraw from the offshore islands, but would only decide whether to attempt to seize the islands after gaining more information. In Mao's words, China should "take one step and watch to take the next step."[137]

By early October, the U.S. response led Chinese leaders to believe that the only way that the United States would forfeit the offshore islands was if the mainland renounced the use of force in settling the Taiwan dispute – a concession China was unprepared to make. During deliberations in the Politburo Standing Committee on how to end the crisis, Chinese leaders suggested that "both China and the United States had been searching for the other's bottom line. Now both sides better understood each other's intentions." Mao summarized that the crisis had achieved its "mission to gauge" American intentions, the same language he had used earlier to describe probing U.S. resolve.[138]

As Eisenhower concluded, the episode also gave the United States leverage in pressuring Taiwan to withdraw forces from the offshore islands. U.S. and KMT military leaders developed a plan envisioning a withdrawal of 17,000 troops from Jinmen, which Chiang accepted in principle.[139] On October 18, 1958, Chiang told his generals that Dulles "might raise the issue of reducing the number of troops on the offshore islands" and asked them to provide an assessment on the matter.[140] Eisenhower also used the episode to seek formal KMT commitment not

---

[134] Ye Fei, *Ye Fei huiyilu* [Memoirs of Ye Fei] (Beijing: Jiefangjun chubanshe, 2007), 663–664.
[135] For the foundational analysis of Mao's domestic motivations, see Christensen, *Useful Adversaries*, 204–225.
[136] Wu, *Yi Mao zhuxi*, 80.
[137] Cited in Chen, *Mao's China and the Cold War*, 180.
[138] Li and Ma, *Zhou Enlai nianpu*, Vol. II, 177.
[139] "Summary Record of Meeting," October 22, 1958; "Telegram from Secretary of State Dulles to the Department of State," October 23, 1958; "Memorandum of Conversation," October 23, 1958. *FRUS 1958–1960, Volume XIX*.
[140] "Minutes of the 27th Military Talks," October 18, 1958. File 602-680200-604, 153. Chiang Kai-shek Collection, Academia Historica.

to take offensive action against the mainland. Despite "considerable difficulty" in getting Chiang's consent, the United States and the KMT signed a joint communique renouncing the use of force.[141] Although Eisenhower had hoped for tougher language, U.S. policymakers felt that KMT acceptance of language foregoing reunification through force as a "major achievement."[142]

Institutional Origins of Eisenhower's Decision. Integrated institutions help explain the accuracy of Eisenhower's assessments during the 1958 Taiwan Strait Crisis. Under integrated institutions, the theory suggests that leaders should be more likely to receive high-quality counsel from bureaucratic advisers. Indeed, each of Eisenhower's assessments was supported by information that integrated institutions produced.

Eisenhower's institutions searched extensively for counsel. In the time leading up to the Taiwan Strait Crisis, U.S. policy toward Taiwan had been routinely reviewed by the NSC system. Between the end of the first Taiwan Strait Crisis in April 1954 and the beginning of the second Taiwan Strait Crisis in August 1958, at least nine NSC sessions considered the costs and benefits of Taiwan and the offshore islands. As early as June 1957, the CIA used NSC meetings to report increased CCP military activity around Jinmen and Mazu.[143] The NSC Planning Board led a routine inter-agency review of the policy in 1957, which included both a military review of proposed changes by the JCS, as well as intelligence assessments from the CIA. The review resulted in a report submitted to the NSC in September and was briefed "in considerable detail" during two NSC meetings on September 23 and October 2.[144]

The NSC itself was central to information provision in the weeks immediately before the mainland began shelling.[145] During a routine NSC briefing on August 7, CIA Director Allen Dulles provided an early warning of a possible Chinese blockade, which would "seek to starve out the

---

[141] "Memorandum of Conversation Between Secretary of State Dulles and President Eisenhower," October 24, 1958. *FRUS 1958–1960, Volume XIX.*

[142] Halperin, *The 1958 Taiwan Straits Crisis*, 531–532; Nancy Bernkopf Tucker, *The China Threat: Memories, Myths, and Realities in the 1950s* (New York: Columbia University Press, 2014), 157.

[143] "Memorandum of Discussion at the 328th Meeting of the NSC," June 26, 1957. *FRUS 1955–1957, Volume III, China.*

[144] "Report by the NSC Planning Board to the NSC on the Review of U.S. Policy toward Formosa and the Government of the Republic of China," September 9, 1957. NSC Series, Policy Papers Subseries, Box 14, Folder 2, DDEL. "Memorandum of Discussion at the 337th Meeting of the NSC," September 23, 1957 and "Memorandum of Discussion at the 338th Meeting of the NSC," October 2, 1957. *FRUS 1955–1957, Volume III.*

[145] "Discussion at the 377th Meeting of the NSC," August 21, 1958. NSC Series, Box 10, DDEL.

offshore islands" while at the same time "refraining from invasion."[146] Information provision through informal channels mirrored the formal process. While Eisenhower opted for informal meetings on occasion during the crisis, he explicitly ordered that all key bureaucratic stakeholders, such as the JCS chairman, attend "any meeting of the statutory members of the NSC."[147] Representation in Eisenhower's informal sessions with bureaucratic advisers afforded access to State, Defense, JCS, and CIA in the weeks before the shelling began.[148] At the interdepartmental level, similarly inclusive meetings between State, Defense, the JCS, and the CIA facilitated information sharing.[149] JCS situation reports on the Taiwan Strait in August 1958 were shared with both the White House and State Department.[150]

Integrated institutions facilitated genuine communication and free exchange of information with and among Eisenhower's bureaucratic advisers. In the NSC's review of Taiwan policy in the fall of 1957, the NSA expressly encouraged both the Department of State and CIA to discuss progress reports, delaying presidential decision until the next NSC meeting so they could provide more detailed feedback.[151] At one point during an NSC discussion, Secretary of Defense Wilson expressly told Eisenhower that "he had a point of view somewhat different from that of the President."[152] OCB meetings on Taiwan in April 1958 similarly included a "broad-ranging discussion" of options facilitated by the NSA,

---

[146] "Memorandum of Discussion at the 375th Meeting of the NSC," August 7, 1958. *FRUS 1958–1960, Volume XIX*.

[147] "Memorandum of Conference with the President," August 11, 1958. Staff Secretary Series, DoD Subseries, Box 4 and 5, DDEL.

[148] See Presidential Appointment Books (August 1958); "Memorandum of Conference with the President," August 11, 1958. Staff Secretary Series, DoD Subseries, Box 4 and 5, DDEL; "Memorandum of Conference with President Eisenhower," August 12, 1958. *FRUS 1958–1960, Volume XIX*.

[149] For example, see "Memorandum on the Substance of Discussions at a Department of State–Joint Chiefs of Staff Meeting," June 27, 1957. *FRUS 1955–1957, Volume III*; "Memorandum from Acting Secretary of State Herter to Secretary of State Dulles," August 15, 1958; "Memorandum of Meeting," August 22, 1958; "Memorandum of Conversation on the Taiwan Straits Situation," September 2, 1958. *FRUS 1958–1960, Volume XIX*; "Memorandum of Meeting between Dulles, McElroy and Twining," September 11, 1958. Dulles Papers, Correspondence and Memoranda Series, Box 1, DDEL.

[150] By the spring of 1955, Eisenhower had established a Watch Committee to monitor the situation in the Taiwan Strait, which kept the senior leadership "well informed." Zhang, *Deterrence and Strategic Culture*, 241. Eisenhower appears to have received special watch reports from the Intelligence Advisory Committee in August 1958. Tucker, *The China Threat*, 237, note 27. See also "Memorandum for the Joint Chiefs of Staff: Summary Situation Report," Staff Secretary Series, DoD Subseries, Boxes 4 and 5, DDEL.

[151] "Memorandum of Discussion at the 337th Meeting of the NSC," September 23, 1957. *FRUS 1955–1957, Volume III*.

[152] "Memorandum of Discussion at the 338th Meeting of the NSC," October 2, 1957. *FRUS 1955–1957, Volume III*.

who noted that the Operations Coordinating Board "had a responsibility to present a realistic paper to the NSC even if such a paper should be objectionable to those who pretend that all is rosy."[153] Members of the NSC staff similarly perceived that the NSA "welcomed any ideas" regarding policy and responded accordingly.[154]

The deliberations that integrated institutions facilitated provided three sets of important information to Eisenhower. The first set of information pertained to the probable outcome if the United States took military action – and the probable outcome if it did not. On August 12, NSA Gray requested a JCS study on possible scenarios in the Taiwan Strait.[155] Immediately before the crisis, NSC meetings in August discussed what various military contingencies would look like if escalation occurred.[156] Representatives from State, Defense, and the JCS met informally on August 8 – over two weeks before the mainland's artillery barrage began – to "think out what steps [the United States] would take" if mainland forces initiated a blockade. State and Defense prepared a set of alternative contingencies for the JCS to initiate military planning. The NSC Planning Board prepared to discuss the situation the following week.[157] The State Department was tasked with examining political aspects of the crisis, the CIA with China's intentions, and Defense with the military balance of power.[158] At the following NSC meeting on August 14, the agenda laid out three questions for members to discuss: the actions the United States should take in the event of a Chinese blockade "with a view to forcing the surrender of the islands without actually landing Communist troops"; the possible response to "a major Chinese Communist assault" on the offshore islands; and the steps the United States could take to signal its policy regarding a Chinese blockade or offensive against the offshore islands.[159] In total, these assessments concluded that air and sea cover would be sufficient to break the blockade.[160] Yet without American intervention, the mainland possessed the capability to seize the offshore

---

[153] "Notes of the Meeting of the Operations Coordinating Board," April 16, 1958. *FRUS 1958–1960, Volume XIX*.
[154] "Memorandum for Gray on the Off-Shore Islands," September 10, 1958. NSC Series, Briefing Notes Subseries, Box 17, Folder 3, DDEL.
[155] Halperin, *The 1958 Taiwan Straits Crisis*, 70.
[156] "Memorandum for the Record," August 14, 1958. *FRUS 1958–1960, Volume XIX*.
[157] "Memorandum of Meeting on the Taiwan Straits," August 8, 1958. *FRUS 1958–1960, Volume XIX*.
[158] Halperin, *The 1958 Taiwan Straits Crisis*, 67.
[159] "Memorandum for the National Security Council: The Situation in the Taiwan Straits Area," August 13, 1958. NSC Series, Box 10, DDEL.
[160] Halperin, *The 1958 Taiwan Straits Crisis*, 86–87.

islands through force.[161] As such, increasing military capabilities in the region was vital to deterrence.[162]

The second set of information centered on China's likely response to limited U.S. military action during the crisis. Specifically, Eisenhower's advisers concluded that China was probing the United States, suggesting that whether China moved to seize the islands would depend on the U.S. reaction. In the spring of 1958, CIA assessments noted that China might "adopt a more aggressive policy toward the Offshore Islands [...] in part to test US intentions in the Taiwan area," noting China "would seek to capture" the offshore islands "by military action" if they "should become convinced" that the United States would not militarily intervene.[163] At an NSC meeting in August, CIA Director Allen Dulles observed that China had "exercised considerable caution" and was "attempting to avoid clashes with Nationalist patrols."[164] Dulles also noted that "Chinese Communist propaganda broadcasts had left the way open for breaking off the Taiwan Straits action."[165] The U.S. intelligence community summarized these assessments in August 1958: "China's principal purpose in stepping up its military pressures in the Taiwan Strait area is to test the intentions" of the United States and Taiwan regarding the offshore islands.[166] Diplomats within the State Department raised similar concerns, noting that it was "highly possible" that China's moves were "the first of a series of probing actions designed to test" the American response.[167] On August 25, just before Eisenhower approved intervention in the crisis, the CIA produced another estimate assessing that China sought to test U.S. intentions with respect to the offshore islands.[168]

These assessments were informed by analysis from diplomatic and intelligence bureaucracies, rather than defense perspectives alone. In NSC meetings, Allen Dulles drew attention to political trends in China and Taiwan, including Mao's speeches and their implications for the

---

[161] Ibid., 87–91, 111–112.
[162] Ibid., 92–93.
[163] "National Intelligence Estimate 13-58: Communist China," May 13, 1958, 19–20.
[164] "Discussion at the 377th Meeting of the NSC," August 21, 1958. NSC Series, Box 10, DDEL.
[165] "Discussion of the 378th Meeting of the NSC," August 27, 1958. NSC Series, Box 10, DDEL.
[166] "SNIE 100-9-58: Probable Developments in the Taiwan Strait Area," August 26, 1958, 1.
[167] "Memorandum from the Assistant Secretary of State for Far Eastern Affairs (Robertson) to Secretary of State Dulles," August 8, 1958. *FRUS 1958–1960, Volume XIX*.
[168] Halperin, *The 1958 Taiwan Straits Crisis*, 111.

Sino-Soviet alliance.[169] State Department officials similarly used NSC meetings to relay the contents of Soviet broadcasts.[170] More broadly, the assessments themselves were likely informed by previous analyses of the political situation in both the mainland and Taiwan.[171] Even in the case of assessing military signals, contributions from the State Department and CIA added additional context. The timing of the PRC deployments during typhoon season, for instance, suggested that China was not immediately moving to seize the islands.[172]

A third set of information pertained to China's likely response to more intensive U.S. military action, such as preemptive strikes. In a meeting between Eisenhower and his advisers on August 29, there was "considerable debate and disagreement" regarding how far U.S. vessels should be allowed to go.[173] It is likely that this disagreement prompted caution on Eisenhower's part, who modified U.S. plans to restrict the escort missions to only three miles of Jinmen.[174] In addition, deliberations led Eisenhower to reject plans for bombing artillery positions on the mainland on grounds that they would be unlikely to succeed and might escalate the situation.[175] Eisenhower's caution was supported by an interdepartmental wargame study, which was included in the NSC briefing materials, calculating the "extent of the U.S. effort required to defeat a Chinese Communist attempt to capture the off-shore islands by force." The logic of this assessment was informed not only by military calculations, but by the observation that the "magnitude of the U.S. attack would have persuaded the Chinese Communist that the U.S. aim was to destroy their regime." Under such circumstances, China might "decide to broaden the conflict," attacking U.S. forces and bases in East Asia. It also assessed that China might "seek expanded Soviet support," raising the risk of general war.[176]

A final set of information centered on costs of maintaining U.S. support for the offshore islands in the long term and, as a result, the advisability of alternative strategies to maintain the KMT regime. JCS

---

[169] "Memorandum of Discussion at the 325th Meeting of the NSC," May 27, 1957; "Memorandum of Discussion at the 327th Meeting of the NSC," June 20, 1957. *FRUS 1955–1957, Volume III*.

[170] "Discussion of the 378th Meeting of the NSC," August 27, 1958. NSC Series, Box 10, DDEL.

[171] For example, see "National Intelligence Estimate 43-2-57: The Prospects for the Government of the Republic of China," August 27, 1957; "National Intelligence Estimate 13–58: Communist China," April 2, 1958.

[172] Tucker, *The China Threat*, 143.

[173] Halperin, *The 1958 Taiwan Straits Crisis*, 204.

[174] Ibid., 198.

[175] Ibid., 206.

[176] "Background Information for Taiwan Straits Discussion," August 13, 1958. NSC Series, Box 10, DDEL. See also Halperin, *The 1958 Taiwan Straits Crisis*, 56–58.

projections concerning force requirements in the event of war prompted "tough questions" about the value of the offshore islands.[177] A JCS analysis given to Eisenhower before his meeting on August 25 explicitly stated that, should the mainland attempt a full invasion of the offshore islands, the military would "require atomic strikes on the Chinese mainland to effectively and quickly stop" mainland aggression.[178] This would have included tactical nuclear strikes on coastal barriers and air bases.[179] As JCS Chairman Twining noted, "if it is our national policy to defend the Offshore Islands, then we must face the possible ultimate consequences of that policy."[180] The intelligence community assessed that such scenarios presented a "grave risk that the Communists would retaliate in kind." Use of nuclear weapons, they predicted, would be "widely condemned by popular opinion, especially in Asia" and that "the adverse reactions would overshadow the favorable effects in most countries."[181] While Eisenhower was unwilling to yield to Chinese pressure during the crisis, bureaucratic counsel informed his choice to lobby Chiang to withdraw once the crisis began to subside.[182] Eisenhower later wrote that while he did not doubt the "total superiority" of the United States, his decisions were informed by the conclusion that "to be successful we might face the necessity of using small-scale atomic weapons" against China. Eisenhower later recalled that, having "recognized the possible necessity of such future use," he decided to proceed cautiously.[183]

Alternative Explanations. Integrated institutions help to explain how Eisenhower formed accurate judgments during the 1958 Taiwan Strait Crisis, but several alternative explanations are worth considering. First, there is limited evidence in support of the interest group model of bureaucratic politics. The most important decisions during the crisis were made by Eisenhower – and did not reflect the view of a single bureaucracy with privileged access. Rather than simply offering a venue for bureaucrats to advocate for policy recommendations, Eisenhower's discussions with his advisers featured debates about the nature of the situation the

---

[177] Accinelli, "A Thorn in the Side of Peace," 119.
[178] Halperin, *The 1958 Taiwan Straits Crisis*, 109–110.
[179] Accinelli, "A Thorn in the Side of Peace," 118.
[180] Cited in Accinelli, "A Thorn in the Side of Peace," 115.
[181] "Special National Intelligence Estimate 100-7-58," July 22, 1958, 1–2. Excerpts from this report were included in the read-ahead briefing materials provided to the NSC prior to its August 14 meeting. See "Briefing Note for the 376th NSC Meeting," August 13, 1958. NSC Series, Box 10, DDEL.
[182] Halperin, *The 1958 Taiwan Straits Crisis*, 117.
[183] Eisenhower, *Waging Peace*, 293, 295.

United States faced, as well as the costs and benefits of the strategies available.

Second, while Eisenhower's generally accurate projections regarding the crisis are consistent with accountability theory, Eisenhower's choices appear to have been shaped more by bureaucratic advice than public opinion. Eisenhower was well-aware of public attitudes through letters to the White House, Congress, and the State Department.[184] State Department summaries of opinion polls "showed that a preponderance of the elite and mass public looked with doubt or outright disfavor on a fight with China over the islands" and preferred "nonviolent resolution through the Warsaw talks or the United Nations and neutralization or demilitarization of the islands."[185] Yet Eisenhower chose to intervene despite a lack of public support for using military action to defend the offshore islands. There was scant discussion of public opinion in Eisenhower's deliberations and, when the president did reference the national mood, he suggested that what citizens valued most was effective policies.[186] In his memoirs, for instance, Eisenhower suggested he felt that once the crisis turned in America's favor, public support would follow.[187]

Finally, there is little doubt that Eisenhower's worldview mattered. Eisenhower was the prototype of the "cold warrior" generation, which strongly believed in domino theory and the efficacy of military force in deterring Communist aggression.[188] Yet even if Eisenhower was predisposed to military action, he sought information from the bureaucracy during the crisis that would help him to determine whether standing firm in Taiwan was likely to succeed or fail.[189]

In fact, Eisenhower's beliefs regarding Taiwan changed dramatically over the course of his presidency. Soon after entering office, he had approved a strategy of "unleashing" Chiang Kai-shek on the mainland, removing restrictions on the Chinese Nationalists to conduct small-scale

---

[184] Eisenhower, *Waging Peace*, 301. See also Tucker, *The China Threat*, 152–153.
[185] Accinelli, "A Thorn in the Side of Peace," 126.
[186] For example, Eisenhower posited that public criticism stemmed from being "shoved into something that [the United States] do not think is correct because of [Taiwan's] intransigence." See "Memorandum for the Record," August 14, 1958. *FRUS 1958–1960, Volume XIX*.
[187] Eisenhower, *Waging Peace*, 303.
[188] Yarhi-Milo, *Who Fights for Reputation*, 82–83.
[189] For a similar argument in the context of the 1954 Dien Bien Phu crisis, see Burke and Greenstein, *How Presidents Test Reality*, 28–52.

attacks against the mainland.[190] Yet Eisenhower's enthusiasm for these more assertive actions waned. During the 1954 Taiwan Strait Crisis, U.S. Defense Secretary Wilson suggested that American policy be changed to eliminate using the offshore islands "to raid Chinese Communist territory and commerce." Eisenhower concurred and suspended such operations and chose to "refrain from assisting or encouraging offensive actions" against China.[191] In short, Eisenhower's flexible beliefs regarding the optimal U.S. strategy toward Taiwan suggests that we cannot attribute his decision-making during the 1958 Taiwan Strait Crisis strictly to the worldview that he brought with him into the White House.

The U.S. Escalation in Vietnam

U.S. commitments in Vietnam trace back to the end of World War II. For the United States, the overarching motivation was to prevent the spread of communism in East Asia. In 1954, the Geneva Accords divided Indochina into North and South Vietnam along the seventeenth parallel. The Communist Party of Vietnam controlled the Democratic Republic of Vietnam (DRV) in the north and was generally aligned with the Soviet Union and the People's Republic of China. An anti-communist regime in the south, the Republic of Vietnam (RVN), aligned with the United States. Although the Geneva Accords called for reunification between the north and south through popular elections, the southern government was not party to the agreement. Knowing the DRV's leader, Ho Chi Minh, enjoyed broad support in the more populous north, the RVN refused to support elections. In response, the DRV pushed for reunification through violence, first supporting Viet Cong (VC) insurgents and then sending its own military forces to escalate the fighting in the south.

By the time John F. Kennedy was assassinated in November 1963, the DRV-backed insurgency was on course to destabilize and topple the RVN regime. Absent a change in U.S. policy, the new U.S. President, Lyndon Johnson, believed that the RVN would not survive for much longer. The fall of Saigon would undermine the credibility of U.S. commitments and risk the spread of communist influence to other parts of the region.

---

[190] "United States Objectives and Courses of Action with Respect to Formosa and the Chinese National Government," November 6, 1953. *FRUS 1952–1954, Volume XIV, China and Japan, Part 1.*
[191] "Memorandum by the NSA (Cutler) to the Secretary of State," September 26, 1954; "Draft Statement of Policy, Prepared by the NSC Planning Board," November 19, 1954. *FRUS 1952–1954, Volume XIV.*

The decisive moments in Johnson's decision-making on Vietnam occurred in the period between November 1964 and February 1965.[192] In the months after entering office, Johnson "deliberately deferred" making significant choices on Vietnam.[193] After the November 1964 election, however, Johnson began devoting his attention to the way forward in Vietnam.

As Johnson began to consider a major change in U.S. policy toward Vietnam, there were two main options available: escalation and exit. As Johnson described it in early February 1965, the choice was between "going forward or running."[194] The first option, which the United States ultimately chose, was to use a combination of strategic bombing and ground force deployments to escalate the conflict. Johnson approved the first phase of the bombing campaign, Operation Flaming Dart, in February 1965, and the next phase, Operation Rolling Thunder, in March. After strategic bombing operations had commenced, the United States quickly began deploying ground forces. Three broad goals underpinned this strategy. First, the United States sought to coerce North Vietnam into accepting American demands to end its support of the insurgency in South Vietnam. Second, the United States hoped to quell the insurgency and ensure an "independent and secure" South Vietnam. Third, the United States aimed to prevent other non-Communist countries in Southeast Asia from falling to communism.[195]

The principal alternative available to the United States was withdrawal. This might have taken one of two forms. The first path was to make the concessions necessary to pursue a negotiated settlement, perhaps through an international conference, such as that which facilitated the Laos settlement in 1962. These concessions might have included ending U.S. military presence in the country, establishing a coalition government that included the Vietcong, and extending diplomatic recognition.[196] A second path was to withhold additional support to South Vietnam and allow the regime in Siagon to collapse. As conditions deteriorated, as U.S. policymakers believed they would, the United States

---

[192] Kaiser, *American Tragedy*, 411; Logevall, *Choosing War*, 335; VanDeMark, *Road to Disaster*, 261–268.
[193] "Memorandum from Bundy to Johnson," November 2, 1964. *FRUS 1964–1968, Volume XXXIII*.
[194] "Memorandum of Meeting," February 8, 1965. *FRUS 1964–1968, Volume II, Vietnam, January–June 1965*.
[195] "Paper Prepared by the Executive Committee," December 2, 1964. *FRUS 1964–1968, Volume I, Vietnam, 1964*.
[196] Robert S. McNamara, James Blight, and Robert K. Brigham, *Argument without End: In Search of Answers to the Vietnam Tragedy* (New York: Public Affairs, 1999), 135–136.

could withdraw from the country by arguing that Saigon was unwilling or unable to sustain itself.[197]

The Logic of Johnson's Decision. What beliefs led Lyndon Johnson to choose escalation over withdrawal? The available evidence suggests that Johnson ultimately concluded that escalation could improve the U.S. negotiating position by imposing overwhelming costs on North Vietnam and the Viet Cong insurgents. In early February, Johnson described that "careful and sustained responses" to North Vietnam would allow the United States to "gain strength essential to stay in South Vietnam or gain an appropriate position for a Conference."[198] Johnson suggested that the United States could "deter, destroy, and diminish the strength of the North Vietnamese aggressors and to try to convince them to leave South Vietnam alone."[199] As Johnson later noted, "I saw our bombs as my political resources for negotiating a peace. [...] our bombs could be used as sticks against the North, pressuring North Vietnam to stop its aggression against the South."[200]

While Johnson's statements at the time suggest a conviction that military coercion would improve the U.S. position, he also harbored reservations. In other words, Johnson felt the odds of success were closer to even rather than a sure win. Johnson's logic for escalation was made more palatable by two complementary assessments. First, Johnson believed that the costs of withdrawal would be overwhelming. Part and parcel of Johnson's assessment was the logic of "domino theory," which posited that the fall of South Vietnam to communism would mean the fall of other countries in Southeast Asia – Thailand, Cambodia, Indonesia, Malaysia – to the Communist bloc as well.[201] If the United States withdrew, Johnson reasoned, the "dominoes would fall, and part of the world would go to the Communists."[202] "Cowardice," Johnson explained, had led to more wars than firm action. Both World War I and II might have been avoided if the United States "had been courageous in the early stages" of the conflicts.[203]

Second, Johnson concluded that there were no alternatives available for a less costly outcome. "I shudder at getting too deeply involved"

---

[197] VanDeMark, *Road to Disaster*, 258.
[198] "Memorandum for the Record," February 8, 1965. *FRUS 1964–1968, Volume II.*
[199] "Summary Notes of the 547th Meeting of the NSC," February 8, 1965. *FRUS 1964–1968, Volume II.*
[200] Goodwin, *Lyndon Johnson and the American Dream*, 264.
[201] Beschloss, *The Johnson White House Tapes, 1963–1964*, 257.
[202] Ibid., 248–249.
[203] "White House Meeting on Vietnam," February 6, 1965. *FRUS 1964–1968, Volume II.*

in Vietnam, Johnson told UN Ambassador Adlai Stevenson. Yet Johnson surmised that escalation was "the only alternative" available.[204] Specifically, Johnson took a dim view of the possibility of a negotiated settlement, concluding that "it was hopeless to expect anything" out of international mediation.[205] Considering a diplomatic conference for a negotiated settlement was, at best, premature.[206] The United States needed, in Johnson's estimate, to first improve its leverage over North Vietnam.

The U.S. Outcome. Contrary to Johnson's assessments, escalation failed both to improve U.S. bargaining position over the DRV or in stabilizing the security situation in the RVN. The costs that the DRV was willing to bear to achieve national reunification proved to be substantially higher than the United States could match.[207] For decision-makers in Hanoi, the conflict was a total war for national unification and independence. For the United States, the conflict was a bid to maintain geopolitical influence in Southeast Asia during the Cold War. As historian Brian VanDeMark summarizes, failure to recognize this disparity was a "fundamental miscalculation."[208]

In fact, escalation had the opposite effect of what Johnson hoped, hardening North Vietnam's position.[209] The bombing campaign immediately mobilized the North Vietnamese masses.[210] Instead of intimidating North Vietnam, British diplomats reported, the U.S. attacks seemed "to have aroused them to still greater efforts" and inspired "a mood of confidence, even of arrogance."[211] While Johnson had intended to deter North Vietnamese support to the insurgency, they instead prompted North Vietnamese decision-makers to escalate in kind.[212]

American escalation also allowed more hawkish leaders within the DRV Politburo to override lingering skeptics who remained open to a negotiated settlement. While there is little doubt that the DRV's ultimate objective was national reunification under communist rule, the

[204] VanDeMark, *Road to Disaster*, 233–234.
[205] "Summary Notes of the 546th Meeting of the NSC," February 7, 1965. *FRUS 1964–1968, Volume II*.
[206] "Memorandum for the Record," February 7, 1965. *FRUS 1964–1968, Volume II*.
[207] William Bundy Vietnam Manuscript (hereafter WBVM), Papers of William Bundy, Box 1, LBJL, Foreword, 4.
[208] VanDeMark, *Road to Disaster*, 231.
[209] Military Institute of Vietnam, *Victory in Vietnam: The Official History of the People's Army of Vietnam, 1954–1975*, trans. Merle L. Pribbenow (Lawrence: Kansas University Press, 2002), 132.
[210] Pierre Asselin, *Hanoi's Road to the Vietnam War, 1954–1965* (Berkeley: University of California Press, 2013), 197.
[211] Cited in ibid., 199.
[212] VanDeMark, *Road to Disaster*, 249.

party leadership had theretofore been divided over how best to achieve it. One group, led by Vietnamese Communist Party General Secretary Le Duan and Politburo member Le Duc Tho, favored a military strategy aimed at rapid unification.[213] A second group led by President Ho Chi Minh and Defense Minister Vo Nguyen Giap, instead favored a combination of military and diplomatic strategies to gradually move toward reunification, possibly through a temporary neutral solution in the South. In fact, roughly half of the North Vietnamese Politburo in 1964 still supported peaceful coexistence, despite increasing political pressure.[214] In late March 1964, the VWP Secretariat called a "special political conference," in which Ho Chi Minh gave a widely publicized speech emphasizing peaceful reunification, suggesting he may have been attempting to "reassert more moderate policy lines."[215]

After the American bombing campaign intensified between February and March 1965, the Central Committee approved more policy measures to expand the war, shifting its "entire economy" to support the war effort and further expanding its military deployments to the South. In the spring of 1965, seven additional infantry regiments, as well as engineers, artillery, logistics, and other special branch units were sent south.[216] Moreover, North Vietnam's interest in diplomatic talks waned. As Fred Logevall notes, North Vietnamese leaders "became much less flexible after the systematic U.S. air strikes began." Between March and April, North Vietnam curtailed its probes of international mediation through French contacts. Vietnamese Prime Minister Pham Van Dong refused to meet with the Canadian diplomat who had previously served as an intermediary with the United States – and told French diplomats that negotiations with the United States were impossible for the time being.[217]

Evaluating Johnson's belief that escalation would prevent the collapse of anti-communist regimes in the region is more complicated. Yet there are many reasons to judge, as Defense Secretary Robert McNamara later reflected, that early disengagement from Vietnam "would have cost the United States far less" not only in terms of human life and material resources, but in terms of the "erosion of [U.S.] containment policy" as well.[218] First, the ultimate collapse of South Vietnam did not trigger

---

[213] Asselin, *Hanoi's Road to the Vietnam War*, 162–164.
[214] Lien-Hang T. Nguyen, *Hanoi's War: An International History of the War for Peace in Vietnam* (Chapel Hill: University of North Carolina Press, 2012), 66–67.
[215] Asselin, *Hanoi's Road to the Vietnam War*, 186–187; Cheng Guan Ang, *The Vietnam War from the Other Side* (New York: Routledge, 2002), 79–80.
[216] Military Institute of Vietnam, *Victory in Vietnam*, 143–144.
[217] Logevall, *Choosing War*, 366–367.
[218] McNamara, *In Retrospect*, 164.

widespread regime change in Southeast Asia. Of the countries commonly identified as the most likely "dominoes" in the region, Thailand, Indonesia, and Malaysia all remained outside the Communist camp. Second, while Vietnam did invade and occupy Cambodia, the expansion of Vietnamese military power in Southeast Asia solidified the rift between China and Vietnam. China opposed further expansion of Vietnamese military support throughout the region as a result. Perhaps the strongest claim that can be made is that some Chinese military support to North Vietnam might have been redirected to other Communist insurgencies in Thailand and Malaysia. Yet the United States could have matched such support with a fraction of the assets it invested in South Vietnam – and could have done so against Communist organizations that enjoyed less domestic support and organization than that in South Vietnam.

Finally, it is likely that Johnson's assessments about the prospects for negotiated settlement were at least partially incorrect. It is plausible that North Vietnam would have agreed to diplomatic negotiations in the window between November 1964 and February 1965, provided that the United States would be willing to commit to withdrawal. A Politburo assessment from November 1964 saw the possibility of a "neutralist peace" that might last for five to ten years before unifying the country.[219] North Vietnamese leader Le Duan noted in early February 1965 that the DRV sought to "encourage Washington to withdraw in the face of the South Vietnamese collapse by proposing a neutral solution in Saigon that is acceptable to both sides."[220] Vietnamese officials later recalled that neutralization was at least part of "the preferred solution."[221] For many, neutralization was "regarded as desirable" precisely because it might present a solution for avoiding a costly conflict with the United States.[222]

During this period, North Vietnamese leaders signaled at least a modicum of openness to diplomacy. After UN Secretary General U Thant called for an international conference in July 1964, Ho Chi Minh responded by indicating that Vietnam was "prepared to send an emissary to meet with a representative of the United States in Rangoon or any other neutral capital in Southeast Asia."[223] In mid-September, North

---

[219] The nomenclature that North Vietnam often used for a negotiated settlement was "neutralization" of South Vietnam. See "Political Bureau's Assessment of the Situation," November 20, 1964, 20. Vietnam Center and Sam Johnson Vietnam Archive (hereafter VCSJVA).
[220] McNamara, Blight, and Brigham, *Argument without End*, 187.
[221] Ibid., 144.
[222] Ibid., 136.
[223] Nguyen Dinh Bin, ed., *Ngoai Giao Viet Nam: 1945–2000* [Vietnamese Diplomacy, 1945–2000], trans. Merle Pribbenow (Hanoi: National Political Publishing House, 2002), 195.

Vietnam accepted a Soviet request for bilateral talks with the United States.[224] The Politburo delayed dispatching some military units until the end of November due to "requirements of our struggle on the diplomatic front."[225] In February 1965, the North Vietnamese leadership continued to press France for an international conference.[226]

One factor that complicated the possibility of a negotiated withdrawal was China's support of the DRV military operations in South Vietnam. Yet even Chinese leaders exhibited some openness to talks during this period. During a conversation with Vietnamese Communist Party General Secretary Le Duan on August 13, 1964, Chinese leader Mao Zedong noted that "you do not want to fight a war, and we do not necessarily want to fight a war" with the United States.[227] Vietnam's openness to negotiations during this window was also reflected in its diplomatic contacts with China. On October 5, 1964, Pham Van Dong told Mao that the Politburo sought to keep the United States from escalating the war. While discussing UN Secretary General U Thant's proposal for negotiations, Mao noted that it was "not a completely bad thing to negotiate." While Mao was unsure whether the talks would be successful, he admitted that the DRV had "already earned the qualifications [i.e., bargaining leverage] to negotiate" with the United States.[228] In early January 1965, both Mao and Chinese Foreign Minister Chen Yi suggested that China was receptive to the idea of an international conference.[229]

Two points surrounding the accuracy of Johnson's beliefs regarding the possibility of diplomatic alternatives are worth clarifying. First, it is likely that any peace agreement would not have lasted. North Vietnamese leaders viewed diplomatic settlement as a temporary solution – referred to as a "transitional phase" – toward securing an American withdrawal before achieving "total victory."[230] North Vietnamese leaders were determined

---

[224] Logevall, *Choosing War*, 212.
[225] Pham Gia Duc, *Su Doan 325* [325th Division], trans. Merle Pribbenow (Hanoi: People's Army Publishing House, 1986), Vol. II, 44.
[226] Logevall, *Choosing War*, 336.
[227] Chen, *Mao's China and the Cold War*, 213.
[228] Odd Arne Westad et al., *77 Conversations between Chinese and Foreign Leaders on the Wars in Indochina, 1964–1977* (Washington, DC: Wilson Center, 1998), 72–74. For an alternative view, see Christensen, *Worse Than a Monolith*, 167–171.
[229] Logevall, *Choosing War*, 365–366.
[230] "Resolution of the 9th Plenum of the Party Central Committee," December 1963. Vu Huu Ngoan, ed., *Van Kien Dang* [Collected Party Documents], trans. Merle Pribbenow (Hanoi: Nha Xuat Ban Chinh Tri Quoc Gia, 2003), 823. See also Nguyen, *Hanoi's War*, 17–47.

to reunite the country and planned to renew military hostilities after the United States had withdrawn. Second, North Vietnam had not clearly defined the terms of neutralization in the fall of 1964 because it believed the United States was not willing to negotiate.[231] In November 1964, Politburo assessments noted that the United States was "not yet prepared for negotiations."[232] North Vietnamese decision-makers did not invest time in defining the terms of a settlement, one official noted, precisely because the United States was "not interested" in negotiations.[233]

Institutional Origins of Johnson's Miscalculation. Fragmented institutions help explain why Johnson miscalculated. A fragmented design both impeded the flow of bureaucratic information and created incentives for bureaucratic advisers to censor the information provided to the president. As such, as historian Fred Logevall summarizes, there was no effort to reassess "the rationale behind the U.S. commitment," to assess "whether such an objective was vital to U.S. security, or whether it was even attainable," much less to clearly identify the "possible solutions to the conflict."[234]

Restricted information search was a deliberate choice. Johnson *chose* to sideline the NSC.[235] Johnson refused recommendations to established a permanent NSC Executive Committee to mirror the institutions the Kennedy administration used during the Cuban Missile Crisis.[236] According to one senior official, Johnson "hated even to have it known that a particular problem [in Vietnam policy] was under intense scrutiny" by his advisers.[237] On December 7, 1964, Johnson issued guidance that he considered it "a matter of the highest importance" that the substance of American policy on Vietnam should be "confined as narrowly as possible" within the Executive Branch.[238] Throughout the decision-making process, Johnson repeatedly told his advisers that he would "fire any leaker" and "stressed the importance of preventing" any disclosure of information to the press.[239]

---

[231] See, for example, "Politburo Directive No. 81-CT/TW," August 7, 1964. Vu Huu Ngoan, *Van Kien Dang*, Vol. 25, 184.
[232] "Political Bureau's Assessment of the Situation," November 20, 1964, 10, 20. VCSJVA.
[233] McNamara, Blight, and Brigham, *Argument without End*, 136.
[234] Logevall, *Choosing War*, 77.
[235] Humphrey, "NSC Meetings during the Johnson Presidency," 44–45.
[236] "Memorandum of the Meeting of the Executive Committee," November 24, 1964. *FRUS 1964–1968, Volume I*; WBVM, Chapter 19, 12.
[237] WBVM, Chapter 18, 4.
[238] "Memorandum From the President to Rusk, McNamara, and McCone," December 7, 1964. *FRUS 1964–1968, Volume I*.
[239] "Notes on a Meeting, White House," December 1, 1964. *FRUS 1964–1968, Volume I*; "Summary Record of the 548th Meeting of the National Security Council," February 10, 1965. *FRUS 1964–1968, Volume II*.

Incomplete and low-quality information stemmed from Johnson's calculation that a more integrated decision-making process threatened to derail his domestic political agenda. For Johnson, if the public understood the level of difficulty the United States faced in Vietnam, it would redirect attention away from the domestic agenda he prized. Johnson later recalled that in 1965 he could "almost touch" his "youthful dream of improving life for more people and in more ways than any other political leader, including FDR" and was "determined to keep the [Vietnam] war from shattering that dream [...] which meant I simply had no choice but to keep my foreign policy in the wings." Johnson argued that "a major debate on the war" would have marked "the beginning of the end of the Great Society."[240]

The first way in which fragmented institutions shaped Johnson's judgments was in the information that reached his desk. The most important counsel supplied during this period came from two people: Secretary of Defense Robert McNamara and National Security Advisor McGeorge Bundy. In a series of memoranda to Johnson, Bundy provided critical advice that pushed Johnson overcome doubts about whether the United States could succeed – and stressed that negotiation would not work. On December 28, 1964, Bundy argued that the Communist regime in Hanoi needed a "reminder" about U.S. "will and determination," noting that reprisal attacks on North Vietnam was would be able to "prevent gradual Viet Cong escalation in South Vietnam."[241] On January 27th, Bundy and McNamara asked for a "very private discussion of the basic situation in Vietnam." In their memorandum, often referred to as the "Y in the road" memo, McNamara and Bundy argued that "the worst course of action" would be to continue on the present course, which "can only lead to eventual defeat and an invitation to get out in humiliating circumstances." They stressed that the preferred course of action was to employ American "military power in the Far East and to force a change of Communist policy."[242]

The January 27th meeting represented an important change in Johnson's thinking on escalation. Whereas as late as December 1964 the president had hesitated to increase American commitments until the South Vietnamese government stabilized, the January meeting persuaded Johnson to declare that the United States would "move strongly" with or

---

[240] Goodwin, *Lyndon Johnson and the American Dream*, 282–283.
[241] "Paper Prepared by the President's Special Assistant for National Security Affairs," December 28, 1964. *FRUS 1964–1968, Volume I*.
[242] "Memorandum From the President's Special Assistant for National Security Affairs (Bundy) to President Johnson," January 27, 1965. *FRUS 1964–1968, Volume II*.

without a stable government in Saigon.²⁴³ In a lengthy memorandum delivered to Johnson on February 7, 1965, Bundy summarized the case for escalation. Bundy argued that the policy would deliver both short-term benefits in stabilizing the situation in South Vietnam and, to a lesser degree, in shaping the DRV's choices in the long term. "Effective and sustained reprisals, even in a low key," Bundy argued, "would have a substantial depressing effect upon the morale of Viet Cong cadres in South Vietnam."²⁴⁴

The analyses provided to Johnson during this period, however, were surprisingly short on detail.²⁴⁵ In early March 1965, Bundy explicitly noted that there would be "no paper work [on contingency planning for sharp deterioration] at all [...] There will be no papers, and this mission [to plan for contingencies] will not exist anywhere except in this memorandum."²⁴⁶ Bundy later criticized himself for not overseeing the "staff work" necessary to assess the "requirements and prospects" for escalation. In Bundy's own view, the process of "decision, explanation, and defense" that he oversaw was unsatisfactory.²⁴⁷

The Bundy-McNamara memorandum, for example, offered few projections about the potential costs of escalations and put forward little evaluation of the alternative options available to Johnson. Bundy's February 7th memorandum, despite its length, similarly offered few detailed projections. Bundy asserted that the overall odds of success could not be estimated "with any accuracy," suggesting that they could fall anywhere between 25 percent and 75 percent. When it came to the expected costs of the conflict, Bundy only noted that the strategy "implie[d] significant U.S. air losses." Bundy's memorandum did not discuss the possibility that bombing raids against North Vietnam would strengthen its determination. Bundy's only projection regarding the duration of the conflict is that, at the "very best," the struggle in Vietnam would be "long." While Bundy supported deployment of small contingents of ground forces to protect U.S. aircraft, there was no discussion of the potential casualties these units might suffer – or whether they could be deployed without being tasked with offensive patrols of the areas surrounding the bases in order to prevent such casualties. Finally, Bundy offered no analysis regarding the potential for withdrawal, instead affirming that there was "no

---

²⁴³ WBVM, Chapter 22, 6; Logevall, *Choosing War*, 318. For an example of Johnson's apprehensions in December 1964, see "Notes on a Meeting," December 1, 1964. *FRUS, 1964–1968, Volume I*.
²⁴⁴ "Memorandum from Bundy to Johnson," February 7, 1965. *FRUS 1964–1968, Volume I*.
²⁴⁵ VanDeMark, *Road to Disaster*, 280.
²⁴⁶ "Memorandum from Bundy to Johnson," March 6, 1965. *FRUS 1964–1968, Volume II*.
²⁴⁷ Goldstein, *Lessons in Disaster*, 218.

way of unloading the burden" onto Vietnam and "no way of negotiating ourselves out of Vietnam which offers any serious promise at present."[248]

What makes these lacunae in the analysis remarkable are the pockets of information answering each of these topics in detail that were scattered across the bureaucracy, but that failed to reach Johnson during the decision-making process.

The first pocket of information suggested that the North Vietnamese regime would not change its bargaining position as the result of strikes. As early as January 1964, analysis from the CIA found that the "principal determinant of DRV prosecution of the war will not be damage suffered from such small-scale operations, but the course of the war in the South and the degree of risk Hanoi believes will be involved in its prosecution."[249] Even large-scale punishment would be insufficient given North Vietnamese resolve. In March, the State Department's Policy Planning Council similarly assessed that strategic bombing against North Vietnam would not work because its decision-makers would persevere even in the face of extensive physical destruction. As such, the primary outcome of escalation would be a deepening of the U.S. stakes in Southeast Asia and an increase in the costs of withdrawal.[250] In October, the CIA released an estimate that found that the best outcome that a bombing campaign could expect was that North Vietnam would accept a ceasefire and negotiation, but "would not be prepared to make any meaningful concessions" to the United States. On the other hand, air strikes risked prompting North Vietnam to "embark on a bold course" that "would carry on the fight and proceed to send its armed forces on a large scale to Laos and South Vietnam."[251]

Wargames conducted in 1964 also pointed to the limited prospects of success. In April and September, the results of two Pentagon simulations showed that bombing would not "cause Hanoi to give up the fight or do much to help matters in the South."[252] White House staff suggested that the wargames might help address the present analytical challenges that the Johnson administration faced.[253] State Department officials queried why the United States was "contemplating an air action

---

[248] "Memorandum from Bundy to Johnson," February 7, 1965. *FRUS 1964–1968, Volume I*, Document 84.
[249] Central Intelligence Agency, "Probable Reactions to Various Courses of Action with Respect to North Vietnam," January 2, 1964. CIA FOIA Reading Room.
[250] Logevall, *Choosing War*, 123.
[251] Central Intelligence Agency, "SNIE 10-3-64: Probable Communist Reactions to Certain Possible US/GVN Courses of Actions," October 9, 1964. The intelligence community was divided over which outcome was more likely.
[252] Logevall, *Choosing War*, 123.
[253] "Memorandum for the Record of the White House Daily Staff Meeting," March 30, 1964. *FRUS 1964–1968, Volume I*.

against the North in the face of a recently played wargame that demonstrated the ineffectiveness of such a tactic."[254] In October, another senior State Department official drew attention to the September wargames, noting that the outcome "reached a point where major ground forces on our side, and/or the use of tactical nuclear weapons, were required to counter a ground reaction estimated as likely from North Vietnam alone."[255] As such, others reasoned that the prognosis for "systematic air attacks" on North Vietnam was "gloomy indeed" and "could not be recommended." These assessments, however, did not reach the president – and there is no evidence that the results of the wargames were passed to Johnson.[256]

Other assessments in the senior ranks of the State Department reflected a similar degree of skepticism about the efficacy of escalation. In late May 1964, Undersecretary of State George Ball sent a memo to Secretary of State Dean Rusk in which he seriously questioned the efficacy of military action against the DRV. "Are we proposing action against the North," Ball asked, "because we are reasonably confident it will, in fact, work, or merely because we are becoming reasonably confident that the present course of action will not work and we are not able to think of anything else to do?" Ball also asked if escalation might, in fact, "lead directly to what we have been seeking to avoid – a conference in which our bargaining position is poor?"[257] In early October, Ball authored a sixty-seven-page report entitled "How Valid Are the Assumptions Underlying our Viet-Nam Policies?" Ball suggested that so long as DRV leaders believed victory was near, "it will probably be willing to accept very substantial costs from United States air action." The SIGMA II wargames in September, Ball argued, showed that "exhausting the 1964 target list presently proposed for airstrikes would not cripple Hanoi's capability for increasing its support of the Viet Cong, much less force suspension of present support levels on purely logistical grounds." On the contrary, Ball assessed that a bombing campaign would not improve America's bargaining position – and might worsen it.[258]

Fragmented institutions curtailed the circulation of Ball's analysis. Secretary of Defense McNamara was "absolutely horrified" by the existence of the memorandum and treated it like "a poisonous snake." In

---

[254] "Letter from the Under Secretary of State (Ball) to the Secretary of State," May 31, 1964. *FRUS 1964–1968, Volume I*.
[255] Bird, *The Color of Truth*, 292.
[256] Ibid., 292–293; WBVM, Chapter 17, 24–25.
[257] "Letter from the Under Secretary of State (Ball) to the Secretary of State," May 31, 1964. *FRUS 1964–1968, Volume I*.
[258] "How Valid Are the Assumptions Underlying Our Viet-Nam Policies?" October 5, 1964. National Security Files, Vietnam Country File Box 222, LBJL.

McNamara's view, as in Johnson's, putting dissenting views "down on paper" was "next to treason."[259] While Ball's memorandum reached National Security Advisor Bundy, it did not reach Johnson until the following year.[260] McNamara later concluded that U.S. policymakers had "seriously erred" by not immediately discussing the memorandum with the president and circulating it for analysis throughout the bureaucracy.[261]

A second pocket of information that failed to reach the president pertained to the costs of a negotiated withdrawal. Specifically, the consensus position in the CIA was skeptical that the costs of losing Vietnam were high.[262] The CIA's Board of National Estimates (BNE) assessed in June that the basic logic of domino theory was flawed. The CIA disagreed with the idea that the "loss of South Vietnam and Laos would be followed by the rapid, successive communization of the other states of the Far East." Besides possibly Cambodia, the CIA believed that "it is likely that no nation in the area would quickly succumb to communism as a result of the fall of Laos and South Vietnam." Moreover, the assessment noted, American strength in East Asia was "based on the chain of islands from the Philippines to Japan, not on the Asian mainland," meaning that it could probably deter China and North Vietnam from "overt military aggression" so long as it could "effectively operate from these bases."[263] A similar report by the CIA's Willard Matthias, who noted that Soviet expansionism had abated after the Cuban Missile Crisis, said that the Sino-Soviet split undermined the potential for monolithic support for communist expansion, and envisioned "some kind of negotiated settlement" in view of the prospects.[264] While the BNE report reached the NSC staff, the available evidence suggests it did not make its way to Johnson.[265]

---

[259] George Ball OHT I, July 8, 1971, LBJL, 10.
[260] A White House routing note attached to the report that Johnson read indicates that the paper "came down from the President's office a few days ago." See "Note from Chester Cooper for McGeorge Bundy," March 2, 1965. National Security Files – Vietnam Box 222, LBJL. See also George Ball OHT I, July 8, 1971, LBJL, 11; Logevall, *Choosing War*, 246; Bird, *The Color of Truth*, 293; James A. Bill, *George Ball: Behind the Scenes in US Foreign Policy* (New Haven: Yale University Press, 1998), 163.
[261] McNamara, *In Retrospect*, 152.
[262] Gelb and Betts, *The Irony of Vietnam*, 230.
[263] "Memorandum from the Board of National Estimates to the Director of Central Intelligence (McCone)," June 9, 1964. *FRUS 1964–1968, Volume I*. While the report did note that the fall of South Vietnam would be "profoundly damaging" to American reputation, it also assessed that the extent to which this should cause individual countries to move toward the Communist camp would be "significantly affected by the substance and manner of US policy in the period following the loss of Laos and South Vietnam."
[264] Logevall, *Choosing War*, 166.
[265] Goldstein, *Lessons in Disaster*, 140. When asked about it later, Bundy did not recall the memo. See Interview with Bundy, cited in Bird, *The Color of Truth*, 446. See also 285. For routing of the report, see *FRUS 1964–1968, Volume I*, Document 209, note 1.

Similar conclusions were detailed in a lengthy memorandum by Assistant Secretary of State for Far Eastern Affairs William Bundy in October 1964. Bundy argued that South Vietnam and Laos were unique cases that most of the world had "written off." While the United States would need to devote special attention to Thailand and South Korea, "a strong case" could thus be made that the "loss of South Vietnam and Laos to Communist control would not shake significantly non-Communist nations in other areas" or excessively embolden the Communist camp.[266] Much like the BNE reports, the available evidence suggests that Bundy's memorandum was not delivered to Johnson.[267]

There was also comparatively little search for information regarding the potential costs of escalation in Vietnam. In the period between August 1964 and February 1965, the senior military leadership did not provide an assessment of force requirements or expected casualties if the American bombing campaign failed and ground troops were required to stabilize the country. In fact, the Pentagon had not even considered the basic logistics associated with the bombing operations, including how many troops would be required to protect U.S. aircraft.[268] This information was available at the time, however. In December 1964, Chief of Staff of the Army Harold Johnson assessed that victory in Vietnam would require five years and 500,000 troops.[269] The Army also assessed that major air strikes against North Vietnam would necessitate ground force deployments by the United States.[270] A JCS study performed by the Marine Corps assessed that it would take 700,000 ground forces.[271]

Instead, Johnson began to approve deployments of ground forces within the insular Tuesday Luncheon group without "work by any staffs outside the Pentagon."[272] McGeorge Bundy later reflected that no one asked "ahead of time what kind of war it will be and what kind of losses must be expected" because Johnson feared the information would leak.[273] One senior State Department official later remembered, the estimated requirements and cost the bombing campaign would ultimately impose on the United States was "infinitely short of the later reality."[274]

---

[266] WBVM, Chapter 17, 17–18.
[267] For the "limited audience" who received a copy of the memorandum, see WBWM, Chapter 17, 15, 26.
[268] VanDeMark, *Road to Disaster*, 271.
[269] McMaster, *Dereliction of Duty*, 247.
[270] Ibid., 225.
[271] Ibid., 261.
[272] WBVM, Chapter 22b, 31; "Telegram From the Chairman of the Joint Chiefs of Staff (Wheeler) to the Commander in Chief, Pacific (Sharp)," February 27, 1965. *FRUS 1964–1968, Volume II*.
[273] Goldstein, *Lessons in Disaster*, 182.
[274] WBVM, Chapter 18, 28.

McNamara later felt that if the Pentagon had done so, it "might have influenced our decisions with respect to the initial deployments."[275]

A third pocket of information that failed to reach the president concerned the availability of alternatives to the United States. In his October memo, Ball noted that "almost no attention" had been paid to date to "the possible political means of finding a way out without further" escalation. Ball noted "conspicuous lacunae" in his own preliminary analysis, but called for the bureaucracy to begin seriously considering the details of a political settlement, such as how specifically the United States might attempt to bolster defense arrangements and assurances to Thailand and Malaysia.[276] Ball's recommendation for additional analytical exploration went unheeded.

Others shared these intuitions, noting that the costs of a graceful exit would not be lower than trying and failing. If the prospects for success were low, the expected reputational costs of escalation in Vietnam were enormous. William Bundy's October 19th memo argued that North Vietnamese leaders would "bend every effort" to have reunification be a Vietnamese solution and would check attempts by China to further export Communist influence in the region. As Bundy noted, even a Vietnam reunited under Communist leadership would still serve as "a buffer against further spread of Chinese influence." The loss of South Vietnam, thus, "could be made bearable." George Ball similarly felt that trying and failing in Vietnam would degrade confidence in the United States. On the contrary, the harder the United States tried and failed, the worse the reputational toll would be. Even Robert McNamara noted that the reputational costs would be higher if the United States escalated but failed.[277]

Other parts of the bureaucracy possessed information about North Vietnam's willingness to enter negotiations under the right terms. A State Department intelligence report from January 1964 suggested that North Vietnam would likely pursue neutralization if it was in "a sufficiently strong bargaining position" and if "Washington wished to drop its commitment to Saigon gracefully." A settlement akin to Laos, the State Department believed, was a "potentially favorable interim solution" the primary attraction of which lay in "getting Washington to withdraw its commitment to Saigon in exchange for internationally recognized neutrality."[278] In March 1964, a CIA assessment observed that

---

[275] VanDeMark, *Road to Disaster*, 271.
[276] "Memorandum from Ball to Rusk, McNamara and Bundy," October 5, 1964. National Security Files – Vietnam, Box 222, LBJL.
[277] *Pentagon Papers* (hereafter *PP*), Part IV-C-2c, 40–41.
[278] Bureau of Intelligence and Research, "Communist Attitudes toward Neutralization for South Vietnam," January 20, 1964. National Security Files – Vietnam, Box 1, LBJL.

North Vietnam's tactics for settlement were "becoming more flexible" in hopes of promoting "a situation where the US would have to accept a face-saving formula for retreat, or be asked to withdraw by a neutralist South Vietnamese regime."[279] In July 1964, the State Department's Bureau of Intelligence and Research noted that both North Vietnam and the Viet Cong had supported a proposal by French President Charles de Gaulle for an international conference to neutralize the peninsula, provided that the United States, France, China, and Soviet Union agreed to "no longer be committed there."[280]

There is scant evidence that North Vietnam's signals of interest in diplomatic was seriously discussed within the White House.[281] Johnson's inner circle did not "properly analyze" nor take "seriously" the prospects for a neutral solution. "It was," as McNamara remembered, "simply rejected."[282] The report of North Vietnam's explicit agreement to enter talks with the United States in September 1964, for example, did not reach the President.[283] McNamara later argued that the Johnson administration never sought "a full explanation" of the North Vietnamese preferences for a negotiated peace process and, if it had, "would have, or should have, jumped at it."[284]

The second way in which fragmented institutions shaped Johnson's assessments was in filtering out information that was incongruent with his prior beliefs. Johnson's desire to win in Vietnam was evident at the time he took office. The President told his advisers that his goal was to "win the war" and that everyone should let "no day go by without asking whether we are doing everything we can to win the struggle there."[285] In February 1964, Johnson said that it was "essential to carry the fight to the enemy" in Vietnam. A "passive position" in response to a deteriorating situation risked "defeatism."[286] In early March 1964, he asked McNamara, "Why don't we take some pretty offensive steps pretty quickly then?"[287] In April, he further wanted "somebody that can lay up some

---

[279] Central Intelligence Agency, "SNIE; The Outlook for North Vietnam," March 4, 1964.
[280] "Research Memorandum From the Director of the Bureau of Intelligence and Research (Hughes) to the Secretary of State," July 25, 1964. *FRUS 1964–1968, Volume I*.
[281] "Telegram from the Embassy in Vietnam to the Department of State," June 24, 1964. *FRUS 1964–1968, Volume I*; Logevall, *Choosing War*, 164.
[282] Ibid., 102.
[283] Gelb and Betts, *The Irony of Vietnam*, 115; Logevall, *Choosing War*, 212.
[284] McNamara, Blight, and Brigham, *Argument without End*, 148.
[285] "Remarks to the National Security Council," December 5, 1963. NSC Meetings File, Box 1, Folder 2, LBJL.
[286] "Memorandum for the Record: Presidential Meeting on Vietnam," February 20, 1964. John McCone Memoranda, Box 1, Folder 3. LBJL.
[287] Beschloss, *The Johnson White House Tapes, 1963–1964*, 258.

plans to trap those guys and whup hell out of them, and kill some of them."[288]

Fear of political survival drove the scope and quality of deliberation that Johnson was willing to permit. Early during his tenure, Johnson asked his advisers to "get together and settle [their] differences" before NSC meetings so that all would be "in agreement" once meetings began. Johnson told them he "deplored the fact that if such a split came before an NSC meeting with 30 or 40 people present, it would immediately become known to the press." Advisers followed Johnson's orders. CIA Director McCone, for instance, assured Johnson that he "would not advance [his] views at an NSC meeting unless specifically requested by the President."[289]

Fragmented institutions shaped the counsel that advisers were willing to relay. At the end of meetings, Johnson had a ritual of going around the room and asking each adviser if they agreed with his decision.[290] Yet few advisers raised any of the doubts that they expressed in private. For instance, George Ball did not raise the concerns expressed in his October memoranda when granted an audience with Johnson in early February.[291] In fact, Ball reversed his position on the possibility of a negotiated settlement, telling Johnson that "any Geneva Conference should only be entered from a position of greater strength" than the United States possessed.[292] Assistant Secretary of State William Bundy similarly did not express the arguments advanced in his own October memorandum. Assistant Secretary of Defense John McNaughton privately noted that bombing would not work and that the best option was to continue "plugging away along present lines," yet chose to censor his dissent during deliberation.[293] Members of the NSC staff similarly chose to keep quiet. Jim Thomson, for instance, privately observed that attempting to bomb North Vietnam "into submission" would not work because "those people we're bombing will survive our taking out everything they've build over these past many years, their infrastructure and so forth."[294] Chester Cooper, another NSC staff officer responsible for the Vietnam portfolio,

---

[288] Ibid., 337.
[289] "Memorandum for the Record: Meeting with the President," March 13, 1964. John McCone Memoranda, Box 1, Folder 3. LBJL.
[290] For example, see "White House Meeting on Vietnam," February 6, 1965. *FRUS 1964–1968, Volume II*.
[291] "Summary Notes of the 545th Meeting of the National Security Council," February 6, 1965; "Summary Notes of the 546th Meeting of the National Security Council," February 7, 1965. *FRUS 1964–1968, Volume II*.
[292] "Memorandum for the Record: NSC Meeting," February 7, 1965. *FRUS 1964–1968, Volume II*.
[293] Logevall, *Choosing War*, 317.
[294] Bird, *The Color of Truth*, 296–297.

wrote in January 1965 that there was "considerable risk" the objective of bombing North Vietnam would not be achieved.[295] Neither staff member expressed these opinions during meetings with the president.

The logic of fragmented institutions are critical to understanding why senior U.S. bureaucrats did not speak their mind on the eve of one of the most important American military actions during the Cold War. William Bundy explained that Johnson's Tuesday Luncheon was "*so* unstructured, so without any opportunity to know what might be discussed." As a result, it was exceptionally difficult for bureaucrats "to see what [they] were doing, and much harder to take a real bite" of questions such as the effectiveness of bombing or the composite strength of the U.S. position.[296] As a result, the administration's analysis of escalation was not "pulled together" because all the "threads ran only to [Johnson] and not sideways to others, or at least too many of them."[297] Chester Cooper similarly noted that the Tuesday Luncheon undermined the ability of bureaucrats to offer dissenting opinions.[298] John McNaughton reportedly did not raise the "extremely tough questions" he was asking in private because there was "a tremendous nervousness that if you expressed an opinion, it might somehow leak out." As such, "there was not much free communication in the government" on the question of Vietnam, which in turn "inhibited to some extent an exchange of information and prevented the President himself eventually from getting a lot of facts that he should have had."[299] George Ball later explained that he chose not to voice dissent because he believed, incorrectly, that he faced a "unanimous view" against his position that left him with "saw no option but to go along" with what Johnson had decided.[300] Fragmented institutions had done their job: Ball was unaware of how many allies he had.

There is some evidence that fragmented institutions shaped the willingness of advisers within Johnson's inner circle to speak candidly as well. McNamara's position on Vietnam changed dramatically before and after Johnson took office. In October 1963, shortly before Kennedy was assassinated, McNamara advocated force reductions in Vietnam. At the time, McNamara argued that the United States needed "a way to get out of Vietnam and this is a way of doing it." Later, McNamara reflected that he believed that "a phased withdrawal beginning in 1963

---

[295] "Paper Prepared by Chester L. Cooper of the National Security Council Staff," January 6, 1965. *FRUS 1964–1968, Volume II.*
[296] William Bundy OHT, June 2, 1969, LBJL, 12–13. Emphasis in original.
[297] Ibid., 10–11.
[298] Cooper, *The Lost Crusade*, 223.
[299] Michael Forrestal, OHT, 30–31.
[300] George W. Ball, *The Past Has Another Pattern: Memoirs* (New York: W.W. Norton, 1982), 390.

and extending into 1965" would allow the United States to complete its training mission in Vietnam.[301] As Johnson came into office, however, McNamara altered his position from recommending phased withdrawal to pressing the importance of domino theory. As one historian writes, "McNamara's abrupt shift reflected his accommodation" to Johnson's beliefs on Vietnam.[302] Another historian similarly concludes that the Defense Secretary's "famed hawkishness on the war" resulted not from optimism about its prospects or conviction about Vietnam's importance, but rather out of an "almost slavish loyalty" to Johnson.[303] Johnson himself noted that if one asked "the boys in the Cabinet to run through a buzz saw for their President, Bob McNamara would be the first to go through it."[304]

While it is difficult to know McNamara's true beliefs on strategic bombing, it is clear that McNamara was opposed to the ground forces that the strategic bombing program eventually required. In May 1964, McNamara stated that "if any action involved the commitment of troops to combat in South Vietnam, we had better forget it because the American people and the Congress would not support such action under any condition."[305] In August, McNamara was "strongly against" deploying "a limited number of Marines to guard specific installations."[306] Between January and February 1965, McNamara was "very much opposed to larger U.S. forces" and believed that the presence of large American forces in Vietnam would be "unacceptable for a variety of reasons."[307] In fact, McNamara had endorsed the bombing program because he felt it would prevent the need for U.S. troops.[308]

Secretary of State Rusk also reportedly harbored "some reservations" about the bombing strategy, but nevertheless did not oppose it.[309] Rusk later reflected that "we in the State Department never thought we could cut off North Vietnamese infiltration and supplies by bombing [...] Nor did we at State think that our Air Force could bomb North Vietnam [...] into submission."[310] Rusk also privately expressed some interest

[301] VanDeMark, *Road to Disaster*, 183–184.
[302] Ibid., 220.
[303] Logevall, *Choosing War*, 127.
[304] Halberstam, *The Best and the Brightest*, 434.
[305] "Memorandum for the Record: Discussion at Dinner at the White House," May 25, 1964. John McCone Memoranda, Box 1, Folder 5, LBJL.
[306] "Memorandum From the President's Special Assistant for National Security Affairs (Bundy) to the President," August 31, 1964. *FRUS 1964–1968, Volume I*.
[307] "Memorandum from Bundy to Johnson," January 5, 1965; "Meeting at the White House," February 10, 1965. *FRUS 1964–1968, Volume II*.
[308] VanDeMark, *Road to Disaster*, 269.
[309] "Memorandum From the President's Special Assistant for National Security Affairs (Bundy) to President Johnson," January 27, 1965. *FRUS 1964–1968, Volume II*.
[310] Dean Rusk, *As I Saw It* (New York: Penguin, 1991), 447–449.

in moving toward a negotiated settlement.[311] Yet when he was in the room with Johnson, Rusk instead argued that negotiations would "simply register the impossibility of a peaceful settlement" and that air strikes would serve "the political purpose" of signaling that North Vietnamese decision-makers "cannot expect to rely upon a sanctuary in the face of their increased infiltration and operations in South Viet Nam."[312] Based on interviews with Rusk, one historian concludes that Rusk deferred because he wanted "no hint of disagreement within the administration" and because "the very format of the Tuesday Lunch was not one that encouraged intellectual exchange."[313]

What might an integrated decision-making process prior to the U.S. escalation in Vietnam have looked like? A plausible counterfactual is found in an ad hoc working group of lower-level NSC representatives that were temporarily allowed to assiduously assess U.S. strategy in Vietnam in November 1964. A diverse array of voices from across the bureaucracy was included.[314] The group was chaired by William Bundy, who described it as the first "full-scale mobilization" of representatives from the relevant bureaucracies. Unlike previous ad hoc working groups that summer, whose participation had been tightly restricted, the papers of the NSC working group were "available to a fairly wide professional circle" who were afforded the opportunity for "extensive comment."[315]

The working group's records show that even at the time, when given an appropriate level of freedom in discussions, deliberation moved assessments toward more pessimistic conclusions regarding escalation in Vietnam, which provide a glimpse into the more accurate assessments that might have been produced under integrated institutions.

First, the working group remained skeptical that strategic bombing would work. The intelligence panel considered the crux of the Vietnam War to lie in "the effect of US sanctions on the will of DRV leadership to sustain and enlarge" the insurgency in South Vietnam – and only to a "lesser extent" on its ability to degrade DRV capabilities. Even if it degraded DRV capacity or morale, the panel assessed, damage to North Vietnam "would almost certainly not destroy DRV capability to continue supporting the insurrection in the South" if the DRV wished to

---

[311] WBVM, Chapter 18, 37; *PP*, Part IV-C-2c, 41.
[312] "Paper Prepared by Secretary of State Rusk," February 23, 1965. *FRUS 1964–1968, Volume II.*
[313] George C. Herring, *LBJ and Vietnam: A Different Kind of War* (Austin: University of Texas Press, 1994), 9.
[314] These included individuals from the Department of State (Michael Forrestal; Robert Johnson; Allen Whiting; Thomas Hughes); Department of Defense (John McNaughton); Joint Staff (Lloyd Mustin), CIA (Harold Ford), and NSC (Chester Cooper; James Thomson).
[315] WBVM, Chapter 18, 3.

do so. While the North Vietnamese transportation and industrial infrastructure were "vulnerable to attack," the economy was "overwhelmingly agricultural and, to a large extent, decentralized in a myriad of more or less economically self-sufficient villages." While air strikes might degrade DRV military capacity to support the insurgency, the panel did not assess that "such actions would have a crucial effect on the daily lives of the overwhelming majority of the North Vietnamese population" nor would attacks "greatly exacerbate economic difficulties as to create unmanageable control problems." Leaders in Hanoi, the panel concluded, "would probably be willing to suffer some damage to the country in the course of a test of wills with the US over the course of events in South Vietnam."[316]

Second, the working group questioned the costs of negotiation. Its early draft reports argued that domino theory was "over-simplified" and would apply only if China were to enter Southeast Asia "in force" or if the United States were to be "forced out of South Vietnam in circumstances of military defeat." While the group felt that Laos would be "extremely hard to hold" and Cambodia might bend "sharply to the Communist side," the United States "could do more" in both Thailand and Malaysia to address the "initial shock wave" that an American withdrawal might create. The United States could similarly do "a great deal" to reassure other countries in Asia – such as Taiwan, South Korea, Japan, and the Philippines – and manage what the group still felt would be "serious effects" that could "unravel the whole Pacific and South Asian defense structures." The group assessed that there were enough "ifs" in their analysis such that "it cannot be concluded that the loss of South Vietnam would soon have the totally crippling effect in Southeast Asia and Asia generally that the loss of Berlin would have in Europe."[317]

In fact, an important component of the working group's original report was that it recommended that the United States expeditiously begin seeking out opportunities for negotiations with North Vietnam. As the *Pentagon Papers* later noted, the assessment revealed "the intensity with which most members of the working group wanted the United States to couple limited military commitments with a negotiated settlement to relieve [its] position in Vietnam."[318] Bundy later recalled that the option partially drew from George Ball's idea of "pull-out" negotiations. Thus, the group suggested circumscribing any military actions against North Vietnam, going so far as to "drop actions against the North Vietnamese altogether if a negotiating situation came about."[319] As recommended,

---

[316] *PP* (Gravel edition), Vol. III, 652–654.
[317] Ibid., Vol. 3, 658.
[318] *PP*, Part IV-C-2c, 30.
[319] WBVM, Chapter 18, 36–37.

the United States would indicate "from the outset a willingness to negotiate in an affirmative sense, *accepting the possibility that we might not achieve our full objectives.*"[320]

As such, the group identified "fallback objectives" that began to analyze what the United States should attempt to achieve if success in Vietnam were no longer possible. The group emphasized that "there was a chance of failure" and that South Vietnam "could collapse, cease to resist, and in some fashion make peace no matter what the US did."[321] The group's fallback positions included: strengthening American positions in other parts of Asia; taking forceful measures such that U.S. posture against Communist expansion was "as little impaired as possible"; and public messaging emphasizing that "failure in Vietnam, if it comes, was due to special local factors" unique to the colonial heritage, geography and resolve of Saigon.[322]

Finally, the working group identified the high costs associated with escalation. It strongly cautioned against a dramatic escalation of the conflict in the form of major air attacks on key targets in North Vietnam. The chances that North Vietnamese leaders would yield to the United States at early stages were "unlikely" – and the likelihood was "significantly greater" that North Vietnam would retaliate with a ground offensive into South Vietnam. Moreover, the working group felt that North Vietnam was likely to be more resolute after major escalation, thereby forcing the United States to "up the ante militarily." The working group cautioned that the plan could very well backfire and "the volume of international noise [...] could reach the point where, in the interest of our worldwide objectives, we would have to consider accepting a negotiation on terms that would relatively but not necessarily be wholly favorable to the attainment of our full objectives."[323]

The working group's independent conclusions regarding Vietnam, however, were not what reached the president. First, early drafts of the group's assessments suggest that it recommended an even more expeditious move toward negotiations, but this recommendation was stopped by Johnson's inner circle. For example, a draft of the group's report from November 18 suggested that the working group believed that the United States should move "early" toward "a Geneva conference" called by the Soviet Union and supported by the United Kingdom, France, and India. While the United States would push for three "minimum

---

[320] *PP* (Gravel edition), Vol. III, 660. Emphasis added.
[321] WBVM, Chapter 18, 11–12.
[322] "Courses of Action in Southeast Asia," November 18, 1964. National Security Files – Vietnam, Box 54, LBJL.
[323] *PP* (Gravel edition), Vol. 3, 661–663.

fundamentals" – an end to North Vietnamese support for the insurgency, an independent and secure South Vietnam, and "machinery" for international verification – the United States would "fuzz the degree of assurance" it required for each. Moreover, the working group identified areas of "give" in the American negotiating position.[324] Bundy's own memo suggests that he was proposing that after the next major strike against a U.S. installation in Vietnam, such as the Gulf of Tonkin crisis, the United States would respond with force but would actively seek a Geneva-style negotiation for a political settlement.[325]

Second, the evolution of the working group's reports strongly suggests that it was discouraged from more forcefully arguing their case. For example, shortly before the working group's analysis was submitted to the NSC principals, William Bundy quietly drafted a paper to "produce a more specific and convincing discussion" that supported the conclusion that "the rest of Southeast Asia would somehow stand, if the United States carried on strongly, even after a Communist takeover in South Vietnam." Bundy later described it to be "as strong a brief for a mild view" as could have been written by "a mind that truly was not made up." Bundy circulated it only to Rusk and McNamara – a sign of the implicit constraints under which the group must have felt they were under.[326] Bundy recalls how McNamara and Rusk reacted would be "decisive for the advice the President would get." Yet McNamara and Rusk told Bundy that the conclusion "won't wash" and, as such, it was omitted from the version that went to Johnson.[327] Moreover, Bundy was reportedly told to retrieve every copy he had generated, presumably so no one else would see it.[328] As Bundy later reflected, the idea of simply "letting go" was rejected "without extensive argument" by Johnson's senior advisers.[329]

Johnson's inner circle restricted the information that Johnson received from the group. At a meeting with the NSC principals on November 24, the working group's recommendation for early negotiations with North Vietnam was abandoned. Johnson's senior advisers devoted little attention in the meetings to "policy issues related to negotiations." McGeorge Bundy explicitly stated that the United States should only let negotiations

---

[324] "Courses of Action in Southeast Asia," November 18, 1964.
[325] Bird, *The Color of Truth*, 295.
[326] One Defense Department official later recalled that "no one would put such a thing on paper without having given it very heavy thought and without knowing that he was taking a real bureaucratic risk." See Bird, *The Color of Truth*, 295.
[327] WBVM, Chapter 1, 7–8.
[328] Bird, *The Color of Truth*, 294–295.
[329] WBVM, Chapter 18, 27.

come into play slowly.³³⁰ The final version of the working group's report was modified to state that the United States "would resist any formal Geneva conference on Vietnam." Instead of pushing toward a negotiated settlement, the United States would "watch and listen closely for reactions from" Hanoi and Beijing.³³¹ Thus, the recommendation that reached Johnson "represented a substantial deviation from the findings" of the working group because it removed the "initially flexible attitude toward national interest and objectives in Southeast Asia."³³²

There is evidence that details regarding the assessment process were misrepresented to Johnson as well. In November, McGeorge Bundy told Johnson that a "devil's advocate" exercise to build a persuasive case for "negotiation and withdrawal under present conditions" had not advanced, but withheld information regarding the existence of Ball's October 5th memorandum, as well as William Bundy's follow-up the same month.³³³ Equally important was the omission of the CIA's dissenting position in the working group. In particular, the CIA cautioned that even though it agreed that limited strikes might cause the DRV to "slack its support" for the insurgency, the United States "cannot be very sanguine" that this would allow it to "firm up" South Vietnam. Rather, the CIA argued that "a likely outcome" of limited strikes would be that North Vietnam would refuse to yield and that the situation would bog down in an "ambiguous result."³³⁴ The CIA's objections, however, were not included in the final assessment that reached Johnson.³³⁵

In a subsequent meeting on December 1, Johnson again met with the NSC principals. When Johnson asked why the United States should not give up in Vietnam, the group offered no substantive answer and instead returned to discussing strategies to improve stability in Saigon. Indeed, the meeting featured no discussion of what the NSC working group had produced.³³⁶ The available records do not suggest that Johnson's advisers communicated the working group's original interest in early negotiations, nor did they present the CIA's dissent regarding the two main estimates regarding domino theory and the likely effect of bombing on

---

³³⁰ *PP*, Part IV-C-2c, 41.
³³¹ *PP* (Gravel edition), Vol. 3, 660. Modification of the portion of the assessment after the November 24th meeting is discussed in *FRUS 1964–1968, Volume I*, Document 418, notes 6–7.
³³² *PP*, Part IV-C-2c, 51–52.
³³³ Rusk and William Bundy corrected that Ball had made "some progress" but had been "preoccupied with other assignments." See "White House Meeting Record," November 19, 1964. *FRUS 1964–1968, Volume I*.
³³⁴ "Memorandum from Harold Ford to Director," November 21, 1964.
³³⁵ Harold P. Ford, *CIA and the Vietnam Policymakers: Three Episodes 1962–1968* (Washington, DC: Central Intelligence Agency, 1998), 70.
³³⁶ WBVM, Chapter 19, 13.

North Vietnam's willingness to compromise.[337] In sum, Johnson's fragmented institutions imparted a toll on the quality of information available during one of the most consequential moments of the Cold War.

Alternative Explanations. Given the complexity of the U.S. escalation in Vietnam, it is unsurprising that several alternative theoretical perspectives also offer some insight into the case. One prominent explanation emphasizes Johnson's deep-seated beliefs, particularly his faith in domino theory. This perspective is compatible with the theory's contention that leader assessments made under fragmented institutions tend to reflect leader's prior beliefs, as there are systematic restrictions on information search and concerns among bureaucrats that impede their willingness to speak candidly. This point helps to contextualize how Johnson's decision-making was so different from Eisenhower's and Kennedy's, even on the sensitive question of Vietnam. As Fred Logevall argues, Kennedy's "decision-making environment," which was "open" compared to that of Johnson's, "would have made the Johnson team more inclined after November 1964 to ask the really fundamental questions about the war, to listen to the many independent voices predicting giant, perhaps insurmountable, obstacles ahead."[338] In fact, just prior to his death, Kennedy had asked the NSC "to organize an in-depth study of every possible option" the United States had in Vietnam, "including how to get out of there."[339]

While speculative, it is possible that Johnson might have arrived at alternative conclusions had a different set of institutions allowed bureaucratic advisers to more forcefully argue their case. After all, Johnson ran in 1964 as the "peace candidate" and one of his advisers described Vietnam as "a venture which ran counter to [Johnson's] basic instincts."[340] At minimum, it is clear that Johnson was apprehensive about escalation up until at least February 1965. In late May 1964, for instance, Johnson privately asked, "What in the hell is Vietnam worth to me? [...] What is it worth to this country?"[341] On December 1, 1964, Johnson told his advisory team that there would be "no point" in attacking North Vietnam if the South Vietnamese government was not in good shape. He noted that the United States might still say, "This is it!" and argued that he did not wish to send "Johnson City boys out to die" if the South

---

[337] "Meeting Notes," December 1, 1964. John McCone Memoranda, Box 1, Folder 5, LBJL; "White House Meeting Notes," December 1, 1964. *FRUS 1964–1968, Volume I*.
[338] Logevall, *Choosing War*, 399.
[339] Reeves, *President Kennedy*, 660.
[340] Berman, *Planning a Tragedy*, 169, note 1.
[341] Beschloss, *The Johnson White House Tapes, 1963–1964*, 370.

Vietnamese government continued "acting as they are."[342] In a memorandum to McNamara on January 7, Johnson stated that opponents of larger American deployments were "right."[343] In short, while he seems to have ultimately concluded that military action would improve his position, there is at least some reason to believe that Johnson's choice was not predetermined by his views on domino theory.

The evidence in support of accountability theory is mixed in this case. There is little doubt that Johnson concluded that the domestic political costs of withdrawal would be high if South Vietnam fell to Communist rule on his watch. The American people did not want to run from Vietnam, Johnson commented, "If I lose it, I think that they'll say *I've lost*."[344] Yet the decision to escalate ultimately undermined Johnson's ability to run for reelection in 1968. To the extent that Johnson's perceptions regarding domestic costs were accurate, the question became whether the domestic political costs would have been lower if Johnson had conceded defeat without escalating in 1965.

Some at the time believed they would have been. "It is always hard to cut losses," Vice President Humphrey noted after Johnson's landslide victory in November 1964, but 1965 might well have represented "the year of minimum political risk" for Johnson.[345] Indeed, between November 1964 and January 1965, there was no broad consensus that the United States should escalate. One Council on Foreign Relations poll in December 1964 found that 25 percent of respondents were unaware of fighting in Vietnam. Of informed respondents, nearly half favored withdrawal and only 24 percent were definitely in favor of using ground forces. Another Harris poll found that only 18 percent favored bombing and 20 percent backed a negotiated withdrawal. A Gallup poll from January 1965 found that 81 percent of Americans supported an international conference to "see if a peace arrangement can be worked out."[346] Private conversations from 1964 suggest that Johnson was aware of this lack of public consensus, noting that "I don't think the people of the country know much about Vietnam and I think they care a hell of a lot less."[347]

For Johnson, the critical calculation was to ensure that he could win the public debate long enough to push his domestic agenda through Congress. "If I don't go in now *and they show later that I should have*," Johnson reflected, "then they'll be all over me in Congress. They won't

---

[342] "Notes on a Meeting, White House," December 1, 1964. *FRUS 1964–1968, Volume I*.
[343] "Memorandum From Johnson to Secretary of Defense McNamara," January 7, 1965.
[344] Beschloss, *The Johnson White House Tapes, 1963–1964*, 401. Emphasis in original.
[345] "Memorandum from Vice President Humphrey to President Johnson," February 17, 1965. *FRUS 1964–1968, Volume II*.
[346] Logevall, *Choosing War*, 282.
[347] Beschloss, *The Johnson White House Tapes, 1963–1964*, 365.

be talking about my civil rights bill, or education or beautification."[348] While fragmented institutions ensured that Johnson could win the debate long enough to pass his domestic agenda, they also meant that he escalated without full information about costs, both strategic and political, that he would pay before he left the White House. As Brian VanDeMark summarizes, this "extraordinary feat of political legerdemain," in the end proved to be a "tragically self-defeating error."[349]

Finally, evidence in support of the interest group model of bureaucratic politics is mixed. On the one hand, Johnson's defense advisers, particularly the Joint Chiefs of Staff, supported escalation in Vietnam. As such, one possible interpretation might suggest that Johnson's choice for escalation was a bargaining concession to avoid public censure by the military for choosing peace.[350] On the other hand, the case clearly shows that Johnson's military advisers were among those whose participation in policy deliberations was curtailed. U.S. military leaders lacked access to and guidance from the White House, which impeded their ability to identify which kinds of information Johnson needed and to plan for the types of campaigns that would accord with Johnson's intent.[351] Thus, even if Johnson's choice for escalation was partly a bargaining concession to the military, this alone would not explain why he received incomplete and vague information regarding the costs of escalation. From this perspective, the price that Johnson paid for protecting himself from bureaucratic criticism was not necessarily the war itself but rather the low quality of information upon which the choice for war was made.

Conclusion

This chapter showed how a political trade-off drove consequential institutional changes in the United States during the early Cold War. Given the comparatively well-institutionalized nature of American democracy, one might expect a strictly integrated institutional design. Yet the chapter shows that institutional changes were substantial enough to shift the United States across institutional types multiple times within less than two decades. While past research suggests that such changes were primarily a reflection of leader personality, the evidence introduced in this chapter illustrates the central importance of cold political calculations.

---

[348] Halberstam, *The Best and the Brightest*, 530. Emphasis added. See also VanDeMark, *Road to Disaster*, 291.
[349] VanDeMark, *Road to Disaster*, 292.
[350] Saunders, "War and the Inner Circle."
[351] For a detailed account, see McMaster, *Dereliction of Duty*.

For Lyndon Johnson, the choice was clear: inclusive decision-making bodies like Eisenhower or Kennedy's NSC were like "sieves." The institutional remedy was equally obvious: insular decision-making processes, like the Tuesday Luncheon, "never leaked a single note."[352]

The effects of these institutional changes were evident both in the medium-n analysis of U.S. crisis performance across this period, as well as the case studies of the Second Taiwan Strait Crisis and the escalation in Vietnam. The competitive dialogue between different bureaucracies with different perspectives proved critical to Eisenhower's judgments. In contrast, fragmented institutions were an important, though underappreciated, factor that degraded the information that Johnson received prior to his most consequential foreign policy decision. In short, fragmented institutions help explain why, as McGeorge Bundy later noted, the analysis Johnson received was so surprisingly thin.[353]

One might rightly wonder what U.S. national security institutions looked like after the Johnson administration. While the scope of this question falls outside what can be considered in detail in this chapter, two points are worth emphasizing. First, the data set analyzed in Chapter 3 suggests that U.S. institutions stabilized after the Vietnam War. While presidential directives setting rules for the NSC modified some structural design features, formal changes were comparatively minor compared to those observed during the Kennedy and Johnson administrations. Second, most of the changes that did occur pertained to the NSC's coordination capacity, such as the composition of coordination bodies or the NSA's authority in these bodies. Such changes tended to occur under less experienced presidents: Jimmy Carter, Ronald Reagan, and George W. Bush. While the magnitude of these changes was not large enough to create a siloed institution according to the cross-national measurement strategy, the marginal changes remain consistent with this book's theoretical intuition that institutional siloing is more attractive to less powerful and less experienced leaders.

Two factors help to explain stability in the U.S. institutional design after the Vietnam War. It may be that bureaucratic threats are usually low in well-institutionalized democracies like the United States, perhaps because of high levels of professionalism and norms against bureaucratic involvement in politics. This would suggest that the uncharacteristically high levels of threat that Johnson faced may have stemmed from the unusual political circumstances under which he took office. Alternatively,

---

[352] Goodwin, *Lyndon Johnson and the American Dream*, 319–320.
[353] Goldstein, *Lessons in Disaster*, 178.

it may be that U.S. national security institutions were more malleable during the early Cold War because the NSC had been established only in 1947. Thus, institutionalization may make these systems more stable over time, such that a president's power to reshape institutions to their liking gradually declines. As discussed in Chapter 9, this process of institutionalization represents an important area for future research.

9 Conclusion

A famous Chinese novella by the twentieth-century author Lu Xun tells the story of a self-deceiving antihero named Ah Q, who would pick fights with his neighbors only to be struck down by those he attacked. Time and again, Ah Q would issue demands to locals and, when they did not comply, start physical altercations that would leave him bested. The tragedy of Ah Q, of course, was that the violence inflicted upon him could have been avoided had he understood the limits of his power.

States behave like Ah Q more often than we might hope. They wittingly charge into international conflicts at the end of which they are no better off – and often much worse off – than when they started. This book has argued that such failed strategies are often the result of miscalculations arising from the design of institutions that connect political leaders to their national security bureaucracies. Leaders generally prefer to avoid conflicts that fail to advance their goals. In an ideal world, leaders adopt integrated institutions that provide them with accurate projections of how confrontations are likely to turn out before they begin. These institutions motivate bureaucrats to search widely for different types of information, help them determine when their information is valuable, and assist leaders in monitoring when bureaucrats are providing low-quality information. Given the informational constraints of the international system, leaders make choices with the most complete and most accurate information possible.

Yet integrated institutions come at a cost. Competent and informed bureaucrats provide better advice, but bureaucrats can also leverage their access to information and expertise to impose political costs on the leader. Leaders resolve this trade-off between good advice and political vulnerability based upon the key characteristics of their political environment. When leaders perceive minimal levels of political threat from the bureaucracy, they are free to reap the benefits of integrated institutions. When bureaucrats possess the capability and intent to politically censure the leader, however, leaders tend to opt for nonintegrated alternatives.

How exactly leaders choose to deviate from an integrated system hinges, in large part, on the issues leaders think will keep them in office. On the one hand, leaders can choose fragmented institutions that reduce information search capacity. Leaders can redesign decision-making bodies to curtail bureaucratic participation, refuse to fill senior bureaucratic positions, and cut staffs that support their decision-making process. By restricting the flow of information between the leader and the bureaucracy, fragmented institutions provide leaders with maximal protection from bureaucratic censure. Leaders tend to need this level of protection when their survival depends on domestic issues, particularly when their agenda includes ambitious policies for transforming their state and society.

On the other hand, leaders can choose siloed institutions, in which they maintain high information search capacity but restrict the ability of bureaucrats to share information with one another. Leaders shut down institutional devices for inter-bureaucratic information sharing (e.g., coordination committees and staffs) and establish rules prohibiting the circulation of information. Such designs are useful to leaders whose survival depends on successfully addressing international security demands. Siloed institutions allow such leaders to strike a balance a demand for the advice the bureaucracy can provide and the political threat that the bureaucracy poses. High information flow between each bureaucracy and the leader helps address the first demand, while ensuring that no one bureaucrat knows too much helps to address the second demand.

These institutional choices shape the quality of judgment that leaders exhibit on the road to war. The patterns of information flow in fragmented and siloed institutions, while sometimes helpful politically, nevertheless undermine the leader's ability to discriminate between those strategies likely to succeed and those likely to fail. Incomplete or low-quality information leads to miscalculation whereby leaders initiate confrontations that seem promising – when in fact the complete array of information the state possesses at the time suggests otherwise. While all international politics is clouded by uncertainty, fragmented and siloed institutions introduce informational deficits of the state's own making. The relationship between political leaders and the bureaucracy is thus central to understanding why states sometimes miscalculate by initiating international conflicts that fail to deliver the benefits that leaders anticipated before the confrontation began.

Summary of Findings

Chapter 3 probed the theory through a cross-national analysis. It developed a strategy to systematically measure differences between national security institutions across time and space. Based on that strategy, it then introduced original data highlighting the fact that states design their national security institutions in fundamentally different ways – and that neither regime type nor leader characteristics predetermine those differences. Exploring these data through statistical analysis showed that states with integrated institutions tend to be less likely to initiate international crises that end without achieving their objectives. This finding suggests that the information that integrated institutions supply leaders allow them to better discern which crises are likely to succeed before the confrontation begins. Further analysis showed that adoption of integrated institutions is associated with political environments in which the bureaucracy is less threatening to leaders.

The subsequent chapters used four case countries – China, India, Pakistan, and the United States – to illustrate the theory's proposed mechanisms in detail. Chapter 4 examined national security institutions in China under Mao Zedong. China's decision-making during the 1962 Taiwan Strait Crisis showed how, even in a dictatorship, integrated institutions can help leaders to arrive at more accurate projections. In contrast, China's decision-making during the Cultural Revolution highlighted how fragmented institutions amplified the decision-making pathologies of strongman rule. Fragmented institutions helped Mao achieve his domestic political agenda: Mao ruled until his death in 1976, chose a successor he preferred, and kept revolutionary ideals embedded into the party's values. Fragmented institutions, however, impaired China's strategic judgment. During the 1969 Sino-Soviet border conflict, information available at the time might have led to much different conclusions about the threat of Soviet invasion and the efficacy of striking preemptively, but Mao's advisers lacked access and standing necessary for providing the information he required.

Chapter 5 turned to cases of miscalculation in China under non-personalist rule. In the years immediately following Mao's death, fragmented institutions arose from perceived bureaucratic threats to Deng Xiaoping's transformative economic reforms. As these economic reforms solidified and Chinese leaders began to perceive greater international challenges, China's institutions shifted toward a siloed design. The chapter then explored two different crises showing how fragmented and siloed institutions engender substantially different paths to miscalculation. The 1979 Sino-Vietnamese War showed how fragmented institutions truncated information search and encouraged Chinese bureaucrats to self-censor in their reporting. These institutional pathologies help to explain why leaders in Beijing mistakenly believed that war with North Vietnam in 1979 would demonstrate China's strength and compel concessions.

328　Conclusion

The 2001 EP-3 reconnaissance aircraft incident instead showed how restrictions on inter-bureaucratic information sharing allowed the military to provide low-quality information shortly after the collision, which led Jiang Zemin to mistakenly believe he could extract concessions from the United States by detaining the U.S. crew.

In Chapter 6, India's defeat during its 1962 war with China demonstrated how fragmented institutions can lead to miscalculation even under democratic rule. Fragmented institutions provided the low-quality information upon which Nehru based his choice to pursue the Forward Policy. Organizational deficiencies were not an oversight. They were a political strategy. The choice for fragmented institutions reflected the perception that India's defense and intelligence bureaucracies posed a threat to the newly established country, as well as Nehru's emphasis on domestic social welfare programs. Moreover, while India's defeat in the 1962 Sino-Indian War motivated a shift away from fragmentation, persisting concerns about the threat posed by the bureaucracy kept India's institutions siloed for several decades after Nehru's death. Indeed, it was only after these fears had subsided that India shifted toward a more integrated model by introducing the National Security Council system.

The discussion of Pakistan in Chapter 7 provided a foil to the Indian case. Both India and Pakistan inherited similar national security institutions from the United Kingdom – and both set them aside in their own ways. Yet India's leaders eventually shifted toward a more integrated system. Pakistan's leaders, preoccupied with the threat of coup for decades after partition, did not. This helps explain why, as late as the 1980s, Pakistan exhibited institutional pathologies characteristic of the Indian system as it was over three decades prior. Even after international threats began to dominate, with the threat of nuclear crisis and transnational terrorism becoming especially prominent, Pakistan's leaders settled for siloed institutions. These institutional choices had tragic consequences during the 1999 Kargil War, which derailed prospects for more peaceful relations with India.

Chapter 8 applied the theory's logic to an institutionalized democracy: the United States. It explored institutional evolution across three American presidencies – those of Dwight D. Eisenhower, John F. Kennedy, and Lyndon Johnson. Despite the fact that all three presidents entered office after the establishment of the NSC system, different political imperatives pushed institutional choices in remarkably different directions. Whereas Eisenhower doubled down on the integrated design he inherited, both Kennedy and Johnson nudged U.S. national security institutions away from an integrated model. For Kennedy, the shift to siloed institutions was short-lived. For Johnson, however, the changes lasted most of his

Summary of Findings

time in office. The evidence presented suggests that the reason these two institutional designs were different had less to do with personality differences between Eisenhower and Johnson, as is commonly assumed. Rather, the motivation was political. Perceiving salient threats to his domestic agenda posed by the national security bureaucracy, Johnson established an insular decision-making body, the Tuesday Luncheon, which effectively replaced the NSC. Cases on the 1958 Taiwan Strait Crisis and the U.S. decision to escalate the Vietnam War illustrated the disastrous consequences of Johnson's institutional choices for American foreign policy.

Table 9.1 compares the performance of the book's political theory of institutional design to alternative explanations considered in the cases. The political theory of institutional design is scored as a success if the observed institutional change matched the predictions in Chapter 2. Leadership style is scored as a success if the institutional change occurred as a new leader entered office and that leader kept the same institutional design across their time in office. Path dependence is scored as a success if the institution persisted across more than one leader. Finally, international diffusion is scored as a success if the evidence presented suggested that the institutional change emulated the institutional design of another country.

The political theory of institutional design successfully predicted the observed design in at least thirteen of the seventeen cases. Kennedy's initial institutional design was a borderline successful prediction, as discussed in Chapter 8. The theory was, however, not able to successfully predict institutional design in China during the mid-1980s (the "lieutenant" period). It was also unable to successfully predict India's and Pakistan's initial institutional design. By comparison, the alternative explanations did not perform as well. Leadership style and path dependence, the two conventional explanations of decision-making process, struggled to explain half the cases considered in the analysis. Several leaders changed their institutional design mid-stream, including Mao Zedong, Deng Xiaoping, and John F. Kennedy. For others, including Jiang Zemin, Hu Jintao, and Rajiv Gandhi, leadership style did not prompt substantial modifications to the institutions they inherited. At best, international diffusion offered some insight into five of these cases. Yet the ways in which both India and Pakistan abandoned the institutions they inherited illustrated the limits of that theory in the context of national security institutions. In short, the analysis suggests that the political environment plays a greater role in the relationships between leaders and their bureaucracies than existing scholarship has suggested.

Table 9.2 provides a similar overview for the analysis of decision-making. The book's institutional theory is scored as a success if (1)

Table 9.1 Summary of case analysis: Institutional design

Country	Period	Institutions	Political design	Leadership style	Path dependence	International diffusion
China	1949–1962	Integrated	Yes	No	No	Partial
China	1963–1981	Fragmented	Yes	No	Yes	No
China	1982–1988	Siloed	No	No	No	No
China	1989–2012	Siloed	Yes	Yes	Yes	Partial
India	1947–1950	Siloed	No	No	No	Yes
India	1951–1962	Fragmented	Yes	No	Yes	No
India	1963–1998	Siloed	Yes	No	Yes	No
India	1999–2015	Integrated	Yes	Yes	Yes	Yes
Pakistan	1947–1948	Siloed	No	Yes	No	Yes
Pakistan	1949–1986	Fragmented	Yes	No	Yes	No
Pakistan	1987–1999	Siloed	Yes	Yes	Yes	No
Pakistan	2000–2008	Fragmented	Yes	Yes	No	No
Pakistan	2009–2015	Siloed	Yes	Yes	Yes	No
United States	1953–1960	Integrated	Yes	No	No	No
United States	1961	Siloed	Partial	No	No	No
United States	1962–1963	Integrated	Yes	No	No	No
United States	1964–1968	Fragmented	Yes	Yes	No	No
Total			**13–14**	**7**	**7**	**3–5**

Table 9.2 *Summary of case analysis: Decision-making*

Period (institutional design)	Case	Institutional theory	Accountability	Leader beliefs	Bureaucratic interests
China (integrated)	Nationalist invasion scare	Yes	No	No	No
China (fragmented)	Sino-Soviet border conflict	Yes	Yes	Yes	No
	Sino-Vietnamese War	Yes	No	Yes	No
China (siloed)	EP-3 reconnaissance aircraft incident	Yes	No	No	No
India (fragmented)	Sino-Indian War	Yes	No	No	No
India (integrated)	Twin Peaks Crisis	Yes	Partial	No	No
Pakistan (siloed)	Kargil War	Yes	No	No	Yes
The United States (integrated)	Second Taiwan Strait Crisis	Yes	Partial	No	No
The United States (fragmented)	Vietnam War	Yes	Partial	Yes	Partial
Total		9	1–4	3	1–2

the leader based their choices on inaccurate projections and (2) the case found that institutional obstructions to information flow shaped those projections. Political accountability is scored as a success if democracy or non-personalist dictatorship is associated with accurate leader projections and high-quality information provision, of if personalist dictatorship is associated with inaccurate leader projections and low-quality information provision. Leader beliefs are scored as a success if the analysis found that the leader possessed strong prior beliefs on the policy and did not change their beliefs during the decision-making process. The bureaucratic interest group model is scored as a success if bureaucratic officials autonomously initiated the crisis or if the leader suggested they had no alternative but to accept the bureaucracy's recommendations.

All cases of institutional siloing and fragmentation – the 1969 Sino-Soviet border conflict, the Sino-Vietnamese War, the EP-3 reconnaissance aircraft incident, the Sino-Indian War, the Kargil War, and the U.S. escalation in Vietnam – showed that leaders chose strategies that incorrectly projected success. In contrast, political accountability theory failed to predict the bulk of the miscalculations considered. Accountability successfully predicted Mao's miscalculations during the Sino-Soviet border conflict, as well as Eisenhower's accurate beliefs during the 1958 Taiwan Strait Crisis. Yet in six other cases, accountability could not explain why the leaders of these regimes miscalculated. As the theory would suggest, leader beliefs proved most pivotal in fragmented settings. Leaders did not update prior beliefs in three of the four crises in which the state possessed fragmented institutions. Yet leaders exhibited flexibility in their beliefs in the remaining five cases considered. Finally, the traditional interest group model of bureaucratic politics fails to predict all but one of the cases considered.

Medium-n analyses of crisis performance across time in each case country lent support to the conclusion that these cases reflect a broader pattern. Consistent with the theory's predictions, the empirical chapters showed that the rate of failure in crisis was systematically lower during periods when leaders sat atop integrated as opposed to fragmented or siloed institutions. Despite the small sample size, the findings were generally consistent with the cross-national statistical analysis suggesting that integrated institutions tend to outperform the alternatives. In sum, the analysis shows that existing accounts offer an incomplete explanation of why states miscalculate and demonstrates that bureaucracy exerts more systematic and less deleterious effects on international politics than the conventional wisdom would suggest.

Implications for International Relations Theory

This book's primary contribution to international relations theory is to advance the argument that bureaucratic participation in foreign policy decision-making may not exert as deleterious an effect on judgment as some suggest it might. On the contrary, the intuition behind integrated institutions is that bureaucracy can be an asset for leaders. What makes integrated institutions helpful to for leaders is not simply that they add more voices to the process. Rather, integrated institutions put specific bureaucracies with different expertise and perspectives into competitive dialogue with one another. The findings show that leaders tend to derive a more accurate picture of the situation they face when such a dialogue pushes bureaucratic advisers to critically examine each other's arguments. Institutions do not determine the quality of judgment, but integrated institutions offer leaders a better chance of avoiding miscalculation. In short, putting bureaucracies at war at home can help prevent leaders from miscalculating on the road to wars abroad.

While the findings help us to move past the important opening salvo that Graham Allison's *Essence of Decision* presented to scholars and policymakers, one core point inherent in that canonical work holds up remarkably well: bureaucracy matters in ways that early critics of the bureaucratic politics model did not appreciate.[1] Just because leaders hold the final say in foreign policy decision-making does not mean that bureaucracies are unimportant. Rather, it is because leaders need help deciding what choices to make that bureaucracies can shape the trajectory of foreign policy.

In addition, the book's theory and findings offer a number of additional insights to the field. First, the findings have implications for theories of the democratic peace, providing a theoretical counterpoint to traditional explanations of how institutions curtail foreign policy risks through political accountability.[2] The logic of accountability theory suggests that democracies and autocracies think more carefully about initiating international confrontations when threats to remove leaders from office are credible. Indeed, the cross-national analysis finds that integrated institutions are associated with democratic regimes. Yet distinguishing between foreign policies likely to succeed is not always readily apparent until it is already too late. The cases of post-Mao China, India, and the United States demonstrate that political accountability does not guarantee good information provision. National security institutions draw attention to the informational dynamics that precede the decision whether to launch

---

[1] For example, see Krasner, "Are Bureaucracies Important?"
[2] Russett and Oneal, *Triangulating Peace: Democracy, Interdependence, and International Organizations*; Reiter and Stam, *Democracies at War*; Weeks, *Dictators at War and Peace*.

foreign policy gambits. Absent effective institutions, even political accountability cannot save states from miscalculation, as leaders choose alluring policies that seem primed to secure their survival in office but end up contributing to their political demise.

This has important implications for how we understand the ways that authoritarian and democratic institutions affect sound strategic judgment. Institutions that help political leaders understand the world are different from those that impose costs for misunderstanding it. As a result, political accountability often proves insufficient for avoiding miscalculation. The book's logic and findings thus point to a less-explored aspect of the so-called democratic peace: the protected position of bureaucratic advisers to convey accurate and well-scrutinized counsel to their political leaders.[3]

Second, the book contributes to an ongoing debate on the relationship between individuals and groups.[4] Scholars and policymakers alike commonly note that human decision-makers are susceptible to bias and misperception. While a seemingly straightforward idea, it is not necessarily obvious how such misperceptions aggregate in group settings. In existing scholarship, one school of thought argues that group decision-making tends to amplify individual-level misperceptions,[5] while others argue that it tends to attenuate them.[6] The theory and findings presented here suggests an answer conditional on the design of institutions. Whether shifting from individual to group decision-making improves or degrades judgment depends on the formal and informal rules shaping the interactions between the group's members.

Third, by looking to institutions that connect leaders and bureaucracies, the book points to one way in which the existing literature focusing on decision-making process might be more fully integrated with the study of international relations.[7] The book finds that leader decision-making is neither assigned at random nor simply an extension of personality.

---

[3] For a similar argument emphasizing the role of societal debate and deliberation in democracy more broadly, see LeVeck and Narang, "The Democratic Peace and the Wisdom of Crowds."

[4] Hafner-Burton et al., "The Behavioral Revolution and International Relations," 2.

[5] Janis, *Victims of Groupthink*; Joshua D. Kertzer et al., "Hawkish Biases and Group Decision Making," *International Organization* 76, no. 3 (2022): 513–548.

[6] Barbara Mellers et al., "Identifying and Cultivating Superforecasters as a Method of Improving Probabilistic Predictions," *Perspectives on Psychological Science* 10, no. 3 (2015): 267–281; Horowitz et al., "What Makes Foreign Policy Teams Tick." For early intuitions on how bureaucracy might improve the efficiency of group decision-making, see Bendor and Hammond, "Rethinking Allison's Models," 311–313, Hafner-Burton et al., "The Behavioral Revolution and International Relations," 20.

[7] For a discussion of the gap between these two literatures, see Kaarbo, "A Foreign Policy Analysis Perspective on the Domestic Politics Turn in IR Theory."

Decision-making processes are regulated by institutions, and the design of those institutions is highly political. This book suggests the importance of looking further back in the causal chain and specifies the political environments that do and do not foster the more effective decision-making processes that existing accounts describe.

Finally, the theory of national security institutions contributes to the literature on civil-military relations, particularly how political leaders establish effective "control" over the military's provision of information and advice. Peter Feaver, for example, argues that effective control comes from greater civilian intervention into military affairs, creating rules and norms that monitor the military's performance.[8] The existing literature on civil-military relations tends to see these monitoring mechanisms as either stemming from generic civilian oversight (e.g., appointing a civilian defense minister) or from competition between military actors. Yet these approaches have their limits. A civilian defense minister, for example, presents a new problem of control for political leaders. In addition, competition between different military actors, such as the pitting of different service chiefs against one another, may not lead to better monitoring if the preferences of these generals and admirals align within one another.

The framework of national security institutions contributes to these rich debates about civilian and military actors. For one, it helps to disaggregate the "civil" in civil-military relations by bringing into focus the relationship between political leaders and a broad range of civilian bureaucrats, including those in defense, diplomatic, and intelligence organizations. This analytical move is important because military organizations are only one of many national security bureaucracies integral to decision-making on the road to war. The political information that diplomats and intelligence officers can bring to deliberations about war and peace is as important as the counsel that the military brass can contribute. Moreover, as the cases showed, siloed and fragmented institutions impeded provision of quality information from a range of civilian advisers and bureaucracies, ranging from Chinese Foreign Minister Chen Yi to Undersecretary of State George Ball, and from Pakistan's Inter-Services Intelligence agency to India's Joint Intelligence Committee. This framework is also important because the differences in perspectives between diplomatic and defense ministries, for example, may be much larger than those between the military services. If more effective information provision stems in part from asking actors with

---

[8] Feaver, *Armed Servants*. See also Huntington, *The Soldier and the State*; Deborah Avant, *Political Institutions and Military Change* (Ithaca: Cornell University Press, 1994); Cohen, *Supreme Command: Soldiers, Statesmen and Leadership in Wartime*.

different perspectives to deliberate, then expanding the range of bureaucratic actors debating before the leader to include diplomatic and intelligence officials offers straightforward benefits.[9] In short, the theory and findings illustrate that subordination of the military is a necessary but insufficient condition for advisory procedures to effectively support a leader's national security decision-making.

Remaining Questions and Future Research

While the scope of this book is broad, it intentionally sets aside numerous questions that may yield interesting topics for future research. One line of inquiry relates directly to the concept of national security institutions themselves. The typology presented in this book need not be the only way of thinking about design differences between institutions. There may be hybrid systems that exist between the ideal types discussed in this book. Future work might also explore other aspects of institutional design, such as the size of the staffs appended to decision-making and coordination bodies.[10] In short, just as there are alternative definitions and measurements of democracy, there is considerable room to widen the analytical aperture for conceptualizing institutions for national security decision-making.

While this book has focused on miscalculation on the road to war, it is plausible that national security institutions might also affect strategic judgment on other issues, ranging from war termination to grand strategy. The theory's intuitions also suggest applications to other policy domains, such as international trade and economic policy. National security institutions in some states have indeed expanded their mandate to include international economic policy. For example, while not discussed in the analysis, the U.S. National Security Council was modified to incorporate the treasury secretary at the end of the Cold War.[11]

More research is also needed on the numerous ways in which political and bureaucratic institutions interact. There are intriguing theoretical avenues to consider. For one, how might higher costs of bureaucratic

---

[9] This adds specificity to Risa Brooks' intuition that strong political leaders can facilitate better information provision through monitoring, but adds an important caveat that not all strong political leaders adopt institutions leading to such outcomes. See Brooks, *Shaping Strategy*, 48–49.

[10] In the United States, for example, the NSC staff size was less than 20 under the Kennedy administration but more than 100 under the Clinton administration. See Karl Inderfurth and Loch K. Johnson, *Fateful Decisions: Inside the National Security Council* (New York: Oxford University Press, 2004), 132.

[11] "Presidential Decision Directive/NSC-2: Organization of the National Security Council," The White House, January 20, 1993.

dissent under authoritarian rule shape foreign policy decision-making? Future research might attempt to develop cross-national measures for institutional protections for bureaucrats – or evaluate what happens to bureaucrats after they leave office.

Another important area for future research pertains to the process of institutionalization. The analysis of the United States in Chapter 8 showed that institutions can change at rapid pace. According to the measures utilized in the cross-national data set, however, U.S. national security institutions have remained integrated in subsequent decades, despite a shifting political climate. Certainly, the data show some institutional perturbations at the margins, but none were large enough to change the coding to a non-integrated type. One possibility is a process of institutionalization that makes it increasingly costly for leaders to move away from integrated designs once they are established.

This pattern suggests that future research might consider how a leader's power to deviate from integrated institutions might be curtailed. If it is true that integrated designs tend to perform better than other alternatives, societies might rightly wonder how to ensure that leaders pay costs for abandoning integrated institutions. The theory's logic implies a set of guardrails that domestic audiences (i.e., voters, legislatures, other elites) might adopt. First, domestic audiences might impose ex ante constraints on the leader's decision-making process, establishing policies that expect leader consultation with the bureaucracy prior to policy decisions. Second, domestic audiences might instead monitor the leader's decision-making process and punish when the leader makes decisions without consulting bureaucratic advisers. Third, states might develop norms of apolitical professionalism within their national security bureaucracy. This does not necessarily mean that bureaucrats cannot hold policy preferences – only that there are clear punishments for bureaucrats who use their position in ways that undermine the leader's political survival. Future research should explore these strategies in more detail.

Finally, while the analysis takes seriously the idea that individual-level attitudes and dispositions within elite decision-making groups are often different, future work can more directly test these intuitions. Past research has attempted to infer beliefs and preferences from elite adviser recommendations. Yet the findings of this book suggest the field needs to interpret such recommendations with caution, accounting for the institutional environment in which such advice is supplied. Future research may attempt to survey elite preferences directly, with a particular emphasis on how attitudes and dispositions are distributed within national security bureaucracies.

Conclusion

This book has drawn attention to the ways in which institutions connecting leaders to their national security bureaucracies affect decision-making. The framework and analysis help scholars and policymakers account for variation in the institutions that we observe across the modern world. It provides theoretical intuitions and empirical support for how these design features affect the way in which states behave. The theory and findings help us think more systematically about how well-designed institutions curb the risk of miscalculation, as well as the political calculations that tragically lead states down the road to pointless bloodshed.

Appendix A National Security Institutions Data Set

Definitions

National security institutions are the formal and informal rules and procedures that define the roles, constraints, and expectations of bureaucracies charged with informing and advising leaders on national security policy. They assist leaders (presidents, prime ministers, and dictators) in deciding and executing national security strategies. Such strategies include but are not limited to: uses of military force, military mobilizations and demonstrations; diplomatic negotiations and communications; and intelligence operations. The data set distinguishes between institutions and organizations/bodies. Institutions refer to the rules governing how specific organizations or bodies are designed. For each country-year, the data set codes the rules and procedures of two types of bodies:

1. *National Security Decision-Making Body*: A body in which the leader may solicit advice, deliberate the advantages and disadvantages of possible national security actions, and/or announce decisions. While decision-making bodies must support the leader's decision-making process, authority need not be shared among body representatives. For example, the US National Security Council is coded as a decision-making body because it advises the president's decision-making, even though body members cannot vote. As such, legislation often refers to decision-making bodies as serving an "advisory" or "deliberative" role. In order to be included in the sample, a decision-making body must meet two criteria: (1) the leader is a member of the organization and (2) the function of the body is to make decisions on national security affairs.
2. *National Security Coordination Body*: A body in which the leader (or designated agent) coordinates national security actions through information exchange with and between defense, diplomatic, and intelligence officials. Coordination bodies are typically subordinate to decision-making bodies in the organizational hierarchy – and may be a subcommittee of the decision-making body.

Basic Information

1. *Name of the Decision-Making Body*: Full name of the body responsible for making decisions on national security.[1]
2. *Name of the Coordination Body*: Full name of the body responsible for coordinating national security.

Institutional Characteristics

1. Composition of the Decision-Making/Coordination Body[2]
    (a) *Total Seats*: Total number of representatives on the body.
    (b) *Defense Ministry Representation*: Is a representative from the ministry of defense a member or adviser on the body?
    (c) *Diplomatic Ministry Representation*: Is a representative from the diplomatic ministry a member or adviser on the body?
    (d) *Intelligence Representation*: Is a representative from the foreign intelligence organization a member or adviser on the body?
    (e) *Senior Military Adviser Representation*: Is at least one of the following a member or adviser on the body: joint staff chairman, chief of staff of the army, air force, or navy? [Note: If the head of state is the senior military adviser, coded as "2." If the senior military adviser is the minister of defense, coded as "0."]
    (f) *Military Representation*: Number of representatives on the body that are active-duty military officers: (0) no military representation; (1) exactly one military representative; (2) more than one military representative but less than all; or (3) all military representatives.
2. Characteristics of the Decision-Making/Coordination Body
    (a) *Staff*: Does the body have a dedicated staff? [Note: If staff support is provided by another organization, such as the foreign ministry or the defense ministry, coded as "0." Also coded as "0" for cabinets, councils of ministers, politburos, and juntas unless there was a dedicated national security staff.]
    (b) *Utilization*: Was the body: (0) aspirational (i.e., existed on paper only); (1) utilized only in crisis; or (2) utilized?

---

[1] If there were multiple, the body with the senior-most membership was coded. All codings are as of July 1. Formally appointed advisers mandated to attend all body meetings were coded as representatives even if they are not an official body member. Other formal advisers who may be invited to select meetings at the discretion of the leader were coded separately as invitees. "Alternates," "observers," and "candidate members," were coded as invitees. In instances in which the formal legislation was available, invitation status is based on whether the legislation specifies certain adviser types. Variables were coded as missing in instances in which relevant documentation is not available.

[2] Decision-making bodies and coordination bodies were coded separately.

(c) *Chairmanship* (Coordination Body only): Is the national security coordination body chaired by: (0) no chairman designated; (1) the leader; (2) the national security advisor; (3) a representative from the defense ministry; (4) a representative from the foreign ministry; (5) a representative from the foreign intelligence organization; or (6) a representative from the leader's executive office (e.g., cabinet secretary)?

Appendix B Archival and Interview Data Collection

Sources

The case studies draw on three types of primary sources: archival documents; interviews; and supplemental sources.

Archives and Document Collections

The first set of primary sources consulted were government documents collected from archives and libraries in China, India, Pakistan, the United States, the United Kingdom, and Taiwan. The analysis also leveraged additional archival records that have been published in compendiums. For cases involving the People's Republic of China, these included chronicles (大事记, 实录, 年谱), as well as speeches and manuscripts (文集, 文选, 文稿) published by the Chinese Communist Party Archives Historical Research Office. For cases involving India and Pakistan, these included the *Selected Works of Jawaharlal Nehru (Second Series)*, *India-China Relations, 1947–2000: A Documentary Study*; and *India-Pakistan Relations, 1947–2007: A Documentary Study*. For cases involving the United States, these included the *Foreign Relations of the United States* series, as well as Public Papers of the Presidents.

China
Ministry of Foreign Affairs Archives
National Library of China
Peking University Library

India
National Archives of India
   Prime Minister's Office
   Cabinet Secretariat

Nehru Memorial Museum & Library
   J. Nehru Post-1947 Papers
   K.S. Thimayya Papers
   S. Dutt Papers
   L.B. Shastri Papers
   Y.D. Gundevia Papers
   P.N. Haksar Papers
   T.T. Krishnamachari Papers
   T.N. Kaul Papers
Institute for Defence Studies and Analyses Library

United Kingdom
The National Archives
The Mountbatten Papers, University of Southampton
Templar Study Center, National Army Museum
   Roy Bucher Papers
   Rob Lockhart Papers

Pakistan
National Library of Pakistan
Institute of Strategic Studies Library

United States
Harry S. Truman Presidential Library
Dwight D. Eisenhower Presidential Library
John F. Kennedy Presidential Library
Lyndon B. Johnson Presidential Library
Richard Nixon Presidential Library
Jimmy Carter Presidential Library
George W. Bush Presidential Library
Fung Library, Harvard University
Rare Book & Manuscript Library, Columbia University

Taiwan
Academia Historica
National Archives Administration

Interviews

Seventy-two semi-structured interviews were conducted in China, India, and Pakistan between 2016 and 2017. Interviewees ranged from academics and mid-level bureaucrats to cabinet-level ministers and senior military officers. The substance of the interview was tailored to fit the individual's position. Interviews with mid-level officials were used to draw inferences about routine procedures in diplomatic, military, and intelligence organizations. Interviews with ministry-level officials were used to draw inferences about the sequence and substance of crisis decision-making. Data biases introduced from strategic nonresponse in politically nonpermissive environments, particularly China, pose two primary challenges for inference: accuracy of information and sample representativeness.[1] To address these concerns, interview responses were cross-referenced with other interviews, as well as with other documentary records. Individuals contacted for interviews did not exhibit systematic patterns in nonresponse based on rank or institutional affiliation.

Finally, the analysis leveraged past interviews with decision-makers. The case on India relied on a set of oral histories maintained by the Nehru Memorial Museum & Library. The case on the United States relied on oral histories available at U.S. presidential libraries, the University of Virginia Miller Center Presidential Oral Histories project, and the Brookings Institution National Security Council project. A list of sources containing records of past elite interviews is provided in Bibliography.

Supplemental Sources

Archival and interview evidence was supplemented with memoirs, official histories, and government reports. In the China case, this includes memoirs written both by senior officials (e.g., Wu Faxian, Liu Huaqing, Tang Jiaxuan) and by junior bureaucrats (e.g., Du Yi, Xiong Xianghui, Zhang Tingdong) who had special access to the decision-making process. Accounts written by Chinese historians with special access (e.g., Xu Yan, Gao Wenqian) were also consulted. In the India and Pakistan cases, the memoirs consulted were primarily written by senior officials (e.g., B. N. Mullik, K. M. Arif, Jaswant Singh, and Sartaj Aziz). Two governmental reports – *History of the Conflict with China, 1962* and *Operations Review of the Sino-Indian War of 1962* – provided details on elite decision-making prior to the Sino-Indian War. In the U.S. case, in addition to published memoirs, a draft of McGeorge Bundy's memoirs is available at the John F. Kennedy Presidential Library. Records of Lyndon Johnson's phone calls are published in *Taking Charge* and *Reaching for Glory*.

---

[1] Erik Bleich and Robert Pekkanen, "How to Report Interview Data," in *Interview Research in Political Science*, ed. Layna Mosley (Ithaca: Cornell University Press, 2013), 84–108; Brian C. Rathbun, "Interviewing and Qualitative Field Methods: Pragmatism and Practicalities," in *The Oxford Handbook of Political Methodology*, ed. Janet M. Box-Steffensmeier, Henry E. Brady, and David Collier (New York: Oxford University Press, 2008).

Micro-Level Institutional Data

Finally, the analysis consulted source materials from crisis adversaries in order to evaluate the accuracy of leader beliefs and bureaucratic information. To code the accuracy of Deng Xiaoping's beliefs during the Sino-Vietnamese War, for instance, the analysis relied on materials from Vietnam. For the 1962 Taiwan Strait Crisis, this included archival material from the Academia Historica in Taipei. For the 1969 Sino-Soviet Border Conflict, this included translated materials available from the Wilson Center Digital Archive, Leonid Brezhnev's diary, and other Russian materials. For the Sino-Vietnamese War and Vietnam War, this included official Vietnamese histories (e.g., *Victory in Vietnam: The Official History of the People's Army of Vietnam, 1954–1975*), chronicles (e.g., *Lich Su Bien Nien Xu Uy Nam Bo va Trung Uong Cuc Mien Nam]*), and memoirs from senior Vietnamese officials (e.g., Huynh Anh Dung, Le Duc Anh). All Vietnamese materials were collected and translated by Merle Pribbenow. For the EP-3 reconnaissance aircraft incident, this included materials collected from the George W. Bush Presidential Library, documents released under Freedom of Information Act requests from the U.S. Department of State and Central Intelligence Agency, as well as memoirs of cabinet officials. For other cases – such as the Second Taiwan Strait Crisis, Sino-Indian War, Kargil War, and the Twin Peaks Crisis – this included source materials referenced earlier in this section.

Micro-Level Institutional Data

As discussed in Chapter 3, three of case studies – China, India, and the United States – examine quantitative patterns in decision-making. There are three sets of archival materials that facilitated the analysis of these "micro-institutional" data.

China

Chapters 4 and 5 analyze a data set on elite meetings compiled from daily activity records (年谱) of twenty senior party officials.[2] Meetings of these bodies offer one important indicator of bureaucratic opportunities to relay information and contribute to policy deliberations.[3] These materials record meetings of formal bodies – such as the Politburo, Secretariat, Foreign Affairs Leading Small Group, and Central Military

---

[2] These included Mao Zedong, Zhou Enlai, Liu Shaoqi, Zhu De, Peng Dehuai, Lin Biao, Luo Ruiqing, Yang Chengwu, Wang Jiaxiang, Ye Jianying, Xu Xiangqian, Nie Rongzhen, Deng Xiaoping, Li Xiannian, Hu Yaobang, Zhao Ziyang, Chen Yun, Liu Huaqing, and Jiang Zeming. For additional details on the data set, see Jost, "Institutional Origins of Miscalculation in China's International Crises."

[3] For a similar approach, see Kenneth Lieberthal, *A Research Guide to Central Party and Government Meetings in China, 1949–1975* (Armonk, NY: M.E. Sharpe, 1978).

Commission – as well as informal meetings between the leader and senior advisers.[4] For each meeting the following were recorded: date of the meeting, the name of the body, the type of meeting (regular, expanded, or standing committee), agenda, the bureaucratic representation at the meeting (Ministry of Foreign Affairs, International Liaison Department, and People's Liberation Army), and whether advisers provided information or reports during the meeting.

India

Chapter 6 analyzes a data set measuring the frequency of correspondence (cables, reports, directives, notes) to and from Jawaharlal Nehru between 1958 and 1962 available in the *Selected Works of Jawaharlal Nehru* (Vol. 44–80). The sample only includes correspondence pertaining to foreign or defense affairs. For each observation, the following were recorded: date, sender name, receiver name, position/affiliation of the sender/receiver, (prime minister, Ministry of External Affairs, Cabinet, Defence Ministry, Home Ministry, Intelligence Bureau, military), and subject (foreign affairs, defense affairs, both).

United States

Chapter 8 analyzes a data set of meetings between the president and national security advisers held between 1953 and 1968. The data set is based on entries in the *Presidential Appointment Books* and *Presidential Daily Diaries* available at the Eisenhower, Kennedy, and Johnson Presidential Libraries. Each record details not only with whom the president met but also the duration of each meeting. Across the sixteen years of records in the sample, there are only seven missing entries.[5] The sample excludes ceremonies, diplomatic visits or preparatory meetings immediately before diplomatic visits, meetings held in transit, meetings with members of Congress or other state politicians (e.g., mayors), and Cabinet or Legislative Leader's Meetings. For each observation, the following were recorded: date, State Department participation (assistant secretary or higher), Defense Department participation (assistant secretary or

---

[4] Meetings of the Central Committee, Party/People's Congresses, work conferences, symposia, diplomatic exchanges and other ceremonial activities were excluded from the sample. All extra-institutional meetings of the supreme leader with central government officials, as well as for all extra-institutional meetings between senior military, diplomatic, and party liaison officials are coded as informal.

[5] The dates of these meetings are February 2, 1964, October 26, 1964, November 10, 1967, November 11, 1967, May 5, 1968, June 12, 1968, and June 23, 1968.

higher),[6] Joint Chiefs of Staff participation,[7] Central Intelligence Agency participation, national security advisor participation,[8] time meeting began; time meeting ended; duration of meeting (in minutes), and meeting type (National Security Council, National Security Council – Informal, National Security Council – Congressional, Tuesday Luncheon, informal).[9]

---

[6] This included the service secretaries (army, navy, and air force).
[7] This included the Supreme Allied Commander Europe (SACEUR) and the Military Representative to the President.
[8] The NSA's meetings with the president are only coded if: (1) another recorded member of the Department of Defense, Department of State, Joint Chiefs of Staff, or Central Intelligence Agency was present; or (2) NSA met alone with the president.
[9] Informal NSC meetings are those in which all statutory NSC members and advisers were present. NSC Congressional meetings are those in which the NSC briefed members of Congress. The LBJ Daily Dairy typically identifies the Tuesday Luncheons explicitly, even when they were rescheduled for other days the week. The coding also includes luncheons not identified as such by the LBJ Daily Diary, but for which there was not a Tuesday meeting that week and which included the typical participants (secretary of defense, secretary of state, and national security advisor).

Bibliography

Published Primary Sources

Beschloss, Michael R., ed. *Reaching for Glory: Lyndon Johnson's Secret White House Tapes, 1964–1965*. New York: Simon & Schuster, 2001.
    ed. *Taking Charge: The Johnson White House Tapes, 1963–1964*. New York: Simon & Schuster, 1997.
Bhasin, Avtar Singh, ed. *India-China Relations, 1947–2000: A Documentary Study*. New Delhi: Ministry of External Affairs, 2018.
    ed. *India-Pakistan Relations, 1947–2007: A Documentary Study*. New Delhi: Ministry of External Affairs, 2012.
Deng Xiaoping. *Deng Xiaoping junshi wenji* [Selected Military Works of Deng Xiaoping]. Beijing: Junshi kexue chubanshe, 2004.
    Deng Xiaoping wenxuan, 1975–1982 [Selected Works of Deng Xiaoping, 1975–1982]. Beijing: Renmin chubanshe, 1983.
Gopal, Sarvepalli, Ravinder Kumar, H. Y. Sharada Prasad, A. K. Damodaran, and Mushirul Hasan, eds. *Selected Works of Jawaharlal Nehru (Second Series)*. New Delhi: Jawaharlal Nehru Memorial Fund, 1984.
Government of Pakistan. *Report of the Hamoodur Rehman Commission of Inquiry into the 1971 War*. Lahore: Vanguard, 2000.
Henderson Brooks, T. B., and Premindra Singh Bhagat. *Operations Review of the Sino-Indian War of 1962*. New Delhi: Ministry of Defence.
Jian, Chen, and David L. Wilson. "All Under the Heaven Is Great Chaos: Beijing, The Sino-Soviet Border Clashes, and the Turn Toward Sino- American Rapprochement, 1968–69." *Cold War International History Project Bulletin*, no. 11 (1998): 155–175.
Jiang, Weimin, ed. *Liu Huaqing nianpu, 1916–2011* [Chronicle of Liu Huaqing, 1916–2011]. Beijing: Jiefangjun chubanshe, 2016.
Jiang Zemin. *Jiang Zemin wenxuan* [Selected Works of Jiang Zemin]. Beijing: Renmin chubanshe, 2006.
Leng Rong, ed. *Deng Xiaoping nianpu, 1975–1997* [Chronicle of Deng Xiaoping, 1975–1997]. Beijing: Zhongyang wenxian chubanshe, 2004.
Li Jie et al., ed. *Jianguo yilai Mao Zedong junshi wengao* [Military Manuscripts of Mao Zedong since the Founding of the State]. Beijing: Zhongyang wenxian chubanshe, 2010.
Li Ping and Ma Zhisun, ed. *Zhou Enlai nianpu, 1949–1976* [Chronicle of Zhou Enlai, 1949–1976]. Beijing: Zhongyang wenxian chubanshe, 1997.

Li Xiannian. *Jianguo yilai Li Xiannian wengao* [Manuscripts of Li Xiannian since the Founding of the State]. Beijing: Zhongyang wenxian chubanshe, 2011.
Liu Jixian, ed. *Ye Jianying nianpu, 1897–1986* [Chronicle of Ye Jianying, 1897–1986]. Beijing: Zhongyang wenxian chubanshe, 2007.
Liu Wusheng, ed. *Zhou Enlai junshi wenxuan* [Selected Military Works of Zhou Enlai]. Beijing: Renmin chubanshe, 1997.
Mao Zedong. *Jianguo yilai Mao Zedong wengao* [The Manuscripts of Mao Zedong since the Founding of the State]. Beijing: Zhongyang wenxian chubanshe, 1987.
Pang Xianzhi and Feng Hui, eds. *Mao Zedong nianpu, 1949–1976* [Chronicle of Mao Zedong, 1949–1976]. Beijing: Zhongyang wenxian chubanshe, 2013.
The Pentagon Papers: The Defense Department History of Decisionmaking on Vietnam. The Senator Gravel edition. 5 vols. Boston: Beacon, 1971–1972.
Vu Huu Ngoan, ed. *Van Kien Dang* [Collected Party Documents]. Translated by Merle Pribbenow. Hanoi: Nha Xuat Ban Chinh Tri Quoc Gia, 2003.
Wang Weicheng, ed. *Li Xiannian nianpu* [Chronicle of Li Xiannian]. Beijing: Zhongyang wenxian chubanshe, 2011.
Westad, Odd Arne, Jian Chen, Stein Tønnesson, Vu Tung Nguyen, and James G. Herschberg. *77 Conversations between Chinese and Foreign Leaders on the Wars in Indochina, 1964–1977.* Washington, DC: Wilson Center, 1998.
White Paper No. VI: Notes, Memoranda and Letters Exchanged and Agreements Signed between the Governments of India and China, November 1961–July 1962. New Delhi: Ministry of External Affairs, 1962.
Xu Zehao, ed. *Wang Jiaxiang nianpu, 1906–1974* [Chronicle of Wang Jiaxiang, 1906–1974]. Beijing: Zhongyang wenxian chubanshe, 2001.
Yan Yongchun, ed. *Xu Xiangqian nianpu* [Chronicle of Xu Xiangqian]. Beijing: Jiefangjun chubanshe, 2016.
Yang Shengqun and Yan Jianqi, ed. *Deng Xiaoping nianpu, 1904–1974* [Chronicle of Deng Xiaoping, 1904–1974]. Beijing: Zhongyang wenxian chubanshe, 2009.
Zeng Dadu, ed. *Zhongguo gongchandang Zhongguo renmin jiefangjun zuzhishi ziliao* [Materials on CCP Chinese People's Liberation Army Organizational History]. Beijing: Changzheng chubanshe, 1996.
Zhang Zishen, ed. *Yang Chengwu nianpu, 1914–2004* [Chronicle of Yang Chengwu, 1914–2004]. Beijing: Jiefangjun chubanshe, 2014.
Zhonggong zhongyang zuzhibu, *Zhongguo gongchandang zuzhi shi ziliao* [Materials on the Organizational History of the Chinese Communist Party]. Beijing: Zhonggong dangshi chubanshe, 2000.
Zhou Junlun, ed. *Nie Rongzhen nianpu* [Chronicle of Nie Rongzhen]. Beijing: Renmin chubanshe, 1999.
Zhu Jiamu, ed. *Chen Yun nianpu, 1905–1995* [Chronicle of Chen Yun, 1905–1995]. Revised Edition. Beijing: Zhongyang wenxian chubanshe, 2015.
Zou Ximing. *Zhonggong zhongyang jigou yange shilu* [Record of CCP Organizational Evolution: 1921.7–1997.9]. Beijing: Zhongguo dang'an chubanshe, 1998.

Diaries and Memoirs

Ahmad, Shamshad. *Dreams Unfulfilled*. Lahore: Jahangir Book Depot, 2009.
Akhund, Iqbal. *Memoirs of a Bystander*. Karachi: Oxford University Press, 1997.
Alexander, P. C. *My Years with Indira Gandhi*. New Delhi: Vision Books, 1991.
Arif, K. M. *Working with Zia: Pakistan's Power Politics, 1977–1988*. Karachi: Oxford University Press, 1995.
  Khaki Shadows: Pakistan 1947–1997. New York: Oxford University Press, 2001.
Aziz, Sartaj. *Between Dreams and Realities: Some Milestones in Pakistan's History*. 2nd ed. Karachi: Oxford University Press, 2020.
Aziz, Shahid. *Yeh Khamoshi Kahan Tak?* [How Long Will This Silence Remain?] Islamabad: Seven Springs, 2015.
Ball, George W. *The Past Has Another Pattern: Memoirs*. New York: W. W. Norton, 1982.
Bhutto, Benazir. *Daughter of the East: An Autobiography*. New York: Simon & Schuster, 2007.
Bo Yibo. *Ruogan zhongda juece yu shijian de huigu* [Reflections on Certain Major Decisions and Events]. Revised Edition. Beijing: Renmin chubanshe, 1997.
Brezhnev, Leonid. *Rabochie i dnevnikovye zapisi* [Work and Diary]. Moscow: IstLit, 2016.
Bundy, McGeorge. *Vietnam Manuscript*. Boston, MA: John F. Kennedy Presidential Library.
Bundy, William. *Vietnam Manuscript*. Austin, TX: LBJ Presidential Library.
Carter, Jimmy. *Keeping Faith: Memoirs of a President*. Fayetteville: University of Arkansas Press, 1995.
Chai Chengwen. "Zhou Enlai lingdao women jinxing ZhongSu bianjie tanpan [Zhou Enlai Led Our Sino-Soviet Border Negotiations]." In *Zhonggong dangshi zhongda shijian shushi* [An Account of Major Events in CCP History], Expanded Edition, edited by Yang Shengqun and Chen Jin. Beijing: Renmin chubanshe, 2008.
Cheng Zhensheng. "Li Xiannian yu gaige kaifang chuqi de duiwai gongzuo [Li Xiannian and Foreign Affairs Work during the Early Reform Era]." *Zhonggong dangshi yanjiu* [CCP Historical Research], no. 6 (2009).
Cooper, Chester L. *The Lost Crusade: America in Vietnam*. New York: Dodd, Meade & Company, 1970.
Cutler, Robert. *No Time for Rest*. Boston: Little, Brown & Company, 1966.
Deng Liqun. *Deng Liqun guoshi jiangtanlu* [Record of Deng Liqun's Lectures on National History]. 2000.
Dixit, J. N. *My South Block Years: Memoirs of a Foreign Secretary*. New Delhi: UBS, 1996.
Du Yi, ed. *Wenge zhong de Chen Yi* [Chen Yi during the Cultural Revolution]. Shijie zhishi chubanshe, Beijing, 1997.
Dulat, A. S. *Kashmir: The Vajpayee Years*. Noida: HarperCollins, 2015.
Eisenhower, Dwight David. *The White House Years: Mandate for Change, 1953–1956*. New York: Doubleday, 1963.
  The White House Years: Waging Peace, 1956–1961. New York: Doubleday, 1965.
Ferrell, Robert H., ed. *The Eisenhower Diaries*. New York: W. W. Norton, 1981.

Fu Xuezheng. "Zai zhongyang junwei bangongting gongzuo de rizi [Days Working in the Central Military Commission Office]." *Dangshi tiandi* [Party History World], no. 1 (2006): 8–16.
Gundevia, Y. D. *Outside the Archives*. New Delhi: Sangam Books, 1984.
Haig, Alexander M. *Inner Circles: How America Changed the World*. New York: Warner Books, 1992.
Huang Hua. *Huang Hua Memoirs*. Beijing: Foreign Languages Press, 2008.
Huynh Anh Dung. *Ghi chep ve Campuchia (1975–1991)* [Notes on Cambodia (1975–1991)]. Translated by Merle Pribbenow. 1995.
Ji Chaozhu. *The Man on Mao's Right: From Harvard Yard to Tiananmen Square, My Life Inside China's Foreign Ministry*. New York: Random House, 2008.
Kasuri, Khurshid Mahmud. *Neither a Hawk Nor a Dove: An Insider's Account of Pakistan's Foreign Policy*. London: Penguin, 2015.
Kaul, B. M. *The Untold Story*. New York: Allied Publishers, 1967.
Khan, Gohar Ayub. *Testing Times as Foreign Minister*. Islamabad: Dost Publications, 2009.
Khan, Gul Hassan. *Memoirs of Lt. Gen. Gul Hassan Khan*. Karachi: Oxford University Press, 1993.
Khan, Mohammad Ayub. *Diaries of Field Marshal Mohammad Ayub Khan, 1966–1972*. New York: Oxford University Press, 2007.
Khrushchev, Nikita Sergeyevich. *Memoirs of Nikita Khrushchev*, edited by Sergei Khrushchev. University Park: Penn State University Press, 2004.
Le Duc Anh. *Cuoc doi va su nghiep cach mang: Hoi ky* [My Life and My Revolutionary Cause: A Memoir]. Translated by Merle Pribbenow. Hanoi: Nha Xuat Ban Chinh Tri Quoc Gia, 2015.
Li Fenglin. "Mosike ershi nian [Twenty Years in Moscow]." In *Dangdai Zhongguo shijie waijiao shengya* [The Diplomatic Careers of Contemporary Chinese Envoys]. Beijing: Shijie zhishi chubanshe, 1996.
Li Peng. *Heping fazhan hezuo: Li Peng waishi riji* [Peace, Development and Cooperation: Li Peng's Diary on Foreign Affairs]. Beijing: Xinhua chubanshe, 2008.
Li Zuopeng. *Li Zuopeng huiyilu* [Memoirs of Li Zuopeng]. Hong Kong: Beixing chubanshe, 2011.
Liu Huaqing. *Liu Huaqing huiyilu* [Memoirs of Liu Huaqing]. Beijing: Jiefangjun chubanshe, 2007.
Lu Fangshang, ed. *Jiang Zhongzheng xiansheng nianpu changbian* [Chronicle of Chiang Kai-shek]. Taipei: Guoshiguan, 2014.
Luo Yisu. "Zai Bolan de suiyue [Years in Poland]." In *Dangdai Zhongguo shijie waijiao shengya* [The Diplomatic Careers of Contemporary Chinese Envoys]. Beijing: Shijie zhishi chubanshe, 1996.
Malik, V. P. *India's Military Conflicts and Diplomacy: An Inside View of Decision Making*. Noida: HarperCollins, 2013.
McNamara, Robert. *In Retrospect: The Tragedy and Lessons of Vietnam*. New York: Vintage, 1996.
Mullik, B. N. *My Years with Nehru: 1948–1964*. New Delhi: Allied Publishers, 1972.
My Years with Nehru: The Chinese Betrayal. New Delhi: Allied Publishers, 1971.
Musa, Mohammed. *My Version: India-Pakistan War, 1965*. Lahore: Wajidalis, 1983.

Musharraf, Pervez. *In the Line of Fire: A Memoir*. London: Simon & Schuster, 2006.
Nie Rongzhen. *Nie Rongzhen huiyilu* [Memoirs of Nie Rongzhen]. Beijing: Jiefangjun chubanshe, 2007.
Nixon, Richard. *RN: The Memoirs of Richard Nixon*. New York: Grosset & Dunlap, 1978.
Palit, D. K. *War in the High Himalaya: The Indian Army in Crisis, 1962*. New York: St. Martin's Press, 1991.
Pradhan, R. D. *1965 War The Inside Story: Defence Minister Y. B. Chavan's Diary of the India-Pakistan War*. New Delhi: Atlantic, 2007.
Raman, B. *The Kaoboys of R&AW: Down Memory Lane*. New Delhi: Lancer, 2007.
Rostow, Walt Whitman. *The Diffusion of Power: An Essay in Recent History*. New York: Macmillan, 1972.
Rumsfeld, Donald. *Known and Unknown: A Memoir*. New York: Sentinel, 2011.
Rusk, Dean. *As I Saw It*. New York: Penguin, 1991.
Singh, Jaswant. *Defending India*. New York: St. Martin's Press, 1999.
——— *In Service of Emergent India: A Call to Honor*. Bloomington: Indiana University Press, 2007.
Sun Hongxian. *Zai Xu Shiyou shenbian de rizi* [Days Beside Xu Shiyou]. Guangzhou: Guangdong renmin chubanshe, 2011.
Tan Jingqiao. "Wuliushi niandai de zongcan zuozhanbu [The General Staff Operations Department in the 1950s and 1960s]." In *Zongcanmoubu: huiyi shiliao, 1927–1987* [General Staff Department: Recollections and Historical Materials, 1927–1987]. Beijing: Jiefangjun chubanshe, 1995.
Tang Jiaxuan. *Jinyu xufeng* [Heavy Storm and Gentle Breeze]. Beijing: Shijie zhishi chubanshe, 2009.
Tang Shubei. "Huiyi Wu Xueqian fu zongli zai Duitai gongzuo shang de zhongyao gongxian [Recollections of Vice Premier Wu Xueqian's Important Contributions on Taiwan]." In *Wu Xueqian jinian wenji* [Selected Works Commemorating Wu Xueqian], edited by Shi Yin. Beijing: Shijie zhishi chubanshe, 2009.
Tran Quang Co. *Hoi Ky Tran Quang Co* [Tran Quang Co: A Memoir]. Translated by Merle Pribbenow. 2003.
U.S. Department of Defense, *The Pentagon Papers: United States-Vietnam Relations, 1945–1967* The Senator Gravel edition. 5 vols. Boston: Beacon, 1971–1972. 12 vols. Washington, DC, GPO, 1971.
Wang Bingnan. *ZhongMei huitan jiunian huigu* [Nine Years of Sino-American Talks in Retrospect]. Beijing: Shijie zhishi chubanshe, 1985.
Wang Guoquan. "Wo de dashi shengya [My Ambassadorial Career]." In *Dangdai Zhongguo shijie waijiao shengya* [The Diplomatic Careers of Contemporary Chinese Envoys]. Beijing: Shijie zhishi chubanshe, 1995.
Wilson, James. "Pakistan Defence: The Early Days." *Army & Defence Quarterly Journal* 121, no. 3 (1991): 303–305.
Wu Faxian. *Wu Faxian huiyilu* [Memoirs of Wu Faxian]. Hong Kong: Beixing chubanshe, 2006.
Wu Xiuquan. *Eight Years in the Ministry of Foreign Affairs: Memoirs of a Diplomat*. Beijing: International Book Trading Corporation, 1985.

Xiong Xianghui. "Dakai ZhongMei guanxi de qianzhou [Prelude to the Opening of Sino-American Relations]." *Zhonggong dangshi ziliao* [Materials on Party History], no. 42 (1992): 56–96.
Yang Dezhi. "Xin shiqi zongcanmoubu de junshi gongzuo [Military Work of the General Staff Department in a New Era]." In *Zongcanmoubu: huiyi shiliao, 1927–1987* [General Staff Department: Recollections and Historical Materials, 1927–1987]. Beijing: Jiefangjun chubanshe, 1995.
Yang Gongsu. *Cangsang jiushi nian: yi ge waijiao teshi de huiyi* [The Vicissitudes of Ninety Years: Recollections of a Diplomatic Envoy]. Haikou: Hainan chubanshe, 1999.
Yang Shangkun. *Yang Shangkun riji* [Diary of Yang Shangkun]. Beijing: Zhongyang wenxian chubanshe, 2001.
Ye Fei. *Ye Fei huiyilu* [Memoirs of Ye Fei]. Beijing: Jiefangjun chubanshe, 2007.
Yew, Lee Kuan. *From Third World to First: The Singapore Story, 1965–2000*. New York: HarperCollins, 2000.
Zhang Hanzhi. *Wo yu Qiao Guanhua* [Qiao Guanhua and I]. Beijing: Zhongguo qingnian chubanshe, 1994.
Zhang Sheng. *Cong zhanzheng zhong zoulai: Liangdai junren de duihua* [Emerging from War: A Conversation between Soldiers of Two Generations]. Beijing: Shenghuo, dushu, xinzhi sanlian shudian chubanshe, 2013.
Zhang Tingdong. *Wo pei Ye shuai zou wan zuihou shiqi nian: yi wei shenbian mishu de huiyi* [Accompanying Marshal Ye for the Last Seventeen Years: A Memoir of a Secretary by his Side]. Beijing: Zhonggong dangshi chubanshe, 1999.
Zhang Zhen. *Zhang Zhen huiyilu* [Memoirs of Zhang Zhen]. Beijing: Jiefangjun chubanshe, 2003.
Zhou Deli. *Yige gaoji canmouzhang de zishu* [Memoirs of a High-Ranking Staff Officer]. Nanjing: Nanjing chubanshe, 1992.
Zhou Wenzhong. *Dou Er Bupo: Zhongmei boyi yu shijie zai pingheng* [Fighting Without Breaking: The US-China Contest and the Rebalancing of the World]. Beijing: Zhongxin chubanshe, 2017.

Oral History Transcripts and Published Interviews

Ball, George. July 8, 1971. LBJ Library.
Brecher, Michael. *India and World Politics: Krishna Menon's View of the World*. London: Oxford University Press, 1968.
Bundy, McGeorge. November 30, 1970. John F. Kennedy Library.
Bundy, William. June 2, 1969. LBJ Library.
Forrestal, Michael V. April 8, 1964. John F. Kennedy Library.
Forrestal, Michael V. July 29, 1969. LBJ Library.
Kaul, B. M. Nehru Memorial Museum and Library.
Komer, Robert. October 31, 1964. John F. Kennedy Library.
Rostow, Walt W. April 11, 1964. John F. Kennedy Library.
Rusk, David Dean. April 27, 1970. John F. Kennedy Library.
Smith, Bromley. July 29, 1969. LBJ Library.
Smith, Bromley. July 23, 1970. John F. Kennedy Library.
Warriach, Suhail. *The Traitor Within: The Nawaz Sharif Story in His Own Words*. Lahore: Sagar Publishers, 2008.

Secondary Sources

Bajpai, Kanti. *Brasstacks and Beyond: Perception and Management of Crisis in South Asia*. New Delhi: Manohar, 1995.

Bajpai, Kanti. "To War or Not To War: The India-Pakistan Crisis of 2001–2." In *Nuclear Proliferation in South Asia*, edited by Sumit Ganguly and S. Paul Kapur. New York: Routledge, 2009.

Bandyopadhyaya, Jayantanuja. *The Making of India's Foreign Policy: Determinants, Institutions, Processes and Personalities*. New Delhi: Allied Publishers, 2003.

Bator, Francis M. "No Good Choices: LBJ and the Vietnam/Great Society Connection." *Diplomatic History* 32, no. 3 (2008): 309–340.

Benner, Jeffrey. *Structure of Decision: The Indian Foreign Policy Bureaucracy*. New Delhi: South Asian Publishers, 1984.

Berman, Larry. *Planning a Tragedy: The Americanization of the War in Vietnam*. New York: W. W. Norton & Company, 1982.

Bian Yanjun, Zhang Wenhe and Yu Lijuan, eds., *Li Xiannian zhuan, 1949–1992* [Biography of Li Xiannian, 1949–1992]. Beijing: Zhongyang wenxian chubanshe, 2009.

Bird, Kai. *The Color of Truth: McGeorge Bundy and William Bundy, Brothers in Arms*. New York: Simon & Schuster, 1998.

Chandra, Satish. "National Security System and Reform." In *India's National Security Annual Review*. New Delhi: Knowledge World, 2005.

Chandra, Satish, and Rahul Bhonsle. "National Security: Concept, Measurement and Management." *Strategic Analysis* 39, no. 4 (2015): 337–359.

Chari, P. R., Pervaiz Iqbal Cheema, and Stephen P. Cohen. *Four Crises and a Peace Process: American Engagement in South Asia*. Washington, DC: Brookings Institution Press, 2009.

Chen Jian. *Mao's China and the Cold War*. Chapel Hill: University of North Carolina Press, 2001.

Chen Xiaolu. "Dangdai jiechu de waijiaojia Chen Yi [The Illustrious Diplomat of Our Era]." In *Huanqiu tongci liangre: Yi dai lingxiumen de guoji zhanlüe sixiang* [It is the Same Temperature Around the Globe: International Strategic Thinking of First-Generation Leaders]. Beijing: Zhongyang wenxian chubanshe, 1993.

Chen Yali. *The PLA in China's Foreign and Security Policy-Making: Drivers, Mechanisms, and Interactions*. PhD dissertation, Johns Hopkins University, 2015.

Chen, King C. *China's War with Vietnam, 1979: Issues, Decisions, and Implications*. Stanford: Hoover Institution Press, 1987.

Christensen, Thomas. *Useful Adversaries: Grand Strategy, Domestic Mobilization, and Sino-American Conflict, 1947–1958*. Princeton: Princeton University Press, 1996.

"Windows and War: Trend Analysis and Beijing's Use of Force." In *New Directions in the Study of China's Foreign Policy*, edited by Alastair Iain Johnston and Robert S. Ross. Stanford: Stanford University Press, 2006.

Worse Than a Monolith: Alliance Politics and Problems of Coercive Diplomacy in Asia. Princeton: Princeton University Press, 2011.

Clark, Christopher. *The Sleepwalkers: How Europe Went to War in 1914*. New York: Penguin, 2012.

Fair, C. Christine. *Fighting to the End: The Pakistan Army's Way of War.* New York: Oxford University Press, 2014.
Fewsmith, Joseph. *China since Tiananmen: The Politics of Transition.* New York: Cambridge University Press, 2001.
Fravel, M. Taylor. *Active Defense: China's Military Strategy since 1949.* Princeton: Princeton University Press, 2019.
———. *Strong Borders, Secure Nation: Cooperation and Conflict in China's Territorial Disputes.* Princeton: Princeton University Press, 2008.
Ganguly, Sumit, and Michael R. Kraig. "The 2001–2002 Indo-Pakistani Crisis: Exposing the Limits of Coercive Diplomacy." *Security Studies* 14, no. 2 (2005): 290–324.
Gans, John. *White House Warriors: How the National Security Council Transformed the American Way of War.* New York: W. W. Norton & Company, 2019.
Gao Wenqian. *Wannian Zhou Enlai* [Zhou Enlai's Later Years]. Hong Kong: Mingjing chubanshe, 2003.
Gauhar, Altaf. *Ayub Khan: Pakistan's First Military Ruler.* Lahore: Sang-e-Meel, 1993.
Gelb, Leslie H., and Richard K. Betts. *The Irony of Vietnam: The System Worked.* Washington, DC: Brookings Institution Press, 1979.
Goldstein, Gordon M. *Lessons in Disaster: McGeorge Bundy and the Path to War in Vietnam.* New York: Holt, 2008.
Gong Li. "Chinese Decision Making and the Thawing of U.S.-China Relations." In *Re-examining the Cold War: US-China Diplomacy, 1954–1973.* Cambridge: Harvard University Asia Center, 2001.
Gong Li, Men Honghua, and Sun Dongfang. "Zhongguo waijiao juece jizhi bianqian yanjiu [Changes and Evolution in China's Foreign Policy Decision-Making Mechanisms, 1949–2009]." *Shijie jingji yu zhengzhi* [World Economics and Politics], no. 11 (2009): 44–54.
Goodwin, Doris Kearns. *Lyndon Johnson and the American Dream.* New York, 1976.
Gopal, Sarvepalli. *Jawaharlal Nehru: A Biography.* New Delhi: Oxford University Press, 1979.
Guo Xiangjie. *Zhang Wannian zhuan* [Biography of Zhang Wannian]. Beijing: Jiefangjun chubanshe, 2011.
Gupta, Arvind. *How India Manages Its National Security.* New Delhi: Penguin, 2018.
Guo Xuezhi. *China's Security State: Philosophy, Evolution, and Politics.* New York: Cambridge University Press, 2012.
Halberstam, David. *The Best and the Brightest.* New York: Random House, 1972.
Halperin, Morton H. *The 1958 Taiwan Straits Crisis: A Documented History.* Santa Monica, CA: Rand, 1966.
Hoffmann, Steven A. *India and the China Crisis.* Berkeley: University of California Press, 1990.
Huang Yao, and Zhang Mingzhe, ed. *Luo Ruiqing zhuan* [Biography of Luo Ruiqing]. Beijing: Dangdai Zhongguo chubanshe, 1996.
Humphrey, David C. "Tuesday Lunch at the Johnson White House: A Preliminary Assessment." *Diplomatic History* 8, no. 1 (1984): 81–101.
Jiang Feng et al., ed. *Yang Yong jiangjun zhuan* [Biography of General Yang Yong]. Beijing: Jiefangjun chubanshe, 1991.

Jiang Hongbin, ed. *Chen Yi zhuan* [Biography of Chen Yi]. Shanghai: Shanghai renmin chubanshe, 1992.

Jin Chongji, ed. *Zhou Enlai zhuan* [Biography of Zhou Enlai]. 2nd ed. Beijing: Zhongyang wenxian chubanshe, 2008.

Kanwal, Gurmeet. "Military Dimensions of the 2002 India-Pakistan Stand-off: Planning and Preparation for Land Operations." In *The India-Pakistan Military Standoff: Crisis and Escalation in South Asia*, edited by Zachary Davis. New York: Palgrave Macmillan, 2011.

Kapur, S. Paul. "Ten Years of Instability in a Nuclear South Asia." *International Security* 33, no. 2 (2008): 71–94.

Keefe, John. *Anatomy of the EP-3 Incident, April 2001*. Alexandria: Center for Naval Analyses, 2002.

Kennedy, Andrew. *The International Ambitions of Mao and Nehru: National Efficacy Beliefs and the Making of Foreign Policy*. New York: Cambridge University Press, 2011.

Khan, Fazal Muqueem. *Pakistan's Crisis in Leadership*. Islamabad: National Book Foundation, 1973.

Khan, Feroz Hassan. *Eating Grass: The Making of the Pakistani Bomb*. Stanford: Stanford University Press, 2012.

Khan, Feroz Hassan, Peter B. Lavoy, and Christopher Clary. "Pakistan's Motivations and Calculations for the Kargil Conflict." In *Asymmetric Warfare in South Asia*, edited by Peter R. Lavoy. Cambridge: Cambridge University Press, 2009.

Lampton, David M. *Following the Leader: Ruling China, from Deng Xiaoping to Xi Jinping*. Berkeley: University of California Press, 2013.

———, ed. *The Making of Chinese Foreign and Security Policy in the Era of Reform, 1978–2000*. Stanford: Stanford University Press, 2001.

Li Danhui. "Zhengzhi doushi yu dishou: 1960 niandai ZhongSu bianjie guanxi [Political Fighters and Rivals: Sino-Soviet Border Relations in the 1960s]." *Shehui kexue* [Journal of Social Sciences] 2 (2007): 146–167.

Li Ke, and Hao Shengzhang, ed. *Wenhua dageming zhong de renmin jiefangjun* [People's Liberation Army during the Cultural Revolution]. Beijing: Zhonggong dangshi ziliao chubanshe, 1989.

Li Lianqing. *Da waijiaojia Zhou Enlai* [The Great Diplomat Zhou Enlai]. Beijing: Renmin chubanshe, 2016.

Leng nuan sui yue: Yibosanzhe de ZhongSu guanxi [Warm and Cold Years: The Ups and Downs of Sino-Soviet Relations]. Beijing: Shijie zhishi chubanshe, 1999.

Lin Hsiao-ting. *Taihai, lengzhan, Jiang Jieshi: Jiemi dang'an zhong xiaoshi de Taiwan shi* [Taiwan Strait, Cold War, Chiang Kai-shek: Taiwan's Hidden History in Declassified Records]. Taipei: Lianjing chuban shiye gufen youxian gongsi, 2015.

Lin Zhengyi. "Jiang Jieshi, Mao Zedong, Kennidi yu 1962 Taihai weiji [Chiang Kai-shek, Mao Zedong, Kennedy and the 1962 Taiwan Strait Crisis]." In *Jiang Zhongzheng yu Minguo waijiao* [Chiang Kai-shek and the Republic's Diplomacy], edited by Wu Zusheng and Chen Liwen. Taipei: Guoli zhongzheng jiniantang guanlichu, 2013.

Liu Xiaohong. *Chinese Ambassadors: The Rise of Diplomatic Professionalism since 1949*. Seattle: University of Washington Press, 2001.

Liu Zhinan. "1969 nian, Zhongguo zhanbei yu dui MeiSu guanxi de yanjiu he tiaozheng [1969, China's War Preparations and its Research and Adjustment in Relations with the United States and the Soviet Union]." *Dangdai Zhongguo shi yanjiu* [Research on Contemporary Chinese History], no. 3 (1999): 41–57.
Logevall, Fredrik. *Choosing War: The Lost Chance for Peace and the Escalation of War in Vietnam.* Berkeley: University of California Press, 2001.
Lu Ning. *The Dynamics of Foreign-Policy Decisionmaking in China.* 2nd ed. Boulder: Westview Press, 1997.
Lüthi, Lorenz M. "Restoring Chaos to History: Sino-Soviet-American Relations, 1969." *The China Quarterly*, no. 210 (2012): 378–397.
Ma Jisen. *The Cultural Revolution in the Foreign Ministry of China.* Hong Kong: Chinese University Press, 2004.
MacFarquhar, Roderick. *The Origins of the Cultural Revolution: The Great Leap Forward, 1958–1960.* New York: Columbia University Press, 1983.
MacFarquhar, Roderick, and Michael Schoenhals. *Mao's Last Revolution.* Cambridge: Harvard University Press, 2006.
Martin, Peter. *China's Civilian Army: The Making of Wolf Warrior Diplomacy.* New York: Oxford University Press, 2021.
Mastro, Oriana Skylar. *The Costs of Conversation: Obstacles to Talks in Wartime.* Ithaca: Cornell University Press, 2019.
Maxwell, Neville. *India's China War.* Revised Edition. Dehra Dun: Natraj, 2015.
McMaster, H. R. *Dereliction of Duty: Lyndon Johnson, Robert McNamara, the Joint Chiefs of Staff and the Lies that Led to Vietnam.* New York: HarperCollins, 1997.
Miller, Alice L. "Hu Jintao and the Party Politburo." *China Leadership Monitor* 9 (2004): 1–12.
Nathan, Andrew J., and Bruce Gilley. *China's New Rulers: The Secret Files.* 2nd ed. New York: New York Review of Books, 2003.
Mukherjee, Anit. *The Absent Dialogue.* New York: Oxford University Press, 2019.
Nawaz, Shuja. *Crossed Swords: Pakistan, Its Army, and the Wars Within.* 2nd ed. Karachi: Oxford University Press, 2017.
Nguyen, Lien-Hang T. *Hanoi's War: An International History of the War for Peace in Vietnam.* Chapel Hill: University of North Carolina Press, 2012.
O'Dowd, Edward C. *Chinese Military Strategy in the Third Indochina War: The Last Maoist War.* New York: Routledge, 2007.
Pradhan, S. D. "National Security System—Evolution." In *India's National Security*, edited by Satish Kumar. New Delhi: Routledge, 2010.
Preston, Andrew. *The War Council: McGeorge Bundy, the NSC, and Vietnam.* Cambridge: Harvard University Press, 2006.
Raghavan, Srinath. "A Coercive Triangle: India, Pakistan, the United States, and the Crisis of 2001–2002." *Defence Studies* 9, no. 2 (2009): 242–260.
War and Peace in Modern India. London: Palgrave Macmillan, 2010.
Raza, Rafi. *Zulfikar Ali Bhutto and Pakistan, 1967–1977.* Karachi: Oxford University Press, 1997.
Reeves, Richard. *President Kennedy: Profile of Power.* New York: Simon & Schuster, 1994.
Rizvi, Hasan-Askari. *Performance of the Defence Committee of the Cabinet.* Islamabad: PILDAT, 2012.

The Military and Politics in Pakistan: 1947–1997. Lahore: Sang-e-Meel, 2013.
Ross, Robert. *The Indochina Tangle: China's Vietnam Policy, 1975–1979*. New York: Columbia University Press, 1988.
Ryan, Mark A., David M. Finkelstein, and Michael A. McDevitt, eds. *Chinese Warfighting: The PLA Experience since 1949*. New York: M. E. Sharpe, 2003.
Saunders, Phillip C. and Andrew Scobell, eds. *PLA Influence on China's National Security Policy-Making*. Stanford: Stanford University Press, 2015.
Scobell, Andrew. *China's Use of Military Force: Beyond the Great Wall and the Long March*. New York: Cambridge University Press, 2003.
Shirk, Susan L. *China: Fragile Superpower*. New York: Oxford University Press, 2007.
Sinha, P. B., and A. A. Athale. *History of the Conflict with China, 1962*. New Delhi: Ministry of Defence History Division, 1992.
Smith, Bromley K. *Organizational History of the National Security Council during the Kennedy and Johnson Administrations*. Washington, DC, National Security Council, 1988.
Smith, David. "The 2001–2002 Standoff: A Real-Time View from Islamabad." In *The India-Pakistan Military Standoff: Crisis and Escalation in South Asia*, edited by Zachary Davis. New York: Palgrave Macmillan, 2011.
Sood, V. K., and Pravin Sawhney. *Operation Parakram: The War Unfinished*. New Delhi: Sage Publications, 2003.
Stolar, Alex. *To the Brink: Indian Decision-Making and the 2001–2002 Standoff*. Washington, DC: Henry L. Stimson Center, 2008.
Swaine, Michael D. "Chinese Decision-Making Regarding Taiwan, 1979–2000." In *The Making of Chinese Foreign and Security Policy in the Era of Reform, 1978–2000*, edited by David M. Lampton. Stanford: Stanford University Press, 2001.
Swami, Praveen. "A War to End a War: The Causes and Outcomes of the 2001-2 India-Pakistan Crisis." In *Nuclear Proliferation in South Asia*, edited by Sumit Ganguly and S. Paul Kapur. New York: Routledge, 2009.
"The Roots of Crisis: Post-Kargil Conflict in Kashmir and the 2001–2002 Near-War." In *The India-Pakistan Military Standoff: Crisis and Escalation in South Asia*, edited by Zachary Davis. New York: Palgrave Macmillan, 2011.
Taylor, Jay. *The Generalissimo: Chiang Kai-shek and the Struggle for Modern China*. Cambridge: The Belknap Press of Harvard University Press, 2009.
Teiwes, Frederick C. "The Establishment and Consolidation of the New Regime, 1949–1957." In *The Politics of China: Sixty Years of the People's Republic of China*, 3rd ed., edited by Roderick MacFarquhar. New York: Cambridge University Press, 2011.
"The Study of Elite Political Conflict in the PRC: Politics Inside the 'Black Box'." In *Handbook of the Politics of China*, edited by David S. G. Goodman. Northampton, MA: Elgar, 2015.
Teiwes, Frederick C., and Warren Sun. *The End of the Maoist Era: Chinese Politics during the Twilight of the Cultural Revolution, 1972–1976*. New York: Routledge, 2015.
Tharoor, Shashi. *Reasons of State: Political Development and India's Foreign Policy under Indira Gandhi, 1966–1977*. New Delhi: Vikas, 1982.

Torigian, Joseph. *Prestige, Manipulation, and Coercion: Elite Power Struggles in the Soviet Union and China after Stalin and Mao*. New Haven: Yale University Press, 2022.

Tucker, Nancy Bernkopf. *Strait Talk: United States-Taiwan Relations and the Crisis with China*. Cambridge: Harvard University Press, 2009.

VanDeMark, Brian. *Into the Quagmire: Lyndon Johnson and the Escalation of the Vietnam War*. New York: Oxford University Press, 1991.

———. *Road to Disaster: A New History of America's Descent into Vietnam*. New York: Custom House, 2018.

Venkataraman, R. *India's Higher Defence: Organisation and Management*. New Delhi: K.W. Publishers, 2011.

Vogel, Ezra F. *Deng Xiaoping and the Transformation of China*. Cambridge: Harvard University Press, 2011.

Wang Dong. "1962 nian Taihai weiji yu ZhongMei guanxi [The 1962 Taiwan Strait Crisis and Sino-American Relations]." *Zhonggong dangshi yanjiu* [Research on CCP Party History], no. 7 (2010): 60–69.

Wang Taiping, ed. *Zhonghua renmin gongheguo waijiao shi* [Diplomatic History of the People's Republic of China]. Beijing: Shijie zhishi chubanshe, 1998.

Wang Xuedong. *Fu Quanyou zhuan* [Biography of Fu Quanyou]. Beijing: Jiefangjun chubanshe, 2015.

Wang Yongqin. "1966–1976 nian ZhongMeiSu guanxi jishi (liandai yi) [Chronicle of Sino-American-Soviet Relations (1)]." *Dangdai Zhongguo shi yanjiu* [Research on Contemporary Chinese History], no. 4 (1997): 112–126.

Wang Zhongchun. "The Soviet Factor in Sino-American Normalization, 1969–1979." In *Normalization of U.S.-China Relations: An International History*, edited by William C. Kirby, Robert S. Ross, and Gong Li. Cambridge: Harvard University Press, 2005.

Whiting, Allen S. *The Chinese Calculus of Deterrence: India and Indochina*. Ann Arbor: MI, University of Michigan Press, 1975.

Wilkinson, Steven I. *Army and Nation: The Military and Indian Democracy since Independence*. Cambridge: Harvard University Press, 2015.

Wu Jianmin. *Waijiao anli* [Case Studies in Diplomacy]. Beijing: Renmin daxue chubanshe, 2007.

Wu Xinbo. *Managing Crisis and Sustaining Peace between China and the United States*. Washington, DC: United States Institute of Peace Press, 2008.

Xia Yafeng. "China's Elite Politics and Sino-American Rapprochement, January 1969–February 1972." *Journal of Cold War Studies* 8, no. 4 (2006): 3–28.

———. *Negotiating with the Enemy: US-China Talks during the Cold War, 1949–1972*. Bloomington: Indiana University Press, 2006.

———. "Wang Jiaxiang: New China's First Ambassador and the First Director of the International Liaison Department of the CCP." *American Journal of Chinese Studies* 16, no. 2 (2009): 137–155.

Xie Hainan, Yang Zufa, and Yang Jianhua, eds. *Yang Dezhi yisheng* [The Life of Yang Dezhi]. Zhonggong dangshi chubanshe, 2011.

Xu Yan. "1969 Nian ZhongSu bianjie chongtu [The 1969 Armed Conflict on the Sino-Soviet Border]." *Dangshi yanjiu ziliao* [Research Materials on Party History], no. 5 (1994): 2–13.

———. *Xu Yan jianggao zixuanji* [Selected Works from Xu Yan's Lectures]. Beijing: Guofang daxue chubanshe, 2014.

ZhongYin bianjie zhi zhan lishi zhenxiang [The True History of the Sino-Indian Border War]. Hong Kong: Tiandi, 1993.

Xue Li and Li Wei. "ZhongYue bianjing zhanzheng: Yuanyin tanxi yu Zhongfang shouyi pinggu [The Sino-Vietnamese Border War: Assessment of the Causes and Evaluation of the Gains]." *Zhanlüe juece yanjiu* [Journal of Strategy and Decision], no. 2 (2015): 67–82.

Yang Kuisong. "The Sino-Soviet Border Clash of 1969: From Zhenbao Island to Sino-American Rapprochement." *Cold War History* 1, no. 1 (2000): 21–52.

Yang Qiliang, et al. *Wang Shangrong jiangjun* [General Wang Shangrong]. Beijing: Dangdai Zhongguo chubanshe, 2000.

You Ji. "China's National Security Commission: Theory, Evolution and Operations." *Journal of Contemporary China* 25, no. 98 (2016): 178–196.

Zaheer, Hasan. *The Separation of East Pakistan: The Rise and Realization of Bengali Muslim Nationalism*. Karachi: Oxford University Press, 1994.

Zehra, Nasim. *From Kargil to the Coup: Events that Shook Pakistan*. Lahore: Sang-e-Mee, 2019.

Zhang Baijia. "The Changing International Scene and Chinese Policy toward the United States, 1954–1970." In *Re-examining the Cold War: US-China Diplomacy, 1954–1973*. Cambridge: Harvard University Asia Center, 2001.

Zhang Baijia and Jia Qingguo. "Steering Wheel, Shock Absorber, and Diplomatic Probe in Confrontation: Sino-American Ambassadorial Talks Seen from the Chinese Perspective." In *Re-examining the Cold War: US-China Diplomacy, 1954–1973*. Cambridge: Harvard University Asia Center, 2001.

Zhang Lili. *Waijiao juece* [Foreign Policy Decision-Making]. Beijing: Shijie zhishi chubanshe, 2007.

Zhang Qingmin. "Bureaucratic Politics and Chinese Foreign Policy-Making." *The Chinese Journal of International Politics* 9, no. 4 (2016): 435–458.

Zhang Shu Guang. *Deterrence and Strategic Culture: Chinese-American Confrontations, 1949–1958*. Ithaca: Cornell University Press, 1992.

Zhang Tuosheng. "The Sino-American Aircraft Collision: Lessons for Crisis Management." In *Managing Sino-American Crises: Case Studies and Analysis*, edited by Michael D. Swaine, Zhang Tuosheng, and Danielle F. S. Cohen. Washington, DC: Carnegie Endowment for International Peace, 2006.

Zhang, Xiaoming. *Deng Xiaoping's Long War: The Military Conflict between China and Vietnam, 1979–1991*. Chapel Hill: University of North Carolina Press, 2015.

Zhou Qi. *Organization, Structure and Image in the Making of Chinese Foreign Policy since the Early 1990s*. PhD dissertation, Johns Hopkins University, 2008.

Zhou Wang. *Zhongguo "xiaozu jizhi" yanjiu* ["Leading Small Groups" in Chinese Politics]. Tianjin: Tianjin renmin chubanshe, 2010.

Zubok, Vladislav M. *A Failed Empire: The Soviet Union in the Cold War from Stalin to Gorbachev*. Chapel Hill: University of North Carolina Press, 2009.

Books and Articles

Alchian, Armen A., and Harold Demsetz. "Production, Information Costs, and Economic Organization." *The American Economic Review* 62, no. 5 (1972): 777–795.

Allison, Graham T., and Peter L. Szanton. *Remaking Foreign Policy: The Organizational Connection.* New York: Basic Books, 1976.
Allison, Graham T., and Philip Zelikow. *Essence of Decision: Explaining the Cuban Missile Crisis.* 2nd ed. New York: Longman, 1999.
Ang, Yuen Yuen. *How China Escaped the Poverty Trap.* Ithaca: Cornell University Press, 2016.
Barnett, Michael N., and Martha Finnemore. "The Politics, Power, and Pathologies of International Organizations." *International Organization* 53, no. 4 (1999): 699–732.
Bar-Joseph, Uri, and Rose McDermott. *Intelligence Success and Failure: The Human Factor.* New York: Oxford University Press, 2017.
Bawn, Kathleen. "Political Control Versus Expertise: Congressional Choices about Administrative Procedures." *American Political Science Review* 89, no. 1 (1995): 62–73.
Bendor, Jonathan, and Thomas H. Hammond. "Rethinking Allison's Models." *American Political Science Review* 86, no. 2 (1992): 301–322.
Betts, Richard K. "Analysis, War, and Decision: Why Intelligence Failures Are Inevitable." *World Politics* 31, no. 1 (1978): 61–89.
Soldiers, Statesmen, and Cold War Crises. New York: Columbia University Press, 1991.
Blainey, Geoffrey. *Causes of War.* 3rd ed. New York: The Free Press, 1988.
Braut-Hegghammer, Målfrid. "Cheater's Dilemma: Iraq, Weapons of Mass Destruction, and the Path to War." *International Security* 45, no. 1 (2020): 51–89.
Brecher, Michael, and Jonathan Wilkenfeld. *A Study of Crisis.* Ann Arbor: University of Michigan Press, 1997.
Brooks, Risa. *Shaping Strategy: The Civil-Military Politics of Strategic Assessment.* Princeton: Princeton University Press, 2008.
Bueno De Mesquita, Bruce, James D. Morrow, Randolph M. Siverson, and Alastair Smith. "An Institutional Explanation of the Democratic Peace." *American Political Science Review* 93, no. 4 (1999): 791–807.
Burke, John P., and Fred L. Greenstein. *How Presidents Test Reality: Decisions on Vietnam, 1954 and 1965.* New York: Russell Sage Foundation, 1989.
Byman, Daniel L. and Kenneth M. Pollack. "Let Us Now Praise Great Men: Bringing the Statesman Back In." *International Security* 25 no. 4 (2001): 107–146.
Carpenter, Daniel P. *The Forging of Bureaucratic Autonomy: Reputations, Networks, and Policy Innovation in Executive Agencies, 1862–1928.* Princeton: Princeton University Press, 2001.
Carson, Austin. *Secret Wars: Covert Conflict in International Politics.* Princeton: Princeton University Press, 2018.
Clary, Christopher. *The Difficult Politics of Peace: Rivalry in Modern South Asia.* New York: Oxford University Press, 2022.
Cohen, Eliot A. *Supreme Command: Soldiers, Statesmen and Leadership in Wartime.* New York: The Free Press, 2002.
Cohen, Stephen P. *The Indian Army: Its Contribution to the Development of a Nation.* Berkeley: University of California Press, 1971.
Colgan, Jeff D. "Domestic Revolutionary Leaders and International Conflict." *World Politics* 65, no. 4 (2013): 656–690.

Croco, Sarah E. *Peace at What Price?* New York: Cambridge University Press, 2015.
Cyert, Richard M., and James G. March. *A Behavioral Theory of the Firm.* Englewood Cliffs: Prentice-Hall, 1963.
Daalder, Ivo H., and I. M. Destler. *In the Shadow of the Oval Office: Profiles of the National Security Advisers and the Presidents They Served.* New York: Simon & Schuster, 2009.
Dahl, Erik J. *Intelligence and Surprise Attack: Failure and Success from Pearl Harbor to 9/11 and Beyond.* Washington, DC: Georgetown University Press, 2013.
Dahlström, Carl, and Victor Lapuente. *Organizing Leviathan: Politicians, Bureaucrats, and the Making of Good Government.* New York: Cambridge University Press, 2017.
De Bruin, Erica. *How to Prevent Coups d'État: Counterbalancing and Regime Survival.* Ithaca: Cornell University Press, 2020.
Debs, Alexandre, and Hein E. Goemans. "Regime Type, the Fate of Leaders, and War." *American Political Science Review* 104, no. 3 (2010): 430–445.
Destler, I. M. "National Security Advice to US Presidents: Some Lessons from Thirty Years." *World Politics* 29, no. 2 (1977): 143–176.
Presidents, Bureaucrats and Foreign Policy: The Politics of Organizational Reform. Princeton: Princeton University Press, 1972.
d'Ombrain, Nicholas. *War Machinery and High Policy: Defence Administration in Peacetime Britain, 1902–1914.* New York: Oxford University Press, 1973.
Downes, Alexander B. "How Smart and Tough are Democracies? Reassessing Theories of Democratic Victory in War." *International Security* 33, no. 4 (2009): 9–51.
Downs, Anthony. *Inside Bureaucracy.* Boston: Little, Brown & Company, 1967.
Drezner, Daniel W. *The Ideas Industry: How Pessimists, Partisans, and Plutocrats are Transforming the Marketplace of Ideas.* New York: Oxford University Press, 2017.
Duelfer, Charles A., and Stephen Benedict Dyson. "Chronic Misperception and International Conflict: The US-Iraq Experience." *International Security* 36, no. 1 (2011): 73–100.
Edmondson, Amy C., Richard M. Bohmer, and Gary P. Pisano. "Disrupted Routines: Team Learning and New Technology Implementation in Hospitals." *Administrative Science Quarterly* 46, no. 4 (2001): 685–716.
Egorov, Georgy, and Konstantin Sonin. "Dictators and their Viziers: Endogenizing the Loyalty-Competence Trade-Off." *Journal of the European Economic Association* 9, no. 5 (2011): 903–930.
Etheredge, Lloyd S. *A World of Men: The Private Sources of American Foreign Policy.* Cambridge: MIT Press, 1978.
Evans, Peter B., Dietrich Rueschemeyer, and Theda Skocpol. *Bringing the State Back In.* New York: Cambridge University Press, 1985.
Fearon, James D. "Rationalist Explanations for War." *International Organization* 49, no. 3 (1995): 379–414.
Feaver, Peter D. *Armed Servants: Agency, Oversight, and Civil-Military Relations.* Cambridge: Harvard University Press, 2003.
Feaver, Peter D., and Christopher Gelpi. *Choosing Your Battles: American Civil-Military Relations and the Use of Force.* Princeton: Princeton University Press, 2004.

Friedman, Jeffrey A. *War and Chance: Assessing Uncertainty in International Politics.* New York: Oxford University Press, 2019.
Fuhrmann, Matthew and Michael C. Horowitz. "When Leaders Matter: Rebel Experience and Nuclear Proliferation." *Journal of Politics* 77 no. 1 (2015): 72–87.
Gailmard, Sean, and John W. Patty. *Learning While Governing: Expertise and Accountability in the Executive Branch.* Chicago: University of Chicago Press, 2012.
——— "Slackers and Zealots: Civil Service, Policy Discretion, and Bureaucratic Expertise." *American Journal of Political Science* 51, no. 4 (2007): 873–889.
Garicano, Luis, and Richard A. Posner. "Intelligence Failures: An Organizational Economics Perspective." *Journal of Economic Perspectives* 19, no. 4 (2005): 151–170.
Garrison, Jean A. *Games Advisors Play.* College Station: Texas A&M University Press, 1999.
Geddes, Barbara. *Politician's Dilemma: Building State Capacity in Latin America.* Berkeley: University of California Press, 1994.
Geddes, Barbara, Joseph Wright, and Erica Frantz. *How Dictatorships Work.* New York: Cambridge University Press, 2018.
George, Alexander L. *Presidential Decisionmaking in Foreign Policy: The Effective Use of Information and Advice.* Boulder: Westview Press, 1980.
——— "The Case for Multiple Advocacy in Making Foreign Policy." *American Political Science Review* 66, no. 3 (1972): 751–785.
Gilligan, Thomas W., and Keith Krehbiel. "Asymmetric Information and Legislative Rules with a Heterogeneous Committee." *American Journal of Political Science* 33, no. 2 (1989): 459–490.
Goldgeier, James M. *Leadership Style and Soviet Foreign Policy: Stalin, Khrushchev, Brezhnev, Gorbachev.* Baltimore: Johns Hopkins University Press, 1994.
Grauer, Ryan. *Commanding Military Power.* New York: Cambridge University Press, 2016.
Gray, Julia. "Life, Death, or Zombie? The Vitality of International Organizations." *International Studies Quarterly* 62, no. 1 (2018): 1–13.
Greitens, Sheena Chestnut. *Dictators and their Secret Police: Coercive Institutions and State Violence.* New York: Cambridge University Press, 2016.
Hafner-Burton, Emilie M., Stephan Haggard, David A. Lake, and David G. Victor. "The Behavioral Revolution and International Relations." *International Organization* 71, no. S1 (2017): 1–31.
Hall, Todd, and Keren Yarhi-Milo. "The Personal Touch: Leaders' Impressions, Costly Signaling, and Assessments of Sincerity in International Affairs." *International Studies Quarterly* 56, no. 3 (2012): 560–573.
Halperin, Morton H., and Priscilla Clapp. *Bureaucratic Politics and Foreign Policy.* 2nd ed. Washington, DC: Brookings Institution Press, 2006.
Haney, Patrick J. *Organizing for Foreign Policy Crises.* Ann Arbor: University of Michigan Press, 1997.
Hassan, Mai. *Regime Threats, and State Solutions: Bureaucratic Loyalty and Embeddedness in Kenya.* New York: Cambridge University Press, 2020.
Herek, Gregory M., Irving L. Janis, and Paul Huth. "Decision Making during International Crises: Is Quality of Process Related to Outcome?" *Journal of Conflict Resolution* 31, no. 2 (1987): 203–226.

Hermann, Margaret G., and Charles F. Hermann. "Who Makes Foreign Policy Decisions and How: An Empirical Inquiry." *International Studies Quarterly* 33, no. 4 (1989): 361–387.

Holmes, Marcus. *Face-to-Face Diplomacy: Social Neuroscience and International Relations*. New York: Cambridge University Press, 2018.

Horowitz, Michael C. "Leaders, Leadership, and International Security." In *The Oxford Handbook of International Security*, edited by Alexandra Gheciu and William C. Wohlforth. New York: Oxford University Press, 2018, 246–258.

Horowitz, Michael C., and Allan C. Stam. "How Prior Military Experience Influences the Future Militarized Behavior of Leaders." *International Organization* 68, no. 3 (2014): 527–559.

Horowitz, Michael C., Allan C. Stam, and Cali M. Ellis. *Why Leaders Fight*. New York: Cambridge University Press, 2015.

Huber, John D., and Charles R. Shipan. *Deliberate Discretion? The Institutional Foundations of Bureaucratic Autonomy*. New York: Cambridge University Press, 2002.

Huntington, Samuel P. *Political Order in Changing Societies*. New Haven: Yale University Press, 1968.

——— *The Soldier and the State: The Theory and Politics of Civil-Military Relations*. Cambridge: Harvard University Press, 1957.

Hyde, Susan D., and Elizabeth N. Saunders. "Recapturing Regime Type in International Relations: Leaders, Institutions, and Agency Space." *International Organization* 74, no. 2 (2020): 363–395.

Iklé, Fred Charles. *Every War Must End*. 2nd ed. New York: Columbia University Press, 2005.

Janis, Irving L. *Victims of Groupthink: A Psychological Study of Foreign-Policy Decisions and Fiascoes*. Boston: Houghton Mifflin, 1972.

Janowitz, Morris. *The Professional Soldier: A Social and Political Portrait*. Glencoe: The Free Press, 1960.

Jervis, Robert. *Perception and Misperception in International Politics*. Princeton: Princeton University Press, 1976.

——— "War and Misperception." *The Journal of Interdisciplinary History* 18, no. 4 (1988): 675–700.

——— *Why Intelligence Fails: Lessons from the Iranian Revolution and the Iraq War*. Ithaca: Cornell University Press, 2010.

Johnson, Dominic D. P. *Overconfidence and War*. Cambridge: Harvard University Press, 2004.

Johnson, Tana. *Organizational Progeny: Why Governments Are Losing Control Over the Proliferating Structures of Global Governance*. New York: Oxford University Press, 2014.

Johnston, Alastair Iain. *Social States: China in International Institutions, 1980–2000*. Princeton: Princeton University Press, 2014.

Jost, Tyler. "Institutional Origins of Miscalculation in China's International Crises." *International Security*, 48, no. 1 (2023), 47–90.

Jost, Tyler, Joshua D. Kertzer, Eric Min, and Robert Schub. "Advisers and Aggregation in Foreign Policy Decision-Making." *International Organization* 78, no. 1 (2024): 1–37.

Jost, Tyler, Kaine Meshkin, and Robert Schub. "The Character and Origins of Military Attitudes on the Use of Force." *International Studies Quarterly* 66, no. 2 (2022).

Kaarbo, Juliet. "A Foreign Policy Analysis Perspective on the Domestic Politics Turn in IR Theory." *International Studies Review* 17, no. 2 (2015): 189–216.

Kenwick, Michael R., and Sarah Maxey. "You and Whose Army? How Civilian Leaders Leverage the Military's Prestige to Shape Public Opinion." *The Journal of Politics* 84, no. 4 (2022): 1963–1978.

Keohane, Robert O. "International Institutions: Two Approaches." *International Studies Quarterly* 32, no. 4 (1988): 379–396.

Kertzer, Joshua D. *Resolve in International Politics*. Princeton: Princeton University Press, 2016.

Kertzer, Joshua D., Marcus Holmes, Brad L. LeVeck, and Carly Wayne. "Hawkish Biases and Group Decision Making." *International Organization* 76, no. 3 (2022): 513–548.

Khong, Yuen Foong. *Analogies at War: Korea, Munich, Dien Bien Phu, and the Vietnam Decisions of 1965*. Princeton: Princeton University Press, 1992.

Kier, Elizabeth. *Imagining War: French and British Military Doctrine between the Wars*. Princeton: Princeton University Press, 1997.

Krasner, Stephen D. "Are Bureaucracies Important? (or Allison Wonderland)." *Foreign Policy*, no. 7 (1972): 159–179.

Krishna, Vijay, and John Morgan. "A Model of Expertise." *The Quarterly Journal of Economics* 116, no. 2 (2001): 747–775.

Kydd, Andrew H. *Trust and Mistrust in International Relations*. Princeton: Princeton University Press, 2005.

Larson, Deborah Welch. "Good Judgment in Foreign Policy: Social Psychological Perspectives." In *Good Judgment in Foreign Policy: Theory and Application*, edited by Stanley A. Renshon and Deborah Welch Larson. New York: Rowman & Littlefield, 2003: 3–23.

Lebovic, James H. *Planning to Fail: The US Wars in Vietnam, Iraq, and Afghanistan*. New York: Oxford University Press, 2019.

Lebow, Richard Ned. *Between Peace and War: The Nature of International Crisis*. Baltimore: Johns Hopkins University Press, 1984.

LeVeck, Brad L., and Neil Narang. "The Democratic Peace and the Wisdom of Crowds." *International Studies Quarterly* 61, no. 4 (2017): 867–880.

Levy, Jack S. "Misperception and the Causes of War: Theoretical Linkages and Analytical Problems." *World Politics* 36, no. 1 (1983): 76–99.

Lewis, David E. *The Politics of Presidential Appointments: Political Control and Bureaucratic Performance*. Princeton: Princeton University Press, 2008.

Lin-Greenberg, Erik, and Theo Milonopoulos. "Private Eyes in the Sky: Emerging Technology and the Political Consequences of Eroding Government Secrecy." *Journal of Conflict Resolution* 65, no. 6 (2021): 1067–1097.

Lindsey, David. "Military Strategy, Private Information, and War." *International Studies Quarterly* 59, no. 4 (2015): 629–640.

Lindsey, David. *Delegated Diplomacy: How Ambassadors Establish Trust in International Relations*. New York: Columbia University Press, 2023.

Lupia, Arthur, and Mathew D. McCubbins. *The Democratic Dilemma: Can Citizens Learn What They Need to Know?* New York: Cambridge University Press, 1998

Malis, Matt. "Conflict, Cooperation, and Delegated Diplomacy." *International Organization* 75, no. 4 (2021): 1018–1057.
March, James G., and Herbert A. Simon. *Organizations*. New York: Wiley, 1958.
May, Ernest R., ed. *Knowing One's Enemies: Intelligence Assessment Before the Two World Wars*. Princeton: Princeton University Press, 1984.
McCubbins, Mathew D., Roger G. Noll, and Barry R. Weingast. "Administrative Procedures as Instruments of Political Control." *Journal of Law, Economics, and Organization* 3, no. 2 (1987): 243–277.
McDermott, Rose. *Presidential Leadership, Illness, and Decision Making*. New York: Cambridge University Press, 2007.
McManus, Roseanne W. "Crazy Like a Fox? Are Leaders with Reputations for Madness More Successful at International Coercion?" *British Journal of Political Science* 51, no. 1 (2021): 275–293.
Mearsheimer, John J. *The Tragedy of Great Power Politics*. New York: W. W. Norton & Company, 2001.
Moffitt, Susan L. *Making Policy Public: Participatory Bureaucracy in American Democracy*. New York: Cambridge University Press, 2014.
Meier, Kenneth John. "Representative Bureaucracy: An Empirical Analysis." *American Political Science Review* 69, no. 2 (1975): 526–542.
Morrow, James D. "Capabilities, Uncertainty, and Resolve: A Limited Information Model of Crisis Bargaining." *American Journal of Political Science* 33, no. 4 (1989): 941–972.
Narang, Vipin. *Nuclear Strategy in the Modern Era: Regional Powers and International Conflict*. Princeton: Princeton University Press, 2014.
Narang, Vipin, and Caitlin Talmadge. "Civil-Military Pathologies and Defeat in War: Tests Using New Data." *Journal of Conflict Resolution* 62, no. 7 (2018): 1379–1405.
North, Douglass C. *Institutions, Institutional Change and Economic Performance*. New York: Cambridge University Press, 1990.
Neustadt, Richard E. *Presidential Power and the Modern Presidents: The Politics of Leadership from Roosevelt to Reagan*. New York: Simon & Schuster, 1991.
Preston, Thomas. *The President and His Inner Circle: Leadership Style and the Advisory Process in Foreign Policy Making*. New York: Columbia University Press, 2001.
Quinlivan, James T. "Coup-Proofing: Its Practice and Consequences in the Middle East." *International Security* 24, no. 2 (1999): 131–165.
Rathbun, Brian C. *Reasoning of State: Realists, Romantics and Rationality in International Relations*. New York: Cambridge University Press, 2019.
Reiter, Dan, and Allan C. Stam. *Democracies at War*. Princeton: Princeton University Press, 2002.
Renshon, Jonathan. *Fighting for Status: Hierarchy and Conflict in World Politics*. Princeton: Princeton University Press, 2017.
Renshon, Jonathan, and Daniel Kahneman. "Hawkish Biases and the Interdisciplinary Study of Conflict Decision-Making." In *Advancing Interdisciplinary Approaches to International Relations*, edited by Steven A. Yetiv and Patrick James. London: Palgrave Macmillan, 2017.
Rosen, Stephen Peter. *Societies and Military Power: India and Its Armies*. Ithaca: Cornell University Press, 1996.

Rovner, Joshua. *Fixing the Facts: National Security and the Politics of Intelligence*. Ithaca: Cornell University Press, 2011.
Sagan, Scott D. *The Limits of Safety: Organizations, Accidents, and Nuclear Weapons*. Princeton: Princeton University Press, 1993.
Saunders, Elizabeth N. "Elites in the Making and Breaking of Foreign Policy." *Annual Review of Political Science* 25 (2022): 219–240.
— *Leaders at War: How Presidents Shape Military Interventions*. Ithaca: Cornell University Press, 2011.
— "Leaders, Advisers, and the Political Origins of Elite Support for War." *Journal of Conflict Resolution* 62, no. 10 (2018): 2118–2149.
— "No Substitute for Experience: Presidents, Advisers, and Information in Group Decision Making." *International Organization* 71, no. S1 (2017): 219–247.
— "War and the Inner Circle: Democratic Elites and the Politics of Using Force." *Security Studies* 24, no. 3 (2015): 466–501.
Schafer, Mark, and Scott Crichlow. *Groupthink versus High-Quality Decision Making in International Relations*. New York: Columbia University Press, 2010.
Schelling, Thomas C. *Arms and Influence*. New Haven: Yale University Press, 1966.
Schub, Robert. "Informing the Leader: Bureaucracies and International Crises." *American Political Science Review* 116, no. 4 (2022): 1460–1476.
Schultz, Kenneth A. *Democracy and Coercive Diplomacy*. New York: Cambridge University Press, 2001.
Sechser, Todd S. "Goliath's Curse: Coercive Threats and Asymmetric Power." *International Organization* 64, no. 4 (2010): 627–660.
Shih, Victor C. *Coalitions of the Weak: Elite Politics in China from Mao's Stratagem to the Rise of Xi*. New York: Cambridge University Press, 2022.
— "'Nauseating' Displays of Loyalty: Monitoring the Factional Bargain through Ideological Campaigns in China." *The Journal of Politics* 70, no. 4 (2008): 1177–1192.
Simon, Herbert A. *Administrative Behavior*. 4th ed. New York: The Free Press, 1997.
Singh, Naunihal. *Seizing Power: The Strategic Logic of Military Coups*. Baltimore: John Hopkins University Press, 2014.
Snyder, Jack. *Myths of Empire: Domestic Politics and International Ambition*. Ithaca: Cornell University Press, 1991.
— *The Ideology of the Offensive: Military Decision Making and the Disasters of 1914*. Ithaca: Cornell University Press, 1989.
Staniland, Paul. "Explaining Civil-Military Relations in Complex Political Environments: India and Pakistan in Comparative Perspective." *Security Studies* 17, no. 2 (2008): 322–362.
Streeck, Wolfgang, and Kathleen Thelen. *Beyond Continuity: Institutional Change in Advanced Political Economies*. New York: Oxford University Press, 2005.
Suleiman, Ezra N. *Dismantling Democratic States*. Princeton: Princeton University Press, 2013.
Svolik, Milan W. *The Politics of Authoritarian Rule*. New York: Cambridge University Press, 2012.

't Hart, Paul, Eric Stern and Bengt Sundelius. *Beyond Groupthink: Political Group Dynamics and Foreign Policy-Making.* Ann Arbor: University of Michigan Press, 1997.

Talmadge, Caitlin. *The Dictator's Army: Battlefield Effectiveness in Authoritarian Regimes.* Ithaca: Cornell University Press, 2015.

Tetlock, Philip E., and Barbara A. Mellers. "Intelligent Management of Intelligence Agencies: Beyond Accountability Ping-Pong." *American Psychologist* 66, no. 6 (2011): 542–554.

Van Evera, Stephen. *Causes of War: Power and the Roots of Conflict.* Ithaca: Cornell University Press, 1999.

Vertzberger, Yaacov Y.I. *The World in Their Minds: Information Processing, Cognition, and Perception in Foreign Policy Decisionmaking.* Stanford: Stanford University Press, 1990.

Walt, Stephen M. *The Hell of Good Intentions: America's Foreign Policy Elite and the Decline of US Primacy.* New York: Farrar, Straus & Giroux, 2018.

Waltz, Kenneth N. *Theory of International Politics.* New York: McGraw-Hill, 1979.

Weber, Max. *Economy and Society: An Outline of Interpretive Sociology.* Berkeley: University of California Press, 1978 [1921].

Weeks, Jessica L. "Autocratic Audience Costs: Regime Type and Signaling Resolve." *International Organization* 62, no. 1 (2008): 35–64.

Dictators at War and Peace. Ithaca: Cornell University Press, 2014.

"Strongmen and Straw Men: Authoritarian Regimes and the Initiation of International Conflict." *American Political Science Review* 106, no. 2 (2012): 326–347.

Weisiger, Alex. *Logics of War: Explanations for Limited and Unlimited Conflicts.* Ithaca: Cornell University Press, 2013.

Weiss, Jessica Chen. *Powerful Patriots: Nationalist Protest in China's Foreign Relations.* New York: Oxford University Press, 2014.

Welch, David A. "The Organizational Process and Bureaucratic Politics Paradigms: Retrospect and Prospect." *International Security* 17, no. 2 (1992): 112–146.

Wendt, Alexander. "Driving with the Rearview Mirror: On the Rational Science of Institutional Design." *International Organization* 55, no. 4 (2001): 1019–1049.

White, Peter B. "Crises and Crisis Generations: The Long-Term Impact of International Crises on Military Political Participation." *Security Studies* 26, no. 4 (2017).

Whitlark, Rachel Elizabeth. *All Options on the Table: Leaders, Preventive War, and Nuclear Proliferation.* Ithaca: Cornell University Press, 2021.

Wilson, James Q. *Bureaucracy: What Government Agencies Do and Why They Do It.* New York: Basic Books, 1989.

Wohlforth, William Curti. *The Elusive Balance: Power and Perceptions during the Cold War.* Ithaca: Cornell University Press, 1993.

Wohlstetter, Roberta. *Pearl Harbor: Warning and Decision.* Stanford: Stanford University Press, 1962.

Woods, Kevin M., Michael R. Pease, Mark E. Stout, Williamson Murry, and James G. Lacy. *Iraqi Perspectives Project.* Norfolk: U.S. Joint Center for Operational Analysis, 2006.

Yarhi-Milo, Keren. *Knowing the Adversary: Leaders, Intelligence, and Assessment of Intentions in International Relations*. Princeton: Princeton University Press, 2014.
  Who Fights for Reputation: The Psychology of Leaders in International Conflict. Princeton: Princeton University Press, 2018.

Zegart, Amy B. *Flawed by Design: The Evolution of the CIA, JCS, and NSC*. Stanford: Stanford University Press, 2000.
  Spying Blind: The CIA, the FBI, and the Origins of 9/11. Princeton: Princeton University Press, 2009.

Index

accountability, theory of, *see also* public opinion
  miscalculation and, 15, 174–175
  Nationalist invasion scare (1962), 110–111
  non-personalist autocracy, 175
  Pakistan, 231
  regime type and, 175
  Sino-Indian War, 178, 214
  Sino–Vietnamese War, 166
  statistical analysis, 60, 67, 72, 74
  Taiwan Strait Crisis (1958), 295
  theoretical summary, 42
  Twin Peaks Crises, 223
agendas, *see* domestic agendas; international vs domestic agendas
Ahmad, Shamshad, 245–246, 254
Aksai Chin, 201–202, 205, 206, 214
Allison, Graham, 5–6, 11, 26, 31, 333
Ayub Khan, 229, 231, 232
Aziz, Sartaj, 226, 239, 246–248, 251, 254, *see also* Kargil War; Sharif, Nawaz

Ball, George, 260, 275, 307–310, 312–313, 316, 319, 335, *see also* Kennedy, John. F; Johnson, Lyndon; Vietnam War, US
Bay of Pigs, 106, 272, 280
beliefs, leader, *see* leader beliefs
Bhutto, Benazir, 237
Bhutto, Zulfikar Ali, 230, 238
border politics, 80, 82–84, 100–102, 111–127, 197–222, 231, 246–257
Brezhnev, Leonid, 24, 51, 62, 115, 159, 160
Brooks, Risa, 12, 40, 227, 336
Brzezinski, Zbigniew, 155
Bundy, McGeorge, *see also* Kennedy, John. F.; Johnson, Lyndon; Vietnam War, US
  information provision, 270, 304, 306, 308, 323
  management of bureaucracy, 259–260, 271
  self-censorship, 309, 319
  strategic assessments, 299, 318
Bundy, William, 309, 310, 312, 313, 315–319, *see also* Kennedy, John F.; Johnson, Lyndon; Vietnam War, US
bureaucracies, powers of, *see also* coups; public opinion
  information, control of, 21, 25–26, 44–46
  institutional choice and, 10, 43–46, 149
  leader experience and, 189, 192–193, 264–265, 268–269, 272
  overview, 3
bureaucratic meetings, *see* meetings, bureaucratic
bureaucratic threat, *see also* bureaucracies, powers of; coups
  case studies, measurement of, 76
  China after Mao Zedong, 86
  China under Mao Zedong, 130, 132–133, 138–140, 175
  defined, 47
  India after Nehru, 189–190, 224–225
  India under Nehru, 178–183
  institutional design and, 46–51, 54, 91–95
  measurement of, 70–72, 76
  Pakistan, 227–230, 232, 236–237
  political punishment and, 47
  US under Eisenhower, 264–265
  US under Johnson, 261, 272–273, 322, 329
  US under Kennedy, 268–269
Bush, George H.W., 24
Bush, George W., 217, 221

Cabinet Committee on Security (CCS), India, 192–194, 219–220, 223
Cambodia, 128, 154–156, 158–161, 163, 165
Carter, Jimmy, 45, 155, 160, 166

370

Index

Central Intelligence Agency (CIA), US, 105, 154, 266, 276, 279, 289–292, 306, 308, 310, 319–320
Central Investigation Department (CID), China, 90
Central Military Commission (CMC), China, 87, 89, 99, 107–108, 112, 124–125, 137–138, 147–148, 162–163
Chen Yi, 302, 335, *see also* Mao Zedong; Nationalist invasion scare (1962); Sino–Soviet Border Conflict
  diplomacy and, 87, 97, 110
  information flows and, 118, 123
  information provision and, 119, 121, 122
Chiang Kai-shek, 103–109, 285–286, 294, 295
Chief Martial Law Administration (CLMA), Pakistan, 233
China, administrations of, *see* Deng Xiaoping; Hua Guofeng; Jiang Zemin; Mao Zedong; national security organizations
China–United States relations, 114–116, 128, 143–144, 152, 160, 168–175, 284–296
Chinese Civil War, 85
Chinese Communist Party (CCP), 84, 90, 94, 128, 130, 133, 140, 141, 144, 201
Chinese Military, 128, 132–133, 135, 137–140, 142–145, 147–148, 151, *see also* People's Liberation Army (PLA), China
civil-military relations, *see also* Brooks, Risa
  China, 90, 98, 142, 147–149, 173
  generally, 55, 335–336
  India, 183, 185, 189
  institutional design, 49–51
  Pakistan, 227–240, 244, 257, 258
Clinton, Bill, 250–251, 253
coercion, 67, 158, 165, 214, 229, 248, 298
coercive diplomacy, 104, 105, 215–217, 221–222, 252, 284–285
Cold War, US, 5, 20, 143, 237, 279–282, *see also* Eisenhower, Dwight D.; Johnson, Lyndon; Kennedy, John F.
Committee on Imperial Defence, UK, 19, 178, 224, 233
communism, spread of, 259, 282, 296, 297, 301, 308, 310, 317, *see also* domino theory, Vietnam War, US
competitive dialogue, 3, 11–14, 31–35, 39, 41, 129, 176, 225, 258, 323, 333
Cooper, Chester, 312
coups
  Agartala conspiracy, 230
  China, 94–95, 133
  coup-proofing, 14
  generally, 46, 70, 72, 76
  India, 178, 183, 192–193, 224
  Pakistan, 226, 228–230, 233, 236, 256, 258, 328
crises, international, *see also* Cold War; EP-3 reconnaissance aircraft incident; Kargil War; Nationalist invasion scare (1962); Sino–Indian War; Sino–Vietnamese War; Taiwan Strait Crisis (1958); Twin Peaks Crises; Vietnam War, US
  casualties of, 1, 158, 177, 226, 259
  costs and benefits, 8–9, 64
  information and, 31, 36
  miscalculation and, 24–25
  overview, 21–23
crisis behavior, *see* decision-making
crisis performance
  analysis of
    EP-3 reconnaissance aircraft incident, 168–172
    general patterns, 79
    Kargil War, 245
    Nationalist invasion scare (1962), 103–110
    Sino–Soviet Border Conflict, 111–117
    Sino–Vietnamese War, 153–155
    Twin Peaks Crises, 216–223, 225
    Vietnam War, 299–303
  charted
    China after Mao, 149–152
    China under Mao, 100
    Cold War, 279–282
    India, 197
    institutional design and, 65–66
  crisis failure
    EP-3 reconnaissance aircraft incident, 171–172
    frequency analysed, 79
    institutional design and, 62, 150–151, 241, 280
    Kargil War, 241
    overview, 1–2
    Sino–Vietnamese War, 157–161
    statistical analysis, 66–67
    Vietnam War, 303–304
  crisis success
    Nationalist invasion scare (1962), 83
    Taiwan Strait Crisis (1958), 286–289
  medium-n coding methodology, 79
Cuban Missile Crisis, 64, 78, 274, 283, 303
Cultural Revolution, *see* Mao Zedong
Cutler, Robert, 265

372 Index

de Gaulle, Charles, 311
decision-making
  China after Mao, 151–153
  Cold War, 280–282
  Kargil War, 245–250, 255–257
  Taiwan Strait Crisis (1958), 285, 286, 294, 296
  Twin Peaks Crises, 216–217
  Vietnam War, 296–299, 304–311
decision-making bodies, *see* national security institutions; national security organizations
Defence Committee of the Cabinet (DCC), India, 180, 185–186, 189–191, 208
Defence Committee of the Cabinet (DCC), Pakistan, 228, 233, 238–239
Defence Ministry, India, 216
Defence Ministry, Pakistan, 227, 228, 238, 252, 255, 258
defense bureaucracies, *see also* national security institutions; national security organizations
  China, EP-3 reconnaissance aircraft incident, 172–173
  China, Hua-Deng Period, 132–133
  China, Jiang-Hu Period, 145–148
  China, Lieutenant Period, 140–142
  China, Sino–Vietnamese War, 162–164
  critical information and, 31–32
  India, post-independence, 180
  India, Sino-Indian War, 178–179
  India, Twin Peaks Crises, 215–216, 219–223
  India under Nehru, 180–183, 185–189, 207–213
  Pakistan, coup d'état, 228–230
  Pakistan, Kargil War, 248, 252–256
  Pakistan and military rule, 232
  US, Vietnam War, 306–310
Defense Department, US, 266, 267, 269, 274, 276, 290–292, 296, 300, 304, 306, 307, 309, 312, 314
democracy, 18, 20, 60, 69, 72–75, 144, 176, 192, 260, 261, 322, 328, 332, 336
Deng Xiaoping, *see also* Sino–Vietnamese War
  crisis decision making, 156–157, 162
  information flows, 78, 91, 98, 151, 163, 164, 166–168
  political environment of, 90, 130, 132–138, 155, 160
design, bureaucratic, *see* national security institutions; political theory of institutional design

Destler, I.M., 17, 52
dictatorial institutions, 27, 39, 57, 68, 73, 74, *see also* integrated institutions; fragmented institutions; national security institutions; siloed institutions
Dien Bien Phu, 282
diplomatic bureaucracies, *see also* national security organizations
  critical information and, 32–33
  diplomatic signals, 110, 119, 120
  Hua-Deng Period, 133, 135–137
  Jiang-Hu Period, 145–148
  Kargil War, 245–248, 253–254
  Lieutenant Period, 142
  Nationalist invasion scare (1962), 110
  Sino-Indian War, 178–179, 206
  Sino–Soviet Border Conflict, 118–121
  Sino–Vietnamese War, 164–165
  Taiwan Strait Crisis, 107
  Twin Peaks Crises, 219
  under Mao, 96–97
  under Nehru, 186–187, 211–212
  Vietnam War, 308–309
domestic agendas, *see also* international vs domestic agendas; transformative economic policy
  after Mao, 134
  China after Mao, 133–135
  fragmented institutions and, 168
  Great Leap Forward, 111
  Pakistan, 230–234
  Soviet Union, 122
  transformative policy, 49, 70, 73–74, 76, 130, 132–134, 171, 175, 183–184, 231–232
  under Johnson, 261, 273
  under Mao, 91, 93–95, 104, 175, 288
  under Nehru, 178, 183–184
domestic vs international agendas, 11, 47, 49–50, 73–74, 76
domino theory, 295, 298, 301, 308, 320, *see also* communism, spread of; Vietnam War, US
Dulles, Allen, 289–293, *see also* Eisenhower, Dwight D.; Taiwan Strait Crisis (1958)
Dulles, John Foster, 285, 287, 288, *see also* Eisenhower, Dwight D.; Taiwan Strait Crisis (1958)

economic policy, *see* domestic agendas; transformational economic policy
Eisenhower, Dwight D., *see also* Cold War; Dulles, Allen; Dulles, John Foster
  as leader, 278
  crisis decision making, 284–289

Index

crisis decision making, alternative explanations, 294–296
information flows, 267–268, 289–294
information search capacity, 266
integrated institutions, 265–266, 328
Planning Board, 267
political environment of, 264–265
elite politics, China, *see also* Hua Guofeng; Jiang Zemin; Mao Zedong
information flows and, 141, 166–167, 175
power struggles and, 130–135
veterans group, 134
victims group, 134–135
Emergency Committee of the Cabinet (ECC), India, 190–191, 205
EP-3 reconnaissance aircraft incident, *see also* Jiang Zemin
alternative explanations, 174–175
background to, 128–129
decision-making, 152–153, 169
institutional design, 172–174
outcome, 127, 171–172, 258
strategic options, 168–169
exchange of information, *see* information flows
Executive Committee (EXCOMM), United States, 270–271, 303

failure, *see* crisis performance
Foreign Affairs Committee (FAC), India, 185, 191
Foreign Affairs Leading Small Group (FALSG), China, 78, 90, 98, 137, 141–142
Foreign Affairs Office, China, 97, 99
foreign ministries, *see* diplomatic bureaucracies
Foreign Ministry, China, 87–89, 91, 93, 95, 97–98, 102, 108–109, 118–121, 123–124, 133, 138, 146, 159, 164–165
Foreign Ministry, Pakistan, 233–235, 238, 240, 243–244, 247–248, 253–255
Forward Policy, 2, 80, 177–204, 206, 208–215
Four Marshals group, China, 121–124
fragmented institutions, *see also* dictatorial institutions; integrated institutions; national security institutions; siloed institutions
appeal of, 11, 168, 178
bureaucratic power and, 47, 49, 130, 211
charted, 27
conclusions, 326
crisis failure and, 68, 79
defined, 9
dictatorial institutions and, 39
domestic agendas and, 50, 54, 73–74, 232
in data set, 57
miscalculations and, 37–39, 81, 205, 261–262, 303, 311–312, 328
functional diversity, 33

Gandhi, Indira, 189
Gandhi, Rajiv, 189, 193, 329
Gang of Four, China, 134–135
George, Alexander L., 13, 23, 37, 43, 52
Gracey, Douglas, 235
Graham, Allison T., 12
Great Leap Forward, China, 91–93, 104, 111, 177, 203, 210, *see also* Mao Zedong
group decision-making models, *see* information quality

Hitler, Adolf, 37
Ho Chi Minh, 296, 300, 301
Hu Jintao, 143
Hu Yaobang, 140
Hua Guofeng, *see also* Sino–Vietnamese War
as leader, 133, 154
crisis decision making, 167
information flows and, 135–137
political environment of, 130–132, 134–135, 138
Huang Hua, 133, 164, 165, *see also* Sino–Vietnamese War
Huang Kecheng, 87
Huang Yongsheng, 117
Hussein, Saddam, 57

India, administrations of, *see* national security organizations; Nehru, Jawaharlal; Vajpayee, Atal Bihari
India–Pakistan, partition of, 184, 245
India–Pakistan relations, *see* India–Pakistan Wars; Kargil War
India–Pakistan War (1947), 241
India–Pakistan War (1965), 102, 191, 241–243
India–Pakistan War (1971), 192, 197, 243, 244
information flows
China, Hua-Deng Period, 135–137
China, Jiang-Hu Period, 147–148
China, late Mao period, 97–98, 118–121, 123
functional failures of, 37

374 Index

information flows (cont.)
  horizontal, 29–31, 86–91, 147–148, 257
  implications of, 334
  India, Sino-Indian War, 206–213
  India after 1962, 191–192
  India after 1998, 194–195
  India under Nehru, 187–189
  institution types and, 4–5, 9–10, 31–36, 38–39
  islands and bridges, 4
  leaders and, 23–25, 34, 38
  Pakistan, early civilian and military rule, 232–235
  Pakistan, late civilian rule, 238–240
  US under Eisenhower, 266–268
  US under Johnson, 275–278
  US under Kennedy, 270–272
  vertical, 26, 39
information quality, 29, see also competitive dialogue
  crisis failure and, 68
  decision-making body size and, 69
  defined, 29
  diverse teams and, 34
  EP-3 reconnaissance aircraft incident, 172–174
  fragmented institutions and, 206–207
  Groupthink, 239
  integrated institutions and, 9–10, 14, 29–31, 34, 43, 102, 107–110
  Jiang-Hu Period, 148
  Kargil War, 255–256
  Nationalist invasion scare (1962), 107–110
  siloed institutions and, 35–36, 38, 271
  Sino–Soviet border conflict, 121–124
  Sino–Vietnamese and EP-3 reconnaissance aircraft incident comparison, 129
  Sino–Vietnamese War, 163–167
  skewing pessimistic, 63–64
  Taiwan Strait Crisis (1958), 289–294
  trade off with political security, 3, 21
  Twin Peaks Crises, 219–223
  under Nehru, 209–213
  Vietnam War, 303
information search capacity
  China, Hua-Deng Period, 135–137
  China, Jiang-Hu Period, 145–147
  China, Lieutenant Period, 140–141
  China, Sino–Vietnamese War, 162–163
  China under Mao period, 86–89, 95–98, 117–121
  dictatorial institutions, 39
  inclusive and insular structures, 27–35
  India after 1962, 190–191
  India after 1998, 193–194
  India under Nehru, 185–187
  measurement of, 55
  Pakistan, early civilian and military rule, 232–235
  Pakistan, Kargil War, 254
  Pakistan, late civilian rule, 238–239
  siloed institutions and, 50
  US, Vietnam War, 303
  US under Eisenhower, 266
  US under Johnson, 275–277
  US under Kennedy, 270–271
information, bureaucratic
  China, Jiang-Hu Period, 146–147
  China, Sino–Vietnamese War, 166
  China under Mao, 87–89, 97–98
  India, Twin Peaks Crises, 219–221
  India after 1998, 194–195
  India before Sino-Indian War, 207
  India under Nehru, 186–189, 208–211, 213
  Soviet Union, Sino-Soviet Border Conflict, 111
integrated institutions, see also competitive dialogue; dictatorial institutions; fragmented institutions; national security institutions; siloed institutions
  assessment and, 15–16, 107–110
  as resource and liability, 10, 44–46, 49–50
  charted, 26
  China under Mao, 86–89, 102
  crisis performance and, 79
  defined, 9
  in data set, 57
  functional diversity and, 31–34
  India after 1998, 192–193
  leader beliefs and, 80
  leader experience and, 72–73
  limited bureaucratic threat and, 46
  miscalculation mitigation and, 31–35, 54
  personalist dictatorships and, 84, 91
  Taiwan Strait Crisis (1958), US, 289–294
  Twin Peaks Crises, India, 219–223
  US under Eisenhower, 263, 265–266
  US under Kennedy, 269–270
Intelligence Bureau (DIB), India, 186–187, 209–213
intelligence bureaucracies
  China, Jiang-Hu Period, 145–147
  China, late Mao period, 97
  in National Security Institutions Data Set, 57
  India, Sino-Indian War, 178–179
  India, Twin Peaks Crises, 219
  information analysis and, 14–15, 33–34

Index

intelligence politicization, 50
Pakistan, Kargil War, 253–254
US, Twin Peaks Crises, 217
US, Vietnam War, 306, 308, 310–311
US under Johnson, 276–277
Inter-Services Intelligence (ISI), Pakistan, 233–234, 240, 253–254
interest group model, 11–14, 30, 40–42, 69–70, 179, 255, 258
   EP-3 Reconnaissance aircraft incident and, 174
   Kargil War and, 257
   Nationalist invasion scare and, 110
   Sino-Indian War and, 213
   Sino–Soviet Border Conflict and, 124–126
   Sino–Vietnamese War and, 166
   Taiwan Strait Crisis and, 294
   Twin Peaks Crises and, 223
   Vietnam War and, 322
international crises, *see* crises, international
international diffusion, 52, 99, 329
   China under Mao and, 148
   India and, 196
   Pakistan and, 240
international vs domestic agendas, 11, 47, 49–50, 73–74, 76
Izvolsky, Alexander, 36

Janis, Irving, 33, 280, 282
Ji Pengfei, 97
Jiang Zemin, *see also* EP-3 reconnaissance aircraft incident
   as leader, 143–144
   crisis decision making, 168–175
   information flows, 128–149, 152, 175, 258
   political environment of, 129–130
Jinmen Island, 104, 284, 285, 287–289, 293
Jinnah, Muhammad Ali, 228, 232
Johnson, Harold, 309
Johnson, Lyndon, 272–324, *see also* Bundy, McGeorge; Bundy, William; Ball, George; Cold War; McCone, John; McNamara, Robert; Rusk, Dean; Vietnam War
   advisory team, 260, 262–263, 273–321
   fragmented institutions, 20, 59, 274–275, 304–306, 329
   Great Society program, 261
   information flows, 277–278
   information search capacity, 275–277
   political character, 260, 278–279, 320–321
   political environment, 272–274

Tuesday Luncheons, 261, 275–279, 313–315
Vietnam War, decision-making, 296–301
Vietnam War, escalation of, 2
Vietnam War, political options, 297–298
Vietnam War and information, 306–315
Vietnam War and institutional design, 303–304
Joint Chiefs of Staff (JCS), US, 266, 276, 289–294, 309
Joint Intelligence Committee (JIC), India, 186, 187, 210

Kaluchak attacks, *see* Twin Peaks Crises
Kargil War, *see also* Pakistan; Sharif, Nawaz
   background to, 221, 226–228, 244–245
   decision-making, alternative explanations, 256–257
   diplomacy, 245–248
   domestic focus, 230–232
   generally, 199
   information, low-quality, 255–256
   information flows, 253, 254
   information search capacity, 235, 252, 254
   Kashmir seizure, 248
   outcome, 225, 250–252
   siloed institutions, 252
Kashmir, 3, 185, 199, 215, 216, 222, 231, 237, 255
Kennedy, John F., 272, *see also* Bundy, McGeorge; Bundy, William; Ball, George; McCone, John; McNamara, Robert; Rusk, Dean; Vietnam War
   as leader, 16–17, 263, 268–269, 275, 280
   crisis decision making, 320
   information flows, 106, 270–272, 275, 276, 278–279, 303, 323
   institutional design, 58, 59, 62, 269–270, 328, 329
   political environment of, 268–313
   political theory of institutional design and, 329
KGB, Soviet Union, 5
Khan, Yahya, 229–230, 233, 240, 243
Khmer Rouge, 154, 155, 158
Khrushchev, Nikita, 5
Kissinger, Henry, 7, 115–116
Korean War, 90, 100
Kosygin, Alexei, 119, 124
Kuwait, Iraq invasion of, 24

Ladakh, 200–203, 207–208, 210
Le Duan, 154, 158, 300

Le Duc Anh, 159
Le Duc Tho, 300
leader beliefs, 133
  Deng Xiaoping, Sino-Vietnamese War, 156–157
  Eisenhower, Taiwan Strait Crisis (1958), 285–286
  Johnson, Cold War, 273–284
  Johnson, Vietnam War, 298–301, 311–312
  Mao, Nationalist invasion scare (1962), 105–106
  Mao, Sino–Soviet Border Conflict, 82–83, 112–114
  measurement, 79–80
  miscalculation and, 24–25, 38, 41, 69
  Nehru, bureaucratic threat, 180–183
  Nehru, Forward Policy, 177–178, 203–204
  political survival and, 76
  shaping beliefs, 80, 82, 105, 133
  Sharif, Kargil War, 227
  silencing bureaucratic information, 121–124, 163–166
  Vajpayee, Twin Peaks Crises, 223
leaders, powers of
  bureaucracies, generally and, 4–5, 10
  international crises and, 22, 42–43
  political experience and, 48–49, 76, 85–86, 138–140, 143, 145, 189, 192–193, 236–237, 264–265, 268–269, 272
leaders, strategies of, 369
  bureaucratic threat and, 46–47, 72, 76
  coercive diplomacy and, 104–106
  crisis initiation and, 22–23, 62
  decision-making, 151–153
  decision-making bodies and, 185–187, 192, 233–235
  institutional design and, 9, 60–62, 95
  overview, 1–2
  projections, 80
  uncertainty and, 25
leaders, trade-offs of, *see also* decision-making
  information vs political security and, 9–225, 261, 312–313
  institutional design and, 10–11, 16–17, 21, 43
  overview, 3
leadership style, 16–17, 52, 329
  China after Mao and, 148
  China under Mao and, 99
  India and, 196
  the United States and, 279

leaks, information, 45, 178, 182, 261, 265, 269, 273–275, 278, 303, 309–313, 323
Lei Yingfu, 108
Li Xiannian, 141, 164
Liaquat Ali Khan, 230–231
Lin Biao, 86, 90, 95, 100, 108, 125, *see also* Mao Zedong; Sino–Soviet Border Conflict
literature review, 42, *see also* research contributions
  accountability theory, 42
  coup-proofing, military, 14
  existing data sets, 54–55
  group decision-making models, 13–14
  institutional design, 52
  institutional miscalculation, and, 41
  intelligence assessments, quality of, 14–15
  interest group model, 11–13, 40–41
  national security institutions, origins of, 16–17
  Vietnam War, crisis failure, 262
Liu Huaqiu, 152
Logevall, Fred, 261, 300, 303, 320
Luo Ruiqing, 90, 107, 140, *see also* Mao Zedong; Nationalist invasion scare (1962)
Lushan Conference, China, 91

MacFarquhar, Roderick, 133
Mao Zedong, 82–127, *see also* Chen Yi; Lin Biao; Luo Ruiqing; Nationalist invasion scare (1962); Sino–Soviet Border Conflict; Sino–Vietnamese War; Wang Bingnan
  as politician
    bureaucratic threat and, 91–95
    as charismatic leader, 85–86
    leadership style, 99
    personalist dictatorship of, 19
    revisionism and, 93–95
  Cultural Revolution
    described, 94
    economic effects of, 154, 158
    military effects of, 128, 139, 163
    political effects of, 95–99, 120, 124–126, 132, 134
  decisions of
    alternative explanations, 110–111
    coercive diplomacy, KMT, 104–106
    Foreign Ministry reorganization, 133
    Nationalist invasion scare (1962), 83
    Politburo Standing Committee, 95
    Sino–Soviet border conflict, 82–83, 124–126

Index

Taiwan Strait Crisis (1958), 287–288
institutional design
  alternative explanations, 99–100
  as self-censorship, 121–124
  crisis assessment and, 107–110
  fragmented institutions and, 83
  information flows and, 89–91, 98–99
  information search capacity and, 86–89, 95–98, 117–121
  People's Republic of China (PRC), 84
  personalist dictatorship and, 84
periods of
  early Mao period, 84–91
  late Mao period, 91–99
McCone, John, 277, 312, *see also* Kennedy, John. F; Johnson, Lyndon; Vietnam War, US
McNamara, Robert, *see also* Kennedy, John. F; Johnson, Lyndon; Vietnam War, US
  information provision, 276, 304–305, 307–308
  management of bureaucracy, 259–260
  other bureaucratic advice, lack of awareness of, 311
  relationship with leader, 269, 311, 321
  self-censorship, 313–314, 318
  strategic assessments, 300–301, 310
McNaughton, John, 312, 313
meetings, bureaucratic
  China, Four Marshals, 121–124
  China, Hua-Deng Period, 135
  China, Jiang-Hu Period, 145–146
  China, Lieutenant Period, 141–142
  China, Nationalist invasion scare, 111
  China, Sino–Vietnamese War, 163
  China under Mao, 87–89, 95–97, 99–102, 118
  India, Twin Peaks Crises, 219
  India after 1962, 191
  India under Nehru, 185–186, 205–206, 210–211
  Pakistan, early civilian and military rule, 232
  Pakistan, Kargil War, 248–249
  US, Taiwan Strait Crisis (1958), 290–291
  US, Vietnam War, 312–315, 319–320
  US under Eisenhower, 265–268
  US under Johnson, 275–276, 279
  US under Kennedy, 270
Mehta, J. S., 206
Menon, V. K. Krishna, *see also* Nehru, Jawaharlal; Sino-Indian War
Menon, V.K. Krishna, 188, 195, 202, 206, 212
Military Council, Pakistan, 233–234

Ministry of Defence, China, 104
Ministry of External Affairs, India, 192, 206, 211
Ministry of Foreign Affairs, Russia, 51
Ministry of State Security, China, 146
miscalculations, *see also* competitive dialogue; political theory of institutional design, Sino–Vietnamese War; Sino–Indian War; Sino–Soviet Border Conflict; EP-3 reconnaissance aircraft incident; Kargil War; Vietnam War, US
  accountability and, 15–16
  alternative explanations, 40–42
  bureaucracies, existing assumptions about and, 6
  defined, 24
  fragmented and siloed institutions, 38–39, 153, 175–176
  fragmented institutions and, 37–39
  information acquisition and, 24–26
  institutional design and, 8–10, 64, 329–332
  integrated institutions and, 31–35
  leader beliefs and, 41, 82
  measurement in cases, 80–81
  overview, 1–3, 325
  siloed institutions and, 35–36
  summary, 53
Mishra, Brajesh, 194, 215, 218, 221–222
Mullik, B. N., 210, 213
Musharraf, Pervez, 217–218, 220, 222, 226, 231, 234–237, 248, 250, 256

National Command Authority (NCA), India, 193
National Security Advisor (NSA), India, 194–196, 215, 218, 221, 222
National Security Advisory Board, India, 218
National Security Council (NSC), India, 5, 179, 192, 193, 195, 328
National Security Council (NSC), Pakistan, 233–235
National Security Council (NSC), US
  Eberstadt report, 263
  generally, 45, 56, 62, 106, 119, 260, 261, 265, 272, 274–282, 289–298, 303, 311–324
  Operations Coordinating Board, 267, 271, 291
  Planning Board, 267–268, 271, 278, 289, 291
  Principals Committee, 56, 59, 318, 319

378   Index

National Security Council (cont.)
  Standing Group, 272
national security institutions
  challenging leadership, 47–48
  coordination bodies, 56
  decision making and, 2, 55, 334–335
  defined, 3–4, 26–27
  expertise in, 13, 25, 44–45, 50
  information flows and, 35
  information search and, 28–35
  institutional design
    change and consistency, 47, 57–60, 148
    consequences of, 79
    crisis performance and, 65–66
    definitions of, 4–5
    overview, 7–8, 26–27
    leader personality and, 16–17, 278–279
    leader trade-offs and, 10–11
    scholarship on, 16–17, 52
    self-censorship and, 37–38, 97–98, 121–124, 186–187, 212–213, 312–315
  inter-bureaucratic information sharing, 9, 12–14, 33–34, 39, 86–89, 107–109, 145–147, 190–191, 194–195, 219–223, 263, 267–268, 271–272
  lack of inter-bureaucratic information sharing, 35, 36, 67, 98–99, 141–142, 163–166, 178–179, 232–235, 239–240, 253–254, 275–278, 306–311
  misconceptions about, 6–7, 35
  overview, 55
  regime type and, 59–60, 225
  self-censoring, 97–98, 121
  United States
    Central Intelligence Agency (CIA), 105, 154
  varied perspectives in, 13–14, 31
national security institutions Data Set, 18, 54–58, 65, 81, *see also* research methodology
National Security Leading Small Group (NSLSG), China, 146
national security organizations, *see also* defense bureaucracies; diplomatic bureaucracies; fragmented institutions; integrated institutions; intelligence bureaucracies; siloed institutions
  China
    Central Investigation Department (CID), 90
    Foreign Affairs Leading Small Group (FALSG), 78, 90, 137, 141
    Foreign Affairs Office, 97, 99
    Foreign Ministry, 87, 91, 93, 95, 97–98, 102, 108–109, 118–121, 123–124
    Ministry of State Security, 146
    National Security Leading Small Group (NSLSG),, 146
    People's Liberation Army (PLA), 86, 98, 132, 138–140, 152, 156–158, 163
    Political Bureau, 86–87, 95–99, 108, 111, 118, 119, 135, 141–142, 145–146, 148, 163–164, 166
    Secretariat, 90–91, 96, 98, 99, 141
    State Council, 90, 91, 97–99, 108, 142
  India
    Cabinet Committee on Security, 192–194, 219–220, 223
    Defence Committee of the Cabinet (DCC), 180, 185–191, 208
    Defence Ministry, 216
    Emergency Committee of the Cabinet (ECC), 190–191, 205
    Foreign Affairs Committee (FAC), 185, 191
    Joint Intelligence Committee (JIC), 186, 187, 210
    Ministry of External Affairs, 192, 206, 211
    National Command Authority (NCA), 193
    National Security Advisory Board, 218
    National Security Council (NSC), 5, 179, 192, 193, 195, 328
    Political Affairs Committee (PAC), 191
    Research and Analysis Wing (R&AW), 193
  Pakistan
    Chief Martial Law Administration (CLMA), 233
    Defence Committee of the Cabinet, 228, 233, 238–239
    Defence Ministry, 227, 228, 238, 252, 255, 258
    Foreign Ministry, 233–235, 238, 240, 243–244, 247–248, 253–255
    Inter-Services Intelligence (ISI), 233–234, 240, 253–254
    Military Council, 233–234
    National Security Council (NSC), 233–235
  United Kingdom
    Committee on Imperial Defence, 19
  United States

Index

Central Intelligence Agency (CIA), 276, 279, 289–292, 306, 308, 310, 319–320
Defense Department, 259, 260, 266, 267, 269, 274, 276, 290–292, 296, 300, 304, 306, 307, 309, 312, 314
Executive Committee (EXCOMM), 270–271, 303
Joint Chiefs of Staff (JCS), 266, 276, 289–294, 309
National Security Council (NSC), 260, 261, 263, 265, 267–272, 274–282, 289–298, 303, 311–324
Operations Coordinating Board, 267, 271, 291
Planning Board, 267–268, 271, 278, 289, 291
State Department, 271, 275, 285, 290–293, 295, 306–307, 309–311, 314
Tuesday Luncheons, 261, 275–279, 313, 315
Nationalist invasion scare (1962), *see also* Mao Zedong; Zhou Enlai
background to, 103–104
decision-making, 83, 105–107
decision-making, alternatives to, 110–111
institutional design and, 107–110
integrated institutions and, 327
strategic options, 104–105
Nationalist party (KMT), Taiwan, 86, 103–109, 144, 284–285, 287–289, 295
Nehru, Jawaharlal, 177–215
as politician, 214
bureaucratic threat and, 180–183
China–India conflict and, 2
domestic agenda focus, 183–185
Forward Policy, 177–178, 202–204, 208–215
information access and, 187–189
information search capacity, 185–187
institutional design, 19, 180, 184–185, 189, 196, 328
political character, 178
political environment of, 177–184
Nicholas II, Tsar of Russia, 50
Nie Rongzhen, 90, 100, 121
Nixon, Richard, 45, 114–116, 121, 122
North Vietnam, *see* Vietnam, Democratic Republic of (DRV)
nuclear weapons, 64, 224, 226, 237, 245–248, 257, 294

Operation Flaming Dart, 297
Operation Koh Paima, 226, 249–257
Operation Parakram (Valor), 216, 217
Operation Rolling Thunder, 297
Operations Coordinating Board, US, 267, 271, 291

Pakistan, *see also* Kargil War; national security organizations; Sharif, Nawaz; Twin Peaks Crises
crisis performance, 241
early civilian and military rule, 228–236
Indian military and, 183, 190, 202
institutional design, 228, 232, 240, 328
nazim system, 231
Pakistan–India relations, *see* Kargil War
Pakistan–India relations, 253
Pakistan–United States relations, 217–218, 237, 250–251, 253
parochial interests, 35–36
path dependence, 16, 52, 60, 329
China after Mao and, 149
India and, 196
Pakistan and, 240
the United States and, 278
path dependence, institutional, 74
pathologies, 6–7, 16, 20, 35–62, 117, 127, 224, 258, 282, 327, 328
Peng Dehuai, 86, 87, 90, 91, 287, 288
People's Liberation Army (PLA), China, 86, 98, 132, 138–140, 152, 156–158, 163, *see also* Chinese military
performance, *see* crisis performance
Pham Van Dong, 128, 158, 300, 311
Planning Board, US, 267–268, 271, 278, 289, 291
policies, economic, *see* domestic agendas; transformative economic policy
Politburo, China, 86–87, 95–97, 108, 111, 118, 119, 135, 141, 145–146, 148, 163–164, 166, 288
Politburo, Soviet Union, 115
Political Affairs Committee (PAC), India, 191
political theory of institutional design
as a relative prediction, 62
conclusions, 329
implications, 333–334
overview, 10–11, 21, 27, 41, 54
prediction, 39, 59, 67, 78–81, 138
qualitative analysis, 86, 107, 149, 167, 190, 197, 205, 225, 237, 241, 265, 323
statistical analysis, 66, 74, 75
testing, 62

380   Index

Powell, Colin, 218
public opinion
  bureaucracies shaping, 44–45
  Cold War, 282
  Kargil War, 249–251
  leader experience and, 72–73
  Sino-Indian War, 178
  Taiwan Strait Crisis (1958), 295
  Twin Peaks Crises, 224, 225
  Vietnam War, 272, 304, 321–322

Qiao Guanhua, 97, 118, 133, 156

Rao, P.V.R., 185
regime type
  accountability and, 66–67
  autocracy, non-personalist, 130
  institutional design and, 59–60, 69, 76, 179, 322
  non-personalist dictatorship, 131, 175, 327
  personalist dictatorships, 38–39, 42, 69
Research and Analysis Wing (R&AW), India, 193
research contributions, 11–20
  bureaucracy, 7–8, 11–14
  intelligence and institutional structures, 14–15
  malleability of national security institutions, 54
  national security institutions, 3, 8–11, 14–17
  National Security Institutions Data Set, 54–62, 81
  overview of cases, 18–20
  summary, 326–332
research methodology
  alternative model specifications and robustness checks, 70
  case selection, 79
  case studies, 18–20, 75–81
  case study coding questions, 76
  case study process, 79–81
  coding questions, 78
  data collection, 56
  data set analysis, National Security Institutions, 18
  micro-level institutional data, 78–79
  overview, 18
  statistical analysis, 66–67, 70–72
Rice, Condoleezza, 218
Roosevelt, Franklin, 38
Rusk, Dean, 119, 271, 275, 276, 307, 314–315, 318, *see also* Kennedy, John. F; Johnson, Lyndon; Vietnam War, US

Russia, Tsarist, 29, 113

Saunders, Elizabeth, 10, 16, 30, 33, 43, 44, 48
search capacity, information, *see* information search capacity
Secretariat, China, 90–91, 96, 98, 99, 141
Shamshad, Ahmad, 254
Sharif, Nawaz, *see also* Kargil War
  as leader, 20, 237, 251
  crisis decision making, 2, 226–227, 245–251, 256
  information flows, 227, 238–239, 252–255, 257–258
  political environment, 234, 237, 238, 256
siloed institutions, *see also* dictatorial institutions; fragmented institutions; integrated institutions; national security institutions
  charted, 27
  China, EP-3 reconnaissance aircraft incident, 172
  China, Jiang-Hu Period, 144–148
  China, Lieutenant Period, 138–142
  China after Mao, 175
  conclusions, 326
  crisis failure and, 68
  crisis performance and, 67, 79
  defined, 9
  historical examples of, 36
  India after 1962, 190–192
  international agendas and, 50–51, 54, 73–74
  logic of choosing, 11, 49–51
  measurement in cases and, 81
  measurement in data set, 57
  miscalculation and, 35–36, 252
  Pakistan, Kargil War, 227–228
  Pakistan, late civilian rule, 237–240, 258
  US under Kennedy, 269–271
Singh, Baldev, 185
Singh, Jaswant, 215
Sino–Soviet Border Conflict, *see also* Mao Zedong
Sino–Vietnamese War, *see also* Mao Zedong
Sino-Indian War, 199–215
  background to, 177–179, 199–201
  decision-making, 1, 199, 203–204
  incomplete information search, 206–209
  outcome, India, 204–205
  strategic options, 201–203
Sino–Soviet Border Conflict, 84
  background to, 82–112
  decision-making, 82, 112–114

Index

decision-making, alternative
  explanations, 124–126
institutional design, 83, 102–124, 126, 327
outcome, 114–116
strategic options, 80, 112
Zhenbao Island attack, 82, 112
Sino–Vietnamese War
  background to, 128–129, 153–155
  decision-making, alternative
    explanations, 166–168
  decision-making logic, 80, 156–157
  incomplete information search, 162–163
  outcome, 157–161
  strategic options, 155–156
Sood, Vikram, 218, 224
South Vietnam, see Vietnam, Republic of (RVN)
Soviet Defense Council, 51
Soviet Union, 296, see also Sino–Soviet Border Conflict
  Cultural Revolution and, 99
  information flows and, 35
  Sino–Soviet split, 2, 3, 177, 203, 210
  Soviet hegemony in Asia, 156, 159, 167
  Soviet Union–Vietnam relations, 153–154, 156–157, 159–160
Stalin, Joseph, 35, 39
State Council, China, 90, 91, 97–99, 108, 142
State Department, US, 271, 275, 285, 290–293, 295, 306–307, 309–311, 314
Stevenson, Adlai, 299
strategies, see decision-making
success, see crisis performance
surveillance, political, 128, 189, 233

Taiwan Affairs Leading Small Group (TLSG), 90
Taiwan Strait Crisis (1954), 296
Taiwan Strait Crisis (1958), US, see also Mao Zedong
  background to, 284
  decision-making, 285–286
  decisions, alternative explanations, 294–296
  information access, 289–292
  institutional consequences, 282
  integrated institutions, 263, 289–294, 323
  outcome, 286–289, 329
  strategic options, 284–285
Talmadge, Caitlin, 14
theory, institutional, see political theory of institutional design

Thimayya, K.S., 207
Thorat, Shankarrao Pandurang Patil, 183
trade-offs, see leaders, trade-offs of
transformative economic policy, 49, 70, 73–74, 130, 132–134, 171, 175, 183–184, 231–232, 327, see also domestic agendas
Truman, Harry, 17, 59, 103
truth to power, speaking, 4, 10, 37–38
Tuesday Luncheons, 261, 275–279, 313, 315, 329
Twin Peaks Crises, 215–223, see also Vajpayee, Atal Bihari
  background to, 215
  decision-making, alternative explanations, 223–224
  decision-making logic, 199, 216–217
  integrated institutions, 219–223
  outcome, India, 217–218
  strategic options, 215–216

U Thant, 301
United Kingdom
  colonial system transplantation, 180
  colonial transplantations, 180
United Nations, 114, 246, 295, 299, 301, 302
United States, administrations of, see Eisenhower, Dwight D.; Kennedy, John F.; Johnson, Lyndon; national security organizations
United States–China relations, 114–116, 128, 143–144, 152, 160–175, 284–296
United States–India relations, 205, 216–218, 221–222
United States–Pakistan relations, 218, 237, 250–251, 253
United States–ROC mutual defense treaty, 105

Vajpayee, Atal Bihari, 248, see also Twin Peaks Crises
  as leader, 192, 245–248, 251–252
  crisis decision making, 216–218, 224
  information flows, 193–195
  political environment, 253
  political options, 215–216
Viet Cong (VC), 296, 298, 304, 307
Vietnam, Democratic Republic of (DRV), 39, 156, 259, 296, 298–304, 306–316, 319, 320
Vietnam, Republic of (RVN), 296, 298–302, 304–306, 308–311, 314–321

Vietnam War, US, *see also* Kennedy, John F.; Johnson, Lyndon
  background to, 259–262, 296–297
  decision-making, 298–299
  decision-making, alternative explanations, 320–322
  fragmented institutions, 303
  generally, 2, 153
  institutional consequences, 282
  low-quality information provision, 311–315
  NSC Working Group assessments, 315–320
  outcome, 299–303
  restricted information search, 303
  scholarship on, 262
  strategic options, 297–298
Vietnam–Soviet Union relations, 153–154, 156–157, 159–160
Vo Nguyen Giap, 300

Wang Bingnan, 108, 109, *see also* Mao Zedong; Nationalist invasion scare
Wang Guoquan, 120
Wang Jiaxiang, 89, 97
Wang Shangrong, 161
Wang Wei, 168
Wang Zhongchun, 115
wargames, 2, 207, 293, 306–307
Warsaw Pact, 160
Weeks, Jessica, 32, 38, 42, 45, 55, 67, 126, 130, 333
Wilhelm II, Kaiser, 28

Wohlforth, William, 23
World War I, 29, 38
World War II, 85

Xu Xiangqian, 121, 163

Yan'an Rectification Campaign, 84
Yang Dezhi, 140
Yang Gongsu, 164
Yang Shangkun, 87, 90, 141
Yaqub Khan, Sahabzada, 234
Ye Jianying, 121, 163

Zardari, Asif Ali, 238
Zegart, Amy, 16
Zhang Wentian, 91
Zhao Ziyang, 140–141, 151
Zhenbao Island attack, 82
Zhou Enlai, *see also* Mao Zedong; Nationalist invasion scare (1962); Sino–Soviet Border Crisis
  as Foreign Minister, 100, 142
  diplomacy, 201, 287
  management of bureaucracy, 87, 89, 91, 92, 98–99, 123, 147
  Nationalist invasion scare and (1962), 108–109
  self-censorship, 98, 206
  Sino–Soviet Border Crisis and, 112, 118, 119
  strategic engagement, 94, 201
Zhu De, 86
Zia ul-Haq, 230, 232

Cambridge Studies in International Relations

160 Rohan Mukherjee
Ascending Order
Rising Powers and the Politics of Status in International Institutions

159 Claire Vergerio
War, States, and International Order
Alberico Gentili and the Foundational Myth of the Laws of War

158 Peter Joachim Katzenstein
Uncertainty and its Discontents
Worldviews in World Politics

157 Jessica Auchter
Global Corpse Politics
The Obscenity Taboo

156 Robert Falkner
Environmentalism and Global International Society

155 David Traven
Law and Sentiment in International Politics
Ethics, Emotions, and the Evolution of the Laws of War

154 Allison Carnegie and Austin Carson
Secrets in Global Governance
Disclosure Dilemmas and the Challenge of International Cooperation

153 Lora Anne Viola
The Closure of the International System
How Institutions Create Political Equalities and Hierarchies

152 Cecelia Lynch
Wrestling with God
Ethical Precarity in Christianity and International Relations

151 Brent J. Steele
Restraint in International Politics

150 Emanuel Adler
World Ordering
A Social Theory of Cognitive Evolution

149 Brian C. Rathbun
Reasoning of State
Realists and Romantics in International Relations

148 Silviya Lechner and Mervyn Frost
Practice Theory and International Relations

147 Bentley Allan
Scientific Cosmology and International Orders

146 Peter J. Katzenstein and Lucia A. Seybert (eds.)
Protean Power
Exploring the Uncertain and Unexpected in World Politics

145 *Catherine Lu*
Justice and Reconciliation in World Politics

144 *Ayşe Zarakol (ed.)*
Hierarchies in World Politics

143 *Lisbeth Zimmermann*
Global Norms with a Local Face
Rule-of-Law Promotion and Norm-Translation

142 *Alexandre Debs and Nuno P. Monteiro*
Nuclear Politics
The Strategic Causes of Proliferation

141 *Mathias Albert*
A Theory of World Politics

140 *Emma Hutchison*
Affective Communities in World Politics
Collective Emotions after Trauma

139 *Patricia Owens*
Economy of Force
Counterinsurgency and the Historical Rise of the Social

138 *Ronald R. Krebs*
Narrative and the Making of US National Security

137 *Andrew Phillips and J. C. Sharman*
International Order in Diversity
War, Trade and Rule in the Indian Ocean

136 *Ole Jacob Sending, Vincent Pouliot and Iver B. Neumann (eds.)*
Diplomacy and the Making of World Politics

135 *Barry Buzan and George Lawson*
The Global Transformation
History, Modernity and the Making of International Relations

134 *Heather Elko McKibben*
State Strategies in International Bargaining
Play by the Rules or Change Them?

133 *Janina Dill*
Legitimate Targets?
Social Construction, International Law, and US Bombing

132 *Nuno P. Monteiro*
Theory of Unipolar Politics

131 *Jonathan D. Caverley*
Democratic Militarism
Voting, Wealth, and War

130 *David Jason Karp*
Responsibility for Human Rights
Transnational Corporations in Imperfect States

129 *Friedrich Kratochwil*
The Status of Law in World Society
Meditations on the Role and Rule of Law

128 *Michael G. Findley, Daniel L. Nielson and J. C. Sharman*
Global Shell Games
Experiments in Transnational Relations, Crime, and Terrorism

127 *Jordan Branch*
The Cartographic State
Maps, Territory, and the Origins of Sovereignty

126 *Thomas Risse, Stephen C. Ropp and Kathryn Sikkink (eds.)*
The Persistent Power of Human Rights
From Commitment to Compliance

125 *K. M. Fierke*
Political Self-Sacrifice
Agency, Body and Emotion in International Relations

124 *Stefano Guzzini*
The Return of Geopolitics in Europe?
Social Mechanisms and Foreign Policy Identity Crises

123 *Bear F. Braumoeller*
The Great Powers and the International System
Systemic Theory in Empirical Perspective

122 *Jonathan Joseph*
The Social in the Global
Social Theory, Governmentality and Global Politics

121 *Brian C. Rathbun*
Trust in International Cooperation
International Security Institutions, Domestic Politics and American Multilateralism

120 *A. Maurits van der Veen*
Ideas, Interests and Foreign Aid

119 *Emanuel Adler and Vincent Pouliot (eds.)*
International Practices

118 *Ayşe Zarakol*
After Defeat
How the East Learned to Live with the West

117 *Andrew Phillips*
War, Religion and Empire
The Transformation of International Orders

116 *Joshua Busby*
Moral Movements and Foreign Policy

115 *Séverine Autesserre*
The Trouble with the Congo
Local Violence and the Failure of International Peacebuilding

114 *Deborah D. Avant, Martha Finnemore and Susan K. Sell (eds.)*
   Who Governs the Globe?

113 *Vincent Pouliot*
   International Security in Practice
   The Politics of NATO-Russia Diplomacy

112 *Columba Peoples*
   Justifying Ballistic Missile Defence
   Technology, Security and Culture

111 *Paul Sharp*
   Diplomatic Theory of International Relations

110 *John A. Vasquez*
   The War Puzzle Revisited

109 *Rodney Bruce Hall*
   Central Banking as Global Governance
   Constructing Financial Credibility

108 *Milja Kurki*
   Causation in International Relations
   Reclaiming Causal Analysis

107 *Richard M. Price*
   Moral Limit and Possibility in World Politics

106 *Emma Haddad*
   The Refugee in International Society
   Between Sovereigns

105 *Ken Booth*
   Theory of World Security

104 *Benjamin Miller*
   States, Nations and the Great Powers
   The Sources of Regional War and Peace

103 *Beate Jahn (ed.)*
   Classical Theory in International Relations

102 *Andrew Linklater and Hidemi Suganami*
   The English School of International Relations
   A Contemporary Reassessment

101 *Colin Wight*
   Agents, Structures and International Relations
   Politics as Ontology

100 *Michael C. Williams*
   The Realist Tradition and the Limits of International Relations

99 *Ivan Arreguin-Toft*
   How the Weak Win Wars
   A Theory of Asymmetric Conflict

98 Michael Barnett and Raymond Duvall (eds.)
    Power in Global Governance

97 Yale H. Ferguson and Richard W. Mansbach
    Remapping Global Politics
    History's Revenge and Future Shock

96 Christian Reus-Smit (ed.)
    The Politics of International Law

95 Barry Buzan
    From International to World Society?
    English School Theory and the Social Structure of Globalisation

94 K. J. Holsti
    Taming the Sovereigns
    Institutional Change in International Politics

93 Bruce Cronin
    Institutions for the Common Good
    International Protection Regimes in International Security

92 Paul Keal
    European Conquest and the Rights of Indigenous Peoples
    The Moral Backwardness of International Society

91 Barry Buzan and Ole Wæver
    Regions and Powers
    The Structure of International Security

90 A. Claire Cutler
    Private Power and Global Authority
    Transnational Merchant Law in the Global Political Economy

89 Patrick M. Morgan
    Deterrence Now

88 Susan Sell
    Private Power, Public Law
    The Globalization of Intellectual Property Rights

87 Nina Tannenwald
    The Nuclear Taboo
    The United States and the Non-Use of Nuclear Weapons Since 1945

86 Linda Weiss
    States in the Global Economy
    Bringing Domestic Institutions Back In

85 Rodney Bruce Hall and Thomas J. Biersteker (eds.)
    The Emergence of Private Authority in Global Governance

84 Heather Rae
    State Identities and the Homogenisation of Peoples

83 Maja Zehfuss
    Constructivism in International Relations
    The Politics of Reality

82 *Paul K. Ruth and Todd Allee*
The Democratic Peace and Territorial Conflict in the Twentieth Century

81 *Neta C. Crawford*
Argument and Change in World Politics
Ethics, Decolonization and Humanitarian Intervention

80 *Douglas Lemke*
Regions of War and Peace

79 *Richard Shapcott*
Justice, Community and Dialogue in International Relations

78 *Phil Steinberg*
The Social Construction of the Ocean

77 *Christine Sylvester*
Feminist International Relations
An Unfinished Journey

76 *Kenneth A. Schultz*
Democracy and Coercive Diplomacy

75 *David Houghton*
US Foreign Policy and the Iran Hostage Crisis

74 *Cecilia Albin*
Justice and Fairness in International Negotiation

73 *Martin Shaw*
Theory of the Global State
Globality as an Unfinished Revolution

72 *Frank C. Zagare and D. Marc Kilgour*
Perfect Deterrence

71 *Robert O'Brien, Anne Marie Goetz, Jan Aart Scholte and Marc Williams*
Contesting Global Governance
Multilateral Economic Institutions and Global Social Movements

70 *Roland Bleiker*
Popular Dissent, Human Agency and Global Politics

69 *Bill McSweeney*
Security, Identity and Interests
A Sociology of International Relations

68 *Molly Cochran*
Normative Theory in International Relations
A Pragmatic Approach

67 *Alexander Wendt*
Social Theory of International Politics

66 *Thomas Risse, Stephen C. Ropp and Kathryn Sikkink (eds.)*
The Power of Human Rights
International Norms and Domestic Change

65 *Daniel W. Drezner*
   The Sanctions Paradox
   Economic Statecraft and International Relations

64 *Viva Ona Bartkus*
   The Dynamic of Secession

63 *John A. Vasquez*
   The Power of Power Politics
   From Classical Realism to Neotraditionalism

62 *Emanuel Adler and Michael Barnett (eds.)*
   Security Communities

61 *Charles Jones*
   E. H. Carr and International Relations
   A Duty to Lie

60 *Jeffrey W. Knopf*
   Domestic Society and International Cooperation
   The Impact of Protest on US Arms Control Policy

59 *Nicholas Greenwood Onuf*
   The Republican Legacy in International Thought

58 *Daniel S. Geller and J. David Singer*
   Nations at War
   A Scientific Study of International Conflict

57 *Randall D. Germain*
   The International Organization of Credit
   States and Global Finance in the World Economy

56 *N. Piers Ludlow*
   Dealing with Britain
   The Six and the First UK Application to the EEC

55 *Andreas Hasenclever, Peter Mayer and Volker Rittberger*
   Theories of International Regimes

54 *Miranda A. Schreurs and Elizabeth C. Economy (eds.)*
   The Internationalization of Environmental Protection

53 *James N. Rosenau*
   Along the Domestic-Foreign Frontier
   Exploring Governance in a Turbulent World

52 *John M. Hobson*
   The Wealth of States
   A Comparative Sociology of International Economic and Political Change

51 *Kalevi J. Holsti*
   The State, War, and the State of War

50 *Christopher Clapham*
   Africa and the International System
   The Politics of State Survival

49 *Susan Strange*
   The Retreat of the State
   The Diffusion of Power in the World Economy

48 *William I. Robinson*
   Promoting Polyarchy
   Globalization, US Intervention, and Hegemony

47 *Roger Spegele*
   Political Realism in International Theory

46 *Thomas J. Biersteker and Cynthia Weber (eds.)*
   State Sovereignty as Social Construct

45 *Mervyn Frost*
   Ethics in International Relations
   A Constitutive Theory

44 *Mark W. Zacher with Brent A. Sutton*
   Governing Global Networks
   International Regimes for Transportation and Communications

43 *Mark Neufeld*
   The Restructuring of International Relations Theory

42 *Thomas Risse-Kappen (ed.)*
   Bringing Transnational Relations Back In
   Non-State Actors, Domestic Structures and International Institutions

41 *Hayward R. Alker*
   Rediscoveries and Reformulations
   Humanistic Methodologies for International Studies

40 *Robert W. Cox with Timothy J. Sinclair*
   Approaches to World Order

39 *Jens Bartelson*
   A Genealogy of Sovereignty

38 *Mark Rupert*
   Producing Hegemony
   The Politics of Mass Production and American Global Power

37 *Cynthia Weber*
   Simulating Sovereignty
   Intervention, the State and Symbolic Exchange

36 *Gary Goertz*
   Contexts of International Politics

35 *James L. Richardson*
   Crisis Diplomacy
   The Great Powers since the Mid-Nineteenth Century

34 *Bradley S. Klein*
   Strategic Studies and World Order
   The Global Politics of Deterrence

33 *T. V. Paul*
   Asymmetric Conflicts
   War Initiation by Weaker Powers

32 *Christine Sylvester*
   Feminist Theory and International Relations in a Postmodern Era

31 *Peter J. Schraeder*
   US Foreign Policy toward Africa
   Incrementalism, Crisis and Change

30 *Graham Spinardi*
   From Polaris to Trident
   The Development of US Fleet Ballistic Missile Technology

29 *David A. Welch*
   Justice and the Genesis of War

28 *Russell J. Leng*
   Interstate Crisis Behavior, 1816–1980
   Realism versus Reciprocity

27 *John A. Vasquez*
   The War Puzzle

26 *Stephen Gill (ed.)*
   Gramsci, Historical Materialism and International Relations

25 *Mike Bowker and Robin Brown (eds.)*
   From Cold War to Collapse
   Theory and World Politics in the 1980s

24 *R. B. J. Walker*
   Inside/Outside
   International Relations as Political Theory

23 *Edward Reiss*
   The Strategic Defense Initiative

22 *Keith Krause*
   Arms and the State
   Patterns of Military Production and Trade

21 *Roger Buckley*
   US–Japan Alliance Diplomacy, 1945–1990

20 *James N. Rosenau and Ernst-Otto Czempiel (eds.)*
   Governance without Government
   Order and Change in World Politics

19 *Michael Nicholson*
   Rationality and the Analysis of International Conflict

18 *John Stopford and Susan Strange*
   Rival States, Rival Firms
   Competition for World Market Shares

17 *Terry Nardin and David R. Mapel (eds.)*
   Traditions of International Ethics

16 *Charles F. Doran*
   Systems in Crisis
   New Imperatives of High Politics at Century's End

15 *Deon Geldenhuys*
   Isolated States
   A Comparative Analysis

14 *Kalevi J. Holsti*
   Peace and War
   Armed Conflicts and International Order, 1648–1989

13 *Saki Dockrill*
   Britain's Policy for West German Rearmament, 1950–1955

12 *Robert H. Jackson*
   Quasi-States
   Sovereignty, International Relations and the Third World

11 *James Barber and John Barratt*
   South Africa's Foreign Policy
   The Search for Status and Security, 1945–1988

10 *James Mayall*
   Nationalism and International Society

9 *William Bloom*
  Personal Identity, National Identity and International Relations

8 *Zeev Maoz*
  National Choices and International Processes

7 *Ian Clark*
  The Hierarchy of States
  Reform and Resistance in the International Order

6 *Hidemi Suganami*
  The Domestic Analogy and World Order Proposals

5 *Stephen Gill*
  American Hegemony and the Trilateral Commission

4 *Michael C. Pugh*
  The ANZUS Crisis, Nuclear Visiting and Deterrence

3 *Michael Nicholson*
  Formal Theories in International Relations

2 *Friedrich V. Kratochwil*
  Rules, Norms, and Decisions
  On the Conditions of Practical and Legal Reasoning in International Relations and Domestic Affairs

1 *Myles L. C. Robertson*
  Soviet Policy towards Japan
  An Analysis of Trends in the 1970s and 1980s

Milton Keynes UK
Ingram Content Group UK Ltd.
UKHW021019091224
452064UK00024B/410